READER'S DIGEST

THE CANADIANS AT WAR 1939/45

COMMEMORATIVE EDITION

Reader's Digest

The Reader's Digest Association (Canada) Ltd.
Montreal

A Note on Style

The Canadians at War 1939/45 consists of writing from many sources, some of it commissioned by Reader's Digest, much of it excerpted from other publications. The various elements have been woven together by Digest editors and every effort has been made to avoid factual error. Nearly every excerpt is condensed and, in most cases, each is introduced with the name of the author. Excerpts of only one paragraph are in quotation marks; the others begin and end with dots. Long excerpts are, in addition, signed with the authors' names.

The Editors

The Canadians at War 1939/45 Commemorative edition

Editor: Andrew R. Byers
Designer: Michel Rousseau
Cover illustrator: Charles Vinh
Rights and permissions: Wadad Bashour
Text preparation: Joseph Marchetti
Picture research: Patricia McGlynn
Coordinator: Susan Wong

Based on the two-volume First Edition

Editor: Douglas How
Associate editors: George Ronald, Charles Smith
Assistant editor: Jeannette Gibbs
Art director: Louis Hamel
Designer: Bill Sharma

Canadian Cataloging in Publication Data
Main entry under title:
   The Canadians at War 1939/45
Commemorative ed.
Includes index.
ISBN 0-88850-321-0 (Commemorative ed.)
ISBN 0-88850-145-5 (2nd ed.)

   1. World War, 1939-1945—Canada. 2. World War, 1939-1945—Personal narratives, Canadian.
I. Reader's Digest Association (Canada).

D768.15.C3 1995   940.54´0971 C94-900818-4

Printed in Belgium
95 96 97 98 99 / 9 8 7 6 5

Contents

The hope that died	Canada plunges into the war she had tried to wish away	6
The black spring	Mobilization—and the shock of Germany's 1940 blitzkrieg	20
Closeup: Over France	The RAF's "Canadian" squadron on the western front	34
All available destroyers	A tiny navy answers Britain's cry for help	35
The Interpreter	Mackenzie King serves as a link between Churchill and Roosevelt	46
They flew with The Few	The epic Battle of Britain	58
Closeup: On guard	McNaughton's Flying Circus awaits invasion in Britain	76
Airdrome of democracy	Canada trains 131,000 men to fight in the skies	77
Closeup: The high, hard road to Britain	Civilians prove that bombers can fly the wintry Atlantic	89
Sheepdog navy	The little ships of the RCN hold the western Atlantic	90
Closeup: The savior of Ceylon	Sqdn. Ldr. L. J. Birchall prevents another Pearl Harbor	102
Hana-Saku Hana-Saku	Two Canadian battalions go down fighting at Hong Kong	103
Closeup: The evacuation	A Japanese Canadian's story of the expulsion of his people	114
The war strikes home	The west coast fears invasion; U-boats range the east coast	116
Dieppe: the day that will not die	The 2nd Division pays a terrible price to learn vital lessons	130
Closeup: Rebel of the skies	"Buzz" Beurling becomes Canada's top fighter pilot	152
Special duty at the War Office	Secret agents in France	154

Closeup: The beautiful agent   Sonia d'Artois fights with the Resistance   165

The dark and bloody winter   The Battle of the Atlantic reaches its greatest crisis   166

The changing face of Canada   The home front   180

Closeup: The tanker   A Vancouver pilot robs Rommel of the oil his army needs   192

They also served   The war works a revolution in the role of women   194

Closeup: Mrs. "Sparks"   Fern Blodgett becomes a sailor   205

The night they broke the dams in Happy Valley   A unique bomb, a famous raid and "dark destruction" in the Ruhr   206

A sailors' place   Halifax survives six years of overcrowding, exasperation, danger   220

Sicily: time of learning   The army goes to war to stay   232

Closeup: Scoop   Ross Munro becomes one of the world's top war correspondents   247

Johnnie's wing   The RCAF adopts Britain's leading ace   248

Ortona: little Stalingrad   The 1st Division whips Germany's crack paratroopers   260

The battle of Germany   No. 6 Group joins the drive to bomb the Reich into defeat   274

Closeup: Life in the giants' shadow   The legendary Andy McNaughton leaves the army he built   286

The deadly destroyer   *Haida* makes dramatic war off the coast of France   288

Closeup: Herbie   Cartoonist "Bing" Coughlin creates the army's most beloved soldier   298

Breakthrough   Canadians shatter the last great barrier guarding Rome   299

A day called D   The Allies land in Normandy   310

**Two nights
in June**   Two airmen make RCAF history   334

**The ones
that got away**   Escape and evasion   344

**Everywhere the pale
upturned faces**   Five thousand Canadians give their
lives to liberate France   356

Closeup: Superspy   A millionaire runs a
secret service organization   376

**The time
of high hope**   Triumph everywhere, and dreams
of an early peace   378

**Cinderella
of the polders**   First Canadian Army makes war
in a "land God had no hand in"   392

Showdown   The toll of battle forces a crisis
over conscription   405

**Closeup: Swift ships
and daring deeds**   Canada's small-ship sailors on
far-flung assignments   414

**A winter
in the trenches**   An officer's poignant diary
of frontline war   416

The indispensables   Tales of the half-forgotten men
of the merchant marine   430

**Closeup: A general
24 hours a day**   Profile of Gen. H. D. G. Crerar   434

**The savage
twilight**   Crerar's Army drives the
Germans across the Rhine   436

**The "angel"
that came too late**   The world's first jet fighter
fails to stop the Allies   448

The lonely years   The grim life of prisoners of war   454

**Closeup: Outfits of quite
superior individuals**   Canada's parachute battalion
and the legendary Force in action   461

**A victory won,
a nation renewed**   As Canada's troops triumph in Europe,
hope and elation seize the nation   462

Index   471

Acknowledgments   479

Picture credits   480

The hope that died

**After a long dream of peace forever,
Canada plunges into the war she had tried to wish away**

The Canada of the late 1930s—not only her people but many of her leaders—suffered from what author Ralph Allen called "an almost epidemic blight of reason, a wish-turned-to-belief that fair words and small deeds could somehow wipe out war." Between 1914 and 1918 she had lost 60,000 men in battle and she wanted no more of it. Through years of economic depression and unemployment, her people watched from afar the march of powerful dictators, the rape of China by Japan, the subjection of Ethiopia by Mussolini's Fascist Italy, the seizure of one neighboring territory after another by Hitler's Nazi Germany. Like other free people, they hoped that amid all this they could live their own lives in peace. In the words of Angus L. Macdonald, the wounded World War I veteran who became navy minister, "We all

longed for peace—everybody. Some longed so deeply that they came to believe that never again would there be war."

The mood of the country was isolationist. "Canada," declared Raoul Dandurand, government leader in the Canadian Senate, "is a fireproof house free of inflammable material." Apart from economic weakness and hatred of war, there were two primary reasons for this attitude. The dictators were thousands of miles away, and the even more isolationist but powerful and friendly United States was right next door. By 1938 President Roosevelt was pledging openly what had long been obvious: if any aggressor attacked Canada his country "would not stand idly by."

Almost alone, John W. Dafoe, renowned editor of the *Winnipeg Free Press,* for years campaigned to have Canada support firm

League of Nations measures against international aggression. Forerunner of the United Nations, the League represented the world's first organized attempt to preserve peace through international collaboration. But in one celebrated episode, in 1935, the new Liberal government of Prime Minister Mackenzie King demonstrated how little it was willing to help give the League the strength it needed. Ralph Allen in *Ordeal by Fire:*

. . . When Italy invaded Ethiopia in October of that year, Canada was on the eve of an election. But its League delegation got Conservative Prime Minister R. B. Bennett's authority to join in condemning Italy as an aggressor. The question of economic sanctions was still being debated when the Canadians learned they were working for a new administration.

The head of the delegation, Dr. Walter A. Riddell, asked the incoming Mackenzie King government for instructions. In reply, the Department of External Affairs cabled the summary of a statement King had given the press: Canada would cooperate in economic sanctions but couldn't consider military sanctions without consulting Parliament. Riddell, who was on a committee debating what goods should

When he learned copper was to be added to the embargo list, Riddell, still without detailed instructions, drew up a resolution of his own, adding the items he felt must be proscribed if sanctions were to work—oil, iron, steel and coal. Copper was not mentioned. "If I left off copper," he explained later, "as the inclusion of copper at the time was not important, it might be more acceptable to my govern-

Hungry and jobless in "a land of plenty," Canadian veterans of the 1914-18 war make a pathetic mid-Depression plea for work and food—as Benito Mussolini's planes (right) dive on African villagers in the prelude to new world conflict. With the League of Nations offering little serious opposition, the Italian dictator (above) easily conquered Ethiopia. By midsummer 1936 Addis Ababa was in Italy's hands and Emperor Haile Selassie was in exile.

be barred to Italy and on what conditions, took this as official guidance. He had learned, though, that aggression or no aggression, sanctions or no sanctions, the world government was crowded with local patriots to whom the lofty avowals of the League's Covenant were less compelling than business-as-usual.

France argued against extending the embargo to iron, steel, coal and oil. Argentina, where a million Italians lived, stressed the possible economic and social damage to Latin America if Mussolini were opposed too zealously. Norway, Poland and Romania demanded to be allowed to send Italy war goods already ordered. Spain argued she ought to be allowed to sell iron ore. Switzerland claimed that to comply with a ban on war goods to Italy would cost the country its best market and throw thousands out of work.

Riddell knew Canada was not immune to temptation. Most of the 27 raw materials described by the League as essential for war purposes were being mined from the Canadian Shield. One was copper.

ment; we were already as much affected as any country by the key-products proposal."

Riddell cabled Ottawa for approval. When no reply came, he felt free to obey his instinct. His motion was clearly in harmony with King's press statement. In any case, the powerful weapon now pointed at Italy had a safety catch: any committee recommendations had to go to individual governments for acceptance.

Riddell's motion sailed through the committee unopposed and a world sickened by Mussolini's bombing of unprotected Ethiopian villages took heart. While others shilly-shallied in the presence of wholesale murder, the courageous Canadians had shown the way. Limited sanctions went into force in mid-November and soon cut Italy's trade by half. If oil was forbidden to him—as now seemed certain—Mussolini's adventure in Ethiopia would be doomed.

Mackenzie King, on vacation in Georgia, had left Justice Minister Ernest Lapointe, his Quebec lieutenant, in charge of external affairs. Lapointe came under heavy pressure. Practically every French-language newspaper opposed action by Canada: what was the difference between Mussolini's foray into Africa and Britain's war of conquest against the Boers? Canada had joined in Anglo-Saxon hypocrisy then; must she repeat the error now? The Roman Catholic Church took no official stand, but to most priests and bishops two facts stood out: Italy was Catholic, Rome was Rome.

No one paid much attention when Fascist Adrien Arcand led his Silver Shirts through the streets of Montreal to deride the League and hail Mussolini, but it was different when Camillien Houde spoke up. "If war should come between Britain and Italy," said the sometime mayor of Montreal and leader of the provincial Conservative party, "French-Canadian sympathies will be with Italy."

Lapointe stood his ground until almost a month after the oil embargo had been endorsed by the League committee. Then, with King's approval, he disavowed all responsibility for the motion to cut off Mussolini's oil, coal, steel and iron. "The Canadian resolution" had represented Riddell's personal opinion, not the views of the government.

The oil embargo had little chance of finding another sponsor. Mussolini went on with his conquest and the committee shoved the embargo into a pigeonhole.

By midsummer the Ethiopian capital was in Italy's hands, Emperor Haile Selassie was in exile and the League was back in session. There was no further talk of an oil-and-steel embargo and the embargo on less important war materials was removed. Said Canada's new delegate, Vincent Massey: "These sanctions having proved inadequate, continuance of the ineffective economic pressure would not secure the original objective and would be worse than useless." . . .

RALPH ALLEN

The officers who headed Canada's three armed forces sensed that the sacrifice of Ethiopia had been a mortal wound to the League—and to peace. In a report to the cabinet, soon after Mussolini's triumph in May 1936, they said: "The possibility of major war is becoming more apparent. Indeed, the realization is growing in many minds that the cessation of hostilities in 1918 was but an armistice. The dispatch overseas of Canadian forces may again be necessary."

But Mackenzie King thought—or hoped—otherwise. Historian A. R. M. Lower wrote in *Colony to Nation:* "The government's refusal to stand by Riddell had removed Canada from the list of countries prepared to uphold the public law by force. When King spoke at Geneva in September 1936, he relegated the League to a medium of conciliation. Thereafter, Canada had no foreign policy except a correct neutrality. Her voice was not raised in international affairs and she left it to the great powers to wreck the world as they deemed best."

In Winnipeg, Dafoe wrote the League's epitaph: "With assurances of the most distinguished consideration, it was ushered into the darkness by Mr. Mackenzie King."

In 1937 King met Hitler, told him that in any general war Canada would stand at Britain's side, and came away reassured. Germany's ruler, he later told journalist Bruce Hutchison, was "a simple peasant." In a confidential memo to Governor-General Lord Tweedsmuir, he said, "I am perfectly certain that the Germans are not contemplating war, either with France or Britain."

In March 1938 the "simple peasant" seized Austria. Canadians were told by London columnist Beverley Baxter in *Maclean's:* "Hitler never wanted war, but

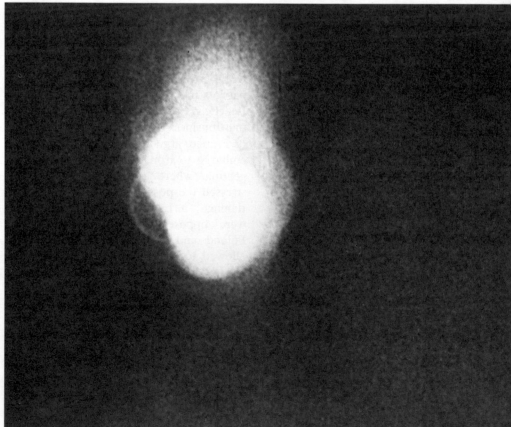

Prime Minister Mackenzie King (left) believed Adolf Hitler was "a simple peasant" with no intention of warring with Britain and France. He believed —or hoped—also, like most Canadians, that Britain's smiling Prime Minister Neville Chamberlain (below left) *had* won "peace in our time." But Winston Churchill told the British House of Commons after Munich: "We have sustained a total and unmitigated defeat. And do not suppose that is the end. This is only the first sip, the first foretaste of a bitter cup."

he overplayed his hand and may be forced to fight." Within a few months, Hitler demanded Czechoslovakia's Sudetenland. He wasn't forced to fight. The British and French gave it to him at Munich, and Prime Minister Neville Chamberlain bore back to London his famous umbrella and his promise of "peace in our time."

Ralph Allen:

. . . The magic word in world diplomacy was now "reality." The companion word "appeasement" had not yet lost face. King referred to appeasement often, and practiced it with diligence and stubborn faith.

When Canadian volunteers enlisted with the Spanish Republicans in the civil war against Fascist Franco—who was actively supported by Hitler and Mussolini—the Canadian government invoked a 60-year-old act forbidding foreign enlistments.

When Chamberlain returned from Munich, King cabled him: "Canada rejoices at the success of your efforts. On the brink of chaos the voice of reason has found a way out of the conflict." King was not alone in his euphoria. In 1935 Bennett's defeated government had handed him a defense budget of $17 million, one half of one percent of the national income. When the new administration sought an increase, it ran into heavy going. Left-wing CCF leader J. S. Woodsworth moved in the Commons that "in the event of war, Canada should remain strictly neutral regardless of who the belligerents may be."

It was significant—and a hint of trouble ahead—that a group of Quebec Liberals abandoned King to support Woodsworth's demand for neutrality. Other voices were raised in alarm. Said the

Chief of Staff, Maj. Gen. A. G. L. McNaughton: "Except as regards rifles and rifle ammunition, partial stocks of which were inherited from the Great War, the country has no reserves of equipment and ammunition." In all Canada there was not a single modern anti-aircraft gun, few operational military aircraft, no aerial bombs. There was ammunition for 90 minutes' fire from obsolescent field guns. "About the only article of which stocks are held," said McNaughton, "is harness. The composition of a modern land force would use very little horsed transport."

Behind the great Atlantic moat, millions of Canadians still practiced mass hypnosis. Day by day in every way the world was getting better and better, and it *would* get better if enough people kept saying so and believing it.

Seeking to harness these mighty forces of autosuggestion and help them to ignore the impending war right out of existence, the country's largest newspaper, the usually sensational *Toronto Daily Star,* embarked on one of the most remarkable performances in journalistic history. All through fateful August 1939 the paper's readers were invited to believe that the day's most important news was: MAN AND WIFE SLAIN, DAUGHTER WOUNDED; or GUNMEN ROB BANK, BEAT TRAIN TO ESCAPE; or BLAST BRIDGES, RUSH TANKS IN U.S. STRIKES; or 2 ROB BALA BANK, NAB ONE AT GUNPOINT. These were the actual front-page news banners the *Star* used on the first four publishing days of the month. Even as late as August 16, 16 days before the shooting started, in the

"This is not peace," said France's Marshal Ferdinand Foch when the Treaty of Versailles was written after World War I. "It is an armistice for 20 years." Adolf Hitler, beaming in the adulation of his Nazi followers, would make Foch's sorry prediction come true and most of western Europe, like a Czech woman forced to salute German troops invading her country, would weep the bitter tears of defeat. But Britain's declaration of war took Hitler by surprise. His interpreter said the Führer was "petrified and utterly disconcerted." Hitler turned to Foreign Minister Ribbentrop and asked: "What now?"

Star's judgment, what mattered most was:

$11,004 NEEDED STILL BY FRESH AIR FUND

On the 18th, Hitler took possession of his erstwhile "protectorate" of Slovakia.

FOIL GRIMSBY BANK HOLDUP, NAB SUSPECT

On the 22nd, Germany announced that Hitler and his greatest enemy, Russia's Joseph Stalin, would sign a ten-year non-aggression pact. Now not two heavily armed dictators would be loose in Europe, but three.

SENATOR O'CONNOR DIES

On the 24th, the Wehrmacht (German Army) wheeled new divisions to the Polish border.

TORONTO MAN NEW SALVATION ARMY HEAD

On the 26th, Mackenzie King cabled peace appeals to Hitler, Mussolini and the President of Poland. The *Star's* main headline:

WOUNDED FATHER AND SON ROUT THREE GUNMEN

On September 1, Hitler attacked Poland. Two days later he was at war with Britain and France.

In Ottawa, Parliament met September 8 to debate what Canada should do. The three-day session marked the end of the career of CCF leader Woodsworth, Canada's most persistent and effective champion of civil liberty and social reform. The little ex-clergyman and stevedore squared his shoulders and went marching down his lonely road again. When he began his brink-of-war speech, he had six followers in the Commons. When he finished, he had none. Not a soul voted with him against the war, nor did he ask that any do so. Woodsworth stated his position firmly and with a trace of sad apology: the last war had settled nothing, the next war would settle nothing. Others could confront him with their realism and logic. They could call him a crank and a hopeless idealist, but they could not make him forget a scene he had witnessed a few days earlier at the Peace Arch between Canada and the United States near Blaine, Wash.: "The children gathered their pennies and planted a rose garden, and they held a fine ceremony in which they interchanged national flags and sang songs and that sort of thing, a beautiful incident."

And then Woodsworth said softly, "I take my place with the children."

King had no more real faith than

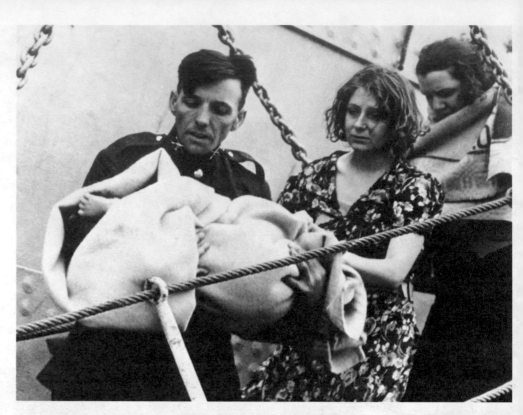

Woodsworth in war's ultimate power to achieve any useful end. But with peace already lost, the option was lost. Unlike Woodsworth, he could no longer meet an impossible problem with an impossible solution. Neither he nor Canada could take a place among the children, so they must take their place among the warring grown-ups.

The problem of Quebec and conscription left no choice either.

[Already there had been anti-war meetings in that province. When a speaker in Montreal shouted that French Canadians would fight before they would be sent overseas against their will, there was wild applause from the crowd. To them, war meant a large army, a large army meant the threat of conscription and conscription meant being forced by the English-Cana-

dian majority to fight the imperialist wars of Britain, the conqueror of New France.]

Conscription had long been an ugly word. It meant, above everything else, that young men of French Canada would be torn from their families to die in a struggle they neither approved nor understood.

When invoked in 1917 to produce desperately needed reinforcements for the Canadian Corps in Europe, conscription had shaken Canada to her foundations. The Archbishop of Montreal, Monsignor Paul Bruchési, had said: "We are nearing racial and religious war." There had been bloody riots in Quebec City. One paper had urged that Quebec withdraw from Confederation: "Our faith, our language, our schools and the future of our children, the well-being of our families, the mission which Providence seems to have confided to our

Britain went to war with Germany at 11 a.m. September 3, 1939. That day, off Ireland, the British liner *Athenia* was sunk without warning by a U-boat. Many passengers were saved, including a baby (left), but loss of life was heavy. One victim was ten-year-old Margaret Hayworth of Hamilton, Ont., and she was mourned as Canada's symbolic first victim of the war. When Prime Minister King (below, left, with Justice Minister Lapointe) broadcast to Canadians September 3, his words suggested Canada too was at war. A number of Ottawa correspondents assumed that, as *The Globe and Mail's* Harold Dingman wrote, "the Dominion of Canada was automatically at war with Germany." Four days later the correction was headlined—as in the Montreal *Gazette* (below), whose F. C. Mears had made the same mistake. On the 10th, to express her autonomy, Canada made her own declaration of war for the first time.

EXTRA The Globe and Mail **EXTRA**

BRITISH EMPIRE AT WAR

His Majesty Calls to Britons 'at Home and Overseas';
French Declaration Follows; Canada's Aid Pledged;
British Cabinet Shuffled; Polish Cavalry Routs Enemy

The Gazette.

Germans Send More Men to West Front, Evacuate Saar as French Bombard Forts; War Not Declared, Premier King Says

hands, to plant on the shores of the St. Lawrence a truly Christian civilization, appear to be passing away. The war came and the majority here again imposed upon us its arbitrary will. We are already crushed by an enormous debt and today they wish to impose by force a law as unconstitutional as it is anti-Canadian, which will send our sons and brothers to the European butchery, like so many cattle, to satisfy the appetite of a master."

In the 1917 federal election, conscription had been overwhelmingly approved everywhere but in Quebec. Canada had lost nearly as much ground in her struggle for unity as she had won in the 158 years since the Plains of Abraham.

And now, after another 22 years, with Parliament about to vote, Mackenzie King faced the same terrible problem. Weighing every word, he said slowly: "The government believes that conscription of men for overseas service will not be a necessary or an effective step. No such measures will be introduced by the present administration."

Justice Minister Lapointe spoke with far greater force and conviction. Constitutionally and morally, he said, it was impossible to remain neutral. As a Canadian, he had a dozen reasons, and the first of these rang forth all the more compellingly because his English was heavy with the accent of the lower St. Lawrence: "Our King, Mr. Speaker, is at war, and this Parliament is sitting to decide whether we shall make his cause our own."

As a French Canadian, Lapointe spoke with equal directness: "The whole Province of Quebec will never accept compulsory service or conscription outside Canada. I am authorized by my colleagues in the cabinet from Quebec to say that we will never agree to conscription and will never be members or supporters of a government that will try to enforce it."

Lapointe's decisive stand, backed by his personal stature in both Canadas, made all that followed superfluous. The proclamation was approved and dispatched by midnight. It reached Buckingham Palace in the early morning, and Canada was officially at war on Sunday, September 10. . . .

RALPH ALLEN

It was an historic occasion. "No onlooker who was present through those brief days in Parliament," wrote Leslie Roberts in *Clarence Decatur Howe,* "will ever for-

get them. The atmosphere was one of deep solemnity and of a unity between parties and racial groups which seldom has existed in Canada, and which could not be expected to withstand the long years of war ahead."

It was almost exactly 25 years since the country had gone to war in August 1914—automatically because Britain had gone. She went this time in a different way, on her own as King had promised, because now she was autonomous. She also went in a different mood.

Historian Lower explained the difference:

"In August 1914, the Canadian people had gone to war in high fighting spirit. In September 1939, they accepted the blow fate had dealt them. Ten years of depression and 20 years' crumbling of old institutions and beliefs did not provide the soil in which buoyant, fighting spirits flourish. There was little jingoism; neither jubilation nor active protest. Canadians reluctantly prepared to accept their fate."

British Columbia's great painter, Emily Carr, sensed the same mood on an outing that week in a Victoria park. "Nobody was smiling," she wrote in her diary. "Everybody spending Labor Day guiltily, in melancholy peace."

When the news of the declaration of war came, just after Sunday lunchtime, the radio network of the three-year-old CBC was carrying an NBC show, *Music For Moderns,* which originated in Philadelphia. Announcer Austin Willis, in Toronto, interrupted "Smoke Gets In Your Eyes" to read a Canadian Press bulletin. Then the network went back to music from KYW in Philadelphia. It was the Kenneth Martin band playing "Inka Dinka Doo." After "Inka Dinka Doo" came "The Man I Love."

"Incredible stupidity," declared *The Financial Post.* "No sense of the sober gravity of the moment seized the CBC."

Eric Hutton, in *Maclean's,* described "The Day Canada Went to War":

. . . If the CBC was inept, the daily press of Canada didn't consider the nation's formal entry into war the day's top news either. Most Monday papers gave it secondary position to what they considered the big news: the Poles were lambasting the Germans on three fronts. Poland was only six days away from total defeat, but there was no hint of that in the optimistic reports of September 11.

In Newfoundland, still a British colony ten years removed from joining Confederation, the mainland's declaration of war was an anticlimax that rated modest space on page 4 of the St. John's *Evening Telegram*. Newfoundland, already at war for seven days, had been the scene of the first "act of hostility" in North America: a German merchant ship had been seized and 30 German prisoners taken. The YMCA in St. John's was converted into a prison.

Newfoundland had rationing and dimouts. Wireless telephones and private radio stations were silenced, mail and cables censored, aliens registered and controlled. Insurance premiums on waterfront property had gone up in less than a week from $1 to $5 for each $1000 of coverage.

A few days before the declaration of war, militia regiments across Canada had been ordered to mobilize. Men flocked to recruiting centers—veterans of World War I and even earlier wars, high-school boys eager for adventure and, above all, the unemployed.

Only near-perfect specimens were accepted. Medical officers rejected far more applicants than they passed, often because of dental defects. During the Depression many had not been able to afford dentists or had used that excuse for neglecting their teeth. Now dentists were besieged by men who had been advised to "get your teeth fixed and try again."

The high ratio of rejections actually increased the unemployment problem. The soup kitchen of the Scott Mission in Toronto found 100 additional hungry men in its lineup. "They left their jobs to join up," said Rev. Morris Zeidman, "and they weren't wanted."

In an overheated Calgary recruiting office a straight-backed veteran with jet-black hair sat waiting his turn. When at last he stood before the sergeant his hair was white and his face streaked with black from the shoe polish he had used for dye. Reluctantly he admitted he was 77 years old and a Boer War veteran.

In a month of recruiting, Canada's forces grew to 70,000 from a professional nucleus of fewer than 10,000. The number would mount to more than half a million by 1941 and to a peak of 740,000 in 1944. Women weren't being enlisted at all in 1939, but 37,000 would be in uniform by October 1944.

Among the earliest to apply were some

unknown men who later would make headlines. Aubrey Cosens, an 18-year-old railway section hand at Porquis Junction, Ont., rejected by the RCAF, got into the Argyll and Sutherland Highlanders and eventually the Queen's Own Rifles. John Mahony, a New Westminster, B.C., newspaper reporter, was one of the first in his community to enlist. Ernest "Smoky" Smith, an unemployed construction worker who lived a few blocks from Mahony, joined the Seaforth Highlanders. Robert Gray graduated from the University of British Columbia into the navy. John Foote, 35-year-old minister of a Presbyterian church in Port Hope, Ont., joined the chaplain corps. These men, typical of Canadians who would serve in World War II, were among the 16 who would win the Victoria Cross.

German troops opened barriers along the frontier and nine armored divisions rumbled into Poland. The Poles replied with 12 brigades of cavalry, the only thing in which they outnumbered the Germans, and Hitler took Poland in 18 days. Canada was in no hurry for war. The navy, recalls Rear Adm. L. W. Murray, at that time a captain and Deputy Chief of Staff, received no direction from the government "so we acted as we thought best, having read the newspapers." Murray obtained permission to assign Royal Navy reservists in Canada and to use any Canadian reservists who volunteered before being called. "Thus," he says, "we committed the first act of war though Canada was not at war until September 10."

Three hours before opening time, would-be airmen line up outside an RCAF recruiting depot in Winnipeg. No one in less than top physical condition was accepted. No one over 45 either, as a white-haired, 76-year-old veteran of World War I found when he tried to join the army in Vancouver. In a month the forces grew from 10,000 to 70,000. Tailors quickly caught up with demand and soon were producing more uniforms than there were men to wear them.

"The greatest single weakness was equipment," wrote Col. C. P. Stacey in an official army history. "Arms were almost entirely 1914-18 pattern. Units possessed virtually no vehicles, although the war would clearly be the most highly mechanized in history. Until 1938 Canada possessed not a single tank. In that year two light tanks were received from Britain. Fourteen more arrived on the eve of war."

The lack of uniforms was even more noticeable. Tip Top Tailors in Toronto, which had made most of Canada's World War I uniforms, put $100,000 into converting the company's cafeteria, bowling alleys and auditorium into a uniform factory before a single government order was received. Tip Top production men were taken aback when they saw the first uniform patterns. "We don't make windbreakers," they objected. But those were no windbreakers. They were the top half of the new battledress—"battle rompers" the soldiers dubbed them. Soon Tip Top was turning out 25,000 a week, faster than the government could enlist men.

Many a uniform-maker slipped a "God bless you" note into a pocket. Most were removed by government inspectors who feared the pious wish might be a coded spy message.

There were other "spy scare" incidents. In Victoria, a 12-year-old girl making a sketch of Government House was chased away by guards when she couldn't produce a permit to do so. Motorists driving past a Toronto hydroelectric substation were stopped and their cars searched; the authorities had been told there would be an attempt to blow it up. Near Red Deer, Alta., a CPR freight engineer sighted heavy timbers across the track just in time to avert a wreck. The RCMP recorded it as the first attempted sabotage by enemy sympathizers.

Patriotism cropped up in unusual places. Rocco Perri, self-styled "king of the bootleggers," asked to be released from jail so he could join up. Harry Baldwin, a German air ace of World War I, enlisted in the RCAF. Three youths who escaped from Toronto's Don Jail were quickly recaptured—at a recruiting office. Members of

nearly all German clubs across Canada pledged loyalty to their adopted country.

Hundreds of Canadians deluged Ottawa with inventions. One was convinced he had a ray that would turn clouds to stone. Beamed on clouds over the enemy lines, it would rain down annihilating boulders.

Temperance forces demanded prohibition. They did not make Canada dry, as they had in World War I, but they came close. In Ontario liquor rationing would reach a low of 12 ounces a month.

The Canadian National Exhibition bought space in U.S. papers to deny that the CNE had closed—only the German exhibit had. Hitler's portrait was a target in midway shooting galleries.

Tourist traffic from the United States decreased. German agents were planting rumors with U.S. hotel clerks, travel-agency employees and gasoline-station attendants: Canadian authorities were seizing cars driven across the border; tourists were kept under police surveillance; Canada was confiscating U.S. money and repaying only 59 cents in Canadian currency. (Actually the U.S. dollar was worth $1.10 Canadian.)

Another rumor said sugar would be scarce. When housewives went on a sugar-shopping spree, merchants tried to stem the panic by selling only to customers who bought other groceries: hamburger at 13 cents a pound, steak 29 cents, apples 10 cents a basket, peaches 19 cents a basket. Simpson's had hand-dipped chocolates at 25 cents a pound, Eaton's offered broadcloth shirts for 84 cents and men's three-piece botany-wool suits for $9.98.

Rumors spread through Toronto: no more marriage licenses. Couples swarmed to the City Hall license bureau, and it was midafternoon before beleaguered clerks could convince all the applicants that marriage wasn't banned.

Even without such false stimuli, war brought a boom in Canadian marriages: 30,000 more in 1939 than in the year before: 80,000 more than in 1932, the deepest year of the Depression. . . .

ERIC HUTTON

Not only was Canada poor—her population was 11,250,000, her gross national product $5.6 billion—but she had doubts

Ontario's Premier Mitchell Hepburn and Quebec's Premier Maurice Duplessis (above left, on the Hepburn farm near St. Thomas) both fought Mackenzie King early in the war, and both lost. With a huge majority in the election of March 1940, King became Canada's unchallenged leader in the fight against Hitler, whose autographed picture he had as a souvenir of their meeting in Germany in 1937. "To Your Excellency," read Hitler's inscription, "with friendly memories." The country King led was woefully weak. On the eve of war Maj. Gen. A. G. L. McNaughton had noted that Canada did have stocks of harness. He added wryly that a modern army would use very little horsed transport.

about the leadership of a Prime Minister who knew nothing of military things, who placed national unity between English and French above all other considerations, who cried that "war would settle nothing, prove nothing, help nothing."

"I never dreamed," King had told Parliament, "that after spending a lifetime to promote and to preserve peace and goodwill, it should fall to my lot to lead Canada into a great war. But that responsibility I assume with a sense of being true to the very blood that is in my veins. I assume it in the defense of freedom—the freedom of my fellow countrymen, the freedom of those whose lives are unprotected in other countries, and the freedom of mankind itself."

Bruce Hutchison in *Mr. Prime Minister:*

. . . King was apparently the last man in Canada to lead a nation at war. But he himself knew that if other men must fight, only he could manage the political process to save the nation from racial fracture and impotence. This happened to be true. Providence had instilled in one unlikely man the exact qualities required, and now that the worst had happened, King set aside all minor concerns and, with new peace of mind, made war.

The nation he could never inspire, but certainly could manage, seemed to rally around him. But he could not be deceived.

He knew that the old racial crisis would erupt again and, in fact, the first installment appeared within a fortnight. Premier Maurice Duplessis called a provincial election on the vague issue of Quebec "autonomy." Everyone knew his meaning: the Quebec government proposed to veto and dislocate Canada's war policy before it could get under way. C. G. "Chubby" Power, a veteran of Quebec politics and federal minister of pensions, told King: "If Duplessis wins, the war is over for Quebec." The chances of defeating Duplessis were no better than 50-50 but the alternative was national havoc. While King hesitated, the decision was made by Lapointe. Quebec's leader in Ottawa realized his own hour had come. There could be no delay, no evasion, no compromise, and no one else could hope to convince his people. He must win or lose everything.

No more important election had ever been called in Canada. No greater triumvirate than Lapointe, Power and Works Minister P. J. A. Cardin had ever fought for Canada together. The work of these three and the defeat of Duplessis was Canada's first victory of the war and made possible all the victories to follow.

But the margin had been close. The triumvirate had won by giving Quebec an absolute guarantee against conscription. If that promise were questioned in the future, the crisis would arise again.

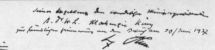

Once he had dealt with those who feared he might go too far in prosecuting the war, King turned to those who charged he was not going far enough. By the end of 1939, he had decided he must have the nation's formal vote of confidence. He needed an excuse for an early election, which the country did not want. As usual, his luck held.

Mitchell Hepburn, the ambitious Liberal Premier of Ontario, rammed through his Legislature a resolution condemning the management of the war as lacking in vigor. King instantly grasped both his danger and his opportunity—the Hepburn he detested intended to replace him, if possible, or at least to create a coalition government. So Hepburn, like Duplessis, must be eliminated.

King assembled Parliament at the end of January 1940, solemnly introduced newly-elected members and, after this masquerade, announced he could not govern under the threat of the Ontario resolution. If Ontario distrusted him, he might be compelled to dissolve Parliament before it could do any business. Hepburn had furnished only the shadow of an excuse for dissolution, since King had promised to conduct another parliamentary session. As King hoped, Conservative Leader R. J. Manion immediately furnished the substance. Leaping to his feet, he denounced King for gagging Parliament, for subverting the constitution and being "unfit to govern."

That was enough for the Prime Minister's purpose. If, he said blandly, the Opposition had no confidence in the government, the people must decide between them.

In retrospect it is easy to see that he could hardly lose the election, but he was by no means sure. The country resented the slaughter of Parliament. Manion might even make inroads into Quebec where he pledged himself against conscription and, surrendering the ancient Conservative label, now called himself the leader of the National Government party which would fight the war and forget partisan politics.

All King's fears were groundless. The nation liked but did not trust Manion. It disliked but trusted King. On March 26, 1940, the government won 181 seats, eight more than in 1935, the largest majority since Confederation, and a solid Quebec. King had his mandate. . . .

BRUCE HUTCHISON

Two views of why Canada went to war:

Hitler and the Nazi regime in Germany have pursued aggressive designs in wanton disregard of all treaty obligations and peaceful methods of adjusting international disputes. They have had resort increasingly to agencies of deception, terrorism, and violence. It is this reliance upon force, this lust for conquest, this determination to dominate throughout the world, which is the real cause of the war that threatens the freedom of mankind. Everything which free men value and cherish, on this side of the grave, is in peril.

The forces of evil have been loosed in a struggle between the pagan conception of a social order which ignores the individual and is based upon the doctrine of might, and a civilization based upon the Christian conception of the brotherhood of man, with its regard for the sanctity of contractual relations and the sacredness of human personality.

The King, speaking to his people at home and across the seas, appealed to all to make their own the cause of freedom. Canada has answered that call.

Prime Minister Mackenzie King

Why was Canada at war? Because Britain was at war, and solely for that reason. Certainly she also fought for a humane cause, against German ambitions and Nazi racism, but those motives were not decisive. Maxime Raymond [a Member of Parliament] made that point once in these cutting phrases: "In September 1938, the [Canadian] government was prepared to declare war if Britain did. Britain did not. We did not. In September 1939, Britain declared war. We declared war. It is as simple as that." Imagine a Franco-Russian war or a Franco-Polish war against the same Hitler. It is certain that Canada would remain neutral.

André Laurendeau in
La Crise de la Conscription

The black spring

Mobilization, plans for a limited war— and then the shock of the German blitzkrieg

Inevitably came the time of parting. As an army unit marches off, a little boy's hand reaches out for one last precious moment in his dad's.

The troop train began to move. The soldier drew his wife to him again. Their kiss, ineffably soft and gentle, seemed to fuse them. Then he turned and sprang on the last car. The train was crowded with faces and he was one of them, but she could not see him. She stood for a long time on the platform, her eyes fixed on the trail of smoke against the sky. Gradually there stole over her the sensation that the flame of her life had left her, and she was only a shell. She felt cold and empty. When she got home, she sat for a long time listening to the silence of the room.

Edward Meade in *Remember Me*

On a raw, gray December morning in 1939, a long troop train pulled into the CNR station in Moncton, N.B. It came out of the west and it bore men from every region of the country. As it neared the platform, the soldiers pushed the windows up and peered out from one car after another. When they spied a khaki column of artillerymen marching to join them, they began to cheer.

Scantily equipped, hastily raised, poorly trained, Canada's 1st Division was going off to war. Moncton's 8th Battery was to go with it.

As the artillerymen swung three abreast down Main Street, traffic stopped and people watched from the sidewalks. Some stood in silence. A few wept. Some cheered a bit or called out to soldiers they knew— to an officer who had for years devoted his spare time to the militia battery, to a genial giant from the slums, to a farmboy from Taylor Village, to a man with a police record, to a teen-ager leaving the prettiest girl in town.

Neither the newspapers nor the radio station had been allowed to say what was to happen. Censorship forbade it. That kept the crowds down but by the time the column reached the station itself, there were scores of people on the platform.

It was like a movie then, the soldiers already aboard shouting greetings, flirting with the girls; the 8th Battery men kissing wives and sweethearts, hugging youngsters, comforting mothers, shaking hands with old friends. Then Moncton's gunners climbed aboard, awkward because of their big packs and rifles. When the train pulled slowly away, they too were at the windows, waving and singing "Roll Out the Barrel," the favorite song of the 1st Division.

They sang or played cards or slept the remaining 200 miles to Halifax. On December 10 they sailed for Britain. It was three months to the day since Canada had declared war.

Four Canadian destroyers led that first contingent of the 1st Division—7400 men —out to sea from Halifax. Behind them, in convoy TC-1, steamed five big liners, *Aquitania, Empress of Britain, Duchess of Bedford, Monarch of Bermuda* and *Empress of Australia*. They were troopships now and soldiers rimmed their rails, cheering, waving and singing their Barrel song. The destroyers shepherded them out to a rendezvous at sea with a powerful Royal Navy escort which took them on to Britain. By year's end 15,911 soldiers had gone this way.

The navy had been actively at war for months, even as it scrambled to build up from a pathetic prewar strength of six destroyers, five minesweepers, two training vessels and 1819 officers and men.

Two weeks before the formal declaration of war, it had set plans in motion to protect the vital merchant-shipping lifeline to Britain.

Joseph Schull in his official navy history, *The Far Distant Ships:*

. . . On August 26 a one-word Admiralty telegram from London arrived in Ottawa: FUNNEL. With that message all British merchant ships passed under Admiralty control. The same transfer took place in Canada the same day. No Canadian-registered ship, no merchant ship in any Canadian port could sail without the authority of the Royal Canadian Navy.

Naval control officers faced an enormous task. All British merchant vessels in North American waters would have to be gathered in from the wide face of the sea, assembled, bunkered, stored, provided with codes and orders. Vessels of every type would have to be formed into orderly fleets, sailed at precise times and by dictated routes with the precision of a crack railway, all in absolute secrecy.

Halifax stirred once again with the grim vitality of a key port in a warring world. Ships put in, their schedules interrupted, their masters angry, demanding explanations they didn't get. Painting parties defiled clean white ships with the dun gray of war. Ancient guns were mounted on merchantmen and a few ships were issued machine guns. Captains proclaimed the absurdity of sailing freighters nose-to-tail. But beneath the grumbling was acceptance of all that had to be done.

On September 16, six days after Canada declared war, the destroyers *St. Laurent* and *Saguenay* moved out through the Hali-

fax approaches. Between them, waddling with a certain untidy gallantry, were the 18 merchant ships of Convoy HX-1, Halifax to the United Kingdom. Awaiting them in the open sea were the British cruisers *Berwick* and *York,* and beyond lay the sleety Atlantic. The bitter battle of the convoys had begun. . . .

While the military forces proceeded with the immediate tasks like convoys and dispatching troops, Ottawa was laying the foundation for the war effort as a whole.

For various reasons, it thought relatively small.

For one, there was little to build on. Not only the navy was tiny. The regular army had 4500 men, an arsenal of 29 Bren guns, 23 anti-tank rifles, five 3-inch mortars, 16 tanks and no modern artillery. The 3100-man air force had 270 largely obsolescent aircraft of 23 types. Only 19 Hurricane fighters were competent for combat. Mili-

tary industrial capacity was low. And national unity was fragile even if, for the moment, it seemed otherwise primarily because of the rejection of overseas conscription.

The result, wrote military historian Col. C. P. Stacey in *The Canadians,* was an "unimpressive beginning. Peacetime ideas of economy and treasury control were dominant, and the war program was tailored to the domestic political situation rather than the menace posed by Germany."

This attitude was soon reinforced by

an atmosphere of unreality both overseas and in the United States. In Europe, Hitler quickly crushed Poland, then stopped. Across western Europe his armies faced those of Britain and France in stalemate. They didn't attack seriously; they didn't retreat. They stood fast behind Germany's Siegfried Line and France's Maginot Line in what grew into an unbelievable hiatus, a fall and a winter of "phony war."

From the neutral United States came reports of worry in high places about the advantages Canada would gain if Britain built up Canadian industries. Britain did little to feed these fears; she kept her war-industry secrets to herself. But Col. Charles Lindbergh, a voice of American isolation, even questioned Canada's very declaration of war. "Have the Canadians," he asked, "the right to draw this hemisphere into a European war simply because they prefer the Crown of England to American independence?"

In this atmosphere, hopes multiplied in Ottawa that Canada could fight a limited war. Finance Minister J. L. Ralston publicly envisaged a program that would be "practical rather than spectacular." Prime Minister Mackenzie King spoke of protecting Canada by sending food and raw materials to Britain and building a navy and air force and a munitions industry. He made no mention of a big expeditionary force like the Canadian Corps of World War I.

Colonel Stacey gave this explanation why: "Because King feared conscription and the adverse effects it would have on national unity—and, doubtless, on his party's chances of staying in power—he was consistently hostile to a large army. He wanted Canada to develop war industry (it would enable Canadians to make ever imagined. It produced more than 131,000 aircrew personnel: Britons, New Zealanders, Australians and a majority of Canadians. But Canada also ended up with a big army, or at least one big enough to fulfill Mackenzie King's political fears.

Its nucleus was on its way overseas that raw, gray day in Moncton in December 1939.

Canada eventually fielded a relatively

Six days after Canada went to war, Convoy HX-1 left Halifax with the first 18 of 25,343 merchant ships to sail from North American ports under Canadian escort. At a conference (left) prior to each sailing, merchant captains went over orders with the navy. Troop convoys started in December 1939 when the 1st Division (left and above) was transported to Britain in five camouflaged luxury liners. One, *Aquitania,* was struck by the liner *Samaria,* outbound for New York, as the convoy entered the North Channel between Scotland and Ireland. No one was injured and damage was superficial—four lifeboats carried away—but it had been a near thing. "Troops aft on the port side were awakened by the crash," wrote Capt. Gillis Purcell. "They rushed into the corridors with life belts and gas masks, believing it was a bombing attack. In other quarters, soldiers slept through the excitement."

money and keep them safely at home); and he wanted military emphasis on the air force and navy, the services which seemed unlikely to make the big manpower demands that might result in conscription."

Indeed, said Colonel Stacey, the 1st Division might not have gone to Britain in 1939 at all if the government had known sooner of the role Canada was to play in the British Commonwealth Air Training Plan.

The original military program, announced within a week of the declaration of war, called primarily for sending the division and building an important but relatively modest air training scheme at home. Then on September 26 the British government proposed that Canada become the site of a much bigger air training scheme that would serve not only Canada but the Commonwealth. Ottawa replied enthusiastically and sought to make this the country's chief military effort.

As things turned out over the long years of war, Canada did run an air training scheme beyond anything Canadians had large army primarily because public opinion wanted one. At Ypres, the Somme, Vimy Ridge, Passchendaele, the four-division Canadian Corps of 1914-18 had covered itself with glory and made by far the country's greatest contribution to Allied victory. The memories of its record were still so vivid that many Canadians instinctively felt that the army must again play Canada's primary military role.

Even before the country was formally at war, the army had begun to mobilize two divisions. Without any special stimulus to recruiting, men enlisted faster than they could be accepted. In the first month, 58,000 enlisted in the army, far more than in either of the other two services.

The 1st Division, earmarked quickly for overseas service, raised three brigades, each made up of three infantry battalions and supporting units like Moncton's 8th Battery of artillery. Three of the nine battalions came from the regular army or Permanent Force; they were the only ones it had. The other six came from regiments of the reserve, the long-neglected Non-Permanent Active Militia.

One reserve outfit was the 1st Battalion of eastern Ontario's Hastings and Prince Edward Regiment. From Farley Mowat's *The Regiment* comes this account of its mobilization and dispatch overseas:

... Picton is a farm town, remote from the world beyond even as Prince Edward County is remote. Almost an island, the county lies with its south face to Lake Ontario, its north shore upon the placid Bay of Quinte. Picton, the largest town, partakes of quietude that in summer is close to somnolence.

The Picton Armories, a rococo monstrosity with red-brick face and foolish little battle towers, has looked out on the main street for decades. Within the iron-

Around noon a boy bicycled down the sleepy main street and stopped at the Armories' door. The telegram he carried read: "Lt. Col. S. Young—KM2—Mobilize." It shattered the peace of Hastings and Prince Edward counties.

Lt. Col. Sherman Young grasped his telephone and he and the adjutant set off a flurry of calls that tied up the local exchange and threw the operator into confusion. In Marmora, Trenton, Madoc and other towns, men threw down shop aprons and stripped off overalls. From the Regiment's five company offices in five towns the telephone calls multiplied. Men drove to back-country farms to pass the news. In poolrooms and beer parlors other men

Within two hours, mobilization had begun. On a beach on Lake Ontario, a 22-year-old company sergeant major was dallying with a pretty girl. A stranger approached and muttered half a dozen words. The young man leaped to his feet, abandoned love, and drove off with the stranger, leaving his maiden marooned and far from home. An hour later, in full uniform, he reported for duty.

In a Trenton rooming house two men who had come into an unexpected windfall were drinking it. When they heard the news they were down to the last half-dozen pints. They eyed each other speculatively, then without a word picked up their unopened bottles and marched off to enlist.

studded doors a drill hall stretches into dimness. Here, between the wars, 20 or 30 volunteers, the men of C company, had gathered one night a week for lectures on how to dig a trench, bayonet an enemy, read a map, keep a rifle clean. The rest of the time the mausoleum stood empty and silent except when the townsfolk needed space for a dance or a chicken social.

On September 2, 1939, it was a hot and dusty vault. In the orderly room a fly buzzed with a shocking resonance in a silence that had become almost tangible.

were silent for one long instant, then crowded to the doors. The word soon reached every corner of the counties.

At the Picton headquarters, men were stunned by the magnitude of the task. In less than 20 days the unit was to turn itself from a peacetime group of 100 civilians into a battalion of more than 900 soldiers. Each man had to be documented, medically examined, provided a place to sleep and three meals a day, given uniforms and boots, paid, and set about the tasks that would make him a fighting soldier.

On a distant farm a man of late middle age heard over the party line. His son drove him to the nearest company headquarters; he could not drive himself, having lost most of his sight and most of his lungs to mustard gas in 1918. He wept when they gently turned him away. The son enlisted.

Men born in Trenton, in Picton, in Bancroft soon heard the news in places as far distant as Wyoming and British Columbia. Before dawn, telegrams were pouring in: "Returning first train east stop hold a

Without even uniforms, let alone modern weapons and ammunition, Canadian Army recruits learn rifle drill—as a well-equipped German armored division, after helping conquer Poland, prepares for the spring assault against France. Army battledress, when it arrived, was in two sizes, wrote the Rev. R. M. Hickey of the North Shore (New Brunswick) Regiment: too big (his trousers) and too small (the jacket they gave him). "A wedge cap three sizes too small completed my trousseau."

place." One man in Toronto, having found his first job in three years, spent his $2 advance pay on gasoline for his motorcycle. In the morning he was waiting at the Picton Armories' door.

Why did they rally so? Not out of the empty patriotism of a bygone age—that much is certain. Perhaps some came simply to escape hard times, some to escape the consequences of failure, some only to escape boredom, ugliness and misery at home. But most came because they couldn't help it, because the Regiment itself

had meaning for them that few could have expressed. They came because it was the hour of their pride, the hour of need.

In Trenton a man who had been a railroad hand now stood behind the cold-storage building, wearing the puttees, breeches and stiff jacket of 1918, shouting drill orders. His platoon wore bright sweaters, jackets, flannel trousers, grease-stained overalls. They carried broomsticks or pieces of wood shaped to resemble the Lee Enfield, for there were not even enough antiquated rifles.

It was a time of enthusiasm such as men seldom know. One sergeant major solved his boot problem by appearing on parade wearing crimson slippers. Most men wore civilian shoes until these disintegrated; then, out of their own pockets, bought farm boots from the Picton stores.

What uniforms were available, from bins where they had lain since 1919, were moth-eaten and shabby, and they never fitted. Some men were issued khaki breeches while their comrades received the tunics. Tailors worked miracles but on parade

25

most men looked like comic-opera soldiers.

A few ancient Lewis machine guns, long since replaced on active service by Brens, represented the sole "heavy" armament. On that memorable day when a real Bren was produced, officers guarding it like a royal personage, the men could only stare in awe in the presence of a shining vision.

Carpenters and masons converted the dungeonlike cellars of the Armories to accommodate nearly 1000 soldiers. Not far away the Tecumseh Canning Factory was converted into a barracks. In early October the outlying companies flooded into Picton and the little town turned khaki overnight. Now the Regiment was whole, its fragments gathered in. There was a formal parade, and for the first time the commanding officer stood at the head of the Regiment. It was also the first time most of the men had participated in anything like it, and they were deeply stirred. Dimly they perceived the existence of that living entity which had no shape and no physical existence, but an infinite capacity to stir men's emotions and claim their loyalty. The spirit of the Regiment was heady stuff. Shortly after that first parade these volunteers were asked to sign a declaration expressing their willingness to go overseas. They were offered time to think it over. "Time, hell!" they cried. "We'll sign the damn thing now!"

The first battledress arrived and the lucky few who received them were envied mightily. The first rifles were issued, stripped, reassembled, stripped again. The first paydays came.

A regimental sergeant major imported from the Permanent Force trained the handful of militia corporals and sergeants and those new soldiers who seemed a little brighter than their fellows. These became the instructors.

One October morning a drill instructor, after much trouble, maneuvered a company into a marching column. Now a company being drilled can be a frightful thing to a nervous commander, for once on the move it does not halt, nor slow, until he so instructs it. That day the instructor saw his column coming perilously close to a building, and in panic he ordered a right turn without pausing to consider his own relative position. As one, the 150 marching men turned on him. He tried to scramble out of the way but tripped and fell, and the company stolidly marched over him without so much as breaking step.

The fact the Regiment was learning next to nothing about how to fight was not of great importance. It was learning to be itself. Off duty, there was acute individual awareness of the state of a man's clothes, the press in his trousers, the cleanliness of his web equipment and, for the lucky ones, the gleam of a cap badge. Badges were a treasure, the one element which could distinguish a man of the Regiment from any other soldier in the army, and they were almost unobtainable. A brisk trade in illicit copies went on, and three or four cents' worth of stamped brass fetched as high as $10. It was a good sign.

The Regiment's spirit soon grew to need something concrete to give it form. A mascot was required. George Ponsford had been eyeing a huge pewter statue of an Indian, presumably Tecumseh himself, that stood in faded majesty on the roof of the canning factory barracks. Close on midnight, Saturday December 16, using a long ladder, George and another man climbed to the roof. The Indian had stood at his post for three decades and it took much labor with a huge pipe wrench to free him. When he was liberated, he slowly keeled over, almost crushing his kidnappers.

Then a third soldier unexpectedly arrived, much the worse for wear, stumbled against the ladder, accepted the challenge and clawed up to the roof. The two men with their trophy were hard put to prevent first the Indian, then the drunk, from plunging over the parapet. Slowly they lowered their two charges to the ground.

Possession of the Indian was one thing, his disposal quite another. But, having bribed the sentry to look the other way, Ponsford and his companion dragged the Chief, complete with spear, to the sergeants' mess, and there set him up with a bottle of whisky in his arms.

In the morning the long-awaited word arrived from Ottawa: the Regiment was to entrain that night, its destination Halifax. That same day the Indian was officially enrolled, issued identification tags, and secreted in the battalion baggage. They named him "Little Chief," in defiance of his great stature and formidable weight, and he became much more than a mere mascot. He became an institution.

On the morning of New Year's Day 1940, a convoy made its way up Scotland's River Clyde. On the decks of HM Transport *Or-*

mande the men of the Regiment thronged the rails.

The Atlantic crossing had been a trying one. The wet and piercing cold of northern seas had penetrated the crowded troop decks with their makeshift bunks and seamen's hammocks; *Ormande* possessed air conditioning to guard against the equatorial sun, but no heating. Neither did she have an easy motion. Most passengers had been seasick all the way across.

There had been near riots when the English cooks served herring at each succeeding breakfast—herring whose sunken eyes stared balefully up from the heaving tables of the messdecks. One man, unable to face the kippers one morning, made an urgent

The Hastings and Prince Edward Regiment found a mascot—a pewter statue —and called it "Little Chief." In Lt. Col. Harry Salmon it later acquired a ruthless commander who restored the unit's pride and didn't mind at all being called "Iron Guts."

dash up the companionway—to be met head-on by a large, cold sea on its way down. Washed back into the messdeck, he bellowed: "Take out, boys, take out! The son of a bitch has sunk!"

Grousing and grumbling, the troops were almost a mob by the time the anchor dropped off Greenock. Soon they boarded trains for southern England and Maida Barracks in Aldershot, Hampshire.

The Regiment found Aldershot a city of frigid barrack blocks with the smell of antiquity and an atmosphere as bleak as Depression labor camps. There were no provisions to defeat the winter cold save for tiny open fireplaces, for which there was no coal.

That first month in England was a dark one. Had officers and non-commissioned officers been able to take hold, all might have been well. But the whole military situation in England was chaotic. Shortages were so chronic they'd become accepted. A single typewriter was issued to the battalion for staff work. Three ancient cars were the transport. A few Bren light machine guns became the main armament. There were insufficient clothes and boots, and the weather was frigid. At one time 300 men had influenza. The food was abominable; men who had taken good victuals for granted were revolted by musty mutton, by Brussels sprouts, by sausages which contained so much bread that they wondered whether to use mustard or marmalade. Mail didn't arrive. Morale dropped lower. Men began to go absent without leave. At a garrison church parade the unit appeared to such poor advantage that the divisional commander called the CO on the carpet. There were ugly rumors the unit was to be used as a work battalion or —bottom of the scale—turned into a pioneer battalion.

Like an unhappy adolescent, sullen, confused and miserable, the Regiment needed a strong man's hand. It got it. On January 30, Lt. Col. Harry Salmon, a Permanent Force soldier who might well have been insulted by the order to take over a militia battalion, took command. Certainly the Regiment was grossly insulted by his appointment. Nevertheless, this man was the catalyst needed to transform magnificent promise into reality. He knew the way, and he was ruthless. A number of officers and senior NCOs were on their way home within a week. Salmon's guiding principle was simple. He believed the pri-

vate soldier was never wrong. If the soldier got in trouble, it was the fault of his officers or NCOs. If officers expected the support of their troops in battle, they had to give the men service during training, and give it unstintingly.

Even Salmon's bitterest enemies came to admit there was reason for his methods; they remembered incidents such as an encounter between Lt. "Fats" Ruttan and one of his men, in Salmon's presence.

The day after Salmon took command, the portly and amiable Ruttan was to escort him through the transport lines. The young lieutenant had warned his men that Salmon was a fire-eater and begged them to play the part of parade-ground soldiers for a while at least. With the tour almost completed, Ruttan beheld one of his drivers approaching. Anticipating a smart salute, he got ready to return it just as smartly. The private, hands deep in his pockets, ambled up and stopped. "Say, Fats," he asked, "you got a match?"

The entire Regiment soon recognized the tiger in their midst. As one private wrote to a friend: "Before that b------came we'd have thought any guy was nuts if he moved at the double. Now if anyone just says your name above a whisper you start to run like you had a bayonet in your rear—just in case old 'Iron Guts' happens to come by!"

But Salmon was not only a breaker, he was a maker of men. The first resentment changed to sullen resignation, then quickened to a stubborn refusal to be beaten by this martinet. This was followed by an awakening pride in the miracle that was taking place. Spit and polish again became matters of individual pride and concern. Men growled at slackers. Little Chief, who had stood at the prow of the troopship crossing the Atlantic and sustained severe abdominal injuries from heavy seas, was taken to a metalsmith and repaired. Resplendent in a new coat of paint, he stood on a dais and critically accepted salutes. The basic training so haphazardly attempted in Canada was begun anew. Men learned for the second time—and this time it stuck.

Even so, they learned only the principles of soldiering, not how to fight a war. The combat training of every regiment in England was still a farce. Each day the companies marched to the broad plains beyond Aldershot and learned about war as it had been. The 1918 pamphlet of field

engineering was the Bible. Fascines, fire steps, revetments, traverses, communication trenches—these were the key words. Miles of trenches grew and spread across Salisbury Plain and the pathetic futility of it went unnoticed. . . .   FARLEY MOWAT

Then the phony war ended. The German Army marched, crushing all opposition. It soon made a mockery of the complacencies of Ottawa. The moment of truth had arrived.

If the western front had held, the 1st Division might well have joined the British Expeditionary Force in France. Instead it lived that memorable spring in disappointment and frustration and finally in spectacular folly. In *Ordeal by Fire,* Ralph Allen tells what happened:

. . . In April, after the German invasion of Norway, the British War Office decided to seize Narvik and Trondheim. Two Canadian battalions, the Princess Patricias and the Loyal Edmontons, were fitted with winter gear, piped aboard trains at Aldershot, drawn up before waiting ships in Scotland—then sent back to Aldershot, their mission canceled. In the end, the War Office dispatched to Norway an inadequate all-British expedition, which was soon withdrawn. One result was the resignation of Neville Chamberlain as Prime Minister in favor of Winston Churchill.

In May Germany struck to the west. Belgium fell. Holland fell. France reeled. With the shattered British Army falling back on its last beachhead in France, its destruction apparently only days away, the War Office summoned the 1st Division's commander, Maj. Gen. A. G. L. McNaughton. The British, cut off from the main body of the French by the pursuing Germans, desperately needed protection for the road and railway on their exposed southwestern flank. McNaughton was asked to provide this, with a British brigade already at Calais and reinforcements from his own division.

By noon May 23 the three battalions of the 1st Canadian Brigade were ready to leave for Dover. By midnight McNaughton himself was across the Channel reconnoitering at Calais and Dunkirk.

He found the situation precarious and confused, and while the brigade waited, he hurried back to London. He told Sir Edmund Ironside, Chief of the Imperial General Staff, that he didn't think the small Canadian reinforcement could materially improve the situation. There seemed little point in throwing the Canadians into a mass of dispirited soldiers and civilian refugees.

The operation was called off. Two days later it was on again. It was called off a second time after McNaughton said his objection "was not based on any timidity but rather on a desire to get the best possible value for the effort made." He added that a brigade group "could go tonight complete with artillery if the Prime Minister and war cabinet decide it should be sent." After this second cancellation Lord Gort, commander of the besieged and retreating force at Dunkirk, appealed for at least one and if possible two Canadian brigades. But Churchill, who had favored sending the Canadians, reluctantly consented to abandoning the project.

Yet while the first ships of a brave and motley fleet nosed into Dunkirk to rescue the British Expeditionary Force, Churchill was planning to send another force to France at once for another purpose.

With 340,000 British and Allied soldiers streaming back across the Channel, disorganized and unarmed, their transport smoking on the beaches of France, there were only two divisions in the United Kingdom ready and equipped to fight. One was the Canadian division, the other the Scottish 52nd. Churchill proposed to send both to France to try to stiffen the crumbling French armies and, more importantly, prevent the utter collapse of the French government and the morale of the civilian population.

It was a far more desperate undertaking than the abandoned sally into Dunkirk. The two divisions, with the remnants of two others trickling back from Dunkirk,

were to deploy across 150 miles of front at the neck of the Brittany peninsula. The object was to delay, somehow, the westward rush of four German armies long enough to permit the fleeing French to rally and form a redoubt and thus save the Allies at least a foothold in Europe.

On June 2, Lt. Gen. Sir Alan Brooke, just back from Dunkirk, was appointed commander of this second British Expeditionary Force. Brooke, who was to become Chief of the Imperial General Staff, wrote: "This was one of my blackest moments. To be sent back into that cauldron with a new force to participate in the final stages of French disintegration was indeed a dark prospect."

When McNaughton had digested Brooke's orders, he drafted an operations instruction which contained the laconic estimate: "A division may have to hold up to 50 miles of front." Then he had his staff bring the division's war diaries up to date and send them to London. As Colonel Stacey wrote: "The 1st Division was, in effect, making its last will and testament— as it had good reasons to do." . . .

RALPH ALLEN

The 1st Battalion of the Hastings and Prince Edward Regiment was one of three that got into France with Brig. Armand Smith's 1st Brigade; the division's other two brigades were stopped before they

On May 10, 1940, the day the Germans invaded Holland, Belgium and Luxembourg by air and land, Winston Churchill became Prime Minister of Britain. "I was conscious of a profound sense of relief," he wrote in *The Gathering Storm.* "At last I had the authority to give directions over the whole scene. I felt as if I were walking with Destiny, and that all my past life had been but a preparation for this hour and for this trial." Three days later, in the House of Commons, Churchill said: "I have nothing to offer but blood, toil, tears and sweat." The goal was victory— "victory at all costs, victory in spite of all terror, victory, however long and hard the road may be; for without victory, there is no survival."

could sail. Farley Mowat takes up the story:

. . . The whole of northeast France was in German hands and the panzer columns were driving southwest, almost unopposed by the disintegrating remnants of the French Army. The Regiment's vehicles had been ordered to proceed independently to France. It was a proud convoy that moved to the embarkation port— more than 50 bright new trucks just received from Canada, ten Bren carriers and a dozen motorcycles. The transport carried with it the unit's two heavy mortars, records and files, battle ammunition, reserve rations, quartermaster's stores and nearly 100 men. It also carried the intelligence files and the unit's entire stock of French maps.

Three days later, when the rifle companies boarded a train in Aldershot, each soldier was equipped with 50 rounds of rifle ammunition and rations for two days. So they went off to war.

On the morning of June 13, the spring sun beat pleasantly down on Plymouth while the Regiment formed up on the station platform in the center of a wildly enthusiastic crowd of civilians. The atmosphere was feverish with false optimism.

Two French ships were at the jetty, one a decrepit passenger boat, *Ville d'Angier,* the other a dirty freighter unloading strawberries for the London luxury trade

—while, almost within sound and sight, France shuddered in the agony of death.

The master of *Ville d'Angier,* an irascible Breton who spoke no English, was not certain he wanted a load of soldiers. As he and the officers argued, the men filched strawberries, smearing faces and uniforms with juice. Lady Astor bustled about dispensing comforts to the troops. Pausing beside one young soldier, she demanded to know his age and, being told he was 19, raised her voice indignantly. "Such children being sent to war! I shall see it is stopped at once!" The boy squirmed.

After some hours the captain of *Ville d'Angier* was persuaded to allow the troops on board, but his attitude remained that of a master whose ship has been chartered for an excursion.

At dawn they came to Brest, and chaos. The town, filling with refugees, was already cluttered with slovenly French soldiers, amiable and without discipline. Marching up the dusty streets, the Canadians were appalled. No flags waved, no bands played. Civilians went about their business.

The military organization was beyond confusion. It was more luck than anything which led the unit aboard its train bound for a point 200 miles inland, where the 1st Brigade was to concentrate. On the afternoon of June 14, the train puffed hesitantly forward, making short dashes between stations, then halting as if to regain courage. In the hot, crowded compartments men drank the cheap wine which flowed at each halting place.

Hour by hour, but unknowingly, they approached the thrusting columns of the panzer divisions. No one gave much thought to the intended purpose of the journey. Each man still had only 50 rounds of ammunition. Several cases of blank training cartridges were in the baggage car.

Their ignorance was appalling. No one had informed the Regiment that the Germans had bypassed Paris, even then entering a state of siege.

The train crawled on and at dawn came into Laval, almost 200 miles inland. There it was halted by a frenzied station master. "Are these Canadians insane?" he cried. "Do they not know Paris has fallen and all resistance is at an end? *Les Boches* are only 40 miles away."

The Canadians did not know, and the shock was so great that at first it could not be believed. France had capitulated. Panzers were even then bearing down on the Channel ports. The CO held a conference. The engineer uncoupled his engine, ran it to the rear of the train, and coupled up again. In this shattering moment when fantasy ended there was no confusion and no dismay. In this, its first vital emergency, the unit responded well.

The holiday mood was at an end. As the train retreated, the face of the country underwent a terrifying change. Every little station was jammed with refugees in panic. A mob crowded against the train at every halt. Laden with absurd articles of

household furniture, most had neglected to think of food. The troops gave their emergency rations to the hungry civilians. Colonel Salmon attempted to stop this dangerous generosity, but was seen to pass his own tin of bully beef to an old farmer and his hungry daughter.

Soldiers manned Bren guns on the train roof to repel expected air attacks. They stared back as if to catch the first glimpse of armored spearheads. When they reached Brest, they found it a hopeless muddle. The men were unloaded along the harbor shore. While the officers tried to find shipping, soldiers waited in the hot sun. Many swam, until a German plane swung over the harbor and the shrapnel from anti-aircraft shells began to hiss down.

Toward evening the companies marched aboard a little Channel pleasure steamer, *Canterbury Belle*. She had been designed to carry 700 passengers but more and more troops swarmed aboard until,

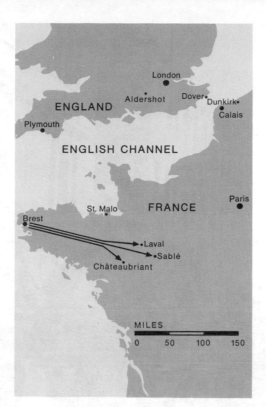

A bomb explodes (left of center) and soldiers dive for cover as German planes and artillery attack the British Expeditionary Force at Dunkirk. From May 27 to June 4 the Royal Navy and a ragtag fleet of small boats rescued 340,000 soldiers, including 120,000 French. After Dunkirk, in a desperate bid to halt the Germans, the Scottish 52nd and 1st Canadian divisions were ordered to Brittany. The Canadians went from Aldershot to Plymouth; two brigades were stopped there but the 1st Brigade reached Brest at dawn June 14, the day the Germans entered undefended Paris. With the French Army disintegrating, the brigade was ordered out after penetrating inland. The Hastings and Prince Edward Regiment's train was turned around at Laval, the Royal Canadian Regiment's near Châteaubriant; they returned to Brest and reached Plymouth early June 17. The 48th Highlanders got as far as Sablé, turned back and sailed from St. Malo on the 16th.

by dawn, there were 3000 — wounded Belgians, parts of French units and two thirds of the 1st Brigade.

A strange inertia settled over the harbor. The war in France was finished, and it seemed this retreating fragment of an army had lost the volition to make the final move to safety. Inexplicably, all that day *Canterbury Belle* lay in Brest and men waited for a new Dunkirk.

sistence, kept its guns out of German hands.

Roberts had explicit orders to destroy his guns but could not bring himself to do so while there was any chance of saving them. He swore he could load them in an hour. The military authorities ashore, thinking he would never finish, gave him two. When the deadline came Roberts had loaded all of his own 25-pounders—and

English women cheered men of the 1st Canadian Division as they marched to ships that would take them to Brittany in a futile 11th-hour move to save France from total defeat. But there was no stopping the Germans. Refugees (below) fled along the tree-lined roads of northern France and town after town, including historic Rouen (right), was overrun. "The long night of barbarism," as Churchill called it, descended on Europe and only Britain and the Commonwealth stood against the Germans. "We are fighting *by* ourselves alone," Churchill said in a world broadcast in July, "but we are not fighting *for* ourselves alone." He pledged that, no matter how long the ordeal, "we shall seek no terms, we shall tolerate no parley; we may show mercy—we shall ask for none." The immediate task of General McNaughton's Canadians was defense of Britain. Four years later they would help restore France's freedom. One city they'd liberate was Rouen.

Then in the evening she made steam for home, and at dawn June 17 the Regiment entrained at Plymouth, for Aldershot. . . .

FARLEY MOWAT

The Hastings' transport section had penetrated deep into Brittany in its own carnival of confusion and had finally returned to the Brest area. There it had been ordered to destroy the Regiment's equipment and vehicles. They were faced with the problem of Little Chief, the 500-pound mascot. There wasn't room to take him back so they buried him in a roadside ditch. Eventually they reached England in a Channel pleasure craft. "At least," sighed Sgt. Basil Smith, "we saw a bit of France."

The whole brigade had been lucky. It is a remarkable fact, says Colonel Stacey, that only six Canadians were left behind across the Channel. One had been killed in an accident. Four were interned but escaped and made their way to England in 1941. The sixth remained a prisoner of war. There were heavy losses in equipment and vehicles but the 1st Field Regiment, through Lt. Col. J. H. Roberts' per-

a number of Bofors anti-aircraft guns that belonged to other units.

"Most of the Canadians," wrote Ralph Allen, "arrived at Aldershot quite unaware of the narrowness of their escape, complaining hotly about the lunacy of the higher brass. But that summer of 1940 soon brought home the unbelievable truth: Britain might be conquered by a hostile army for the first time since William of Normandy. If this were to be prevented, the job might fall squarely on the Canadians, the closest approach to a mobile, armed and fully manned ground division in all the British Isles."

General McNaughton said in a letter: "We are now squarely set for what I have long thought was the important task, the defense of these islands."

Over France

Stan Turner, whose first two kills as a fighter pilot were over Dunkirk on May 25, 1940, was a group captain in command of an RCAF wing in northwest Europe by the end of the war. He fought in the battles of Britain, Malta and the North African desert and was a wing leader in Italy. One of the few Allied airmen to fly in so many theaters of war, Turner shot down at least 14 planes, won the DSO and the DFC and Bar.

On June 14, 1940, as the Canadian Army's 1st Brigade moved out of Brest to try to form a last-ditch redoubt in Brittany, another group of Canadians flew their Hurricanes into Nantes, some 100 miles southeast. They were pilots of the RAF's 242 "All-Canadian" Fighter Squadron—every man a prewar volunteer who had gone to England to enlist. One was FO. Stan Turner of Toronto, who in three weeks over France had already destroyed the five aircraft that qualified him as an "ace." A reminiscence:

. . . By the time we reached Nantes we were pretty bushed. Although the squadron had done well—we'd shot down 30 aircraft—we had also been badly mauled. Seven pilots had been killed, two wounded, one had had a breakdown and our CO was missing. Most of the patrols were now being led by myself or Willie McKnight, who had just won a DFC. Willie was 21, a wiry, dark-haired little guy from Calgary, and absolutely fearless.

After the Dunkirk evacuation we'd been sent to France to operate from an airfield south of Paris. The battle by then was so confused it was often difficult to tell friend from foe. One evening, just before dusk, my wingman and I went after a Dornier bomber. It was too far ahead to catch, but by the time we turned back, we didn't have enough fuel to reach our base at Châteaudun. We landed in a wheat field and, as we climbed out in the dim light, a bunch of French farm workers sprang out of the hedgerows and came at us, yelling and brandishing scythes and sticks. It was touch-and-go to convince them we were on their side. Another night we had trouble with fifth columnists. A couple slipped past our guards and turned on the yellow lights in the Hurricane cockpits. We couldn't see the glow from the ground, but it was visible from the air. Jerry came over and dropped incendiaries, but fortunately there was no damage.

On June 14—the day the Germans held a victory parade in Paris—we flew to Nantes on the west coast with two other squadrons. Our job was to fly cover over the evacuation ports of Brest and Bordeaux, keep tab on German movements and destroy supply dumps and other targets. Our ground crews had been evacuated so we had to fuel and arm our own aircraft, do spot servicing, then get back in the air. At night we slept under our planes and took turns on guard. One evening we went into Nantes, and soon wished we hadn't. As we came out of a bar we were sniped at—probably by another fifth columnist. We beat it back to the airfield and found the canteen tent abandoned.

It was loaded with liquor, so we had a party. Willie McKnight, I remember, refused to drink from a glass. Whenever he needed a drink, he reached for a bottle, smashed the neck and took it straight.

The day France surrendered, French soldiers set up machine guns along our runway. "All aircraft are grounded," an officer told us. "There's to be no more fighting from French soil." We saw red. A brawl was threatening when I felt a tap on my shoulder. Behind me was a British Army officer, who had come out of the blue. "Go ahead and take off," he said, "I'll look after these chaps." He pointed to his platoon which had set up machine guns covering the French weapons. The French officer shrugged and left.

Time was running out. The Germans were over the Loire River and heading toward us. On June 18 we flew a last patrol over Brest and made a couple of sorties inland. Flying back from one, I saw a small British armored car racing down a road. It stopped at a crossroads, seemed to hesitate a moment, then took up a defensive position. It was all alone. The only troops near were in a German armored column advancing toward the crossroads.

At 1 p.m. we got orders to evacuate—the second to last RAF squadron to leave France. We destroyed several Hurricanes that no longer had pilots and then set fire to the canteen. All that booze—it was heartbreaking. We armed and fueled our aircraft and climbed in. We were a wild-looking bunch, unshaven, scruffily dressed, exhausted, grimed with dirt and smoke. We were also in a pretty Bolshie mood. After weeks of fighting we were all keyed up. Now that the whole shebang was over, there was a tremendous let-down feeling. As we headed for England we felt not so much relief as anger. We wanted to hit something, and there was nothing to hit. The skies were empty—not a German in sight—and the ground below looked deserted too. It was all very sunny and peaceful, and quite unreal. As if the war didn't exist. But we knew the real war had only just begun. . . .

STAN TURNER

All available destroyers

**From across the sea, a desperate cry for help—
and a tiny Canadian Navy answers as best it can**

For three hours the Canadian minister to France, Lt. Col. Georges P. Vanier, had been tossing on the Bay of Biscay, his head swimming as oil smoke belched from the stack of a dirty little sardine boat named *Le Cygne*. "Never," he was to say later, "have I seen a boat which looked less like a swan in line or in color. Never have I been as ill."

In *Le Cygne* with Vanier were Sir Ronald Campbell, British ambassador to France, and Colin Bain Marais, the South African minister. It was June 1940, France had surrendered to Germany, and the three envoys were trying to get to Britain.

"The Canadian government had authorized me to go," recalled Vanier when he was Governor-General years later, "but it was my duty to choose the proper moment. I decided not to remain after the armistice as Canada was continuing the fight, so I asked to take leave of Marshal Pétain, the new Prime Minister. He was too tired and I was received by his deputy, General Weygand.

" 'General,' I said, 'I am leaving France.' He asked why. I answered, 'My government is not keen that I should be captured by the Germans.' (Nor, as a matter of fact, was I.) I inquired, 'Can you give me a guarantee that the Germans will not come here to Bordeaux?' He said, 'I cannot. The Germans may come at any time.' "

Campbell, Bain Marais and Vanier left for Arcachon, on the Biscay coast some 40 miles south of Bordeaux. There they boarded *Le Cygne* and headed for the open sea, where they hoped to rendezvous with the British cruiser *Galatea*.

After three hours of wet and miserable waiting, and no sign of the cruiser, they were about to return to shore.

"Then," said Vanier, "the destroyer appeared. When I looked up after being hoisted aboard, I recognized an old friend, Comdr. Wallace Creery.

35

Three young lieutenant commanders (left) were captains of the first Canadian destroyers to reach Britain: Harry DeWolf of *St. Laurent,* H. N. Lay of *Restigouche* (opposite page) and J. C. Hibbard of *Skeena.* They left Halifax on such short notice, DeWolf says, that "I wasn't even allowed to phone my wife." *St. Laurent* rescued some 850 men after the sinking of the British liner *Arandora Star*—and learned most were enemy prisoners. Lt. Col. Georges P. Vanier, the Canadian minister to France (below, inspecting French troops), was evacuated by a fourth destroyer, *Fraser.*

"'What are you doing here, Creery?' I asked. 'This is my ship,' said Creery. And I replied, 'What, is this a Canadian ship?'"

She was, the destroyer *Fraser*. She was there in response to a desperate cry from Britain for help in the face of mounting disaster and the likelihood of a German attempt to invade England. To retain mastery of the English Channel was the task of the Royal Navy. It needed all the help it could get.

From London to Ottawa late in May had gone an urgent request for "all available destroyers." The cabinet agreed, even though it meant virtually stripping Canada herself of naval defenses. The navy mustered four destroyers. Joseph Schull, in *The Far Distant Ships,* told of their departure:

. . . In Halifax, on the afternoon of May 24, *Restigouche, Skeena* and *St. Laurent* were preparing to go to sea on an unscheduled voyage. Leaves had been canceled, libertymen recalled. The messdeck "buzz" gave promise only of another local convoy run. But, in early evening, as the destroyers nosed out of harbor, men on watch noted that there was no convoy.

The explanation came several hours later. *Restigouche, Skeena* and *St. Laurent* were on their way to Britain. *Assiniboine* and *Ottawa,* in refit, would not be operational until mid-June. *Saguenay* could not make the crossing; she, too, badly needed refit. *Fraser,* en route to Bermuda, had been ordered to continue, refuel at Bermuda and proceed to the United Kingdom.

The first wartime passage of the three destroyers was uneventful but scarcely monotonous. By day and night the men went through intensive air raid and anti-submarine exercises. When they secured at Plymouth on June 1 the evacuation of Dunkirk was at its height.

Fraser, from Bermuda, reached Plymouth on June 3. A week later the four RCN destroyers joined the great RN force fending off U-boats and E-boats and salvaging the melancholy remnants of defeat as German infantry and armor poured into France.

Restigouche and *St. Laurent,* on June 9, saw from 30 miles out the flames of Le Havre rising 600 feet into the night sky. On June 11 they were off St. Valéry-en-Caux near Dieppe, helping a British destroyer embark wounded. Part of the Brit-

ish 51st Division was holding a six-mile line in the vicinity but reported itself "in no immediate need of evacuation."

About 8 a.m. on the 12th five salvos splashed into the water 100 yards from *St. Laurent* and *Restigouche.* A German battery had taken up position on the cliffs behind St. Valéry. The destroyers engaged the battery, but were unable to observe the fall of their shells behind the cliff. For the first time, Canadian ships had exchanged fire with the enemy. . . .

JOSEPH SCHULL

On June 21, the day of France's degrading surrender at Compiègne, *Fraser* was sent far down the west coast, near the Franco-Spanish frontier, to land a Royal Navy evacuation party and to patrol off St. Jean-de-Luz, one of the last remaining exits from France. At dawn on the 23rd she was ordered 90 miles north to Arcachon to pick up some diplomats.

"Shortly before noon," Rear Admiral Creery wrote years later, "as I started to turn *Fraser* toward the entrance to Arcachon, a lookout shouted 'Object in the

water bearing red one-double-oh, about half a mile, might be a fishing boat.' It was a sardine boat with the party we sought. We rigged scramble nets and the boat came alongside. Whenever the roll of the sea caused its deck to rise flush with ours one of the party would jump and be seized by a sailor clinging to the nets. Thus we got them all on board one by one. Colonel Vanier's artificial leg, a legacy of World War I, was no small hindrance to the acrobatic feat required of him. However, it was achieved without mishap."

"I was so seasick," recalled Vanier, "that the problem of how to transfer to the destroyer hardly interested me. I did not take a very active part in the transfer. I was treated as if I were a precious bundle to be conveyed somehow from boat to ship.

"*Fraser* later put us aboard *Galatea,* which next morning turned toward England at 30 knots. At 3 a.m. I went on deck. A full moon shed a silver light over the sea and the sky was clear, save to the east, where great clouds like a symbol were weaving a shroud over France. Our victory was her only hope that she would rise again from the humiliation of defeat."

Fraser returned to St. Jean-de-Luz and was joined by *Restigouche* and several British destroyers.

The tumult of evacuation was fully under way. Boatloads of defeated soldiers and destitute civilians streamed out to liners, tramps, trawlers and pleasure craft jostling in the rough waters of the harbor. Some destroyers threaded dangerously among the merchant ships, marshaling them into convoys for escort to England. Other destroyers zigzagged outside on anti-submarine patrol. In the dreary 48 hours of the St. Jean-de-Luz evacuation 16,000 soldiers escaped.

Admiral Creery described the final evacuation:

. . . The Germans occupied Bordeaux and swept on south. By the morning of June 25, they were within 25 miles of St. Jean-de-Luz. The French, to conform to the armistice terms, had advised that all evacuation must cease by 1 p.m.

Fraser had been ordered to remain in harbor during the final evacuation but we had difficulty finding a safe anchorage. We had to re-anchor twice. On the last attempt we held firm—for a reason we were not to discover until later. We decided to remain where we were until all evacuees had been embarked and until the return of Sub-Lt. William Landymore, who had been sent away in our motorboat to try to persuade some Belgian trawler skippers to sail to England instead of Spain.

Suddenly the officer of the watch, who had a slight stammer, exclaimed, "G-G-Good G-G-God, there's a g-g-gun!"

I looked where he was pointing. On a hill a small force had appeared with a field gun and a tank. We couldn't make out their nationality, but ships in harbor are sitting ducks and there was only one thing to do.

We ordered the merchant ships to proceed to sea and had to watch several boatloads of evacuees turn sadly back to shore.

Our motorboat returned and Landymore sent the boat's crew swarming up the falls but remained in the boat himself. I was anxious to go to action stations and weigh anchor but it took all hands to hoist the boat. All was going reasonably well until a steadying line parted, the boat canted sharply outboard and Landymore was catapulted into the sea.

At one time between the wars, says Rear Adm. L. W. Murray, he felt the Canadian public "would be quite pleased if someone would take the whole navy out to the middle of the ocean and sink it without trace or memory." Only a tiny force survived the government's peacetime economies but A. V. Alexander, First Lord of the Admiralty, told the captains of four Canadian destroyers sent to Britain in 1940: "You come at a time when destroyers are worth their weight in gold." This photo of *Fraser,* commanded by Comdr. W. B. Creery, was made the morning of June 25 as she evacuated soldiers and civilians from St. Jean-de-Luz near the Franco-Spanish border. The Germans were 25 miles away. Twelve hours later, after colliding with a British cruiser, *Fraser* sank with a loss of 47 men.

Just as this happened I was told the anchor had apparently fouled a cable on the bottom of the harbor and could not be hoisted. And the officer of the watch reported there now were several guns on the hill, all apparently trained on us!

So we fished Landymore out of the water, slipped our cable and departed in haste if not in dignity.

The merchant ships headed for England, escorted by several RN destroyers. *Fraser* and *Restigouche* were ordered to join the British cruiser *Calcutta* in a sweep

north in search of an enemy ship of which there had been a vague report. No enemy was sighted and toward dusk the flag officer turned his small force toward home. . . .   W. B. CREERY

Joseph Schull continues the narrative:
. . . At 10 p.m., with a fresh breeze blowing, a moderate swell and visibility of one and a half miles, *Fraser* was slightly ahead of *Calcutta* and to her right, *Restigouche* a bit behind the cruiser and to her left. They had been in action for a week, under threat of submarine and air attack. Creery had had one night's sleep in ten.

Calcutta signaled "single line ahead": the two destroyers were to form up behind her. *Fraser* swung left, intending to make a 180-degree turn and run back along the right of the cruiser and come into station behind her. But *Calcutta* thought *Fraser* intended to cross in front of her and pass down her *left* side. *Fraser* would have had little room to cross in front, so *Calcutta* made a sharp turn to the right, thinking to avoid collision.

But the cruiser's right turn and the destroyer's left turn had put them, at a combined speed of 34 knots, on courses that made collision inevitable. Engines were put astern and wheels reversed but no order could take effect in time. *Calcutta* sheared through *Fraser*. The destroyer's forepart broke off and floated away. Her bridge, with the bridge personnel, was lifted onto *Calcutta's* bow and remained there, swaying and groaning.

["The eight of us," said Creery, "hastily climbed over the front screen of

Fraser's erstwhile bridge and dropped six feet or so onto *Calcutta's* deck. It was pitch-dark and I couldn't see any part of *Fraser* but I heard shouts from the forepart and then, a little later, voices singing 'Roll Out the Barrel.' A large portion of the ship's company had been in their hammocks when *Calcutta's* bow plowed through the messdecks. Some must have been killed outright but those who survived found their way up onto the forecastle and were rescued by boats from *Calcutta* and *Restigouche* before the forepart finally filled and sank."]

Restigouche raced alongside *Fraser* and, rocking in a swell which threatened to dash her against the jagged steel, brought her stern around. While the hulls of the two ships ground perilously together, 60 of *Fraser's* crew, including one stretcher case, were transferred. For the men in the water, *Restigouche* and *Calcutta* lowered boats, floats and scramble nets.

Sixteen officers and 134 men were rescued; 47 Canadians and 19 British sailors died.

The loss of *Fraser,* heavy blow though it was, was a minor incident of those disastrous days, one of the casualties as certain to occur under conditions of prolonged and incessant strain as under direct shellfire. Nor could it be lingered upon.

Not only was Britain threatened with invasion by a triumphant army, but the supply lines on which her life depended were imperiled as never before. *Skeena, Restigouche* and *St. Laurent* now turned with scores of British ships to a desperate battle for the convoy routes through the southwestern approaches to England. U-boats moved in for the slaughter; the Luftwaffe was everywhere over the Channel and far out to sea. The great ports of the south and east were under constant attack. In their hours in harbor between U-boat hunts and rescue of survivors from sunken vessels, the Canadian destroyers landed men to help the British during air raids.

By early July the hard necessity of revising the whole supply system was conceded. The ports of the south and east were out of action so far as convoys were concerned. There remained only the ports on the Mersey and Clyde rivers. Cargoes from North America must be landed in the west and north. The great ocean convoys must be sent up through the north-

western approaches. And where the retreating convoys went, the escort forces followed. *Skeena, Restigouche* and *St. Laurent* sailed north with British destroyers to operate from Liverpool, Greenock, Rosyth and later Londonderry. . . .

JOSEPH SCHULL

In these northerly waters, two major adventures were in store that July for the nine-year-old, 32-knot destroyer *St. Laurent,* nicknamed "Sally Rand" after the celebrated fan dancer. Torpedoes were the cause of both.

The first was fired by German U-boat captain Gunther Prien, who in October 1939 had astonished the world by sneaking into the British Home Fleet anchorage at Scapa Flow in Scotland and sinking the battleship *Royal Oak.*

In this *Maclean's* account, told to Terence Robertson, Vice Adm. Harry De-Wolf—then a commander and skipper of *St. Laurent*—describes what happened when Prien struck again:

. . . On a fine July day, Prien's U-47 was returning to her Biscayan base after a three-week Atlantic patrol. His only remaining torpedo was defective and his crew worked all night in the hope it could be put to good use before they reached harbor. At 4 a.m. July 2 the torpedo was repaired. Two hours later, Prien brought U-47 to periscope depth 100 miles west of Northern Ireland for his dawn check around the horizon.

To his astonishment, a liner was steaming smack into the crossed hairs of his periscope lens—and she was alone.

The 15,305-ton British liner *Arandora Star* had been one of the most luxurious cruise liners in the world, with elegant ballrooms, cocktail bars and swimming pools. When war broke out she was transformed into a troop carrier, stripped of expensive furnishings, painted a functional battleship gray and equipped to carry nearly 2000 troops in quarters originally designed to please 400 passengers.

British authorities were rounding up enemy aliens who had lived and worked in England for years without bothering to become naturalized. Among them were famous chefs and maîtres d'hôtel from the finest clubs and restaurants in London's West End, stage and screen celebrities and respected businessmen. It was decided to move them to Canada.

The first 1500 were sent to Liverpool and herded aboard *Arandora Star.* By mischance they were joined by nearly 100 prisoners of war—Nazi merchant seamen and U-boat personnel—who were regarded as dangerous. To prevent trouble at sea, 200 British Army guards were put aboard and barbed-wire fences were strung down both sides of the ship and across her decks. They not only formed an impregnable barrier between the prisoners and the liner's crew but also barred access to the lifeboats.

Arandora Star became an escape-proof floating prison. Her captain protested that the barbed wire would make a death-trap of the ship if she were torpedoed, but his protests went unheeded. *Arandora Star* sailed for Canada on July 1. She had no naval escort, relying instead on speed and zigzag to avoid attack.

When Prien saw her, his submarine was in perfect position to attack with its last torpedo. "I prayed it would work," he said later. "After I gave the order to fire we waited, counting the seconds. Suddenly, right amidships, a column of water rose above the target's masthead and we heard the crash of the detonation."

Most of the prisoners, the guards and the *Arandora Star* crew were asleep. The torpedo crashed through the thin steel hull on the starboard side and exploded in the engine room. In two minutes the engine room was flooded to sea level, the main generators were out of action, the ship was in darkness and all communications were broken. Five hundred men died in their bunks.

Bulkheads buckled as water streamed through the ship. Frantic prisoners scram-

bled up iron ladders toward the boat deck. Their flight came to an abrupt halt at the barbed wire. The front ranks were pushed against the fences, which they tried to tear down with their hands. Dozens of men, overwhelmed by panic, thrashed at the wire and became hopelessly enmeshed.

The British guards behaved magnificently, hacking down the fences with bayonets and channeling the prisoners to where the crew were trying to launch the lifeboats that had escaped damage. Only ten got away, each with about 60 men. The liner's crew threw about 40 rafts over the side and shouted to the prisoners to jump. The internees, numbed and afraid, refused. At 7:20 a.m. *Arandora Star* lurched to starboard, tossing hundreds of prisoners into the sea, and slid beneath the surface.

Not quite 100 miles south, my ship *St. Laurent* was part of a destroyer screen protecting the British battleship *Nelson*. We picked up wireless messages reporting the sinking and at 11 a.m. *Nelson* ordered us to the scene. It would take *St. Laurent* 2½ hours at full speed to reach the position last signaled by *Arandora Star*. I was sure other ships would be there before us.

As we neared the position, an RAF Sunderland signaled that the sea ahead was littered with survivors. The flying boat had been circling for two hours, dropping ration kits, first-aid outfits and cigarettes and

The bigger the Allied ship, the richer the prize for some U-boat captain and his torpedoes. Canadian Pacific Steamships' 42,000-ton *Empress of Britain,* one of the ten largest in the world, had been in the convoy which took the 1st Canadian Division to Britain in December 1939. Ten months later, steaming alone and relying for safety on her 26-knot speed, the British-registered *Empress* and her largely British crew were bombed and machine-gunned by a German aircraft off the west coast of Ireland. Forty-five persons died. The rest of the 643 passengers, mostly British servicemen and dependents, abandoned the ship. Aflame, she was taken in tow but two days later, on October 28, 1940, soon after this photograph was made, she was torpedoed and sunk.

matches in watertight bags. The pilot directed us till we found a huge patch of oil-covered water about three miles in diameter in which hundreds of black blobs floated in dazzling sunlight.

I later wrote in my official report: "*St. Laurent* was stopped in the center of this area. All boats were sent away to pick up individuals while the ship was maneuvered among the rafts and heavier wreckage, picking up groups of three and four. This part of the work was painfully slow. Very few survivors were able to help themselves to any extent and in many cases it was necessary to put a man over the side to pass a line around them and hoist them bodily inboard. Some were very heavy. Many were covered in oil.

"During this time the lifeboats were making their way toward the ship. First

to arrive was a powerboat, well filled. This was quickly cleared and supplied with a fresh crew and sent away to pick up more. *St. Laurent's* coxswain and a seaman from *Arandora Star* remained in the boat and brought in at least 100 survivors."

Most survivors were elderly men, too weak to swim, kept afloat by their cork life jackets. The Atlantic can be bitterly cold, even in summer, and these men had been immersed for at least seven hours.

One who climbed aboard by himself stood on deck in his pajamas and asked to see the captain. He was Major Dury, commander of the military guard. He asked that the "most dangerous" of the Germans and Italians be confined under guard. So our No. 1 boiler room became a jail packed with some 40 prisoners of war.

The RAF flying boat circled above us during the rescue. We signaled that we were picking up enemy prisoners. He replied: "How bloody funny!"

All the crew emptied lockers, suitcases and kit bags of personal clothing and distributed it among the shivering survivors. There was not nearly enough. The ship was overflowing. Survivors filled all messes, officers' quarters, one boiler room and the engine room. Many remained on deck and were made as comfortable as possible under canvas screens. As the cooks started to ladle out hot stew, using every conceivable container, Italian chefs made their way to the galley and volunteered to help. They gaped at the rows of pots filled with chunks of meat, and concluded that we had performed a second Miracle of the Loaves and the Fishes.

None of us disillusioned them by telling the truth. Early that morning our refrigeration gear had broken down and without it our entire supply of fresh meat would have gone bad. I had given orders for the meat to be cooked and the galley staff had filled every pot and pan they could find. It had been simmering ever since.

By 4 p.m., with 850 survivors aboard, *St. Laurent* felt dangerously overloaded. When she rolled one way, there was a pause before she started to roll back again —quite different from the normal lively roll of a destroyer. Movement on deck was dangerous, with men packed tight on decks covered with oil and filth. Ropes were slung to prevent the weaker survivors from slithering overboard.

When we docked in Scotland at 6:30 a.m. the next day what looked like a whole regiment lined the dockside with bayonets fixed. This ludicrous situation developed into pure comedy with the sound of singing from the wardroom. Throughout the night one of my officers had been comforting the prisoners there with rum. Now they were ready to sign armistice terms with anyone. As they prepared to go ashore they were inspired to signify their appreciation to the ship and could think of no better way than with several choruses of "There'll Always Be an England." . . .

HARRY DEWOLF and TERENCE ROBERTSON

The torpedo in *St. Laurent's* second adventure was one of her own. Just prior

one lad in an excess of zeal would loose a torpedo against the ship itself?

We had landed the *Arandora Star* survivors at Greenock, on the west coast of Scotland, and were ordered to Rosyth, a naval base on the east coast.

On a fine Sunday afternoon, in company with the Canadian destroyer *Skeena,* we were steaming up the west coast en route to Rosyth by way of the Minches and Pentland Firth. *Skeena* followed on our starboard quarter, about 300 yards distant. Sailing inside the Western Isles, we were in relatively safe waters and at a relaxed state of readiness. The torpedomen were cleaning, polishing and painting the torpedo tubes. All tubes were loaded, but

The *Arandora Star* incident (above), one of the largest individual rescues of the war, was not the only time *St. Laurent* plucked the enemy from the sea. Left: the veteran Canadian destroyer takes aboard survivors from a U-boat which sank after being attacked by the U.S. escort carrier *Bogue* in May 1943.

to the *Arandora Star* incident, DeWolf had been promoted commander and ordered to Halifax to report for a new assignment. This is his own account, from *Reader's Digest,* of a hair-raising episode that happened before he could get to Halifax:

. . . My relief was to be Lt. Comdr. Herbert S. Rayner, a torpedo specialist. In the busy week that followed, the men of our torpedo department had no time to spruce up their weapons for his inspection. And who could suspect that when they did,

they had safety devices to prevent accidental firing, one being a simple hand-operated latch.

A battery of four tubes is normally trained fore and aft, and is pivoted outboard before a torpedo is aimed and fired. An explosive charge then catapults the 24-foot-long, ton-and-a-half steel "fish" out of its tube and safely clear of the launching ship's side. The torpedo's engine starts as the missile leaves the tube.

At the tail two counter-rotating propellers, powered by gas and compressed air, drive the torpedo toward its target at speeds up to 45 knots. The 600-pound warhead of TNT is comparatively safe until the rushing sea water spins a four-bladed propeller down a threaded stem inside the nose to unwind a safety device. Now the torpedo is armed and will explode at the slightest contact with any of the four blades.

At 1805 on that fine July day, a young seaman-torpedoman, intent only on his painting and finding the firing lever in his way, lifted the safety catch and pulled back the lever. His brush never reached its mark. With an explosive WHOOMP! the torpedo leaped free.

I was in my sea cabin on the starboard side of the bridge when I was aroused by a terrific clatter. I rushed out and saw a torpedo loose, its propellers racing madly and making a shattering noise on the steel deck.

Since it had been fired toward the stern, it struck first the steel ladder to the high-angle gun platform, then knocked over some ready-use ammunition boxes, struck the anti-aircraft gun a glancing blow and crashed head-on into the after superstructure. From there it rebounded to the starboard side of the deck. When I sighted the torpedo from the bridge, it appeared to be charging the superstructure for the second time.

I yelled to the bridge, "Tell *Skeena,*" then hurried aft. *Skeena* could see what was happening and shifted smartly to our port quarter, keeping on the lee side of *St. Laurent.* If the torpedo went over the side, *Skeena* would be in more danger than we.

Another sight greeted me: a stream of sailors racing forward, on the opposite side of the ship, at top speed. They were headed sensibly for the forecastle, as far forward as they could get. But a torpedo that could crush a battleship's hull as if it were a beer can made any spot on *St. Laurent* unattractive.

As I headed aft, I had no idea what I might do when I reached there. Fortunately, the torpedo gunner's mate, Chief Petty Officer Sam Ridge, who did know what to do, arrived at the same time. *St. Laurent* had just a gentle roll on, or we could have done nothing. The torpedo was rolling with each motion of the ship. It would lurch forward with each heave of the deck; then, as the deck came level, the torpedo would stop, like a bull in the ring, undecided in which direction to make its next charge. When it rolled against the guardrails, we advanced and held it there momentarily by bracing our legs against its

Comdr. Harry DeWolf (right) and the torpedo tubes of a River Class destroyer. "One thing he left out of his story," says Rear Adm. L. W. Murray, "was the danger involved in having a torpedo loose with the equivalent of half a ton of TNT on the front of it. As he went to see what he could do, he said to the people on the bridge: 'Tell my wife I was thinking of her.' " DeWolf's calm showed in his ship's log: "1805—fired one torpedo inboard accidentally, altered course 315 degrees, reduced to 16 knots. 1810—altered course 010 degrees and increased to 22 knots."

Wartime Germany had no heroes quite like its ace U-boat commanders. One of the top three was Gunther Prien (below), who penetrated Scapa Flow in September 1939 and sank the battleship *Royal Oak.* Here he acknowledges the cheers of admiring Berliners as he rides to an audience with Hitler. In March 1941, while attacking a convoy, Prien's U-47 was sunk with all hands by a British destroyer. That same month the two other top aces were lost. Joachim Schepke too was killed. Otto Kretschmer, who sank 300,000 tons of Allied shipping, was captured and imprisoned at Bowmanville, Ont.

flank and holding onto the top guardrail. Ridge ran to get a key to turn off the compressed air that was driving the propellers.

I straddled the torpedo and held onto the guardrail. With the next roll of the ship the torpedo rolled away from the ship's side. I let go the rail and galloped along with it, my feet on the deck and my hands on the torpedo's slippery surface. My only concern was to keep clear of the propellers, which were close behind me. The torpedo rolled across the deck and back, about ten feet each way. When it reached the guardrail again, Ridge had returned with the key.

He and the torpedo gunner, R. L. Ellis, were able to wrestle the torpedo steady until we could turn off the air. Once the noise of the propellers was stopped, the situation became less tense, more help arrived, and the torpedo was securely lashed in place against the guardrails.

The crash against the after deckhouse had pushed the torpedo's pistol back into the warhead, and so damaged the whole front end that it could not be safely touched. We were able to remove the warhead

from the torpedo, but even so the warhead and its pistol remained a problem, a quarter ton of sensitive explosive.

There was no help readily available at dockside when we arrived in Rosyth the next day. I went directly to the local headquarters to report for orders and also to note that I had a damaged torpedo and wanted a replacement. I received instructions to sail at once with a convoy. My torpedo problem, I was told, would be taken care of by another department!

When I returned to the ship, I found my crew had hoisted the torpedo and the damaged warhead onto the jetty without dockyard help. I reported by signal, briefly, how the torpedo had been damaged and where it had been left, and so to sea with the convoy.

On my return to the United Kingdom —fortunately not to Rosyth, but to Liverpool—I was met by Lieutenant Commander Rayner, who took over the ship. I was safely back in Canada by the time the very angry Rosyth dockyard authorities caught up with the "Sally Rand," which had left them holding such an awkward baby.

I had in the meantime written a report suggesting a court of inquiry would be unnecessary, because there was nothing to be learned. The young torpedoman admitted what he had done and that was that.

The Rosyth dockyard was understandably put out, because nobody wanted to touch the damaged warhead, let alone move it. Lieutenant Commander Rayner was able to fend off their furious inquiries by referring to my written report, which answered everything except what to do with the remains. In the end, we learned, they secured it to a ground mine and laid it in a North Sea minefield. . . .

HARRY DEWOLF

As summer passed and winter came, the U-boats struck mainly between Britain and Iceland. The hard-pressed escort ships scored few victories. In one three-hour hunt St. Laurent and the British destroyer Viscount dropped 80 depth charges; when U-boat diesel oil bubbled to the surface they were sure the sub had been sunk. The Admiralty, cautious even in those desperate days, credited them with a "probable."

The interpreter

In this unwarlike man, wrote Bruce Hutchison, were all the qualities Canada needed in a wartime leader. By no means the least of Mackenzie King's achievements was his role as a link between Prime Minister Churchill and President Roosevelt (opposite). Churchill had written in the *Saturday Evening Post* in 1930: "Canada is a magnet exercising a double attraction, drawing both Great Britain and the United States toward herself and thus drawing them closer to each other. No state, no country, no band of men can more truly be described as the linchpin of peace and world progress." It was not a new role for Canada but in 1940 it was an important role.

In the last days before France capitulated in June 1940, the Canadian cabinet sat in Ottawa's East Block—aghast. When Mackenzie King told his ministers he had appealed to French Premier Paul Reynaud to fight on, they seemed unable to believe how bad things were.

Small wonder. Few periods in human history match the tragic and turbulent drama of that spring and summer.

When France did go down, a deeply troubled and divided United States remained neutral. President Roosevelt gave every help he could but he was hobbled by isolationist sentiment, by a Neutrality Act which limited his scope for action, and by doubts among some of his countrymen that Britain could survive.

For Canada, there was no such alternative. As the cabinet now knew, every-

thing had changed. It was an entirely different war and it would have to be fought in an entirely different way than they had planned. With men of all three forces in the front line across the sea, Canada suddenly had become the strongest ally of a besieged Britain. But after nine months of war she was still poorly equipped to fill the role.

It was a time of tumult, not least in the hearts of French Canadians. Ernest Lapointe wept publicly over the collapse of France. In the streets of Montreal, journalist André Laurendeau was struck by "the dismal sorrow of the people. I hadn't believed France was so real to them. For days, even weeks, they had an air of mourning. They felt grief, deception, maybe a little shame because the French name, of which they felt so sure, was shaken. Later they would hear of the weaknesses and faults of France, but not then. June was dominated by her distress."

It was a time of doubt. The oratory and defiance of Winston Churchill stirred the free world but at one point Mackenzie King recorded his private belief that Neville Chamberlain would have been a safer guide for Britain in the long run. When Roosevelt announced all possible aid for Britain, King wondered "if it is not coming just too late."

It was a time of cracking down. Shortly before Italy stabbed France in the back even as she fell, the Royal Canadian Mounted Police went into action. Before the war, according to C. W. Harvison, later a commissioner of the force, the Mounties had penetrated the ranks of Nazi and Fascist organizations, had detected their leaders and plans for espionage and subversion. In September 1939, they had interned hundreds of potential Nazi sympathizers. Now, facing a new threat, they took in hundreds of Italian sympathizers. Among them was tall, eloquent Adrien Arcand of Montreal, Canada's No. 1 Fascist, who had boasted in 1939 that he had 12,000 followers and once issued thousands of dollars worth of special currency to be redeemed when Canada fell under his control. Commissioner Harvison, in his book *The Horsemen,* reports one major result of the detentions and years of earlier underground work: "Not one case of enemy sabotage occurred in Canada during the war."

It was, above all, a time to prepare as never before. There could be enemy raids; some thought there might even be invasion. If Britain fell, the Royal Navy would probably make Canada its headquarters. Defense headquarters began to prepare for that eventuality. There was even consideration of what would happen if Churchill's government moved to Ottawa.

The Americans ordered conscription and turned to arms production in a major way. For the first time, Canadian military leaders went to Washington to seek arms and to discuss continental defense. It was a mark of the American public mood that it was done in secret. It was a mark of Roosevelt's mood that he asked railway officials how they would move 300,000 U.S. troops into the Maritime Provinces if needed for defense. The two countries had pledged in 1938 that they would stand together if North America were attacked. Now they went much further; they drew up a continental alliance which has been pivotal in Canadian military arrangements ever since.

For Canada, in short, the war really began in the spring of 1940. The number of authorized army divisions was doubled to four. She scraped the barrel and sent Britain four destroyers, a fighter squadron, elements of the 2nd Division, plus whatever small arms and artillery she could find. She suddenly realized not only that the original plan to train Commonwealth aircrew must be enlarged but that Britain could no longer help; she took it on alone. She set up navy and army commands on the Atlantic coast, with Newfoundland as an added responsibility. She sent troops to Newfoundland, Iceland and the West Indies, and would have sent them to Greenland if the United States had not intervened; in Washington there were suspicions that imperial ambition lay behind the Canadian urge to do so now that Greenland's master, Denmark, was in German hands.

Canada hadn't even been able to arm herself. Now she was asked to arm herself and others. Britain had kept blueprints, tool designs and patents at home, in the belief that the war would last but three years and that her own industry should reap its benefits. Abruptly, she began to flood Ottawa with orders. A new Department of Munitions and Supply was created and its minister, Clarence Decatur Howe, was asked to work an industrial revolution. In the year Canada remained Britain's ranking ally, he built an apparatus that, among other things, could equip an army division every six weeks.

Armed with the powers of a legal dictator, Mackenzie King put together the team that would fight this new, all-out war. He himself was its most enigmatic member. A bachelor, he was given to depressions and to working his staff to thankless exhaustion. The shrewdest political manipulator Canada had ever known, he was also given to consultations with mediums who he believed brought him into contact with the other world, including the mother he had worshipped in life. A number of his cabinet ministers disliked or even despised him but as a team they were superb.

Howe masterminded not only military production but also the expansion of air-training facilities. Norman Rogers was killed in a plane crash and his place as defense minister was taken by James Layton Ralston, a decorated hero of World War I, an eminent corporation lawyer. Ralston's ministry was broadened to take in the ebullient C. G. "Chubby" Power as air minister and Angus L. Macdonald, former premier of Nova Scotia, as navy minister. James Lorimer Ilsley, another Nova Scotian, succeeded Ralston as finance minister and launched the country into unprecedented taxation and economic restrictions. There was enormous talent and integrity in this team; it led the country into an enormous achievement, far beyond anything it had ever done.

The government demanded sacrifices, but in 1940 the country wanted nothing less. In relative quiet, it lived through the first phase of a drama of conscription which would come to one climax within two years and to a far bigger one in 1944. Under a new National Resources Mobilization Act, men were drafted for one month's training for home defense. The following spring this was increased to four months, later to as long as the war should last. The one major public objection came from Camillien Houde, now mayor of Montreal. When he urged French Canadians to refuse to register for military service, Justice Minister Lapointe interned him. Lapointe's opposition to overseas conscription remained; conscription for defense of the homeland was something else again.

At the summit of all this activity, Mackenzie King lived through what he came to consider the greatest days of his life.

Winston Churchill years before had called Canada "the linchpin of peace" as the interpreter between the United States and Britain. King now undertook to play that role as no Canadian ever had, as a liaison between Churchill and Roosevelt.

He had known Roosevelt for years; the President called him "Mackenzie." King had first met Churchill and been appalled by his arrogance when, as a young man, the Briton came to Canada on a speaking tour. Later, in 1908, they met again and Churchill said he guessed he'd made an ass of himself at the time. King grinned agreement, and they became friends.

Bruce Hutchison in his biography, *The Incredible Canadian,* describes King's relationships with Churchill and Roosevelt:

"A bizarre and ill-assorted triumvirate began to take shape that spring. Publicly it was King's misfortune to be matched on either side by a spectacular personage who outshone him. His position was fixed by the dimensions of his nation. But he was not a minor partner. He had a far larger effect on the other two than the public ever guessed. To his last days King treasured nothing more than Churchill's cables testifying to that work which, though the most secret, may well have been the most important he ever did."

King and Roosevelt became confidants. In the Canadian, says Hutchison, the President found an unprejudiced consultant who brought a fresh view of world problems, a man to whom he could talk

freely. In Churchill, King soon realized, there were prodigious qualities he had once underestimated.

As the Germans crushed western Europe and mustered their forces on the French coast, there was an important role for an interpreter. Churchill began to beseech Roosevelt for aid. Roosevelt was willing to help but there were limits to what he could do. King was drawn into the act.

His own story of that period is told in his diary, published as *The Mackenzie King Record* with editing and comments by his wartime aide, J. W. Pickersgill.

It shows him caught up in what he considered British bargaining for American entry into the war and in working out a deal to strengthen Britain and enlist U.S. help in the defense of Canada.

In mid-May, as France tottered, King turned to Roosevelt to provide planes for the British Commonwealth Air Training Plan now that Britain couldn't do so. Roosevelt said he couldn't either. But he soon was turning to King about the fate of the British Navy. He feared France was doomed and that Britain would be unable to survive German attack. He wanted King to persuade the other dominions to bring pressure on Churchill not to yield to any soft peace, not to surrender the fleet even if it meant destruction. The fleet, Roosevelt urged, should make its base elsewhere; King George VI should go to Bermuda. U.S. bases would be made available for repairs. In time, a cordon would be thrown around Germany.

King was "revolted" at first because "it seemed to me that the United States was seeking to save itself at the expense of Britain." Nor would he try to pressure the other dominions; he felt Australia and South Africa would "misinterpret or resent our attitude." He would be accused of being pro-American. He would be prepared to pass on the U.S. view to Churchill on his own but "whatever I did should be done direct with Churchill and the President and not through others." Back from Roosevelt came the request that King present the President's views to Churchill as though they were representative of Canadian opinion.

A condensed version of the *Record's* story:

...King spent a good part of May 30 drafting a message to Churchill. "The difficult part," he wrote, "was to try and meet

the President's wishes of having the message appear to be from myself while taking care that it was wholly his point of view I was putting over. I wish it could have gone much sooner. However I believe it will be really deeply appreciated by Churchill, and come at a moment that will be helpful to him. If it does, it may well be the most significant message that has crossed the ocean in this war. Hitler cannot be defeated nor the Empire saved without the aid of the United States. Taken in the right way, they are a generous and warmhearted people and will help. Dealt with in any superior way, every instinct of cooperation will be chilled."

In this message, sent May 31, King

Adrien Arcand (above, under sign, with detectives) and ten other leading Canadian Fascists were arrested in 1940 when Italy entered the war. The RCMP had long since penetrated Nazi and Fascist organizations, and rounding up their leaders was easy. But even as Hitler's Canadian admirers were interned, the Führer himself was at the height of his success. He had danced with delight as France signed Germany's humiliating surrender terms, then posed triumphantly with the Eiffel Tower as a Paris backdrop.

stated the President's views on the British fleet in these terms: "The President feels it would be unwise to ignore the grave possibility of France being overrun and Britain being unable to repel mass air attacks. As long as there is any possibility of defense, the British fleet should be left in action. If the British Isles can withstand air bombardment, it is possible that a blockade can be made so effective that Germany and Italy can be defeated. If it became apparent, however, that hope of successful resistance was gone, the President fears the United Kingdom might be called on to make a hard choice between a cessation of hostilities based on surrender of the British fleet and parts of the Empire on terms the Germans might or might not observe, or prolonging the war with a merciless attitude on the part of Germany.

"The United States cannot, it is considered, give immediate belligerent aid. If, however, Britain and France could hold out for some months, aid could probably then be given. If further resistance by the fleet in British waters became impossible before that, the President believes it would be disastrous to surrender the fleet on any terms, that it should be sent to Canada and elsewhere. He would also deem it wise that, in such a contingency, vessels that cannot be moved should be destroyed.

"Were this course adopted, the United States would open its ports to the British fleet and help in the building up of bases at Halifax and elsewhere. It would extend the provisions for the defense of the western Atlantic, and its fleet would hold the Pacific and defend Australia and New Zealand.

"As soon as grounds could be found to justify active American participation (and neither Roosevelt nor State Secretary Cordell Hull believes this would be more than a few weeks), the United States would participate in a stringent blockade of Europe.

"Both believe that if Germany should threaten any vicious action against the United Kingdom as punishment for allowing the fleet to escape, U.S. public opinion would demand intervention. If, for example, the Germans should attempt to starve Britain into ordering the fleet to return, the United States would send food ships under naval escort to the British Isles. Interference with such ships would mean instant war."

On June 4 [as the Dunkirk evacuation was completed] King recorded that "the greatest feature of the day was Churchill's speech" which concluded: "We shall never surrender, and even if, which I do not for a moment believe, this island or a large part of it were subjugated and starving, then our Empire beyond the seas, armed and guarded by the British fleet, would carry on the struggle until, in God's good time, the New World steps forth to the rescue and liberation of the old." King wrote: "When I saw his concluding words, I recognized that the dispatch I had sent him had been helpful. Skelton [O. D. Skelton, external affairs undersecretary] was filled with delight. I am quite sure Churchill prepared that part of his speech in the light of what I sent him. As Skelton said, there is good reason for me to be happy at what has been accomplished as a result of direct personal effort in the past fortnight."

On June 5, Skelton brought a message from Churchill which King felt would help advance matters with the President. Churchill said: "We must be careful not to let Americans view too complacently [the] prospect of a British collapse, out of which they would get the British fleet and the guardianship of the Empire, minus Great Britain. If United States were in the war and England conquered, it would be natural that events should follow the above course. But if America continued neutral, and we were overpowered, I cannot tell what policy might be adopted by a pro-German administration such as would undoubtedly be set up.

"Although the President is our best friend, no practical help has (reached us) from the United States yet. Any pressure you can apply would be invaluable."

King sent an emissary to Washington June 6 to deliver this message to Roosevelt along with his own interpretation of Churchill's reference to a pro-German administration. King's memo said the reference had to be read "in the light of the knowledge of Mr. C's character, his public utterances and above all his scrupulous regard for constitutional procedure. Mr. C. will never consider surrender. The only way in which negotiations could take place with the enemy would be by such a division of opinion within Britain itself that there would grow up a demand for surrender. Mr. C. would never take the responsibility for such a step. If he saw

Mackenzie King's key cabinet ministers included, from left, top: Angus L. Macdonald, Norman Rogers, James Lorimer Ilsley; bottom: C. G. "Chubby" Power, James Layton Ralston, Clarence Decatur Howe. Mayor Camillien Houde (right) — Montreal's "part court jester, part *paterfamilias*, part beloved scalawag," Ralph Allen called him — was interned when he urged French Canadians not to register for home-defense military service.

public opinion become so strong that his government were in the minority, he would ask the King to call on the leader of the surrender party to form a government. To Mr. C's way of thinking such a government would be pro-German. It would have the responsibility of arranging surrender and, as Mr. C. says, no one could tell what policy the pro-German administration might adopt.

"Anyone who knows Mr. C. and understands the British fighting spirit will realize that Mr. C. has set forth a sincere statement of what would take place were the point to be reached while Mr. C. is at the head of the government, where any demand for surrender might come from the British people as a consequence of fears of annihilation. He [King] does not believe this is put forward as either bluff or

for the purpose of bargaining but solely to make the position clear to Mr. R."

Hugh Keenleyside, King's emissary, saw Roosevelt and Hull June 7 in Washington and, on his return, reported that they did not accept King's interpretation of Churchill's reference to a pro-German administration and felt that if the telegram really represented Churchill's attitude it was "alarming and distressing." All they wanted, according to the President, was for Churchill to stick to the program outlined in his speech. Both expressed the hope that King would continue the discussions with Churchill not on the basis of "an American plan" but primarily "to save the Empire."

On June 16, sure French resistance would collapse, King "felt I should get off to Churchill a communication which would end the kind of bargaining for entry of the United States into the war which has been going on. When a communication came from Churchill giving his own appreciation of the position, I took advantage of it to write out a dispatch which gave it as my opinion that the United States should get bases at Iceland, Greenland, Newfoundland and the West Indies and supply the inadequacy of the defense of our own coasts, etc. The problem over the French fleet, at the moment (the prospect of its surrender), gave a chance to show that the United States' surmises and representations which I sent along some weeks ago, were only too well founded." King also reiterated Roosevelt's concern about the British fleet and urged that no time be lost in working out plans for the transfer, if resistance became impossible, of surviving units before there was any possibility of surrender. The telegram envisaged joint plans by the United Kingdom, the United States and Canada for all eventualities.

Churchill replied June 24: "If you will read again my telegram of June 5 you will see there is no question of trying to make a bargain with the United States about their entry into the war and our dispatch of the fleet across the Atlantic should the Mother Country be defeated. On the contrary, I doubt very much the wisdom of dwelling upon the last contingency. I have good confidence in our ability to defend this island, and I see no reason to make preparation for or give any countenance to the transfer of the British fleet. I shall never enter into peace negotiations with Hitler, but obviously I cannot bind a future government which, if we were deserted by the United States and beaten down here, might very easily be ready to accept German overlordship. It would be a help if you would impress this danger upon the President."

On June 28, King "was much distressed when Howe told me of increasing feeling in the United States that it was almost wasting material to send much to the United Kingdom; that the feeling there had changed greatly since France had dropped out. This is really appalling and most unfortunate. If the United States does not help Britain, we will have to pray pretty hard for the Lord to hear the prayer that will save the rest of the English-speaking world." . . .

THE MACKENZIE KING RECORD

As the perilous days went by, Britain urged King to help get an understanding with Washington on finances and purchasing; arrangements were made at King's behest for Canadian military chiefs to visit Washington secretly to work out plans for joint defense; Roosevelt sent word he'd like to discuss personally with King "a common plan of defense for North America, including the Atlantic islands, with a view to getting the British government to join in the plan." The Prime Minister threw his weight behind a proposal that the Americans get air facilities from the British in the West Indies and Newfoundland.

At this stage, Maj. Gen. H. D. G. Crerar returned from London to become Chief of the General Staff. Britain's military leaders, he reported July 26, thought the chances were 60-40 that Germany would seek to invade Britain within six weeks. If England fell, the Royal Navy would make its headquarters on this side of the Atlantic and Canada "should do all possible to get our harbors and coast defenses ready to cooperate." Crerar favored working out plans with the United States, having this done openly with Britain. "I told him," recorded King, "that I only wished we could get Britain to meet the United States and ourselves on that ground."

By August 3, King was informed that Britain was, in fact, offering Washington air facilities in the West Indies and Newfoundland and that there were suggestions in Washington for exchanging 50 overage U.S. destroyers for them. He sent word to Roosevelt that the destroyers could be of "decisive importance." But he wanted the strengthening of naval defenses on this side of the Atlantic to be discussed too, even though the British Channel was still the "first line of defense for democratic peoples."

On August 15, Sir Gerald Campbell, Britain's high commissioner in Ottawa, gave King "very confidential communications regarding arrangements which will ensure Britain getting some of the destroyers at once and the United States the assurance the President has wished that the British fleet will be brought to this side should England be crushed. Also an undertaking by Britain to let America have bases in some of the Atlantic islands." "These," wrote King, "are the things I proposed to the [British] government and

have been trying to get them to agree to for months."

For weeks, various emissaries—Canadian, American and British—had been acting as intermediaries. The time had come for Roosevelt and King to meet personally. *The Mackenzie King Record* goes on:

. . . King noted that on August 16 "the girl at the switchboard said the President wished to speak to me. He said: 'Hello, is that you, Mackenzie? I am going tomorrow night in my train to Ogdensburg. If you are free, I would like you to have dinner with me there. I would like to talk about the destroyers, and they (the British) are arranging to let us have bases on some of their Atlantic possessions for our naval and air forces. Are you free?' I said: 'Yes.' The President said: 'We can talk over de-

fense matters. I would like you to stay the night with me in the car and, on Sunday, I am going to a religious service, and I think it would do both of us good. We could attend it together.' I said I would be pleased to accept."

King motored to Ogdensburg, N.Y., the next day with Pierrepont Moffat, U.S. ambassador in Ottawa. Before leaving Ottawa, Ralston gave him a list of supplies the Canadian forces were trying to procure in the United States and suggested he enlist Roosevelt's support. They reached the President's car at seven o'clock. Roosevelt was "sitting in a corner in his white suit enjoying lemonade" along with War Secretary H. L. Stimson and one or two

of his staff. "The President greeted me with his usual smile and hearty handshake, calling me 'Mackenzie' and telling me he had had a very busy day reviewing troops. He looked exceedingly well. Was in a very happy mood." King later "was astonished to see the President eat a huge steak for dinner. Neither Stimson nor I could have taken one eighth of it."

After dinner, Roosevelt and King quickly agreed in principle on the establishment of a board to study common problems of defense and make recommendations to the two governments. After that, the President read messages from Churchill regarding the destroyers and Atlantic bases. King had copies of most

gress, which public opinion would accept as fair. Up to the last few days, he had almost despaired of being able to meet the British on this request. That the United States itself had become so alarmed after French collapse, they did not wish to part with any of their own security."

Roosevelt said only legal technicalities were holding up the transfer of the vessels. He said King "could tell Churchill that and could advise him to begin to get crews across at once unless we had crews we could send." Roosevelt also told him of other things he planned to make available to Britain.

King continued, "the President said he did not like having conferences between

When Italy declared war on June 10, 1940, Mussolini's legions (left) joined Hitler's for the final subjugation of France. "Future generations," Winston Churchill wrote in *Their Finest Hour,* "may deem it noteworthy that the supreme question of whether we should fight on alone never found a place upon the war cabinet agenda. It was taken for granted." A Canadian brigade served in Iceland (above) that summer and one battalion spent the winter of 1940-41 on the island.

of them from Churchill. When he came to the end of a dispatch referring to Canada, the President said: "This is where you come in." King replied "that Churchill had already communicated with me and that I had sent word to him that we were wholly agreeable to the United States being given bases on the islands of the Atlantic and that, as he knew, I had put this forward to Churchill. As to Newfoundland, I said both the British and our government would probably have to do with that matter as well as the United States." King added that Air Minister Power had left for Newfoundland that day and that Canada was about to spend a million on facilities at Gander airport.

The President seemed "most anxious to meet the British and to get a *quid pro quo* for destroyers without consulting Con-

the two countries carried on in secret. I was exactly of his mind. It was a tremendous relief to have everything in the open, apart from the effect the joint board itself would have."

On Sunday morning, after church, King gave Roosevelt the Ralston memo on war supplies. The President and Mr. Stimson said they would have difficulty with the defense services.

While King and Stimson were looking at the list on the sofa, the President began to draft a joint press statement. "He did this on a sheet of paper which he took from the basket and with a pencil in his hand. Read aloud the draft. I questioned him as to the use of the word 'permanent.' He said he attached much importance to it. I said I was not questioning the wisdom of it but was anxious to get what he had in mind." Roosevelt felt the board should not be designed "to meet alone this particular situation but to help secure the continent for the future." King concurred. The title agreed on was the Canada-United States Permanent Joint Board on Defense.

King and Moffat left Ogdensburg Sunday afternoon and, on reaching Ottawa, the Prime Minister dictated a telegram to Churchill on his talks. He let Churchill know that Roosevelt hoped to arrange, before that week ended, to begin supplying Britain with destroyers. The President hoped to arrange all this without authorization from Congress, on the ground that he was obtaining a defense *quid pro quo*

Roosevelt's concern for a *quid pro quo* for the destroyers and a querulous attitude to the joint board. Meanwhile, on Monday he "had a talk with Skelton who said, if I did nothing for the next five years for the country, I should be satisfied with what was now done."

On August 26, the joint board had its first meeting in Ottawa. King welcomed the American members. "A few minutes before," he wrote, "I had received an alarming message. It disclosed so completely the wisdom of the establishment of the board that I read it." This message from the British Admiralty reported that a convoy had been attacked by a U-boat westward of the normal U-boat area, an

in the bases. King also indicated that the President was arranging to make available other planes and ships and that he believed he could let the British have 250,000 rifles.

King referred to large expenditures by Canada in Newfoundland and indicated there would probably be the necessity for cooperation by the three governments there.

After outlining the agreement for the joint board, King observed that the President had suggested that some of the 50 destroyers might remain in the Canadian Navy but King wanted Churchill to have the final word.

He was elated by the outcome of his conversation with the President and was hurt when the reply from Churchill on August 22 indicated impatience with

escorting vessel had been sunk and five ships were missing. The Admiralty thought the U-boat might be on her way to operate off the Canadian coast.

That same day Sir Gerald Campbell, the British high commissioner, showed King the terms of the proposed lease of the bases in Newfoundland and asked Canadian concurrence. King showed him the Admiralty message "to illustrate how more than ready I was to have this granted without delay, pointing out that our coasts had been left bare of defense by sending destroyers to help the British at a critical moment." He told Campbell he had been "surprised at the message from Churchill, particularly that part which referred to the board. It showed how much appreciation was given in British quarters to anything that did not suit their mood. When mat-

President Roosevelt and Prime Minister Mackenzie King (left, with U.S. War Secretary H. L. Stimson) at Ogdensburg, N.Y., in August 1940. They helped speed the transfer of 50 U.S. destroyers to Britain and set up the Canada-United States Permanent Joint Board on Defense (right). The board's co-chairmen were Col. O. M. Biggar (seated, second from left) and New York's Mayor F. H. LaGuardia (seated, center). Canadian members included Dr. Hugh L. Keenleyside, Air Commodore A. A. L. Cuffe, Capt. L. W. Murray, Lt. Col. Georges P. Vanier and Brig. Kenneth Stuart.

"Not charity but an investment"

William Stephenson, the Canadian-born head of British secret intelligence in the Americas, played a key role in the destroyers-for-bases bargaining in 1940 because, as he said years later, in his efforts to procure aid for Britain, he "instinctively concentrated" on William J. "Wild Bill" Donovan.

At a time when Joseph Kennedy, U.S. ambassador in London, among others, was predicting Britain's defeat, Donovan was convinced she would survive—granted sufficient aid from the United States. And President Roosevelt knew, liked and listened to Donovan, a prominent New York lawyer. Stephenson set out to furnish Donovan with evidence that "American assistance would be not charity but a sound investment." From H. Montgomery Hyde's book *The Quiet Canadian:*

. . . Stephenson suggested Donovan visit Britain in the summer of 1940 so he could give the President a first-hand report on the country's chances against Hitler. Roosevelt agreed Donovan should go as his unofficial personal representative—without Ambassador Kennedy being told. "I arranged every opportunity for him to conduct his inquiries," Stephenson said. "He was received by the King, had ample time with Churchill and members of the cabinet. He visited factories and military training centers. He spoke with industrial leaders and representatives of all classes. He learned that Churchill was no bold façade but the very heart of Britain which was still beating strongly."

After Donovan returned home, Stephenson cabled London: "Donovan greatly impressed by visit. Has strongly urged our case *re* destroyers and is doing much to combat defeatist attitude in Washington by stating convincingly we shall win."

At midnight August 22 Stephenson was able to report that the figure of 50 destroyers had been agreed on by the President. . . .

ters were going badly, Churchill had been ready to appeal urgently to the United States for help and to ask my cooperation. When it looked as if the British might still win because of their air force, they were ready to pull away from U.S. cooperation."

King read Churchill's message at the cabinet war committee meeting on August 27. Ralston, [T. A.] Crerar and Lapointe "were indignant." King said he "had thought of ignoring it. They felt an answer should be sent which would let Churchill see his reply had not been appreciated, and make clear how exceptionally wise our action was in the light of the approach of a U-boat." They noted the contrast between Churchill's messages to the President when he said the fate of the war might depend on being supplied with destroyers, and the latest one "saying he would rather go without destroyers than to have experts haggle."

On August 30, King went to the Seigniory Club at Montebello, Que., to dine with U.S. Treasury Secretary Henry Morgenthau. Morgenthau told him "he had had a telephone message from the President, who said to give me his love and to let me know that everything had been worked out satisfactorily between Churchill and himself. That 99-year leases for military bases were to be given free of charge in Newfoundland and Bermuda. On the other islands, leases were to be given in exchange for the destroyers. It would be a *quid pro quo*. In this way the President would get over the legal difficulty of not being able to sell destroyers. He could exchange war material for even more than its equivalent."

Next day King received from Sir Gerald Campbell "the statement that Churchill has communicated to the President as the basis of the exchange. It comes around completely to what I had mentioned in my cable to Churchill and what I thought would be necessary to secure the destroyers without the President going to Congress. Churchill has ingeniously saved his face by having part of the bases given free. It is an immense relief that this had all been so successfully accomplished."

On September 11, King noted that something seemed to be holding him back from replying to Churchill before listening to his broadcast on that day. He found this broadcast with its forecast of invasion and tribute to the RAF [the Battle of Britain

Between farm fields near Houlton, Me., a U.S. Navy aircraft heads for the Canadian frontier. U.S. neutrality law prohibited war planes from being flown across the international boundary so they were landed at airports near the border, then towed into Canada. If this procedure met only the letter of the law, it did provide aircraft at a time when Canada's and Britain's need was desperate.

was at its peak] "intensely moving, an address to the people informing them of the probable immediate invasion of Britain, and asking them to stand firm. I question if ever in history anything comparable has taken place. I felt strongly that I should send a message to Churchill."

The message read in part:

"I ask you at this time of intense anxiety to give the people of the United Kingdom the assurance that Canada was never more proud of the privilege of having her forces so closely associated with those of the United Kingdom and the Commonwealth in the magnificent stand against ruthless aggression and for the preservation of the liberties of men. Britain may count on our support to the utmost of our strength."

On September 13 King was delighted to receive a message from Churchill which gave him "more pleasure than almost anything that has happened. It made so clear my part in bringing together the English-speaking peoples and an appreciation by Churchill of my own efforts; also, the significance of what I have striven to do on this continent."

King wrote that he felt "Churchill had realized he had not sent the sort of message he should have with reference to the defense board agreement and the agreement re destroyers and was anxious to make amends which he did in magnificent fashion."

Churchill's message read: "I am touched by the personal kindness of your telegram and all our people are cheered and fortified to feel that Canada is with the Mother Country heart and soul. The fine Canadian divisions which are standing on guard with us will play a notable part should the enemy set foot on our shores.

"I am very glad to have this opportunity of thanking you for all you have done for the common cause and especially in promoting a harmony of sentiment throughout the New World. This deep understanding will be a dominant factor in the rescue of Europe from a relapse into the Dark Ages.". . . THE MACKENZIE KING RECORD

Precisely how much influence King wielded as a linchpin in 1940 is difficult to say. In his war histories, Churchill quotes telegrams he sent urging King to support and explain Britain's case in Washington. He gives no indication that he considered the Canadian's role especially significant.

Certainly what King did was only part of a larger pattern which included direct communications between Churchill and Roosevelt. It is also true, however, that four years after the events of 1940 Churchill told King personally that "we [British] all look to you as the link with America. You alone could have done it. We look to you above all else to keep the two together. Canada is the interpreter."

Canada's role as interpreter, says Bruce Hutchison in *The Incredible Canadian,* reached a peak at Ogdensburg:

. . . Without a word in Congress, the United States had signed its first military alliance with a nation of the Commonwealth. Without a word in Parliament, Canada had bound herself to stand with her neighbor in the defense of North America.

But the secret purpose of Ogdensburg reached beyond that. Roosevelt was proposing to rescue Britain, so far as that lay in his power, with the 50 destroyers. Under the American Constitution and the Neutrality Act it was a tricky business, even for Roosevelt. He could manage the Constitution and Congress, but not Churchill. That was why he called in King.

Roosevelt felt he could give away the destroyers in exchange for military bases only on a *quid pro quo* basis. The British were happy to transfer the bases, but not eager to do it as a straight swap. It was for the honest Canadian broker to make sure that they accepted a *quid pro quo* deal.

In smoothing the way, King probably exercised a greater influence on world events than any Canadian before him. For in his mind, and doubtless in Roosevelt's, the United States had bypassed the Neutrality Act, had made a fiction of neutrality, had committed itself to the survival of Britain. . . .

Churchill, in *Their Finest Hour,* indicates that he resisted a *quid pro quo* or outright swap arrangement because there would be "vehement opposition" if the issue were presented "as a naked trading away of British possessions for the sake of 50 destroyers." He did eventually tell Parliament, however, that "these measures are linked together in a formal agreement." In his history he adds this final comment:

"Thus we obtained the 50 destroyers. We granted 99-year leases of the air and naval bases. I repeated my declaration about not scuttling or surrendering the British fleet, in the form of an assurance to the President. I regarded all these as parallel transactions, and as acts of goodwill performed on their merits and not as bargains. The President found it more acceptable to present them to Congress as a connected whole. We neither of us contradicted each other, and both countries were satisfied."

They flew with The Few

Canadian airmen in the epic Battle of Britain

The Battle of France is over. I expect that the Battle of Britain is about to begin. Upon this battle depends the survival of Christian civilization. Upon it depends our British life, and the long continuity of our institutions and our Empire. The whole fury and might of the enemy must very soon be turned on us. Hitler knows that he will have to break us in this island or lose the war. Let us therefore brace ourselves to our duties, and so bear ourselves that, if the British Empire and its Commonwealth last for a thousand years, men will still say, "This was their finest hour."

WINSTON CHURCHILL, JUNE 18, 1940

Britain stood alone in the front line, alone and suddenly majestic. Her only allies, the faraway countries of the Commonwealth, worked frantically to help avert disaster, thankful that at least some of their strength was in the British Isles. Canada had her 1st Division there and in August sent part of her 2nd. To two army cooperation squadrons of tiny Lysanders she added the Hurricanes of No. 1 Fighter Squadron of the RCAF. Off the coasts of Britain, a few Canadian destroyers prowled.

Hitler hoped that, with France conquered, Britain would be convinced of the futility of fighting on. He put out several peace feelers. All were rejected for he had completely misjudged the British. Fortified by Churchill's bitter medicine of "blood, toil, tears and sweat," they were ready for a fight to the finish.

In the face of such defiance, Hitler ordered Operation Sea Lion to be readied for September 15. As the German invasion fleet assembled in ports from Brest to Hamburg, the British dug in. The countryside erupted in a rash of tank traps, roadblocks, machine-gun nests, pillboxes and barbed wire. Weapons ranged from pitchforks and muskets to caches of fuel to be set ablaze off the Channel coast.

Because the British Army had lost so much equipment at Dunkirk, General

McNaughton's 1st Canadian Division was for a period the only whole and reasonably well-equipped infantry division in the country. Even it had suffered heavy equipment and transport losses in its foray into Brittany in June. The Canadian division was given the task of multiplying itself into an army for the benefit of German Intelligence. Its men were marched and countermarched across southern England to create the illusion of vast forces on the move, and the weary soldiers came to call themselves McNaughton's Flying Circus.

Britain's epic battle was to be fought not on the ground, however, but in the air. Before Sea Lion could be launched, the RAF had to be wiped from the skies. Only by achieving air supremacy could the Germans hope to transport their invasion fleet

across the Channel and keep it supplied. Sea Lion planners counted on winning the air during the summer, then invading in mid-September when the moon was full and the tides high. While the Luftwaffe was destroying the RAF, the German

Britain would fight, Churchill told the House of Commons, "whatever the cost may be . . . we shall never surrender." Throughout the island men of peace like this vicar (left) learned how to kill Germans if need be. The skies blossomed (lower right) with balloons to keep German planes high and away from prime targets. Luftwaffe commanders in France could look across the narrow English Channel to the white cliffs of Dover. Reichsmarshal Hermann Göring, their leader, is third from the right.

Navy would have two months to organize the invasion craft and the German Army could practice amphibious assault.

The air battle over Britain was fought in three overlapping phases. From July 10 to mid-August the Luftwaffe hammered at shipping in the Channel and at the docks and harbor facilities of southern England. From August 13 to September 6, it concentrated on fighter airfields and aircraft factories. The Germans might have won if they'd kept at this. Instead, in the third phase, they turned on London and other cities, hoping to break the will of the British people.

In quality of pilots and aircraft, Britain and Germany were evenly matched, but the RAF was outnumbered in fighter aircraft. In early August, the Luftwaffe had 2550 planes including 1029 fighters, 998 bombers and 261 dive-bombers. To oppose them Britain's Fighter Command had 708 Hurricane and Spitfire fighters, and some 40 two-seater Blenheims and Defiants. In addition, the British had a crucial weapon—a chain of radar stations that gave early warning of raids and indicated where to intercept the enemy.

By far the largest number of defenders were Britons, but fighter pilots of many other nations flew with them, including some 80 Canadians. Of these, 26 were in the RCAF's No. 1 Squadron, which arrived soon after Dunkirk; 16 flew as a team in the RAF's 242 "Canadian" Squadron; the rest were scattered among a dozen other RAF squadrons. These last included men such as PO. Johnnie Bryson, an ex-Mountie; Flt. Lt. Johnnie Kent of Winnipeg, who flew with the Poles in 303 Squadron; and FO. W. H. Nelson, who served in 74 Squadron with the South African ace Adolph "Sailor" Malan. Another 200 Canadian airmen fought in RAF Bomber and Coastal commands, which throughout the battle pounded at German invasion ports and other targets; 27 of them gave their lives.

On July 11, the second day of the battle, the Canadians suffered their first fighter casualty. In a Luftwaffe attack on the naval

base at Portland, PO. D. A. Hewitt of Saint John, N.B., hurled his 501 Squadron Hurricane at a Dornier bomber and was hit himself. Gushing smoke, his plane plunged into the sea.

Another Canadian pilot, Richard Howley, died eight days later; two more, A. W. Smith and Hugh Tamblyn, had narrow escapes. All were in 141 Squadron and flew the Defiant, a two-seater hunchback with a large power-operated gun turret which bulged its lines and crippled its speed. One pilot said later: "The Defiant should not have been used as a fighter. It had no guns up front and when the pilot put the aircraft into a tight turn, the gunner was forced down until he couldn't see his gunsight."

Over Folkestone that day, 20 Messerschmitt 109s came out of the sun from 15,000 feet and dived on nine Defiants. Two of four machine guns in Tamblyn's plane couldn't fire: the squadron had scrambled while the guns were being re-armed. Within five minutes, only two of the nine Defiants remained. They survived largely because of Hurricane pilots who dived to the rescue. Five Defiant crews, including Howley and his gunner, were killed. One Me 109 was shot down.

biography, *Reach for the Sky,* by Paul Brickhill:

. . . The pilots were all down at the dispersal huts, on readiness, when he arrived. At A flight's hut, Bader pushed the door open and stumped in unheralded. From his lurching walk the Canadians knew who he was. A dozen pairs of eyes surveyed him coolly. No one got up. Hands stayed in pockets. The room was silent. Watchful.

At last Bader said, "Who's in charge here?" No one answered.

"Well, who's the senior?" Again no answer, though men looked at one another inquiringly.

"Isn't anyone in charge?" A large dark young man said: "I guess not."

Radar held the key to Britain's victory. German aircraft were detected and tracked by stations near the coast (below), then plotted by WAAFs in Fighter Command operations rooms as Hurricanes (right) and Spitfires climbed to intercept. With members of his No. 1 RCAF Squadron is Sqdn. Ldr. Ernest McNab (front center), the first RCAF pilot to shoot down a German plane in the Battle of Britain. The others, from left: FO. Bill Sprenger, FO. O. J. Peterson, Flt. Lt. W. R. Pollock, FO. Paul Pitcher (behind McNab), FO. Phil Lochnan, Flt. Lt. E. M. Reyno, FO. Eric Beardmore, FO. S. T. Blaiklock and FO. R. W. Norris.

After their fighting in France, the pilots of the badly-mauled RAF 242 "Canadian" Squadron were re-forming at Coltishall, near Norwich, where they became part of 12 Group guarding the industrial Midlands; 11 Group held the front line to the south. The Canadians were awaiting a new CO, Douglas Bader. A peacetime RAF pilot, Bader had lost both legs in an air crash in 1931, had been fitted with artificial limbs and had taught himself not only to walk without a stick but also to play golf, tennis and squash. When war came, he'd badgered his way back into the RAF and proved he could fly as well as any pilot. Now, in his first command, Bader was determined to make 242 the best squadron in the RAF. But it might be a battle—the Canadians, he was told, were a wild lot and a tough bunch to lead. From Bader's

Bader eyed them a little longer, anger flaring, turned abruptly and went out.

In B flight dispersal the eyes again stared silently. "Who's in charge here?" he asked.

After a while a thick-set young man with wiry hair and a face chipped out of granite rose slowly and said, "I guess I am." He wore the single ring of a flying officer.

"Isn't there a flight commander?"

"There's one somewhere but he isn't here," said the young man.

"What's your name?"

"Turner." And then, after a pause, "sir."

Bader walked out. A dozen yards from the door a Hurricane crouched with the humpbacked, bowlegged look of all Hurricanes. Over the airfield for half an hour he tumbled it round the sky, one acrobatic merging into another. When he taxied in

the pilots were standing outside watching, but he climbed out unaided, got into his car and drove off.

Later he called the pilots to his office and silently eyed the rumpled uniforms, the preference for turtle-neck sweaters instead of shirts and ties, the long hair and general untidy air. At last he spoke: "You're a scruffy lot. A good squadron *looks* smart. I don't want to see flying boots or sweaters in the mess. You will wear shoes and shirts and ties. Is that clear?"

It was a mistake. Turner said unemotionally, in his deep, slow Canadian voice: "Most of us don't have any shoes or shirts or ties except what we're wearing."

"What d'you mean?" Bader said aggressively.

"We lost everything in France." With a trace of cynicism, Turner explained the chaos of the running fight, how they had apparently been deserted by authority, shunted about, welcome nowhere, separated from their ground staff till it had been every man for himself, each pilot servicing his own aircraft, and sleeping under his own wing. The squadron had suffered nearly 50 percent casualties. When the end had come they had flown back across the Channel. Since then things had not greatly improved and they were drifting. There was no self-pity in Turner's story, only a restrained anger.

"I'm sorry," said Bader. "I apologize for my remarks." A silence. "Have you claimed an allowance for loss of kit?" Apparently they had, and it was assumed, with more cynicism, that the claim was drifting along the proper channels. "Right," Bader said. "Tomorrow go into Norwich, to the tailors. Order what you want. I'll guarantee it's paid. Meantime, beg or borrow shoes and shirts. I've got some shirts and you can borrow all I've got. Okay?"

"That's fine, sir," said Turner.

"Right! Now take it easy. What fighting have you had?" The next half hour was a lively discussion on various aspects of the trade.

After lunch Bader led them into the air in twos and was pleased to see they knew how to handle their Hurricanes, though their formation (by his standards) was rather ragged. That night he turned his charm on them. Finally one pilot put down his empty pint pot and said, "Hell, sir, we were scared you were going to be another

With the German Army set to invade Britain, the Luftwaffe flew more and more missions across the Channel (top). Among the defenders were Douglas Bader and his 242 "Canadian" Squadron—above, from left: Crowley-Milling, Tamblyn, Turner, Saville (on wing), Campbell, McKnight, Bader, Ball, Homer, Ben Brown. Right: Bader and McKnight, with 242 booting Hitler. Top right: Mark "Hilly" Brown, a Manitoban who had downed 15 planes over France with No. 1 RAF Squadron. Shot down August 15, he wrote home: "I suffered facial burns but they have healed very well and I expect to be flying in a day or two. The next time you send me anything, you might include some Spanish peanuts. I was just thinking yesterday how I would like to have a chew at some."

goddam figurehead." The evening progressed with great hilarity.

Next morning people were neater and earlier—and busy. The new CO was everywhere, at dispersals, in the maintenance hangar, the radio hut, instrument section. Two English flight commanders arrived; Eric Ball took over A flight and George Powell-Sheddon B flight. The squadron was becoming a team.

The Hurricanes were hardly ever out of the air, ranging over Norfolk in formation and cloud flying, climbing on practice interceptions, tangling in mock dogfights. The first time Bader did dawn readiness he slept as usual with the rostered pilots in the dispersal hut, taking his legs off and parking them beside his iron cot, complete with shoes, socks and trousers so he could be ready for action before the others.

It was the first time they'd seen him with his legs off and surreptitiously they eyed them, fascinated. It was uncanny to see that a man so vital *did* have artificial legs. The legend was true.

Within a fortnight 242 Squadron was a cohesive unit. Bader lived for his squadron and expected all his men to do likewise. His swashbuckling figure was likely to appear anywhere as undisputed head of the family. As Turner said to West, the squadron engineer officer: "Legs or no legs, I've never seen such a goddam mobile fireball."

The muscular Stan Turner himself was not a mild man, having a large capacity for beer and a penchant for firing off a revolver in public. The wing commander had suggested: "You ought to get rid of that chap. He's too wild." But Bader saw eye-to-eye with Turner, a first-class pilot, fearless and decisive. In fact, he made him a section leader and found that responsibility curbed his wildness.

Already he had his eye on several pilots as section leaders, in particular Hugh Tamblyn, who'd been posted here from 141 Squadron and its clumsy Defiants. The handsome Tamblyn had an air of reliability about him, and so did Noel Stansfeld and Laurie Cryderman. Two years before Cryderman had been leading a jazz band. Another Canadian, Norrie Hart, had painted on his Hurricane a chamber pot with swastikas falling into it. John Latta was a dark, slight young man with the dourness of his Scottish ancestors. Ben Brown was very handsome, very brave and a very bad shot. Neil Campbell was even more handsome. Bob Grassick was blithely imperturbable. All the Canadians seemed fearless, none more so than Willie McKnight, a flinty-eyed little dead-shot who had already won a DFC in action over France. He was a tough little man with a weakness for soft music; he had a large collection of Bing Crosby records and played them endlessly in the evenings.

Apart from Bader and the two flight commanders, the only English pilot on the squadron was Denis Crowley-Milling. There was also Roy Bush, a New Zealander. Yet no one noticed nationality; they were too busy training and life under the new CO was stimulating, though no fighting seemed in sight. One never saw a German aircraft up there in the Midlands. Pity, in a way. . . .   PAUL BRICKHILL

To the south, action was building up as the Battle of Britain went into its second phase. On August 13—*Adler Tag,* the Germans called it, Eagle Day—the Luftwaffe launched mass attacks on airfields. Save for a five-day respite, this assault lasted until September 6 with high casualties on both sides. At the outset, PO. Joseph Larichelière of Montreal, with 213 Squadron, shot down six planes in two days. A day later he was killed.

PO. Harry Mitchell of Port Hope, Ont., chalked up a triple in one day in action with 87 Squadron on August 14.

By now the RCAF's No. 1 Squadron was about to be committed to battle. Its men had moved to Croydon airfield, just south of London, in early July for six weeks of operational training. While the battle raged overhead, they flew each

morning to nearby Northolt for instruction with the Air Fighting Development Unit. For Sqdn. Ldr. Ernest McNab those weeks of July and early August were intense with worry. Were his men qualified to meet the Germans? Of their flying skills he had no doubts; his squadron had some of Canada's most experienced aviators, both career RCAF men and a band of keen young "Sunday pilots," mainly well-to-do Montrealers from No. 115 Auxiliary Squadron. Two of the latter, Gordon McGregor and Deane Nesbitt, had won peacetime flying trophies. But this was not peacetime flying.

The 26 pilots were aware of this. As a group they were sometimes kidded about being "old men." McNab, McGregor and Hartland Molson were in their late 30s. Most were in their late 20s. Only four, Dal Russel, Arthur Yuile, Bev Christmas and Tom Little, were really young. Yet this had its advantages: the squadron trained with a maturity others didn't have.

To gain combat experience, McNab arranged for himself and McGregor to go on operations with 111 Squadron. They could not have chosen a better day. On August 15, the Luftwaffe hurled almost its entire operational strength—more than 2100 aircraft—at Britain. McNab's flight intercepted one formation over the Thames estuary, and he shot down a Dornier bomber.

His kill drew first blood for the RCAF. Two days later No. 1 Squadron was posted "operational" and moved to Northolt. The battle was at its height. Since August 8, RAF Fighter Command had lost 98 pilots and 60 wounded. To meet the shortage, 53 volunteers from other commands were called in as reinforcements.

"This was the lowest point in my life," McNab later recalled. "I didn't think my men were ready for combat." They had fired at a moving target only once. Their aircraft recognition training had consisted of an instructor hastily shuffling a pile of silhouettes.

For several days no aircraft came their way. Then on August 24, in the confusion of battle, there occurred one of those inevitable and tragic incidents of war. Richard Collier records in his book *Eagle Day:*
. . . McNab's Canadians, 12 strong, were bulling west toward Chichester harbor, eyes squinting against the blinding afternoon sun. German bombers were reported heading north across the Isle of Wight, and at HQ 11 Group the controller feared the worst: the raiders must be bound for

Tangmere sector station. The Canadians were to intercept the Germans over Selsey Bill, the southernmost part of the west Sussex coastline.

Nine miles northwest, at Thorney Island, three RAF Blenheim patrol planes of 235 Squadron, Coastal Command, were sent on the same mission. Now the controllers spotted the German intention: a mass strike against Portsmouth harbor. Over Selsey, McNab's Canadians realized it, too; black oily puffs of smoke hung in the sky to the west. At 4:40 p.m., at 10,000 feet, the Canadians swung toward Portsmouth. For the first time, they became aware what fear could do. McNab's palate was "as dry as cotton wool." Dal

the white flash on the fins. British! His section broke violently to port and didn't attack. But the following planes saw what they took to be long yellow spears of tracer curving toward them, and opened fire, not realizing the Blenheims were firing yellow and red Very pistol flares, the recognition signal.

Tires holed, undercarriage wrecked, one Blenheim escaped the point-blank fire by crash-landing. A second got down too—starboard engine holed, windscreen starred with thick opaque blotches. It was pure tragedy that the third Blenheim never made it. Smoke streaming from its tail plane, its starboard engine on fire, it spiraled toward the sea. Then another burst

climbed, shifted the formation to sections to starboard, and dived out of the sun from 16,000 feet with throttles wide open, his leader's cry of "Tally-ho!" crackling into the earphones.

McNab fired his eight guns at one Dornier but even as he watched it burst into flame, his own aircraft was hit, forcing him to land. Now FO. R. L. Edwards, No. 2 in McNab's section, wheeled to attack. Opening up at a Dornier at almost point-blank range, he shot off its tail assembly. Then Edwards was hit, and his Hurricane went down out of control. The sky was a twisting maze of snarling aircraft, and in the delirium of the fight, each man was on his own, singling out a target, jockeying

Russel, chewing gum, felt the wad cleave to the roof of his mouth; later he had to prise it clear.

Ahead, at 6000 feet, three aircraft were flying in line astern, heading away from Portsmouth. Through the ack-ack puffs, McNab saw them as Junkers 88s. To Flt. Lt. Gordon McGregor, "Those planes were black—black against the sun."

McNab, leading his section of three, called, "Echelon, starboard, go!" and they put the Hurricanes' noses down and their right thumbs on the gun buttons. Then they were diving at 300 miles an hour, too fast for all to hear McNab's scream in their earphones: "Break, break! Don't attack!"

From 3000 feet above the dark silhouettes, McNab had seen the gun turrets which Ju 88s conspicuously lacked—and

came. It fell apart, blazing, before it struck the water.

Even now the Canadians didn't appreciate what had happened. Back at Northolt, the station commander broke the news gently. McNab cried: "My God, what have we done? What can I do?" The commander was compassionate: "There's nothing you can do; these things happen. The one thing you must do is fly down and explain." . . .　　　　RICHARD COLLIER

Within 48 hours the squadron had made amends. On August 26, it flew to North Weald to relieve a RAF unit and that afternoon was ordered to intercept 30 Dornier bombers approaching across Essex. While a Spitfire patrol drew off the fighter escort, McNab led his 12 Hurricanes into the sun in line astern. He

into position, cursing, firing. Then away into a tight turn, tighter and tighter, till the blood seemed to turn to lead and vision blurred.

In a few minutes it was over and the sky was clear. Ammunition spent, the Canadians returned to base to tally the score: three Dorniers destroyed, four damaged. Then the grim news: Edwards was dead, the first RCAF pilot to die in action. In his diary, he had noted that the prettiest, most peaceful place he had seen in England was Woking, in Surrey. He was buried in its cemetery.

The squadron saw more and more action. On August 31, patrolling the Dover coast at 22,000 feet, they were attacked out of the sun by Messerschmitts. So rapid was the attack, so deadly the fire, that only two Canadians could bring their guns into

Ju 87s, Stuka dive-bombers which made a fearsome whining noise in plunging to attack, head for a target in Britain. They had been highly successful over Poland and France but were so badly mauled over Britain that they had to be withdrawn. In air force slang all German aircraft were bandits. Here Canadian pilots scramble—race for their fighters—after radar and plot have established the course of enemy attackers.

action. Three Hurricanes were badly damaged and the pilots bailed out, two of them —FO. George Hyde and FO. Vaughn Corbett—burned about the face, hands and legs. As Corbett jumped, his parachute harness failed. At 300 feet a second, he fell headfirst for a mile until his parachute opened and wafted him into a hospital garden. When Bill Sprenger was hit, the instrument panel started exploding in his face. Controls shot away, his Hurricane dropped a mile before he could slip from the emergency hatch. With two mates circling protectively, he drifted to earth in his parachute. Another Canadian, Eric Beardmore, discovered that enemy fire had carried away his air-speed indicator and elevator controls and riddled his tail plane "like a piece of Swiss cheese." He nursed his Hurricane home.

That afternoon the score was evened when the Canadians intercepted over Gravesend. Flying Officers Little and Bev Christmas each shot down an Me109 and FO. Ross Smither was credited with another damaged. Flying Officer Kerwin sent a Dornier diving headlong into the sea and FO. Dal Russel damaged another. The Canadian loss was one Hurricane; its pilot, FO. Jean-Paul Desloges, badly burned, parachuted to safety.

All that August, Bader and the Canadians of 242 Squadron waited impatiently. Paul Brickhill in *Reach for the Sky*:

. . . It was 11 Group's battle and 12 Group was held back. Burning for the fight, Bader pleaded with 12 Group's commander, Air Vice-Marshal Trafford Leigh-Mallory. But Leigh-Mallory told him: "You've got to hang on. The enemy would be delighted

London (right) was bombed—and took it—for 57 consecutive nights as the air force "gave it 'em back." In this sequence a Messerschmitt 110 is attacked from astern and takes hits (1) on the rear of the cockpit. The starboard engine bursts into flame (2), smoke envelops the plane (3) and (4) it begins its dive to destruction in the sea.

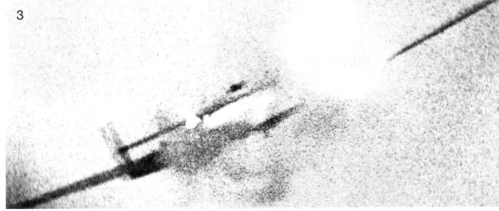

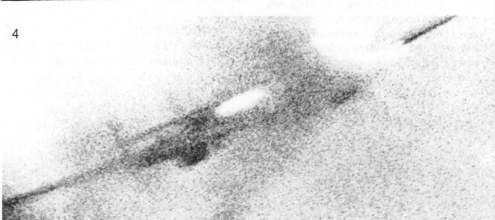

to draw our fighter cover away from the Midlands. I can't send you in until 11 Group calls for you."

It was hard waiting. Then, on the morning of August 30, the order came: "242 Squadron take off immediately for Duxford!" Duxford lay south, not far from London. Whooping wildly, the pilots ran for their Hurricanes.

By 10 a.m. the planes stood round the Duxford field and Bader's men waited in a restless knot. And waited. From Ops they heard that the Luftwaffe was storming over southern England, but still 11 Group sent no call. Bader sat by the phone, seething. At 4:45 the phone rang: "242 Squadron scramble! Angels 15 [climb to 15,000 feet]. North Weald."

As the wheels folded into the wings and the rest of the pack thundered behind, Bader flicked the R/T switch: "Laycock Red Leader calling Steersman. Am airborne." A measured voice answered: "Hallo, Laycock Red Leader, Steersman answering. Vector [course] one-nine-zero. Buster [full throttle]. Seventy-plus bandits [enemy aircraft] approaching North Weald." He rec-

ognized the voice of Wing Comdr. A. B. Woodhall, Duxford station commander.

Behind Bader the 12-Hurricane squadron slid into battle stations, four vics—V-shaped formations of three planes each—in line astern. They climbed steeply south through haze. Holding a map on his thigh, Bader saw that 190 degrees led over North Weald fighter station. The sun hung over the starboard wing and he knew what he would do if he were the German leader: come in from the sun! From the southwest. This was no good. He wanted to be up sun himself. Disregarding the controller's words, he swung 30 degrees west. At 9000 feet he was boring steeply up over the haze in steady air, eyes probing to the left, seeing nothing.

"B-b-blue Leader calling Laycock Leader. Th-th-three aircraft three o'clock below." It was Powell-Sheddon's stuttering voice.

Over the rim of the cockpit he saw three dots well to the beam. They might be anything.

Then came the order: "Blue section investigate." Powell-Sheddon peeled off to

starboard, followed by his two satellites. Nine left against 70-plus.

Southwest of North Weald a glint, then another and in seconds a mass of little dots; too many to be British. The skin tingled. The blood pulsed. Bader shoved his throttle forward and called tersely: "Enemy aircraft ten o'clock level."

Now the dots looked like a swarm of bees droning steadily northeast, stepped up from a vanguard at 12,000 feet. The bombers were in tidy lines of four and six abreast, and he was counting the lines: 14 lines—and above and behind them about 30 more planes that looked like Me 110 fighters. Above them still more. Over 100. The Hurricanes were above the main swarm now, swinging down on them from the southwest out of the sun, a good spot to start a fight if the 110s had not been above. The main swarm were Dorniers. Must go for them. Too bad about the Messerschmitts above. Have to risk them. He called:

"Green section take on the top lot." FO. Pat Christie of Westmount, Que., led his three up and away to the right.

There were thousands of scrambles (left), hundreds of air battles big and small, and heavy casualties on both sides. Below, at left, a British pilot plunges to his death, his plane framed by the silhouette of a German machine gun. Nearby is a second enemy aircraft. Flt. Lt. J. A. "Johnnie" Kent (right), from Winnipeg, was a Battle of Britain flight commander with the RAF's 303 (Polish) Squadron—"Kentowski," they called him. By the end of the war Kent was credited with 13 aircraft destroyed, two "probables" and three damaged. Below: Fighter pilots, ready for immediate takeoff, await the order to scramble.

Bader again: "Red and yellow sections, line astern, line astern." From 1000 feet above he dived on the swarm of 70 followed by the last five Hurricanes, and now among the Dorniers saw more Me 110 fighters. Rage shook him. A demonic compulsion told him to dive into the middle of that smug formation and break it up. He aimed into the middle.

Black crosses! Glinting perspex! Wings that spread and grew hugely, filling the windscreen. He was on them and suddenly the drilled lines burst in mad turns left and right out of the sights, out of the way. He swept under and up, swinging right. A ripple was running through the great herd, and then it was splitting, scattering. Glimpse of Willie McKnight hunting left, Crowley-Milling lunging ahead, three 110s wheeling in front. The last was too slow. Just behind, he thumbed the button and almost instantly, as the bullets squirted, pieces flew off the 110. Fire blossomed into long flames as it heeled over.

The blood was fired, nerve and muscle taut, the brain racing. Above to the right another 110 was slowly curling out of a stall-turn and he reefed his nose up after it, closing fast. A hundred yards behind, he fired for three seconds; the 110 rocked, and he fired again. Flames burst along the starboard wing and the 110 was going down, blazing.

Full of the fire of the kill, he looked for others and suddenly his exultation chilled; in the mirror above his eyes a 110 poked its nose above the rudder, slanting in. He steep-turned hard and over his shoulder saw the 110 heeling after, white streaks of tracer flicking from its nose past his tail. The Hurricane turned faster and the 110 dived and vanished under his wing. Bader spiraled steeply after, saw the 110 well below, streaking east, and chased it, but the 110 was going for home like a bat out of hell and it was hopeless. He was startled to see he was down to 6000 feet. Sweating and dry-mouthed, he pulled up, but the fight was over. The sky was empty and he wondered again, as all pilots wondered, that a mass of raging aircraft could vanish in seconds.

A lone Hurricane appeared on the left, and he ruddered toward it till he saw the emblem painted on its side—a picture of Death holding a big scythe, dripping blood. Willie McKnight! He raised two fingers to indicate he had got a couple. The Canadian nodded vigorously and then three of his fingers spread above the cockpit rim. Three! And they headed home.

When all the Hurricanes were back, the pilots came in hanging on the sides of the flight trucks, cheering and yelling: "Did you get one?" Drunk on high spirits, they pieced the battle together: a Dornier had crashed into a greenhouse, another into a field, a 110 into a reservoir, a Dornier into a plowed field. Turner got one, Crowley-Milling shot the belly out of a Heinkel, Ball had one . . . several others. They totted up the score, 12 confirmed and several damaged. The rest had fled. Not a single bullet hole in any Hurricanes. Not a bomb on North Weald.

Bader led the squadron back to Coltishall, turning in his cockpit to make rude and hilarious gestures. . . . PAUL BRICKHILL

Action had given Bader an idea: meet strength with strength, build wings of three

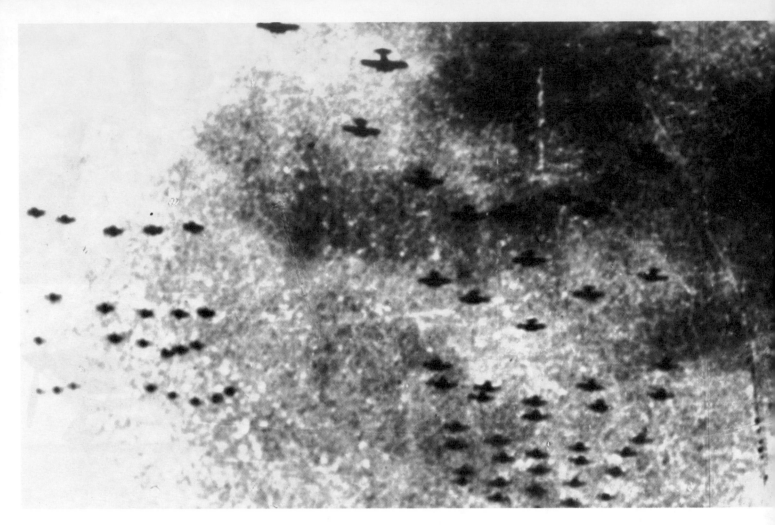

or more squadrons to combat the large German formations. He got the green light, and 242 found itself part of the experiment. On September 7, they tried it but the scramble call came too late. Of the three squadrons, only 242 got into action. Two days later the wing was back at Duxford again, and this time they all made it. When the fight was over, 242 had knocked down 11 planes, including two to McKnight. The other squadrons had destroyed nine.

But two men were missing. One had bailed out and eventually got back. The other, Pat Sclanders of Saint John, N.B., was dead.

September 9 had been a successful day also for the RCAF's No. 1 Squadron. In a dogfight with Messerschmitts escorting Dorniers over southeast London, it had downed four aircraft. FO. O. J. Peterson had attacked a Dornier so close that, as he fired, pieces flew off and shattered the windscreen of his Hurricane. His face cut and his eyes filled with tiny pieces of plexiglass, Peterson fell 11,000 feet before he could regain control.

After three hectic weeks the Canadian pilots were weary. Most days they reported for duty at 4 a.m. On waking, some pilots simply pulled their flying suits over pajamas; in the evening they had merely to slip off their suits and fall into bed.

At first light, the pilots reported to the dispersal hut, slipped on Mae West life jackets, fitted parachutes in their planes—and waited. Dispersal was a shack with a coal stove to ease the morning chill. Its walls were adorned with posters and girlie pictures, and on one wall was a telephone. This was the nerve center. The first ring was a warning that radar had picked up enemy bandits. The second was the scramble call: get up and intercept!

"Every time that phone rang, your stomach rolled over," recalled FO. Paul Pitcher of Montreal. "Mostly because of the hour, we would be lying down when that first ring came. So all of us would get up and stroll about, trying to look nonchalant. This was the worst moment, waiting. Things were different in action; you were so busy you couldn't remember later what happened."

When the scramble came, the 12 duty pilots raced for their machines, already started up by ground crews. The hum of idling engines changed to a roar as the formation took off. At the head of the leading vic was McNab. Bringing up the rear, weaving from side to side to protect the squadron from surprise attack from astern, were the Tail-end Charlies. It was not a popular position. Said one pilot: "You were either promoted from this spot, or you were buried."

By the second week of September, when the raids on London were reaching their height, the Canadians were veterans. They had learned that the best way to break up a large bomber formation was to hurl themselves at it head-on so the Germans would scatter. They had discovered how to deal with the Germans' "circle of death," a defensive gambit used by the twin-engine Me 110s which were often sent into action as fighter-bombers. On sighting British fighters, the Me 110s would form a circle, flying propeller-to-tail in a defensive ring against fighters. The Canadians had come up against this tactic

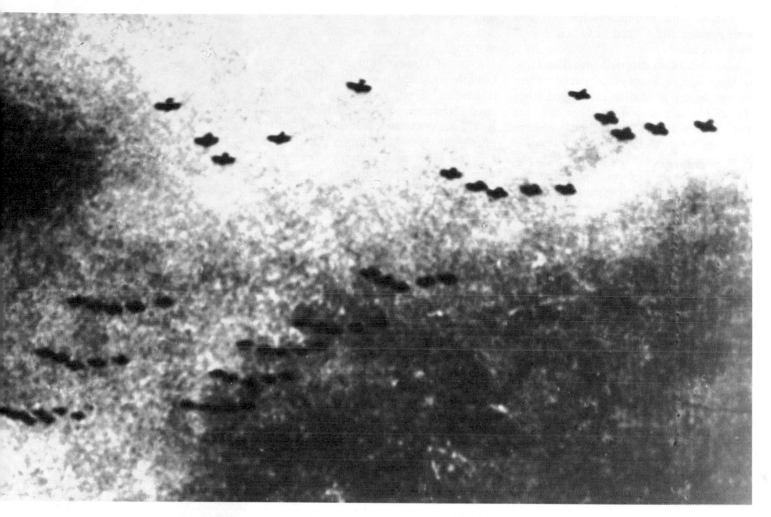

Bandits over Biggin Hill: the German air force heads for London—and defeat. Londoners, said Churchill, had in their bones "the confidence of an unconquered people."

on September 4 when McGregor was leading the squadron. Instead of attacking from outside the circle, McGregor led his Hurricanes 3000 feet above the Germans. Then, one by one, they dived out of the sun. As they reached the circling Messerschmitts, they wheeled *inside* the ring, flying in the opposite direction so each Canadian could deliver a near head-on attack on each German plane in turn. The Me 110s, unable to bring their fixed forward guns to bear on the Canadians circling in their midst, were forced to break formation. The squadron's score: two aircraft shot down, one probably destroyed, six damaged, and not one Canadian casualty.

As the air war built up, so did the tension. Some pilots sought relief in sleep; others tried to unwind at late night parties in town. From Northolt they would drive to London in a 1911 Rolls Royce, complete with a liveried chauffeur named Sebastian. They learned that a few whiffs of oxygen through a pilot's mask would not only give a man a boost in the air, but helped on the morning after an all-night celebration.

Almost every fighter pilot felt a sense of doom in those razor-edged days when a newcomer often would die before he had qualified for a change of sheets. Some tried to blot it out in liquor; others couldn't drink at all. At 242 Squadron, Roland Dibnah found the tension so great that even one jigger of liquor nauseated him. Douglas Bader, however, seemed almost insensitive to danger. With his infectious exuberance, he designed the squadron's emblem, a figure of Hitler being kicked in the breeches by a flying boot labeled 242. The design was painted on all 242 Hurricanes.

The climax came Sunday, September 15, the day now officially known as the anniversary of the Battle of Britain. Said Air Vice-Marshal Keith Park, 11 Group commander: "It was one of those days of autumn when the countryside is at its loveliest."

Richard Collier in *Eagle Day:*

... The morning began with a conference at 11 Group headquarters at Uxbridge. At 10:30 a.m. Park was startled to see Winston Churchill. He'd no wish to disturb anyone, he said, but he and his wife had been passing and looked in to see if anything was afoot.

Churchill often dropped into The Hole at Uxbridge, a bombproof nerve center 50 feet below ground, camouflaged from above into a golf course. This was the first focal point of every battle, where the duty controller, sifting information from radar stations and observer posts, allotted raids by sectors, planning the opening gambits like a gigantic game of chess. As Churchill's party trooped down to the Ops room, Park warned, "I don't know whether anything will happen today, sir."

All over southern England, the pilots shared Park's feelings: if trouble was afoot, there was no sign of it. Squadron after squadron sought distraction in music—nostalgic, ragtime—any familiar music. At Hornchurch, PO. "Razz" Berry's phonograph was forever grinding out "Sweet Violetta" and "She Had to Go and Lose It at The Astor." At 242 Squadron's dispersal at Duxford, a doggerel pop of the day, "Three Little Fishes," grated interminably over the loudspeaker. Bader, making the rounds of his now five-squadron fighter wing, quietly assured the Poles of one squadron: "You'll soon be back in Warsaw."

At 11 Group headquarters, Wing Comdr. Eric Douglas-Jones watched the six telephones linking him with the fighter sectors and the six bulb-lit panels charting every sector's squadrons. By now trouble *was* imminent. The plotters at the map were piloting the colored disks with their long croupier's rods: 40-plus coming in from Dieppe, corrected swiftly to 60-plus. Seconds later, 80-plus, direction Calais. Even Douglas-Jones, a seasoned controller, now felt a brooding sense of crisis.

A dead cigar gripped in his teeth, Churchill broke silence: "There appear to be many aircraft coming in." Park reassured him: "There'll be someone there to meet them."

Along the coast of southern England, 50,000 men and women of the Observer Corps, binoculars leveled, peered toward the mist-shrouded sky. As the faint, far specks grew in number, their officers, prone among yellow gorse on the chalky cliff tops, lifted their field telephones. Their warnings lent weight to the radar reports. At Pevensey, Rye, Swinggate and Poling, the German formations had swum

into focus: wide, deep, steadily-beating echoes, arising from the mists of the morning.

From Rye radar station, Cpl. Daphne Griffiths reported urgently: "Hostile Six is now at 15 miles, height 15,000." At once Stanmore queried, "How many, Rye?" and the answer flashed back: "Fifty-plus." Still, in 11 Group's Ops room, Douglas-Jones made no move. The squadrons needed height and sun. But supposing this was a feint?

At 11:03 a.m. he could wait no longer. He reached for a telephone and automatically, 35 miles away, a bulb glowed on the desk of Sqdn. Ldr. Roger Frankland, controlling at Biggin Hill.

As Douglas-Jones, using the direct secret line, ordered "72 and 92 squadrons to patrol Canterbury, angels 20," Frankland seized his microphone; simultaneously identical instructions, further coded to fox German fighters, volleyed across Biggin Hill airfield: "Gannic squadron, scramble."

To the first pilots airborne, it seemed that the Luftwaffe, as never before, held the sky. Twenty thousand feet over Canterbury Cathedral, PO. Anthony Bartley, 92 Squadron, noted cotton-wool puffs of flak staining the sky; a vast gaggle of bombers was winging inland, evading the guns with ease, closely escorted by Me 109s, 3000 feet below and astern. Awed, he muttered, "Where the hell do we start?"

At 11:25 a.m., learning that every 11 Group squadron was in action, the RCAF's No. 1 among them, Duxford sent Bader's 12 Group wing speeding to London.

The Luftwaffe streamed across the Channel, slim logger-headed Dorniers, glinting shark-nosed 109s, slow, scantily-armed Heinkel 111s, many decorated with insignia as colorful as any air force had ever boasted ... the green dragon signifying Hauptman Hans von Hahn's 1st Wing, 3rd Fighter Group ... Major Adolf Galland's Mickey Mouse, armed with gun and hatchet, puffing a cigar like Galland's own ... the eagle's head of Werner Mölders ... Major von Cramon-Taubadel's jet-black ace of spades. Minute by minute the swarm grew denser.

Now, as the two forces locked in battle, the sky became filled with darting aluminum shapes and billowing parachutes. All of the 21 British squadrons airborne since

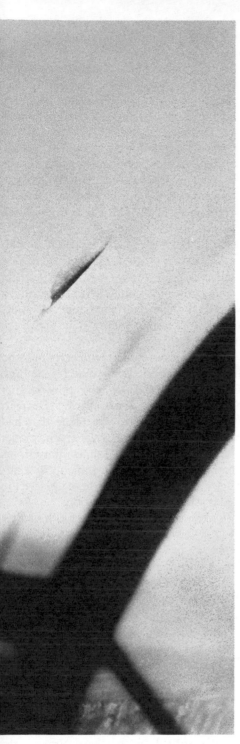

11 a.m. had intercepted, though not all had met with marked success.

At 18,000 feet over Biggin Hill, Mc-Nab's Canadians never saw the 109s that slashed at them from the sun. Their formation broken up by the attack, only two of the Hurricanes closed with the raiders. At close range, Deane Nesbitt shot one Me down in flames, then had to bail out of his burning Hurricane. He drifted to earth with back injuries. Ross Smither was dead, shot down in the first seconds of attack.

Now, as Big Ben boomed noon, 148 German bombers broke through undeterred to central London, landing one bomb, unexploded, in King George's back garden at Buckingham Palace. Arriving late from the north, Bader's wing spotted the bombers five miles distant, "like black flies sliding toward the naked city." As they gave chase to the west, they little by little gained height and sun—and suddenly, unbelievably, the bombers turned, sweeping into their sights.

By now the radio-telephone was pandemonium; at the spearhead of 302 Squadron, Sqdn. Ldr. Jack Satchell heard Bader shout, "Weigh-in, everyone for himself." Ten thousand feet above, where 12 Group's Spitfires waited to tackle the fighters, Flt. Lt. Jack Leather chuckled to hear Bader explode: "Let's get the bastards." Promptly, Woodhall's soothing voice sounded from Duxford: "Douglas, remember there are ladies in the Ops room."

At 11 Group headquarters, one lady didn't mind; while Churchill remained tensely on the controller's dais, his wife, tuned in to a nearby radio-telephone link-up, heard a flood of oaths as the Poles sighted the bombers. When a shocked staff officer made to switch off, Clementine Churchill restrained him: "It's lovely, I wouldn't have missed it."

Twenty-seven thousand feet over London, Sqdn. Ldr. James McComb of Bader's force throttled back with mounting

At the height of the battle: (above left) a RAF pilot, his parachute, his Hurricane and its severed port wing fill the sky in front of a German Dornier over the Channel; (left) a Dornier plummets toward London's Victoria Station on September 15; (above) a dead bandit; (right) a London newspaper seller watches a dogfight high over the British capital.

Children huddled in trenches in parks and gardens but, as Hitler did his worst, thumbs-up Britons still could laugh and dance. "While the defeat of the Luftwaffe in the air incurred an unrepayable debt to The Few," Edward Bishop wrote in *Their Finest Hour: The Story of the Battle of Britain 1940,* "the stoicism of civilians carrying on under the inspiration of Winston Churchill incurred an almost equal debt." Hundreds of British children were eventually evacuated to Canada.

impatience. At this height the intense cobalt blue of the sky, the sun's fiery radiance, his breath condensing like frosted glass on the cockpit canopy were exhilarating sights. But though his Spitfire had waited for seven long minutes to engage the hovering 109s, the German fighters had made no move.

Most were watching their fuel gauges, knowing that the moment to break for the Channel must soon come. But though McComb didn't divine this, he saw Bader's Hurricanes below had the monopoly of the action. He broke radio silence: "To hell with this—we're coming down! Squadron echelon port—St. George for Merrie England."

And down they went. The sky became a wheeling, snarling saraband of warplanes—"the finest shambles I'd ever been in," said Bader.

Few men could know with certainty who fired at whom, or with what results. Sgt. Ray Holmes, a Hurricane pilot of 504 Squadron, hot on the trail of a Dornier, was convinced it was the plane that had bombed Buckingham Palace; no sooner had it blown up than Holmes himself, his Hurricane hit, bailed out. Landing in a garbage can, he phoned his base: his victim had crashed at Victoria Station.

Unknown to Holmes, PO. Keith Ogilvie of Ottawa was just then making this same report to 609's intelligence officer, a feat which earned him a personal commendation from Queen Wilhelmina of the Netherlands. A Palace guest, she was anxious to thank the Canadian for guarding her so zealously.

By 12:29 p.m. the Observer Corps at Bromley, Kent, could report no further raids coming in. Though the sky was scarred with contrails, the last great wave had receded.

The lull would not last long. Even now, on the airfields of northern France, the Germans were refueling and bombing up for the biggest sortie of all. When it came any RAF plane still serviceable was airborne. At 11 Group headquarters Churchill asked Park, "What other reserves have we?"

Park answered: "There are none."

Sector controllers all over southern England marshaled squadrons as 11 Group instructed them. Radio-telephones crackled with call signs: "Hello, Garter, this is Caribou (No. 1 RCAF), your message received and understood" . . . "Hello, Turkey Leader, this is Runic, patrol Maidstone, angels 20" . . . "Laycock Red Leader, this is Dory . . . about 40 bandits heading for Lumba . . . will you patrol?"

By 2:25 p.m. came the last classic interception of the Luftwaffe by Air Chief Marshal Hugh Dowding's fighters: tiny black specks, flashing silver in the sun's rays, machine guns rattling, white parachutes drifting, like the first giant flakes of a snowfall.

To Maj. Adolf Galland, the spearhead of this mighty German force whose task was to clear the skies over Maidstone, it seemed that fresh squadrons had suddenly been conjured from the ground. For ten hectic minutes, Galland wheeled in battle . . . and achieved precisely nothing. Then, sighting Hurricanes 2500 feet below, he swooped at the last plane on the port flank, closing to within ramming distance. Chunks of molten metal beat on his windscreen and, for one fearful instant he was penned in on all sides by Hurricanes. He attacked, an onslaught so stunning that not one Hurricane opened fire, and then the whole formation had burst apart and 1500 feet down Galland saw two pilots bail out.

Fully 3000 feet below, a third Hurricane loomed, and again Galland dived, firing until flames burst from the cowling. Yet still the RAF pilot seemed undaunted; his machine glided serenely on. Three times Galland banked, opening fire—then stopped abruptly. The Hurricane was still spiraling down. The pilot sat relaxed, stone dead.

With German aces like Galland bemused by the whirl of fighters, it was small wonder the bombers paid a bitter price: almost a quarter of all those engaged, with many more seriously damaged. The crucial two-hour delay had given the RAF time to refuel and rearm.

At 2:30 p.m. over southeast London, McNab's No. 1 RCAF dived like angry eagles on 20 Heinkel bombers. A strong Me 109 fighter escort above made little effort to intervene. The 11 Canadian Hurricanes cut the bombers to ribbons. To McNab, the white plumed exhausts of the wheeling aircraft were suddenly "like skywriting gone mad." From the carnage, FO. Phil Lochnan of Ottawa emerged to fulfill ambitions of his own. Belly-landing his Hurricane beside a crashed bomber he had shot down in the mud flats of the Thames estuary, he personally escorted the crew

from the aircraft and became one of the few fighter pilots ever to take a prisoner.

Everywhere now the battle was a clawing, stalling mass of fighters bent on destruction, battling within a cube 80 miles long by 30 broad, more than five miles high: a battle that within 30 minutes would number above 200 individual combats. So crowded was the sky that PO. Patrick Barthropp felt awed. In the morning, he'd noted in his logbook: "Thousands of them." That afternoon, he noted: "*Still thousands.*"

Dowding's Fighter Command was still some 170 pilots under strength, but at this 11th hour a fierce elation had seized every man. Some had bizarre experiences. Stan Turner of 242, his Hurricane's tail afire, was about to bail out over the Thames when he realized there was no necessity. A heavy rain cloud he'd just flown through had extinguished the flames. One Polish pilot, intent on finishing off a Dornier, flew so close that one German bailed out into his propeller, smashing it to pieces. Somehow, the Pole force-landed his bloody Hurricane.

Later, a few perfectionists would see September 15 as a day of failure. At Duxford, Bader was cursing like a trooper. His afternoon scramble had come too late; the Germans had had the height on his wing all the way, the controlling had been inept. Given expert guidance, he maintained, his pilots could have shot down every raider that crossed the coast—and from now on this was Bader's insatiable ambition.

To the newsmen, by contrast, it seemed a day for tributes. *The New York Times'* Robert Post reported: "The German loss of aircrews is tremendous." The London *Daily Express* was sardonic: "Göring may reflect that this is no way to run an invasion." The London *Times* was cautiously confident: "The figures give grounds for sober satisfaction."

What were the figures? On the evening of September 15, the RAF and Anti-Aircraft Command claimed 183 enemy aircraft destroyed. Records later established it as 56 destroyed against a loss of 26 British planes. What is certain is that September 15 marked the turning point. Although the daytime raids continued into October, that day broke the back of Göring's offensive.

On September 17, Germany's Gross Admiral Raeder dictated for the war

diary, "The enemy air force is by no means defeated. On the contrary, it shows increasing activity. The Führer therefore decides to postpone Operation Sea Lion indefinitely."

Within two months, Hitler's resolve was crystallized. An onslaught on Russia assumed full priority.

But on the evening of September 15, nobody among Dowding's pilots thought in terms of final victory. If many messes held parties that night, it was because the nerves demanded one. It was the same across the Channel. Adolf Galland was in Lille, playing ragtime on a café piano. His pilots had hijacked every military road sign for blocks around, and carted them to the café; one officer was swinging from a chandelier. It was long past midnight, but when the provost men strode in to check his papers, Galland just played faster than ever, black cigar clenched in his teeth. He said, "Just look in the *Berliner Illustrierte,* front page." It featured his latest decoration. At this moment, he hated anybody who wasn't a pilot, the whole stinking war.

It was late when Winston Churchill, back home, at last left his study. His bodyguard, Inspector Walter Thompson, was almost out on his feet, and Churchill said, "You're tired out, Thompson." It was the first time the Prime Minister had ever put an arm round his shoulder. Then Churchill said: "It will be worth it in the end. We're going to win, you know." . . .

RICHARD COLLIER

They did. When the Battle of Britain ended the overall score was 1733 German aircraft destroyed for a loss of 915 British fighter aircraft. The 42 Canadian fighter pilots of No. 1 RCAF and 242 Squadron had destroyed an estimated 60, had at least another 50 probably destroyed or damaged. Canadians flying with other fighter squadrons had done equally well. From July 10 to October 31, the dates officially recognized as the opening and closing of the battle, 20 Canadian fighter pilots died in action. Of these, three served with No. 1 Squadron RCAF, three with 242 Squadron the remainder with other RAF squadrons.

As Churchill wrote: ". . . the stamina and valor of our fighter pilots remained unconquerable and supreme. Thus Britain was saved. Well might I say in the House of Commons that 'never in the field of human conflict was so much owed by so many to so few.'"

On guard

Ben Malkin was one of roughly 25,000 Canadian soldiers in Britain in mid-1940. This is his recollection of that time:

... In my regiment, the 3rd Field, Royal Canadian Artillery, confusion was probably no more compounded than in any other unit of the 1st Division during the British Army's retreat to Dunkirk, and after. To a soldier, the army is always confused, faceless, inscrutable, faintly comic. The phrase "situation normal, all fouled up," expressed in the acronym "snafu," is as militarily standard as the incomprehensible order, "don't just stand there, do something!"

We were domiciled on Salisbury Plain that May, completing our training, which meant firing a few rounds of live ammunition from our guns. Until then, we had only pretended to fire them. Upon finishing our 10-day course, we were to proceed to France to engage the Wehrmacht, win the battle for freedom, then go home. Those were our orders.

We arrived on Salisbury Plain three days after the German attack on the Low Countries started. By the time we had fired our guns, the Germans had overrun Holland and Belgium, and were driving the British to the sea. Our own travel plans were canceled after a 48-hour period during which a bemused general staff ordered us to France several times, only to cancel the order each time. About then, we began to lose the amateur standing of volunteers, citizen soldiers with trust in their leaders and their cause. The evident chaos was instilling in us a thoroughly professional attitude—cynical, amused, wholly resigned to our fate, clinging to each other for comfort and morale.

This attitude took sharper form as we engaged in the strange events of the next two months. Shortly after the Dunkirk evacuation, we were sent to Northampton, a manufacturing town on the edge of the Midlands. A motley assembly, we mustered a large number of World War I weapons and civilian trucks, the factories not yet having been fully geared to war production.

Our regiment, and perhaps some others, drove through Northampton several times. There was speculation that we were trying to convince any spies in the area that there were three times as many of us as there actually were. But I have always believed the commanding general, in the lead, was trying to pretend we didn't belong to him and was trying to lose us.

After a few days billeted with civilians, in whom we didn't appear to inject either enthusiasm or confidence, we were taken to Blenheim Castle, about eight miles from Oxford. The whole 3rd Brigade (Royal 22nd, Carleton and York, and West Nova Scotia regiments, ourselves, engineers and medicals) was bivouacked on the grounds and, for undisclosed reasons, a heavy guard was posted at all gates.

Many of us managed to get out anyway, some with passes, some without, for a visit to Oxford. We were bushed after several weeks on the road, and wanted only a little beer and a kindly word. But after being short-changed in fish-and-chip shops and pubs, and being told by the people of Oxford that we were a scruffy-looking lot, we broke up the place. It was the nearest approach to war we'd seen.

We were at Blenheim only a few days when again to horse, for destinations unknown. The prevailing and most reliable rumor originated with the battery commander who said we were probably bound for the south of France, where we could make a landing virtually unopposed, then fight our way north. In the context of some of our other activities of the past month, this plan sounded reasonable.

But we ended up in the middle of a wood, a common near Guildford, south of London, and were told our division was the entire mobile reserve of the British Army. We rolled on the ferns and laughed uncontrollably.

It was not long after, in August, that the Germans began their daylight attacks on the nearby RAF flying fields. We had a view of much of the aerial fighting, as we spent most of our time on maneuvers in the region. The maneuvers were designed mainly to acquaint us with every road in the south of England, so that we of the mobile reserve could get to the invasion point as quickly as possible, or (our professionalism was gaining force as our romanticism died) retreat as rapidly as possible. Since most of our time was spent sitting at the side of a road, waiting for trucks to move, we had no trouble watching the dogfights. They were exciting, but far off. It was hard to feel involved in them. . . .   BEN MALKIN

Airdrome of democracy

Canada trains 131,000 men to fight in the sky

After dinner on the evening of September 26, 1939, Prime Minister Mackenzie King went to his study to leaf through official dispatches from London. He came across one from Prime Minister Neville Chamberlain, a proposal to set up in Canada a large-scale plan for training British, Canadian, Australian and New Zealand aircrew.

"We hope," said Chamberlain, "that you will agree as to the immense influence such a great project may have on the whole course of the war. It might even prove decisive."

King liked the idea. He saw it as a way to lessen pressures for a large army. His government had been thinking of an air-training scheme anyway. And he'd been awed by German airpower in the swift conquest of Poland.

By September 28, he had general cabinet endorsement of a scheme that, 18 months later, Winston Churchill would call "one of the major factors, and possibly the decisive factor, of the war."

That opened the way for detailed discussions, and it wasn't long before King was

indignant over the "railroading, taking-for-granted style" of Britain's chief negotiator, industrialist Lord Riverdale. Always suspicious of British tendencies to want to centralize Commonwealth power, he told his diary it was "amazing how these people from the Old Country seem to think that all they have to do is tell us what is to be done. No wonder they get the backs up of people on this side."

This didn't prevent the broad plan from emerging by early December: 20,000 aircrew would be trained annually under

RCAF direction, with staffs from all four countries. Since the cost to Canada would be much higher than had been foreseen, Britain would buy more Canadian goods and would state publicly that air training would be the most effective contribution Canada could make to the war. Total cost was estimated at $660 million. Britain would pay her way with trainer aircraft, air frames, engines and spare parts. Canada would pay for initial and elementary flying training and for 80 percent of remaining costs.

Financial arrangements were one thing; Canadian identification was another. The British, wrote wartime Air Minister C. G. "Chubby" Power in *A Party Politician,* saw the future of the war almost entirely in terms of airpower, and they wanted control of all the Commonwealth's airmen. "The British idea was essentially to train men from all parts of the Empire and leave their allocation to the RAF."

Canada wanted her own squadrons and, says Power, the discussions "almost collapsed in bitterness" before the issue was settled. To King, the British were engaged in "a recruiting scheme for the British Air Force rather than any genuine attempt at cooperation." They were, he felt, trying to keep the Canadians under their thumb as they had in World War I.

The British countered with one proposal after another, all setting limitations on the number of specifically Canadian squadrons. King and his cabinet ministers rejected them all.

Then something happened that has since become part of the folklore about the Prime Minister's passion for anniversaries. With two days to go, King became determined that the final agreement should be signed by December 17, his 65th birthday. How he wound up the affair is recounted in *The Mackenzie King Record,* his diaries as edited by J. W. Pickersgill, his wartime assistant:

. . . "Ralston [Finance Minister J. L. Ralston, later to be defense minister] kept coming back to the question of command and care of our men. That when enlisting large numbers of pilots in Canada, they would ask whether they could expect to be in Canadian squadrons rather than squadrons commanded by British officers. Ralston pointed out that, unless there was clear understanding on these matters, there would be fear among our men that they would be sent into such places as Pass-

chendaele in the last war, and their lives unnecessarily sacrificed. I stated that I would have to give Parliament assurance that we had guarded against this kind of thing.

"I heard Air Chief Marshal Sir Robert Brooke-Popham [Lord Riverdale's chief technical adviser] say that, as service [ground] crews were so much larger than aircrews, if Canadian squadrons were serviced by British crews, it would mean a larger number of 'Englishmen' under the command of Canadians. I said nothing, but made a very careful note of the remark, which really let the cat out of the bag. As we had thought, what is really in the minds of the British is to keep command in their own hands."

King worked all next day (the 16th) on his broadcast announcement of the training plan and on getting Riverdale to sign. That afternoon he had word from Ralston that Sir Gerald Campbell, British high commissioner in Ottawa, and Brooke-Popham were in his office going over a statement. King told Ralston to let Riverdale know that tomorrow was his birthday and that he "would immensely appreciate it if this matter could be cleared up before this old year of my life was out." He wanted to make the announcement about the air agreement before that of the landing of the 1st Division in Britain, which was to be made December 19 or 20.

Ralston gave Riverdale this message and reported that Riverdale would come to see him later in the day. Somewhat later, Ralston telephoned Riverdale again but could not reach him. King then told Ralston to leave for Montreal, where he had an appointment, and "I would look after matters myself."

By this time King's principal secretary, Arnold Heeney, had discovered that Riverdale was dining with Sir Shuldham Redfern, secretary to Governor-General Lord Tweedsmuir. It was nearly nine o'clock but King was determined to get the matter settled that night.

"I decided I would ring up Lord Riverdale at Redfern's and ask him to see me at once; also that I would ring up the Governor-General and ask him to see me immediately and get the whole situation placed before him as representative of the King. When Riverdale came to the telephone I told him I was most anxious to see him as soon as possible. He said he would be along in the morning. I said that would be too late; we must get this plan settled tonight. He said he could not get his team together. Some had gone to a game of hockey, others were at dinner. I said I was not in the least concerned about the team; it was he I wanted to speak to.

"I spoke about the formula worked out with Ralston. He said he thought it ought to be accepted. I told him he would have to take responsibility if it were not settled, and that if further time were lost, the King should know where the responsibility lay. I was therefore going immediately to see the Governor-General. Riverdale said: 'I will do my best to get the team together.' I said: 'Never mind the team, come yourself.' "

When King called Government House, he was told that "it was thought the Governor was in bed. I said I wished to see the Governor whether he was in bed or not."

King reached Government House about ten o'clock. Redfern took him to Lord Tweedsmuir's bedroom.

"The Governor was propped on his pillows looking pretty frail. He extended greetings on my birthday tomorrow. I said I had come on the most important matter I had ever had occasion to speak to him of. In our talk, the Governor said it was insanity on the part of these men to delay the matter for a moment. I told him what Brooke-Popham had said about Canadian aircrews being identified as Canadian while serviced by English crews—that a Canadian might command a much larger number of Englishmen. The Governor said that was perfectly outrageous. I told him, too, how Brooke-Popham had contended it was essential to have ground crews as well as aircrews of the same force. The Governor said that was ridiculous, that there was no reason why Canadian aircrews should not be serviced by English ground crews.

"On every point the Governor was 100 percent with me. He asked if there was anything he, himself, could do. I said I thought I would not be suggesting anything out of the way if I asked him to send for Brooke-Popham and have a word with him.

"He said: 'I will have him come in the morning.' I looked at the Governor and said: 'In the morning? I am afraid that will not do. This matter must be settled tonight.' He said: 'I will get him at once.' "

King went to his office, where Riverdale arrived just before eleven o'clock. He told Riverdale he thought they "must settle this matter at once ourselves." Riverdale felt the statement "prepared by Ralston and himself was quite correct." That statement read: "On the understanding that the numbers to be incorporated or organized at any time will be the subject of discussion between the two governments, the United Kingdom government accepts in principle

that the Canadian pupils, when passing out from the training scheme, would be incorporated in or organized as units and formations of the Royal Canadian Air Force in the field. The detailed methods by which this can be done would be arranged by an inter-governmental committee."

Riverdale confided that "he had had a lot of trouble with his own people and it would help a lot if I could get Ralston to drop the word 'the' in front of the word 'Canadian.' Brooke-Popham seemed to feel it had a sinister significance, that Canadians could not go unless all were in Canadian formations."

King pointed out that the numbers affected had to be discussed between the two governments and this "made it quite clear that it was not expected that every individual should go in." He added that he personally "thought whether the 'the' was in or not, the sentence meant exactly the same." However, King would not make the change without consulting Ralston.

Riverdale left the room while King telephoned. Ralston agreed to drop the "the," providing King held that the two things meant the same. "I then had Lord Riverdale return and said I would agree to the 'the' being struck out. Lord Riverdale agreed he would sign on that understanding but would like to have a word with his men first.

"I said to him: 'We must take no chances on that.' However we waited for Brooke-Popham. When he did not come, I had them phone Government House, where he was with the Governor-General, to let him know Lord Riverdale was waiting for him. As we got on toward midnight, I said we could not wait—must not wait any longer."

They were about to begin signing the agreement when Brooke-Popham arrived as "twelve o'clock was striking. Arnold Heeney was with him, and was the first to shake hands and wish me a happy birthday. Lord Riverdale was next, and Brooke-Popham also extended his wishes. We then had a word as to whether the agreement should be dated the 16th or 17th. Lord Riverdale said to fix whatever date I wished. I said as it was now exactly the 17th I would prefer to date the documents exactly on the day on which they were signed."

King noted that, when Brooke-Popham arrived, "Riverdale told him that the Prime Minister had agreed to strike out the

word 'the.' Brooke-Popham said, 'That makes the agreement satisfactory as far as I am concerned.' I said I had done so because Lord Riverdale agreed with me that the meaning was the same whether the 'the' was in or not.

"Brooke-Popham looked as if he had been spanked. His face was very red and his manner very crushed. I think having the Governor-General speak to him was something he had never anticipated, and having been governor of a Crown colony himself, he would realize the significance of the word of a governor in a self-governing dominion, given in the name of the King."

The final diary entry for the day reads: "After all had left the office I phoned Ralston to let him know that the agreement had been signed. I do not recall ever having heard anyone laugh more heartily. He was really joyous, tremendously relieved."

King spent his birthday working on a broadcast which included these words: "The United Kingdom government has informed us that participation in the air-training scheme would provide for more effective assistance toward ultimate victory than any other form of military cooperation Canada can give."

its history. Wrote Leslie Roberts in his RCAF history, *There Shall Be Wings:*

. . . Approximately 40,000 trained personnel would be required. They would administer, instruct and provide ground crews at 58 aviation-training schools. The first flying schools were to open by May 1940 and the entire scheme was to be in operation by the end of April 1942, turning out a minimum of 20,000 aircrew a year. Ad-

000 just to run the air schools? But progress was made from the very first days.

Canada's 17 civilian flying clubs agreed to handle elementary flight training. Commercial operators of bush routes and charter flights said they would run schools where observers could be trained by RCAF men. From air force reserves came administrators and instructors. These men, led by members of the permanent RCAF,

That evening King wrote in his diary: "It was certainly a memorable birthday. I suppose no more significant agreement has ever been signed by the government of Canada." . . . *The Mackenzie King Record*

The crisis was over but, wrote Chubby Power, the men who settled it "little dreamed of the legacy of trouble left to the poor unfortunate who was called upon to interpret their understanding." As things turned out, thousands of Canadians would end up as members of the RCAF but in RAF squadrons. And the problem of their control would haunt Power for years.

When details of the agreement became known, newspapers said Canada's responsibility was staggering. It was. The country was tackling the largest single enterprise in

ministration, repairs, equipment and the training of instructors would occupy schools and depots to a total of 74, exclusive of the command organization. Some 3500 new planes would be required at once, together with 6500 engines and ample spare parts.

Many Canadians asked where these would come from, and where the pilots would be trained. The RCAF had two well-equipped training stations at Trenton, Ont., and Camp Borden, Ont., but the rest of its equipment was far below requirements. Many people believed Canada's share of the cost, estimated at $350 million, could better be spent raising infantry divisions. Where, they asked, were you going to find enough men to take flight instruction and to supply army and navy needs when it was proposed to tie up 40,-

After midnight December 16-17, in the early hours of Mackenzie King's 65th birthday, he and Lord Riverdale (facing) sign the air-training agreement. Soon from coast to coast over a million miles a day were being flown by instructors and students in planes like these Harvard trainers. In building airfields, enough cement was poured to have made a 20-foot-wide highway from Ottawa to Vancouver.

were the foundation on which the flying schools were built.

The astounding success of the plan belongs to three men. The first was Air Minister Power, whose department recruited flying trainees by the thousands, raised all the ground personnel and trained young fliers from the four Commonwealth countries.

None of this could have happened, however, without the second man, C. D. Howe, who organized airdrome construction and found the aircraft. First as minister of transport and the cabinet member responsible for the War Supply Board, then as minister of munitions and supply, Howe worked miracles. The third man in this remarkable trinity was Ralph P. Bell who, after joining Howe's executive committee, directed the aircraft program.

A group in Howe's Department of Transport, working under J. A. Wilson, director of civil aviation, found the airfield sites. A number of satisfactory coastal fields were excluded because they were in defense areas. Mountains ruled out most of British Columbia. The prairies were ideal, as were the more lightly populated areas of Ontario, Quebec and the Maritime Provinces. By the time the four governments had worked out their agreement, Wilson's engineers had chosen most of the sites, using the Canadian National Railways real estate department as its negotiator.

Ottawa was a madhouse. Contractors sweated it out waiting for instructions to build airfields near remote prairie villages. Lined up in the same government buildings were representatives of firms seeking contracts to build airplanes. Men borrowed from private firms initialed purchase orders demanding immediate delivery of everything from jeeps to jigsaws. In other offices sat expediters whose job was to make sure that these supplies arrived on time. Behind them all, working a minimum 14-hour shift, was Clarence Decatur Howe, a man of action who had the power to enforce his decisions. ("If you can't produce, we will take your plant and put somebody there who can.")

In all this confusion, the plan began to take shape. The first instructors' course started at Camp Borden. Buildings arose on a score of new airfields. Then, just as the first 169 pilot trainees mustered at Toronto, the Germans struck through the Low Countries and across France.

One of the first repercussions was news that Britain couldn't fulfill promises to provide 1500 twin-engine Ansons as advanced trainer aircraft. A shipload of Ansons, already on the high seas, was returned to the United Kingdom.

["This," wrote Air Minister Power, "sent most of us in Ottawa into a bit of a panic, and there was some question whether the plan would be abandoned." But Britain insisted that the training continue; planes would have to be found elsewhere.]

The Air Ministry hoped to be able to buy a number of single-engined Harvards in the United States; 600 were subsequently acquired.

Britain, standing alone in Europe, needed arms, planes, fighting ships and men from every corner of the Commonwealth. Canada's greatest immediate decision was to take over the air-training plan almost completely and even to try to telescope two years' construction into one. Money no longer mattered. What was important was to find advanced aircraft for students to fly once they had qualified on the Tiger Moth and other "elementaries." Twin-engine machines must, as well, be found in which middle-aged bush pilots might train observers, navigators, gunners and wireless operators. The solution to these problems lay with C. D. Howe.

Few Canadians would have exchanged jobs with him in 1940. Howe was building merchant ships, ordering guns, making commitments for ammunition, uniforms and boots, taking factories away from irresponsible or unpatriotic owners, and keeping his word to Air Minister Power that he would equip the air plan and open the schools on time.

As fast as the schools could receive them, Power's men were calling up recruits, breaking them in on the drill square, sending them to initial training school and on from there to elementary flying. But classes were being held back because the Anson training planes from Britain were no longer arriving.

Howe decided to have the Anson redesigned to take new engines. In the United States he contracted for 5000 Jacobs engines with the proviso that Canada must get the entire factory output until the order was filled. To produce Ansons in Canada, Howe formed a Crown company called Federal Aircraft. Its first task was to redesign the Anson to take the Jacobs engine, then to farm out contracts. In addition,

Federal was to turn out the first mock-up of the new machine and flight-test it.

Meanwhile, Howe and his men shopped for anything airworthy which might qualify as a twin-engine advanced trainer. To help out, the British managed to ship a few Ansons. For the training of fighter pilots, single-engine Harvards were needed; Howe soon had Noorduyn Aviation of Montreal producing more than 100 a month.

Despite all the problems, 31 flying units were in operation by the end of 1940. The first pilot class, 39 men, graduated September 30 at Camp Borden and all were kept in Canada as flying instructors or staff pilots. The first observers received their wings October 24 at Trenton and all but one went overseas the following month. On the 28th more than 50 air gunners graduated at Jarvis, Ont. More graduated in December at Mossbank, Sask. In its original form, the plan had not anticipated any graduates at all in 1940. Thus Canada was well ahead of schedule, and had met the challenge created by the collapse of France. . . . LESLIE ROBERTS

But a political storm was brewing, and it grew into a nasty one. In February 1941, the Conservatives charged in the Commons that the Anson program had bogged down and that Federal Aircraft should go. Finally Howe rose to answer the Opposition charges.

Fitness was stressed (above right) no matter which of eight aircrew categories a man was in. Embryo pilots trained in Link trainers (top), steering by cyclorama landmarks. The George Cross was awarded posthumously to two students: LAC K. M. Gravell of Vancouver, who went to the aid of a pilot in a burning plane, and LAC K. G. Spooner of Smiths Falls, Ont., a navigator who took the controls of an Anson in an emergency, enabling three men to bail out safely before the plane crashed.

Federal Aircraft's program, he admitted, was in trouble. It had underestimated the job. But he could "see nothing to indicate we would get more planes by upsetting the Federal applecart." With Britain forced to halt Anson deliveries, the full weight had fallen on Canada at a time when the country lacked plants and trained manpower. It was a "mushroom industry." What did the Opposition expect?

In the final analysis the best answer lay in results. By June 1, 1943, 1850 Canadian-built Ansons were flying—350 more than the initial target. Canada had produced 2360 elementary trainers at de Havilland and Fleet Aircraft, 3578 advanced training machines and 2076 service aircraft—a grand total of 8014 from an industry which had been virtually nonexistent before the war.

As 1941 opened, aircrew trainees were being enrolled by the thousands and individual Canadians were helping out in many ways. They entertained the trainees, ran canteens. In some cases, the entire costs of elementary flying schools were borne by local flying clubs or by donations from the community concerned. Vancouver citizens paid for 14 training planes. Bush pilots came down from the north to act as instructors.

The trainees themselves came from farms, university campuses and business offices, from all trades and walks of life, from all parts of the globe. Among them were an Australian sheep rancher, a young English earl, a New York band leader, a clerk from Argentina, a teacher from New Zealand, an Ontario bond salesman, a Czech farmer, and a young, golden-tongued Welshman named Richard Burton—as unknown then as another young British trainee named Arthur Hailey. The U.S. magazine *Fortune* reported that the plan was "the most conspicuous and universal expression of Canada at war." It added:

. . . From the Maritimes to Vancouver Island, from Windsor to Saskatoon one sees the brass-buttoned blue of air force uniforms, and hears day and night the drone of yellow-winged Harvard trainers and box-kite-like Tiger Moths taking off, circuiting, landing in endless repetition. Youngsters—kids of 18, 19, 20—on the trains and in hotel lobbies and taverns, strutting a bit because of the white tabs in the caps that set them apart as aircrew students (as distinct from ground trades). Youngsters from England, homesick and tense, who sometimes weep uncontrollably the first day they sit down to mountainous stacks of food. Youngsters from Australia, rawboned and rambunctious, easily spotted by their distinctive dark blue uniforms ("passionate purple," they call it), who can down a bottle of ale at a gulp and chase it with another. Youngsters from New Zealand who howl for beefsteak at breakfast. Youngsters from the United States, breezy and self-assured, who would not take their own air corps' "No" as a reason for staying out of the war. And most of all—seven out of ten—youngsters of Canada, proud and determined, full of consciousness that in World War I four Canadian airmen shot down more enemy planes than any other four Allied aces; and that one of them, "Billy" Bishop, wears the uniform of air vice-marshal today.

They are everywhere in Canada. At Mossbank, a station so remote that it serves as a place of banishment for the unruly. At Jarvis, on Lake Erie, dubbed the "banana belt" because the winter blasts there are a few degrees less congealing than at most stations. At Uplands, handy to Ottawa's fancy Château Laurier, where newly-fledged graduates, chest buttons popping, joyfully "wet their wings"— as often with beer or Coca-Cola as with whisky. At Penfield Ridge, N.B., where navigation students learn that "the Maritime Provinces treat you swell"; and whence they move, shortly, a step farther east to Halifax and embarkation for service overseas. . . .

Aircrew were the glamour boys of the war and competition to become one was keen. Len Morgan, born in Terre Haute, Ind., was one of hundreds who came up from the United States. In his book *The AT-6 Harvard,* a story about the famous aircraft used to train fighter pilots, he tells what it was like to be 19 years old and "on your way to realize a lifelong dream":

. . . A truck drove along a country road near St. Catharines, Ont., on a summer morning in 1941. In the back, a dozen boys faced each other over a pile of kit bags. They wore blue uniforms and made a great deal of noise laughing, shouting and waving at pretty girls. The truck turned into a narrow lane leading to a gate over which hung a sign, "No. 9 Elementary Flying Training School." It stopped and the driver spoke to the guard.

"Another load of Americans come to save us from the Nazis."

"Winston will be relieved. I'll call him right away."

A short, red-faced British sergeant waited for the noisy riders to climb down. Noticing him, they formed a rough line. The sergeant regarded this pitiful effort with an expression of utter disdain. Finally he spoke to himself quietly: "My bloody nerves." He shook his head the way people do at funerals.

He walked around his new charges, peering into every face. He paused to sight along the uneven row of heads, closed his eyes and shuddered. Suddenly he strode to the front and bawled, "Tennnnnnn-shun!" An uneasy minute passed before he spoke.

"If *this* is what His Majesty's air force has come to, God help us. My name is Flight Sergeant Maxwell and you chaps are going to get to know me very well indeed." He paused for emphasis.

"I know you're here to learn to handle these bloomin' airplanes but first you're bloody well going to learn how to march." He regarded the recruits with fresh distaste. "You look like a lot of sloppy navy people! This is the Royal Canadian Air Force, and we expect much more than the navy. Is that clear?"

Receiving no reply, he pulled a paper from his pocket.

"All right then, answer to your names. Woods?"

"Here."

"Morgan?"

"Here."

"Vogel?"

"Here."

"Wendt? . . . Vogel? Wendt? Are you sure you're reporting to the right station?"

Len Morgan (below) was one of a dozen American youths in a class of 41 RCAF recruits at an elementary flying school near St. Catharines, Ont. The Fleet Finch and de Havilland Tiger Moth (right) used for basic training "approximated in size, general appearance and performance the fighter aircraft of World War I." Morgan's class moved up to Harvards at Aylmer, Ont. —and to an instrument panel (below right) that was "a hopeless confusion of black-faced dials and toggle switches."

We laughed and this pleased him for he imagined himself to be—and indeed he was—a man with a genuine sense of humor. Old Bloody Nerves was all right and we knew it that moment. He was no one's fool, mind you, but a fair man and all that a good disciplinarian should be.

The clumsy scene we played before him that day had its bizarre twist. We were Americans, citizens of a nation at peace, enlisted in the service of a nation at war. We were never asked to swear allegiance to the King. We signed agreements to serve "for the duration and a period of demobilization of up to one year," contracts from which we were immediately released when the chance came later to join our own country's forces. About 5500 Americans took this quicker way into the air. We were there because we were too young for

the peacetime U.S. Air Corps, or too old, or did not have the required two college years—or something. We were there for one reason, to learn to fly. None of us, at that stage, had strong feelings about the war.

Our dozen men were joined at No. 9 by Canadians, Australians and Englishmen who did have strong feelings about the war. Each new load of arrivals was promptly dressed down by Sergeant Maxwell and sent off to wax the barracks floor.

Our class of 41 was nearly a third American and the sign over the main gate was altered one night to read "Royal California Air Force," a stupid stunt that cost us, including the puzzled English, two hours of extra drill.

"California? Where's this California, Rodney?" one Englishman asked.

"One of the islands we own in the Pacific, old boy, somewhere near Pitcairn, I'd say."

"Of course, one of the colonies."

The class was split into two groups. One attended ground school while the other flew. If you flew in the morning you took signals, navigation, aero engines, parachutes, instruments and other studies in the afternoon.

Elementary flight training in Canada then utilized the famous de Havilland Tiger Moth and the Fleet Finch. Both approximated in size, general appearance and performance the fighter aircraft of World War I. Our grass field with its single hangar and row of small biplanes was almost a copy of a 1918 airdrome in France. This obvious similarity was not lost on boys who had devoured yarns about Spads and Nieuports. As soon as the barracks floor had been waxed to the satisfaction of Old Bloody Nerves, we went down to the hangar.

Our instructors were civilians, Canadian and American. I drew Mr. Al Bennett, a quiet fellow. He showed me how to adjust my parachute and 30 minutes later we were pounding along at 3000 feet. Fleet students rode in the front seat, and when Mr. Bennett banked the ship I looked between the wings and wondered why we did not slip right into the farms below. Leveling out, he said, "All right, you have control." I grabbed the stick and left my fingerprints there for all time.

"Relax, son, relax. It won't bite you. Fly it with two fingers—and don't stand on the rudders."

I marveled at his skill and, by the time that the first flight was over, I was exhausted, somewhat discouraged, but absolutely determined to learn how it was done.

Ten days later Mr. Bennett said, "Make one more circuit and landing just like the last one, but drop me off at the hangar first." The first solo, just like that. On the downwind leg I twisted twice to look into the empty backseat and laughed loud enough to hear myself above the engine.

My logbook shows 65 hours and 50 minutes flown at St. Kitts. Our class dwindled to 22 in six weeks. Washouts and ground-school failures got 19. There was the fellow who wouldn't land. Thirty or more times he executed a beautiful approach, then climbed just before touchdown. They grounded the rest of us while an instructor flew alongside him, trying to lead him to earth. It didn't work. Finally, just at dusk, the frightened boy dropped to the grass in a perfect three-point landing. Next day he was on his way to gunner's school.

At St. Kitts we learned the fundamentals of navigation, engines, meteorology and related subjects—and a little bit about flying. On August 16 we packed our kit bags, shook hands with our instructors and climbed aboard trucks. Not one of us failed to seek out Old Bloody Nerves.

"Thanks again, Sarge, for getting me off the hook with the Old Man."

"Very good, lad, and mind that it doesn't happen again." Then, marching importantly around us, "What is this, a bloomin' tea party? You're slopping about like a lot of navy people! Into the lorries, come along. My bloody nerves!"

We had maintained the perfect safety record Old Bloody Nerves was so proud of. No one said much as we lost sight of him standing under the sign at the gate.

The surviving members of our class were split into two groups, half going to multi-engine training in Ansons, the rest of us to Harvards. My crowd reported to No. 14 Service Flying Training School at Aylmer, Ont. We were divided into units, ours—13 Americans and 14 Canadians— becoming C flight. Civilian-operated St. Kitts had been a quiet little grass field with one small hangar and a row of wood barracks. Aylmer boasted a long line of steel hangars, concrete runways and a sprawling camp area. The place was strictly air force and all business. It was outfitted with Harvard IIs.

After unloading our baggage, we inspected one of the planes at close range. It was a huge, all-metal creation with a tremendous 600 horsepower Pratt and Whitney nine-cylinder radial glistening darkly under an enormous cowl. After the simple cloth-covered Fleet, the Harvard looked massive, rugged, heavy, complex.

American military schools of this era led the flying student gradually through primary training in Stearmans to basic school in the Vultee Vibrator and finally to the big, powerful Harvard. By the time a cadet stepped into his first AT-6 Harvard he was a reasonably accomplished pilot.

The Canadians elected to bypass the intermediate (basic) stage and move the 65-hour student from Fleet or Moth school right into the final stage of training. Some experts thought this was going too fast. A 60-hour pupil couldn't handle 600 horsepower, they argued. Looking back we can see that the Canadians were right. The Harvard was eventually to become the USAF's primary trainer, the first plane a recruit flew!

Sgt. Bob Campbell, my instructor, took me for a hop the first training day and I immediately fell in love with the Harvard. I observed the wild instrument readings with amazement, listened carefully to his description of the ship's operation and watched the trees streak by. It was tremendous. We raced for the field in heavy rain, touched down on the wet concrete at an impossible velocity and somehow stopped before we ran out of airport. I hadn't learned much in the Fleet.

Next morning Sergeant Campbell started teaching me how to handle the Harvard. Most of it we learned the hard way. Landing after a dual period, the nose swung left. I hit the rudder hard and felt the tail wheel come unglued. Around we rushed in a slewing one-wheel turn, one wing tip pointing at the sky, the other dragging through grass alongside the runway. I thought we'd never stop. Finally we slumped back onto all three wheels, facing across the runway, engine still ticking. We had turned 450 degrees. I taxied in feeling like an utter fool.

After four hours of dual, I was sent up with the officer commanding our flight. He kept me in the circuit 30 minutes, chewed me out—I had it coming—then signed my solo permit. I flew the howling monster alone for the first time or, to be more honest about it, I hung on tight

By September 30, 1941, training aircraft were flying 1,429,000 miles per fatal accident. But in one six-month period there were 50 air collisions—these Avro Ansons landed safely—and one month 20 aircraft were damaged because pilots forgot to lower the wheels on landing. In another month accidents put 500 planes out of action for periods ranging from half a day to forever. Disobedience, carelessness and pilot error caused 70 percent of the mishaps and many of the air-training plan's 856 deaths.

while it took me on a wild ride through the sky.

As the days flew by, we learned to think faster, to react instinctively, to work on two problems at the same time, to anticipate trouble. We were awkward: right part of the time and scared most of the time—but we were learning.

On solo hops we were assigned certain practices to perform. It might be a cross-country one day and routine air work the next. There was ample time for experimentation. Dogfighting was discouraged but not exactly forbidden. At the noon mess Vogel might mutter, "You're flying solo this afternoon, aren't you? Meet you over Tillsonburg at 8000 feet."

"I'll be there at two o'clock."

The main thing was not to get caught. There was no secret about what was going on, for the air on a sunny afternoon was filled with Harvards trying to shoot each other down. There was no sport like it. I recall one experience vividly.

mile behind him and the accumulated speed reduced the distance between us rapidly. I gave him a quick squirt and rolled away to his left—but not before I got a horrifying glimpse of *two* heads in the canopy. I had jumped an instructor and student. I rolled into a vertical dive for the nearest cloud. He couldn't have taken my number; it was all over too fast. Shaken, I swore I'd spend the rest of my time doing what Sergeant Campbell had sent me up to do.

Then something made me look over my shoulder. There, not 50 feet behind, was a big fat 600 horsepower Pratt and Whitney engine. There were two helmeted heads in the cockpit. I opened up and away we went. For five minutes I tried every stunt I thought I knew. The big black engine followed me like a shadow. At last I permitted them to come alongside. Two faces regarded me coldly and then banked away.

I waited all evening for a summons to

ending. More than one honeymooning couple on International Bridge at Niagara Falls was unnerved by a Harvard roaring beneath their feet and disappearing before any numbers could be copied down.

When these things happened we would be mustered for parade in full dress. The Old Man would appear.

"Does anyone have any knowledge of two Harvard aircraft flying low over Buffalo yesterday at (looking at his telegram) approximately 1630 hours?"

Silence.

"Thirty-two of our machines were airborne at that time. No information on this from any of you?"

Silence.

"Very well, then. Sergeant Major, dismiss the parade."

And, later in the mess: "I say, Rodney, did you hear the squadron leader and that sticky business about airplanes flying over Buffalo?"

I got off the ground early, scrambled above the agreed level of engagement—this was not considered dishonorable—and lurked behind a big cumulus, waiting for my prey. Right on time and right on altitude, he appeared. Craftily working my way around the cloud I got behind him with the sun at my back. Then, mentally flicking on the gun switch, I rolled on my back, Hell's Angels style, and dived for his tail.

I was McCudden, he was Von Richthofen. I pulled out a quarter of a

the CO's office. None came. Next day Sergeant Campbell remarked, in passing, "Did you ever stop to think that a Harvard with one man in it should be able to *outclimb* a Harvard with two men in it?"

The U.S. border, a few flying minutes away, was too much of a temptation for some. One Harvard trainee dropped in at Detroit's airline terminal, enjoyed a coffee and was gone before anyone realized who he was. There were phone calls from Washington to Ottawa, stern lectures, warnings. This sort of thing was never-

"It couldn't have been any of our chaps, of course. Probably some Canadians. They can't find their way to the bathroom."

Of course, we all knew who had buzzed Buffalo.

Nineteen is an impressionable age. Put a boy who has never wanted to do anything but fly in a big, hefty, fully-aerobatic 600 horsepower fighter-type airplane and he soaks up this new world like a sponge. The heady aroma of gasoline, the spine-tingling sound of aircraft

'The sunlit silence . . .'

The war inspired many a Canadian serviceman to write poetry. Much of it was sentimental verse about home and loved ones and the loneliness of separation. There were also reams of doggerel about soldiering overseas, like this verse from "Buster, 8NBH" that was published in the army newspaper in Italy, The Maple Leaf:

The barrel never ever shrinks
Although the contents alter;
Some criticize and say it stinks
Yet many soldiers falter.
Some say it's stepping nearer doom
While others shout "Supremo-o!"
A little gas, paint and shellac—
You've got some Itie vino.

But there was serious work, too. One of the memorable poems to come out of the Canadian forces was a sonnet written not by a Canadian but by one of the Americans who came north to join them. John Gillespie Magee, Jr., was born in Shanghai in 1922, the son of American missionary parents. In 1940, he won a scholarship to Yale but turned it down to join the RCAF. Magee was killed as a pilot officer in Britain in December 1941, while flying a Spitfire on practice maneuvers. He was 19.

HIGH FLIGHT

O, I have slipped the surly bonds of
  earth
And danced the skies on laughter-
  silvered wings.
Sunward I've climbed and joined the
  tumbling mirth
Of sun-split clouds—and done a
  hundred things
You have not dreamed of—wheeled
  and soared and swung
High in the sunlit silence. Hovering
  there,
I've chased the shouting wind along
  and flung
My eager craft through footless halls
  of air.

Up, up the long delirious, burning blue
I've topped the windswept heights
  with easy grace
Where never lark, or even eagle, flew,
And, while with silent, lifting mind I've
  trod
The high untrespassed sanctity of
  space,
Put out my hand and touched the
  face of God.

engines coming to life at sunrise, the utterly indescribable sensation at the top of a loop, the talk of those who speak your language, the snug feel of parachute straps, the entire overwhelming atmosphere. I remember it all. That was living.

In later years I often compared notes with U.S. Army and Navy pilots to see how our training stacked up. Ours was hurried but it covered the essentials thoroughly. Looking back, I am surprised that such a sensible approach could have been devised by any military service.

Our ground-school subjects were for the most part pertinent; flight training was strictly no-nonsense. We were taught to take off and land without damaging His Majesty's property, to navigate by day or night, to fly on instruments and handle our ships in any average situation. That's about it.

The American cadet was better trained when he got his wings but only because the Commonwealth plan intended that its graduates receive further schooling at operational training units in Britain. Boiled down, the RCAF student got his wings at an earlier stage than his American counterpart. The final product in either case was reasonably competent and able to carry his weight in a frontline outfit.

In spite of our accelerated training there was time for "outside activities." As long as we passed the weekly exams and weather did not delay flying, the weekends were free. Toronto, Detroit and Buffalo were the usual targets. To stand on the highway in an RCAF uniform was to get a lift from the first car, which helped when you earned $70 a month. The Canadian people could not have been more friendly or generous. I have the most pleasant recollections of footloose weekends and the warmth and friendliness of the people I met.

At last the course ended. Three from C flight got the axe and were posted to navigator's school. The rest of us received our wings on November 21 and were given ten days leave before going overseas.

"You'll look back someday and know that these were the best days of all your flying," Mr. Bennett had said. In a way he was right. Any pilot thumbing through his old logbooks will catch himself thinking, *these* were the best days though I did not know it then. The sum total of impressions, the hazy swirl of in-

dividual recollections, punctuated by vivid memories of inexpressible pleasure, fear beyond description or sudden tragedy—this is the memory that pleases him and haunts him. The Harvard is at once the wondrous vehicle that unlocked a new world, and a hideous, mud-spattered heap of yellow aluminum that snuffed out the life of a luckless friend. This is the way we remember it. . . .

LEN MORGAN

In June 1942, after more than 22,000 aircrew had graduated, it was decided to extend the training plan to 1945 and increase the number of training schools to 67 (including 21 double schools). Ten new specialist schools were also added for operational training, training flying instructors, and other functions, and Canada also assumed administration of 27 RAF schools which had been set up in Canada. When the plan reached its peak in 1943 there were 97 flying schools operating with 184 other units in support, and a staff exceeding 100,000 was helping to turn out more than 3000 graduates each month. In addition to aircrew, tens of thousands of men were trained in ground trades.

The final cost was $2231 million. Canada's contribution in money and equipment was $1589 million—more than four times the original estimate. For this the plan produced 131,553 aircrew graduates in eight categories ranging from pilots to gunners: 42,110 from the RAF (mostly from Britain but also from France, Belgium, Holland, Norway, Czechoslovakia, Poland and India); 16,608 from Australia and New Zealand; and 72,835 from Canada.

Of the Canadians, Air Minister Power said: "We have taken the very cream of our youth. As a body, they are more Canadian than even the House of Commons. These boys are mainly third, fourth and fifth-generation Canadians, bred in Canada, schooled in Canadian schools and with an intensely Canadian viewpoint. They are the future leaders of this country, and the destiny of Canada will some day be in their hands."

When this stirring speech was made November 6, 1941, 90,000 Canadians were already serving in the RCAF. In the words of President Franklin D. Roosevelt, Canada had truly become "the Airdrome of Democracy."

The high, hard road to Britain

Even as the Commonwealth air-training program was beginning, another response to Britain's desperate situation sprang from the dynamic mind of Canadian-born Lord Beaverbrook. Once he became Churchill's minister of aircraft production in May 1940, he not only broke all the rules to produce the planes that won the Battle of Britain: he also pursued his own unorthodox plan to fly bombers across the North Atlantic. Up till then, bombers for Britain went over by ship.

In 1937 Britain's Imperial Airways had inaugurated a two-way transatlantic air-freight service. But it was a summer service only. Flying the North Atlantic in winter was considered dangerous and impractical—even without the perils of war.

Then Germany's invasion of the Low Countries and France created a new need for planes. Beaverbrook sent for Capt. D. C. T. Bennett, an Australian who had launched Imperial's service. Said Beaverbrook: "We're going to fly the Atlantic with American bombers. You're going to do it."

Beaverbrook appointed Morris Wilson, the Royal Bank of Canada president, to organize the air-ferry service. By July 1940, Wilson had persuaded the CPR to set up an air-services department. Its first task was to handle the delivery of 50 Hudson bombers from the Lockheed Aircraft Corp. in Burbank, California.

Flying the war planes to Canada would have contravened the U.S. Neutrality Act, so other means of delivery were devised. The first two Hudsons, for example, landed at Pembina, N.Dak., just a stone's throw from the border. They were then towed into Canada and flown to Montreal by Bennett and another pilot. Meanwhile, Beaverbrook was hiring airmen from both sides of the Atlantic. Because pilots were scarce in Britain and Canada, many early recruits were Americans, who got $1,000 a trip.

As the Hudsons arrived in Montreal, Bennett planned his first transatlantic crossing. Because only a few recruits could navigate, he decided that the Hudsons must fly in formation under his leadership. He calculated that the maximum number of aircraft that could maintain formation on an Atlantic flight was seven. Newfoundland's lonely Gander airfield, recently opened, became the takeoff point. It was accessible only by air and rail, and the only buildings were a control tower and one hangar. The fliers lived in train coaches and pondered the dangers they would face.

Atlantic weather was often unpredictable and forecasting was rudimentary. Radio reception was often nonexistent. The worst enemy would be extreme cold, and the planes were ill-equipped for icing. Mechanical failure and human error were critical possibilities. And on the far side of the Atlantic, German planes might be lurking.

On a dark November night the first seven Hudsons squatted in arrowhead formation on the runway at Gander, ready to go. The band of the Queen's Own Rifles of Canada, a unit on garrison duty, was on hand. Because the light was too poor for reading music, the leader chose a piece his men knew by heart. As the airmen climbed into their twin-engine, twin-tail planes, the Queen's Own played them on their perilous way with the strains of "Nearer My God To Thee."

Soon the seven crews—the Australian leader, nine Americans, six Canadians and six Britons—were airborne for Northern Ireland. If only one or two planes survived, or none, the plan to fly aircraft to Britain would be dropped. But Britain's need was such that, if even three of the seven arrived safely, the plan would survive.

Ten hours and 17 minutes after takeoff, Bennett's plane touched down at Aldergrove, near Belfast. Some of the other aircraft were up to an hour behind him but

In November 1940, the Lockheed Hudson (above) inaugurated the air-ferry service across the wintry North Atlantic. The first Hudsons were unarmed; the later models were larger and carried guns.

all seven eventually made it, despite cold, ice, rain, severe turbulence and assorted mechanical problems.

Soon bombers were crossing the ocean in a steady stream. One of history's great air transportation operations had begun, one that would eventually fly nearly 10,000 planes to Britain.

In 1941 the Royal Air Force took over direction of the service and the whole concept broadened. To get fighters and short-range bombers overseas, a new staging route was developed. The Americans built airfields in Greenland and Iceland; the Canadians built one at Goose Bay, Labrador, in six hectic months. It went on from there. In time, planes were taking off from remote northern airfields enroute not only to Britain but also to Russia, which needed them too.

Sheepdog navy

The only thing that ever really frightened me was the U-boat peril... The Battle of the Atlantic was the dominating factor all through the war. Never for one moment could we forget that everything happening elsewhere—on land, at sea or in the air—depended ultimately on its outcome, and amid all other cares we viewed its changing fortunes day by day with hope or apprehension. WINSTON CHURCHILL

Just before 4 a.m. December 1, 1940, a flare shot up out of the dark Atlantic near a convoy 300 miles west of Ireland and was seen by lookouts on the destroyer *Saguenay*. As her crew raced to action stations, she abandoned her 12-knot zigzag, increased speed and wheeled to investigate. Where the flare had been fired the Canadians now saw a submarine—and a moment later, as one of *Saguenay's* 4.7-inch guns opened up on the enemy, a torpedo smashed into the destroyer's port bow. The U-boat dived. *Saguenay,* the first Canadian warship to be torpedoed, seemed mortally wounded. Wrote Joseph Schull in *The Far Distant Ships:*

... The seamen's messdecks were fiercely ablaze and the forepart of the ship had to be cleared. Smoke and flame compelled evacuation of the bridge. Inflammable materials in the paint shop forward of the messdecks added to the flames. Salt water pouring through the jagged gash in the ship's port side ignited calcium flares, which fed their choking fumes into the inferno.

A fire party was beaten back. As the forward magazine was flooded, the forepart, for some 60 feet back from the bow, began to bend, then a great section of the smashed hull broke off and sank. The blazing forecastle, relieved of this dead weight, began to lift. Engineers and stokers kept *Saguenay* moving at about two knots, with the ship being steered from an emergency position. An attempt to go astern was abandoned when terrific vibration told of a bent

propeller shaft. Five officers and 85 men were transferred to the British destroyer *Highlander* to reduce casualties in case of another torpedo attack; and throughout the night and most of the next day a skeleton crew fought *Saguenay's* fires.

That evening tugs arrived, but the destroyer now was working up to six knots and considered she was doing as well by herself as she could in tow. She continued under her own power with one tug standing by. At noon the next day she was rounding the north of Ireland with all fires out and her steering gear back in operation. As she approached Barrow-in-Furness, across the Irish Sea from the Isle of Man, she set off an enemy mine. With new damage to her stern and her remaining fuel contaminated by salt water, she had to accept a tow, and reached harbor December 5....

For a year and more, *Saguenay* and a handful of other River Class destroyers had conducted Canada's naval war virtually alone. Since summer they had fought beside British warships against submarines prowling the coasts of Britain. When the

"Long after the passions of battle have cooled," Capt. John M. Waters, Jr., wrote in *Bloody Winter,* "the bravery, the fighting spirit and the dedication of the men who fought in the U-boats compel the respect of other fighting men. That they served a government bent on an evil design was their misfortune and later shame but, like us, most of them fought for their country and their people."

The first Canadian warship torpedoed was *Saguenay*, one of the first destroyers built specifically for Canada. She survived the December 1940 torpedoing and a collision in November 1942 which detonated her depth charges and blew off her stern (right). The battered destroyer was later anchored in Nova Scotia's Annapolis Basin, offshore from HMCS *Cornwallis,* and used for training recruits.

ships and RAF Coastal Command planes made things too hot there, the U-boats moved west. With Iceland as a new base, the destroyers and planes went out into the Atlantic after them.

There, with a loss of 23 men and grievous injury to herself, *Saguenay* had done the job she was supposed to do: the speed with which her guns went into action, said an Admiralty report, forced the U-boat under and prevented it from attacking the merchant ships. In the classic Battle of the Atlantic, now in its early stages, that would be the classic role of Canada's sheepdog navy: to sink U-boats if possible, but above all to save the convoys.

Now *Saguenay* would be out of action for several months, and the navy needed not fewer ships but far more. There had been only six destroyers in the beginning. A seventh had been added from the Royal Navy and renamed *Assiniboine*. But *Fraser* had been lost by collision in June. *Margaree,* obtained from the British to replace *Fraser,* was herself sunk in collision with a freighter on a squally North Atlantic night in October, with a loss of 141 of her 175-man crew. Now, two months later, *Saguenay* was out—and the Battle of the Atlantic was expanding.

It was a dark prospect. But *Saguenay's* loss coincided roughly with the end of an era. Help, at last, was on its way from two sources: the arsenal of an ally and the production lines of Canada herself. Joseph Schull writes:

... The "four-stackers," the 50 overage destroyers given by the United States in exchange for 99-year leases on British bases in the Western Hemisphere, began to arrive in December. Canada received seven, six of which were named for Canadian rivers: *Annapolis, Columbia, Niagara, St. Clair, St. Croix* and *St. Francis.* The seventh, *Hamilton*, saw RN service before coming to Canada.

As the U.S. ships arrived in Canadian ports en route to England, the new crews were struck by American generosity; every inch of storage space was crammed with provisions now only a memory in England. There were bunks instead of hammocks; there were typewriters, radios, coffee-making machines.

There were also defects which became apparent at sea. The lean, four-funneled destroyers, emergency vessels laid down during the last year of World War I, had been built in haste for a less technical conflict. They were not sufficiently maneuverable against U-boats and their sea-keeping qualities left much to be desired. Narrow beam and shallow draft made them difficult to handle in rough weather. The messdeck bunks, for all their pleasant appearance, made exorbitant demands on the men's crowded living space. Their steering gear was flimsy and cranky.

With all their faults, four of them were sent to bolster the small Canadian destroyer force operating with the British. Com-

Efficiency, not comfort, got top priority in Canada's growing navy: messdecks seemed always overcrowded. The corvette *Moose Jaw* (opposite, being launched at Collingwood, Ont.) shared a submarine kill in September 1941. The RCN's tiny force of destroyers was augmented by ex-American "four-stackers," this one (opposite) camouflaged to look like several ships.

Rear Adm. L. W. Murray (above, at sea in the destroyer *Assiniboine*) describes the ships of the Newfoundland Escort Force he commanded: "They worked a 35-day cycle to and from Iceland, leaving overnight, picking up an eastbound convoy the first day out, escorting it to a point off Iceland and turning it over to another escort. In Hvalfjord there were no fresh provisions and very little rest: bridge and engine room were manned day and night against the possibility of the anchors dragging as the wind roared in the fjord. About four days of that, until a westbound convoy came past. Then the long beat back, covering slow ships probably insufficiently ballasted and against the prevailing wind, with about seven days in St. John's again before repeating the dose."

modore L. W. Murray took command of Canadian ships and establishments in the United Kingdom.

During the last months of 1940, 14 small, half-equipped, sketchily manned steel warships passed down the St. Lawrence. They were the first Canadian corvettes, unsampled fruits of a building program well in arrears but nonetheless under way. The little vessels, 190 feet in length, 33 in beam, with a speed of 16 knots and a planned armament of one 4-inch gun, two machine guns and a stock of depth charges, were designed for a complement of 92 men. Out of necessity, their armament would grow, the number of their anti-submarine devices would be multiplied by gadgets yet undreamed of; and for all this equipment and for the men to operate it, room would have to be found or made. The corvettes would never be handsome or comfortable ships. They would, some wit cracked, "roll even on wet grass." Yet the captains who took them over, mostly former merchant officers, soon felt a grumbling affection for them. With all their limitations, the corvettes performed like thoroughbreds under the knowledgeable hand of a seaman.

On the slipways of the Canadian coasts and the Great Lakes, other corvettes were taking shape. Improved designs were in the blueprint stage. But the passage of the first 14 down the St. Lawrence demonstrated that the nation, with no evidence yet of what the ships would be worth, at least could produce them.

Both they and the four-stackers were badly needed to meet a mounting scale of attack. During the last week of February 1941, 150,700 tons of Allied merchant shipping were sunk; in the first two weeks of March, 245,000 tons; and this rate of loss continued into April and May. Three or four ships and their cargoes were being sunk daily.

The war was entering what Churchill called "one of the great climacterics." On June 22, Hitler invaded Russia and soon had her reeling. A Soviet collapse would enable Hitler to attack across the Channel and across the Atlantic, with enormous resources at his command. Even if Russia held Germany to an exhausted stalemate, there could be no Allied victory without an attack supplied by sea and mounted from the British Isles. Whether for ultimate defense against a mightier Germany or for our own seaborne assault, Allied resources

down for every one replaced. Eight submarines were coming into operation for every one sunk. U-boats swarmed in the Mediterranean. They were off Gibraltar, off the Cape Verde Islands at the bulge of Africa, off Cape Town far to the south.

In the Atlantic, where the U-boats could strike a mortal blow, the need was for many more small ships. Because of their limited range, they would have to be operated in relays from base to base. To meet this need, St. John's, Nfld., became the key to the western defense system. By its position alone, it bridged nearly a quarter of the gap between the Canadian seaboard and Iceland.

In June, Canada's Commodore Murray returned from Britain to become Commodore Commanding Newfoundland Escort Force. From Liverpool, the RN's Commander-in-Chief Western Approaches, Adm. Sir Percy Noble, directed the whole Atlantic battle, but Commodore Murray exercised autonomy within his own zone.

The Newfoundland force was made up of 6 Canadian destroyers and 17 corvettes, plus 7 destroyers, 3 sloops and 5 corvettes of the Royal Navy. Soon more ships— French, Norwegian, Polish, Belgian and Dutch—were allotted to Commodore Murray. His authority extended to all local escorts operating from St. John's and to convoys and their escorts while in Newfoundland waters. Canadian ships, formerly distributed among British escort forces, now became components of a separate force under Canadian command. . . .   JOSEPH SCHULL

When the western Atlantic became Canada's domain, there were 25 U-boats on patrol south of Greenland and east of Newfoundland. It was the RCN's responsibility to shepherd convoys past the submarines to the mid-ocean meeting point south of Iceland where British ships took over. The RCN did it mainly with corvettes.

In design, they were "really improvised whalers," wrote Rear Adm. W. S. Chalmers in *Max Horton and the Western Approaches*. They were "thrown into the battle because it was thought that catching whales and killing U-boats had something in common. They were originally intended for coastal work, but sheer necessity caused them to be used as ocean escorts."

At 16 knots, they were too slow and "of little value from an offensive point of

had to be turned into munitions of war and stockpiled in the United Kingdom.

The resources were more than sufficient, but between the promise of the future and the need of the present lay a perilous gap of space and time that could be bridged only by ships—all the ships now available and hundreds more. Many convoys arrived at British ports each week and the tonnage unloaded was enormous. Yet a great percentage of it was what the island required simply to exist. Only the margin above that daily necessity represented the power to

wage war—munitions, aircraft, guns, tanks and, above all, aviation gasoline and fuel oil. If oil stocks fell below the point of safety, the operation of ships and planes would have to be curtailed. If U-boat attacks could not be met effectively, more ships would be lost, creating further shortages which would again reduce operations. The increasing demands of the war had to be met by a corresponding increase in the flow of cargo.

But the U-boats imposed a steady drain. Three merchant ships were going

"Make no mistake," says Rear Adm. L. W. Murray, "the real victors in the Battle of the Atlantic were not navies or air forces but the Allied merchant seamen." In bitter cold and icy water, few could expect rescue (left) when a merchant ship was sunk. Two (above) who were picked up by the destroyer *Ottawa* survived a second time when she was torpedoed a few hours later with a loss of 114 men, including the captain, Lt. Comdr. C. A. Rutherford, who gave his life belt to one of his crew.

view," said Admiral Chalmers, but "they filled the gap in convoy defense for over two years, while providing experience in a very tough school."

The corvettes were long on endurance and seaworthiness, short on looks and crew comforts—and occasionally more serious things. Terence Robertson, in *Maclean's,* described his first look at one:

. . . She was Canadian-built, Canadian-manned and named *Windflower.* When the destroyer in which I was serving met this newcomer to the Atlantic battlefield in

January 1941, we not unnaturally approached for a closer look. We saw on her foredeck a 4-inch gun with a wooden barrel that drooped. Then we were warned to keep clear of her stern with the immortal signal: "If you touch me there, I'll scream."

Windflower and *Mayflower* were the first corvettes commissioned in Canada and, because the navy was short of suitable weapons, both had been fitted with dummy guns for their maiden voyages to England. *Mayflower's* gun must have warped too.

K was for corvette, the duck-tailed little ship that would "roll even on wet grass." Off Halifax (below) on May 23, 1941, corvettes set out for St. John's to form the nucleus of the Newfoundland Escort Force. In the lead is *Chambly,* which four months later played a major part in the first sinking of a U-boat by a Canadian corvette. Most corvettes bore the names of Canadian cities and towns, among them Wetaskiwin, Alta. The crest (below) on *Wetaskiwin's* gunshield was a playing card: a leggy Queen of Hearts seated wetly in a puddle—all this deriving from a deliberate and obvious mispronunciation of the ship's name.

When she met the huge battleship *Rodney* in the Irish Sea, the British admiral was so appalled by the droop in her gun barrel that he signaled: "Since when are we clubbing the enemy to death?"

This irrepressible pair were the forerunners of 122 Canadian corvettes which, in the next four years, would carry thousands of farmers, miners, students and white-collar workers to victory over the elite professionals of the U-boats. Their exploits were rarely spectacular, almost never heroic. But in the Battle of the Atlantic, the most protracted and bitterly fought campaign ever waged at sea, the names "Canadian" and "corvette" became almost synonymous and the little ships created legends of courage and endurance.

One of the most colorful men in this operation was Comdr. J. D. Prentice, captain of the corvette *Chambly.* He had retired from the Royal Navy in 1934 to manage his ranch in British Columbia. In 1939, at 41, he returned to sea.

"The enemy," he told his officers, "is not destroyed by untrained ships." He proceeded to ensure that *Chambly* was a trained ship.

While exercising at St. John's on September 3 with the newly commissioned corvette *Moose Jaw,* Prentice received permission for both corvettes to steam to support convoy SC-42, then being threatened south of Greenland by one of the first U-boat wolf packs, submarines fighting in disciplined groups.

En route Commander Prentice grinned

at Lt. Edward T. Simmons, his first lieutenant. "When we get there we'll not have to worry about the convoy," he said. "Our job will be to find the enemy and kill him."

Convoy SC-42 consisted of more than 60 ships spread over 25 square miles of ocean. Sweeping ahead was the destroyer *Skeena.* Her captain, Lt. Comdr. J. C. Hibbard, was senior officer of the escort. Astern and on the beams were the corvettes *Orillia, Kenogami* and *Alberni.*

The U-boats attacked at dusk on September 9. In the first 24 hours, they destroyed ten merchant ships. On the night of the 10th, *Chambly* and *Moose Jaw* crossed the convoy's line of advance ten miles ahead of it and turned to sweep toward the leading ships. The operator of *Chambly's* asdic [detection equipment] reported: "Echo bearing oh-two-oh degrees. Range 700 yards. Submarine."

Prentice gave his orders quietly. "Tell *Moose Jaw* we're attacking. Full ahead. Stand by depth charges." The corvette vibrated wildly as she gathered speed and ran over the target, dropping six depth charges.

Two hundred feet below, U-501 listed heavily. Steam filled the control room and from the battery room came a shout: "Chlorine gas. We've got to go up."

The U-boat surfaced. *Moose Jaw,* 400 yards away, increased speed to ram. As the corvette bore down on them, the Germans on U-501's deck jumped overboard. With the enemy no longer able to escape, *Moose Jaw* swerved away, her bow grinding into the U-boat's outer casing and her stern swinging around to brush against the U-boat's conning tower.

Chambly's Prentice sent a boarding party under Lieutenant Simmons to prevent scuttling. Leaving his men on U-501's deck, Simmons, accompanied by Stoker William Brown, climbed to the conning tower and beckoned two Germans to lead the way inside to close the seacocks. They refused. As Simmons turned to go down alone, there was a shout from Brown. The lieutenant swung about, glimpsed an upraised arm holding a huge monkey wrench and hit the German on the jaw, knocking him overboard.

Starting down the conning-tower hatch, Simmons found his gas mask impeding him. He took it off, accepting the risk of chlorine, and went in unprotected. As he reached the bottom of the ladder he saw a wall of water rushing at him—a bulkhead must have given. He climbed back to the conning tower and ordered his men to abandon the U-boat.

"I remember being dragged under," he said. "I struggled to get clear of the conning-tower rigging and floundered about trying desperately to reach the surface. There was a hopeless feeling of not being able to last. I completely forgot my Mae West. When I did reach the surface, I popped out like a champagne cork. I was almost alongside our lifeboat, which had already picked up our boys and some Germans."

Stoker Brown, despite the gas and in-rushing water, had persisted in trying to find and close the seacocks. He went down

with the U-501, the first submarine sunk by a Canadian corvette.

By December 1941, 64 corvettes were in commission; 60 more were ordered for the next two years. Evidence of German respect for Canada's sheepdog navy appeared in a Berlin news report quoting U-boat commanders as "boiling with rage at being unable to attack as often as in earlier days owing to increased convoy protection by corvettes."

Winter voyages were made in icy darkness, and in certain knowledge that survivors of a sinking ship would freeze to death within five minutes. Mountainous seas crashing against slender steel hulls

made life in the engine rooms a series of frightening alarms. The engineers were always conscious of the devastation that would follow a torpedo hit.

Fogs were even more dangerous than Atlantic gales. On December 7, a freighter loomed out of one such fog, reared high above *Windflower* and cut into her engine room. The corvette that had steamed into enemy-infested waters with a wooden gun 11 months before died without ever using her real one. Her boilers burst, spreading scalding steam over the wounded, and she sank with a loss of 60 men.

From tragedies and triumphs there emerged a corvette character—a small-ship man, careless of discipline, contemp-

tuous of pomp, heedless of gold braid, an amateur warrior with unexpected skill. This *esprit de corps* expressed itself in the ships' self-designed crests: *Moose Jaw* displayed a fire-belching moose in hot pursuit of Hitler; *Calgary,* a cowboy riding a bucking corvette; *Galt,* a corvette spanking a U-boat. And it was vividly apparent at sea. One corvette signaled another in the middle of a hurricane: "Have just seen down your funnel. Fire is burning brightly." A corvette fired star shell and reported: "Am illuminating enemy." The senior ship replied: "That's me." A British destroyer leaving a Canadian corvette in charge of a convoy signaled: "Good luck." She received the reply: "Thanks. Actually, we rely on skill." . . .   TERENCE ROBERTSON

The Canadian Navy had grown to 20,000 men by the end of 1941. Of these 12,000 were at sea, many in corvettes manned by men not long out of civilian clothes. "In *Moose Jaw,"* recalls Lt. Harold Lawrence, "we were lucky. We had *two* prewar navy men on board: the captain and a leading seaman."

A few captains, like Alan Easton, had been in the merchant service before the war. They knew the loneliness of command and the bond between a captain and his ship. In *50 North,* Easton tells of the time he saw the first corvette he was to command:

. . . She was resting on the blocks of a dry-dock in a St. Lawrence River shipyard. I stood on the wall and looked down at this sturdy vessel which was to take me many miles over the ocean. HMCS *Baddeck* was mine; we were to spend a part of our lives together.

I was elated at being given command. When anyone is put in charge of something he thinks important, he feels he has been

After asdic listening gear had detected an underwater target at 700 yards, depth charges (left) from the corvette *Chambly* brought U-501 to the surface the night of September 10, 1941. As the corvette *Moose Jaw* raced in, her stern touched 501's conning tower. Some Germans (above, going ashore later at Greenock, Scotland) jumped overboard; the captain, Hugo Förster (extreme right) stepped to the corvette's quarterdeck without getting his feet wet. Says Lt. Harold Lawrence, who was in *Moose Jaw:* "He wanted to surrender and save as many of his men as he could." U-501, writes Joseph Schull, "had come to grief on her first operational cruise; which was fair enough since most of the men in the two corvettes had never been to sea before." In *Moose Jaw* the average age was 21. The captain, Lt. F. E. Grubb, was 26.

singled out as being above the crowd. But in my case the authorities probably had no alternative. There was no one else handy. In the navy during the first half of the war, there were not enough people to go around. Often you got the job whether you deserved it or not.

I could see that the ship had been built after the fashion of a big steam trawler, but with a longer and sharper bow. In her nakedness, her fat belly seemed to bulge over the floor of the dry dock, suggesting an ample capacity for, among other things, a large engine. Her rounded stern was inclined to turn up like a duck's tail.

The first sight of a ship in which one is going to sail is always exciting, that first

glimpse which creates an immediate impression—perhaps of size or strength or just lowliness, and a sense of curiosity, sometimes of disappointment.

This time I was not disappointed. It was Sunday and everything was quiet—no hammering or riveting, no trail of steam from the machine shop. What was her character? Was her spirit yet born? Would she stay young like this or grow old quickly? I was glad it was quiet because this was my private introduction.

It was a month before I had an opportunity to try her on the broad St. Lawrence below Quebec. She had been fitted out by then, her crew had come on board and she had been duly commissioned.

Some of the men felt strange. But this alien environment was what others expected, even sought, when they joined the navy. Most of them—for most were new to this—felt a twinge of concern and a little ache of homesickness. But these were hidden by an extra swing of the shoulder and more noise than necessary.

When we left at last for Halifax there was no fanfare. No "off to war" business.

Just a farewell hoot of the whistle as we pulled into the river.

Of the three officers, only the navigator had been in a ship before. Of the 50 men, about five had been professional seamen or fishermen and, below, no more than six were experienced with engines and boilers. With such a complement, it was hard to keep steam up, avoid the shoals or even steer a straight course. Had anything warlike occurred there would have been a shambles.

The few who knew their profession taught the others. Boats were lowered many times and rowed and hoisted; men swung the lead for soundings; they were taught lookout-keeping; they learned to put out fires, read a swinging compass and compensate with the wheel, stoke the furnaces without belching smoke, handle the guns in a choppy sea and throw a heaving line. But all this was not learned easily.

One day, coming into Halifax from a patrol, we were going alongside a jetty, which could be observed from the admiral's office. The admiral was known to be fond of watching his ships docking. A strong offshore wind was blowing. It was now or never with the heaving line as the bow of the ship drew parallel to the jetty at a nice throwing distance. An able seaman heaved, but his line went up like the first act of the Indian rope trick instead of across the gap. It came down in the water on the lee side. Another man heaved a spare line. It reached the jetty and was caught—but the thrower let go his end of the rope. The ship drifted away, while the admiral looked down from his window on the performance.

But the crew of *Baddeck* learned quickly and well. A few troublemakers—sea lawyers, the navy called them—were drafted off the ship and a new team of "corvette men" was ready. One windy, early October day, with the sun shining fitfully, we set out for the Battle of the Atlantic. On the jetty in Halifax were a small number of women, two or three together, some alone. As the ship cast off her ropes, the women seemed to take turns waving. They looked bitterly forlorn. An officer on the forecastle, a petty officer amidships, waved back. One or two others waved their caps to their wives.

There were few sailors, if their homes were far away, who could afford to bring their wives east. Fewer who had wives to bring. But one felt sorry for that solitary

group as they grew smaller in the distance, and most of the crew must have been glad that their families did not have to go through all that.

We sailed to Sydney, N.S., topped up with fuel and stood out of the harbor to await the convoy. Many ships of many nations were lying at anchor in the fine land-locked harbor, the assembly port for the eastbound slow Atlantic convoys in those days. Off the harbor mouth, I examined the ships as they came out at intervals of three or four minutes. The more weatherbeaten and decrepit the ship, the more attractive to me; she had a story to tell and I could sometimes discern a part of it by just looking.

The newest might have been 10 years old, the oldest perhaps 40 or 50. Some were built of iron, the inch-thick plating of the 1880s, before the days of steel. They were large and small, from about 900 tons to 9000. You could tell almost at a glance their nationality, or the country in which they were built, by the shape of their hulls and the construction of their upperworks. They were all heavily laden, only a few were not down to their Plimsoll marks and some had little freeboard, perhaps four feet between the water and the well deck.

The first ship moved slowly to allow the others to take their stations, so that the whole could form into three columns. When the commodore was satisfied that all were in place he ran up a flag hoist: the speed of the convoy was seven knots. When every ship had signified that she understood his signal, the commodore hauled his flags down and the engines of this hetero-geneous collection of vessels simultaneous-ly moved faster, although to the onlooker there was no perceptible change in speed.

On that voyage I became convinced it was the merchant seamen who suffered most. They could not really fight back—or even maneuver quickly to avoid attack. They presented the best targets and never knew when they would be singled out for extinction. The suspense must have been awful.

These men tramped from Cape Town to Rio alone and unprotected save for an old heavy gun, crossing an ocean where power-ful German surface raiders roamed. Up the Brazilian coast and through the Indies, still alone, to North America. Then in convoy across the North Atlantic, their lives in constant jeopardy. Off the United King-dom they would be haunted by E-boats and mines and hunted by bombers.

Comments on corvettes and the North Atlantic:

The suggestion to call the new breed corvettes came from Rear Adm. Percy Nelles, Canadian Chief of Naval Staff.

Rear Adm. L. W. Murray

The name is famous in history. The first corvette was a flush-decked wooden vessel with only one tier of guns, resembling a frigate.

Wartime press release

The corvette was not a true man-of-war but an offspring of the small whaling vessel.

Capt. John M. Waters, Jr., in Bloody Winter

Again we sailed to the same old routine: seas bursting down our funnel, men blaspheming, others praying, while the little ship shuddered.

Comdr. Peter MacRitchie in The Legionary

The old corvette sailor, the shivering wretch who year after year climbed out from sodden blankets to face again the misery of a midnight watch in a midwinter gale.

Orillia Daily Packet and Times

Once I had loved being at sea. Now I hated the Atlantic: the ugliness of it, the gray dreariness, the eternal whine of the wind in the rigging.

Alan Easton in 50 North

Bread grows green mold. Dry clothes are forgotten. Exhausted men sleep where they can. But there is pride, even exhilaration, in a small ship beating a powerful adversary. The sea is neither cruel nor kind; it is indifferent.

Lt. Harold Lawrence

Few knew the colossal tasks these unsung heroes achieved. They were overshadowed by the epics of fighting men who had done no more and probably less. Only their families really knew. If they came home—which thousands failed to do—they soon had to go out again and face the same conditions.

We navy men did not go through the torments they did, nor did the other fighting services. A merchant seaman could fortify himself with nothing but hope and courage. Most of them must have been very afraid, not for days and nights but for months and years. Who is the greater hero, the man who performs great deeds by swift action against odds he hardly has time to recognize, or the man who lives for long periods in constant, nagging fear of death, yet carries on?

This war the merchant seamen fought, this war we fought beside them, could be terribly tiring. Once, in the 56 hours after a first ship had been torpedoed in one con-

voy, my snatches of sleep totaled about 3½ hours. Perhaps it was not surprising then, as we straightened away with the job over, that I could speak, coherently, only about half a sentence as I tried to give the navigator my final instructions. My words would dwindle into nonsense. I struggled against this and by standing erect and moving about a little on the bridge I thought I eventually conveyed my wishes to him. Then I went below and collapsed into my bunk.

Two years later I met the navigator and asked: "Do you remember when we turned north for Reykjavik after that action? It was a bit after lunch and I was going down to turn in."

"Yes," he answered. "I remember turning north and taking over."

"Do you know," I said, "I was so tired that I was falling asleep as I was speaking to you. I felt embarrassed in case you noticed it. Did you?"

"Did I?" A broad grin. "No, sir. I was too sleepy to know what you were talking about."

Our enemies were fatigue, U-boats and the weather. One dark night, making for port after leaving the convoy and running before a high quarterly sea, the ship was pitching and rolling deeply, slowly; too slowly—the waves almost synchronized with her speed. At times she rode like a surfboat before the rollers with her nose pointing down.

At 2045 the stern rose high and the ship rolled 50 degrees to port and hung for an interminable time until the great sea relented and plowed forward along the keel. When the leading seaman of the watch was able to check several minutes later, the after-lookout man was not on the high gun platform. The bulwarks on the starboard quarter were bent inboard, the protective plating on the gun platform almost flattened and the large raft on the port side gone—damage that told that the lookout had been swept overboard. The great sea must have buried the whole after end of the ship.

We turned to search but as we rose and dived into the steep seas we knew we could never find him. His close friend and shipmate cried for days and nights. . . .

ALAN EASTON

Closeup:

The savior of Ceylon

Although their country was not to play a major role in the Pacific war, Canadians got into it in many ways as individuals or in small groups. The most crucial figure of them all was an RCAF pilot who fought there only briefly and didn't know for years what he'd achieved.

In early 1942 the Japanese surged forward. Malaya was overrun. Singapore fell. The Philippines, Burma, Java, Borneo, Sumatra were invaded. As April opened, a large Japanese naval force sped west across the Indian Ocean toward the strategic island of Ceylon with its British naval base.

At the same time a Catalina flying boat, piloted by Sqdn. Ldr. Leonard J. Birchall of St. Catharines, Ont., was flying to Ceylon on a posting to the tropics. Only a few weeks before, his 413 Squadron had been patrolling off the Norwegian coast in freezing weather.

On April 4, the squadron was ordered out on reconnaissance over the Indian Ocean. From Birchall's diary:

. . . Our task was to be in a position approximately 250 miles southeast of Ceylon at first light and to patrol this area during daylight to ensure that no enemy shipping, especially carriers, approached close enough to run in during the night and launch an air strike at first light against Ceylon.

During the day we received a message to change course to due south of Ceylon. About one hour before our patrol was finished, the moon came up and we decided to extend our patrol time to get an exact astro fix by using moon and sun shots. This took us about 350 miles due south of Ceylon.

As we were preparing to return, we noticed to the extreme south a small dot on the horizon. With lots of fuel, we turned

to identify it. Just as we got close enough to identify it with binoculars, we noticed several more ships. Our identification proved them to be Japanese: battleships, aircraft carriers, cruisers, destroyers and troop carriers in convoy. Being at a low altitude, we

had managed to get under the enemy outer air screen and close enough to identify all the ships, their position, course and speed.

We immediately coded a message and started transmission. During this time, Japanese aircraft spotted us. We were halfway through our required third transmission when a shell destroyed our wireless equipment and seriously injured the wireless operator. There was no cloud cover or other protection, and we were now under constant attack. Shells set fire to our internal tanks. We managed to get the fire out, and then another started, and the aircraft began to break up. Due to our low altitude it was impossible to bail out but I got the aircraft down on the water before the tail fell off.

All the time we were under constant strafing. The crew managed to evacuate the aircraft with the exception of one air gunner whose leg was severed. He, unfortunately, went down with the plane. Eight of us swam away from burning gasoline spread out over the water. Two were seriously injured and unconscious and we had them in life jackets. The strafing continued and we had to dive each time the enemy fired. The two in life jackets could not do this and were killed. This left six of us and we stayed in a group until a destroyer put out a boat to pick us up. Three were badly wounded. The rest of us, although we had several wounds, were fairly well off.

The Japanese had picked us up to find out whether we had been able to send a warning, and to obtain information on the defenses of Ceylon. We denied having gotten a message away and said we had only arrived in Colombo the day before and had no knowledge of the defenses. Despite severe beatings we stuck to our story and it

appeared to be accepted. We were then placed in the forward paint locker where three could lie down, two could sit and one had to stand. We remained like this for three days during the attack on Ceylon. We were given no medical treatment and only a cup of soup each day.

Following the attack we were transferred to the aircraft carrier *Akagi*. We arrived at Yokohama the day after the famous Jimmy Doolittle air raid on Tokyo. We were paraded before the populace who vented their anger on us. It was not until the end of the war that I found out our message had gotten through and had been of value. . . .

LEONARD J. BIRCHALL

It had indeed. On receipt of Birchall's message, Ceylon went into a fever of activity. As Leslie Roberts records in *There Shall Be Wings*:

. . . Merchantmen in Colombo harbor were ordered to sea to escape. Defenses were mounted. Thirty-six Hurricanes, recently arrived, were put on instant alert. A second Catalina, sent out to keep watch on the Japanese fleet, did not return but reported the enemy's changed position.

When the Japanese launched a great air attack on the city on Easter Sunday, with 50 bombers and as many Zero fighters, it was repulsed with great losses to the enemy, though the port and city suffered substantial damage and the Royal Navy lost two cruisers and a destroyer to low-flying bombers.

It was the first check to the Japanese drive through the Far East; they retired and did not come back. A single Canadian Catalina and its crew had averted a second Pearl Harbor. Birchall was awarded the DFC as "the savior of Ceylon.". . .

He was later awarded the Order of the British Empire for his conduct as a prisoner. He took brutal treatment because he repeatedly intervened when the Japanese beat prisoners or denied them medical treatment.

But Birchall's greatest tribute involved no award at all. Someone once asked Winston Churchill what he considered the most dangerous moment of the war. He said his greatest alarm came when he heard the Japanese fleet was heading for Ceylon at a time when the Germans were threatening to seize control of Egypt. Ceylon would give the Japanese control of the Indian Ocean. This, added to enemy control of Egypt, would "close the ring" and make the future black indeed. Disaster was prevented, said Churchill, by the man who spotted the Japanese fleet. His was "one of the most important single contributions to victory."

Hana-Saku
Hana-Saku

**Hopelessly outnumbered and ill-prepared,
two Canadian battalions go down fighting the Japanese at Hong Kong**

For two years the army had been marshaling the bulk of its strength in Britain. For two years there had been rumors that Canadian soldiers were going into action in France, Norway, the Middle East, in an invasion for the liberation of Europe—almost anywhere but where action finally came.

When it came—briefly—in December 1941, it involved neither the liberation of Europe nor the four divisions mustered in Britain for that ultimate purpose. It involved the defense of an Asiatic outpost of the British Empire by two battalions that belonged to no division at all.

Hong Kong was a disaster. Ian Adams, in *Maclean's,* compared it to the Charge of the Light Brigade, "an act of stupidity and folly" that sent inadequately trained and ill-equipped men to defend an island that was indefensible.

Britain requested the two infantry battalions in September 1941. This reinforcement of the Hong Kong garrison, said the British government, would "reassure Chiang Kai-shek as to our intention to hold the colony and have a great moral effect throughout the Far East."

Unmentioned was the view Winston Churchill had dictated to his Chief of Staff on January 7, when such a possibility was first broached: "This is all wrong. If Japan goes to war there is not the slightest chance of holding Hong Kong or relieving it. It is most unwise to increase the loss we shall suffer there. Instead of increasing the garrison, it ought to be reduced to a symbolic scale. We must avoid frittering away our resources on untenable positions. Japan will think long before declaring war on the British Empire, and whether there are two or six battalions at Hong Kong will make no difference to her choice. I wish we had fewer troops there, but to move any would be noticeable and dangerous."

Churchill was accurate in his appraisal of what would happen in the event of attack. And by late 1941, with Britain's for-

tunes at a low ebb, Japan was nearing the end of her long thinking. She had been ravaging China for years; she had made no secret of her dreams of ruling Asia, and more than Asia. She had joined Germany and Italy in the Triple Alliance. Her plans for conquering Hong Kong had in fact been laid as early as July 1940. The code word for attack was *"Hana-Saku, Hana-Saku,"* literally "flowers abloom, flowers abloom." The three divisions that would answer it were massed within 30 miles of Hong Kong when the Canadians sailed.

Only nine days before the Canadian force did sail, the rabid militarist Gen. Hideki Tojo became Prime Minister of Japan. Lord Halifax, British ambassador in Washington, promptly warned London and Ottawa that this made war inevitable and that it would be absurd to commit more men to Hong Kong. He suggested Ottawa re-examine its policy. According to his war histories, Winston Churchill himself, in approving the request for Canadian troops, had "allowed myself to be drawn from" his position in January. But he had called for "a further assessment before the battalions sail." A day before departure, London told Ottawa war in the Far East was "unlikely at present."

Ottawa stuck with its decision. Lt. Gen. Maurice Pope, then Assistant Chief of the General Staff, says in *Soldiers and Politicians:* "I heard a member of the government say they had been actuated solely by two ideas: (a) it was unthinkable that Canada should seek to fill only the comfortable roles and (b) Britain was in a difficult spot and frankly seeking a helping hand. In these circumstances, any thought of refusing the request had never occurred to them."

It was hoped the Canadians would see only garrison duty. But the directives to their commanding officer also said they would "participate to the limit of your strength in the defense of the colony should the occasion arise."

The need for secrecy and speed was considered so vital that the entire expedition was whipped together in little more than two weeks. Its core was the two infantry battalions, both classified by army headquarters as "in need of refresher training or insufficiently trained and not recommended for operations." One was Quebec's Royal Rifles of Canada under Lt. Col. W. J. Home; it was just back from garrison duty in Newfoundland. The other was the Winnipeg Grenadiers under Lt. Col. J. L. R. Sutcliffe; it was just back from garrison duty in the West Indies. In addition, there was a brigade headquarters with a signals section and other specialists. The entire force of 1975 men was under Brig. J. K. Lawson.

They sailed from Vancouver the night of October 27, in the converted passenger ship *Awatea.* Her departure was secret. Her destination was unknown to most of those aboard. Her fate was to deliver the Canadians into one of the most tragic episodes of the country's war.

One of the Canadians was a signalman named William Allister. Now a Montreal writer and painter, he is the author of *A Handful of Rice,* a novel about Canadians captured at Hong Kong. Here is Allister's account of the expedition and the battle, based on his own diary, on interviews he made for CBC broadcasts and on material from official records:

... As a member of the headquarters signals section, I was among the hundreds who had assembled in Ottawa in an atmosphere of tense speculation. My diary reads:

"Left home for the last time. Couldn't tell them it was embarkation leave. Goodby's were hasty—which is best. Mom is sure I'll be back weekends. The notice said: 'You are wanted for special duties overseas.' Sounds important and frightening. But what the hell, anything official is always ominous. All kinds of rumors flying. Startling and exciting. Then we're told to pack and issued summer uniforms. We are going in a day or so, and to a hot climate. Africa? Jamaica? Could be. More probably China. And I've never been farther west than Winnipeg. It's too fantastic! The depot's jumping, crowds pouring in and all hush-hush."

Within a few days we were speeding across the country. When we got aboard the *Awatea* in Vancouver, things began to go awry. Our vehicles were late; they came on another ship and never did reach us. There was immense confusion and no fanfare. The soldiers unwittingly began to echo Churchill's prophetic words that this was "all wrong." A sense of doom seemed to creep through our ranks. Resentments flared.

Awatea zigzagged across the Pacific to avoid submarines. It was anything but pleasant; nauseating conditions for the men, rumors of submarines, doubts of what lay ahead. Our lone escort, the armed merchant cruiser *Prince Robert,* often fell so far behind she was out of sight.

A few days out of Hong Kong we were told of our destination and that we should be ready for anything, even fighting our way ashore. A corporal: "I guess they felt Tojo's hoopla about conquering the world was grounds for suspicion. When I watched the briefing I said, 'My God, another Dunkirk!' And someone answered, 'No, fella, at Dunkirk they had somewhere to go.' "

My diary: "Before we landed on November 16 our brains were addled with precautions about everything from sexual diseases to the customs of Indian soldiers who would train with us. But how could anyone prepare green Canadian kids for the impact of the Orient? Our first shocker was seeing crowds following the ship in sampans, eating garbage we threw overboard. The waterfront stench made it almost impossible to breathe. It was an odor you could practically taste.

"On landing, we found that our main positions were on the island of Hong Kong but our barracks on the mainland nearby. We route-marched through Hong Kong's sister city of Kowloon to our barracks at

Canadian troops disembark at Hong Kong. Their main positions were on Hong Kong island, their barracks on the mainland. Brig. J. K. Lawson (above) commanded the Canadian force.

Sham Shui Po. All the pomp and ceremony made us feel like an army of occupation amid the teeming Chinese. The filth, poverty and verminous atmosphere hung over us like a pall. I wanted to pull on gloves and a gas mask when I thought of the cholera, dysentery, malaria, typhoid, venereal disease around me. Barefooted old women bent low under huge loads while coolie bosses bellowed behind them. We saw filthy shops and slabs of meat black with flies; harmless beggars, their diseased legs half eaten away; white men in Panama hats riding rickshas right out of a Hollywood movie. Neon in Chinese. Nothing connected. Time seemed to be motionless. A weird sensation.

"Slept under mosquito netting like Clark Gable in *China Seas,* nearly eaten alive by bedbugs the first night. Hired a valet for 28 cents a week. He shines our shoes and buttons, presses our uniforms, gets an *amah* to do our laundry, makes our beds, runs errands, serves tea in bed. U.S. fags ten cents a deck. Beer ten cents a bottle. Bills stick out of our pockets. The beggars mob us—it's hard to walk. We get shaved in bed while we sleep—for five cents a week! What a time! Gals galore. Thousands of refugees fleeing ahead of the Japanese at Canton. Prostitution seems to be a national sport. But the girls are often just nice kids sold by their parents for about $200 to keep the family alive."

Everything was dirt cheap. Servants waited on us hand-and-foot. There was a kind of hysteria in the air. Who could believe there were 50,000 to 60,000 seasoned Japanese troops only 30 miles away? That spies were all around us in this colony of 1,500,000 people?

Posing as barbers, tailors, dentists, these Japanese spies and a Chinese fifth column were everywhere, even inside our barracks. Warehouses were leased by fifth columnists and used to construct foundations for heavy artillery. The popular barbershop in the Hong Kong Hotel was their intelligence headquarters and the top brass in the colony were among its clientele.

We did some training and got to know a bit about the countryside, but the three weeks we had were tragically inadequate for what lay ahead. The island of Hong Kong we had to defend was 29 square miles in area, a rugged, confusing mass of mountains, hills and valleys with almost no flat ground. It was only a half mile across to the mainland peninsula of Kowloon. Beyond that to the north lay more mountainous land called the New Territories, which stretched 30 miles to the border of China.

Information on the defenses was not reassuring. There were 36 guns, but the mobile artillery had none of the latest models. There were 20 early model anti-aircraft guns but no radar equipment. There were six old-fashioned RAF planes but no hope of more. Most naval units had been withdrawn, leaving only a few small vessels.

We stood alone. Still the Governor, Sir Mark Young, and the military commander, Maj. Gen. C. M. Maltby, appeared to believe Hong Kong could be defended. There was food for 130 days. The total defense force added up to fewer than 14,000, including nurses and civilian volunteers. Besides the Canadians, there were three regiments of the Royal Artillery containing many Indian troops, one Indian regiment with British officers from the Hong Kong

and Singapore artillery, two engineer companies, one British infantry battalion (Royal Scots), one British machine-gun battalion (Middlesex Regiment), two Indian infantry battalions (7th Rajput Regiment and 14th Punjab Regiment) and the Hong Kong Volunteer Defense Corps, a militia outfit.

My diary: "We were camping out in tents at Waterloo Road (cheery name), setting up signal offices, exploring the Chinese mansions, singing, laughing. We drove north into the New Territories and saw lots of pillboxes and gun emplacements, nice and solid-looking. It looked like a cinch that Japan wouldn't dare start a fight; she had her hands full with China. The boys were on a tourist spree, bringing back kimonos, dressing gowns, pajamas. Steaks at Jingles were two inches thick and a foot and a half long, all for two bucks. What a life."

"Nothing to worry about," I wrote home. "Those poor guys in England getting bombed and living on rations—and us living like kings. You can rest easy, Mother me dear, the war is thousands of miles from your darlin' boy." The letter went off on the China Clipper on December 8, and was shot down by the Japanese. Time had run out.

On the morning of December 8, Hong Kong time—December 7 in North America—some of us were shaving when we heard the air-raid sirens. We paid no attention. "The usual rehearsal," my diary says. "We heard this booming and figured it was artillery practice. Jenkins went out on the balcony to look at the harbor and saw planes swooping down. He came in very surprised. 'They're dropping bombs,' he said. We just laughed. We nearly died laughing! The windows were blown in and we hit the deck. They were aiming at our building—they seemed to know where everyone was. We beat it out of the building. Ronny and Fairley were hit. Shrapnel was flying and Rutledge hollered for us to lie flat. We saw a Chinese coolie get his head blown off. At the camp gates there were about 50 dead Chinese piled up. We had the distinct impression that there was a war on."

The news of war filled the airwaves. Sneak attack on Pearl Harbor. Much of the U.S. Pacific fleet wiped out. Emergency sessions of Parliament. Declarations of war by the United States, Canada, Britain. But we were in Hong Kong, isolated and far from home. Our two infantry battalions were already in their positions on the island and our signals section with the defenders of the Kowloon Peninsula and the New Territories.

The closer we looked the more impossible the situation seemed. The six tiny aircraft were bombed on the ground, giving the Japanese *carte blanche* in the air. And their planes could fly too low for anti-aircraft guns to take aim. The garrison was vastly outnumbered and outgunned. There was no hope of reinforcement. Britain's two great battleships, *Prince of Wales* and *Repulse*, were sunk by aircraft off Malaya within a few days. The U.S. fleet had been crippled; the Chinese armies could offer no help. We found ourselves pawns in a huge power play, caught in the center of a hopeless, suicidal frontline position.

The enemy we faced was made up of tough veterans seasoned by years of war in China. Our Canadian force was deemed adequate only for garrison duty. You couldn't compare us to the trained Canadian divisions in England. Neither of our battalions had trained in anticipation of battle and to make matters worse, many reinforcements sent to the two infantry units were raw recruits or little better.

A private: "I had exactly 30 days' training. I learned how to left turn, how to right turn, how to salute—all the usual things. But I never fired a shot till I got to Hong Kong."

A corporal: "I taught one fellow how to load and discharge his rifle behind battalion headquarters in the hills. He was killed before he even got to fire it."

On December 10, as Japanese troops (below) pushed down the Malayan peninsula, off the coast Japanese aircraft destroyed the British battle cruiser *Repulse* and battleship *Prince of Wales* (left, just before sinking). Austin Willis recalls how the news was broadcast in Canada: "I was on duty in the booth in Toronto, feeding the CBC radio network. Lorne Greene rushed in and read the short tragic bulletin about the ships, with a staggering loss of life from drowning. I burst in right after with a commercial: 'Buy your son in the service a Bulova watch—they're watertight.' I sure remember *that* one —and the subsequent uproar too!"

A lieutenant: "Some of these soldiers were just too damn young. I remember one who was wounded—I suddenly realized that he was only a child of 16 or 17."

A private: "There was a case where the Japanese were attacking and these fellows were throwing hand grenades without knowing enough to pull out the pins." One furious British sergeant yelled: "What are y' tryin' to do—'it 'im on the 'ead with it?"

The Japanese first sent thousands of shock troops pouring across the New Territories. They met one British and two Indian battalions to which our signals section was attached. So we might claim to be Canada's first soldiers to see action in the war. At first the advance outposts on the frontier held the attackers at bay, but they came on in waves all day and all night. There seemed no end to them.

My diary: "Wallie had to ride back and forth to the front lines. Said it's blood-curdling to hear the Japs' battlecries. They came charging right into the machine guns. Our men used their machine guns—the Lewis, the Bren, the Vickers—till the barrels were red-hot. The Japs went down like wheat and still they kept coming, climbing over hills of bodies. The pillboxes turned out to be deathtraps. The Japs climbed on the roofs and lobbed grenades down the air vents. Our guys set their guns up on the roofs after that and the hell with the pillboxes. The Indians loved it all. They'd hold their fingers down on the trigger and never stop, happy as hell. They wept when they were ordered to retreat."

The defenders fell back to their main defenses, the so-called Gin-Drinkers Line, a series of pillboxes stretching across the isthmus about five miles behind Kowloon. They were surprised to find the World War I tactic of holding one long line outmoded, surprised that the propaganda stereotype of the Japanese as myopic barbarians who couldn't see in the dark was fatally wrong. They proved to be excellent night fighters. On the 9th, the Japanese sealed the fate of the Gin-Drinkers Line.

D company of the Grenadiers was brought over from Hong Kong to help and saw action briefly on the 11th. By then the Royal Scots and Rajputs holding the front were fighting on nerve alone. The order came to retreat to Hong Kong. D company was ordered to cover the Royal Scots' withdrawal that night, while the 7th Rajputs were left to hold Devil's Peak Peninsula, a last mainland defense.

Withdrawal sounded fine on paper, but it reckoned without the chaos of half a million Kowloon citizens scrambling to escape across the half-mile of water. Panic and hysteria swept the waterfront. Fifth columnists fired at soldiers and civilians alike. Boats, sampans, junks, ferries, jammed with terrified refugees, were pounded by bombs and sprayed by machine guns. Mobs looted warehouses. Police fired into crowds. Soldiers destroyed vehicles and ammunition. Last-minute demolition squads blew up harbor installations. Our signals section were kept at our posts until the last day, the 12th, and then ordered to get away as best we could.

My diary: "We got our equipment on two trucks and went roaring through the streets, rifles cocked for snipers. Riotous confusion everywhere. The civilians had no arms. Families were split. An old lady stretched out a hand for help as we passed. We couldn't help. They all had to be left behind. Bombs falling everywhere. One blew a crater in front of us. We backed up and took a side street. People running everywhere. At the dock we had to carry the signal sets—they felt like pianos— through the mobs and load them on a boat. Ha—what boat? Bedlam. Everyone trying to get a boat—prices crazy. Every floating board under hire. Looters being shot all around us. One drunken police sergeant, giggling happily, was shooting at anyone, looter or not, as long as he was a coolie. Good clean fun. One guard at a warehouse was letting looters inside, then shooting them down.

"We took a ferry at gunpoint but its engine kept stalling. Just as we got into the water, planes dive-bombed us. The shore was lined with people with no way to cross. They knew what happened when the Japs took a city. One munitions boat blew up. We had no life belts and I couldn't swim.

"We finally made it across and got a truck to Victoria barracks, just in time to run into the worst shelling ever—we were next to a munitions depot they were trying to hit. We lay along the cement passage and each time I heard the split-second hiss I flung my hands over my helmet—silly reflex. One shell blew my helmet off and through the smoke I saw Blackie waving it on the end of his bayonet where it had landed."

A private: "The guys that had been beaten off Kowloon came back full of fear, with stories of horror—the Japs were hanging people from lampposts and cutting throats and raping."

My diary: "We all lay down to sleep exhausted. But I couldn't sleep. We sat up and smoked and talked in low voices. Finally the question was asked: 'Do you think we'll ever get out of here alive?' Penny said, 'I don't think so.' And there was silence."

The island dug in. The Canadians were divided: the Royal Rifles went into an East Brigade with the Rajputs, under Brigadier Wallis; the Grenadiers, with our signals, the Punjabs and Royal Scots, into a West Brigade under Brigadier Lawson with headquarters at Wong Nei Chong Gap. The Middlesex machine guns were to cover the coast from pillboxes. Morale was high among those who had not met the enemy. One battle-weary Royal Scot, listening to the Canadians merrily singing songs like "Silent Night," said: "The puir daftees. They think it's Christmas comin'. Gawd help us."

Japan's flag was hoisted over Kowloon by the 13th. A demand for surrender was refused. Planes and artillery began to pound the island. Fires were started, guns knocked out. Crowds ran to and fro in the streets or lined up for rice while bombs fell. On the night of the 15th, a landing was beaten off with a Royal Rifles platoon getting in the first shots. The enemy was behind schedule and impatient. On the 17th they again demanded surrender with a threat of indiscriminate bombardment. It was rejected. Time was important to both sides. Our orders were to fight to the last man.

The final, most important and tragic phase was about to begin. On the 18th a devastating barrage was leveled point-blank across the harbor against the northeast coast and the area leading up to Wong Nei Chong Gap.

My diary: "We're shooting messages back and forth about landings. The shelling is murderous. We lie flat on the pillbox floor and count the booms when they go off and when they land. The second part's a cinch because they're landing on *us*. Fires

Casualties among civilians (left) were high as the Japanese struck south through Asia. The fall of Singapore on February 15, 1942, "is a sort of anthology of all that is worst in British military history," writes Peter Young in *World War 1939-45*. "It is a tale of complacency, unpreparedness and weakness, relieved only by isolated tactical successes and the firmness of a handful of units and individuals." Hong Kong (below, Japanese soldiers attack) was another disaster, "an act of stupidity and folly," wrote Ian Adams in *Maclean's*. He compared it to the Charge of the Light Brigade.

Police station

Brigadier Lawson's body found here

Brigade HQ shelters

Mount Nicholson

Kitchen shelters used as hospital

Ammunition storage

Company shelters held by Grenadiers' D company

started down below in the oil dumps. Smoke obscuring the shore. Are they landing? How many? It this the night?"

It *was* the night. As soon as darkness fell, 7500 Japanese began crossing in small boats, ferries, homemade rafts, sampans; some even swam. They landed at several points on the north side of the island. The Rajputs and Middlesex manning the pillboxes on the beaches took a heavy toll before they were overrun.

A Grenadier: "They came running ashore firing from the knee. They came in waves of 30 or 40 and there was no stopping them—the more we hit with artillery and machine guns, the faster they came."

Past theories haunted the situation. In the conviction that any attack must come from the south, from the sea, most of the island's guns faced the wrong direction. Was this merely a feint to cover a landing from the south? Wait till daybreak, some advised, then we'll clean them out.

But the Japanese weren't waiting for daybreak. Noiseless in rubber shoes, they fanned out east, west and south. To try to plug a gap around Jardine's Lookout, a

company of the Winnipeg Grenadiers was thrown in. Its platoons were split up. One, under Lieutenant Birkett, was to cover the front from the Lookout's summit. Of their wild night in rain and darkness, Sgt. Tom Marsh recorded: "We had been told to stay where we were for the night and report at Wong Nei Chong Gap in the morning. We had settled down when orders came to occupy Jardine's Lookout, about a mile away. Lieutenant Birkett had a Volunteer, a militiaman, as a guide. Although we were unaware of it, the Japs had already passed our destination and we were walking right into the middle of them. We reached a pillbox occupied by Hong Kong Volunteers. They tried to dissuade Birkett from going on because the enemy were all around, but he decided to carry out orders."

They were soon pinned down by enemy fire. They answered with Bren and tommy guns. Mortar shells were bursting; bullets and chips of rock flying. Confusion was intensified by the darkness. Patrols crisscrossed. Lieutenant Corrigan and his men ran flush into the enemy. By the light of one bursting flash, Corrigan suddenly saw

a Japanese officer rushing at him, waving a sword. He caught the blow with one hand and with the other grabbed the sword, wrestled the officer to the ground and killed him.

Marsh: "Lieutenant Mitchell of A company made his way over to us and wanted to know what unit we were. He said he thought we were firing at his company. This was possible in the confusion but we didn't think so."

Meanwhile, to the east, the Royal Rifles were strung out along a 15-mile line from Lye Mun Passage south to the Stanley Peninsula. They were already exhausted from a round-the-clock alert. As the Japanese struck through the Rajputs, virtually wiping them out, they ran into the Rifles' C company, sent in to defend Sai Wan Hill under Maj. W. A. Bishop. The company drove the enemy off the slopes but could not take the crest. For three hours a savage seesaw battle raged till the Canadians were ordered back to avoid encirclement. At the same time, other Rifles were trying to prevent the Japanese from seizing 1700-foot Mount Parker or to evict them from positions they had reached. One entire Rifles platoon and two sections were trapped and either killed, wounded or captured.

When dawn came, the Japanese were on the summit of Mount Parker. The Rifles and what else was left of the East Brigade were ordered to withdraw south to occupy a line across the Stanley Peninsula in the vicinity of Stanley Mound, to concentrate for counterattacks. The Japanese soon cut them off from the Grenadiers and the rest of the West Brigade.

I had spent part of that first night at West Brigade headquarters at Wong Nei Chong Gap. My diary: "Our captain knew we'd be trapped. He left four men to keep communications going and told the rest of us to start hoofing it. Where to? Anywhere—any way. At first we took the sets but later gave up and smashed them. We stumbled through the dark and rain, challenged by nervous sentries, and got lost in the hills. Ended up in a wrecked car and tried to sleep till dawn. At the first gray light firing started all around us. Couldn't find any Canadians so we joined an English officer. Killed my first men. Three. I often wondered how I'd feel. I felt nothing. Just numb with fright. We were encircled and had to run in front of their machine guns to get away. I've never known such terror."

A private: "Everything got mixed up. You'd find yourself under a different officer. We didn't know where anyone was. We didn't know D company was supporting Brigade HQ from our left and when fire came from there we returned it. We were actually engaging our own men."

Marsh: "At one point I crawled toward two men to warn them to pull back with their Bren light machine gun. I laid on my stomach and called. H. yelled that S. was shot and helpless. I could hear S. pleading not to be left and his friend consoling him. Just then a Japanese officer jumped up, waving a sword and screaming 'Banzai! Banzai!' I shot. He spun and collapsed. We decided to try to get S. out. They were at the bottom of a six-foot drop. I unfastened my sling and passed my rifle down, and H. put S's belt through the sling. We waited till a burst of fire stopped and then H. heaved S. up and I pulled and dragged. He dropped behind a rock beside me amid a hail of bullets. H. threw the Bren up and followed. But getting S. up the rugged slope was the dangerous job. We turned him on his back. He was semiconscious and I didn't think his chances were good but H. was set on saving him. We dragged him by the shoulders, taking advantage of every bit of cover. We had just reached an open space and Corporal Darragh had crawled down to help when all hell broke loose. A machine gun had us in its sights. H. was killed. S's body was riddled. Darragh's hand was smashed. A bullet hit my leg and I dived back. I was shot in the head and lost consciousness."

When Marsh came to he found blood flowing from his mouth. He managed to bandage his head, then crawled up to Jardine's Lookout. "Several of the platoon lay dead or desperately wounded. Lieutenant Birkett was still on top of the pillbox manning a machine gun. By this time they had us under artillery fire. There was a terrific explosion, a direct hit. I blacked out again. I awoke in the afternoon to find a corporal lying across me, badly wounded. He motioned me to lie quiet. The Japs had wiped out all resistance and were bayoneting the wounded. I lost consciousness again and awoke to the drizzle of rain in the darkness. All was quiet. Only the dead remained. My left arm was broken. I could see bodies all around me. They had probably taken me for dead and not bothered to finish me."

Other Grenadiers were fighting desperately around the Lookout and Mount But-

Canadian soldiers fought and died and were captured in Wong Nei Chong Gap (left). Below: Japanese bombs fall on Hong Kong. "This Christmas of 1941," Stephen Leacock wrote in *New World Illustrated*, "may seem to us the most distressed, the most tragic of the ages—Christmas in a world of disaster never known before. But yet it's Christmas. And we ought to keep it so—the old, glad season of goodwill and kindliness and forgiveness toward everybody. Notice, toward everybody—even toward Adolf Hitler. What? You say you'd rather boil him in oil. Oh, but, of course, I *include* that; boil him, and then forgive him boiled."

ler. A platoon under Lieutenant French had stormed Mount Butler but had been driven back, its officer wounded and later killed. Then A company, under Maj. A. B. Gresham, was ordered to clear the two hills. It was split up and those under 42-year-old CSM. John R. Osborn reached Mount Butler, took the summit at bayonet point and held it for three hours. At last they were driven back toward Wong Nei Chong and, along with other elements of A company, were encircled.

A Grenadier: "Our ammunition was running low. Enemy fire was terrific. We did what we could with a couple of Brens and six or seven tommy guns. There were nine or ten of us in a huddle when I saw a grenade sailing over, high in the air. It landed next to Osborn. He'd thrown others out but there was no time to throw this one. Something had to be done instantly or several men would be killed. Osborn did it. He deliberately rolled over on top of the grenade and took the full charge."

To protect several of his countrymen caught in the battle for Hong Kong, CSM. John R. Osborn rolled on top of a grenade and died saving the lives of several other Winnipeg Grenadiers. He was awarded a posthumous Victoria Cross. The 17-day battle cost Canada 290 dead, 493 wounded. Nearly as many died later in prison camp as were killed in battle.

But no amount of bravery could save a hopeless situation. They were soon overrun. In the other group from A company Gresham and others were killed, the rest wounded or taken prisoners.

The enemy poured through Wong Nei Chong Gap. Brigadier Lawson's headquarters was cut off and he was trapped. An attempt to relieve him proved fruitless. As the enemy lobbed grenades down the air vents, bodies piled higher and higher in the pillboxes. One group of 12 decided to break out. Seven were cut down, but five reached cover and held off the attackers till nightfall. Then they crept through the enemy lines and rejoined their own forces. At 10 a.m. Brigadier Lawson telephoned General Maltby that his headquarters was surrounded and he was going outside to fight it out. He rushed out firing and was riddled by bullets.

The exhausted Rifles, to the east, were now the core of the force in the Stanley Peninsula. Only a few detachments of Middlesex and Volunteers were left to help them. In the days that followed, the Rifles fought under every conceivable disadvantage. The astonishing fact is that they not only clung to their positions so long, inflicting heavy losses, but actually were able to mount numerous counterattacks. In the few hand-to-hand fights that took place, the Japanese lost. After that, they relied on grenades and their deadly skill with mortars.

For the Rifles, each desperate battle meant more irreplaceable losses. Yet somehow they held on day after day. Food and water were cut off. Sub-units were broken up, slaughtered, captured.

A corporal: "When the Japs captured the island's reservoir the only water we had was in our bottles. Word came that Churchill expected us to fight to the last bullet and the last drop of water and I thought: "This is me. I'm the guy he's talking about!"

Nor was it any better where the Grenadiers fought. The Royal Scots had tried an unsuccessful counterattack on Wong Nei Chong Gap on the 19th with heavy losses. Still there was no thought of surrender.

The Grenadiers' D company was led by Captain Bowman who, someone said, "was so exhausted he was talking gibberish." Ordered to attack a Japanese strongpoint on Mount Houston, Bowman was last seen charging them with a blazing tommy gun. Two more officers were wounded

and two platoons almost annihilated before the third managed to seize ground vitally needed by the enemy. Its men commanded the one north-south road across the island and stopped the enemy advance till December 22 when their shelter was finally smashed by shellfire. The survivors were taken prisoner. When the Japanese officer heard how few men had held them off, he slapped the Canadian officer for lying about their numbers.

While that fight was going on, headquarters company, with parts of C company, had obtained a foothold at the Gap, fighting under Maj. E. Hodkinson, who was wounded. B company under Major Hook joined C company on the 20th, and that night in heavy rain and fog attacked Mount Nicholson. They were driven off, leaving 20 men and two officers on the slope. They renewed the attack at dawn. The casualties included all the officers, seven NCOs and 29 men.

My diary: "Finally caught up with my unit near Wan Chai Gap. Many of them had just been killed. From sheer inexperience, they had set up signal sets on the exposed side of a house and got a direct hit. My closest buddies. We got a ration of rum and went up to dig their graves. After two nightmarish days, the sight of their mangled bodies was too much and I cracked up."

As the fighting raged on, those who were taken prisoner were marched off, shot or left in exposed positions to be blown up by their own fire. The wounded were generally bayoneted.

Cpl. Bud Dicks: "They lined us against the wall and took our wallets, etc. I was trying to figure out which I preferred—to be shot or have my head cut off. They made a real drama of it. They put up a firing squad and the officer stood beside them with his sword ready to come down. To me it was like cutting an artery. Hope goes out of your whole being. You're limp. And then he stopped and all the time we could feel the bullets that didn't come. The officer took us to a cement ledge overlooking a cliff and lined us up again. He put his revolver in a sergeant's back and shot him. At that we threw ourselves over the cliff. They opened up on us from above. In falling I smashed my face on a rock and lost consciousness. When I woke I thought I was dying but I found out you don't die that easily."

Tom Marsh: "I was dizzy from head and

leg wounds and they flung me into a shed crammed with prisoners—whites, Chinese and Indians. Many were wounded or dead. The floor ran with blood. There was no room to lie down, no food, no water. Thirst for a wounded man is acute torture. A few tried to help but most sat huddled, waiting. A big gun was planted beside our building and I could hear our mortars trying to get its range. Then it came, a blinding flash, shrieks and moans. I owe my life to the fact that we were so closely packed."

Everywhere now the defenders were fighting with their backs to the wall, in shrinking positions. The colony rejected a third surrender demand even though 25,000 enemy troops were pouring across the island, and more stood behind them. The exhausted Allies tried to hold a last desperate line to the west to protect the towns of Victoria and Aberdeen with all their helpless civilians. Hospitals crammed with wounded threw themselves on the mercy of the invaders.

In the south, shortly before six o'clock Christmas morning, about 150 to 200 Japanese broke into the emergency hospital at St. Stephen's College and started to bayonet the wounded in their beds. Two doctors who tried to stop them were shot, then bayoneted repeatedly. Before the massacre ended 56 patients had been stabbed to death; three British nurses were murdered and their bodies mutilated. Four Chinese nurses were raped again and again.

A Canadian padre, Capt. James Barnett, was just preparing to administer Holy Communion when the Japanese stormed in. He was herded with 90 others into a room so small they could not all sit down. "A Japanese soldier came to the door and made us put up our hands and took my watch, my ring and some money," Barnett recalled later. "Another Japanese entered with a sack of ammunition and threw cartridges in our faces. A third later removed two riflemen. Immediately afterward we heard screams from the corridor outside. The men in the room asked me to tell the Christmas story and say some prayers. We all thought it was the end."

After the main force of Japanese left, some of the wounded survivors were taken to another hospital. A Canadian nurse: "Every time you heard footsteps you wondered: Is this it? Is it the Japs?

Then the door opened and a Canadian lad was wheeled in on a stretcher. There was only a bit left of his arm. He'd been a patient at St. Stephen's when the Japs came in and he was bayoneted and bayoneted, always in the arm. They tried to destroy the nerve center. When he tried to crawl away they'd go after him. Then he played dead and they left him alone. But his arm had to be taken off. Next evening he said: 'Sister, what can you give me for pain in an arm that isn't there?' "

Marsh: "We were tied together in pairs with barbed wire around our wrists and around our throats. I staggered along with wounds in the head and knee and a broken arm. Japs were passing along a road above us. When they saw us they came bounding down the slope with fixed bayonets and obvious intentions. Their own officers beat them off with swords. Our march continued. Men were falling or being dragged by others. Those who couldn't go on were cut loose, dragged aside and bayoneted."

My diary: "Ernie was one of those we left behind at Wong Nei Chong. When they finally surrendered they were tied up with barbed wire and marched for what seemed an eternity. He couldn't make it because of his wounds. When at last he fell and couldn't rise a Jap orderly picked him up on his back and carried him the rest of the way."

Dicks: "When I came to after throwing myself over the cliff, my face was caked with blood. For two days I crawled toward Stanley where I thought our fellows were. I found it swarming with Japs. Hunger and thirst were killing me. I roamed the hills behind the Jap lines for four or five days. The last night I fell asleep in a ditch. When I woke a Jap was standing over me. He handed me some flowers and said: 'Peace. War over.' "

It was, for us. At 3:15 p.m. Christmas Day, General Maltby ordered a ceasefire. There was no point in continuing the slaughter. Mobs were rioting in the towns. There was no water. Communications had broken down. A few pockets of resistance continued, but for the rest the silence of defeat settled over the hills. We lay down our arms, some shocked, some relieved, some fearful of being killed or tortured. About four o'clock, a Japanese soldier put his head in the door of the room at St. Stephen's College where Captain Barnett and 90 others were held.

"Through sign language," said the padre, "he told us that we could all be friends now."

A Grenadier: "We watched the Union Jack come down and the Rising Sun go up. It was a very empty feeling."

The battle had lasted 17½ days. The Japanese had suffered 3000 casualties, roughly 1000 more than the defenders. We Canadians counted 290 men dead, 493 wounded. But for those of us who had survived, the worst was yet to come. We were to find that this was merely the first act in a long and terrible crucifixion.

We were packed into a Chinese refugee encampment on the island and later into barracks on the mainland. For months there were no accurate casualty lists for anxious families in Canada. For three years and eight months the indescribable ordeal of imprisonment continued, full of death, disease, beriberi, epidemics, starvation, brutality. Dragging our sick bodies to labor in the tropic heat at bayonet point, we were truly a legion of the condemned. Like slaves, 1184 of us were locked in the hold of a ship and sent to Japan to do forced labor in mines, shipyards, coal yards. We watched our comrades die or go mad, watched pride and manhood ground in the dust. Of the 1975 Canadians who sailed from Vancouver that October night in 1941, 555 never returned. Nearly half of this number died in prison camps.

At home, controversy raged over the Hong Kong affair. George Drew, Ontario Conservative leader, charged that the whole expedition was mismanaged and ill-prepared. A Royal Commission study by Chief Justice Sir Lyman Duff found a number of things to criticize but "no dereliction of duty on the part of the government or its military advisers." This was branded "whitewash" by the Opposition in Parliament and by others.

For CSM John Osborn there was a posthumous Victoria Cross. For the rest of us, a mixture of bitterness and pride, salted over the years by the knowledge that many are dying too young and that most of the remainder are in poor health from wounds or malnutrition diseases. But, in one sense, many of us feel strangely grateful for the experience. In the twin hells of action and imprisonment, we were able to discover the heights and depths of the human soul. . . .

WILLIAM ALLISTER

The evacuation

When Japan attacked Pearl Harbor and Hong Kong in December 1941, there were cries that she would invade Canada and arguments that, if she did, her forces *could* be aided by the Japanese Canadians of British Columbia. The fears, fueled by long-standing racial animosity, produced a climate of suspicion and hate, described by one official as "mass hysteria and prejudice."

For its part, Ottawa beefed up its forces in preparation for an invasion it didn't really expect. As it turned out, Japan's only strike against Canada was a submarine shelling of a Vancouver Island lighthouse in June 1942.

What the federal government did about Japanese Canadians, however, was another matter and one that has stirred argument ever since. Because of the prevailing paranoia, Ottawa's actions affected not only enemy aliens and naturalized citizens but native-born Canadians, too.

Frank Moritsugu was a Vancouver 19-year-old when he and six other young *Niseis* (Canadian-born children of Japanese immigrants) heard a radio broadcast about Pearl Harbor. This is his story of what happened then and later:

... We looked at one another, numb, terrified. Then we ran for our homes. There was one question in all our minds: "What's going to happen to us?" One thing was certain: our little world had collapsed; nothing would ever be the same again.

British Columbia had conditioned us for this reaction by the paradox of our lives. On the one hand I was, I believe, typical of my people in my love for this magnificent province and for Canada. My parents, both Japanese born, had insisted that I learn the ways of my own native land. My feeling for the Union Jack and the British Crown was profound. My pride in the victory of the Battle of Britain was immense. On the other hand I lived in a Japanese neighborhood, spoke Japanese, used judo in school fights that usually divided on racial lines, and

knew all too well that anyone of Japanese stock was made to feel unwelcome in this province.

There were some 23,500 of us in Canada in 1941, 95 percent of us in British Columbia, mostly along the coast. Of that total, 6700 were Canadian born, 7000 were naturalized citizens, the rest were nationals of Japan. But to white British Columbians we were all second-class citizens, clustered in "Little Tokyos," pursuing work that law or custom left open to us—farming, fishing, gardening, running small businesses. Against a backdrop of racial hatred, we couldn't vote, become lawyers or pharmacists, hold municipal public office, or work on construction jobs involving government contracts, among other things. We were pushed into a narrow economic sphere, then accused of endangering white living standards by our low wages and poor living conditions. For years politicians used us as scapegoats and whipping boys and people accused us of being a fifth column for "the yellow peril."

When the war broke out in 1939, we weren't allowed to enlist. The RCMP registered all of us as Japanese and gave us special identification cards, formal tokens of our second-class status.

Given that background, Pearl Harbor had to be crucial to us, and things began to happen fast. Within 24 hours, our three daily Japanese-language schools were closed by the police, and some 40 Japanese-Canadians were interned. The only newspaper still al-

After the war, the Canadian government passed, then rescinded, an order for the deportation of Japanese Canadians. Thousands, including this little girl, left anyway.

lowed in our community, *The New Canadian*, an English-language weekly, had to publish three times a week to serve a people hungry for information about its fate.

The newspaper took me on staff—and gave me a ringside seat for the next two months of anti-Japanese anger and hysteria. There were telephone reports from Japanese disturbed about hate incidents—a brick thrown through a store window, a "Dirty Jap" slogan scrawled overnight on a storefront. And bitter Japanese Canadians came with stories of a world falling apart. One day a man came into the office almost weeping in fury. His boat had been among the hundreds of Japanese-Canadian fishing vessels rounded up by naval officers "for security reasons."

When Hong Kong fell on Christmas Day, Canadian troops were captured by the Japanese and British Columbians reacted violently. On December 30, Maj. Gen. R. O. Alexander, head of the army's Pacific Command, told Ottawa there was a danger of "interracial riots and bloodshed," and advised moving the Japanese Canadians from the coast. Politicians and labor, service and church organizations echoed his call.

Like other Niseis, I protested to anyone who'd listen that I should be treated as a Canadian citizen. I clung to my faith in British justice, a basic part of my ideal of Canada. Canada was our country, the only country many of us knew. To me, Japan seemed foreign and alien, a country which in recent years had done all the wrong things. I didn't expect justice from British Columbia, but I did expect Ottawa would help us.

What Ottawa did do came in two phases. On January 14, 1942, it ordered the evacuation of Japanese nationals, those without Canadian citizenship, from a "protected area" 100 miles deep along the coast, barred all persons of Japanese origins from fishing, directed evacuees to turn over their belongings for safekeeping, and promised us all we'd be protected. A month later, the fall of Singapore produced panic all around us. Vancouver city council and scores of organizations demanded Japanese Canadians be removed from the Pacific Coast. In short order Ottawa bowed to the outcry: all of us, citizens or not, were to be evacuated.

My father, an alien, was evacuated on February 23, leaving his landscaping business to my brother Ken and me. I was shocked to see how beaten my father looked as he boarded the train for Yellowhead, B.C. The first breakup of our close family shocked all of us—parents and eight children. And now, our family would be split three ways: The nationals or aliens were to be in one group, women and children in another, and all males over 18 were to be sent to highway-construction camps.

Bitterness spread through our ranks. Some wanted to flout the orders, mainly because they feared what would happen to the women and children. Others, myself included, opposed this *gambari* (resistance) stand. I said we should put our trust in Ottawa. A poison swept through our ranks, turning friends into enemies. Once, even I was accused of being an *inu,* a spy for the authorities. Then on April 10 I was on my way on a train, under police guard. There was a sense of finality in me, of cutting forever the roots I'd grown in the only place I thought of as home. It would, in fact, be 19 years before I saw Vancouver again.

For the next 17 months I was in the Yard Creek camp near Revelstoke, B.C. We were paid 35 cents an hour for working on what would become part of the Trans-Canada Highway. There was no barbed wire, but we had sentries guarding us from a pillbox. With its beautiful scenery, Yard Creek in other circumstances would have been a delightful place; to us it was a symbol of shame.

When orders came for married men to depart for the towns where families were to relocate, Dad left Yellowhead to help build

a new settlement called Tashme, near Hope. The other family settlements were mostly in small mining ghost towns, in the Slocon and Kootenay valleys.

The only Japanese left in the "protected area" were those married to persons of other races. Even World War I veterans were removed, and the *gambari* supporters were moved farthest of all, to barbed-wire internment in Ontario. They wore prisoner-of-war uniforms and were cut off from other Japanese Canadians for months.

Eventually Ken and I got permission to visit the family in Tashme. The camp was a raw, makeshift settlement of hundreds of shacks about 14 by 25 feet. My family was jammed into one tiny shack, yet they were comparatively well-off. Small families had to share shacks and facilities, and those irritations caused many vicious fights. Over everything there was a mood of hopelessness, of strong, vital people in an environment without aim or purpose.

My parents had become convinced they must leave Tashme for their children's sake. The B.C. Department of Education refused responsibility for teaching them. Young Niseis without training were teaching in the primary grades. Small wonder that my parents wanted to leave. But to go where?

British Columbia urged interned families to move east out of the province. Few were willing to go; to them, the world beyond the Rockies was a forbidding, unknown place, full of communities which openly insisted they didn't want us either. But that was the course my parents chose.

I had my own reasons for wanting to leave Yard Creek. I was involved in camp strikes, and my foreman warned me that if it kept up I'd "be sent east." Luckily, something better happened. *The New Canadian* began publishing in the Kootenay Valley ghost town of Kaslo, and asked for me. I spent the fall and winter of 1943-44 there, an idyllic time of sports, girls and parties. Then, in March, I joined my family on a farm near St. Thomas, Ont. Our new home was on the estate of former Ontario Premier Mitchell Hepburn.

Even this far from the coast and long after Japan had ceased to be a threat, our movements remained restricted. We still had to carry our registration cards, and we were forbidden to enlist in the armed services. That changed in January 1945. There was a special reason. As the war in Asia wound down, the British Army needed language experts to deal with Japanese prisoners, and Canada was the only place in the Commonwealth with a concentration of people of Japanese origin.

Ottawa changed its policy toward Japa-

nese-Canadian enlistment without publicity. Once that happened, I knew I had to go. It took me two days and nights to beat down the arguments of my parents. "If I go, it will prove we are Canadian. The whole family will benefit. We'll finally be accepted." I enlisted in April and, a month later, without even basic training, joined 21 other Niseis heading for India. En route, a strange thing happened. Polling for the federal election took place on the troopship, and we Niseis voted like anyone else. No Niseis had ever voted in British Columbia.

The British wanted us to assist in Allied takeovers after Japanese surrenders. But few Niseis in our special force could speak, read or understand Japanese well enough to be of much help. I found myself teaching others, and it was one indication of what had happened to our links with Japan. I got another shock when I did deal with Japanese prisoners. We spoke the same language but had little else in common.

When I returned to Canada in the spring of 1946 I was filled with a love of country that only seems to come by leaving it. Soon after my discharge from the army, an RCMP constable came to our St. Thomas house with the hated registration card I had turned over on enlistment. "Your photo looks pretty weather-beaten," he said. "Better get new ones taken. And send us two copies for our files." I took the envelope and the card and threw them at him.

The evacuation was a nightmare we Japanese Canadians will never forget. Nor was it helped by events after the war. For several years we still had to report to the RCMP if we traveled more than 50 miles. Even Japanese-Canadian veterans still had to carry registration cards. British Columbia didn't want us back. Ottawa passed an order for our deportation to Japan and, even though it was eventually rescinded, some 4000 went. Hundreds of our people were bitter over the small sums they got for property held "in trust," and sold without their consent.

But by 1949 the barriers were gone. Even British Columbia granted the vote to Orientals. The pattern of Japanese-Canadian settlement had changed. The tight little ghettos our people had known were broken up. Toronto became the largest center of Japanese Canadians in the country, and they avoided living in clusters. Once granted full citizenship, many of our people did well indeed.

The passing years have brought regrets and apologies. Yet the memory of the evacuation is a reminder to all Canadians that the denial of human rights can happen here . . .

FRANK MORITSUGU

The war strikes home

World War II had been raging for 27 months when the Japanese attacked Pearl Harbor and Hong Kong without warning December 7, 1941. On that "date which will live in infamy," as President Roosevelt called it, the conflict took its ultimate shape. It now encompassed the earth, embroiling every major power and many lesser ones.

In Canada, apart from concern and then grief over the fate of two battalions at Hong Kong, the reactions ranged from fear to consolation.

There was fear, for the first time in living memory, that Canada might be attacked. Within a few weeks, this fear multiplied in British Columbia to something close to panic. It led to demands for stronger and stronger defenses and to evacuation of Japanese Canadians from the coast.

There was consolation that the United States now was an outright belligerent. But even that brought complications. The fact that the United States conscription allowed for military service anywhere in the world reinforced long-smoldering demands that Canada should adopt a similar program. Within a month of Pearl Harbor, this pivotal political issue was aflame.

Senator Arthur Meighen, former Conservative Prime Minister, resigned from the Senate and entered a Toronto by-election. His aim was to win a seat in the House of Commons where he would become Opposition leader. He called for coalition government and "compulsory selective service over the whole field of war."

Prime Minister Mackenzie King was appalled—first because he detested Meigh-

en and feared him as a parliamentary foe, second because he had given Quebec a pledge in 1939 against the very thing Meighen advocated, conscription for overseas service. And he had renewed the pledge in 1940 in getting parliamentary approval of conscription for service at home only.

Now King tried a flank attack that would drain away the support of people who might vote for Meighen if they thought he represented the one hope for overseas conscription. He announced a national plebiscite to free him from his pledge. Not, he said, that conscription for overseas would inevitably be applied. But he wanted to be free to use it if he had to: "Not necessarily conscription but conscription if necessary."

King's tactics helped defeat Meighen in the February by-election, only to have the

116

Public Works Minister P. J. A. Cardin, Quebec's strongest cabinet voice since the death of Ernest Lapointe, objected violently. He had gone along with the plebiscite to help calm the conscriptionists. But parliamentary action to open the way for potential overseas conscription was to Cardin a betrayal of the pledge to Quebec. If, as King said, conscription was not necessary, "then why in the name of God authorize it?"

By the time King had steered his cabinet and an aroused country around the issue, Parliament had approved overseas conscription "if necessary," Cardin had resigned and Ralston had handed in a letter of resignation. Ralston wanted it understood that if conscription did become necessary it would be ordered at once, without any reference to Parliament. King wanted to go to Parliament first. Typically he worked out a compromise that kept Ralston in the cabinet: the cabinet would, if it became necessary, order conscription first and then lay its case before Parliament.

Nobody tried to define what "necessary" meant. But King kept Ralston's letter anyway, just in case. In another 2½ years, he'd have use for it.

America's role in the 1942 conscription controversy was indirect, but Pearl Harbor pushed her into another role that had a much more direct influence on wartime Canadian life.

Washington ordered major measures to strengthen the defenses of Alaska. Thousands of American servicemen and civilians came flooding into Canada to build a highway from northern British Columbia into Alaska, to use a string of Canadian airfields to ferry planes to Alaska and Russia, to start an oil pipeline from the Mackenzie River Valley to Whitehorse in the Yukon, to build airfields to ferry planes to Britain. Edmonton, for one, became a boom town, the gateway to the wilderness where much of this was going on.

Ottawa, meanwhile, tried to soothe British Columbia's fears that, if the Japanese did attack North America, they would attack more than Alaska. The fears turned out to be groundless. Paradoxically, for Canada, the most important development arising from Pearl Harbor came not on the Pacific coast but along the Atlantic coast. And it was launched not by the Japanese but by the Germans.

Prime Minister Mackenzie King signs autographs after voting in the conscription plebiscite of April 27, 1942. Fourteen days later the slaughter in the St. Lawrence began. Left: torpedoed merchant ships in the Gulf. Only Quebec voted against overseas conscription "if necessary." Mackenzie King recorded in his diary: "The returns show clearly the wisdom of not attempting any conscription through coercion and in violation of pledges. Whatever is done now will be done with the will of the majority, expressed in advance, and if proceedings are taken in the right way, will be gradually acquiesced in by those in the minority."

later plebiscite bring new problems. English-speaking Canada voted overwhelmingly to free him to implement overseas conscription "if necessary"; French-speaking Quebec voted overwhelmingly not to. The very division King most feared stood crystallized before him, and it soon was at work in his cabinet.

Despite an overall majority that gave him power to do so, the Prime Minister had no intention of imposing overseas conscription and splitting the nation, especially when the army wasn't even in action. Nevertheless, Defense Minister J. L. Ralston and other ministers insisted that, if conscription were not to be imposed at once, the law forbidding it must at least be amended. When King agreed rather than risk a cabinet revolt, he was at once in trouble again.

With the United States in the war, submarines were no longer restrained by any niceties of U.S. technical neutrality. Said German Grand Adm. Karl Dönitz: "The whole American coast is now open for operations by the U-boats."

There were no U.S. coastal convoys (and no plans for any), and few warships or aircraft for anti-submarine patrol. U.S. merchant ships and tankers were unarmed. Lights in seaboard cities and towns burned as brightly as ever. Samuel Eliot Morison wrote in *The Battle of the Atlantic* that "Miami and its luxurious suburbs threw up six miles of neon-light glow, against which the southbound shipping was silhouetted; ships were sunk and seamen drowned in order that the citizenry might enjoy business and pleasure as usual."

But Pearl Harbor had at least changed the rules of war for American seamen in the Atlantic. For months, wrote Joseph Schull in *The Far Distant Ships,* it had been an undeclared and ill-defined war: . . . They had fought with one hand tied behind their backs. First there had been the neutrality patrol, in which U.S. warships warned the ships of belligerent powers away from combat in the Western Hemisphere. The warnings had become sharper and the Nazi tendency to disregard them more pronounced. In September 1940 had come the exchange of American destroyers for British bases. The Lend-Lease Act had

The St. Lawrence defense force, wrote Joseph Schull, was "the merest fraction of the navy's strength: two corvettes, five Bangor minesweepers and a few Fairmile motor launches." Above: two Bangors and a corvette (middle). Adequate protection of shipping in the St. Lawrence would have meant stripping the Atlantic convoys (right) of some of their badly needed escorts. This the navy refused to do.

been passed in March 1941; later the same month an agreement between the British and American navies had brought new cooperation in the Atlantic.

Three U.S. battleships, three cruisers, an aircraft carrier and two squadrons of destroyers had been transferred from the Pacific to the Atlantic by the end of May. In July, U.S. naval and air forces relieved British forces in Iceland. In August, the U.S. Navy took over strategic control of operations on the western side of the Atlantic. Still not at war, the United States had determined that trade convoys carrying enormous tonnages of American-made war supplies were going to get through. The U.S. Navy would be responsible for their protection as far as Iceland.

A big American base was built at Argentia, Nfld., and authority in the western Atlantic was delegated to the American admiral there. Canada's Newfoundland Command, and her other commands along the eastern seaboard, came automatically and abruptly under American control.

The first HX (Halifax to Britain) convoy to sail under the protection of a U.S. naval task group left September 16, 1941. Thereafter all HX convoys were to be under American escort as far as mid-ocean SC convoys from Sydney, N.S., were to be escorted to the same area by Canadian groups. British ships would take over all convoys at the mid-ocean meeting point

The Newfoundland Command's Canadians had been fighting the war for two years; the U.S. forces had little experience. The Canadians were placed under an admiral whose country was not even a belligerent. Fortunately, Adm. A. L. Bristol at Argentia and Commodore L. W. Murray at St. John's were realists and diplomats. Relations between their staffs were excellent and soon the combined forces were operating as one.

But Pearl Harbor meant that American strength in the Atlantic had to be diverted to the Pacific, at a time when British responsibilities had vastly increased. The Japanese reduced Allied naval strength in the Pacific and Indian oceans to insignificance. Singapore was lost; Australia, India and all the Eastern bastions were threatened. The Mediterranean and Red Sea, if controlled by the Axis, would permit the linking of Japanese naval strength with German land power in an overwhelming combination. The Royal Navy, its strength diluted since August for convoys to Russia's far-northern Murmansk, must be diluted again for the Pacific.

U.S. ships had to be withdrawn from the western Atlantic in such numbers that by February of 1942 only a few modern escorts remained on convoy duty. The long-looked-for accession of a mighty ally meant, for the escort forces of the western Atlantic, an almost fatal loss of strength.

December 1941 and January 1942 were a nightmare. Hundreds of ships, unable to keep station in the incessant gales, were driven far beyond the range of escorts and left to struggle on alone. Wide alterations of course, made necessary by the weather as often as by the U-boats, added extra days and hundreds of extra miles to convoy voyages. The escorts were under almost unendurable strain and continually under strength. Men might carry on up to some not-yet-determined point without sleep or rest, but ships were machines whose limits of endurance were fixed. The number of escorts out of action from enemy damage, weather damage or breakdown was increasing. The entire system showed signs of cracking.

The Royal Canadian Navy at this time formed the main strength in the western Atlantic, with 13 destroyers and 70 corvettes. In February 1942, ships running between Halifax and Newfoundland became the Western Local Escort Force; their journey was extended by setting a west-ocean meeting point at which their convoys were taken over by mid-ocean groups, 700 miles from Halifax.

The mid-ocean groups were increased from six to seven by reducing the number of ships in each. Their eastern terminal was moved 500 miles east and south, from Iceland to Londonderry in Northern Ireland. On her first run under the new sys-tem, one Canadian corvette did not make Londonderry. *Spikenard* was lost with heavy casualties the night of February 10, south of Iceland. She was zigzagging to starboard of the convoy when a torpedo hit the tanker *Heina*. Almost simultaneously another struck *Spikenard*. The other escorts were unsure whether two ships or one had been torpedoed. *Chilliwack,* a corvette to port of the convoy, was attacking at the time *Spikenard* was hit. *Dauphin,* three miles astern, saw one explosion and what she thought was a second. She moved toward the blazing *Heina* and spent two hours getting all the survivors out of the oily water.

Throughout the night, the two corvettes tried to call *Spikenard* by radio-telephone —and thought her silence perhaps due to equipment failure. No wireless signal was made for fear of homing other U-boats onto the convoy.

Next day the British corvette *Gentian* searched along the track of the convoy and came upon a float with eight *Spikenard* survivors, all who were ever found. None of them had been on *Spikenard*'s bridge and none could say exactly what happened. They remembered that action stations had been sounded and speed increased. Then a torpedo struck *Spikenard* between bridge and forecastle. Part of the ship's side and part of the deck were blown away, and fire destroyed the bridge and wireless office.

Flames reached petrol stowed beside the mast, climbed to the superstructure and reached down into the bowels of the ship. Men racing from the messdecks fought to the forecastle through a curtain of flame. Some fell into the flooded forepart of the ship through a gaping hole in the deck. As *Spikenard* began to sink, her whistle blew an eerie requiem. Five minutes later the sea closed over her.

Spikenard disappeared before the first corvette reached *Heina's* position. Light from the flaming tanker fell far short of the *Spikenard* men struggling in the water. In the black, windy night their shouts were lost, and they had no flares to attract attention. Twice they saw a corvette in the distance; each time it passed them by. . . .

JOSEPH SCHULL

About the time *Spikenard* was lost in mid-Atlantic, U-boats were moving inshore for what they called "the American hunting season." Their kill was enormous: 2,500,000 tons in six months along the unprotected Atlantic seaboard. Many of the 500 ships they torpedoed were tankers waddling north with precious oil and aviation gasoline.

The U-boats massacred Allied shipping from Newfoundland to Panama. They roamed the Gulf of Mexico, the Caribbean and the Florida Keys and torpedoed within a few miles of Halifax and Miami and Cape Hatteras. Between Boston and Key West alone, more than 200 ships went down within ten miles of land. The submarines had so many targets that they often headed home for lack of torpedoes rather than shortage of fuel. Not much could be done to stop them. Every escort assigned to halt this seaboard slaughter would be one less for the vital, vulnerable transatlantic convoys. The real hope lay in new ships and aircraft and new and better anti-submarine weapons and tactics.

The losses were almost more than the Allies could take. Gen. George C. Marshall, U.S. Chief of Staff, said they threatened the entire war effort. "I am fearful," he said, "that another month or two of this will so cripple our means of transport that we will be unable to bring sufficient men and planes to bear in critical theaters to exercise a determining influence on the war."

In June 1942 the rate of sinkings was one ship every four hours. In the first half of 1942 only 21 U-boats were sunk—and

Public outcry over sinkings like these raised the possibility that Maj. Gen. F. F. Worthington's 4th Armored Division, in training at Debert, N.S., would be sent to the St. Lawrence. Larry Worthington, in *Worthy,* describes what her husband did: "He had a troop of reconnaissance cars fitted with sheet iron to look like armored cars and on them mounted wooden guns covered with canvas covers. Under a bilingual lieutenant, the troop toured the St. Lawrence district, passing word that the whole division was providing protection. At the end of the week Defense Minister J. L. Ralston told Worthy: 'I'm glad to say the flurry has died down.' "

for every one sunk, five were being built. Wrote Schull:

. . . They lay submerged in shallow water by day, and surfaced at night to operate in groups. Night after night the dull roar of explosions at sea was heard ashore and the flames of exploding tankers lit the sky. Sometimes oily smoke hung heavily above U.S. coastal cities and towns. The noise of battle at sea was followed on land by the sight of maimed and exhausted survivors.

The attack was deadly, and not only to the United States. Britain's oil sources were being cut off one by one. The route from the Middle East through the Mediterranean was nearly closed. Borneo and the Dutch East Indies were lost to Japan. Oil from the Persian Gulf, brought through the Indian Ocean and around the Cape, was menaced by Japanese surface raiders and submarines. Britain's war machine now depended mainly on tankers from Trinidad, Aruba, Curaçao and Maracaibo. If that stream of shipping were cut, the machine would grind to a stop. . . .

Imperial Oil, whose motorship *Canadolite* had been captured by a German raider off West Africa in March 1941, lost three more ships and many Canadian crewmen in 1942. *Montrolite,* en route from Venezuela to Halifax, was sunk in February with loss of slightly more than half her crew. *Victolite,* on the same run, was torpedoed a few days later. None of her crew of 46 survived. *Calgarolite* was sunk that May but all hands survived.

A Canadian corvette helped destroy one of the preying U-boats. *Oakville* was part of an eight-ship escort for a convoy of 29 tankers south of Haiti on the moonlit night of August 27. As action-stations bells jangled men from their hammocks on *Oakville's* upper deck, a U.S. patrol plane circled above a submarine it had bombed and forced to submerge. *Oakville* steamed up to depth-charge the already damaged sub, then prepared to ram as the U-boat surfaced, her crash dive frustrated by the corvette's quick attack. But so sharp was *Oakville's* turn that she missed. U-94 bumped down the corvette's port side. The Canadians' guns hammered at the enemy, blowing away his main gun and sweeping the German gunners from the slippery decks. *Oakville* rammed a second time, and again U-94 passed down her side—so close that *Oakville's* guns could not be

brought to bear. Canadian sailors, in their frustration, hurled Coke bottles at the enemy. More depth charges, and the battered U-94 wallowed astern. She lay stopped on the surface and her crew prepared to abandon ship. *Oakville* came alongside. Sub-Lt. Harold Lawrence and Petty Officer A. J. Powell leaped to the enemy deck. Two Germans emerged and were ordered below, but came forward to make a fight of it. Lawrence and Powell shot them. The rest of the crew began to emerge and soon 20 were lined on deck. Going below, Lawrence found water seeping into the smashed interior; the boat had been scuttled. Lawrence ordered the captives overboard. The two Canadians and the Germans were picked up by a destroyer.

Oakville was serving in the Caribbean at a time when the RCN could have used her elsewhere.

Mid-ocean and local escort forces could barely maintain their cycles. Halifax-Boston convoys had been formed in March with Canadian ships as escorts—not new ships but ships withdrawn from other local escort forces. For weeks Canadian naval officers worried over the prospects of a Battle of the St. Lawrence which would have to take second place to the defense of ocean convoys and the provision of oil.

In May 1942 it began.

One night early that month a German U-boat captain—a Lieutenant Commander Thurmann—decided not to risk his U-553 against the new coastal convoys off Boston. They were too well protected for the sure kills he wanted. He turned north for the Gulf of St. Lawrence.

By May 9 he was skirting the south coast of Newfoundland. Watchers near Cape Ray saw his submarine at dawn on the 10th. Later that day, about 65 miles south of Anticosti Island, an aircraft drove him under but did no damage.

U-553 spent the night of May 10 on the surface near the western end of Anticosti Island, her crew on deck to enjoy the spring air. Thurmann, through binoculars, could see the lights of the village of Port Menier. He submerged at dawn, lay on the bottom all day, surfaced that night and headed west toward Gaspé. Just before midnight he sighted a merchant ship headed straight for him. The Battle of the St. Lawrence was about to begin.

For many months Canadian authorities would disclose little about it despite pub-

lic clamor for information and for countermeasures.

A wartime navy officer wrote later that there had been good reasons for keeping the facts quiet at the time. Lt. Jack McNaught in *Maclean's:*

. . . In five months 23 ships were torpedoed and 700 people killed—more than the Canadian Army would lose in Sicily.

That was the truth. The rumors were something else again. For example: three small transports carrying U.S. personnel and supplies to the great new airport being

built at Goose Bay in Labrador were torpedoed in the Strait of Belle Isle. Two ships sank and more than 250 lives were lost. A week later, in Scotland, a Canadian officer was told that a convoy of huge troop carriers had been cut to pieces and 6000 soldiers drowned.

Strange tales reached Montreal from summer resorts on the St. Lawrence: German U-boat officers and men were landing in dinghies. They were dressed in Canadian naval uniforms, spoke perfect English, and had themselves a wonderful time dancing with local girls. The facts: now and again, Canadian sailors came ashore for a few hours.

A small schooner put in for supplies at a north shore port. Next day it was common knowledge for hundreds of miles that a German submarine had tied up at the jetty in broad daylight and her commander had walked boldly up to the general store and bought canned fruit for his crew.

The truth about the war in the St. Lawrence was grim enough.

The ship Thurmann sighted the night of May 11 was the 5000-ton British steamer *Nicoya,* with a crew of 76 and ten passengers: a mother and her baby and eight seamen from a ship sunk in the Caribbean. Thurmann fired point-blank into *Nicoya's* bow, smashing two lifeboats and tearing a great hole below the waterline. A second torpedo hit amidships. Nine minutes later

Nicoya went to the bottom, the first ship sunk by enemy action in Canadian inland waters since the War of 1812.

Seventy of *Nicoya's* men and the ten passengers took to the boats and made for the coast, 12 miles away. The other six of the crew went over the side in a raft and were never seen again. The boats couldn't keep together and came ashore at various places. The mother and baby, alone in one boat, were mercifully carried in by the current.

The villages of Chloridorme and St. Yvon gave the 80 survivors hot drinks and clothes and next day cars and ambulances took them to a hospital and hotels in Gaspé.

Framed in the eye of a submarine periscope (right), a ship dies. Plucked from the awesome waste of the sea, a survivor lives.

U-553 turned northwest and at 2:40 a.m. May 12, about 20 miles from where *Nicoya* had gone down, sank the Dutch cargo steamer *Leto*. Twelve men were killed and the ship sank in six minutes. The survivors were picked up by a British merchant ship which escaped attack because U-553, as soon as *Leto* went down, turned and headed out of the St. Lawrence for home.

Radio Berlin announced with a special chime of bells that the two sinkings had caused consternation in Canada. They hadn't—not the kind of panic the Germans meant—but there was shock and surprise and uneasiness that the war could be brought so close to Canada. Some Cana-

dians demanded all-out protection for St. Lawrence shipping. The navy knew—but couldn't say—that this was what the Germans wanted.

U-553 made no more attacks and was undetected as she worked her way out of the Gulf to safety. Quebec-Sydney convoys were started under the protection of a small escort force based at Gaspé, but there was no further submarine activity in the river or the Gulf during May and June.

On July 6 another U-boat torpedoed three ships in a convoy ten miles from Cap-Chat. A few days later a British liner went down off Cap-de-la-Madeleine. In these four ships 12 men were killed but more than 100 survived. Then came an-

other lull and it looked as if the Battle of the St. Lawrence was over. But U-517 and Lt. Comdr. Paul Hartwig were still to come. They showed up the same night that *Oakville* sank her sub in the Caribbean, and for six blazing weeks contemptuously defied the navy.

In bright moonlight August 27 Hartwig sighted a convoy of six American ships and three U.S. Coast Guard escorts close to the Labrador shore just west of the Strait of Belle Isle. They were bound from Sydney, with men and stores for a U.S. station in Greenland.

U-517 attacked at once. Her first torpedo hit the army transport *Chatham* and 13 of the 562 on board died. Hartwig's

second target was *Arlyn,* a small merchant ship on charter to the U.S. Maritime Commission. Three of her 54 people were killed instantly. Six disappeared and were never found. The rest, except 14 men of the gun crew who had to swim (they were picked up eventually, half-dead with cold), swarmed into boats and rafts and made for the barren shore. The next day they too were picked up and taken to Sydney with the 312 survivors from the transport. A third ship, *Laramie,* was torpedoed but not sunk, and by skillful seamanship was brought to harbor.

Hartwig lay for the rest of the night and all next day on the bottom. At dark August 28 he surfaced and slid south along the Labrador coast. On the night of September 2, he saw a wonderful target outlined against the northern lights: two Canadian convoys, one outward-bound from Montreal to Goose Bay, the other running from Goose Bay to Montreal. They were about to pass. . . .   JACK MCNAUGHT

Hartwig struck first at a small Canadian steamer, *Donald Stewart.* Her story is told

In June 1942 the submarines were sinking an Allied ship every four hours —and for every U-boat sunk, five were being built. This time of death by explosion and drowning and exposure was one of the best of all the submariners' "happy times." What sort of men were U-boat officers? Wolfgang Ott in *Sharks and Little Fish:* "They were lean, wiry, thin-hipped, weatherbeaten, moving with easy grace. They could drink—and hold—stupendous quantities of liquor. They seemed remarkably well balanced, going about their business in a quiet, good-natured way, without waste motion, useless talk or heroics. They did not talk about the war. They took the losses quietly, without fuss, just as they took the victories. They kept their spirits up and twitted death. They were the elite, and all through the war they bore themselves as such—when success smiled on them and, later, when they had become little more than cattle going to slaughter."

by Paul W. Tooke, then a wheelsman on the old 244-foot canaller:

... We had cement for the Goose Bay airport runways and the main deck was covered with drums of aviation gasoline. On top of this was a three-foot layer of dressed lumber. On top of the lumber were lashed nine dump trucks.

With us were two other freighters, *Canatco* and *Ericus* of Canadian National Steamships, and the Canadian corvettes *Trail* and *Shawinigan*. We were running five abreast, with the escorts at each edge, *Shawinigan* being at the right and *Donald Stewart* next to her. We passed Anticosti about 10 p.m. and altered course up toward the Strait of Belle Isle. It was a typical Gulf night—dark, fog patches, poor visibility, a damp southeast breeze. We were all running blacked out, of course, and Capt. Dan Nolan was leaning out the wheelhouse window, straining his eyes and ears.

Suddenly: "Hard-a-starboard!" I rapped the wheel over. As the convoys approached each other, a huge black shape loomed close to port, the noise of her propeller clearly audible. "Now hard-a-port!" Another black shape slid down the starboard side. We did this for a hair-raising 15 minutes and finally cleared the inbound convoy—none of us and none of them showing a light.

At midnight, Chief Officer Frank Shaw took over the bridge. After an hour Captain Nolan returned, saying he thought he smelled diesel fumes—that could only mean a submarine—but nobody else smelled them, so the skipper went back to his room, muttering.

At 1:55 a.m. September 3 a torpedo crashed into our starboard side amidships. I'd been asleep in the alleyway outside my room, having left my bunk to the bedbugs. As I rushed on deck I saw the first explosion of aviation gas. The lumber caught fire and the flames set off more fuel. One explosion threw gasoline up the mast and its heavy wire stays, and the flames followed it, outlining the whole lot like a giant Christmas tree. The wind fanned the flames across the ship, cutting us off from the lifeboats aft.

Shaw released the port wing life raft, and when it came tight on its rope, it was in the middle of the fire. "Let's go, boys," said Captain Nolan, and he climbed down. At that moment another explosion sent a mass of flames across the ship and nobody else dared try for the raft. Cool as ice,

Shaw saw that our only hope lay in getting off in a 14-foot sailing dinghy that he and Second Officer André Lacroix had built. It was stowed on No. 1 hatch. But what about Nolan?

"Paul," Shaw said, "nip up to the bridge and release that life-raft rope before the Old Man gets burned to death." I rushed to the bridge, and found the rope spliced to the rail. This was an axe job, but in my panic I couldn't remember where the nearest fire-axe was. I started down the bridge ladder and saw the axe through the open steps. When I chopped the rope clear, the skipper was face down on the raft, close to the ship's side. Flames were roaring three feet above him and 100 feet downwind, because the ship was still moving ahead. The raft drifted clear of the flames and Captain Nolan stepped off into a lifeboat just as the second engineer and his oiler lowered it into the water.

When I got back to the main deck it was deserted and the dinghy was gone from the hatch. I thought they'd forgotten me but the sound of Shaw's level voice reassured me. He was over the side on a ladder with one foot in the dinghy and only his head showing above deck. "Get some loose boards to paddle this thing," he snapped. I ran toward the holocaust on deck, grabbed three or four boards, threw them into the boat and clambered down the ladder after Shaw. I was the last man off her, and not a minute too soon.

Under Shaw's guidance, we just managed to skirt the flames without anyone getting burned, and we stopped to watch *Donald Stewart* dying amid the biggest mass of flames I've ever seen. She settled in the middle, her back broken. Then her bow and stern tilted up for a moment, and she slid under. The whole thing had taken only three minutes.

I marvel that any of us got off, especially us 12 up forward who were cut off from the lifeboats. We lost three men from the engine-room gang but it was a miracle there weren't more. Frank Shaw's cool leadership is all that saved us. I guess he was getting used to it: at 27, this was the fifth time he'd been sunk.

Donald Stewart was gone, and her bedbugs with her, but not the flames. Aviation gas burned over a huge area and 70-foot flames lit up the low-lying clouds for miles around. When *Shawinigan* came racing up, the flames were higher than her mast. She slammed full astern alongside us and we

127

lost no time climbing aboard, well aware that she was a sitting duck, silhouetted against the great wall of fire.

Ten days later we were landed at Quebec. Two years after that, in this same Gulf of St. Lawrence, *Shawinigan* was lost, either torpedoed or iced up and overturned. They never knew which because there were no survivors. . . . PAUL W. TOOKE

Jack McNaught takes up the story:
. . . After torpedoing *Donald Stewart,* Hartwig spent several days on patrol and was repeatedly attacked by aircraft. One dropped a bomb on the U-boat's deck— it was a dud. Hartwig helped heave it overboard. On September 6, near Cap-Chat,

tell the difference. *Arrowhead* followed the pillenwerfer long enough to let U-517 escape.

There were two more explosions that night and *Raccoon* was never seen again. The body of one of her sailors was washed ashore on Anticosti; 36 other men disappeared, like the yacht, without trace.

Hartwig followed the convoy down the Gaspé coast and on the evening of September 7 got past the inadequate escort and into position for an astonishing feat. Ahead were the Greek *Mount Pindus* and her sister tramp *Mount Tayegetos,* astern the Canadian *Oakton.* Hartwig ordered three torpedoes fired within seconds. With one volley he sank three ships and killed nine

he sighted a convoy bound for Sydney. It was escorted by two corvettes, two Fairmile motor launches and *Raccoon,* a small steam yacht the navy had converted into a makeshift escort vessel with a gun mounted forward and a crew of 37 officers and men.

Hartwig fired a torpedo at the Greek merchant ship *Aeas,* killing two men. The rest of the crew took to the boats.

Comdr. E. G. Skinner, in the corvette *Arrowhead,* found Hartwig by asdic, attacked with depth charges and almost got his man: U-517 hadn't been able to dive deep enough. The Germans could hear *Arrowhead*'s propeller thumping dangerously near. Hartwig released a *pillenwerfer,* a gadget about the size and shape of a can of soup which gave off a mass of bubbles and sounded so like a U-boat that only the most talented asdic expert could

men; a total of 75 men survived.

U-517 lurked in the Gaspé Passage, between the mainland and Anticosti Island, waiting for another Quebec-Sydney convoy. Instead, on the foggy night of September 11, Hartwig sighted the corvette *Charlottetown* and the minesweeper *Clayoquot,* heading home to Gaspé. He fired two torpedoes into *Charlottetown* and she sank in three minutes.

Clayoquot went after U-517 but didn't find her, then picked up 55 survivors from the corvette. Ten men had died. Shortly after noon September 15, Hartwig attacked a convoy eight miles off Cap-des-Rosiers in the neighborhood of Gaspé town. He sank two ships in six minutes, then dropped astern and followed at a safe distance. Once more, he escaped detection by the RCAF. . . . JACK MCNAUGHT

"The morale of the merchant seamen." Drab official phrase though it was, wrote Joseph Schull in *The Far Distant Ships,* "it stood for the rock on which the convoy system was securely based." Above: survivors approach a rescue vessel. Right: Canadian sailors help an injured merchant seaman ashore.

Early next morning, 150 miles upstream and only about 200 miles from Quebec City, two more ships in the same convoy were torpedoed—apparently by another U-boat, since Hartwig did not claim them. Hartwig himself was depth-charged that day and U-517's firing gear was damaged and her capacity to distill fresh water cut from 50 gallons a day to 10. But he still had four torpedoes and the urge to use them.

On October 3 he followed three lighted ships but decided they were neutrals and let them go. (They were Swedish freighters sailing from Montreal with grain for Greece.) A day later he sighted a convoy of 21 ships and fired his last salvo at long range. All four torpedoes missed.

Weaponless now, Hartwig nosed out of Cabot Strait on October 5, with 31,101 tons of Allied shipping to his credit. He calculated 27 bombs and 118 depth charges had been dropped near enough to cause him discomfort. A month later, on his next outward voyage from Germany, he was caught by a seaplane from the British carrier *Victorious*. U-517 went to the bottom but Hartwig survived and was soon telling all for the Admiralty records.

U-boats sank two more merchant ships in the Gulf in October. The heaviest blow came when the passenger vessel *Caribou*, plying between Sydney and Port-aux-Basques, Nfld., was torpedoed with a loss of 136 lives.

That ended the Battle of the St. Lawrence. It had been, wrote Joseph Schull, "an almost unmitigated defeat for Canada, a defeat deliberately and unavoidably accepted, just as the disastrous losses along the American seaboard had been accepted. Adequate defense of the St. Lawrence would have meant recall of many Canadian ships from the Atlantic. This would have been of far more benefit to Germany than all the achievements of Hartwig and his companions. It was in the Atlantic, along the convoy routes, that the pattern of defeat or victory had still to be resolved. It was there that Canada could best serve her own interests and make her greatest contribution to the Allied effort."

Dieppe: the day that will not die

The 2nd Division pays a terrible price to show how *not* to launch an invasion

In the spring of 1942 most of the 2nd Canadian Infantry Division disappeared from their camps in Sussex. At first no one gave it much thought. It was nothing new for the Canadians to move out to strike at some imaginary enemy on the South Downs behind Brighton or in the farmlands of Kent. But this time they didn't come back to The King's Head and The Black Horse for beer on Saturday night. When they'd been gone a month, Sussex was sure the Canadians had been sent to fight in the Middle East. But, in fact, as war correspondents soon learned, they hadn't left the south of England.

Ross Munro in *Gauntlet to Overlord:* ... On June 5 I was told to drive to a certain map reference. I was met there, then taken to a town near the English Channel where it turned out the 2nd Division had been training for several weeks. At divisional headquarters most officers knew an operation was planned but the work was always referred to as training. Ostensibly this was what I had come to cover for The Canadian Press.

The story I could not write was that the Canadians, with some British troops and a few French and Americans, were going to assault a French port. It would be a raid, nothing more. The force included the Essex Scottish from Windsor, Ont., the Royal Regiment from Toronto, the Royal Hamilton Light Infantry, the Cameron Highlanders of Winnipeg, the South Saskatchewan Regiment and les Fusiliers Mont-Royal. The Calgary Tank Regiment, with 40-ton Churchill tanks mounting the new 6-pounder gun, was in the force, and there were detachments of Montreal's Black Watch and Régiment de Maisonneuve, the Calgary Highlanders and Toronto Scottish—and British paratroopers.

On June 27 the divisional commander, Maj. Gen. J. H. Roberts, outlined the plan to his officers, giving every detail except the name of the town. They were impressed. I heard one say: "This'll be a piece of cake." In my diary I made these notes:

July 2—We go aboard ships.

July 3—It looks as if H-Hour will be 4:15 a.m. tomorrow. It depends on the weather. We need calm seas and little wind. Lord Louis Mountbatten, Chief of Combined Operations, and Gen. Dwight Eisenhower, American commander in the European Theater of Operations, come aboard. Eisenhower chats with the American Rangers attached to us for experience. I buttonhole him as he leaves and he says, "These boys of ours are just the first of thousands who'll eventually go into Europe." That sure is second front talk. The troops are briefed. Everyone has maps and now knows the target area well. They know every street by name—and the name of the town: Dieppe. Then we get a message: "Operation postponed 24 hours due to weather."

July 4—Another 24-hour postponement.

July 5—The weather is still not good. The sea may make it tough for the small

boats to hit the beaches. There is too much wind for the paratroopers to land to attack the coastal batteries on our flanks.

July 6—A fourth postponement.

July 7—The news comes at 10:30 a.m.: "The operation has been canceled." God, what a blow! Men break down and cry, they take the disappointment so hard.

I went to the CP office in London and confessed I had come back empty-handed from what would have been one of the great stories of the war. I had never been so depressed. . . . ROSS MUNRO

Lt. Gen. Bernard Montgomery, then chief of Britain's Southeast Command, was anything but depressed. The military authority responsible for the raid, he said later he was "absolutely delighted" by the cancellation and recommended that the assault be "off for all time." Long after the war Montgomery said in a CBC interview: "I'd never been happy about this very difficult operation being done by such inexperienced commanders and troops. Bravery is no substitute for battle experience."

But his delight didn't last long. Despite the fact that thousands of soldiers might have talked about the original plan, despite the risk that the Germans might have learned of it, the operation was revived July 14 by Combined Operations (the commandos, experts in coastal raids). The

Dwarfed by cliffs like those along the north coast of France, Canadian soldiers splash toward a Sussex beach near Seaford during exercises in May 1942. The army commander, Lt. Gen. A. G. L. McNaughton (opposite page), had by then given the go-ahead for a raid on Dieppe by the 2nd Division, led by Maj. Gen. J. H. Roberts (left). Years later McNaughton said: "The responsibility was mine and nobody else's. The final decision was mine. I said yes. And I say quite frankly that if I were in exactly the same position I would do exactly the same thing tomorrow."

British Chiefs of Staff approved it July 20. This time Montgomery was not involved; he was soon to go to North Africa. Military responsibility was handed to Lt. Gen. A. G. L. McNaughton, Canada's senior officer in Britain; he delegated it to Lt. Gen. H. D. G. Crerar, commander of the 1st Canadian Corps.

The problem of security was met by not concentrating the force in advance of the raid. Instead, units were moved direct from their camps in England to ports of embarkation, believing they were going on a large-scale exercise. Just prior to embarkation the troops were issued with weapons and ammunition.

On August 19, when the 2nd Division did go to Dieppe and Ross Munro got his story after all, it was the story of the bloodiest nine hours in Canadian military history, a battle whose purpose and worth are still questioned.

For instance, why were the Canadians sent on this mission? They were picked because they were clamoring for action after 2½ years in Britain, and because, even though inexperienced, they were consid-

ered among the best-trained troops in the world. When Montgomery asked whether the Canadians wanted the job, Crerar told him: "You bet we want it." McNaughton, who could have vetoed Canadian participation, accepted the plan drawn up by Combined Operations. He cabled Ottawa that the objective was worthwhile, the land forces sufficient, the sea and air forces adequate, the arrangements for cooperation satisfactory. Crerar agreed that "the plan is sound. I should have no hesitation in tackling it if in [General] Roberts' place."

Why was the raid planned in the first place? The British view was that before the Allies could invade Europe they had to learn how. A full-scale, for-real "exercise" was the only way. "This operation," said Gen. Sir Alan Brooke, Chief of Britain's Imperial General Staff, "is quite indispensable. If we ever intend to invade France it is absolutely essential to mount a preliminary operation on a divisional scale. This is it."

But there were other factors too. "The public in all the Allied countries," says historian Col. C. P. Stacey, "was calling loudly for action." To this were added political pressures from Britain's allies. General Crerar said after the war that he felt the raid was revived because of prodding from the Russians and Americans; they brought "great pressure on the British particularly to create some diversion that would take German pressure off the Russians," then fighting for survival.

"The only way they could do it," said Crerar, "was to use the same troops and the same techniques as originally planned. Except that commandos would be used on the flanks instead of paratroopers, the plan for August 19 was the same as that for early July."

In fact, the Russians and Americans had been pressing for something far bigger than a raid. Ralph Allen in *Ordeal by Fire:*
. . .Russia was demanding of Churchill and Roosevelt that spring that they come to the Soviets' help—and of course their own—by launching an immediate second front in western Europe. Although the United States was heavily engaged with Japan and was still in a relatively primitive stage of its military buildup, Roosevelt—against the advice of his chief military and diplomatic advisers—gave Russia what amounted to an undertaking that the second front would be opened in 1942. Churchill agreed to a tripartite communiqué that "full understanding" had been reached "with regard

Before such an attack took place, there "would have to be the strongest reasons" for believing it would succeed. If it failed, "there would be no saving of Britain thereafter, with the consequences that would flow therefrom."

The American commanders remained adamant. When the British planners remained equally so, U.S. War Secretary H. L. Stimson joined his top subordinates, Gen. George C. Marshall and Adm. Ernest J. King, in suggesting the President lay down an ultimatum: either the British would agree to a Channel crossing in 1942 or the United States would withdraw its agreement that Germany must be defeated before Japan. Roosevelt refused to accede

The ancient city of Dieppe, clustered around its small sheltered harbor, lies in a break in the limestone cliffs of Normandy at the mouth of the River Arques. Photos taken from destroyers during the raid (above and left) show the high cliffs; a prewar aerial photo (above left) shows the inner town. At the top of this photo are the east and west harbor moles; at the upper right, the east headland. To the left of the moles, between the sea and the town, lies the esplanade with its lawns and paths. A tobacco factory (twin chimneys) lies at about the middle of the mile-long beach. Out of the picture at the left is the casino, a feature attraction in a town that before the war had been called "the poor man's Monte Carlo."

to the urgent tasks of creating a second front in Europe in 1942." But he added in an *aide-mémoire* that no one could yet be sure whether the operation would prove feasible so soon and therefore Britain could give no promise that it would actually be undertaken.

American military planners continued to press for an almost immediate assault on western Europe. When Mountbatten visited Washington in June, Roosevelt suggested the possibility of at least a "sacrifice" landing before the year was over. Churchill said the Allies should make "no substantial landing in France unless we are going to stay [or] unless the Germans are demoralized by another failure against Russia. If Russia is in dire straits, it would not help her for us to come a hasty cropper on our own."

Canada was on the periphery of the argument, but Prime Minister Mackenzie King's instinctive position was similar to Churchill's. He feared the President was "crowding matters pretty strongly" and made it clear that Canada was not agreeing to "an immediate attack on Germany."

to what Stimson later admitted was a "bluff."

When, at last, the decision against a 1942 invasion of Europe was taken on July 22—after the Dieppe raid was "on" again—General Eisenhower thought the date might well go down as "the blackest day in history." Later he changed his mind and concluded that the decision to make substitute landings in North Africa late in 1942 had been a wise one.

Aside from mollifying the United States and Russia and spreading confusion among the Germans, the chief object of the Dieppe raid was to gain experience in an amphibious assault against a strongly held and fortified enemy coast. The total front to be attacked covered ten miles of cliff and beach and five major strongpoints, including Dieppe itself. At least half a dozen questions about tactics and weapons would have to be answered at Dieppe if the eventual second-front landings were to have a reasonable chance:

Which was better—to prepare the way for an initial landing or to dispense with bombardment and try for surprise? Could a major, well-defended port be seized from the sea without so badly damaging it that it would be of no value in the critical first days of the buildup? Could tanks be landed in the first wave and what chance had they of getting across the beaches and seawalls? What new equipment and weapons would be most useful? Was it best to work to split-second timing and a fixed plan? How much discretion should be left to the officers on the ground?

The Germans had detected the first concentration of ships around the Isle of Wight and were reasonably certain some sort of cross-Channel attack was coming that summer, but where and when they learned only when it began.

Hitler had taken the declaration in favor of a 1942 invasion to mean more than it said and had strengthened the Channel defenses and thickened the reserves behind them. Between March and August, German strength in France, Belgium and Holland was increased by nine divisions. Nearly half the Luftwaffe was in western Europe or the Mediterranean.

Dieppe not only had its share of this strength but also had the natural obstacle of high cliffs overlooking the beaches. It was protected by concrete pillboxes and artillery positions and barbed wire. There were nearly 50 field and coastal guns and howitzers, from French 75s to German 150-millimeters, plus three anti-aircraft batteries and a few anti-tank guns. Although the 302nd Infantry Division, the area's first-line defender, had to stand sentry on a frontage of 50 miles, there were ample reserves behind it. . . . RALPH ALLEN

Against this strong position were sent untried troops supported only by fighters, fighter-bombers and light bombers and the four-inch guns of eight destroyers. Two things might have made all the difference: a battleship and heavy bombing. There was no battleship because the Admiralty, desperately short of ships, wouldn't risk a big one in the Channel on an expedition which promised no help for the war at sea. And it was decided not to subject Dieppe to heavy bombing either. "Mr. Churchill decided we could bomb Dieppe if we wanted to," said General Roberts, "but the RAF said the chances of even hitting Dieppe looked small, let alone specific targets. So I said I wouldn't take a chance. All they would do was block the streets and my tanks would never get through."

And so, without adequate support, the raid began on Dieppe, a resort town that was sometimes called "the poor man's Monte Carlo."

General Roberts, sailing in the Royal Navy destroyer *Calpe,* had 4961 Canadian soldiers, 1075 British commandos and 50 U.S. Army Rangers under his direct command. The air commander, RAF Air Vice-Marshal T. L. Leigh-Mallory, back in Britain, could count on 60 squadrons of fighter aircraft and 7 of light bombers and fighter-bombers; he hoped the raid would prod the Luftwaffe into a major confrontation. The naval force, commanded by RN Capt. John Hughes-Hallett, consisted of *Calpe,* six other RN destroyers, one Polish destroyer and numerous smaller war craft manned by Britons, Canadians and a few Free French.

Each of the eight beaches to be assaulted was given a color. From east to west:

Beach opposite Berneval	Yellow 1
Beach at Belleville-sur-Mer	Yellow 2
Beach at Puys	Blue
Beach at Dieppe (east)	Red
Beach at Dieppe (west)	White
Beach at Pourville	Green
Beach at Varengeville	Orange 1
Beach near River Saane	Orange 2

The raiders were to destroy German defenses, airdrome installations, radar and power stations, dock and rail facilities and fuel dumps, get German invasion barges for Allied use, seize documents and capture prisoners.

The deputy commander of the operation, Brig. Churchill Mann, outlined the plan:

"H-Hour was 4:50 a.m. Because of lack of sea room and of trained landing-craft crews, the four flank attacks (Yellow, Blue, Green and Orange beaches) had to be launched half an hour ahead of the frontal attack across the main Dieppe beaches (Red and White). This was the plan for H-Hour:

"On the far left British commandos were to destroy the gun battery at Berneval. Landing at Puys, the Royal Regiment and a company of the Black Watch were to destroy guns on the east headland overlooking Dieppe harbor.

"On the extreme right commandos were to destroy the Varengeville battery. At Pourville the South Saskatchewan Regiment was to land astride the River Scie. Thirty minutes later the Cameron High-

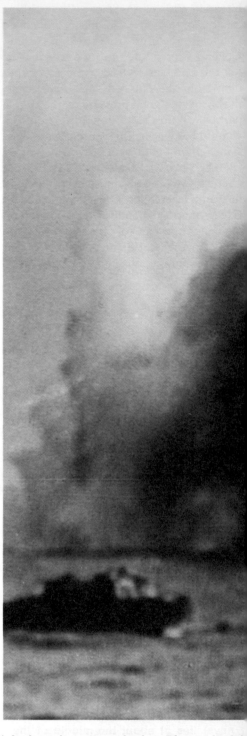

It doesn't matter whether Dieppe had any point or whether it was badly planned or whether some of us were cowards or maniacs or brutes. What is important is that a lot of good men believed in something enough to die for it. You can't belittle that and you shouldn't try to.—Maj. Brian McCool, Royal Regiment of Canada, beachmaster at Dieppe, quoted in *Maclean's.*

landers would advance through the Saskatchewans' beachhead, move inland, join tanks from Dieppe and assault an airdrome and a German divisional headquarters believed to be at Arques.

"There were to be two other attacks at H-Hour plus 30 minutes. On the left half of the beach at Dieppe the Essex Scottish and tanks of the Calgary Regiment were to land simultaneously and advance rapidly into the town to secure the harbor area for engineer demolitions. On the right half of the Dieppe beach the RHLI would land

with other Calgary tanks and move through the town to secure exits for other tanks to proceed inland where they would join the Camerons.

"Les Fusiliers Mont-Royal were to land later, occupying the perimeter of the town after the Essex and RHLI had seized it. All Canadian units were to withdraw across the main Dieppe beaches, with the FMR serving as rearguard.

"The British commandos on the extreme left and right flanks would withdraw from the beaches on which they had landed."

Wrote R. W. Thompson in *Dieppe at Dawn:*

. . . At 12:15 p.m. August 18, two minesweeping flotillas sailed from Portsmouth to open channels through the German minefields. Under cover of smoke, 24 tank landing craft received their Churchill tanks. Throughout the afternoon and evening, 6086 men were embarked. Just under 5000 were Canadians.

That night 252 little ships moved out of Portsmouth, Southampton, Shoreham and Newhaven. They planned to speed un-

seen, unheard and unheralded across 70 miles of narrow seas and make their assault. By nightfall August 19 the expedition planned to be safely home again.

At 11:30 a hand grenade exploded in the infantry landing ship *Invicta,* wounding 17 men of the South Saskatchewan Regiment. That was the only incident until at 2:55 the landing ships began to put their assault craft into the water. The armada was safely assembled, its presence unsuspected, within easy reach of the enemy-held coast. There were no sounds of aircraft overhead. The radar screens were clear. The wireless silence remained unbroken. The timings were according to plan. . . .

At 3:47 a.m., 63 minutes before H-Hour, the raiders ran out of luck. As the assault troops made the last ten-mile run in to the coast, 23 landing craft and their three escorts ran into a small German convoy and its escorts. A short, indecisive battle followed, alerting German shore batteries on the east and scattering part of the landing fleet.

As a result, fewer than a third of the Yellow Beach commandos got ashore at Berneval and Belleville-sur-Mer. Instead of knocking out the Berneval battery, they were pinned down and either killed, wounded or captured by midmorning. A few commandos managed to snipe at the gun crews, seriously interfering with the battery for more than 90 minutes during the time of the main landing at Dieppe.

On the far west, at Orange Beach, other commandos unaffected by the encounter with the German convoy achieved their full objectives. They retired on schedule after

capturing and destroying all the guns and killing most of the gunners in the Varengeville battery.

Elsewhere the raid was an almost unrelieved catastrophe. What follows are excerpts from various accounts of the fighting on the four Canadian beaches:

BLUE BEACH (Puys)

Royal Regiment of Canada

Ross Munro in *Gauntlet to Overlord:*

. . . We were seven or eight miles from Dieppe when to our left there was a streak of tracer bullets, then the clatter of automatic guns—the chance encounter, as we later learned, with the German convoy. We kept our heads down but our little craft was so jammed that even to crouch was to crowd someone. I sat on a cart of three-inch mortar bombs. More tracer swept ahead of us. Some pinged off our steel sides. A sailor rigged his Lewis gun through a slit at the stern and answered with a few bursts. An enemy ship—likely an E-boat, a small motorboat—was less than 200 yards away. From other directions came more German tracer. There might have been four ships intercepting us.

There wasn't much we could do. There's no armament on these assault craft for a naval action and our support ships didn't seem to be about. It looked as if we were going to be cut up piecemeal; more tracer whistled past, then there was a great flash and a bang of gunfire behind us: a destroyer speeding to our assistance. It fired at the enemy ships and they turned and disappeared.

The interception slowed our flotilla greatly and it was apparent we were going to be late. We had to make it before day-

light or we wouldn't stand much chance. Surprise was all-important.

Our planes were overhead now. German flak spouted from Dieppe and the sky was a spectacular flaming chandelier of colored lights and flashes. Searchlights fingered the sky. There were a dozen sharp flashes of bursting bombs. Now I could see a long stone pier at Dieppe, a red navigation light burning at the end. Our flotilla was off course and we shifted to hit Puys.

The Royals and the company of Black Watch were very late. They should have been on the beach before dawn and it was gray morning now. The air force, spotting our trouble, dropped a ton of smoke bombs on the headland east of Dieppe harbor. This smoke curled down to the sea and covered us temporarily for the run-in. But the smoke was spotty and the last 30 yards was in the clear. Geysers from shells shot up in our path. The German ack-ack and machine guns on the cliff were deafening.

The men in our boat crouched low. Then the ramp went down and the first infantrymen poured out. They plunged into about two feet of water and machine-gun bullets laced into them. Bodies piled up on the ramp. Some men staggered to the beach.

I was near the stern and to one side. Looking out the open bow, I saw 60 or 70 bodies, men cut down before they could fire a shot. A dozen Canadians were running along the beach toward the 12-foot-high seawall, 100 yards long. Some fired as they ran. Some had no helmets. Some were wounded, their uniforms torn and bloody. One by one they were hit and rolled down the slope to the sea.

I don't know how long we were nosed down on that beach. It may have been five

A plane flies a few feet above the stony beach of Dieppe, laying smoke to try to help Canadian infantry and tanks through the barbed wire, across the esplanade and into the town. Only a few riflemen got into Dieppe; none of the tanks got off the esplanade. Intense enemy fire killed many attackers in their landing craft. Correspondent Ross Munro, an eyewitness to the Royal Regiment slaughter at Puys, described a boat like the one below: "The bottom was covered with soldiers. Everyone who had tried to leave the boat had been cut down."

we gotta beat 'em!" He was dead in minutes.

I could see sandbagged German positions and a large house on top of the cliff. Most of the German machine-gun and rifle fire was coming from the fortified house and it wrought havoc. They were firing at us point-blank. There was a smaller house on the right and Germans were there too.

The men from our boat ran into the terrible German fire and I doubt that any even reached the stone wall. Mortar bombs were smashing on the slope to take those not hit by machine-gun bullets that streaked across the tiny beach. Now the Germans turned their anti-aircraft guns on us. The bottom of the boat was covered with sol-

last look at the grimmest beach of the Dieppe raid. It was khaki with the bodies of Canadian boys.

We limped a few hundred yards out to sea in the brilliant sunshine, numb with shock. Of the 80 we had taken in, 20 were left and more than half of them were wounded. Some boys had been hit a dozen times. Nobody had counted on casualties like this. . . .   ROSS MUNRO

Only one party of Royals even got off the beach. Twenty officers and men led by Lt. Col. D. E. Catto cut through the wire at the west end of the seawall, reached the cliff top and cleared two houses, but machine-gun fire on the gap in the wire cut them off from support. When it was obvious the raiding force had withdrawn and there was no hope of being picked up, they surrendered.

The regiment was virtually wiped out. One of every two of its 554 officers and men died on the beach or later from wounds. Only 65 Royals got back to England and of these only 22 were unwounded. In the three hours between landing and surrender, the unit suffered 96 percent casualties.

GREEN BEACH (Pourville)
South Saskatchewan Regiment
Cameron Highlanders

Two miles west of Dieppe—and four miles from the slaughter at Puys—two other battalions had better luck. The navy put the Saskatchewans ashore at Pourville on time and they weren't fired on until they landed. But in the semi-darkness the landing craft had not beached on target: instead of being astride the River Scie, most of the unit landed west of it. The companies assigned to take high ground to the east had first to work through the village and cross the main highway bridge.

The company west of Pourville occupied all its objectives and killed or captured many Germans. But the companies trying to cross the bridge came under heavy fire from the heights.

War correspondent Wallace Reyburn, in a CBC broadcast:
. . . The bridge was about 200 yards long, really a kind of causeway. It was wide and had no balustrades. That made it very exposed. On the hill across the river was a huge concrete fort, its guns all trained on the bridge. The river was in flood and the bridge was the only way to get across apart from swimming.

minutes. It may have been 20. It was brutal and terrible and you were shocked almost to insensibility to see the piles of dead and feel the hopelessness. One lad crouched six feet from me. He had made several attempts to rush down the ramp but each time a hail of fire had driven him back. He had been wounded in the arm but was determined to try again. He lunged forward, and a streak of tracer slashed through his stomach. I'll never forget his anguished cry as he collapsed on the bloody deck: "Christ, we gotta beat 'em,

diers. An officer was hit in the head and sprawled over my legs. A naval rating had a gash in his throat and was dying. A few who weren't casualties stood up and fired back at the Germans, even when they knew the attack was a lost cause.

Orders were to land the troops, then pull back to sea. It was useless to remain a sitting target. Everyone who had tried to leave the boat had been cut down. Our naval officer ordered the craft off the beach. Ponderously we swung around. Through an opening at the stern I got my

I saw the first men try to cross. Great chunks of concrete flew in the air—mortar shells exploding. Bullets pinged off the road. In a minute or two, what had been a smooth concrete road was gashed with craters and pockmarked with bullet holes. Our men were mowed down.

Striding up the road unhurried, revolver dangling from his hip, came Lt. Col. Cecil Merritt, the Saskatchewans' CO. As he reached us he took his tin hat off and wiped sweat from his forehead. It was a hot, steamy day. He asked what the trouble was. Someone said: "This bridge is a hot spot, sir. We're trying to get across it."

"Now men," he said, "we're going to get across. Follow me. Don't bunch up together, spread out. Here we go!" Erect and bareheaded, he strode forward onto the bridge. His helmet hung from his wrist as

he walked. As I watched him lead his men through that thundering barrage, I felt a quiver run up and down my spine. I'd never seen anything like it. . . .

Merritt led a series of attacks which took several of the positions commanding the bridge and the village. But in spite of his bravery—for which he was awarded the Victoria Cross—and the efforts of his own men and Cameron Highlanders now mingled with them, the high ground could not be cleared. Col. C. P. Stacey in *The Canadian Army 1939-45:*

. . . The enemy had every approach covered by mortar and machine-gun fire and our thrusts were all beaten back, although small parties got close to a heavily wired radar station and one reached the edge of the Four Winds Farm trench system.

Firing from well-prepared positions, German gunners kept many Canadians from landing and frustrated every bid to launch a full-scale push into Dieppe. Only small groups of men, in bitter hand-to-hand fighting, achieved any success on the main beaches. West of Dieppe, at Pourville, the South Saskatchewan Regiment and Cameron Highlanders of Winnipeg attained some of their objectives. The Saskatchewans' Lt. Col. Cecil Merritt (left) was awarded the Victoria Cross for valor in leading his men through heavy fire across a key bridge.

The Camerons were to pass through the Pourville bridgehead and operate against an airdrome in conjunction with tanks from Dieppe. They were landed late. As the landing craft drove into the shallows, the Camerons' bagpipes answered the whine of shells and the rattle of machine guns.

Lt. Col. A. C. Gostling leaped onto the beach. There was a burst of fire and he fell dead. Maj. A. T. Law led the Cameron column inland two miles, destroying small parties of Germans. It reached Petit Appeville, overlooking the bridges across the Scie, which it must pass to reach the airdrome. But no tanks were to be seen. The Scie crossings were held in strength by

enemy troops and time was growing short. The unit withdrew, suffering and inflicting casualties on the way. It had penetrated farther inland than any other battalion that day.

The Saskatchewans and Camerons lost heavily during the evacuation. The Germans raked the beach from lofty positions east of Pourville and from high ground to the west—from which a Saskatchewan company had retired due to a misunderstanding of orders. Naval craft came in through a storm of steel; the Germans, who showed little stomach for close fighting, were held off by a courageous rearguard under Colonel Merritt. The greater part of both units was re-embarked, though many men were wounded. The rearguard surrendered when ammunition was running low and it was clear there was no pos-

sibility of evacuation or of doing further harm to the enemy. . . .

RED AND WHITE BEACHES
(Dieppe)
Essex Scottish and RHLI
Calgary Tank Regiment
Les Fusiliers Mont-Royal

In the main assault on the mile-long beach at Dieppe itself, surprise was neither hoped for nor intended. This landing had been deliberately scheduled for half an hour later than those on the flanks. The Essex Scottish would go ashore on the eastern half (Red Beach), the Royal Hamilton Light Infantry on the adjoining western half (White Beach).

Beneath guns on cliffs at either end— the east and west headlands—a wide beach of stones climbed steeply from the sea to a four-foot-high seawall. Between the wall and the town was a broad esplanade with no cover—except for a casino near the western end of White Beach. With its seaward side on the beach and its inland side only a few yards from a row of hotels, the casino would give some protection to troops trying to cross from beach to town.

Terence Robertson in *Dieppe: The Shame and The Glory:*

. . . The Germans had razed buildings to give their guns unobstructed fields of fire. Hotels had been transformed into sandbagged machine-gun nests and sniper hideouts. Even the casino had been partly demolished and concrete pillboxes built among the debris. Halfway up the sloping

beach was barbed wire six to ten feet thick; more was strung along the top of the seawall and still more crisscrossed the esplanade.

The harbor entrance at the east end of the beach—the Essex Scottish end—consisted of two large piers or moles 300 yards long. It lay under the shadow of the east headland, which was pitted with caves. On both headlands guns the attackers knew about enfiladed the entire beach; other weapons they knew nothing about were concealed in the caves: anti-tank guns, machine guns and light artillery which could be run out to fire and withdrawn in the face of bombardment.

Particularly dangerous were the big guns on the headlands, the machine-gun emplacements in the battlements of an old castle on the west end, a tank cemented into a harbor mole and a fortified tobacco factory facing the beach.

Gen. Konrad Haase, the German divisional commander, had brought his sector to maximum alert at 5 a.m. The assault was planned for 5:20.

The first naval salvo was fired at 5:12 a.m. Simultaneously, the RAF laid smoke screens over the east headland to neutralize the defenses, attacked gun emplacements with cannon fire and strafed the seafront. Most German gun crews bolted for cover when the fighter-bombers arrived and were still hiding when the assault came in. The fire that greeted the infantry was bad enough, but not nearly as heavy as it might have been.

Mortars in the landing craft lobbed smoke bombs to cover the touchdown. The men hit the beach in near-perfect formation and within a three-minute bracket, the first at 5:20, the last at 5:23 a.m., and scrambled up the steep beach.

Lt. Col. Fred Jasperson of the Essex Scottish was first out of his boat, urging on men who were beside him one second, dead the next. He threw himself against the seawall. What remained of his battalion headquarters staff had kept up with him and he ordered a Bangalore torpedo, a long, thin explosive, placed under the barbed wire. As it exploded, the group swarmed over the wall. But the wire had parted to a depth of only three feet, leaving another three intact. As the Essex tried to cut through, the snipers and machine gunners in the hotels and tobacco factory cut them down.

On White Beach Lt. Col. Robert Labatt of the RHLI came out of his boat and

On Blue Beach, at Puys, the Royal Regiment was all but annihilated. From positions up the cliff (photo at left) and behind the seawall the Germans laced the beach with mortar and machine-gun fire. In this photo (above) from a German propaganda film Canadian dead sprawl below the wall at Puys. Of 554 Royals embarked for Dieppe, 65 got back to England. "It was a massacre," said one survivor, "a bloody mess."

slithered over a ridge of pebbles 25 yards to the left of the casino. To each side his companies were spreading out, blasting their way through the first wire.

Men in a hollow ahead of Labatt fired at a pillbox on the left corner of the casino and at the windows above it. The pillbox was protected by barbed wire, and Labatt was transfixed at the sight of a soldier crawling under the lower strands. All sense of personal danger vanished. He ached to shout encouragement.

The solitary soldier cleared the last strand, squatted to pull a grenade from his belt, stood up and casually shoved it through the gun slit. Labatt recognized Pte. Hugh McCourt. The pillbox belched smoke and flame. A tin hat on a bayonet bobbed behind the destroyed position, and the grinning McCourt reappeared to beck-

on others to join him. They couldn't. In those few minutes all had been killed or wounded.

When the Calgary Regiment and its Churchill tanks came in late, they found a beach where already 200 soldiers lay dead or wounded.

[Twenty-nine tanks left their landing craft. Two were "drowned" in deep water. The rest, due to a navigating error by the destroyer leading their landing craft in, reached the beaches ten minutes late. The infantry, instead of having tanks land simultaneously to cover them over the esplanade, went ashore alone. When the tanks did land, many were stopped by the seawall or bogged down in sand and stones. Some got around the low ends of the wall onto the esplanade, but none could get past the concrete obstacles the Germans

had erected to bar the way into the streets of Dieppe. Nor could the engineers destroy the obstacles. But the Churchills remained in action nonetheless, firing on German positions and providing protection for the infantrymen pinned down on the beach.]

The two beachmasters, Maj. Brian Mc-Cool for the army and a Royal Navy commander, had set up near the junction of Red and White beaches without having too much to be masters of. There was no traffic to control other than the collection and disposal of the wounded, so McCool became an extra communications link between the various commanders, summoning fire support where it was most urgently needed.

Little information reached *Calpe*. The headquarters destroyer, festooned with wireless aerials, should have been able to maintain contact with every unit ashore or afloat. It didn't, chiefly because naval signalmen with the first assault waves were picked off by snipers. Most signalmen who landed were killed; many others failed to reach shore. General Roberts' receivers crackled and sputtered but rarely spoke.

And some of the reports he did get misled him.

Pinned along the seawall, Colonel Jasperson realized the Essex Scottish were in a trap from which few could escape. But CSM. Cornelius Stapleton exploded a Bangalore torpedo under the wire on the seawall, let out a mighty battlecry, and charged through the gap with about 15 men at his heels. They crossed the Boulevard Maréchal Foch, made a crouching, zigzag dash for more than 100 yards across the promenade and stormed over the Boulevard Verdun, throwing grenades at the windows of buildings facing them, firing guns from their hips and bellowing their hate. At the seawall a section of men, shouting encouragement, stood up and fired incendiary grenades, attempting to cover the charge by setting fire to the buildings. The tobacco factory exploded into flames as Stapleton and his men broke into a building east of it, blowing down doors, blowing out shuttered windows and leaping into smoke-filled infernos of their own creation.

Some of the group splintered off to another building, exacting terrible retribution for the slaughter on the beach. A third party reached the east end of the boulevard and mowed down enemy troops debussing from trucks. Their ammunition all but expended, the tattered party rejoined the housecleaning group, then raced across that fire-filled esplanade.

Almost 30 minutes after their exodus from behind the seawall, Stapleton was back. His brief foray would greatly influence the operation. Shortly after 6 a.m. Jasperson had used the only walkie-talkie still working to inform the RHLI: "Twelve of our men in the buildings. Have not heard from them for some time." *Calpe* intercepted this signal. Placed in the context of reports from elsewhere, it suggested occupation of buildings facing Red Beach and partial consolidation of the beach itself. General Roberts wanted the east headland. At 6:10 the intercepted message was reinforced by solid evidence that he might get it via Red Beach. This was a report from the destroyer *Fernie* saying: "Essex Scot across beaches and in houses."

DAILY NEWS FINAL

BROOKLYN QUEENS LONG ISLAND

NEW YORK'S PICTURE NEWSPAPER

Vol. 24. No. 48 — New York, Thursday, August 20, 1942 — 52 Main + 12 Brooklyn Pages — 2 Cents

YANKS IN 9-HR. RAID ON NAZIS

Allied Commandos Storm Dieppe on French Coast

200 REICH PLANES DOWNED

Stories on Pages 2 and 3

Canadian casualties included 1874 men captured, 568 of them wounded. Of the 6086 troops sent to Dieppe, close to 5000 were Canadians. Despite what the New York *Daily News* implied, only about 50 of the raiders were Americans—men of the 1st U.S. Ranger Battalion. A year later, on August 19, 1943, *The New York Times* said in an editorial:

"Men afoot and men in tanks were exposed to a fire that no valor could withstand. Hundreds of them went as far as they could and died, but these deaths achieved nothing except to prove what was already known—the high quality of the Canadian troops and of the small units of [other nations] who accompanied them. Someday there will be two spots on the French coast sacred to the British and their allies. One will be Dunkirk, where Britain was saved because a beaten army would not surrender. The other will be Dieppe, where brave men died without hope for the sake of proving that there is a wrong way to invade. They will have their share of the glory when the right way is tried."

It was an inexplicable magnification of Stapleton's skirmish that provided Roberts with news of a success he could reinforce, news so grossly exaggerated that it enticed him toward the fatal assumption that even limited success warranted exploitation.

At 6:15 his hopes were given further encouragement when Labatt reported the RHLI were at the casino. Five minutes later Roberts received a distorted signal from the naval beachmaster with the Royal Regiment at Puys: "Impossible land troops." The words "any more" preceding "troops" had been omitted. After a brief conference with Hughes-Hallett, Roberts decided to commit the Royals—whom he now thought to be lying off Puys in assault boats—to Red Beach, from where they might still assault the east headland. In fact, the Royals had already been decimated. The FMR, Roberts' reserve battalion, still had not been committed.

It may be that Roberts read too much into the fragmentary information that reached him. But time had become a predominating factor. If Dieppe were to be taken, the reserves had to be committed by 7 a.m.—a time limit set by the anticipated rate of German reinforcement. If the town did not fall by 9 a.m., an overwhelming counterattack could be expected. Withdrawal would have to begin by 11.

Having tried to exploit the limited success he *thought* he had on Red Beach, Roberts now made a similar decision about White Beach: the report of limited RHLI success at the casino led him to order in the FMR. They were to land near the casino, to the RHLI's right. Critics later said Pourville was the only success warranting exploitation. They forget that Roberts knew nothing of the beachhead there until 90 minutes later.

The FMR, under Lt. Col. Dollard Ménard, landed strung out along the beach, most of them so far to the west that even White Beach was to their left. Nearly 200 reached the base of the west headland and huddled under the overhang against the face of the cliff. They were so far west they had found a beach of their own, a

new one bared by the ebbing tide and on the right fringe of the battle.

One boat which touched down under the cliff was commanded by Lt. R. F. McRae, senior Canadian naval officer at Dieppe. He and his crew worked among the wounded giving morphine, bandaging and whispering words of hope. The Germans came to the edge of the cliff and saw that the stricken boat was little more than a stranded first-aid post. It was not fired on again.

Assault troops, tanks and reinforcements now were ashore. But Dieppe had become a battle of independent groups, of platoons intermingling, companies breaking up and coalescing, men fighting alongside strangers and dying in their arms. Because wireless and radio-telephone sets were smashed, commanders used runners — who were almost always killed. Pebble splinters caused as much havoc as bullets. No organized assault could be made. The troops were reluctant to leave shelter and go forward without the tanks; the tanks could not go forward until the engineers had blown the roadblocks; many of the engineers were dead; the rest, loaded with 60-pound charges, could not go forward until the troops had secured the immediate vicinities of the roadblocks.

Only at the casino were the Canadians able to launch any real attacks. Capt. Denny Whitaker and one section of RHLI stormed into the building. They stopped, hugging the walls of the entrance, blinking to adjust their eyes from sunlight to sudden shade. A rifle fired and one soldier collapsed, fatally wounded. Pte. T. W. Graham, knowing he would be silhouetted against the light outside, moved quickly from the wall, throwing grenades in rapid succession. When the swirling smoke receded, five Germans had their hands in the air. Rifle fire from upstairs chipped the paneling near Whitaker's head and the stalking began, down long, narrow corridors, across balconies, from room to room.

Pte. A. W. Oldfield and three other soldiers started up a wide, circular staircase and met four Germans running down. The enemy turned in sudden flight. Grenades blew them to pieces. Oldfield found a sniper and went after him with his bayonet. For the first time in his life he killed a man while looking into his face, watching him die, trying to free the bayonet before he vomited over his victim's head.

Pte. F. E. A. Jenner reached the third floor. "The only two Germans I ran into I shot because they wouldn't come out of their hiding place," he reported. Pte. R. W. Wilkinson found himself at one end of a corridor, a German at the other; both had tommy guns. The fact neither could win occurred to them at the same time. Both dodged back to shelter. Other soldiers, as a team, crept stealthily to one closed door after another, one throwing it open while the others poured fire in. Their score mounted steadily. By 8 a.m. 20 prisoners were hunched along a wall.

The casino was never quite cleared of the enemy. More than 100 RHLI, FMR, engineers and signalers occupied the first two floors, although enemy snipers continued to fire from the third floor and the roof.

But the ground floor was available for sections trying to get through to the town.

Engineer Sgt. George Hickson, with 18 men, used that route to attempt to destroy a telephone exchange. In the Rue de la Martinière snipers and machine guns pinned them against buildings and it seemed they were trapped. Most French civilians in the vicinity wore an insignia like a swastika. "We watched for some time before deciding these 'civilians' were really collaborators giving away our positions to the Germans," said Hickson. A Bren gunner aimed a long burst. The "civilians" scattered, running, the slower ones bowled over by bullets.

The sniper fire grew erratic and the Canadians retreated toward a cinema— but they didn't get far. Fifty yards away a German patrol occupied a house they would have to pass. The only way to do so would be to storm the place. They rushed the house, broke down the door, sprayed the hall with tommy guns, threw grenades and plunged into the clouds of smoke and dust with bayonets ready. A dozen Germans attacked with bayonets as the Canadians came up the stairs. When the fight ended every German was dead, every Canadian wounded.

Among the FMRs who landed just west of the casino was Sgt. Pierre Dubuc. He ran 100 yards up the beach to a depression where he stayed for "a long hour." Two pillboxes set into the seawall fired continuously over his hollow. Pte. N. Daudelin crawled in beside him, dragging a smoke-making machine. At Dubuc's order, Daudelin furiously cranked the handle of

the machine. Germans in the pillboxes fired, but soon smoke hid him from sight. Then Dubuc and Daudelin wriggled on their stomachs to the sides of the pillboxes, stood up and dropped grenades through the gun slits.

Beckoning Daudelin to follow, Dubuc ran and crawled 150 yards to an abandoned tank, and both men vanished inside. For 20 minutes they fired the tank's 6-pounder at enemy guns on the west headland, until there was no more ammunition.

Now they split up. Dubuc waved to a group of Fusiliers against the western cliff face. Eleven followed him about a mile through the streets of Dieppe to the inner harbor docks, Bassin Duquesne and Bassin du Canada, so named because the harbor had been for years the loading port for ships taking freight and French settlers to the New World.

At the Bassin du Canada they found two large barges tied up alongside a quay. Four of Dubuc's men boarded the barges while the rest stood guard on the quay and fought a spirited duel with sailors firing from below decks. When ammunition was all but

expended, the party withdrew to look for cover and await the arrival of Royal Marines assigned to seize German invasion barges. "Just then," Dubuc said later, "15 Germans rushed us. We had no ammunition for the automatic weapons and little for the rifles. We surrendered. We were taken into a courtyard behind a house where the Germans shouted orders we couldn't understand."

An exasperated German burst out in English: "Undress or we shoot." Dubuc, speaking French, said that as French Canadians they could never accept an order given offensively in English. One German eventually confronted Dubuc to say curtly, in French: "Undress."

The Canadians stripped to their underwear and were told to stand with faces to a wall, their hands raised. All but one of the Germans departed, taking the clothes and equipment. The lone guard was a boy about 17. In German, Dubuc asked:

"Do you speak English or French?"

"English a bit, I speak."

"I suppose you're as hot and thirsty as we are. How about a drink of water?"

The German turned to look for a tap and the Canadians sprang upon him. Someone lifted a short length of iron piping. The boy died.

The Canadians ran, each man for himself, heading back to the beach. As Dubuc scampered down one street after another, Frenchmen stared, girls squealed. He ran into a German patrol, swerved round them, his heart pounding. The sight of a man galloping through town in his underwear convulsed the Germans no less than the French. German catcalls followed him as he vanished into another street.

There was a pause in the gun duel between Canadians in the casino and Germans in the seafront buildings as the sweating figure in white underwear sprinted across their lines of fire. Dubuc cleared the seawall and lay panting on the beach, nursing the ache in his side and dripping wet from his run. A voice said: "Who are you?" He looked up into the smoke-blackened face of an RHLI sergeant and weakly replied: "Sergeant Dubuc, FMR."

"Then where the hell have you been out of uniform?". . .   TERENCE ROBERTSON

Some badly wounded men drowned as Dieppe's 22-foot tide swept in during the battle. In the chaotic withdrawal, the Rev. John Foote (above), chaplain of the Royal Hamilton Light Infantry, helped many wounded men into boats. As the last boat headed for England, Foote returned to the beach and was taken prisoner, believing "the men ashore would need me far more in captivity than any of those going home." He later received the Victoria Cross. In a message (left) from his headquarters ship off Dieppe, Maj. Gen. J. H. Roberts reported the "sad decision to abandon" a large part of his force. Roberts said later that Dieppe "certainly finished" his active career. He felt he was made the scapegoat for the disaster.

The landing of the reserves had done no good. The Germans still held the Dieppe headlands and continued to sweep the main beaches with murderous fire. General Roberts ordered the raiders to withdraw at 11 a.m. He later sent this message to General Crerar by pigeon:

"Very heavy casualties in men and ships. Did everything possible to get men off but in order to get any home had to come to sad decision to abandon remainder. This was joint decision by force commanders. Obviously operation completely lacked surprise."

Only a few landing craft could get to the RHLI on White Beach, hardly any to the Essex Scottish on Red Beach. Altogether only about 500 men were evacuated. *Calpe* alone took home 278 wounded.

Colonel Labatt in a CBC interview:

. . . Each unit was responsible for its own withdrawal. The navy sent in one flight of craft on which 300 or more were re-embarked under cover of a smoke screen from the air. This smoke blew away at the critical moment, leaving these ships within range even of rifle fire and they were simply blown out of the water. No more craft came in after that because, I suppose, there were no more to come.

The groups on the beach were by that time in small blobs, some under the west cliff, some near the casino, some farther east, others down by the pier. They were fighting independently. The ones under the west cliff were mostly wounded; they had very little ammunition left and very few weapons. Many had been in the water and had swum back again without their weapons; a Mae West will not keep a man and his weapons and ammunition afloat.

Dieppe has a 22-foot tide and now this tide was rolling in and drowning many of the wounded. Chaps were going out from cover to pull these men above the high-water mark—but they themselves were sitting ducks. We saw that things were getting extremely tough for the people on the right and they had to give up. A naval officer assured us more craft would be coming in. We kept going until only we were left. All the others had to give up.

We had some German airmen who'd been shot down and taken prisoner. When it became apparent there was nothing further we could do and that we were losing so many men through drowning, we sent some of these Germans out toward the seawall. They waved to their pals, who

147

came up to the edge of the seawall and wire. We ordered the tanks to stop firing and then we marched through the wire to join our comrades.

I was allowed to send men to the beach to help rescue the wounded. After dusk we were not allowed to approach the beach again. I'm afraid it's inevitable that some of the wounded were left. There were so many we couldn't rescue them all, but we did what we could. . . .

One of many who had helped rescue the wounded when boats were still available was the Rev. John Foote, RHLI padre. Terence Robertson wrote that Foote saved at least 30 lives. He lifted one man on his back, walked into the water, waded to the nearest boat and, despite the crowd around it, persuaded men to help him transfer the wounded man on board. He waded back to shore, walked to the LCT, lifted another wounded man to his back and turned toward the beach. So it went for more than an hour, the incredible padre seeking out boats and calling to all who could hear: "Every man carry a man." When only one boat remained, two men pulled him into it. The boat had moved astern when suddenly the padre leaped into the water and returned to the beach because, he said, "It seemed to me the men ashore would need me far more in captivity than any of those going home." Foote, a prisoner until May

1945, was subsequently awarded the Victoria Cross.

The army, which did no fighting for so long before Dieppe, did no more fighting for months after. In this new time of waiting Canada counted and recounted the staggering losses—and blamed and accused and rationalized and tried painfully to understand why. This exercise in anguish and doubt has never ended. For it has always been obvious, in retrospect, that this was how *not* to go about an invasion. The haunting question is whether the lessons learned were worth the enormous price.

Nearly 60 percent of the 6086 Canadian, British and U.S. troops engaged were casualties. The Germans, on their side, admitted 591. Among the nearly 5000 Canadians the casualty rate was close to 70 percent. More than 900 Canadians died —almost a third as many as all the Allied dead on D-Day in Normandy two years later. Close to 2000 Canadians were captured—more than the army lost as prisoners in the 11 months of the northwest Europe campaign or the 20 months in Italy. Fewer than half the Canadian assault force got back to Britain, many of them wounded.

Of 582 men of the RHLI, 217 got back; of 554 of the Royal Regiment, 65; of 553 Essex Scottish, 52. Two colonels were killed, four captured. One of the two brigade

A few hours after the raid the smoke of battle still hung over Dieppe. From the west headland (right) Germans looked down on the harbor moles, main beach, casino (tall building) and tobacco factory (chimneys). A German officer said of Canadian prisoners (above): "The way they got hold of themselves and went into captivity was excellent." Some assessments of the raid:

The casualties may seem out of proportion to the results. It would be wrong to judge the episode solely by such a standard. It was a costly but not unfruitful reconnaissance-in-force.
Winston Churchill

The raid taught the enemy more than it did us.   U.S. historian S. E. Morison

Let no one tell you the Dieppe affair was devoid of valuable results. I know of no other single incident that did so much to confirm convictions that the coastal fortifications in France could be successfully breached on a large scale.   **Gen. Dwight Eisenhower**

I have no doubt that the Battle of Normandy was won on the beaches of Dieppe. For every man who died at Dieppe at least ten or more must have been spared in Normandy in 1944.
Lord Mountbatten

commanders was taken prisoner, the other severely wounded. One destroyer and all 29 tanks were lost.

Eighty-eight fighter planes, ten tactical reconnaissance aircraft and eight bombers were destroyed—for the raid did produce a tremendous air battle. Of 67 squadrons dispatched from England, 8 were RCAF. Twenty-three U.S. Flying Fortresses attacked the German aircraft base at Abbeville to keep it inactive during the withdrawal.

Against Allied losses of 106 aircraft, the Germans lost only 48 destroyed and 24 damaged. It was hardly the crippling blow the RAF had hoped to deal the Luftwaffe. It was, instead, a substantial defeat. Yet it has received little attention in the decades of controversy which have made August 19, 1942, a day which refuses to die. Discussion is almost invariably about the ground attack.

Some of the survivors try to see Dieppe in perspective. Forbes West, battle adjutant of the Royal Regiment, told the CBC nearly a quarter century after the raid: "If you were one of the people concerned, the loss was pretty big; but in terms of global war, it's not very big."

Lord Mountbatten of Combined Operations said: "It's impossible to overestimate the value of Dieppe. It was the turning point in the technique of invasion. Many vital lessons were learned." The men who

died at Dieppe, said Mountbatten, "gave to the Allies the priceless secret of victory. For every man who died at Dieppe in 1942, at least ten or more must have been spared in the invasion of Normandy in 1944."

But among the men who survived Dieppe are some who bitterly insist they were shortchanged. Eric Maguire, in *Dieppe: August 19,* quotes an unidentified "survivor of Blue Beach": "Every man knew his job and was eager to get a crack at the enemy. We wanted to give a damn good show, to the world, to Canada and to the Germans. We were not afraid despite the odds, and we would do our jobs whatever we ran into when we landed. You can imagine our feelings when we were spotted and knew we were sitting ducks at the mercy of God and the Germans. We landed in terrific fire, in broad daylight with no smoke cover. Everything seemed to go wrong. I'll always remember the faces of the survivors, after the surrender, officers and men sitting on the beach among our dead, crying. We felt robbed of the chance to fight and show what we could do. We had the right kind of men and equipment to put up one hell of a fight, but the whole affair was a failure because we were not given the chance to land as an organized unit. Instead we were a confused, bewildered bunch of men seeking shelter and defending our lives as best we could. On the beach where the Royal Regi-

ment landed, it was a massacre, a bloody mess."

Combined Operations said at the time that the paramount lesson of Dieppe for landings yet to come was "the need for overwhelming fire support, including close support, during the initial stages of the attack." This should be provided "by heavy and medium naval bombardment, by air action, by special vessels or craft working close inshore, and by using the firepower of the assaulting troops while still seaborne."

R. W. Thompson commented in *Dieppe at Dawn:* "Surely this lesson about firepower did not need to be learned as late as August 1942. Had it not been learned at Gallipoli and in a thousand land battles? Was it not known to every brigadier who had ever commanded an infantry brigade? And if firepower and close support are necessary in a land battle, why not in a land battle launched from the sea and against an enemy with known heavy artillery support? It is bad enough in the cause of tactical surprise to be deprived of a preliminary bombing or bombardment, but to be left with totally inadequate fire support thereafter seems inexcusable."

The raid showed that no major port could be captured quickly or intact, so the Allies determined that when they invaded the Continent they'd take their own port, the two Mulberry artificial harbors. When they went to Normandy they also took a weird collection of special vehicles developed as a result of Dieppe: bulldozer tanks, flail tanks to cut through minefields, amphibious tanks, flame-throwing tanks.

On D-Day, June 6, 1944, the assault troops went in with overwhelming fire support and a host of new equipment, and close behind came the artificial harbors. On D-plus-1 General Crerar told a group of Canadian officers: "Until Dieppe proved otherwise, it had been the opinion in highest command and staff circles that an assault against a heavily defended coast could be carried out on the basis of securing tactical surprise, and without dependence on overwhelming fire support.

"If tactical surprise was to be the basis of the plan, then bombardment, prior to imminent 'touchdown,' obviously had to be ruled out. Dependence on tactical surprise also implied an approach under cover of darkness and landing at first light. Adequate air superiority, after surprise had been achieved and throughout the operation, was, of course, essential.

"From the study of Dieppe emerged the technique and tactics adopted for the vast combined operation which took place yesterday. When this war is examined in proper perspective, it will be seen that the sobering influence of Dieppe on existing Allied strategical conceptions, with the enforced realization of the tremendous preparations necessary before invasion, was a Canadian contribution of the greatest significance to final victory."

Brig. Peter Young, a military historian who was with the commandos at Berneval wrote "the raid did nothing to persuade Stalin that his allies were trying to help him." But, in his book *Storm from the Sea*, Young wrote: "What did Dieppe prove? To the Germans it proved that their system of coast defense was sound, and in the two years that followed they continued to plan with the intention of repelling invasion on the beaches. If we made a mistake in attacking such a strong place without adequate fire support, at least the enemy were lulled into a sense of false security. Thereafter, they pursued a policy of coastal defense which was to be their undoing in 1944. In war the right things often happen for the wrong reasons."

Did the Germans know the Canadians were coming?

"No," said Colonel Stacey, "they did not. We can be quite definite about that."

The noise of the fight at sea after the chance encounter with the German coastal convoy did alert Luftwaffe radar operators at Berneval and the defenders at Puys. But, said Colonel Stacey, the German convoy escort apparently made no report of landing craft and the convoy fight "did *not* result in a general loss of the element of surprise." It is questionable, he said, whether it affected the main operation at all.

What happened at Puys was later explained by Maj. Richard Schnösenberg, the German commander there. He had order-

Soldiers taken off the beaches, many of them wounded, kept stumbling into the jammed wardroom of the destroyer. It was strange how alike they looked. Fear, pain, fatigue seem to paint a universal expression. Their faces were not white but grayish. Their eyes were staring and they moved jerkily, like robots, like punch-drunk fighters. A fighter gets that way when his brain has received too many shocks. These men had received too many shocks.

Quentin Reynolds in *Dress Rehearsal*

ed a routine "drill alarm" and all units at Puys were in position when "we heard a spectacular shooting at sea." He simply kept his men at their posts.

"Some Germans," said Colonel Stacey, "told our prisoners they had been tipped off but this, I think, is due to the fact that the moon and tide were right for a raid and the whole German garrison along the coast was in a state of alert. We have many German documents for this raid and there is no evidence that they were tipped off. There's lots of evidence they were not. This is probably the major misconception about Dieppe and I don't think you'll ever eliminate it from most people's minds. They'll go on believing that the Germans were waiting for us. And the basic reason is, of course, *the fact that we lost the battle.*"

For his part in the raid, General Roberts was decorated for "ability, courage and determination to a high degree"—then transferred to head reinforcement units in the

in which the lessons of Dieppe were brilliantly and successfully applied—but for Dieppe itself, a nine-hour calamity of staggering losses and unattained objectives.

Ross Munro called it a disaster and a triumph. *Saturday Night* called it "another Passchendaele," reviving memories of one of the worst and most pointless bloodbaths of World War I. To Ralph Allen it was "a magnificent fiasco." He wrote that the politicians and generals made so much of Dieppe's "lessons" right after the raid that "many people felt they were simply trying to cover up a senseless blunder with a retroactive excuse." But Allen agreed with the consensus among Dieppe students: the raid was *necessary* and it *did* pay off, not only in Normandy but also in the landings in North Africa, Sicily and Italy and the Salerno and Anzio assaults.

Ironically, the defeat itself and the ghastly price the Canadians paid was another important thing about the raid. R. W. Thompson, in *Dieppe at Dawn,* asks: "Did

spring of 1943. General Crerar denied making him the scapegoat and official histories say there was no connection. But Roberts said "my active career was certainly finished" at Dieppe. He never got another field command.

Just as Roberts was not allowed to forget Dieppe, so Canada could never forget. This is the World War II battle for which Canadians are best remembered. Not for Ortona or the Scheldt, not for Falaise or the Hochwald or the Hitler Line or the Rhine—not even for Normandy's D-Day

the failure at Dieppe contribute in itself to the success of the Normandy landing in June 1944? Would success that day at Dieppe have deprived us of many valuable lessons and led to failure afterward? Was, in fact, failure necessary?

General Crerar had no doubt. "If Dieppe had been a success," he said years later, "the Allied invasion would have been launched far too soon, with inadequate preparations, and I think it would have been a disaster. Dieppe saved us from that."

Closeup:

Rebel of the skies

We seemed to have blown right into the middle of hell. You knew you'd come to a war that was running 24 hours a day. Bombs were liable to come whistling around your ears any minute. You'd see fighter planes all over the sky, and every once in a while some poor devil spinning down in flames. From the ground, you heard the din of ack-ack (anti-aircraft fire), up high the clatter of machine-gun and cannon bursts. You saw erks (ground crew) scurrying about, patching bomb craters in the tarmac, engineers detonating time bombs, rescue launches rushing to sea to pick up floating parachutists. Never a dull moment, day or night. That was Malta in the blitzes.
"BUZZ" BEURLING *in Malta Spitfire*

From late 1940 to late 1942 the island of Malta stood alone, under siege, defying the German and Italian forces that dominated the Mediterranean. Britain hoped to thwart their domination by using the island as a base from which bomber and torpedo squadrons could attack convoys supplying the enemy armies in North Africa. These air and sea strikes proved disastrous to the Axis and, in October 1941, Hitler ordered his planes to bomb Malta into rubble.

Among the besieged island's defenders were Canadian airmen attached to the RAF. By the summer of 1942, never less than one fighter pilot in four was a Canadian, and the most colorful and controversial of them all was 20-year-old George Beurling from Verdun, Que. Beurling had two nicknames, "Buzz" and "Screwball," and, as Edmund Cosgrove wrote in *Canada's Fighting Pilots*, when fellow fliers "called him 'Screwball' it was sometimes in friendship but more often in anger tinged with envy. He was the greatest fighter pilot Canada produced, a lonely, tragic figure who could anger superiors and antagonize wingmates. 'He was a very difficult man to understand—he got your back up,' said a pilot who flew with him. But Air Vice-Marshal C. M. 'Black Mike' McEwen called him 'a man without ambition for promotion who just wanted to do the things he did best, fly and fight.' "

Beurling's days of glory began on June 9, 1942, when he flew to Takali airport on Malta from a British aircraft carrier off the Algerian coast. For the next five months, he fought victoriously in the skies over the island, downing 29 enemy planes. Later, after he'd become a national hero back home, he would say he'd give up 10 years of his life to relive those months. As he said when George VI presented him with four medals for his combat achievements in Malta, "I enjoyed every minute of it." But Beurling's fate was that he would never find in peace a challenge to match his wartime experiences.

The son of highly religious parents, Beurling could quote the Bible at length, but what he wanted to do most of all was fly an airplane. As Edmund Cosgrove wrote:
. . . When other teenagers dated, he studied a preflight manual. Even boyhood hunting contributed to his deadly skill as a fighter pilot. "I was always thinking of angles of fire," he once explained. The flight of a bird before his shotgun taught him to lead a target and make lightning calculations on speed and trajectory.

He first flew at nine when a pilot at an airport near his home took him up in exchange for doing chores around the hangars. He built and sold model aircraft and spent the money on flying lessons. He first took the controls of a plane at 14 and soloed at 16. He received his pilot's license just before the war and qualified for a commercial license—which was refused because he was considered too young.

When the war started the RCAF turned Beurling down for lack of education—he had a year to go to complete high school—so he planned to enlist with the Chinese Air Force to fight Japan. He got to the United States but was picked up for illegal entry and sent home. Then he tried to get to Finland to fly in its war against Russia but his parents refused permission. Again he tried the RCAF and was refused. Then he hit on the RAF. He heard the Chilean cargo vessel *Valparaiso* needed sailors. Submarines sank seven ships in her convoy but she made it to Scotland, and Beurling hurried to an RAF recruiting office.

"Sorry, son, but you haven't even got your birth certificate," an officer told him. Beurling crossed the Atlantic two more times, came back with the certificate he needed.

"You again!" the RAF officer said, and signed him up immediately . . .

EDMUND COSGROVE

During training, Beurling fell in love with the Spitfire. But when he was posted to a fighter squadron he was soon at odds with his fellow pilots. Cosgrove's words: "In the era of team flying, he flew and fought best as an ardent individualist." He shot down two planes but was accused of breaking formation to do it. Ostracized, frustrated, he asked for a transfer—and ended up in Malta.

Brian Nolan in *Hero, the "Buzz" Beurling Story:*
. . . He was assigned to Takali, a dusty airfield in the middle of an island. When he first landed there were so many bomb craters it seemed as if he were about to touch down on the moon. But there was a frontier atmosphere about the place that Beurling found exciting.

P. B. "Laddie" Lucas, his flight commander in the RAF's 249 squadron, was warned that he was trouble, that "he gets separated from the squadron." But when Lucas called him in, he took a liking to this man with the strange gentle smile and the penetrating ice-blue eyes: "I felt I was in the presence of a very unusual young man . . . champing at the bit to have a go."

Lucas warned Beurling not to repeat his lone-wolf tactics, and sent him into battle. A week later he asked the pilot assigned to fly as a two-man team with Beurling how they were getting on. "God Almighty," was the reply, "he's quick and he's got the most marvelous eyes, but he's a hell of a chap when it comes to keeping up with us."

Lucas immediately called for Beurling. At the interview, the pilot began to speak candidly of how he despised sticking to formation: "I'm a loner, and I've got to play it that way." Lucas exploded: "You've got to stick to the guy you're flying with. That's why we're alive. If you let me down, you're on the next goddam airplane out of here."

Beurling sensed this was no idle threat. "Boss," he said slowly, "that's good enough for me." Within a month of this showdown, he had become a legend.

As his score mounted, other pilots grew eager to know what made this strange man so deadly. There were many reasons. Everyone who ever flew with Beurling knew he possessed "super vision." He almost always spotted the enemy before anyone else. Few fighter pilots could match his shooting skill, and his airmanship was just as impressive. He was a "natural" pilot who kept his moves to a minimum in combat.

On July 6 his score of three hits took a dramatic turn. He was aboard one of eight Spitfires that were scrambled to intercept three Italian Cant bombers and 30 Macchi 202s, Italy's top fighter. The Spitfires dived straight into the formation from 20,000 feet. Beurling opened fire, damaging a bomber. Then suddenly he was on the tail of a Macchi whose pilot, spotting him, plunged into a dive. Beurling chased him for 15,000 feet and when the Italian pulled up at 5000 feet Beurling let go a two-second burst from 300 yards. It was a perfect hit.

Although he wasn't aware that he himself had been fired on, when Beurling inspected his plane at Takali, he found it riddled with bullets. Before the day ended he bagged a second Macchi and that same evening in failing light he fired one shot at a German Messerschmitt fighter which plunged into the sea. His total for the day was four, and it was only the beginning of his fame.

July 27 was another memorable day. In a morning sortie he dispatched two Macchis and a Messerschmitt, and damaged a third plane. Gassed and rearmed, he was soon back in the air again, this time to take on 20 Messerschmitts. At 17,000 feet, moving like a cattle wrangler, he herded two of them out of the pack, drove them down to 1000 feet and blasted one into the sea, leaving the second streaming smoke.

But by now Beurling was losing weight rapidly. Weakened by the tension of battle and the lack of proper diet, he collapsed with a case of dysentery which left him incapacitated. As he lay in his bunk, a signal from London ordered him to do something he had refused to do: accept an officer's commission. He didn't feel like an officer, he'd said, but now he received the honor in silence, too weak to protest.

By September Beurling's weight was down from 175 to 125 pounds, and he was skeletal and gaunt. But he insisted on flying. He seemed to be everywhere, hair all over the place, eyes glinting, a frightening sight. By October he was talking constantly, one of the first symptoms of battle fatigue.

October 14 dawned as another apparently routine day. At 1300 hours the scramble order came. Today's show was to the east where 50 fighters and 8 bombers were headed in. In the melee Beurling bagged three German planes, but made the mistake of forgetting his own tail. Suddenly his Spitfire was rocked with cannon hits, and shrapnel struck his ribs, left heel and leg. His controls shattered, the aircraft pitching into a 16,000-foot plunge, Beurling was certain he was going to die. But at 2000 feet, with flames engulfing the cockpit, he managed to crawl out onto the wing and at 500 feet pulled the rip cord of his parachute and floated to the sea.

When a rescue launch reached him, he was sitting in his rubber dinghy in a pool of blood. Surgeons removed as much shrapnel as they could and patched him up, but he had lost part of the heel, a wound that would plague him for the rest of his life.

His remarkable odyssey on Malta was over . . .   BRIAN NOLAN

Ottawa had asked that he be sent home to take part in a recruiting campaign and a war bond drive. En route, he was aboard a Liberator bomber, one leg in a cast, when he had one more close shave. The plane hit a thunderstorm as it neared Gibraltar, and Beurling sensed danger. He hobbled to an escape hatch, and as the plane crashed into the sea, he jumped. Despite the heavy cast on his leg, he swam 160 yards to safety.

In Canada, he was lionized from coast to coast. In his home town, 10,000 people packed a rink to cheer him repeatedly, but when the time came for him to speak he said, "This is no place for me. I'm a fighter pilot, not a speech-maker." When 29 young girls each gave him a red rose—one for each of his kills—they may have awakened memories of an episode that had haunted him since leaving Malta. His eyes had met those of an Italian pilot just before Beurling blew his head off and saw blood stream red down the side of the cockpit. At times he would joke about it but, said his brother, it left him with nightmares that made him "cry all night."

At his own request, his Canadian tour over, Beurling was transferred to the RCAF, then was posted to one of its squadrons in England. He was glad to be back in operations, but it just didn't work out. He shot down one plane but broke out of formations, grew sour and uncommunicative, and defied orders three times by flying too low. He was shifted to a different squadron, shot down another plane, but found flying in support of lumbering American bombers an unsatisfactory substitute for freewheeling Malta-style combat. In March 1944 he proposed that he become a sort of airborne privateer, be given three wingmates who would fly protective shotgun for him as a lone ranger in a long-range Mustang fighter. He was turned down, and three months later resigned from the RCAF.

The war went on without him. He married, and that didn't work out either. Nor did the peace. He tried several things. None amounted to much. He wanted to be a fighter pilot in China's civil war but was refused a visa. "Combat is the only thing I can do well," he'd say. "The only thing I ever really liked." In 1948 he was offered the opportunity to find another Malta.

He made arrangements to fight for the new state of Israel against the Arabs who wanted it killed at birth. Brian Nolan:

. . . In Rome on Thursday, May 20, he was to take a Canadian-built Norseman freighter on a practice flight prior to his departure for Israel. He was paired with Leonard Cohen who had also served in Malta as an RAF pilot. They made two circuits of the airfield, then banked to come in for a landing. The plane was 300 feet from the ground when a flicker appeared along the bottom of the fuselage. It became a sheet of flame. The plane was seen to turn violently toward the Tiber River. It didn't make it. As the wheels kissed the ground, flames engulfed the fuselage. There was a thunderous explosion.

"Buzz" Beurling had walked away from crashes in the past. This time he had run out of luck . . .

153

Special duty at the War Office

With a courage denied most men, secret agents like Guy Bieler and Frank Pickersgill obey Winston Churchill's order to "set Europe ablaze"

On the evening of November 10, 1942, a black-haired little man of five feet seven strode up the walk to a red-brick house in the London suburb of Ewell, as he had done many times before. He was Gustave "Guy" Bieler, a captain in Montreal's le Régiment de Maisonneuve. The house, his *pied-à-terre* since his arrival in Britain in September 1940, was the home of his sister Madelaine (Mrs. Hartas Dale).

For some months Bieler had been "on special duty at the War Office"—that's all he would say. "He wasn't allowed to talk and my husband and I knew it," Mrs. Dale said years later, "so we didn't ask any questions. But I'd guessed, even when he'd been in uniform. That night in November, for the first time, he wore civilian clothes. I looked in his overcoat and there was no indication of where it had been made. That was the kind of thing that happened when people went to occupied France, and I guessed this was a last visit."

Mrs. Dale cooked her brother a meal and when he left he said casually, "See you soon." A month later, the War Office sent her Captain Bieler's suitcase for safekeeping. "In it," she said, "was a map of Paris. And a poppy. I took this to mean Guy had left England on Remembrance Day, November 11, and was in or near Paris. Now I was *certain* he'd gone to France as some kind of secret agent."

Her guess was a good one. Bieler was working for Britain's Special Operations Executive (SOE), a secret and unorthodox organization whose job was to coordinate Resistance operations in occupied Europe with Allied strategic needs, to sabotage and to train and arm patriots to strike when invasion came. SOE had a single basic order from Winston Churchill: "Set Europe ablaze."

To accept that order was to face extraordinary danger; an enemy agent in disguise was liable under international law to be executed if caught, and the Germans used their own brutal interpretation of the law. If trapped by the dreaded Gestapo or SS, an agent could expect torture first, then lonely and often barbaric death in concentration camps like Buchenwald, Dachau or Flossenbürg.

Of 480 agents SOE sent to France, 130 were captured—and only 26 of those survived. Twenty-eight of its agents came from the Canadian Army: Guy Bieler, Frank Pickersgill, Gabriel Chartrand, Roger Caza, François Deniset, John Macalister, Roméo Sabourin. . . . Many details of the experiences of these and other agents have never been disclosed. Men who lived by secrecy committed little to writing—and destroyed records as soon as the war was over. Some still insist the story must remain secret.

It is known, however, that several score Canadians of various racial strains were Resistance organizers, wireless operators, arms instructors and saboteurs. They saw duty in the Balkans, North Africa, the Dodecanese Islands, the Far East—but mainly in France. Of the 28 Canadian Army men who went to France, eight died.

Guy Bieler was the first of these to leave England. The day his sister got his suitcase he *was* in Paris, as she'd guessed, with a crippling spine injury suffered when he parachuted from an RAF bomber. His Resistance contacts wanted to signal SOE to send a small plane to a secret rendezvous and fly him back to England. Bieler refused. He was determined to do the job he'd come to do. And he did, with distinction and a rare courage that makes Frenchmen still talk of him with awe.

Bieler was born in France of Swiss parents and came to Canada in 1924 at the age of 20. Thoroughly bilingual, he taught school in Pointe-aux-Trembles, near Montreal, and later became chief of translation for the Sun Life Assurance Company of Canada. He was a quiet, pipe-smoking man who played the piano, liked practical jokes and loved canoeing. He preferred casual clothes and, his friends say, had a comfortable, lived-in look about him.

He joined the University of Montreal contingent of the Canadian Officers Training Corps in 1939 and was given a commission in le Régiment de Maisonneuve in June 1940. Three months later he said good-by to his wife and two children and went overseas.

In time, Bieler became the Maisonneuves' intelligence officer. This led to contacts at the War Office and a chance meeting with Col. Maurice J. Buckmaster, head of SOE's French Section. Buckmaster soon persuaded Bieler to join SOE. He left the Maisonneuves June 4, 1942, and was sent to Wanborough Manor, SOE's "preparatory school" in Surrey. There he underwent four weeks' basic training and a going-over by psychologists and sergeants.

In this red-brick Tudor mansion near Guildford, classes were in French and trainees were bidden to behave as Frenchmen in France. They were under constant observation: Could they hold their liquor? Were they argumentative after a few drinks? What irritated them? What put them off guard? When surprised, did they exclaim in French or English? When suddenly awakened, what did they say and in what language? If they talked in their sleep, was it in French or English?

At 38, by far the oldest member of his class, Bieler was affectionately called "Granddad." But Wanborough's CO found him "the best student we've had. He is conscientious, keen, intelligent, a sound judge of character; good-natured, absolutely reliable, outstandingly thorough, a born organizer."

Next, in Scotland, came a month of "silent killing," knife work, boat work, rope work, pistol and machine-gun training, fieldcraft, map-reading, elementary Morse. Then parachute training near Manchester and advanced training near Beaulieu in Britain's southern New Forest. Bieler was taught the importance of looking natural and ordinary while doing unnatural and extraordinary things. He learned how to spot a follower, when to change an address, how to conceal a personality. He was interrogated roughly by Beaulieu staffers dressed in German uniforms.

Gabriel Chartrand, a friend of Bieler's, was accepted for SOE training about the time Bieler completed his. He found Bieler a hard man to follow: "The CO at Wanborough told me, 'If you're half as good as Guy, you'll be magnificent.' He'd made a fantastic impression. Everywhere I was told, 'Guy was here,' and there was a sort of awe about the way they said it 'Guy,' of course, was all they knew him by: he'd adopted his nickname as his code name."

Bieler was the one agent everyone at every SOE school felt would be superb in the field. Vera Atkins, Buckmaster's chief assistant, briefed him on conditions he'd find in France—curfews, restricted zones,

rationing, documents. She remembered him for "his mature outlook, his calm, kindness, poise and beautiful voice." Guy, she said, was "a man among boys."

Placide Labelle, then with Canadian Army public relations in Britain, knew Bieler briefly during leaves in London. "He was pretty hot on grammar and syntax," said Labelle. "We'd have a beer in a pub and talk about the differences between Anglo-Saxon and French thinking, and how the French people had evolved differently in Canada and Switzerland and Belgium. He loved language and history. He'd talk about how English was influenced by Latin through French, how calf became *veau* and then veal, and sheep

Lt. Gustave "Guy" Bieler of le Régiment de Maisonneuve during the Canadian Army's long wait in Britain. He volunteered to serve with Special Operations Executive and in November 1942 he parachuted into France.

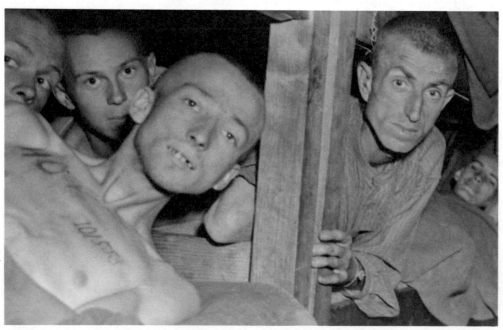

became *mouton* and finally mutton. Language fascinated him."

After the November 10 visit to his sister in Ewell, Bieler went to an SOE "operational holding school" and on November 18, when the weather was right, to an airfield for his flight to France. He knew what he was getting into: against the Gestapo and SS, he told Chartrand, "we probably have a 50-50 chance of coming out alive."

"He was a fatalist," said Chartrand, "the kind who says, 'I'm going to die the day I'm going to die.' But he believed in the importance of man, the *grandeur* of man. I told him once, 'Guy, we're 'way on in our 30s; we could have stayed home.' He looked at me and said very simply, 'You *cannot* permit what these Germans are doing to spread.' Then he said something more: 'I have people in France, don't forget—my brother and others. I'm a soldier and I'm here because I want to help save people from being pushed around.' "

Bieler could tell no one any details of his work but he wrote to his wife Marguerite in Montreal: "It will be my great fortune and privilege, I think, to see the very best in men." He knew, but didn't say, that he might also see the worst.

Two other men parachuted into France with Bieler: Capt. Michael A. Trotobas, an Anglo-Frenchman ten years younger than he, and an English wireless operator,

Lt. A. A. G. Staggs. Trotobas and Staggs were to establish a sabotage circuit at Lille. Bieler was to do the same at St. Quentin, a city of 60,000 about 80 miles north and east of Paris. But he was to do it alone. SOE's shortage of wireless operators was severe; Bieler would have to communicate with London through other agents' operators.

He and Trotobas were to fight their clandestine war deep in pro-British, anti-German northeast France, a main battlefield of World War I. Their zone was from Armentières, near the Belgian border, south to Soissons and Senlis, astride railway lines that would be vital to German supply when the invasion came. Railways would be their main targets, railwaymen their chief helpers.

Trotobas, Staggs and Bieler parachuted to earth about 65 miles south of Paris—it was too risky to land in the more heavily defended northeast. Bieler landed on rocky ground and suffered a bad back injury. For hours he lay helpless, but Trotobas and Staggs eventually got him to Paris and the "safe house" of 74-year-old Mme Marie-Louise Monnet. He hid there for months, in intense pain. But he made contact with many Resistance people, among them his brother René-Maurice. He and his Czech-born wife Mania had joined the movement early in 1942 and, like Madame Monnet, took great risks to shelter SOE agents.

On April 7 Guy felt strong enough to travel to St. Quentin. Word had been sent to a middle-aged land surveyor named Eugène Cordelette and he met him at the railway station. Cordelette found Bieler in "a precarious state of health," limping badly. Together they walked the eight miles to Cordelette's house in the village of Fonsomme, Guy leaning heavily on the older man's arm.

"He was a week without going out," recalled Madame Cordelette, an incurious woman who guessed her husband was "involved" but never presumed to ask.

After that week's rest, Guy went to work. Wearing the blue trousers and jacket of a workman, he sat at a table under a tree behind Cordelette's house, soaking up the strengthening sun of April, recruiting men and building his network—*le réseau* "Tell"—into a strong, aggressive force. Bieler's strength slowly returned but he remained handicapped: he walked with his head to one side and one shoulder slightly hunched because of his pain.

Bieler got in touch with officials of the French National Railways to select targets. He received 16 parachute deliveries of arms and explosives and soon 25 Tell teams armed with submachine guns went to war as saboteurs. They destroyed a German troop train, derailed 20 other trains, damaged 20 locomotives with abrasive grease, wrecked an engine repair shop and 11 other locomotives and cut the Paris-Cologne rail line 13 times. They were hurting the Germans greatly and the French not at all, if they could help it.

"Air bombing of railways," said Cordelette, "sometimes severely tried the civilian population. Guy asked that destruction of railway lines be entrusted to saboteurs. On

One name Bieler used was Maurice Alfred Léger (identity card, opposite page). With Eugène Cordelette (above) he built a sabotage network at St. Quentin. Weapons and ammunition came in canisters (left) dropped from aircraft. SOE equipment (extreme left) included: (1) radio receiver, (2) transceiver, (3) switchblade knife, (4) shortwave transmitter, (5) silk map, (6) silent gun, (7) compasses, one in a collar stud, (8) lapel knife. Agents like Bieler knew capture would mean torture, concentration camp (left, bottom) and almost certain execution.

one occasion, to avoid loss of civilian lives, he refused to blow up an important munitions train on a siding near many houses. He made up for this by having another munitions convoy blown up in the uninhabited countryside."

The testimony of those who knew Bieler in France shows that he became a deeply loved and respected man. He was careful, deliberate, thorough—but lonely, a lonely man doing an intensely lonely job. Nobody—not Cordelette, not even Trotobas up in Lille, whom he saw occasionally—knew he was Guy *Bieler*. Just *le commandant Guy,* the stranger-leader with the hunched shoulder, a man who loved Beethoven records and sometimes shyly showed snapshots of a faraway wife and children.

For Madame Cordelette *le commandant Guy* was a calm and deliberate man who

seemed to take in stride whatever life handed him. He smiled a lot, she said, and his conversation in her hearing was about unimportant things. He traveled by bicycle most of the time but sometimes went by train to Paris.

Ben Cowburn, an agent who knew Bieler in Paris, remembered him talking about the problem of names: should he use a common name like Dupont or an unusual one? A common name got you into trouble because the police were always looking for someone called Dupont and you'd get rounded up by mistake. But if you used an unusual name, it would stick in people's minds. Either way was dangerous.

One name Bieler used was Guy Morin—an in-between name like Charles Jackson or Peter Walker. He also had a card identifying him as Maurice Alfred Léger, four

years older than he really was, and describing him as five feet seven or eight, with dark hair, brown eyes and oval face.

The Germans didn't know who Bieler was, or where he was. But each new act of sabotage brought them closer to the SOE agents causing so much trouble. The Gestapo got Trotobas in November—shot him to death in a dawn gunfight in Lille. Bieler plunged into deep despair but, overworked and exhausted though he was, he helped keep Trotobas' Lille network going.

By now Bieler had a wireless operator of his own—"Mariette," a 32-year-old Anglo-Swiss woman whose real name was Yolande Beekman. They made an effective team: Mariette received and transmitted, Guy did the encoding and decoding. He shared with no one the contents of messages from SOE in London; nor did he disclose the wider implication of Tell's acts of sabotage.

Few of Fonsomme's 450 people were curious about Guy, even though he had no job and came and went at all hours, sometimes being absent a day or two or a week. Nobody asked where he'd been and he volunteered no information.

Bieler and Yolande spent Christmas Eve 1943 with Resistance man Camille Boury and his wife at the Bourys' house in St. Quentin.

"Guy arrived," said Boury, "carrying two Santa Clauses stuffed with candy for our children and under each arm a few good bottles. We listened to the BBC messages from London and then the wonderful Christmas music. We had the traditional pine tree. Guy recited to us (as he could so well) the beautiful poetry of Verhaeren and Victor Hugo. We sang Canadian and French choruses.

"At midnight, the moment of Christmas, we were suddenly quiet and Guy put his head in both hands for a long time. When he finally looked up he seemed quite overcome. He asked for a pencil and on the back of a photograph he wrote, 'Chief, French Dept., Sun Life Assurance Company, Dominion Square, Montreal.'

"Then he said to us, 'If misfortune overtakes me, write to this address. You will find my wife there. Tell her how I spent Christmas. Describe this evening to her. Tell her how I thought of them.'"

Then Bieler did what he had done many times. "His greatest pleasure," said Boury, "was to go and look at my little boy and girl sleeping. They never saw him for he did not want them to be able to chatter. (We had to take so many precautions against the accursed Gestapo.) Each time he could, he went to see them asleep. He stood there in the darkness that night and puffed on his pipe in a way we remember so well, and we felt that seeing our children in some way helped him think of his own boy and girl with greater intensity."

Bieler's mood was rooted in more than homesickness. By that Christmas the Germans were getting very close. London didn't know this, but Bieler and Yolande Beekman and Cordelette certainly did, and they almost certainly knew why. "More casualties are caused," an SOE security officer had warned, "by detection of wireless operators than by penetration by *agents provocateurs*." Every message Yolande sent tightened the noose.

In October, she had started transmitting from the attic of Mlle Odette Gobeaux's house in St. Quentin. One day in December a German car with wireless-detection and direction-finding equipment passed by and it was decided to move the wireless to Boury's. On January 11, 1944, a man was seen in the street outside Boury's house, his collar turned up and what looked like earphones on his head. Three days later Guy and Yolande were at le Café du Moulin Brûlé, with the proprietors, Georges Tixier and his wife. Two Gestapo cars pulled up

Bieler's *réseau* "Tell" destroyed a German troop train, derailed 20 other trains, damaged many locomotives and cut the Paris-Cologne rail line 13 times. Georges Tixier (above, with Madame Tixier) ran the café where Bieler was arrested. Tixier died in Buchenwald; his wife survived concentration camp. Bieler (right, with his son Jean-Louis) knew by Christmas 1943 that the Gestapo was closing in on him.

and a dozen men rushed in. "We were all taken away," said Madame Tixier. "I never saw them again." There were many more arrests in St. Quentin. Altogether more than 40 members of the Tell network were arrested and 26 were eventually executed.

It was 19 months since Guy Bieler had started "special duty at the War Office" and 14 months since his parachute drop and crippling injury.

That night, in a corridor of the St. Quentin prison, Cordelette saw him being taken from the first of a long series of brutal Gestapo interrogations. "He was chained hand and foot," said Cordelette. "His face was horribly swollen but I could read in his eyes this order: 'Whatever happens, don't talk.'"

There were ground rules about talking. Some agents were less able than others to stand interrogation by ruthless German secret police. "The understood rule," wrote M. R. D. Foot in *SOE in France,* "was to hold out, say nothing, for 48 hours. During that time all people who had been in contact with the arrested agent were supposed to move and cover their tracks. When the two days were past, the agent was at liberty to say what he liked if the pressures were no longer bearable. The best died silent or, if they had to talk, said nothing the enemy wanted to hear."

Cordelette didn't talk. Nor did the man he knew as *le commandant Guy.* "In spite of all torments," said Cordelette, "he showed no weakness."

Bieler's torments lasted for months. He was moved from prison to prison for one interrogation after another. In April he was sent to an extermination camp at Flossenbürg in Bavaria, battered but not broken, determined to survive. At this same time, in other prisons, another Canadian was fighting for his life too. He was Frank Pickersgill of Winnipeg, a scholarly six-footer who talked in English or French of philosophy, religion, history and the arts. He was in his mid-20s, a student at the Sorbonne in Paris, when the war started. He was a cynic then; "I suspect," he had written in July 1939, "that it will be war this time. It has ceased to have any connection with democracy or any other ideological considerations and it's just a naked question of interest. As a Canadian I feel like sneering." He was captured by the Germans in 1940 and interned near Paris

for 15 months. He escaped and was trapped for many months in Vichy France. In October 1942, as a noncombatant with a deaf ear, he was permitted to leave. In Lisbon he received joyful cables from his brother Jack, assistant to Prime Minister Mackenzie King, entreating him to return to Canada. But Frank by now had seen too much of German methods. His cynicism was gone.

"I'm afraid," he replied, "that I'm in the war up to the neck. There are certain jobs I can do better than others." He flew to London and in November, the month Bieler parachuted into France, was commissioned in the Canadian Army and seconded to SOE. His radio operator was John Macalister, a 29-year-old Canadian Rhodes Scholar. They were to set up a network near Sedan, on the Franco-Belgian border.

SOE's main Paris network, "Prosper," in its eagerness to prepare for a possible Allied landing in the summer of 1943, had expanded greatly—and soon would pay a

The Gestapo (opposite) caught Frank Pickersgill (above), and his radio operator, John Macalister, only days after they dropped into France in June 1943. Another Canadian, Maj. J. R. "Ray" Wooler, was for 18 months chief instructor at the SOE parachute school near Manchester, England. He made 201 training jumps in Britain and North Africa, another 35 in Southeast Asia. His 237th jump was behind the Japanese lines in Borneo in 1944. Many Canadian airmen risked their lives to deliver weapons and ammunition to agents in France.

heavy price for indiscretion and bad luck. Pickersgill and Macalister would pay for it too. By the spring of 1943, the Gestapo was hot on Prosper's trail.

Real trouble, wrote M. R. D. Foot in *SOE in France,* blew up in the second half of June:

. . . On the night of the 15th, Pickersgill and Macalister were parachuted to a subcircuit in the Cher valley north of Valençay. They stayed a few days with agents Pierre Culioli and Yvonne Rudellat and on June 21 all four set off by car to catch a train for Paris. In the village of Dhuizon they were arrested.

Three nights later, the Germans made some still more important arrests and decapitated the Prosper circuit. The Canadians had brought with them several messages for other agents, which the London staff had been trusting enough to send in English, addressed to each agent by his field name. Culioli had done these up in a parcel addressed to a fictitious prisoner of war in Germany. The Germans found the parcel in the car, and many arrests followed. Into the bag went several hundred members of various circuits in and around Paris, substantial quantities of parachuted arms and two wireless sets—one of them Macalister's—complete with codes. For ten months the Germans ran four *Funkspiele* (wireless games) with captured transmitters, leading London to believe various smashed networks were still operating. In one unlucky month several agents were dropped to three different Gestapo-controlled circuits. Two had been enemy-operated for five months; the third—"Archdeacon"—the subcircuit Pickersgill and Macalister were to have set up—had never worked in the Allied interest at all.

The Germans had not only Macalister's radio set and codes but also the correct security checks, presumably because Macalister had written them down. They discovered what Archdeacon's area was to have been. A German policeman, Joseph Placke, who spoke good French and a little English, toured the area impersonating Pickersgill and formed a number of reception committees of genuine French resisters. Fifteen large drops of stores were made to this bogus circuit during the ten months London believed it to be flourishing. Placke's Frenchmen did not know that the trucks he provided to remove the stores were driven by Germans in plain clothes. . . .

One of six agents dropped to Placke's bogus Archdeacon was Roméo Sabourin, a Canadian. He and another agent parachuted the night of March 2-3, 1944. In a moonlight gunfight near the field where they landed, they killed two Germans but were wounded and taken prisoner. Neither was any use to the enemy but Sabourin's capture helped tip London to the Pickersgill-Macalister disaster. When neither Sabourin nor another operator who had jumped that month came on the air with prearranged messages to indicate they were safe, SOE headquarters at last became suspicious. E. H. Cookridge in *Inside SOE:*

. . . London signaled that an SOE officer would fly over a certain field and try to contact Pickersgill in person by S-phone from the aircraft. The Gestapo, not even sure Pickersgill was alive, asked Berlin to locate him and return him to Paris. But when London repeated the order to Pickersgill, the Gestapo could stall no longer. A radio expert, von Kapri, and Placke were sent to the rendezvous. From the plane Maj. Gerry Morel of SOE called over the S-phone. Von Kapri replied in French, then Placke in English. Morel concluded neither voice was Pickersgill's and the aircraft flew off. As a final check, London sent a signal with personal news of Pickersgill's family. It required an answer but, without eliciting information from Pickersgill, the Germans could not reply.

The sick, emaciated Canadian was extracted from the mass of "subhumans" in a concentration camp at Rawicz in Poland. In Paris the Gestapo promised him he would spend the rest of the war in comfortable detention if he cooperated. So enraged was Pickersgill by the proposition that he grabbed a bottle from his interrogator's desk, attacked his guard and ran into a corridor.

There he met two SS men, aimed the broken bottle at the neck of one, severed his jugular vein and killed him. The other was so badly slashed that he died two days later in hospital. Pickersgill jumped from a second-floor window and ran, with SS men in pursuit. Hit by four bullets, he was recaptured. . . .

On August 8, 1944, two weeks before the liberation of Paris, Pickersgill and Macalister and 35 other Resistance prisoners were shipped to Germany. Among them were Sabourin, the 20-year-old Canadian

who had been captured when he landed, and Wing Comdr. F. F. E. Yeo-Thomas, a Briton who was one of SOE's best agents.

"Pickersgill and Macalister," said Yeo-Thomas, "were in the worst shape. Pickersgill was in agony from his wounds."

Wrote McKenzie Porter in *Maclean's:*

. . . On August 18 they reached notorious Buchenwald. All around were men shambling blindly through the dust, holding out empty bowls like beggars, staggering away from snapping dogs. In this nightmare, according to Yeo-Thomas, Pickersgill seemed possessed of superhuman spirit. When a ragged section went to draw rations, Pickersgill would march at its head, chin up, shoulders back, singing. His followers would be too miserable to fall into step or take up the refrain. Then the poignant loneliness of Pickersgill's bearing and voice would shame them and they too would march and sing.

Buchenwald rules said every military prisoner should salute all German officers.

On sighting an officer, Pickersgill would order his section to disperse behind huts. When the officer had passed, he would re-form the section and march on. Thus, said Yeo-Thomas, "Pick helped our men to hang on to the last shreds of their pride."

Fifteen of the 37 prisoners were executed September 6. Three days later another 16, among them Pickersgill, Macalister and Sabourin, were summoned. They fell in in threes, with Pickersgill at the head of one file. At his command they marched off, a forlorn little band trying to march like guardsmen. Pickersgill, a cracked husk of a man, but unbroken, limped and occasionally staggered as his unhealed wounds, malnutrition and slight deafness combined to unsteady him.

He began beating time. And back to the few remaining in the hut drifted the quavering notes of "Madelon"—for a Frenchman who marched at Pickersgill's side. And "Alouette" for Sabourin. And, for Yeo-Thomas (who was soon to escape by

assuming the identity of a dead prisoner), "Tipperary."

That night the marchers were thrashed and flung into a bunker. An emaciated French priest was refused permission to administer the last sacraments to the Roman Catholics. He prayed all night outside the bunker and managed, via a guard who began to show a sense of shame, to slip wafers of the Sacred Host to the captives.

The following night the 16 were taken to the crematorium. Once more the priest knelt outside and prayed. He heard scuffling noises and faint cries of *"Vive la France!" "Vive l'Angleterre!"* and *"Vive le Canada!"*—the cries of men being hung by hooks, men the Germans would let perish by slow strangulation. Their corpses were burned and the chimney belched smoke all night. . . . MCKENZIE PORTER

Guy Bieler's brother René-Maurice (left) was arrested, then fatally wounded in an Allied bombing raid. Twenty-six members of *le réseau* "Tell" were executed amid the despair and degradation of German concentration camps. The map shows Montargis, near where Bieler parachuted into France; Fonsomme and St. Quentin, the center of his *réseau's* activities, and Lille, where his friend Trotobas was slain in a gunfight. Also shown is Valençay, where Pickersgill and Macalister parachuted.

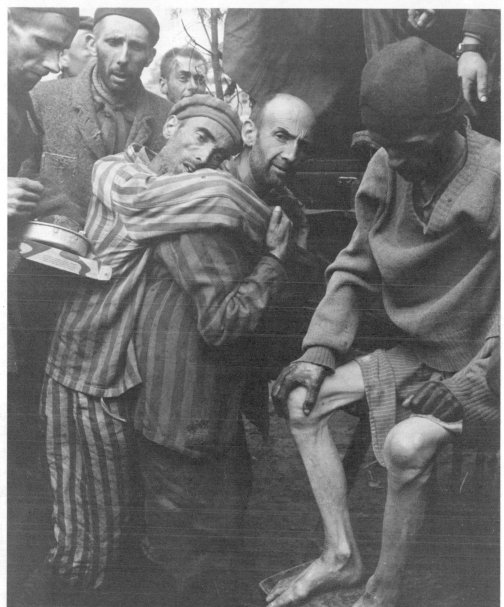

That same month—perhaps the same week—in the little Bavarian town of Flossenbürg, Guy Bieler was executed. Since April, he and 14 other British agents had been kept in solitary confinement in tiny windowless cells, denied exercise, writing materials and reading matter. Their diet: black ersatz coffee in the morning, soup at midday, bread and coffee at night. Most prisoners were eventually taken from their cells, led barefoot into a courtyard and hanged.

Bieler was in pitiful condition. A Danish officer who survived Flossenbürg said that torture, on top of his back injury, had wrecked him physically. But he had told nothing. His courage and dignity had so impressed the Germans that when the gaunt little man limped his last painful steps and went fearlessly to his death, he did not go alone—he was accompanied by an SS guard of honor.

They spared him gas or hanging. Guy Bieler stumbled to a wall in the prison courtyard and was shot. His body was cremated. "This is the only instance known to us," said Colonel Buckmaster, "of an officer being executed in such circumstances by a firing squad with a guard of honor."

The day Guy Bieler died, aged 40, his old regiment, the Maisonneuves, having helped close the Falaise Gap, were fighting not far from St. Quentin. Gaby Chartrand, who'd sneaked into France by Lysander plane in March 1943 and returned to Britain by motor torpedo boat in December after sabotage assignments around Rouen and in the Sarthe region, was back in France again, as an army censor.

Bieler's brother René-Maurice was dead, captured by the Gestapo and fatally wounded in an Allied bombing. René-Maurice's wife, Mania, was in a concentration camp. So were old Madame Monnet of the "safe house" in Paris and Madame Tixier of le Café du Moulin Brûlé. Georges Tixier was in Buchenwald and would die there. In another camp, Eugène Cordelette was barely alive.

About the time Bieler was killed at Flossenbürg, Yolande Beekman was being executed at Dachau. She and three other women agents, wrote M. R. D. Foot, "were called out into a sandy yard and told to kneel by a wall. They saw bloodstains in the sand and knew their fate. They knelt two and two, each pair holding hands; an SS man came up behind them and shot each of them neatly, through the back of the neck."

The people Bieler had gathered close to him were decimated. Yet his work and theirs went on. Despite the wholesale arrests, Tell had survived: men and explosives were poised at strategic places on the railways around St. Quentin, others with submachine guns were in position to attack road convoys, still others were ready to cut the Paris-Lille telephone. From D-Day on, they carried out their assignments.

One day in 1946, Guy Bieler's 11-year-old son Jean-Louis put on his Wolf Cub uniform and with his mother and sister went to Rideau Hall in Ottawa. There, from Governor-General Viscount Alexander, Mrs. Bieler received the DSO awarded posthumously to "this most valiant gentleman," her husband. Later, the son wrote a composition about the father he hardly remembered:

"After the war was over and the sound of the last shot faided out, the details of what this man had done started seeping out. . . ."

Quoting from the DSO citation, Jean-Louis described Guy Bieler's work in St. Quentin, his arrest, his imprisonment. Then he went on in his own words:

"He was dilivered from this treatment in Sept. of 1944 when he was taken into the camp yard and shot. . . He was awarded 11 medals. . . France awarded Major Bieler the highest award it can which was the Crois du Guare and the Distinguished Service Order is the second highest medal the King could award.

Briggs, were overwhelmed by the love felt for their father. They were shown, almost with reverence, where he had slept and where he had sat in the sun and built his *réseau*, where he was when the Germans rushed into the café. In the village of Bohain they found a war memorial bearing the names of the two Bohain men who died as prisoners of the Germans—and a third, the name of an honorary citizen of Bohain: "Cdt. Guy."

Mrs. Briggs said after her pilgrimage to the streets and fields where Tell thrived: "My heart is very full. To spend two weeks being loved by so many people is a great privilege. I think it is the most wonderful gift a father could leave his children."

Gabriel Chartrand, who calls Bieler "*the* great Canadian war hero," named his eldest son after him. And long after the war he said: "I still weep for Guy—not, mind you, that he would want me to. He told me once, 'Either you serve or you don't. If you do serve, you give it all you've got.'"

"In conclusion, I would ask you to remember that these men fought that others might live and so that you could be free, and not to forget our war Heros."

For those who had known Jean-Louis Bieler's father, there was no forgetting. The little town of Fonsomme, not knowing his full name, nonetheless called a street after him. In time the people did learn Guy was Guy Bieler—but left the street name as it was, rue du commandant Guy. Not only does Fonsomme have a rue du commandant Guy but St. Quentin and Morcourt both have a rue du commandant Guy Bieler, named after the liberation. In Canada too, his name is perpetuated: a lake on Baffin Island in the Arctic now is Bieler Lake.

On visits to St. Quentin long after the war, Bieler's son and daughter, Mrs. David

On a war memorial in Fonsomme:

> **39-45**
> **DALONGEVILLE Maurice**
> **FALENTIN Emile**
> **JOUBE Marcel**
> **MAROLLE Ambroise**
>
> **Cdt GUY**
>
> **GOSSOIN Simon**

And from his house at 25 rue du commandant Guy in Fonsomme, old Eugène Cordelette wrote: "No day passes without us speaking of him."

The beautiful agent

Sonia "Tony" Butt met Guy d'Artois (right, hatless, with cigarette, behind the German lines) at an SOE school in Britain. Some of the preparations for her mission are described by McKenzie Porter: She had forged identity and ration cards and would pose as the daughter of a French couple killed in a bombing raid. All records in the town where her fictitious parents were supposed to have lived were destroyed by the Maquis. She was given a bundle containing four frocks, two sports outfits, six pairs of silk stockings, wedge shoes and fluffy underwear, all made in France and in keeping with the upper-middle-class standards to which she supposedly had been raised. They also gave her 200,000 francs (at that time $4000). The bills were undetectable forgeries made by currency printers in England.

Canada had no woman secret agent of her own in World War II but did acquire one through a marriage in the Special Operations Executive (SOE) family. She was Sonia "Tony" Butt, a slender 19-year-old English blonde who had been educated in France and spoke French like a native. She became Mrs. Guy d'Artois just before she and her husband parachuted into France in 1944. A friend called her "a mixture of Jeanne d'Arc, Mata Hari and Mrs. Miniver."

In *Maclean's*, McKenzie Porter told of this "youngest and perhaps most beautiful secret agent" and the colorful Canadian Army captain she met in an SOE school:

... When they went to the parachute school near Manchester, they knew their training was nearly finished. For Guy, who'd won his paratrooper's wings before joining SOE, the jumping was easy. Sonia found it hairraising but never balked. As she was about to make her fifth and final practice jump she gave Guy a wicked wink. When they hit the ground Guy proposed and Sonia accepted.

They wanted to go to France together and, with the idea of clinching this, they married. It was the worst thing they could have

done. SOE's Col. Maurice J. Buckmaster informed them a joint mission was out of the question: the Germans would have no compunction about torturing them in front of each other for information. The lives of hundreds could be jeopardized.

A few days later Guy disappeared. Not long after, in April, Sonia jumped from a bomber—and dropped almost on top of a German truck convoy. But she quickly changed into an attractive sweater and skirt and the first German who came close shouted the equivalent of "Hiya, babe!"

By D-Day, around Le Mans, she and agent Christopher Hudson had trained a Maquis force of 500 men to cut telephone wires, blow up railway tracks, bridges, factory installations and locomotives, and to harass German troops. When U.S. troops entered Le Mans they found Maquisards

under Hudson and Sonia containing a German battalion defending an airfield. The two agents went under American command and were put to work interrogating prisoners. But they went behind the German lines again, posing as French collaborators.

Sonia was reunited with her husband at an advanced SOE headquarters in Paris. Guy d'Artois had commanded 3000 Maquisards near Lyon in central France and built the best communications system in the whole underground. Scores of secret switchboards in farmhouses had been connected by miles of telephone wire stolen from the Germans. Guy had kept tabs on German troop movements over a wide area and, able to phone orders at long range, had launched many effective attacks. . . .

Guy d'Artois is still remembered affectionately in places like Charolles, Cluny and Mâcon as *le Canadien*, a man of great courage who trained Frenchmen to use and maintain weapons sent from England.

Wrote Colonel Buckmaster:

... D'Artois traveled from farm to farm where arms were stored and held training sessions for more than 50 groups. It was too much to hope such an intensive program could continue undisturbed indefinitely and, soon after D-Day, when his work was virtually completed, he was ordered to leave the region.

His next assignment was in the center of France, in the path of German reinforcements straggling up through the ambushes of the Resistance to the Normandy battlefront. Here his task was to delay and harass troop concentrations; sever rail, road and telephone communications; inflict the short, sharp guerrilla attacks, then fade unseen into the landscape.

He was outstandingly successful and was awarded the DSO. Not only was his military prowess remarkable, but he had the good sense and good fortune to marry Tony Butt. . . .

The dark and bloody winter

The grimmest battles of the war's longest campaign are fought in the bitter North Atlantic

Here, 240 miles east of Cape Race, Nfld., the sea was calm in the black summer night. It was just after eleven o'clock; the moon wouldn't be up for another two hours. There had been a submarine attack earlier, and escort ships were hovering around two crippled merchantmen. The corvette *Sackville* was screening them. The convoy had made a 90 degree turn to starboard and gone on.

On *Sackville's* crowded bridge, seven men peered into the night. The captain, Alan Easton, thought for a moment of the pathetic sight of a hurt, stopped ship. It looked like a frightened animal, crouching, resigned to its fate. To a submarine commander, it had to be an inviting target. With two crippled ships in the vicinity, there might soon be another attack.

The captain heard the navigator acknowledge a report from the radar operator. In his book *50 North,* Easton later told what happened:

. . . "Radar contact red four-oh, mile and a quarter, sir."

"Hold it." I had my glasses on the dark water beyond the port bow. Then, to the man on the wheel: "Port 15. Steady on oh-three-five."

"Red one-oh, one mile," came a new report from radar. Ten degrees on the port bow.

"Steer oh-two-five."

"Object's small but getting larger," called the navigator, repeating the radar report.

"Can you see anything, Number One?" I asked.

"Not yet, sir," replied Black, the first lieutenant.

"Stand by for star shell," I said. Black passed the order.

"There it is! A bit to starboard! Submarine, I think, sir." I looked hard. Surely, I thought, that's a trawler. High in the bow and high aft. Then I realized that it wasn't her stern. She's high amidships. It's her bridge, her conning tower! Now I can see

her stern. It's low. It's a submarine! Beam on.

"Full ahead. Fire, Number One!"

After what seemed a long wait the star shell burst. There she was! The U-boat lay broadside on, 400 yards away. Her bow was pointing across our course. She had obviously just got underway and was working her propellers at full speed. I altered course five degrees to starboard. Was that enough? Too much? Was she diving? Yes.

"Fire again!"

The U-boat was barely a ship's length away. But only the upper part of her conning tower was showing.

"Stand by to ram!" Then: "Set pattern A." Back on the quarterdeck, men made the depth charges ready.

Our bow was almost in the luminous whirlpool where the U-boat conning tower had been, the great white wake showing the short straight course she had steered. She had had no time to turn before she dived and she could not dive and turn as well.

In three seconds the bow cut the disturbed water. I waited for the crash. Another 30 feet. The streak of foaming

water was beneath the gun deck now. I heard no grind of steel nor did I feel the keel touch. Now it was beneath the foremast.

"Fire!" The ship shook violently as our depth charges exploded.

I was shaking badly. I felt weak. My mouth was dry. I had failed even to hit her.

"How far have we gone since firing?"

"A thousand yards."

"I'll turn now and see if you can pick her up," I said to Collins, the asdic officer.

We turned and steamed back and Collins' detection gear reported underwater contact. We ran in and fired five more charges. A strong smell of diesel oil came to us, obviously from the U-boat. The torpedo officer appeared on the bridge, breathing fast.

"What are you doing here?" I asked. Why had he left his post when we were using depth charges?

"Finest thing I ever saw, sir! We're wasting ammunition now."

"What do you mean?"

"Didn't you see what happened on the first attack?" Then he told the story. The depth charge from the starboard thrower must have touched the U-boat as it exploded. The sub broke surface a few feet astern, rose to an angle of 40 degrees, exposing one third of her long slender hull. Her momentum was carrying her forward at right angles to our course. As she hung poised for an instant, a charge dropped over the stern rail exploded immediately beneath her and she disappeared in the

whole German Navy, called it: "Being as strong as possible in the right place at the right time. U-boats are the wolves of the sea: attack, tear, sink!"

The odds in the Atlantic were slowly changing in favor of the wolf packs. Since the end of World War I, Admiral Dönitz had believed that the best way to attack a convoy was to hit it with a large number of U-boats simultaneously, preferably on the

huge column of water. I heard a voice: "She'll never surface again, sir."

We resumed patrol.... ALAN EASTON

That happened on August 3, 1942, in the midst of a five-week period that saw Canada's destroyers and corvettes sink four U-boats, get credit for probably killing another and for damaging a sixth. It was a time of good hunting for the sheepdog navy. It was also a deceptive prelude.

The Battle of the Atlantic was shaping toward its greatest crisis. The U-boats' time of easy victories along the American seaboard was over. The Battle of the St. Lawrence was waning. Across the sea, in Britain's Western Approaches, planes and escort ships were punishing the German submarines as never before.

But in mid-ocean—beyond the range of aircraft from Canada, Newfoundland, Greenland, Iceland and Britain—U-boats prowled in bigger and ever bolder concentrations called wolf packs by the Allies and *Die Rudeltaktik* (pack tactics) by the Germans. Adm. Karl Dönitz, renowned submarine tactician, soon to be head of the

surface at night. But for many months in World War II he had no chance to prove his theory. Capt. John M. Waters, Jr., in his book *Bloody Winter,* summarizes the war the U-boats had fought:

...The first year they operated singly, much in the fashion of World War I. Not until the early fall of 1940 did Dönitz have enough boats to put his new tactics to use. They caught the British and Canadians unprepared and convoy after convoy was slaughtered. This was the U-boats' first "happy time." Most convoys fought through but losses were appalling.

With 1941 came radar, able sometimes to detect surfaced U-boats at night. Then the entry of the United States into the war brought a second "happy time" as U-boats rampaged along a nearly undefended American coast, sinking nearly 2½ million tons of shipping before belated countermeasures drove them away.

But *the* crisis was still to come. American men and war products had to be transported to Europe, most of them in great merchant and troop convoys. Only U-boat Command could stop them. But in January

1942, only 91 of Germany's 249 submarines were operational. So she threw all her shipbuilding resources into a mighty U-boat buildup: 90 boats joined the fleet between July and October. Dönitz believed that with 300 he could win.

The decision lay ahead on the stormy North Atlantic convoy lanes. October 1942 to May 1943 would see the Battle of the Atlantic reach its ultimate fury....

One of the earliest victims of the stepped-up U-boat campaign was the destroyer *Ottawa,* torpedoed September 13 with a loss of 114 men, including the commanding officer, Lt. Comdr. C. A. Rutherford, who gave his life belt to a seaman. William H. Pugsley, in *Saints, Devils and Ordinary Seamen,* recounted the *Ottawa* story as told him by a petty officer who survived:

...The first torpedo came in through the port shell room and the signalmen's and stokers' messes. It wiped out all the signalmen and all but four of the stokers. About 6 of 40 or so asleep in the mess one deck above were still alive, in a mad pile of broken tables and twisted metal.

I went in to do what I could. All around were men dead from concussion alone, not a mark on them. One man blown down into the stokers' messdeck just hung there, his face shaved off by the jagged steel. An asdic rating was sleeping right above where the blast came. He wasn't hurt at all, but a smashed oil pipe had whipped around his leg and we couldn't get him free.

The men in the asdic cabin, we couldn't get them out either. It was waist-high in muck and debris and the door opened outward. We swung frantically with axes to try and break it down. The men inside were alive and unhurt. They were shouting up the voice pipe to the bridge. But the door was four or five inches thick and copper-sheeted. We weren't making any impression on it and we all expected a second torpedo. The explosion had blown a carbide float over the starboard side and it lighted up the whole ship.

Ten minutes after the first torpedo, the second one hit the starboard side in No. 2

boiler. It killed all the stokers on watch and part of the engine-room staff.

The ship began to list heavily to starboard and we had to give up trying to free that chap trapped in the twisted oil pipe and the men in the asdic cabin. It was grim having to leave them, but the ship started to go fast.

When we got on deck she was almost on her starboard side. Guys were climbing down the port side into the water. One had been operated on for appendicitis a day or so before and was still very weak. Two fellows said they'd stick by and help him. We never saw them again. The ship went over on her side, then broke in two. The bow came up, then the stern, and she slid slowly under. Five or six floats got away. I was on one with 19 others. Eleven of us came through. The convoy went right on, but the destroyer *St. Croix* stayed. So did two corvettes. They dropped depth charges till about 4 a.m. Then *St. Croix* circled while the corvettes picked up survivors.

The wind had risen and so had the sea, and the worst was not having enough clothes on. Jelly fish wrapped around our bodies and poisoned us. It was painful even at the first, a severe burning sensation and then later terrific swelling and running sores. Some guys were attacked in the groin and were in agony for days. It was too rough to lower boats, and we had to make our own way to a corvette. They couldn't maneuver for fear of cutting down the swimmers. Many were so weakened by the long exposure—we were about five hours in the water—that they just couldn't make it. They were lost in the heavy seas right beside the corvettes. Only 65 of us survived, out of 179.

It still haunts me, having to leave that kid trapped with the oil pipe round his leg. And those men in the asdic cabin, the place filling slowly as the ship got far enough under for water to come down the voice pipe from the bridge. . . .

WILLIAM H. PUGSLEY

Admiral Dönitz maintained a day-and-night offensive and in the last six months of 1942 his boats sank over two million tons of shipping. In November alone, 117 ships of over 700,000 tons were sunk; 72 were in convoy. The killing and dying was worst in the great Greenland Air Gap where the escorts were on their own, with no help from aircraft. The Germans called it the Devil's Gorge; the Canadians and British used another name: the Black Pit. Navy veteran Hugh Garner, in *Storm Below,* told what war was like there that winter: . . . It is a silent war, the corvette captain thought. A war of ambush and shooting fish in a barrel. Jerry lies out here somewhere, knowing we're approaching, able to hear us with his sound gear. He sits just above the surface of the water, his tubes trained on a ship in the convoy, and waits until he can't miss. We try to pick him up on radar or sight him; then we attack, with gunfire if he's above water, with depth charges if he's below. If he dives we follow

For sighting a U-boat which his ship, *St. Croix,* sank July 24, 1942, a seaman receives a $10 award from Rear Adm. L. W. Murray—a prize put up by the destroyer's captain, Lt. Comdr. A. H. Dobson. Four times *St. Croix* dropped patterns of depth charges (as above left). The final result, Joseph Schull wrote in *The Far Distant Ships,* "was a nasty, oily litter of timber, clothing, pocketbooks, cigarettes, food packages and bits of human flesh. *St. Croix* triumphantly gathered her grisly remnants, which were later found to include a once-filmy brassière labeled *Triumph, Paris.*" To destroy submarines was important. To get the convoys through was a must. Left: a convoy makes a turn to port as it nears the United Kingdom.

Adm. Karl Dönitz, who emerged as commander-in-chief of the German Navy in January 1943, was heart and soul a submarine man with a fanatical belief that his U-boats could win the Battle of the Atlantic. With three million square miles of shipping lanes to hide in and an endless procession of targets, the submarines almost did win. German and Allied naval men alike maintained superb morale; the Canadian Navy bolstered its own with "The Barber Pole Song," which became almost a shanty in its ships. Written by Surgeon Lt. W. A. "Tony" Paddon of the corvette *Kitchener,* it was the song of Escort Group C5, whose striped funnel markings had earned the nickname "Barber Pole Brigade." Ships joined the group, did their stint of mid-ocean duty and left, but the song remained. It was sung to the tune of "Road to the Isles." Part of the chorus:

From Halifax or Newfiejohn or Derry's
   clustered towers,
By trackless paths where conning
   towers roll,
If you know another group in which
   you'd sooner spend your hours
You've never sailed beneath the Barber Pole!

him with asdic, and plot his turns and evasions. He plots us too, and he knows where we are. He can hear our screw churning the water above his head; we can tell where he is by the magic of a detection gear which sends us his position.

His job is completed when he has fired his torpedoes; all he wants then is to hide. But our job is only starting. We follow him, if we can, as though he were a cockroach running evasive action beneath a man's boot. When we find him we drop our charges and hope he'll be destroyed.

This war is submarine against ship, the ship against submarine. It is a pattern of 14 depth charges, each containing 350 pounds of high explosive, being dropped where the submarine is believed lying. It is the explosive warhead of a torpedo ripping into a plodding ship.

Only when the stunned, frozen, oil-smeared survivors are lifted from the boats and rafts, only when the sullen, deafened Jerry prisoners are hoisted aboard does the thought occur that there were real men in those steel things.

It is a war of strangers. A mile to starboard lies the convoy. There are men aboard all the ships and they have been traveling with us for 11 days, and yet they're strangers to us. Just as much strangers as the men in the submarines.

A mean way to wage war. No preliminary barrages, no attacks over the top of a trench. A war of deceit and deception; a battle of the sharpest eyesight.

If the ship belongs to the enemy, sink him. Blow the guts out of him. Kill every man aboard with hot steel and concussion, with the caress of live steam from blown-up boilers, with the slow strangulation of the Atlantic, with the zut-zu-ut of small-arms fire as he tries to surface and swim for his life. If he is smaller than you are, ram him. Cut him in half.

If a handful of seamen scramble into a raft, shoot them for the glory of the Third Reich. If 50 men float in their life jackets and a submarine is hiding beneath them, fire your charges and sink it. Even though it means the death of the 50 swimmers. Even though it means the tremendous shock of sea water through every pore and orifice of their bodies. Even though they scream to you to pick them up. . . .

HUGH GARNER

Alan Easton wrote that everything bad about the Battle of the Atlantic seemed worse at night:

. . . It was worst of all on the black nights when a man could see virtually nothing. Eyes might have been shut for all the use they were in knowing what was before the ship. I was ashamed one night when I came on deck and jumped as I caught sight of the moon out of the corner of my eye. My pulse had quickened. I had thought, for an instant, it was a rocket from a sinking ship.

It seemed silly that I could have arrived at this state of nerves, surprising that only three or four fairly intensive months could have replaced reasonable fearlessness with anxiety. Lack of sleep had something to do with it. I rarely slept for more than three hours at a stretch, usually less; there were signals and the inevitable false alarms, and the weather had to be watched and the behavior of the merchant ships. But as soon as daylight came my worries left and I was free until dusk. Then I was back on that desolate ground once more. All night the wind would moan over the bleak, rugged, inhospitable hummocks, and the sea became a directionless space, treacherous at every step. . . .

It was in the black Atlantic nights that the Dönitz wolf-pack tactics worked best. Time and again they were too much for the always under-strength convoy escorts. Typical was the ordeal of Convoy ONS-154—46 ships bound from Britain to America with an all-Canadian escort, the destroyer *St. Laurent* and five corvettes. On the night of December 26, 1942, the escort attacked two surfaced U-boats with gunfire and depth charges. One sub fired a torpedo which *St. Laurent* dodged, then both U-boats withdrew to join others for the inevitable wolf-pack attack. It came soon after midnight. What happened was described in *Maclean's* by a wartime navy officer, Lt. Jack McNaught:

. . . One after another, torpedo hits sounded in the convoy. Flames broke out on four merchant ships and all sank quickly. About 3 a.m. *St. Laurent* spotted a surfaced U-boat and opened fire with 20-mm. guns and 4.7s. The U-boat, 1000 yards away, went to periscope depth. The destroyer closed in and dropped charges. Sunk or not, that U-boat gave no more trouble that night. Other subs were driven off, for the time being, and 180 survivors were picked up.

By dawn the wolf pack was ahead, safely out of range and waiting on the surface for other U-boats to join them. For the Canadians, trouble was piling up. Only *St. Laurent* and *Chilliwack* had been able to refuel. The tanker *Scottish Heather* had been torpedoed and forced to turn back to Britain. The oil-starved escorts had to fuel as quickly as possible from the remaining tanker, *E. G. Seuber*. Then the rescue ship *Toward,* 18 miles astern, reported: "Have insufficient food and water for survivors on board. Request another rescue ship be detailed." In the whole of ONS-154, no suitable ship could be spared.

U-boats closed in again and the Admiralty ordered the convoy's course altered sharply southward when dark came. Lt. Comdr. Guy Windeyer of *St. Laurent* answered the welcome order: "To C-in-C Western Approaches: Psalm 119, Verses 97 and 98." In Liverpool, the admiral read in his Bible: "Oh how love I Thy law! It is my meditation all the day. Thou through Thy commandments hast made me wiser than mine enemies: for they are ever with me."

There were certainly 20 U-boats, possibly 25. One quarter of all the submarines in the Atlantic had gathered to attack one convoy, and the change of course didn't help. The escort raced among the plodding columns of merchant ships, attacking where they could, turning from one threat to another. U-boats were everywhere. "At one stage," the captain of the corvette *Shediac* reported later, "torpedoes were so numerous that one officer remarked, 'Here comes ours now, sir,' as if groceries were being delivered."

Rockets and star shells lit the ocean. White tracer poured from machine guns in U-boat conning towers, crisscrossing the red-and-white tracers from the escorts and the convoy, the orange flashes of heavier guns and the livid blasts of torpedo hits. Pinpointing this nightmare were the little red lights on the life jackets of men floating in the sea and the flashlights of men clinging to rafts or crowded into lifeboats.

The escort ships had to press the hunt for U-boats and could do nothing to help the men in the water. "It's a terrible thing," *St. Laurent's* medical officer wrote in his diary, "to have to pass survivors and be unable to pick them up. This was the most demoralizing experience of all."

The attack ended suddenly, a little before midnight. In four hours, the U-boats had sunk ten ships, the heaviest loss in a single attack during the whole Battle of

the Atlantic. It might have meant the heaviest loss of life. Instead, 500 of the 600 crewmen were saved by the salt-stained and cockroach-ridden old tramps that brought up the rear of ONS-154.

All the next night the escorts criss-crossed through and around the merchant ships, but no serious attack was made. Here and there depth charges were dropped over a U-boat creeping under the convoy, but once again no submarines were definitely sunk. Yet no merchant ships were sunk either, and no escort hit. The night's work could be reckoned a success.

Next day ONS-154's situation became desperate. *Shediac,* short of oil, headed for the Azores and *Battleford,* almost as starved for fuel, left with her in case she had to be towed. This, in fact, happened the next morning when the two corvettes were still five hours from port.

At 7:30 p.m. *St. Laurent* found a surfaced U-boat two miles ahead of the convoy. The enemy dived and was not seen or heard again. There were no more attacks.

Fourteen ships had been sunk. More than 100 seamen had died. That was a disaster and defeat. But 32 ships were brought into port with 2000 people aboard alive. That was victory....

JACK MCNAUGHT

There might be pride that small, over-worked, under-equipped escorts could wrest any measure of victory from the wolf packs. But pride could not dispel the gloom of that winter of crisis and the sense of impending catastrophe.

During 1942, U-boats destroyed eight million tons of merchant shipping. Imports into the United Kingdom fell to two thirds of the tonnage received in 1939. And the wolf packs kept gaining in strength. By the end of 1942 Dönitz had 212 operational U-boats, more than twice as many as he'd had a year before.

The American contribution to mid-ocean protection of the merchant convoys, wrote U.S. Coast Guard Capt. John M. Waters, Jr., was pitifully small: five Coast Guard cutters and several World War I destroyers. Captain Waters wrote in *Bloody Winter:*

"For Canadians," wrote Ralph Allen in *Ordeal by Fire,* "World War I reached its depth of misery and entrapment in the trenches of Ypres and Passchendaele. In World War II the trenches were the cold, dark, rumbling bellies of the escort ships and the merchant vessels." Above: a corvette's bridge in dense fog. Right: survivors of a torpedoed ship await rescue. "A man floating or swimming or clinging to a raft after a winter sinking in the North Atlantic," wrote Allen, "had a life expectancy of five minutes. It seldom took longer for the subarctic wet and cold to paralyze and kill him."

"The dearth of American escorts was not due to the U.S. Navy dragging its feet. With the outbreak of the Pacific war, many modern destroyers had to be transferred to reinforce the hard-pressed Pacific Fleet. Most of the modern destroyers left in the Atlantic were assigned to escort fast troop convoys, which by virtue of their speed rarely encountered U-boats. The remaining fleet destroyers were withdrawn from the North Atlantic in the early fall of 1942 for the North African invasion, and afterward remained in the Mediterranean or on the central Atlantic convoys running between the United States and Gibraltar. In the winter of 1942-43, there were no modern U.S. destroyers in the northern ocean; the defensive actions around the slow merchant convoys were fought by the RN and RCN, a handful of Polish, Norwegian and French escorts and the American flush-deck destroyers and Coast Guard cutters."

Captain Waters wrote of the Canadian Navy: "Most of the crews of its small ships had never seen the sea until they reported aboard. Their mistakes were many but

they proved to be one of the most important factors in keeping the Atlantic sea lanes open. Had they failed, the results would have been catastrophic. In their expansion, the emphasis was at first on numbers rather than quality, and their mistakes as they learned were sometimes painful; but any sailors who cruised those waters in the year of crisis should gratefully salute the RCN ensign whenever they see it."

Nonetheless, the Canadian Navy's defeats that winter forced it to face facts: it was sending men and ships to sea ill-prepared.

Gilbert Norman Tucker, in *The Naval Service of Canada, Its Official History,* said the disasters suffered by Canadian ships during the last four months of 1942 were "so grave as to reflect very unfavorably on their fitness for active duty." He cited sinkings in the St. Lawrence, the torpedoing of four merchant ships at anchor in Wabana harbor in Newfoundland, the loss of 15 ships in Convoy SC-107 and 14 in ONS-154, all without destruction of one submarine.

Inferior equipment was a chief reason for the failure, Tucker wrote, and this was "in the main the result of delays in manufacturing and fitting improved radar and anti-submarine gear." He added:
... Canadian ships were generally six months or a year behind their sisters in the Royal Navy. Canadian production of equipment usually did not begin until after the equipment was put into use by the RN.

In addition, the Canadian force in the North Atlantic was considerably reduced to release some escorts for badly needed refit and to provide 17 modernized corvettes (16 Canadian, 1 British) for the invasion of North Africa. The success of the corvettes in the Mediterranean—they sank three submarines in January and February 1943—emphasized the need for improved equipment in other ships.

When liaison with the Royal Navy was improved, the Canadians received information and technical improvements from the earliest plans through experimental design and prototype trials to acceptance.

RCN authorities could study each piece of equipment in its early stage and investigate the feasibility of producing it. In the final stages of the war, Canadian ships were on even terms with their British consorts in equipment and this was reflected by their growing success against U-boats. . . .

But in the winter of 1942-43, the navy still had to battle shortages and delays and had to improvise and compromise and do without. The battle and the weather still ran in the Germans' favor. "On all but ten days of December, January, February and March," wrote Joseph Schull in *The Far Distant Ships,* "gales raged somewhere over the convoy routes. In January, 4 merchant ships went aground, 8 foundered and 40 were heavily damaged by weather. One

ships of 282,000 tons. Of 85 ships sunk after 20 days of March, 67 had been lost in protected convoys, and only four U-boats had been sunk.

Capt. S. W. Roskill, the RN historian, wrote: "One cannot look back upon that month without feeling something approaching horror over the losses we suffered." The U-boats, said the British Admiralty, were "very near to disrupting communications between the New World and the Old."

Unlike the escort ships, the German submarines could find peace from the Atlantic weather. But when they ran on the surface, they had to battle wind and waves and cold just as their enemy did. Wolfgang

In the winter of 1942-43, merchantmen and warships battled the worst Atlantic weather since the start of the war. Some vessels foundered, many had to heave to and ride with the wind and sea. Iced-up ships could become top heavy and capsize. Life for German submariners like the gun crew below was "an ordeal uncomfortable even to imagine," wrote Joseph Schull. "In the cramped interiors of the steel shells which might well be their tombs, they spent as long as three months with only an occasional glimpse of stormy sunlight or a breath of fresh air."

rescue ship turned over and sank with her weight of ice. The commodore's ship of another convoy split her seams in a gale and went down with no survivors."

Of the 196 Canadian and 35 British escorts under Canadian operational command, less than 70 percent could be kept in operation.

At least 110 of Dönitz's U-boats were in the Atlantic, and the appalling Allied losses continued. In the last ten days of February 1943, 21 ships of 183,650 tons were lost; in the first ten days of March, 44

Ott, in *Sharks and Little Fish:*

. . . It went on and on. The cold was bitter. The steel sides seemed like walls of ice. When the first watch returned to the bridge, hungry, frozen and dead-tired, their clothes sopping wet, it was still dark. The storm was still raging. By 1000 hours there was a pale cold light which turned the world a dirty, depressing gray and sapped strength and courage.

When relieved at noon, the men again collapsed in the control room. For an hour they hurtled from side to side. They tried

to remove their outer clothes but were too tired, the leather too heavy. They staggered into the engine room, a few degrees less cold, and dozed. In the afternoon they went back on watch, fortified by two slices of canned bread with a little butter, but desperately sleepy, frozen, utterly indifferent, fiercely irritable.

At night there was not one single star, only the white foam on the seething sea. If you gave in to weariness, you were done. When the boat heeled, it took forever to right itself.

Bloody welts formed on the men's necks where their frozen jacket collars scraped as they drew in their heads before the on-rushing seas and cutting wind.

A shudder ran through every one of them when the chief quartermaster reported, "Shadows bearing two-four-zero."

"Here we go," said Langen, the control chief. The distance was 4000 yards. The convoy could be discerned only by its color, blacker than the night sea.

"Battle stations," the captain called. The command was passed along, and a moment later the reports: "Motor room manned and ready. . . Engine room manned and ready . . . Control room manned and ready." Then the engineering officer: "All ready below." And the exec: "Torpedoes ready."

A new batch of orders from the captain: "All ahead flank, course one-two-zero. Tubes one to five, stand by for surface fire. Radio room send this message: 'Convoy sighted, course two-one-zero, speed eight knots. Am attacking.' Chief quartermaster, request target bearing."

Each man knew what to do. Each was practicing his trade. The men on the bridge could feel the change: the wind whistled louder, spray fell on their binoculars, the deck trembled. The bow wave rose high, the foam took on a lighter color, the forward section of the boat seemed to rise. All this gave the men a glorious feeling that nothing could diminish.

The exec reported, "On target." The captain said, "Fire at will." The hearts of the bridge watch pounded; their breath came in jerks and for seconds—when they thought they'd been sighted—they stopped breathing altogether.

They made out three corvettes at the head of the convoy, a destroyer circling like a dog guarding sheep. They couldn't fire. The convoy speeded up and by the time the correction was fed into the torpedoes, the target bearing exceeded 140 degrees and the range had increased.

"Secure from battle stations. We move up again and attack submerged," said the captain. The engineering officer trimmed the boat and went to periscope depth. Then they heard the ships.

The corvettes passed over, amid the high whir of their speeding screws. Then the lumbering freighters, their propellers slow and irregular, the tone an octave lower than that of the corvettes. But before they could pass over, Captain Lüttke fired.

175

Those who could not see a stopwatch counted softly, and at 52 there were four explosions in quick succession. The men nodded as though to say, that's Lüttke's precision work.

The ships had been hit. The sound room reported sinking noises. "Depth 30 meters. Retract periscope," said the captain.

The convoy passed overhead, an endless armada. Then without warning the first depth charge struck—a roar and shock as though a volcano had erupted beneath the submarine. Not too close, but bad enough. It was a long while before they relaxed and some, chiefly among the older men, remained frozen for the duration of the attack. They waited. Aside from the captain, the engineer, the radioman and the helmsmen, they had nothing to do. That was the worst part of it. "They just dropped that one for the hell of it," said Langen. But this was not true, and they knew it. The "sweeper"—the destroyer astern of the convoy—must have located them. And a moment later the finger was on them. Every man felt that tapping on the side was a death sentence.

"Sound beam," cried the radioman. The men gritted their teeth. They felt like guinea pigs, imprisoned in a steel tube.

"Take her down slow to 80 meters," said the captain. Then the destroyer was over them and eight depth charges exploded close by. Everything made of glass

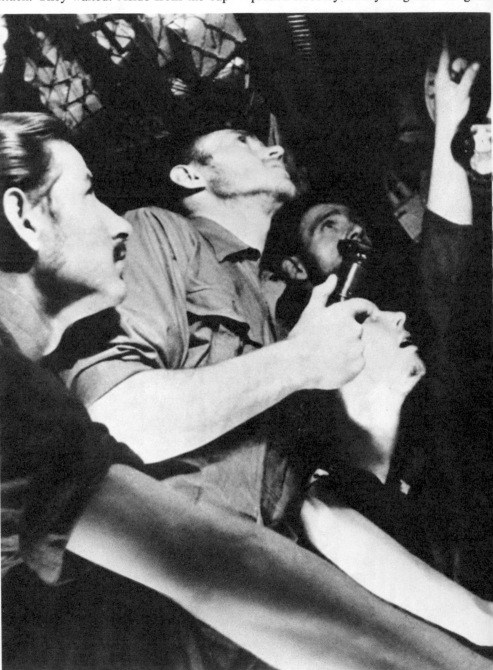

smashed. Water seeped through the hatches. The lights went out. The men, except for the few who stood up to the shock, differed from corpses only in degree. They were finished; only their hearts were functioning. The noises had been louder than human ears can bear. The pressure hull saved their eardrums, but not their nerves.

Lüttke ordered hard right rudder and both engines ahead emergency. The submarine was now 330 feet down. Then the destroyer splashed more depth charges in the water. The explosions lasted half a minute. Several rivets had sprung in the engine room and water spurted, hissing on the hot engines. Steam spread through the boat. The hull began to strain.

The first to crack was Langen. He had managed to raise the boat by pumping; 20 depth charges went off at intervals of three seconds and hurled her down again. Water drove through the valves. The pressure hull creaked. Rivets sprang. The steel tube writhed. And when the crashes had ceased and the hull stopped quaking, there was the dull sound of Langen banging his head against the floor. All they could do was hit him, drag him aft and lock him up.

The boat was going down. Down. Down. But the end did not come. The straining, creaking pressure hull held. They passed the 750-foot mark.

The radioman cracked. He screamed instead of reporting the sound bearings; then

up the shells. No one spoke. The steaming air made it hard to breathe. There was hardly any oxygen left, and every moment seemed to drain their remaining willpower.

"We're going up now," said the captain. He called for the sound bearing.

"The enemy is not moving."

"But I hear his engines," the captain replied.

"I know, sir, but the bearing does not change."

When the boat had risen to 120 feet, the miracle became clear: the boat was rolling slowly. "Try to hold us where we are," said the captain. "Maybe a storm's blowing up. When it's dark, we'll surface."

In the next two hours the boat went

They were going down quickly. Six hundred feet of water now was weighing on the hull. That was what made those hideous sounds. The sound beam searched again, then the destroyer started on a new run. The men whimpered, then screamed, as if to drown the sound of the destroyer's screws. But the sound persisted. And still the sound beam prodded.

It was an unequal contest. The destroyer was faster and more heavily armed; she had plenty of time and an unfailing technical eye. Against such odds bravery was useless. The men on the surface needed only to stand by and wait.

More and more water poured in, and the engineer struggled to keep the boat from sinking farther: 750 feet was the limit. The chief quartermaster counted so many depth charges that he finally gave up.

he burst out sobbing, tore off his earphones and lay in the passageway outside the sound room. The exec took up the phones. The boat rose 300 feet, then 12 depth charges drove her down; she rose again and 9 more sent her down again; she rose and 16 more depth charges flung her back. Several other men cracked up. They were not needed. She rose again; 5 charges sent her back to 600 feet. The boat stood almost on her head, the men had to cling to bars, levers, wheels, valves. It went on for 11 hours and 40 minutes. Then the batteries were spent.

The captain: "All hands stand by for surface battle. There are three warships up there. We are going to sink them one after the other."

Flashlights snapped on. The ammunition ready box was opened, the men passed

down only 100 feet and only 27 depth charges were dropped. Some were not very close. Then for 35 minutes nothing happened at all, except that the sound beam touched the side a few times as though to make sure the sub was still there. After another half hour Lüttke went up to periscope depth and took a look. "It's a black night," he said. "They're hove to. We surface."

When the men were on the bridge and their eyes accustomed to the darkness, they saw a destroyer 300 yards away. In this weather she was, for practical purposes, unmaneuverable; she had to attend to her own business to keep from capsizing.

The storm carried off the wave tops, as though to plane the sea smooth. Visibility was no more than half a mile. The men on the bridge clung fast and held their faces into the storm, and laughed when the sea broke over them. They loved the sea. . . .

WOLFGANG OTT

Joseph Schull takes up the story:

. . . In March 1943, about 70 U-boats were in the northwest Atlantic, in three great lines of patrol: one between Labrador and Greenland, another running due south and to seaward of Newfoundland and Nova Scotia, a third paralleling the Nova Scotia coastline to a point below New York. They barred every exit and entry for the ocean convoys. Eastward, to the fringe of British coastal waters, were 40 more U-boats.

This North Atlantic force of 110 U-boats was by no means the total. On one day, March 9, five convoys were attacked simultaneously: two transatlantic convoys, a north Russia convoy, a convoy bound from Brazil to Trinidad, and one on passage from Britain to Gibraltar.

But the North Atlantic was still the crucial area. There escort groups, struggling to keep convoys together in the great gales, had the impossible task of warding off attackers who came from many directions at once, often outnumbering the defenders two to one, sometimes more heavily than that. Evasive routing was practically useless in view of the number of U-boats at sea. Every sailing was made with the virtual certainty of encountering a large German concentration. Losses were outpacing the entire shipbuilding efforts of the Allies. So many escort vessels were laid up for repair or weather damage in March that the group system was in danger of disorganization. It began to seem that the convoy system, after all the years of effort, could not be maintained.

March losses were 627,000 tons of merchant shipping. It was not the highest figure of the war, but the ominous fact was that, for the first time, 75 percent of the ships had gone down while protected in convoy.

In April the U-boats closed in on the western side of the ocean. Several groups of 10 or 12 patrolled 600 miles from Newfoundland, sweeping the convoy routes from northeast to southwest of St. John's.

But by then the worst was over, even if no one quite realized it. There were various reasons. With the improving weather, shore-based planes flew more patrols and remained longer over the convoys; soon their wide arcs would intersect over mid-Atlantic. From American and British shipyards came fast merchantmen transformed into aircraft carriers, their planes equipped with detection gear, guns and depth charges. Five new British support groups set sail within a few days of one another. Led by destroyers, they included frigates, new twin-screw anti-submarine ships larger and faster than corvettes. These groups were hunters. Free of convoy responsibilities, they sought out known U-boat concentrations or, when a convoy was in danger, provided a far-ranging outer screen of ships to reinforce the close escort. When the danger had subsided they moved off to other areas, always on the hunt.

Better radar came into service and a weapon called hedgehog, a battery of two dozen 65-pound bombs, appeared forward of the bridge on some Canadian ships. Whereas depth charges were dropped astern and the target submarine often escaped because the explosions broke asdic contact, the hedgehog bombs were thrown ahead and there was no break in contact. If a U-boat lay anywhere within the 100-foot oval pattern of bombs, it would be killed. If not, the bombs would sink harmlessly to the bottom while the ship, still in contact, prepared for another attack.

In May, in one of the first uses of hedgehog, a U-boat kill was shared by the Canadian corvette *Drumheller*. A merchantman had been torpedoed in mid-ocean, and *Drumheller* had just picked up 15 survivors when her lookouts observed a shore-based Sunderland flying boat about six miles away, circling low and flashing that she was over a submarine. Ten minutes later, *Drumheller* saw the U-boat running on the surface and putting up a hot barrage against the Sunderland and a plane from the escort carrier *Biter*. *Drumheller* opened fire and the submarine dived.

Drumheller dropped depth charges, then regained contact in time to guide the British frigate *Lagan* into position for a hedgehog attack. The sea's heaving blackness rumbled upward, churning white and green with the explosion. Oil followed, then a litter of debris, then a huge bubble of air 60 feet in diameter from the U-boat's shattered pressure tanks. It had been sunk through effective use of four Allied arms: shore-based aircraft, carrier-based aircraft, ships of the close escort and ships of the support groups.

The U-boats fought back. They took advantage of any circumstances which weighed in their favor. When gale conditions prevented effective air support of one convoy, 12 ships of 43 were torpedoed. Yet merchant ship sinkings for May fell to 157,000 tons and U-boat losses totaled 37 sunk and 32 damaged. At last, the monthly total of U-boats destroyed or knocked out of action was above the total of new submarines coming into service. . . .

JOSEPH SCHULL

In April there had been an adjustment in command which had significance for Canada. Since late 1941, the U.S. Navy had exercised strategic control in the western Atlantic, even though its ships escorted only a minor fraction of the trade convoys. Since Canada now was clearly a full partner in those waters, she was given full control of all convoys and escorts north of New York and west of Greenland. Authority was vested in Rear Adm. L. W. Murray, Commander-in-Chief Canadian Northwest Atlantic, with headquarters in Halifax. South of his area the United States retained control; east of it the Royal Navy had authority.

At roughly the same time, Canada got back 24 corvettes she could well use: 7 which had been lent to the U.S. Navy for service in the Caribbean, the other 17 from the Mediterranean. The RN added further to Canada's Atlantic strength by transferring six overage destroyers to the RCN.

The Allies sank 17 submarines in June. In July they killed 46 as surfaced U-boats tried to fight it out with the planes that now seemed to be everywhere. By August these German tactics were proved a failure and there was a general withdrawal of the wolf packs. Deprived of surface mobility, they could no longer group in overwhelming numbers.

The turning point, it was later agreed, had come in May. By then, said Dönitz, "we had lost the Battle of the Atlantic."

Captain Roskill, the British historian, wrote in *The Navy at War,* that "because convoy battles are marked only by latitude and longitude and have no names that ring in the memory, the victory of May 1943 is scarcely remembered. Yet it was in its own way as decisive as the Battle of Britain in 1940; for never again was the German Navy able seriously to threaten our lifeline."

Wrote Captain Waters:

. . . The immensity of the Battle of the Atlantic dwarfed all other sea battles of

Merchant seamen and navy men, survivors of two torpedoings, reach St. John's, Nfld., in September 1942. In the winter that followed, merchant seamen again earned the navy's admiration. "I remember addressing the captains," says Rear Adm. L. W. Murray, Commander-in-Chief Canadian Northwest Atlantic, "and trying to reassure them that all would be well. But they knew, and they knew I knew, that the probabilities were that 25 percent of them would not reach the United Kingdom in their own ship and that half that number might not arrive at all. For months this loosely disciplined service stood up to casualties like that and never faltered. No ship missed a convoy from Halifax because of malingering."

history and its pivotal effect in many respects exceeded Waterloo, Trafalgar, Gettysburg or the Marne.

Not only in its broad strategic implications, but in the number of ships involved, it was gigantic: 85,775 ships in 2889 escorted merchant convoys ran to and from the United Kingdom across the transocean routes. Of these, 654 ships were lost from the convoys, 1578 others while sailing independently, a total of 11,899,732 tons of shipping on the North Atlantic alone. Over half were British, and 30,248 British merchant seamen gave their lives that Britain might continue to fight.

Credit for the victory must be largely given to the RN and RCN, which for most of the 45 months before the spring of 1943 fought alone, with support from the Americans coming only in the last third of the crisis. A few hundred warships and aircraft and the fewer than 50,000 men of the escort forces were the fulcrum on which the free world's cause was so precariously balanced. Few of their countrymen knew and even fewer now remember the desperate fight waged on the cold and cruel northern seas. But had it failed, the results would have been catastrophic. The clear measure of the devotion and courage of these men shall always be that in that dark and bloody winter of crisis they did not fail. . . .

The changing face of Canada

On the home front: boom towns and zoot suits, rationing and regulations and industrial revolution, Victory Bonds, Victory gardens and Victory stockings

One spring morning in 1942 an old sourdough named Charlie Johnson was patrolling his trapline in the Yukon when he heard a terrible crashing in the woods. "I looked up and saw big trees toppling and thought I'd gone crazy," he recalled later. "When I saw a bulldozer, and some Yank soldiers told me they were building a road to Alaska, I realized *they* were crazy. Hadn't I heard of the road? I hadn't even heard of the war."

Charlie Johnson was one in a million. By 1942 there was hardly a man, woman or child in Canada whose life had not been affected by the war. The road he'd stumbled on—the Alaska Highway, or Alcan as it was known then, from Dawson Creek, B.C., to Fairbanks, Alaska—was part of the reaction to fears of a Japanese invasion. But it was only part of a vast transformation that had already brought dramatic change and was setting the stage for even greater change after the war. The streets were alive with people in uniform. Daylight saving time had come for the duration. Tens of thousands of Canadians were working harder and longer than ever before. Hamilton's steel mills were running three shifts a day, seven days a week; so were Toronto munitions plants, Montreal aircraft factories, Vancouver shipyards. In towns across the land machine shops were turning out the tools of war on government contracts of every kind.

Shipbuilding was typical. In 1939, Canada's 14 shipyards and 15 boat plants had employed only 3400 men, almost all on repair jobs. By 1942, more than 40,000 men and women were at work on contracts worth $500 million, and by October 1944 this force would more than double. By then Canada's 90 shipyards had launched almost 3000 cargo ships, naval escort vessels and other special purpose craft.

Automobile plants, switched exclusively to war production in early 1942,

were soon producing 3800 military trucks and 250 armored vehicles a week. The country was producing 315 aircraft, 2,300,000 shells, 16,000 rifles and 98,000,000 rounds of ammunition a month and launching a 10,000-ton cargo ship every four days. The list went on and on, through tanks, guns, mines, warships, TNT, cordite and depth charges. In Sarnia, Ont., government plants were built to turn out Canada's first synthetic rubber. With about one-half of one percent of the world's population, we had become the fourth largest producer of armaments among the Allied nations.

The transformation operated not only at the industrial level. It also had social, financial and psychological dimensions, and it was directed by government to a degree the country had never known. Ottawa in midwar was busy, crowded and loaded with talent. Everywhere, wrote *Maclean's,* "are dollar-a-year men, and $10- and $20-a-day men; controllers of this, that and the other; business executives; buying experts; technical advisers. The Château Laurier lobby, Ottawa's clubs, Wellington Street and Sparks Street are full of strange faces, men who have come from all parts of Canada to run some branch of the war effort."

The wartime cabinet under Prime Minister Mackenzie King was probably the greatest in Canadian history. Its powers were enormous, its political opposition weak. It was backed by a civil service staffed by many of the ablest men in the land. It was backed, too, by a public mood which had replaced the uncertainties and doubts of the Depression with belief in a single national purpose. The result, said *The New York Times* in November 1941, was a war effort that "is one of the little appreciated miracles of the war." It was, said Winston Churchill, "surpassed by none."

"When you consider," said the U.S. magazine *Fortune,* "that prewar Cana-

dian industry had never made a tank, a combat airplane or a modern high-caliber rapid-fire gun, the speed with which industry was organized and production started ranks as an industrial miracle."

The miracle workers were ordinary Canadians from Glace Bay to Port Alberni, led by a few hundred key men in Ottawa. It had taken the fall of France and the siege of Britain to accomplish this transformation. From then on the country was truly at war. When blueprints, tool designs and assignments of patents poured across the Atlantic from Britain, C. D. Howe's Department of Munitions and Supply sprang to life. Contract after contract specified production for which the country had neither plant nor personnel. But under Howe's dynamic direction they were met. He did it by tapping industry for top men—"men of experience, men who know values, men of absolute integrity"—and freeing them of red tape to get done what had to be done.

Probably no group in Canada's history, said *Fortune,* ever wielded such power as Howe's department in revolutionizing the nation's industry. It could tell businessmen what to make, where to sell raw materials and when to deliver. For failure to obey, it could commandeer factories and schedule production as it saw fit. Canada, said the magazine, had a planned economy; the people had surrendered their simple rights.

Howe was the hardest-worked man in the cabinet, said *Maclean's,* and also the toughest:

. . . He lets contracts for staggering figures; builds vast, streamlined factories; looks on a million-dollar order as small change. How he stands up under the strain of 14 hours of work a day, his meal hours incidental to conferences, is a mystery. Yet on weekends he finds time to play golf, occasionally 36 holes.

So it is with Defense Minister J. L. Ralston, a prodigious worker whose

weakness is his slavishness to detail. He must hear and read everything, understand everything himself. Those who work with him swear by his earnestness and industry and swear at his propensity to smother himself with trifles.

The antithesis of Ralston, and the surprise of Ottawa, is Air Minister C. G. "Chubby" Power. Twenty years ago, a broth of a lad back from the Great War, he was the playboy of Ottawa. Today he is a brilliant, driving minister, resourceful and innovating at his desk, decisive and masterful in cabinet, a red-tape cutter irreverent of military formula.

Angus L. Macdonald, the poetic Gael and former premier of Nova Scotia, is

We're Holding the Cards Now Axis!

LET'S SHOW 'EM
BUY VICTORY BONDS

Under the impact of war, the capacity of Canadian industry expanded rapidly. A nation with few factories geared for war production suddenly made everything from Bren guns (above) to military vehicles. Canadians supported this wartime industrial expansion by spending vast sums on Victory Bonds. When the first bond drive brought in $807 million, Finance Minister J. L. Ilsley said "each Canadian should stand on his toes and cheer and then get back to work."

By 1942 the aircraft industry was producing 315 planes a month. "Thanks to the skill and devotion of our men and women," Prime Minister Mackenzie King said in a speech to the British Parliament in 1944, "Canada is a granary, an arsenal, an airdrome and a shipyard of freedom."

finding his sea legs as navy minister, becoming meanwhile the orator of the cabinet. . . .

In addition to these men who built and armed the military forces there was another, equally important breed, the men who managed the delicate financial machinery which made modern war possible. Their leader and their symbol was, like Ralston and Macdonald, a Nova Scotian—the austere James Lorimer Ilsley, a red-haired lawyer from the Annapolis Valley. He succeeded Ralston as finance minister at the age of 48. Brilliantly aided by his deputy minister, W. C. Clark, Ilsley bore crushing responsibility and wielded proportionately awesome power, but used the streetcar to save gasoline and unsmilingly ordered hash or macaroni at Bowles Lunch. He dealt in billions of dol-

lars yet once was seen going back to a phone booth to check whether he'd forgotten a nickel in the return slot. Such was his burden that he once told a friend he awoke every day wishing he could die.

He was no friend of Prime Minister King. Bruce Hutchison said Ilsley deplored King to the point of laughter and tears, but nonetheless served him faithfully. "He must be numbered among the great," said Hutchison, this man who

"shattered his health in mastering the almost insoluble problems of wartime finance."

"He has shown no aptitude for coating bitter pills," wrote Grant Dexter of the *Winnipeg Free Press.* "There are no sugarplums or silver linings in his budgets. He is immune to flattery. He can't be wheedled. He has no ambition for place, power or money. But he has the things that count: character, warmth of heart, sincerity, fidelity to principle." Indeed *Saturday Night* once assured Ilsley that "the country loves him for his common sense almost as much as for his courage and his honesty."

By 1941 he was finding $3.9 billion a year to run the war, including $2 billion from taxes, $95 million in enforced savings, and $1.75 billion from borrowing. But he was running into serious trouble for two major reasons.

The first was an ever-growing shortage of American dollars. To build its war machine, Canada bought more and more from the great arsenal beginning to emerge in the United States. Finally the need for U.S. dollars became a crisis. Ilsley's experts tried to secure Washington's assistance, but within existing laws—the United States was not yet at war—there seemed no way to do it.

At this point another chapter was written in the friendship of Mackenzie King and President Franklin Roosevelt. Bruce Hutchison in *The Incredible Canadian:*
. . . King saw this dollar shortage as essentially a political problem, to be solved by politicians. It was solved by the two foremost politicians of America on April 20, 1941, at the Roosevelt family home at Hyde Park, N.Y. Believing as he did, King did not attempt to explain the economics of the crisis to Roosevelt. Besides, as they drove about the estate in Roosevelt's little hand-manipulated car, the President admitted he could never get his mind around foreign exchange.

So King simply told his friend that Canada would go broke unless she could earn more American dollars. The United States could postpone the debacle by forcing Canada to liquidate her last reserves of gold and what assets she still held in the United States, but only for a while. What would be the result? Canada would turn on her neighbor in anger. Even if the United States lent Canada money, the sense of charity would rankle.

Roosevelt might not understand foreign exchange but he understood people. He was shocked at any possibility of a rift. How could the thing be fixed?

Quite easily, said King. Let the United States buy from Canada roughly as much as Canada bought from the United States. Let the United States pay Canada in American dollars for materials that would be supplied free to Britain under the American Lend-Lease Act. Let the United States use Canada's productive machinery to support Britain and, in the process, provide Canada with dollars needed for her own support. In other words, let the economies of the two North American nations be geared together for defense purposes.

A swell idea, said Roosevelt. The two politicians had applied a political solution to an economic problem too big for the economists. They jotted their thoughts on a slip of paper, the Hyde Park Declaration. Roosevelt scrawled a postscript: "Done by Mackenzie and F.D.R. on a grand Sunday in April." It was a good Sabbath's work.

In operation, the declaration proved technically difficult. But when the technicians raised detailed objections, Roosevelt thundered: "This is what I want done! Do it!" It was done. . . .

C. D. Howe sent businessman E. P. Taylor to Washington as head of War Supplies Limited, the Crown agency charged with putting the Hyde Park Declaration into effect. Under Taylor's direction, more than a billion dollars' worth of Canadian goods were sold in the United States. He became the most important link coordinating the industrial war efforts of Canada, the United States and Britain.

One vital problem had been brought under control, but another quickly took its place. By late 1941 the slack had largely gone out of the economy. Only Britain had come closer to the ideal of full employment. It had meant numerous restrictions: fewer radios, refrigerators and phonographs, no more aluminum kitchenware, not many silk stockings, higher and higher taxes, enforced savings, gasoline rationing. It would mean no new cars. It would mean more rationing: sugar, coffee, tea, butter, meat, beer, whisky, wine. No worker would be allowed to change his job without approval by a government agency called Selective Service. Industries not essential to the war would be drained of labor.

But in a booming economy none of these things struck vitally at the real threat. Prices were going up. Demand was exceeding supply. Ilsley and his financial experts could see an inflationary explosion directly ahead. Bruce Hutchison wrote:

. . . The experts had relied on taxation, the borrowing of real savings and credit policy. They knew direct wage and price controls would mean an almost impossible task of administration and virtually total state control. But if the economy were not to explode and sink, the last desperate measure must be taken.

Mackenzie King, the economist, pronounced total price and wage control impossible to enforce. Partial controls might work—were already working in certain commodities—but a horizontal ceiling would soon be smashed or submerged by a black market.

For many days the struggle continued behind the scenes in Ottawa. In the end, not entirely convinced, King agreed to try. Now that he had accepted the policy, he announced it to the people as his own. . . .

What King said on October 18, 1941, was simply that all prices were frozen. Nobody could sell anything at a price higher than the one he charged for the same goods between September 15 and October 11. Customary or prevailing discounts or price differentials had to be retained. The lid was on to stay.

It was a unique experiment. Canada's allies watched with skepticism and U.S. experts at first dismissed it as unworkable. But the price ceiling was part of a larger scheme, correlated with wage and salary ceilings and a bonus to be paid if the cost of living rose. The man in charge of this vital part of Ilsley's financial mechanism was 40-year-old Donald Gordon, moved from his post as deputy governor of the Bank of Canada to chairman of the Wartime Prices and Trade Board. Before long his U.S. counterpart, Leon Henderson, was calling him "the best damned price controller in the world."

Gordon's first move, wrote Peter Newman in *Flame of Power,* was to call a press conference:

. . . It was short and in character. "Some of you probably think inflation is the only healthy answer," Gordon said. "We'll break for ten minutes and give those who feel that way a chance to leave." No one moved. "All right, then, we'll go ahead on the assumption that everybody accepts the credo of controls and ceilings. Now you might as well go home while I think this through. I don't know anything about price ceilings, or how to make them work."

Gordon's job was not only to flatten prices but also to allocate essential materials through civilian rationing. He recruited top business brains. To Douglas Dewar, a leading Vancouver accountant, he wired: DOUGLAS I NEED YOU. Dewar replied: WHERE AND WHEN? Gordon: HERE AND NOW. Dewar was working in Ottawa 48 hours later.

Gordon enlisted the most respected man in each commercial and trade group to become a prices board administrator. No industry could thus object—the orders came from a man who understood its problems, language and techniques. Prices board lawyers who drew up woolly worded regulations were chastised by Gordon: "I'm the corner grocer, and this doesn't make a damn bit of sense." When a file of undertakers protested restrictions on cotton in casket linings, Gordon threw them out. "If I die," he boomed, "the regulations will be relaxed!"

Angry Toronto unionists once challenged Gordon to defend his rulings. He told them, "Gentlemen, where I come from, a blackhearted bastard is a term of endearment." The tension vanished. . . .

Just as Canada's defense and dollar problems could not be solved solely in Canada, so inflation could not be halted long if it were allowed to develop in the United States. It was more than a Canadian problem. Bruce Hutchison, in *Fortune,* described "Canada Under the Lid" some six months after the ceiling had been imposed:

. . . Gordon's job was twofold—to peg prices in Canada and to show the American people, solely by example, that a democracy could control prices and operate a wartime totalitarian economy within the framework of free capitalism. The feasibility of the scheme has been demonstrated. The United States has largely followed it.

In Canada the very simplicity of an overall ceiling caught the public's imagination and hardly anyone stopped to realize the difficulties ahead. Gordon, knowing this first fever of enthusiasm would soon burn out, proceeded to scare the daylights out of Canada. On radio he described the danger of inflation in words the housewife could understand—in terms of budgets, savings, life insurance and the Sunday roast. He called newspaper publishers together—at their expense—and threatened them with economic chaos if the ceiling broke.

Mackenzie King had indicated an intention to peg all prices—manufacturing, wholesale, retail. The board's first act was to throw this plan overboard. It pegged only the retail price and allowed for limited flexibility in manufacturing and wholesale prices.

This was necessary because of a squeeze which developed this way: when the ceiling came into effect December 1, retailers could afford to sell goods already on their shelves at the basic-period price.

But they had also ordered goods in advance at higher wholesale prices. This loss had to be absorbed somehow; by law it could not be handed on to the consumer.

The squeeze, said Gordon, must be rolled back from the retail to the wholesale, then from the wholesale to the manufacturing level—a complicated process. How could it be absorbed fairly? When many basic costs had increased how could the squeeze be absorbed at all?

Gordon's reply was simple: retail prices were *not* going up. If they did, someone was going to jail; business would have to solve its problem somehow. The board's machinery went to work. Each administrator called in key men from his industry—manufacturers, wholesalers, retailers. They decided among themselves how much of the squeeze each level of business should absorb. In general, the manufacturer absorbed 50 percent, the wholesaler and retailer the remainder.

To cushion the shock of the squeeze and to save labor and materials, many models and styles were eliminated, deliveries reduced, fancy packaging outlawed. The board used subsidies to help handle business that could not operate under the ceiling.

Donald Gordon puts it this way: "The fact business was intelligent enough to take temporary losses to avoid something infinitely worse, the fact the Canadian people were willing to sacrifice their right to struggle for increased income, is the most stirring demonstration of democracy I have ever seen. In the pinch, democracy works—if you give the people the facts." . . .   BRUCE HUTCHISON

Through the combination of price and rental controls and rationing—plus severe taxes, enforced savings and sales of Victory Bonds to siphon off demand for goods—Canada excelled in keeping her economy healthy and in check. Her cost of living rose only slightly from 1942 to the end of the war. The official *Canada Year Book* for 1945 published figures which showed that the country's record was the best in the world.

And as the cost of living was held down, the standard of living climbed. The population increased by 7 percent during the war; the consumption of goods and services jumped 78 percent. In 1942 Ottawa correspondent Grant Dexter reported that "alongside our war effort has developed the greatest boom in our history."

The Ottawa that masterminded this remarkable economic achievement was itself transformed by the war. By 1942 the old 10-to-4:30, two-hours-for-lunch, time-out-for-golf, pause-for-afternoon-tea-then-dress-for-dinner Ottawa was a thing of the past. Restaurants were packed and many a meal was taken standing up. You fought for a place on a rush-hour streetcar and pondered whether this boom was to be enjoyed or suffered.

Maclean's painted this picture:

. . . The Ottawa civil service total is 18,000, up 65 percent over prewar. Thousands of people have moved here and they're still pouring in. For soldiers and airmen in training the government has provided food and shelter. Others have to shift for themselves.

The government has built temporary

wooden office buildings. Famous private residences have been converted to provide living space. Sir Clifford Sifton's mansion, now Bromley Hall, provides something approximating hotel service and its dining room is open to the public. In such hostelries a room without private bath rents for $40 a month; but there are not many and they are all full. The luxurious 200-suite Roxborough Apartments—average rent $150—is full too.

An astonishingly large number of private homes have been converted into rooming houses. Some serve meals, others offer rooms only. Boarding houses sleep guests two and three in a room and feed them at three sittings. Rents are pegged and sternly regulated by the local rentals committee, so there is little downright profiteering. But the house hunter finds there isn't an empty residence in the city. Official Ottawa is widely scattered. Government departments are in warehouses and over tobacco shops—wherever there is floor space. The typical worker shares a crowded office with a dozen others. A secretary gets no more than a table, but an executive rates a desk, a telephone and sometimes a beaverboard partition. When a fresh appointee arrives they shift the furniture, install a telephone and run up another partition.

Expenditure is cautiously pared; taxes, rationing and controls have made the public sensitive about Ottawa. Any hint of extravagance brings angry mail. You wonder if anybody has any comfort or fun. A capital which houses 18 foreign legations has a retail section almost like the main street in a small town. . . .

That was Ottawa, the shabby, unlikely center of a national revolution. And the longer the war went on, the more its authority was felt across the land. "Use it Up, Wear it Out, Make it Do, and Do Without," preached the prices board. "Conserve your tires," said one edict in May 1942. "They're probably the last you'll get until the war is over." All usable tires had come under control and "no person may buy or sell, borrow or lend, barter or exchange, mortgage, give away or receive as a gift, burn, cut, destroy or otherwise dispose of a usable tire or tube." C. D. Howe signed that one.

And a mere month later: "No employer hereafter shall hire any person, male or female, without the approval of a Selective Service officer." Break that law and you could be fined $500 and jailed for a year.

Canada got no U.S. free aid under Lend-Lease. Instead, in Mutual Aid, it ran its own equivalent. It felt that as a nation in a favored position, free from the ravages of war, it should meet its own needs and share in aiding less fortunate allies. Its total war aid to other countries amounted to $3.4 billion, compared with its total military cost of $15.5 billion.

ALL USABLE TIRES NOW UNDER CONTROL

Regulations announced on May 15 prohibit all but essential vehicle owners from obtaining usable pneumatic tires or tubes for their cars or trucks, or from obtaining retreading services. Apart from such legal sales, no person may buy or sell, borrow or lend, barter or exchange, mortgage, give away or receive as a gift, burn, cut, destroy, or otherwise dispose of a usable tire or tube.

FOR DETAILS OF THE NEW REGULATIONS SEE YOUR TIRE DEALER

THE DEPARTMENT OF MUNITIONS AND SUPPLY
Honourable C. D. Howe, Minister

CONSERVE YOUR TIRES . . . They are probably the last you'll get until the war is over

Donald Gordon (left), the blunt-talking boss of the prices board, urged Canadians to "live the frugal life." Announcing a voluntary sugar ration of 12 ounces a week, he said: "Anything in excess is not only against the law but an offense against decency." Gordon believed people "want to be told what to do in this war. We're telling them." Restrictions on car tires (above) were typical. Right: a Canadian Aid to Russia Fund shipment is loaded aboard ship.

Canada could help others because, above all, it had worked its own economic miracle: a threadbare nation had become a vast arsenal and farm. Private industry had done much but, where there were gaps, C. D. Howe never hesitated to create government-owned Crown companies—eventually there were 28. These organizations were involved in mining and refining, aircraft production, the manufacture of explosives and synthetic rubber and—although the public didn't know—the search for uranium. These enterprises reported to Howe, not to Parliament.

Lord Beaverbrook described Howe as "one of a handful of men of whom it can be said, 'But for him the war would have been lost.' " It was Howe who led industrial Canada to a place behind only the United States, Russia and Britain. With the possible exception of Britain, wrote Leslie Roberts in his Howe biography, Canada's per capita production was the highest of all the Allied nations. And of its 1943 war production, only 30 percent went to the Canadian forces, the rest to Canada's allies. Britain and Russia were getting more per capita from Canada than from any other nation.

"Never again," said Howe that year, "will there be any doubt that Canada can manufacture anything that can be manufactured elsewhere." The remark went almost unnoticed at the time. But not long after, in the postwar boom years, Canadians realized how right he'd been.

By 1942 Canadian farms were producing record quantities of food for the armed forces, the home front and Britain, even though 200,000 men had left the land to enlist and the output of new farm machinery had dropped markedly. Farmers made use of the machinery they had and got help where it could be found. When the prairies came up with a record grain crop of 1.2 billion bushels it became known as the year everybody went west. To gather the bumper harvest, school openings were delayed, small towns closed up shop, students flocked out from the east by train, Indians came down from the north.

"A trip through the west this summer is a heartening experience," wrote Carlyle Allison in the Winnipeg *Tribune.* "The land is green again. It is almost unbelievable if you know anything about Saskatchewan in the long dry years when even five-year-old children had never seen rain."

Various kinds of war work had uprooted thousands and sent many to remote corners of the country to work on vital and sometimes secret projects. On Quebec's Saguenay River construction crews toiled through sub-zero weather to complete one of the world's largest hydroelectric developments, the 1,200,000-horsepower Shipshaw project. They were changing the course of the river, and moving it from a valley to the top of a ridge to meet the power demands of the Aluminum Company of Canada's giant Arvida smelter as it poured out ingots for the booming aircraft industry.

At Steep Rock in northwestern Ontario an army of workers was building dams and diverting the Seine River to drain part of a 15-mile-long lake. The treasure they sought was one of the world's richest iron-ore beds—in the lake under 380 feet of glacial sediment. Ninety million cubic yards of muck, clay and gravel had to be removed, a task bigger than dredging the Panama Canal.

In northern British Columbia and the Yukon, the country was being revolutionized by the road that had amazed trapper Charlie Johnson. After the Japanese attack on Pearl Harbor, Canada gave the United States permission to build the road. Its construction hit little Dawson Creek with "an impact like a second Klondike gold rush," wrote Edwin Guillet in *The Story of Canadian Roads:*
... Quonset huts and supply dumps sprang up. Waterlines and a sewage system were built. Prices skyrocketed. Soon American troops were joined by thousands of American and Canadian civilian workers. "This is no picnic," said the poster advertising for workmen, but the pay was good and there were plenty of willing hands.

The roadbuilders spread out from Dawson Creek to Fort St. John, B.C., and Fort Nelson, B.C. At the other end they worked from Fairbanks in Alaska and Watson Lake and Whitehorse in the Yukon. No time was wasted on engineering niceties. The dirt road was looped over hills and rammed through forests. A 20-ton bulldozer led the way, with others following to clear debris. Strung out 30 to 50 miles behind the bulldozers were men felling trees, building culverts, hauling gravel. Overhead, reconnaissance planes took photographs of the next stretch of muskeg and forest to be attacked. Work went on seven days a week, day and night, in temperatures which ranged from sub-tropical heat to 50 below zero.

On November 20, 1942, The Road was ceremonially opened at Soldiers' Summit, overlooking Kluane Lake. Canadian and American flags were hoisted as the band played "God Save the King" and "The Star-Spangled Banner." Then the first convoy of trucks from Dawson Creek pushed on to Fairbanks. Ten thousand soldiers and 6000 civilian workers had produced a 24-foot roadway at an average speed of eight miles a day, completing in eight months a stupendous piece of construction that would normally have taken more than five years. . . .

After the Japanese invaded Alaska's Aleutian Islands in 1942, supplies rolled north in great volume. Edna Jaques reported in *Maclean's:*
. . . Of all the ripsnortin', hell-raisin' towns that ever mushroomed to fame overnight, Dawson Creek heads the list. It's a hundred boom towns rolled into one, a hundred army camps, a stampede, a madhouse. It's a bedlam of activity where the noise of trucks blasts the air by day and night and old-timers are wrought to such a pitch that they don't know whether they are coming or going.

A quiet family life is a faraway dream of the past that seems unreal now, and teachers almost have to tie the children to their desks to keep them in school at all. Water is more precious than gold; a tarpaper shack is a king's palace and "rooms just ain't to be got," as one woman angrily put it.

The trains roll in loaded with food, implements of war, bulldozers, army vans, lumber, steel for bridges, pipe for oil lines, guns, ammunition, soldiers, plane parts. Dawson Creek is packed with soldiers, truckers, engineers, freighters, bridgebuilders, stockmen, police. You can find roustabouts, hangers-on, sharpers, gamblers, bootleggers—the fighting, drinking scum that follows in the wake of every boom. Vice prowls the streets after supper and no woman dares go out alone at night. Mothers watch their daughters like hawks.

From morning to night people talk trucks. One company has a thousand on the road day and night and wishes it had a thousand more. Men who were begging for jobs a few years ago now make more money than they ever dreamed of, some as much as $1000 a month. . . .

In more subdued surroundings at Port Radium in the Northwest Territories, miners were working a thousand feet below the surface of Great Bear Lake, tunneling for pitchblende, the host rock of uranium, the raw substance of atomic power. None of the workers knew that the black rock would play a part in two massive explosions that would end the war.

In the cities, with thousands on the move, it often was hard to find a place to live. Canada had had a housing shortage for years. When war came, construction of homes took second place to barracks, airfields and munitions plants. The problem was increased still more by the large number of wartime marriages and the great movement of workers to war jobs in congested cities.

Nevertheless people muddled through, and some faced the situation with humor. An ad in an Ottawa paper read: "Have you ever lived with your mother-in-law for six months? Army officer and wife seek rescue in form of small central apartment." In booming, overcrowded Edmonton, one desperate couple advertised: "Wanted by American couple with two small children, 4- or 5-room furnished house or suite. If you don't like children, we will gladly drown them."

For some, the situation was desperate. In Saint John, N.B., social workers found a couple and their six children sleeping in one room, mainly on chairs.

Rent controls put a ceiling on what landlords could charge, and special tribunals were available to tenants who felt they were being gouged. In Vernon, B.C., a judge termed four shacks "unfit for human habitation" and reduced the rent to 25 cents a month each. But there were ways to get above the ceilings: some landlords demanded the tenants "purchase" keys before moving in.

Far removed from the problems of the crowded cities and booming projects were the thousands of Canadians "doing their bit" at home. One woman in Clive, Alta., resolved to knit a sweater and two pairs of socks for each Clive man who went to war. By the end of 1943 she had made 64 sweaters and 128 pairs

U.S. Army engineers (left) reconnoiter the route before bulldozers begin smashing through bush and muskeg to build the Alaska Highway, linking Dawson Creek, B.C., and Fairbanks, Alaska. Ten thousand soldiers and 6000 civilians did the job in eight months. Below: a contractor's warning to men seeking jobs on the Alcan Highway, as it was then called.

JUNE 15 42

THIS IS NO PICNIC

WORKING AND LIVING CONDITIONS ON THIS JOB ARE AS DIFFICULT AS THOSE ENCOUNTERED ON ANY CONSTRUCTION JOB EVER DONE IN THE UNITED STATES OR FOREIGN TERRITORY. MEN HIRED FOR THIS JOB WILL BE REQUIRED TO WORK AND LIVE UNDER THE MOST EXTREME CONDITIONS IMAGINABLE. TEMPERATURE WILL RANGE FROM 90° ABOVE ZERO TO 70° BELOW ZERO. MEN WILL HAVE TO FIGHT SWAMPS, RIVERS, ICE AND COLD. MOSQUITOS, FLIES, AND GNATS WILL NOT ONLY BE ANNOYING BUT WILL CAUSE BODILY HARM. IF YOU ARE NOT PREPARED TO WORK UNDER THESE AND SIMILAR CONDITIONS DO NOT APPLY

Bechtel Price - Callahan

of socks. Backyards everywhere sprouted vegetable patches. Community garden leagues discussed soils, bugs, worms and fertilizers. Victory gardeners in one league in Montreal grew vegetables worth $500,000 in one year alone.

Wherever there were large numbers of servicemen there were canteens run by volunteer women. Some Canadians collected for victory. One Nova Scotia woman began gathering pennies and after 22 months turned 10,000 of them into a Victory Bond. Toronto launched a campaign in 1942 to conserve power for war production. Street lights were dimmed, store-window display lights were turned off and people were asked to work close to their windows and delay turning on house lights as the sun went down. Outdoor Christmas lighting was banned.

Taxes were the talk of the country. In 1938, Ottawa's revenue from personal income taxes was $42 million. By 1943 it had risen to $815 million. A married man with no children and an annual income of $2500 was taxed $651, more than a quarter of his pay; $250 of this was enforced savings, to be returned after the war. If taxes were high, there were also more people now in a position to pay them. In December 1939 there had been only 2.2 million salary and wage earners; two years later there were 3.1 million, the biggest boom in Canadian history.

The films Canadians saw, the books they read and the songs they sang were mostly foreign. Top movie stars doubled as pin-up girls: Veronica Lake, Lana Turner, Rita Hayworth, Betty Grable, Alexis Smith, Hedy Lamarr. Moviehouse favorites included "Mrs. Miniver" with Greer Garson and Walter Pidgeon; Noel Coward's "In Which We Serve," a story of the Royal Navy; "Corvette K-225," about Canada's Navy, and the National Film Board's "Canada Carries On" series about the country at war.

Important Canadian books were written during the war. Hugh MacLennan's *Barometer Rising,* about Halifax in World War I, was published in 1941 and he soon was at work on *Two Solitudes.* Bruce Hutchison's *The Unknown Country* came out in 1942. Mazo de la Roche produced three Jalna chronicles during the war: *Whiteoak Heritage, Wakefield's Course* and *The Building of Jalna.* Gabrielle Roy wrote *The Tin Flute* and Gwethalyn Graham *Earth and High Heaven.* Canada's great poet E. J. Pratt hit his stride with *Brébeuf and his Brethren* in 1940, *Dunkirk* in 1941 and *Still Life and Other Verse* in 1943.

There seemed to be new songs every week. A few of the best survived long after the war: "The White Cliffs of Dover," "We'll Meet Again," "I'll Walk Alone," "A Nightingale Sang in Berkeley Square"—and one of Gracie Fields' great ones, "Now is The Hour." In 1942, big bands such as Glenn Miller's and Tommy Dorsey's were playing "Paper Doll," "Brazil," "Don't Get Around Much Anymore," "I'll Be Around," "That Old Black Magic"—and "White Christmas," an Irving Berlin/Bing Crosby hit that would eventually sell more than 45 million records.

On CBC radio, in concerts and at Victory Bond rallies, Canadian performers played and sang all the Hollywood, New York and London favorites. Canadians danced to music played by the orchestras of Lucio Agostini, Jack Arthur, Rex Battle, Trump Davidson, Geoffrey Waddington, Samuel Hersenhorne, Mart

Kenny, Roy Locksley, the Niosi brothers and Denny Vaughan. On radio, it was the heyday of Toronto's Happy Gang: Bert Pearl, Blain Mathé, Joe Niosi, Eddie Allen, Kathleen Stokes and Jimmy Namaro; of Edgar Bergen and Charlie McCarthy, The Lone Ranger, Amos 'n Andy, Don McNeill's Breakfast Club, and soap operas such as Ma Perkins and Big Sister. Canadian entertainers included Wayne and Shuster, Percy Faith, Wishart Campbell, Robert Farnon, Wally Koster, Norma Locke, James Milligan, Ruby Ramsay Rouse, Carl Tapscott, Ernest Dainty, Claire Wallace—and Don Messer.

Entertainers made a big contribution to the war effort: music made it easier to take the uncertainties, the separations, the heartbreaks—and some of the relatively minor irritations, such as rationing.

Food rationing was introduced in 1942, and more than 11,000,000 ration books—one per person—became part of national life. But rationing never reached

the scale it did in Britain. In fact, British servicemen were surprised by Canada's relative bounty. For most Canadians the rationing of sugar, coffee, tea, butter and meat was more nuisance than hardship. But there were shortages. Housewives were urged to beat milk into their butter. Restaurants observed meatless Tuesdays and Fridays; some displayed signs such as: "Use less sugar and stir like hell. We don't mind the noise!" Liquor was scarce; people waited outside vendors' stores to offer $15 to $20 "for whatever you have, mister."

People had more money to spend, but such things as new cars and appliances were unavailable and used ones were not always easy to get. In April 1942, when gasoline was rationed, some Canadians put their cars away "for the duration."

The war dominated not only the news columns but also the advertisements in Canadian papers and magazines. This page from a 1943 issue of *Maclean's* (below) featured the story of a U-boat kill by the corvette *Ville de Québec* and an appeal for support of The Overseas League Tobacco Fund (400 cigarettes for $1). In Toronto (right) and Galt, now Cambridge, Ont. (below)—and across the country—war on the home front was often a struggle to find adequate housing. Registries appealed to well-housed people to share their dwellings with servicemen's families and with war workers and their children. All Canadians were registered (below, left) in 1940.

WEDNESDAY, AUGUST 13, 1941

Acute Housing Situation In Galt Worries Family Service Bureau

Others soon had to: when parts broke or tires went bald, there was no replacing them unless you could prove your driving was "essential." A weekend trip became a luxury and business in some holiday resorts fell off badly.

Before the war, three of ten Canadians had driven to work. Now car pools were encouraged by allowing pool drivers extra gas coupons. But public transport soon became overburdened. Office and plant hours were staggered, and seats in buses and streetcars were changed to allow more passengers. Bus stops were reduced to save gas.

Conserving gasoline became almost a national pastime. One service station notice read: "No smoking near gas pumps—maybe your life is not worth saving, but gasoline is!" Drivers fine-tuned their cars to ensure maximum mileage. Switching off the gas and coasting downhill became a common—if dangerous—practice. R. S. McLaughlin, president of General Motors of Canada, set the nation a frugal example by driving to work in a horse and buggy. Others built strange gas-saving vehicles, such as bicycles powered by washing-machine engines.

Occasionally shortages, real or imagined, brought on panic buying, and inevitably there was some counterfeiting and conniving with ration books. Women coped with rationing without much diffi-culty, but they were less happy about fashion regulations. In mid-1941, when it was announced that no more silk would be imported, women rushed to buy all the silk stockings they could get. Once these were gone, they wore "mixtures" or "Victory stockings." Said the magazine *New World Illustrated:* "Victory stockings are made from yarn in which filaments of silk are twisted with those of artificial silk. They wear well and look well, but are not so elastic as all-silk. But a 'mixture wrinkle' is a badge of honor."

Restrictions on men's fashions brought about a strange sartorial revolt, caused riots and introduced a new term into the Canadian vocabulary: zoot suit.

Zoot-suit mobs appeared in 1943, when 50 "drape-shape, stuff-cuffed and reat-pleat hoodlums," as one writer described them, broke up a street dance in Montreal. Anybody was suspect who wore a wide collar with a loud tie, baggy pants with tight cuffs, tightly draped jackets hanging to the knees, gaudy socks and Cuban heels. Other zoot-suiter hallmarks were "a Tarzan hairdo, a loud sports coat, huge shoulders and a long watch chain dangling almost to the knees." Knuckle-dusters and lead pipe were optional.

In June 1944, 200 zoot-suiters attacked 30 soldiers returning to the army depot in the Montreal suburb of Longueuil. This led to a weekend of bloody fights concentrated in a dozen nightclubs and some other locales in downtown Montreal. Some 400 sailors appeared on St. Catherine Street, hunted zoot-suiters and stripped many of their fancy apparel.

One result of the fighting and the attention it focused on zoot-suiters was the conviction of a Montreal manufacturer for cutting cloth and selling suits contrary to government regulations. He was fined $400.

Across the land the war changed the character of cities and towns. Moncton, N.B., bristled with air force life, both Canadian and British, for it was here that the RAF mustered its air trainees coming into Canada and going out. Prince Rupert, B.C., was a growing, defended port, hectic with cargo for Alaska. Windsor's car plants worked round the clock. But many smaller places became quieter than ever. When Sgt. Jack Scott visited Kemptville, near Ottawa, he was struck

by the silence of its streets. A local inhabitant explained: most of Kemptville's young people had gone to war.

In Newfoundland, St. John's became a throbbing naval base, a crucial port in the Battle of the Atlantic. Thousands of Canadian, American and British servicemen brought profound changes to the colony's insular life and exposed its people to higher living standards. Unknowingly, they helped prepare Newfoundland for its entry into Confederation four years after the war ended.

Rural Manitoba faced a teacher shortage so chronic and severe that school boards didn't bother to advertise. Six hundred high-school graduates took a six-week cram course to help fill the gap, at salaries of roughly $700 a year.

In Winnipeg, as elsewhere, children felt the war in various ways. The fathers of many were overseas. Some of their friends were British children evacuated to Canadian homes. Children filled utility bags ("No used toothbrushes, please") to be sent to bombed-out Britons. They collected old woollens to be turned into blankets and sent overseas. They put out the salvage and hoed Victory gardens. They saved nickels that now were five-sided and made of zinc. They saved quarters to buy War Savings Certificates, miniature versions of Victory Bonds. If they got some hard-to-find foolscap, they wrote on both sides of it.

Thousands of homes entertained servicemen, mostly trainees from the many air schools. Before the war was over, Mr. and Mrs. Augustus Cannell of Winnipeg had had 350 airmen as weekend guests, among them a young Welshman named Richard Burton who was later to become an actor and a household name.

Winnipeg women ran a central bureau, the first of its kind, for the city's 10,000 volunteers. They registered both people and organizations, got the Junior League to underwrite expenses and pledged themselves to a community-and-war effort. Women in Hamilton and Vancouver followed suit.

In between feeding their families and war guests, these Winnipeg volunteers drove sick children to hospitals, cleared homes to receive evacuated children from overseas, kept the city's welfare clinics going and took airmen's children to the circus. They set up food conservation classes and used their extra preserve sug-

ar for a canning operation that sent fruit to overseas troops.

The bureau ran a huge salvage operation to collect paper, rags, iron, aluminum, bottles, rubber, bones and fat that could be used for war production. It even collected a coffin; it was sold to someone who wanted a flower box. By 1943 the salvage organization had 56 leaders, 1800 block captains, 60 transport workers, 1000 schoolteachers and 30,000 schoolchildren, 238 women selling in stores, 68 committee members and 32 executive members. Its earnings reached $378,359, representing a profit of $112,847.

The women smoked out toothpaste tubes, tinfoil, newspapers and hot water bottles; they drove and maintained second-hand trucks and underwrote their overhead by selling what wasn't melted down for munitions; they appealed to World War I veterans and got hundreds of tin helmets and sent them to London's air raid workers. They organized a warehouse for clothing and shipped 70 tons overseas, paying for the shipping charges by selling Christmas cards. They held rag drives to collect clean cloths for tank repairs, scrounged furniture for leave centers, canvassed for the Red Cross, Community Chest, the Salvation Army and blood donor service. They coordinated dozens of hospitality services into a single United Services Center, whose low-priced home-cooking canteen brought in nightclub entertainers and gave out movie passes, short-order laundry and shoe-repair information.

Then there was Montreal, the nation's unofficial escape valve. Jim Coleman wrote in *Maclean's* in 1944:

. . . Montreal is a bountiful oasis in a land of rationing. There is enough demon rum here to float the entire fleet. You can buy cigars in handfuls. Inquire about this apparent anomaly and the Montrealer shrugs his shoulders and looks significantly toward heaven.

Night life in "The Paris of America" is booming. Tired businessmen, expatriates who have fled briefly from more arid sections, money-heavy war workers and men and women in uniform keep the merry wheels spinning.

The boom dwarfs even the lush days of the Torrid Twenties, when the stock market was on a bender. There are two reasons: more people have more money and Montreal is the only major city in Canada where a person may drink in public without risking arrest.

The pleasures of Montreal are gustatory and just plain gusty. Its French cooking is ranked with the finest in the world and eating isn't necessarily expensive. For many years Café Martin and Drury's English Grill have catered to a discriminating clientele and an extremely satisfactory *table d'hôte* dinner can be had in either for as little as $1.15. At the Mount Royal Hotel's Normandie Roof, where crowds form early each evening to eat, dance and see a floor show, dinner is $2.50 a person. The average drink cost 65 cents, plus a cabaret tax of 25 percent and a provincial tax of 5 percent.

There is a notable elasticity in the city's "closing laws." The largest bars in the Mount Royal and the Windsor Hotel adhere to a schedule. But the nightclubs set their own rules—the basis of which seems to be: "Don't close if there's a good spender in the house." The formal night spots close Sunday, but bootleggers do a flourishing business.

There are rumors that some of the nightclubs are fronts for gambling establishments. In any event you can find ample outlet for gambling in Montreal—dice, roulette, barbotte and betting on the horses.

The inexhaustible liquor supply in the nightclubs is interesting to a visitor. Apparently anyone with proper connections can obtain liquor by the bottle or case without possessing a permit.

Hockey games, wrestling matches and theaters are besieged. Restaurants and hundreds of taverns are packed. No matter how you feel about such things in wartime, entertainment in Montreal is booming as never before. . . .

JIM COLEMAN

Montreal was so wide open—and its venereal disease rate so high—that by 1944 military authorities were threatening to put the entire city out-of-bounds to all servicemen not stationed there. City police staged an anti-vice drive. A number of brothels were closed—only to be reopened a few months later.

The liveliness of Montreal stood in sharp contrast to what another journalist found in Victoria. As part of the deep apprehension which spread through British Columbia after Pearl Harbor, a detailed plan had been worked out to evacuate the entire populace of Vancouver Island and to speed troops to likely Japanese landing spots. Hundreds of trucks, cars, yachts and powerboats had been earmarked for the job. A bustling naval base throbbed at Esquimalt.

What effect, journalist Lionel Shapiro wondered in 1942, had all this had on the traditional reserve of Victoria? Had it become as rowdy as San Diego, as hectic as Honolulu? The answer, he wrote in *Saturday Night,* was no:

. . . Victoria is a crowning example of how to withstand the impact of military necessity. Many military and naval newcomers are here, to be sure, but Victoria hasn't changed. Promptly at ten o'clock Billy Tickle and his ensemble play the national anthem in the lounge of the Empress Hotel and Victoria's candle is snuffed out for the night. Neither an urchin's hoot nor an auto's rumble rends the atmosphere until the next morning.

The serviceman does not wither or collapse in Victoria, however. There are dances for him under local auspices. The Victoria Hostess Club, for instance, has a handsome hall in operation nightly where dancing and refreshment (light) may be obtained at little or no cost. There is joviality and jitterbugging but everything stops at an eminently respectable hour. Victoria is war-conscious; vibrantly so, to be sure. But not after 10 p.m. . . .

Victoria was an exception to the one overriding fact of wartime life across Canada: change. Bruce Hutchison detected it at work in Quebec. In his 1942 book *The Unknown Country,* he said:

. . . Ideas are flowing in here, into the towns and smallest villages. What these ideas are doing to Quebec, how they are changing the old values and the old virtues, how much they are helping to unite the two races of Canada and break down old barriers—this is one of the great imponderables of Canadian life.

Young men are learning to compete with English-speaking Canadians in business, in manufacturing, in modern techniques. Here is the basic change that sweeps the old French province.

Up and down the St. Lawrence, the smoke of English-Canadian capital billows up beside French-Canadian church spires, hard by the little narrow farms. In the hills, streams are dammed for power by English-Canadian corporations. Rural Quebec is being industrialized by the enterprisers of other provinces. French people leave their farms to live in the new industrial towns and cities, and there they find that life is not what they used to think. It is infinitely more complex and difficult and glittering. There are pleasures they never heard of and economic, class and wage problems unknown back in the village, where the curé could settle anything. Here agitators stir them up against the owning class and against English-speaking Canadians. Soon Quebec begins to develop a self-conscious proletariat, where it had once only a carefree peasantry.

The Church grows worried. Some of the people in the towns are skeptical and question the old teachings. The ruling classes are worried. The politicians find all sorts of new pressures, new cries and new notions. What is happening to Quebec, the most conservative, peaceful, innocent part of the whole New World? Civilization is coming to Quebec. The civilization of machines. . . .

The long-range implications of what this meant are immense. To a substantial extent, the war prepared the way for the momentous things that happened later. But at the time these implications were lost in a larger phenomenon. The whole country was changing. It would never be the same again.

Every Canadian was urged to make some contribution to the war effort. Many men and women, like this farmer's wife, were volunteer aircraft spotters. Children played a part too. In Winnipeg (left) they line up to contribute pots and pans in a drive for aluminum to be used in the manufacture of weapons.

The tanker

In a mobile defensive action, a shortage of petrol means disaster.

FIELD MARSHAL ERWIN ROMMEL

The situation for Rommel's Afrika Korps was desperate. On the night of October 23, 1942, British Eighth Army had launched a long expected attack on the Axis front at El Alamein and, after two days of battle, had punched deep holes in the defenses. Rommel, on sick leave in Germany, had immediately flown to Egypt to take command, but even the Desert Fox could do little. Fuel was so short that there was scarcely enough to keep a mobile battle going for two or three days. Unless he could deploy his tanks as he wished, his hands were tied.

On the 25th Rommel signaled Hitler that the battle would be lost unless he received fuel immediately. To his annoyance, he had learned that his supply ships were being sent to Benghazi to keep out of range of RAF Beaufort torpedo bombers which had been harassing Axis convoys. From Benghazi it would take days for the fuel to reach the front—and Rommel couldn't wait. He therefore insisted that a convoy containing the 5000-ton tanker *Proserpina*, with 3500 tons of fuel aboard, be diverted to Tobruk which was much nearer.

By the afternoon of October 26 *Proserpina*, with two freighters and an escort of four destroyers, was in sight of the Libyan coast. But the convoy had been spotted, and an RAF strike force of eight torpedo-carrying Beauforts, five Bisley light bombers and six Beaufighters was quickly assembled at Gianaclis, southeast of Alexandria. The crews were told: "The tanker is the primary target. The battle is approaching a critical stage and Rommel must get this tanker

through to stand a chance. The Bisleys will go in first and create a diversion by attacking the freighters. The Beauforts will go for the tanker. Fighter cover will be provided by the Beaufighters. By the time you get there the convoy will be well within cover of shore-based flak and fighters."

One of the Beaufort pilots was PO. Ralph Manning, a quiet Canadian from Vancouver. In an account he wrote shortly afterward, Manning reconstructed what happened to himself and others on the mission:
. . . Out to the aircraft for a quick takeoff. Just before we board, Hal Davidson of Winnipeg, a Beaufort pilot on his first operational mission, yells good luck. We are going to need it. As we head out to sea I try not to think what it will be like at the other end.

Two hours later we make a landfall. Our navigation is a little out and we are slightly east of Tobruk—a pity since Jerry will know we are here and have time to get fighters in the air. We follow the coast west and just past Tobruk see 12 power-driven barges below. Up comes the flak, and the shore guns open up too. Charlie Bladen starts firing at the barges with a side gun and my other gunner, "Nimmy" Nimerovsky, tells him in a bored voice to save his ammunition.

Up the coast we go, and then ahead we sight two aircraft circling some ships below. It must be the convoy. The ships are hugging the coast about a mile offshore—a small merchant ship and a destroyer, then a large merchant ship and a couple of destroyers. No sign of the tanker but I think I see something else farther along.

At this moment our formation leader, Flt. Lt. "Auntie" Gee does a steep turn toward the ships, followed by the other aircraft. I pull upward sharply. I am surprised and irritated, because I am *sure* there is no tanker among these ships. Since we have not passed it, it must be farther along. I decide to fly on, feeling a little scared because there are some Italian fighters overhead now. Soon after, thank God, two of the Bisleys catch up and, unknown to us, another Beaufort, piloted by Norman Hearn-Phillips, is also following. Ahead there's a plume of smoke. We come abreast of it—and sure enough it *is* the tanker with one destroyer on its port beam.

Meanwhile, as I learned later, the main formation is making its attack on the other ships. Three Bisleys go in first, striking for the leading vessel, the small merchant ship. As they drop their bombs the flak is fierce. One Bisley is hit and crashes. The Beauforts go in next—four dropping their torpedoes at the lead ship and one at the larger merchantman. A Beaufort staggers as a shell shoots half its rudder away, but somehow the

pilot regains control and climbs away. Hal Davidson is not so lucky. After dropping his torpedo, his aircraft is hit, hovers for a moment, then flicks over and falls to the sea. The rest of the formation, realizing that it has attacked the wrong target, now heads west to give us support.

Hearn-Phillips is already on the scene. But as he starts his run-in on the tanker, his aircraft is hit by flak. The shell pierces the fuse box, shorting the electrical system—and the torpedo releases itself and falls harmlessly into the sea. Now ours is the only torpedo left.

We turn toward the tanker to make our run and are almost in position when the tanker realizes its danger and turns head-on, spoiling our approach. I am strongly tempted to drop the torpedo, but decide to attack from the other side. The destroyer turns inside of us, firing all the time. We turn and come in on the tanker from the landward side. At about 700 yards I press the button to release our torpedo. Almost at the same time a Bisley streaks toward the ship, drops its delayed-action bombs and pulls up sharply, but a fraction too late. Its wing strikes the tanker's foremast and shears off, just as a second Bisley flies in over the tanker to attack. Up in the nose of our aircraft my navigator, Norm Spark, records the scene on his camera.

As we speed forward, I see out of the corner of my eye puffs of white smoke on the destroyer as a Beaufighter dives in and gives it a burst. So much is happening that I forget the danger from the exploding bombs and, at the last second, I pull hard on the stick and gain height. There's a hell-uva explosion and jar, and for an awful moment I wonder whether we have engines or not. But we are still flying. I have had no chance to observe the run of our torpedo but suddenly there's another great explosion and a shout from Nimerovsky: "It's a hit!" Evidently our torpedo gave the tanker a glancing blow on the port bow, failed to go off, and then ran along the side of the hull and finally exploded just before reaching the stern. It is soon shrouded in smoke.

Over the radio there's a lot of excited talk. Then I hear Nimmy yelling for me to take evasive action as there is more flak coming up at us. I see some of our aircraft to port and make for them. Soon there is a good party of us and we speed out to sea.

On the run home someone sights a formation of Messerschmitts heading northwest but we are flying low and luckily escape their attention. Then, tragedy. I notice a bright flash to our rear and yell to Nimmy asking what it is. In a shocked voice he tells me that a Bisley and Beaufort have collided and crashed into the sea. We fly on and eventually the pink skyline of Alexandria comes in sight. On landing we find that one of our petrol tanks is holed and the mainspar damaged by bullets, and we figure we must have been hit by one of the Italian fighters during the attack.

At dusk a force of Wellington bombers is sent to finish off the convoy. They sink the large merchant ship, with two torpedoes. There's no sign of the small merchantman. But the tanker is where we left it, still burning from stem to stern. . . . RALPH MANNING

For the Axis troops the loss of *Proserpina* was devastating. On November 2, Eighth Army launched a massive attack and by November 4 the enemy was in full retreat after one of the key battles of the war.

PO. Ralph Manning (left) piloted the Beaufort whose torpedo hit the tanker *Proserpina*. His navigator, Flt. Sgt. Norm Spark, captured the action on film (below). The Bisley at the top of the photograph has dropped its bombs and pulled up sharply —but a fraction of a second too late. Its wing has struck the tanker's foremast and sheared off—just as a second Bisley (bottom) moves in to attack.

They also served

The war works a revolution in the role of women in the armed forces, in industry and in the home

The Canadian commodore, an old seadog, was adamant. "I will not have women in my command," he shouted. "I don't want them, and I won't have them."

The representative of the Women's Royal Canadian Naval Service stood her ground. "But Commodore," she replied, calmly tapping her forehead, "our Wrens have something up here."

"I don't care where they've got it," snapped the commodore. "My sailors are sure to find it."

There were Colonel Blimps in Canada, too—old-school commanding officers like the commodore who couldn't tolerate the thought of women in the armed forces and couldn't imagine that they'd be anything more than a nuisance.

The Blimps lost. Before the war was over 45,000 Canadian servicewomen were performing almost every non-combatant job a man could do, and often doing it better.

The Blimps' reaction was only part of the story of resistance to this revolutionary change. Britain had been recruiting women since 1938 but the war was nearly two years old before the Canadian government would accept the idea. Canada didn't need women to run her war, Ottawa said; she had more than enough male volunteers. A nurse, of course, was different. Nursing sisters were a Canadian military tradition. Ten of them were in the Boer War. From 1914 to 1918 some 2800 Canadian nurses served—and 47 died as a result of enemy action. When World War II began, there was no question that nurses should serve again. By June 1940 the first contingent of 129 was on its way to Britain.

But other women, it seemed, were not wanted. Undaunted, some decided to mobilize anyway. Unofficial women's service groups sprang up across Canada, teaching members first aid, how to repair vehicles, how to drill like soldiers. In Victoria, ten women started the B.C. Women's Service Club; another group formed

Women helped win the war as CWACs, WDs, Wrens, nurses, riveters, welders, bus drivers, munitions makers. . . . Whatever her wartime job, the Canadian woman helped improve the status, morale and working conditions of her sex more than any social legislation had ever done.

the Canadian Women's Service Force; *Toronto Daily Star* columnist Ivy Maison inaugurated the Canadian Auxiliary Territorial Service, taking its name from Britain's ATS. Women were so eager to serve that the CATS quickly grew to a force of more than 3000. Their theme song enthused:

> We will fight for the might that we know is right,
> And even Mussolini knows that CATS can fight. . . .

If Mussolini knew, Ottawa still professed not to. The voluntary organizations lobbied for acceptance of women in the military forces but not even the manpower shortage that developed early in 1941 could change things.

Then Britain suggested sending some members of her Women's Auxiliary Air Force (WAAFs) to Canada to work at RAF training schools. This led Ottawa to reconsider. In May 1941 the cabinet authorized enlistment of "female auxiliary personnel." On July 2, an order-in-council established the Canadian Women's Auxiliary Air Force (later the RCAF Women's Division—the WDs). A month later the Canadian Women's Army Corps (CWACs) was created. The navy—whose authorities first thought a "maximum of 20 women would suffice"—held out one more year, then established the Women's Royal Canadian Naval Service. Eventually the Wrens recruited not 20 women but 6500.

Reported author Robert Collins:

. . . By early fall of 1941, recruiting was underway. Posters proclaimed, "You Can Personally Help Win This War." Women volunteered by the hundreds. A few came because they were bored but most because they were patriotic. Many enlisted because they had sons, brothers, husbands or fathers in uniform. One girl checked in with "We Have To Kill the Germans and Japs" painted on her suitcase.

There were farm girls and debutantes, showgirls and university grads. The CWACs, at one time or another, had a hospital assistant who spoke ten languages, a full-blooded Cree Indian from Saskatchewan and a professional knife thrower. The WDs had a bronco buster, a parachute jumper, a New Jersey model and a girl who had walked 19 miles to a recruiting center in the north.

Officials were confronted with strange new problems. Would ladies' jacket pockets be expandable? Yes, to accommodate Kleenex and compacts. Would greatcoats be belted in front? Never! That would only make stout girls look stouter. What about pay? The women would get two thirds a man's pay; later this was raised to four fifths. . . .

While the other services turned to Britain for help, the army organized the CWACs on its own. Col. Elizabeth Smellie, nursing matron-in-chief, was made temporary administrator, and toured the country to select the first officers. Mrs. Joan Kennedy, commandant of the B.C. Women's Service Club, was appointed director, and by September 1 the CWAC was ready to enroll its first volunteer.

Like male recruits in 1939, the early CWACs had to wait weeks for uniforms. Meanwhile they drilled in civvies. Irene Vivash, a volunteer from Peterborough, Ont., who later won a BEM, recalls that "one of the recruits, Alice Pruner, used to march in front of me with a set of fox collar pieces that flipped up and hit me in the face whenever the sergeant major called halt. It caused me to sneeze, her to giggle and the sergeant major to bellow."

There were two basic training centers for CWACs: one in a former residential school in Vermilion, Alta., the other in an army camp at Kitchener, Ont. By 1943 Kitchener had a staff of 200 and was teaching not only discipline, drill and army routine but more than 25 trades. Many were trained to become clerks, stenographers, cooks, storewomen, tailors, laundry workers, telephone and wireless operators. Others learned to be cipher clerks, radar operators, medical and dental assistants, drivers, armorers, draftsmen, mechanics, fitters, welders.

Lotta Dempsey, who visited the Kitchener camp in early 1943, reported in *Maclean's*:

. . . The women live in 35 tar-paper huts. They sleep in long, bare bunkhouses, each with 40 or more Spartan upper and lower bunks. They wash in bleak "ablution rooms" equipped with rows of metal washbowls and cement-floored showers. They eat in large mess halls, 500 at a time, cafeteria style. And they have learned to work in teams, at everything from repairing wireless sets to drilling with gas masks.

But all through the camp there is a sense of womanliness, as pungent as the *eau de cologne* in the sergeants' mess, as real as the cold-cream jars in the washrooms.

I watched the CWACs do "man jobs" well and efficiently, and while they worked I heard a patter of woman-talk: a new boyfriend . . . a letter from home . . . a spring hat glimpsed in a window (they talk about them even if they don't wear them) . . . a movie or a love story.

Once I came upon a briskly marching column, and instead of the strains of "Roll Out the Barrel" or "Mademoiselle From Armentières" they were singing in a high, sweet chorus, "As Long As You're Not In Love With Somebody Else, Why Don't You Fall In Love With Me?" . . .

Roughly 21,000 women passed through the CWAC training centers. Some were chosen to go on to officer training at Ste. Anne de Bellevue, Que.—one of them for an unusual reason. She was called before a selection board and told to be seated. As she sat down her chair collapsed. Looking calmly up from the floor she said, "Is this part of the test?" The board passed her on the spot, convinced that anyone that unflappable had to be a good officer.

The RCAF appealed to Britain for help in forming its Women's Division, and in the summer of 1941 five WAAF officers arrived to help two Canadian appointees, Kay Walker and Dr. Jean Davey. One of the first jobs was to select and train what soon was known as the "First 150"—all of whom became officers or NCOs. Their commanding officer was Sqdn. Ldr. G. P. Hedges.

An ex-CWAC, Gladys Taylor, wrote that "every women's service had its 'mother hens'—sergeant majors and others who, under violent protests at first, were entrusted with imparting military drill, discipline and esprit de corps to the ladies. They held a special place in the hearts of the women they trained. Poems were written to them. Socks were knit for them. But few got quite the devotion of Sgt. Maj. Fred Purkis whose CWAC girls at Vermilion presented him with a bouquet of flowers and a rocking chair on Mother's Day."

The "First 150" became the backbone of the RCAF's 17,000-strong Women's Division. Its motto was "We serve that men may fly." Recruits at Toronto's No. 6 Manning Depot, under Hedges' command, were taught trades which included such specialist jobs as parachute packing, photo-interpretation and air traffic control.

The navy organized in much the same way as the RCAF. As director it appointed Adelaide Sinclair, a former Wartime Prices and Trade Board official. "One day," she recalled, "I was called in by Navy Minister Angus L. Macdonald. He talked to me about everything except the Wrens. If it was a test I must have passed it." To assist her the British Admiralty lent Superintendent Joan Carpenter and two other senior Wren officers. They toured Canada to pick the first 67 recruits, 22 of whom became officers. A basic training center called HMCS Conestoga, commanded by Lt. Comdr. Isabel Macneill, was opened at Galt, Ont., in October 1942. A record of the ceremony says: "The chaplain closed his prayer book. The bugle sounded the general salute. A new white ensign was raised by the halyardmen and another ship had been commissioned in the service of the RCN. But this ship did not slip down the ways. It would never hear the firing of guns or the roaring of angry seas. HMCS Conestoga was a stone frigate and the first ship in our navy to be captained by a woman."

When Wrens left Conestoga for their first posting, they were sternly lectured on behavior. It was like that in all training centers. Graduates were told that on them rested the reputation and future of all women's services. To smooth the way, the WDs sent a training command staff officer, Willa Magee, to "indoctrinate station commanders in the reception of airwomen."

She found that although most male commanding officers were enthusiastic about having airwomen in their command, they were unsure as to how to handle them. Some seemed to regard the WDs as "a strange new religious order which should be cloistered for the duration. They variously suggested the construction of high walls around our barracks, rigid partitioning in the mess halls, separate parades for airmen and airwomen, and a general program of ascetic monasticism. This attitude stemmed from typical male uneasiness in the face of things feminine rather than from deliberate hostility. By contrast, other commanders persisted in spoiling the WDs. So anxious were they to welcome the women that they would have no hand in their discipline except to ensure that they suffered no undue hardships. WDs were not permitted to parade too early in the morning for fear they would catch cold; airmen's canteen funds were spent for WD canteens when airmen themselves had dreary ones."

In practice the problems were soon sorted out. As Robert Collins wrote:

... When the first contingent of trained WDs reached Moncton air station in January 1942, they peered warily from their bus windows, wondering if it was permissible even to look at the men. But no airman was in sight.

"Suddenly we realized they were all inside peeking out at us," remembers Fran Richardson. "They had repainted an entire barracks block for us, laid on a fancy dinner and then taken cover. There were 60 men in my section. They screened my dates, told me who not to go out with and acted like big brothers."

Naturally not all servicemen regarded the women as sisters. But the women soon learned to cope with this problem. When applicable, they pulled rank. Sometimes they used force: one Peeping Tom fled from a London, Ont., CWAC barracks before an onslaught of boot-wielding lady privates.

The real problem often was the wolf in officer's clothing. Wren Jean Danard waited one night while two senior officers flipped a coin to see who'd take her home. "Neither dreamed of consulting me," she says. "Luckily, the nice guy won." Another time she was called into a commander's office for dictation. As she began to take notes the officer seized her left hand in an amorous grip. Wren Danard studied the gold rings on his sleeve and did the only thing she could: kept taking dictation with her right hand. The bewildered officer hung on but made no further advances. He never called her back for dictation either.

By late 1942 the RCAF's Air Marshal L. S. Breadner spoke for commanders of all services when he told a group of WDs: "The experiment is over. You are no longer a novelty to the service. The WD has become an integral part of the RCAF and soon we shall wonder how the service ever got along without you."

A year later there were 32,000 Canadian women doing jobs that would have been unthinkable for women two years before, and sometimes doing them with outstanding resourcefulness and courage. In Manitoba a 21-year-old CWAC ambulance driver drove three sick soldiers 62 miles through a blizzard, ran out of gasoline, scrounged more and reached Winnipeg triumphantly behind a snowplow in the middle of the night. In the Maritimes another CWAC private crawled out of the wreckage of a truck, gave first aid to four companions and the driver, hobbled half a mile to a telephone on a sprained ankle and won the British Empire Medal. By war's end 244 servicewomen had won decorations. . . . ROBERT COLLINS

The ambition of many servicewomen was to be posted abroad, and some 2900 CWACs, 1400 WDs and 1000 Wrens were. Most went to Britain but some CWACs worked in headquarters jobs in Italy and northwest Europe. Other women served on Canadian military staffs in Washington and New York.

Canada's 4172 nursing sisters got around too. On March 8, 1941, one of them became the toast of London. Petite, pretty Helen-Marie Stevens, a physiotherapist on leave, was dining in West End London's posh Café de Paris that night when a German air raid struck. A bomb exploded on the dance floor and turned the nightclub into a shambles. Dead and wounded were everywhere. In an eerie darkness lit by flashlights and flames, Lieutenant Stevens worked for hours, binding wounds with tablecloths and serviettes, putting makeshift splints on broken limbs, using champagne as an antiseptic. She was in nerve shock from the explosion but she was the last woman to leave. Her only comment: "I did what any Canadian nurse would do."

The London press disagreed. One headline after another called her a heroine. Canadian Press war correspondent Ross Munro found her next day for an interview. It led to courtship—and marriage two years later.

Some nurses were posted to remote places. In *Checkmate in the North,* W. G. Carr recalls:

... At first there were no white women at the new air base at Goose Bay, Labrador. Then six nursing sisters were flown in when the RCAF hospital was opened. Told they would be the only women among several thousand men, one nearly fainted. Another shouted, "Oh Lord, this must be paradise!"

Soon another five Canadian women arrived, then eight American nursing sisters. All were a credit to the services they represented. They played no favorites. They were about as jolly and carefree a bunch of girls as one could meet. They attended Saturday night parties in the mess and danced until everyone who wanted to had danced at least once. Then chairs were drawn up in front of the fire and everyone sang the old songs. They were like 19 sisters in a big family of unruly boys. . . .

The nursing sisters got closest to the front lines. Two of them, Kathleen Christie

Drummers beat time for recruits in training at HMCS *Conestoga,* the navy's "stone frigate" at Galt, Ont. Drumming was a sideline; these Wrens' main duties were as sick berth and wardroom attendants and clerks. Specialist training for air force women (above) included parachute packing and photo-interpretation.

and Maye Waters, went with the Canadian force sent to Hong Kong. They nursed the sick and wounded during the December 1941 battle and in prison camp. They were repatriated in November 1943. Canadian nurses served in western Europe, Africa, Sicily and Italy. Twelve were wounded in an air raid on Catania, Sicily. Another 99 survived when the troopship *Santa Elena* was torpedoed in the Mediterranean on November 6, 1943.

Santa Elena was carrying 1800 Canadian Army personnel to Italy, including the staff of No. 14 Canadian General Hospital. About 20 miles off the North African coast, the convoy was attacked just after sunset by German torpedo-bombers. In the fading light the raiders flew low and released their torpedoes almost at mast height. They struck three ships.

Most of the nurses were in their cabins or the dining room when an explosion ripped through *Santa Elena*. The lights went out and the vessel took on a list. There was confusion but no panic. When the "abandon ship" was sounded the nurses climbed into lifeboats and were lowered away. In some the ship's crewmen seemed incapable of taking charge so the nurses took over and manned the oars themselves.

While the rest of the convoy moved on, two ships stopped to take on survivors while several destroyers guarded against submarine attack. Some lifeboats made for the destroyers, others pulled toward the nearest ship, the liner *Monterey*.

To get aboard *Monterey* the exhausted nurses had to climb almost 60 feet up a rope net in the dark. Waiting for the lifeboat to rise in the swell, each nurse in turn leaped to catch the net, then hauled herself up. One, Elsa Turnbull, lost her hold almost as she reached the top; she fell to the water, narrowly missing a cluster of rafts and boats. A man dived in and pulled her out. Another nurse, Ida MacKay, fell from 15 feet up and was rescued too.

The nurses were taken to a wardroom. "We were a sorry-looking sight," remembers Agnes Lovett. "None of us had any kit but we found a lipstick and a few combs and soon made repairs." Within an hour she was called to duty: a soldier required an emergency operation and she was asked to assist.

No lives were lost in the sinking of *Santa Elena* but the staff of No. 14 General Hospital landed in Italy without equipment,

which had gone down with the ship. It was soon replaced and the staff went to work.

In Italy the narrow roads often made casualty evacuation so difficult that hospitals had to be moved as far forward as possible, often within sound of gunfire and exposed to air attack. Casualty clearing stations, field dressing stations and field surgical units to which nursing sisters were attached were often set up ahead of the gun sites and sometimes under observation of enemy positions.

Nursing Sister Evelyn Pepper of No. 5 Casualty Clearing Station wrote in *The Canadian Nurse:* "In the 18 months our unit was in Sicily and Italy, we moved forward with the fighting troops 16 times. Once we set up our unit in a small apartment block ahead of a heavy gun site. Almost certainly we were being observed by the enemy. Before we were really ready to receive them, the casualties were on our doorstep, and we were working like beavers. One of the operating-room nurses, on hearing a scratching sound on the roof, looked up. 'There must be mice or bats up

there,' she said quietly through her mask. 'That's neither mice nor bats,' the surgeon replied, 'that's shrapnel!' The operations continued throughout the night."

On the Ortona front casualties were constant, wrote Lt. Col.W. R. Feasby in *The Canadian Medical Services.* "Troops lived under indescribable hardships, and the nursing sisters shared these conditions with a cheerfulness never to be forgotten by the men. In spring 1944, as the fighting shifted to the Cassino area, the nursing sisters followed closely behind the advancing troops. They slept in ambulance cars, under canvas and in bomb-torn buildings. They worked at top speed and in some cases almost to the point of exhaustion. In 20 days of May and June, more than 2000 Canadian casualties were cared for by our nurses."

For many other nursing sisters, first contact with battle casualties came soon after D-Day when the first wounded arrived back in England. As soon as the Normandy beachhead was large enough to contain casualty clearing stations and general hospitals, the nursing sisters were

The first CWACs to serve overseas went to Britain in November 1942. Soon some were training as fire fighters in London's blitzed areas. One CWAC in a later draft made headlines when she removed her cap so she wouldn't have to salute, then kissed Lt. Gen. E. W. Sansom—her father. Charmian Sansom became a lieutenant, an announcer on a BBC program beamed to Allied troops in Europe. Enchanted by her voice, men wrote letters like the one below, begging her to send a photo. "I'm not allowed to," said Charmian. But when the program closed down in July 1945 everybody saw Charmian Sansom on the cover of *Picture Post*.

sent over. One of the first contingents to go belonged to No. 7 Canadian General Hospital. Attached to it was Red Cross welfare officer Jean Ellis. In *Face Powder and Gunpowder* she writes:

. . . Approaching shore, we could see a mass of people on the beach. They waved and shouted and surrounded us the minute we landed. Canadian soldiers swarmed in. French boys in berets gaped at us; gendarmes beamed: abbés in long robes smiled at us. Everyone cheered and tried to shake our hands.

Soon we were loaded into open trucks and set off, driving through village after village amid lines of cheering lads. French people leaned from windows to throw

kisses, calling out, *"Vivent les Canadiennes!"* As we passed troops in fields along the way, we sang "The Maple Leaf Forever" and "O Canada" to let them know that 60 Canadian girls had come to share their job.

Many times our convoy was forced to stop and soldiers would dash over to shake hands.

"Girls! They're Canadians."

"How far are you going, girls?"

"What's your hospital?"

We saw many tears. Before long a lot of us were feeling them trickle down our own faces. We knew that we reminded the boys of their womenfolk at home . . . and they reminded us of boys we would never see again.

Our convoy drove up to a British hospital near Bayeux and 35 girls were dropped off to "board" until our own equipment arrived. The rest, including myself and my Red Cross friend Connie Harrison, were driven five miles forward to No. 75 British General Hospital, a collection of tents in a field.

On our second morning there the matron told us, "A huge convoy is coming in with hundreds of casualties. My staff cannot handle them all. Will you girls help?" The nursing sisters ate and reported for duty.

Connie, Betty Hanlon, the laboratory technician, and I were the only laymen in our party, but we hoped there would be jobs for us too. When we asked for orders, the matron said: "Meet all the incoming patients at the A and D (Admission and Dispatch) tent. Do what you can for them while they await admission to wards."

Casualties usually did not go directly from the front line to a general hospital. But this was the day Caen was taken. Ordinary facilities could not handle all the cases, so hundreds of wounded were brought in with little previous treatment.

Wounded men on stretchers were placed in rows in the big A and D tent. All were badly hurt, many unconscious. Some had arms and legs almost severed. Some had already undergone emergency amputations. Yellow field dressings covered wounds and the men all wore their mud-caked, bloody uniforms. All were mercifully under the influence of drugs. The heat was stifling, smells were terrific and millions of flies came swarming around.

Connie and I went down the rows of stretchers with cigarettes, trying to be

we must know what you look like. We must have some link between this evanescent Charmion that we know and the everyday world of tangible mortals. We think, in view of the impossibility of asking you to join us here, that a photograph of you would accomplish this.

In this world of many ills there are few things that truly bring joy to men. You, in your radio form have been many things to us at many times. The gayety in your voice, the lilt, your charming laughter have all been things that have lightened our hearts and for this we have been in your debt. Now we ask one more thing- this photograph. You have

PICTURE POST

cheerful though it was a struggle not to burst into tears. Saying things like "Hi. Anything we can do for you?" sounded silly, but the boys appeared to like it. We lit cigarettes for those who couldn't light their own. We had tea for all who were allowed it, and was it ever welcome! Once the doctor said they could have fluid, they gulped down everything brought to them.

"Will you take my boots off, Sister?" one boy said faintly. He was very pale and his eyes were closed. I had to tug hard before the boots came off; the poor lad's feet were horribly swollen. His socks were so rotten with perspiration that they practically fell off; the smell was indescribable. I washed some of the blood and dirt off his face, then wiped his feet. "Thanks, Sister, that feels wonderful," he smiled, still not opening his eyes. "I haven't had my boots off for two weeks." I removed many boots that day; the expression on the men's faces was touching. Even those who were unconscious would wiggle their toes in relief.

After the first convoy of 200 patients had been admitted to wards, I went to the matron for further orders. "Go into any ward and offer your services," she said. I was assigned 25 beds and told to remove the patients' clothing, bathe them, keep them from getting chilled and have them ready for further examination by the MO. Everything I had ever learned about first aid came in handy but it wasn't nearly enough. Parts of uniforms had to be cut off and I was so afraid of hurting the men that my fingers were all thumbs and I shook like a leaf at times.

Water was very precious and one basin was used over and over until it simply could not be used again. Even when it was almost mud, some poor lad's feet were soaked in it to make him relax.

The heat, flies and smells had made me more than a little dizzy when the nursing sister asked for help with a delirious patient while she adjusted the bandage on his head. I remember saying through a sort of haze, "What is all that gray stuff on the pillow?"

"Brains," she said.

Everything started to go black. I dashed out of the tent and was violently sick. After the first spasm I looked across to the next tent and there was Connie in the same situation. When we could, we waved limply to each other and went back to work. In the next two days, 600 casualties came in. . . .

JEAN ELLIS

Most Canadian women served their country out of uniform. By 1944 there were almost a million of them working in war plants and civilian industry. Robert Collins in *Maclean's:*

. . . Fully half were doing what had always been considered men's work, and doing it well. With fingers sensitized by years of stitching buttonholes and shelling peas, women excelled at such intricate jobs as filling fuses, assembling radio tubes and operating small machines. But they were good at almost anything: paint spraying, auto assembly, spot welding, light punch-press work and riveting. Women ran streetcars, operated gas pumps, trimmed meat in packing plants, bottled beer in

The women's services: below, a Wren sick berth attendant, supervised by a nursing sister, assists at an operation; right, an RCAF Women's Division band; below (opposite page), CWACs arrive in Naples in June 1944.

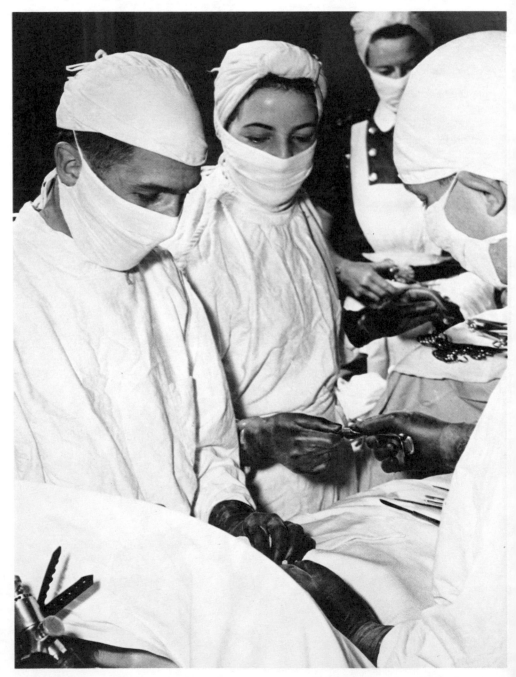

brewerics and moved log booms at pulp mills.

The Steel Company of Canada at Hamilton had them cleaning plant railway tracks and loading freight cars. Canadian National Railways in Toronto assigned them to oiling engines, cleaning ashes from pits and firing up boilers. The CNR liked them because, says an ex-superintendent, "to our great surprise they did exactly as they were told!"

Thousands went into the major war plants of Ontario and Quebec, making aircraft, rifles, ammunition, anti-aircraft guns and radar equipment. Others worked everywhere from Nova Scotia shipyards to B.C. salmon canneries. Eighty percent of them were between 18 and 40, but they also included schoolgirl farmerettes who pitched hay on summer holidays and a 72-year-old woman who rose at 4 a.m. daily to be on time for her job as an inspector in a Toronto arsenal. They were housemaids, housewives, students, Junior Leaguers—women from every background. The Bren-gun assembly line at the John Inglis plant in Toronto included Margaret "Kitty Cat" McDonald, wife of Mickey, then public enemy No. 1. In Flin Flon, Man., the wife of a British diplomat worked as a supervisor for a mining-smelting company; a Toronto sculptress, Merle Foster, helped build Lancaster airplanes; a Hollywood starlet, Helen Gray Fraser, was a transport driver with de Havilland Aircraft.

Such jobs gave some women a sense of purpose for the first time in their lives. For each, the war was a rare adventure that somehow sharpened one's sense of awareness. The female war worker became a sort of national heroine. Her turbaned head,

with curls billowing out in defiance of safety regulations, looked down from billboards almost as often as the rock-jawed airman who kept inviting young men to become World Travelers at 21. Every city had its Miss War Worker contest, with contestants roundly and firmly packed into form-fitting coveralls. For women on night shifts, movie houses ran morning films. There was an Anti-Noise Week to help

A Red Cross girl is the first glimpse of home for Canadian seamen just released from prison camp. They were captured after surviving the sinking of the destroyer *Athabaskan* in 1944. Women worked the same long hours as men but, said one nursing sister, "we played hard too." Left: a CWAC officer catching, a nursing sister at bat. Above: war correspondent Ross Munro of The Canadian Press and Nursing Sister Helen-Marie Stevens on their wedding day in Britain. They met when Munro went to interview Lieutenant Stevens about her care of the wounded in the bombing of London's Café de Paris in March 1941.

them sleep and everyone hummed "Milkman, Keep Those Bottles Quiet."

The pay was good. Employers were willing to pay a woman almost as much as a man. A female aircraft production worker in 1944, for example, averaged 79 cents an hour in most provinces, three cents less than a man.

Before the war women had worked in a few roles such as stenographers and telephone operators. The idea that they should go to work in multitudes and into many other jobs was a revolutionary thing. But by 1942 manpower was so short that Ottawa was telling single women what jobs they should or should not take, establishing day nurseries for working mothers and setting up an emergency vocational training program.

Appeals for women workers were made on radio, in magazines and newspapers. Employers were no longer fussy about age or education. Indeed, they had discovered that the old were as good as or better than the young. They were steady, dependable and careful, which was all-important in munitions work.

Male heckling drove many women workers to tears. But sooner or later the women brought the men to heel. Sometimes they fought fire with fire. One shipyard had a sign that said NO SWEARING, PLEASE. THERE MAY BE GENTLEMEN PRESENT. In a Manitoba plant one girl swore so fluently and frequently that a man on a neighboring machine complained. She was moved.

Women workers found that strategic tears could transform a snarling 250-pound foreman into a meek, apologetic man. They demanded and got coffee breaks, piped-in-music and washrooms with dressing tables, wide mirrors and pastel colors. They brought potted plants to work. They filled factory newspapers with items like this: "The girls look smart in their new beige-and-green overalls. How about snapping up the men's appearance? Why couldn't they wear shorts?"

Snug-fitting colored coveralls became standard female attire in most plants, for reasons of both morale and safety. On the whole, women workers were not particularly accident prone. At first they refused to tuck their curls under their headgear or remove rings and costume jewelry. But whenever a worker was scalped or lost a finger there was a noticeable increase in safety consciousness.

And the women did a superlative job, particularly where tedious detail was involved. At the General Engineering Company of Scarborough, Ont., 4500 women filled 41 different types of fuses and other explosive units under strictest safety regulations. They did a job so intricate, says a GECO official, that "it simply wasn't for men's hands." GECO did not have a single fatal explosion during the war. . . .

ROBERT COLLINS

One woman who worked in such a plant was writer Edna Jaques. In a wartime *Maclean's* article she told what it was like:

. . . Around our benches works a varied group—a soldier of the last war who was turned down for this one; a little Irish girl whose husband is overseas; a young Bulgarian boy; a bitter, middle-aged woman whose life has gone awry. A strange loyalty has grown up among us; it flares up suddenly if any of us are snubbed or laughed at by some other shop.

We take our shifts as they come, day or night. The night hours drag. We talk and laugh and sing old favorites, new hits, hymns, battle songs. Sometimes there is just one worker singing softly to himself, sometimes two or three, and then suddenly we all burst forth joyously, as if responding to a common chord.

I remember one dreary night when the Bulgarian boy started "Land of Hope and Glory" and in a second everyone in the shop was singing, loudly, tunefully, as if it had been rehearsed. "—Mother of the Free, How shall we extol thee, who are born of thee?" The little Bulgarian was leading, his head thrown back, his hand raised like a choirmaster. "Wider still and wider, shall thy bounds be set, God Who made thee mighty, make thee mightier yet. . ." Up to the white ceiling the song floated and down the glistening corridors.

There is a huge 1500-seat canteen where we crowd like hungry wolves at noon hour or on night shift at about 2 a.m. Looking across the canteen at 2 a.m. is like looking at a slice of life. You'll find every sort of woman here, their white hands stained with gunpowder or yellow as saffron from tetryl. Some of their faces have broken out in festering sores from the acid fumes that drift in the air like poison gas.

For two years now we've worked with feverish haste and infinite care. We've

sweated and sworn and vowed we'd quit (but we haven't). The infernal din of the machines is in our ears day and night. The whine of presses, the grumbling ear-shaking noises of the vibrator drive through every nerve and cell of our bodies, until at dawn we creep exhausted and gray-faced to the waiting buses and go home. Too tired to eat or wash or speak, we crawl into bed and sleep like the dead until the alarm goes off to start another day or night.

When they tell us that in the London blitz they had to stop the guns because there were no more shells, we set our teeth and go at it harder than ever. For we know that we're fighting for our country just as truly as if we stood on the cliffs of Dover. . . . EDNA JAQUES

"What did you do in the war, Mummy?" For the first time in history, tens of thousands of women have been asked that question since 1945. The general answer is that women helped win the war in many ways, and in doing so won a victory in their own long fight for emancipation and recognition. They proved their worth in the armed forces. They invaded male worlds such as banking, and they came to stay. They improved the status, morale and working conditions of their sex more than any social legislation had ever done. They proved beyond doubt that they had the intelligence, skills and stamina to tackle almost any job men could do. Although the high wall of male prejudice was not finally breached, by the end of the war it was at least significantly cracked.

But perhaps the development with the most marked effect was the emergence of the working mother. Says Dr. F. H. Knelman of Montreal, a professor in the history of science and a student of the role of women in society:

"The war started the movement of mothers out of the home in large numbers, and there have been numerous repercussions. A revolution in shopping, for instance. The stores had to come up with something for women who didn't have the time they'd had before. So we got convenience foods.

"What it did to the home itself is historic. Over the centuries a number of things have gradually whittled away the authority of the father. When he left the home to work in the factories created by the Industrial Revolution, he had to start sharing his authority with his wife. When compulsory education took his children away from home, he began the long process of sharing his authority with the state. But he was still the financial backbone of the family. When his wife left home and went to work in World War II, even the financial bulwark of his authority began to go. The implications are profound for the whole future of the family."

Hundreds of women acquired new skills and went to work alongside experienced tradesmen in Canada's shipyards. For some (above left) it was a lot like home—wielding an iron, but on the fabric of motor torpedo boats under construction at the Canadian Power Boat Company in Montreal. Edna Watson of Toronto (above) went to Halifax to be married and stayed on to build destroyers after her soldier husband was sent overseas.

Mrs. 'Sparks'

The time had come for the Norwegian cargo ship *Mosdale* to sail from Montreal and the captain, 30-year-old Gerner Sunde, was anxious to get away. But there was a difficulty that day in June 1941. Fern Blodgett, 22, had just reported aboard as the new wireless operator—and nobody seemed to know whether a wartime ship *could* sail with a woman in the crew.

Canadian and Norwegian authorities could find no regulation which said a ship could. Nor could they find one which said a ship couldn't. So it was ruled that, if the captain was willing to take her, Miss Blodgett could go. The captain had no alternative. She was the only wireless operator available. By the time a counter-order came through, it was too late. The girl who had wanted to be a sailor all her life was on the high seas.

that I was not a little boy, and I'd go unhappily back to my dolls. But I never got over wanting to be a sailor.

When the war came, I thought I saw a slim chance. I was a stenographer in Toronto but I had my evenings free—and surely there would eventually be a need for seagoing wireless operators. I applied to three schools that gave wireless training. Two said they had never had a woman student and they didn't intend to start now. The third accepted me. After 18 months of night classes, I was a trained operator.

Not long after that, the school principal phoned me. "You once told me you'd like to go to sea," he said. "Did you mean it?" That night, Friday, June 13, I was on a train to Montreal.

My life in *Mosdale,* a 3000-ton ship with a crew of 35 and room for 12 passengers, took some getting used to. I got violently seasick. I had hoped to fix up my cabin as any girl would but I had to give up. It was too small. I loved it anyway. I wondered what I'd be like in a crisis if we were attacked by submarines or surface raiders or bombers. I wondered whether I would be a woman

But *Mosdale* was a lucky ship. She was one of a half dozen Norwegian fruit carriers that started the war—and the only one to survive. She could make 15 knots and for a long time that was enough to let her sail alone because she could outpace any submarine. None of us liked it when she was assigned to convoys and had to reduce speed.

My mother and sister sometimes tried to persuade me to stop going to sea. I couldn't. I liked it too much. I liked the crew. I enjoyed the passengers we carried: correspondents, technical experts, an African explorer, servicemen, merchant seamen who had been torpedoed. Besides, it wasn't at sea but on land that I had my worst frights—trying to pick my way back to the ship through blackouts in British ports.

I finished the war as *Mosdale's* "Sparks" and remained with her for another six months. Then I went ashore to stay. I've made my home in Norway ever since. Occasionally I meet other Canadian women who followed my example, not only in going to sea in wartime ships but in marrying Norwegians they met on board. But so far as I know I was the first. . . .   FERN SUNDE

She remained there through most of the Battle of the Atlantic. *Mosdale* made 98 wartime crossings, more than any other Allied ship, and Fern Blodgett was aboard for 78 of them. But from July 1942 on she sailed as Mrs. Gerner Sunde. She married the captain in Saint John, N.B., and promptly went back to sea for her honeymoon. She recalls:

. . I grew up in Cobourg, Ont., and as a young girl I'd go down to the shores of Lake Ontario to watch the lake boats pass. They fascinated me. I even loved the sound of their whistles. Then it would come over me

or a wireless operator if we were torpedoed. As a woman, I could be expected to head for the lifeboats. As a wireless operator, as the ship's "Sparks," I'd be expected to remain on duty. I decided I'd be a wireless operator.

Fortunately, I never had to test my decision. There was always the threat of danger and toward the end of the war our nerves got pretty frayed. Submarines chased us. We had torpedoings around us, passed through storms which scattered the convoy, once changed course unexpectedly and passed through a minefield our charts didn't show.

Wireless operator Fern Blodgett Sunde meets Norwegian King Haakon aboard the cargo vessel *Mosdale* in the summer of 1943, after the ship's 51st wartime Atlantic crossing.

The night they broke the dams in Happy Valley

**An elite squadron and a unique bomb
combine in the most celebrated air raid of the war**

It was Sunday evening, May 16, 1943. Outside 617 Squadron's hangars on the RAF bomber base at Scampton near Lincoln, the aircrews gathered around the trucks that were to take them to the big Lancaster aircraft parked on the far side of the field. Some of the men stretched out on the grass, smoking a last cigarette. Others stood around talking, their expressions, as the squadron adjutant noted, ranging from "the grim and determined to the 'don't care a damn.'" Dave Shannon, a baby-faced pilot of 20, who was growing a large mus-

tache to look older, chatted casually with his fiancee, a WAAF officer serving on the station. Underneath, most were thinking the same thing: for God's sake let's get started.

They had good reason to be keyed up. For eight weeks they had been training for this mission and it was likely to be the most difficult and dangerous they had ever flown: a low-level attack on the Möhne, Eder and Sorpe dams. Those three giant ramparts controlled the main water and power supplies of the Ruhr, the massive

German industrial area Allied airmen ironically called "Happy Valley" because of its vicious defenses.

At 8:50 p.m. Wing Comdr. Guy Gibson, a short and ruggedly handsome Englishman of 25, glanced at his watch. "Time to go," he said and then turned to his friend John Hopgood and made the remark he always did before a mission: "Well, Hoppy, tonight's the night; tomorrow we'll get drunk."

Gibson watched the men clamber into the trucks. There were 133 of them—19

7-man crews—and he had handpicked every man. Although their average age was only 22, almost every crew member was a veteran of one tour of operations and many had come through two. Since it was rare to survive the 60 sorties that made up two tours, these were among the most experienced—and luckiest—in Bomber Command. None was luckier than Gibson who had lived through 172 missions and had won the DSO and Bar and DFC.

The men came from Britain, Australia, New Zealand and Canada, a typically "mixed" Commonwealth squadron. And, also typically, roughly one out of four or five—30 of them—were RCAF men. Gibson, as he later wrote, had a soft spot for Canadians. "I like their ways and manners, their free and easy outlook. Even when they chew gum."

He had two of them in his own crew. FO. T. H. "Terry" Taerum was a quiet-spoken man from Calgary, in love with a pretty WAAF girl from Ireland. As navigator of the lead aircraft, Taerum had a heavy responsibility. But Gibson was confident: Terry had already made 35 trips and knew exactly what he was doing. PO. G. A. "Tony" Deering of Toronto had been brought in to replace Gibson's front gunner who had gone sick.

As the trucks pulled up beside the four-engined Lancasters, Canadian navigator FO. Danny Walker noticed that someone had chalked on one of the bombs: "Never in the field of human conflict have so many been shaken by so few." This Churchillian misquote was a joke only the crews could appreciate. For the one bomb each aircraft carried was unlike any they had ever seen before. It had no nose or fins, but was shaped like an oversize oil drum and suspended *crosswise* below the bomber's belly between two protruding V-supports. A pulley and belt drive connected the bomb to a small motor. Shortly before the target was reached, the motor was to be switched on to set the bomb spinning backward. As the five-ton missile gathered momentum, the whole aircraft would shake madly until the bomb reached 500 revolutions per minute. Then the vibrations would level out. It was, Walker reflected, a most unusual weapon. But then the entire mission was extraordinary.

The dambusting raid was the brainchild of Barnes Wallis, a British aircraft designer and inventor. In 1939 Wallis had started

wondering where and how bombing could hurt Germany most. He decided the best way was to strike at its sources of power and water, the hydroelectric dams. Of these, three stood out: the Möhne, Eder and Sorpe. They contained nearly all the water supply of the Ruhr. Deny the Ruhr industries power and water and there would be no production.

That was the Wallis theory. But how were such colossal structures to be knocked out? The Möhne dam had a solid concrete and masonry base 112 feet thick, towered 130 feet high and was topped by a concrete roadway 25 feet wide. The Eder dam was even bigger. The heaviest RAF bomb at the time, a 1000-pounder, would hardly scratch the concrete. To do the job, Wallis calculated, a 30-ton bomb containing 30,000 pounds of explosive would be needed. But no bomber was big enough to carry such a load. There had to be some new kind of weapon.

What Wallis eventually came up with

after months of research was a cylindrical missile with a "shock-wave punch." It was about five feet long and four feet in diameter, carried 6500 pounds of the new explosive RDX, and weighed five tons—light enough to be carried by a Lancaster modified to hold it. But to be effective the bomb had to be dropped from low altitude at an exact position so that it would explode 30 feet under water and right against the dam wall. With millions of tons of lake water acting as a giant tamp, the full force of the explosion would be expended against the

wall. Several bombs exploded in the same place would, with the help of the water pressure, shift the cracked wall back until it toppled.

But how was the bomb to be aimed so that it would explode in the right position and also surmount anti-torpedo nets a short distance in front of the dams? Wallis's answer was simple. The bomb would bounce across the lake like a flat stone skipped over the surface of the water. To make it bounce, it would be given a backspin before release. When it hit the water,

Wing Comdr. Guy Gibson (standing on ladder) and his crew, about to enter their Lancaster bomber. Canadians are G. A. "Tony" Deering (third from left) and T. H. "Terry" Taerum (extreme right).

the spin would send the bomb bounding forward over the lake, and the torpedo nets, until it hit the dam. It would rebound, but the spin would force the bomb back again against the dam wall. And when it sank to a depth of 30 feet, a pressure-activated fuse would set off the explosion.

The authorities were skeptical but Wallis wrote a detailed treatise and sent copies to 70 influential men. In February 1943 he was given the go-ahead.

There was not a moment to lose. The best time to smash the dams was the week of May 13-19 when their water level would be highest. In the meantime the bombs had to be produced and tested, the men who were to drop them gathered and trained.

Air Chief Marshal Sir Arthur Harris, chief of Bomber Command, chose Guy Gibson to lead the raid. But at first not even Gibson was told the targets. He was simply ordered to pick the crews, form them into a new squadron and train them in low-level night flying.

Canadian Danny Walker was in Stratford-on-Avon resting after a tour of oper-

for bravery. Dave Rodger, another Canadian gunner, thought the squadron resembled an all-star NHL team.

As they waited for Gibson to speak at their first briefing, the crews speculated. The betting was that they were going to attack the German battleship *Tirpitz* or U-boat pens. Gibson could offer no help. "I can't tell you the target," he said. "All I can say is you'll have to practice low flying day and night until you can do it with your eyes shut. Security is essential. You've got to keep your mouths shut. If we can surprise them, everything'll be fine. If they're ready for us . . ." He looked at the men in silence.

The training began. Low flying, with its temptations to go under bridges or skim over rooftops, was normally forbidden; so Gibson's men were delighted to do it on orders. As they roared over the countryside at treetop height, people would dive for ditches and sheep would scatter in the fields. Hugh Munro, a Montreal technical sergeant, was out one day when his pilot headed straight toward a castle on top of a hill. The plane passed so low that Munro could look through the castle windows. Another time, at dusk, Danny Walker's crew just missed a power line.

To simulate moonlight and enable the crews to train by day as well as night, the aircraft windows were fitted with amber screens and the men wore blue glasses. They ranged over Britain from Cornwall to the Hebrides.

They needed all the practice they could get. Never before had crews been asked to handle their equipment so precisely in action. To reach the dams they would have to fly at night at rooftop level over a devious route planned both to gain surprise and to avoid known German flak concentrations and night-fighter airfields. On reaching the target they would have to fly over the lake at exactly 240 m.p.h. and at exactly 60 feet above the water, and then release the bomb precisely 425 yards from the dam wall.

There was a further technical problem: normal bomb-aiming and altimeter equipment would not do. Air Vice-Marshal Ralph Cochrane, in charge of planning the raid, set the "backroom boys" to work on that. Soon an expert from the Ministry of Aircraft Production visited Gibson. "I think I can solve your bomb-aiming problem," he said. "There are a couple of towers on top of the wall of each dam. We've measured them from aerial photographs and they're 600 feet apart. Now this is how we do it." He produced a small triangle of plywood with a peephole at one angle and a nail stuck in each of the other two corners. "You look through the peephole. When the towers are in line with the nails, you are about 425 yards from the dam. You press the trigger and the bomb will then drop in the right spot."

It worked. Gibson's bomb-aimers tried it on an English dam equipped with dummy towers. On the first trial, eight practice bombs were dropped with an average error of only four yards.

But there was still the problem of maintaining height. Another expert called on Gibson. "Put a spotlight under the Lancaster's nose," he said, "and another under the belly, both pointing down and inward so they converge at 60 feet. When the two spots come together on the water, there you are!"

It, too, worked beautifully. But there was a drawback. The lights would provide a perfect target for the German gunners defending the dams. Reconnaissance photographs had shown that there were at least six gun positions around the Möhne alone, and some of the guns were in the towers the planes would have to fly between. Nevertheless, the defenses were surprisingly light for such important targets—especially since at least one German had anticipated such an attack.

In August 1939, Oberbürgermeister Dillgardt had written from his office in the Ruhr to the Wehrmacht chiefs in Münster about the dams' defenses. He, like Wallis, thought that a large bomb exploded deep in the water close to the dam wall might blow a large hole in it by compression. He was a layman and he admitted that experts did not agree with him, but he painted an ugly picture of what might happen. He even predicted that any attack would be made in May when the dams were full.

The military authorities said the matter would be given careful consideration, but little was done. Dillgardt kept on. Finally he received a terse note: "There is no further need for regular reports to this office regarding storage level of these dams. Heil Hitler!" Later the generals threw him a last crumb by sending some searchlights and 20-mm. guns.

Then, shortly before the raid, aerial photographs revealed that the anti-torpedo boom in front of the Möhne dam was being repaired, and the dark shapes of five new

tions when Gibson wired to ask if he would join the squadron. Walker had served with Gibson before; he was on his way to Scampton the next day. So was Joe McCarthy, an American pilot in the RCAF who considered Gibson "a gentleman and as far as operations are concerned—the King."

On March 21 the crews assembled for the first time. Harry O'Brien, an air gunner from Edmonton, took one look around and knew immediately something big was on. Almost every other man wore a decoration structures were rising on top of the dam itself. There seemed to be only one explanation: new gun positions.

On May 15 all was ready. That afternoon the pilots, navigators and bomb-aimers were told of their targets for the first time and shown scale models of the dams. As Danny Walker walked back to the mess, he reflected on Gibson's lighthearted final words: "You'll all be given posthumous V.C.'s."

That night the squadron doctor doled out pills to help the crews sleep.

The day of the attack arrived. In this adaptation of his famous book, *The Dam Busters,* Paul Brickhill tells the story:

. . . Toward noon a Mosquito reconnaissance aircraft touched down with the latest photos of the dams. The water in the Möhne was four feet from the top—just right. After lunch the headquarters meteorological officer walked into Cochrane's office and predicted clear weather.

"What?" said Cochrane. "No ifs, buts and probablies?"

"No, sir. It's going to be all right."

The loudspeakers sounded about four o'clock, ordering all 617 Squadron crews to the briefing room. Soon the hushed young men were sitting on the benches. Gibson repeated the briefing he had given the others the previous day, and Wallis told them about the dams and what their destruction would do. Cochrane finished with a short, crisp talk.

The final lineup was:

Formation 1. Nine aircraft in three waves, taking off with ten minutes between waves: Gibson, Hopgood, Martin; Young, Astell, Maltby; Maudslay, Knight, Shannon. They were to attack the Möhne, and after the Möhne was breached those who had not bombed would go on to the Eder.

Formation 2. One wave in loose formation: McCarthy, Byers, Barlow, Rice, Les Munro. They were to attack the Sorpe, crossing the coast by the northern route as a diversion to split the German defenses.

Formation 3. Townsend, Brown, Anderson, Ottley, Burpee. They would take off later as the mobile reserve.

Supper in the mess was quiet. No one said much, although Melvyn "Dinghy" Young said to Gibson, "Can I have your next egg if you don't come back?" That was the usual chestnut and Gibson brushed it aside with a few amiably insulting remarks.

Some Dambusters flew east from Scampton, then across the Zuider Zee. Others went southeast across East Anglia to the Dutch coast, then east on a bearing which took them close to Eindhoven.

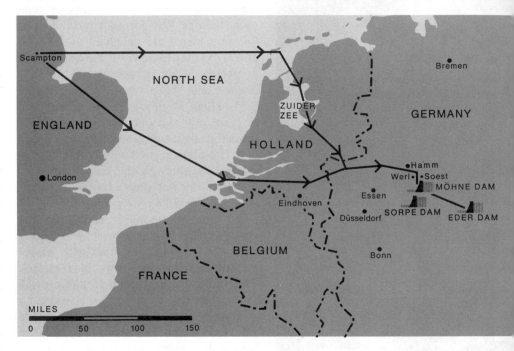

In twos and threes they drifted down to the hangar and started to change. Mickey Martin, an Australian, stuffed his toy koala bear into a pocket of his jacket. It was a gray furry thing about four inches high with black button eyes, given to him by his mother as a mascot. It had as many operational hours as he had.

Around nine o'clock the crews of the first two formations boarded their aircraft. In Gibson's G for George, navigator Terry Taerum again checked the flight plan, memorizing once more the major landmarks and German flak defenses. Then he laid aside his navigation instruments and looked out at the Lincolnshire countryside. There was nothing to do now but wait for the take-off signal.

At exactly 9:10 a red Very light curled up from Gibson's aircraft, the signal for

the second formation to start; the northern route was longer and they were taking off 15 minutes early. Then there was a hitch. Big Joe McCarthy, a former Long Island lifeguard, found his Lancaster out of action with leaking hydraulics. While he and his crew raced to take over a spare plane, the rest of Formation 2 took off behind New Zealander Les Munro.

At 9:25 Gibson in G for George, Martin in P for Popsie and Hopgood in M for Mother punched the buttons of the booster coils and the engines whined and spun explosively. G for George waddled forward, taxied to the south fence, swung its long snout to the north and waited. P Popsie turned slowly in on the left, M Mother on the right. They took off and at 200 feet turned slowly on course with the sun low behind.

McCarthy eased T for Tom off the runway 20 minutes late and set course on his own. At 9:47 Dinghy Young led Astell and Maltby off. Eight minutes after that Maudslay, Shannon and Knight were in the air. The final five, the reserve aircraft, did not take off till two hours later. By the time they arrived in the target area Gibson, if still alive, would know where to send them.

As England faded behind, Gibson's G George dropped down to 50 feet and on each side Martin and Hopgood came down too, putting off the evil moment when German radar would pick them up. But they couldn't put it off indefinitely; about 20 miles from the Dutch coast the blips would be flicking on the radar screens and the orders would be going out to the German flak batteries and night-fighter fields.

Martin ranged up alongside Gibson and there was a light winking as he flashed his Aldis lamp at them. "What's he saying, Hutch?" Gibson asked his wireless operator.

"He's saying we're going to get drunk tomorrow night," said Hutchison. Hutchison didn't drink but his Aldis winked back, "You're damn right."

Terry Taerum told Gibson: "Our ground speed is exactly 203½ miles an hour. We will be there in exactly one hour, 10 minutes and 30 seconds. We ought to cross the coast dead on track. Incidentally, you're one degree off course." The last part was the standing joke. The pilot who can fly without sometimes yawing a degree or two off course has yet to be born.

In the Ops room of the RAF's 5 Group HQ at Grantham, Cochrane was walking a jittery Barnes Wallis up and down, trying to comfort him. Sir Arthur Harris came in. "How's it going, Cocky?"

"Nothing to report yet, sir."

They talked quietly. Every now and then Wallis looked at the big operations map on the wall. The route had been penciled in and he was counting off the miles the planes should be traveling. At 0:35 Cochrane looked at his watch and said, "They ought to be coming up to the Dutch coast now."

The sun had gone and the moon was inching higher, lighting a road across the water for the planes. The Dutch coast came up ahead, a black line dim on the water. Then from a couple of miles out on the port side a chain of glowing little balls climbed into the sky. "Flak ship," said Martin laconically. The shells were way off. The sparkling moonpath ended abruptly and they tore across the white line of surf and were over enemy territory.

The northern wave made landfall about the same time, sighting Vlieland, Holland, and turning southeast to cut across the narrow part and down over the Zuider Zee. Les Munro led them across the dark spit and then, without warning, there were flashes below. Munro felt the shock as fiery little balls hit the aircraft. He called to see if the crew were all right but the earphones were dead.

Percy Pigeon, his Canadian wireless operator, came up and shouted into his ear,

"No radio. No intercom. Flak's smashed it. I think everyone's okay." Munro flew on several miles but it was no good and he knew it. Without radio he could not direct the attack on the Sorpe, could not even direct his own crew or get bombing instructions. Swearing, he turned for home.

Inside the Zuider Zee the water was dark and quite flat, treacherously deceptive for judging height. Geoff Rice slipped down to level at 60 feet by his belly lights, but the lights were not working properly and lured him lower as he tried to get a fix. A hammer seemed to hit the aircraft and there was a roar above the engines. Rice dragged her off the water but the belly was torn out of her and the bomb had gone with it. The gutted fuselage had scooped up a couple of tons of water; it was pouring out of her and the rear gunner was nearly drowning in his turret. Marvelously, she still flew but was dropping back. When they found the bomb was gone Rice turned back toward England.

The remaining two pilots, Flt. Lt. Barlow of Australia and PO. Vernon Byers of Canada, skirted their turning point on the cape at Stavoren and ten minutes later crossed to the enemy land again at Harderwijk. No one knows exactly how soon the flak came up at them, but it got them both. There is a report that as Barlow's aircraft hit the ground the bomb went off with a blinding flash. Among his crew was Canadian gunner Harvey Glinz. It was either then or soon after that Byers and his crew, including Canadian James McDowell, died too. Now only McCarthy was left of the Sorpe team, flying 60 miles behind.

Over Holland, Gibson, Martin and Hopgood were down as low as 40 feet, playing hide-and-seek with the ground, the bomb-aimers calling terse warnings as houses and trees loomed up. Four miles to port they saw the flare path of Gilze-Rijen, German night-fighter field, and a few miles on they passed to the left of the night-fighter airdrome at Eindhoven. They could expect fighters now. Martin and Hopgood closed in on each side of Gibson for mutual protection.

The other two groups in Formation 1 were on course, too. Dinghy Young flew over the canal at Rosendaal and turned delicately to lead his group between the fighter fields, but Bill Astell did not seem certain of the exact turning point. He bore off a little to the south and then turned

back, but had fallen half a mile behind. Young and Maltby did not see him again, nor did anyone else. Astell and his crew were lost, among them three Canadians, Frank Garbas, Abram Garshowitz and Floyd Wile.

Fourteen aircraft left.

The leading three slid across the border into Germany and saw no light or movement anywhere. Taerum thought they were too far south so they edged to the north, a little nervily because this was the treacherous leg—they were coming up to the Rhine to sneak between the guns of Huls and the Ruhr. Just short of the river some light flak guns opened up without warning; the aircraft gunners squirted back at the roots of the tracer, and then they were out of range. No one badly hit. The Rhine was rushing at them and up from a barge spat a thin line of tracer. They were past before the bullets found them.

Two minutes later more guns opened up and three searchlights lit on Gibson. Toby Foxlee in Martin's aircraft and Tony Deering, Gibson's Canadian forward gunner, shot at the searchlights. One of them popped out but the two others held; the air was full of tracer. The rear gunners came into action. The searchlights switched to Martin, blinding him. Every gun was firing, the aircraft shuddering with the recoil, and then they were through.

They worked themselves back into formation. Hutchison tapped out a flak warning; back in Grantham the powerful group radio rebroadcast it to all other aircraft.

Gibson swung them north around Hamm. Taerum said, "New course, Skipper, 165 magnetic," and then they were hugging the ground on the last leg, slicing between Soest and Werl. Now the moon was high enough to light the ground and ahead loomed the dark hills that cradled the water. They climbed to clear the ridge that rimmed the horizon; then they crossed over the valley. Down below lay the flat sheet of Möhne Lake.

It was like looking down on the model they had memorized. The same saucer of water, the same dim fields, and across the neck of the lake the squat rampart hugging the water, crowned by the towers. In the half-light it looked like a battleship, but more impregnable. Reinforced concrete over 100 feet thick.

"God," Martin's bomb-aimer said, "can *we* break that?"

The dam came suddenly to life. Lines of angry red meteors streamed into the sky as the German gunners hosed the area.

The aircraft swung away and cruised in wide circles round the lake. There seemed to be about ten guns, some in the fields near the dam, some in the towers on the dam itself.

Gibson started calling the other aircraft in his formation and one by one they reported. Except Astell—he had been dead for an hour. After a while Gibson gave up calling him. Over the intercom Gibson said soberly: "Well, boys, I suppose we'd better start the ball rolling."

He flicked his transmitter switch: "Hello all Cooler aircraft, I am going in to attack. Stand by to come in in your order when I tell you. Hello M Mother. Stand by to take over if anything happens."

"Okay, Leader. Good luck." Hopgood's voice was a careful monotone.

Gibson turned wide, hugging the hills at the eastern end of the lake. He said tersely: "Bomb on!" "Spam" Spafford, the bomb-aimer, flicked the switch to start the motor. The aircraft shook violently as the bomb turned faster and faster until it reached 500 revolutions per minute. They came out of the hills and slammed across the water, touching 240 m.p.h.

Gibson rattled off the last orders: "Check height, Terry! Speed control, Pulford! Gunners ready! Coming up, Spam!"

Taerum flicked the belly lights on and, peering down from the blister, started droning: "Down . . . down . . . down . . . up a bit . . . steady, stead-y-y." The lights were touching each other. G George was at 60 feet exactly and the flak gunners had seen the lights. Streams of glowing shells were whipping toward them, seeming to move slowly at first like all flak, then rushing madly at their eyes as the aircraft plunged into them.

Gibson held steady, pointing the plane between the towers. Taerum was watching from the blister, Pulford had a hand on the throttles. Spafford held the plywood sight to his eye and the towers were closing in on the nails. Gibson shouted to Pulford, "Stand by to pull me out of the seat if I get hit!" There was a sudden snarling clatter up in the nose; Deering had opened up, his tracer spitting at the towers.

The dam was a giant rushing toward them, the cockpit stank of cordite and

thought was nothing but a cold alarm shouting, "In another minute we'll be dead." Then Spafford screamed, "Bomb gone!" and they rocketed over the dam. A red Very light soared upward as Hutchison pulled the trigger to signal "Attack successful." Then they were corkscrewing down the valley, hugging the dark earth.

Gibson, turning steeply, lifted the plane out of the hills, and looked back. A voice in his earphones said, "Good show, Leader."

The black water between the towers suddenly rose and split and a huge white core erupted through the middle and climbed toward the sky. The lake was writhing. As the white column of water

reached its peak and hung 1000 feet high like a ghost against the moon, the sound of the explosion reached the aircraft. They saw sheets of water spilling over the dam and for a wild moment thought it had burst. But the white column died slowly as the fury of the water passed. The dam was still there.

In a few minutes Gibson thought the lake was calm enough for the next bomb and called: "Hello M Mother. You may attack now. Good luck."

"Okay, Leader. Attacking." Hopgood was lost in the darkness over the hills at the end of the lake while the others waited. They saw his belly lights flick on and the two little yellow pools slid over the water

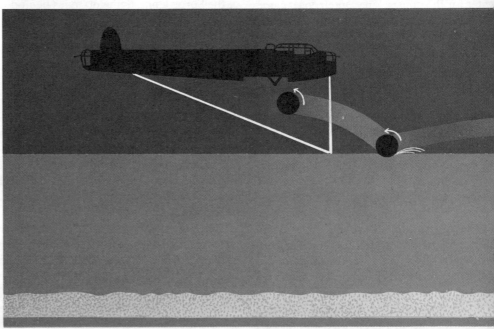

closing and joining as he found his height. He was straight and level on his run; the flak saw him and the venomous fireflies were darting at him. He plunged on and was closing fast on target when the shells hit him.

A red glow blossomed round the inner port wing tank. Then a long ribbon of flame trailed behind M Mother. The bomb-aimer must have been hit, because the bomb overshot the parapet onto the power-house below. M Mother passed the dam, nose up, straining for height so the crew could bail out. Then the tanks blew up with an orange flare, a wing ripped away and the bomber spun to the ground in burning, bouncing pieces. The bomb went off near the powerhouse like a brilliant sun. It was all over in seconds.

Gibson radioed: "Hello P Popsie. Are you ready?"

"Okay, Leader. Going in."

"I'll fly across the dam as you make your run and try and draw the flak off you."

Martin was turning in from the hills and Gibson headed across the lake, parallel to the dams and just out of effective range of the guns. As Martin's spotlights merged and sped across the water, Gibson back-tracked and Deering and the rear gunner, Trevor-Roper, opened fire. Six lines of tracer converged on the towers, drawing the Germans' attention so that for some seconds most of the guns did not notice Martin rocketing over the water. He held his height and speed. They were tracking straight for the middle of the dam between

the moon-bathed towers when the gunners spotted them and threw a curtain of fire between the towers, spreading like a fan so they would have to fly through it. Martin drove straight ahead.

A sharp "Bomb gone!" and in the same instant a shudder as two shells smacked into the starboard wing. Over the radio Martin shouted, "Bomb gone, Leader."

"Okay P Popsie. Let me know when you're out of the flak. Hello A Apple. Are you ready?"

"Okay, Leader."

"Right. Go ahead. Let me know when you're in position and I'll draw the flak for you."

Martin called again, "P Popsie clear now, Leader."

"Okay. Are you hit?"

"Yeah. Starboard wing, but we can make it."

The lake boiled again. More water cascaded over the dam, but it cleared soon and the dam was still intact.

Dinghy Young was on the air again. "A Apple making bombing run."

Gibson headed back over the lake to harass the flak gunners. Martin did the same. As Young came plunging across the lake Gibson and Martin came in on each side, higher up, and the flak did not know where to shoot. Young swept past the dam and reported he was all right. The great explosion was up against the dam wall again, beautifully accurate, but the dam still held.

Again Gibson waited till the water was calm, then called Maltby and ordered him

The "bouncing bomb" resembled a huge oil drum or a depth charge. When in place under the fuselage, said Guy Gibson, it made his Lancaster (left) look "like a pregnant duck." It was carried between two callipers and could be revolved. Ten minutes before attack the bomb was set spinning backward at 500 revolutions a minute—by belt drive from a motor in the fuselage. Below: with the use of two spotlights to determine height, the aircraft drops the bomb. Its backspin (note arrows) makes it skip forward, over the torpedo nets (parallel vertical lines). The spin keeps it against the dam. As the bomb sinks, a fuse activated by water pressure sets off the explosion. The "earthquake" effect of the shock waves breaches the dam.

in. As Maltby came across the water Gibson and Martin came in with him, firing with every gun and flicking their navigation lights on this time, hoping to draw the flak gunners to the wrong target. The red cartridge soared up from Maltby's aircraft: "Attack successful."

The spray from the explosions was misting up the whole valley and it was hard to see what was happening. Gibson called Shannon to make his attack; the words were barely out when a sharp voice filled his earphones: "Hell, it's gone! Look at it for Christ's sake!" Wheeling round the valley side, Martin had seen the concrete rampart abruptly split and crumble under the weight of water. Gibson swung in close and was staggered by what he saw. A ragged hole 100 yards across and 100 feet deep split the dam and the lake was pouring out of it, 134 million tons of water crashing into the valley in a jet 200 feet long, smooth on top, foaming at the sides where it tore at the rough edges of the breach and boiling over the scarred earth where the powerhouse had been.

Gibson told Shannon to "skip it."

The others flew over, awed into silence. In the moonglow they watched a wall of water, 25 feet high, rolling down the valley at 20 feet a second. The silence was broken as they went mad with excitement. The only man not looking was Hutchison; he sat at his keyboard tapping out the code word for success.

At Grantham the phone rang and in the silence they all heard the Morse crackling in the receiver. The operator printed the message letter by letter on a signals pad and let out a cry: "It's gone."

Wallis danced round the room. The austere face of Cochrane cracked into a grin. He grabbed one of Wallis's hands and started congratulating him. Harris grabbed the other hand and said: "Wallis, I didn't believe a word you said about this damn bomb but you could sell me a pink elephant now."

Two miles down the valley from the Möhne lay the sleeping village of Himmelpforten, which means Gates of Heaven. The explosions had wakened the village priest, Father Berkenkopf, and he guessed instantly what was happening; he had been afraid of it for three years. He ran to his small stone church and began tugging grimly on the bell rope, the signal he had arranged with the villagers. In the darkness the clanging of the bell rolled round the

valley and then it was muffled in the thunder moving nearer. Berkenkopf must have heard it and known what it meant, but he was still pulling at the bell when the flood crushed the church and the village and rolled them down the valley. It went for many miles and took more villages, a maelstrom of water and splintered houses, beds and frying pans, the church chalice and bell, the bodies of cattle and horses, pigs and dogs—and human beings.

As the Lancasters circled over the destruction of the Möhne dam, the crews could see the glow from the wreckage of M for Mother still burning below. Unknown to them, two of Hopgood's crew were alive. One was John Fraser, the Canadian bomb-aimer. Fraser had been by the front escape hatch when the aircraft was hit and caught fire. Over the intercom

The Möhne before and after the attack. Right: most of the lake has poured through the 100-yard breach in the dam. The powerhouse below the dam is obliterated in foam and white water. The Dambusters saw a wall of water 25 feet high plunge down the valley at 20 feet a second.

214

he heard Hopgood tell the crew to bail out and that he would try to gain height to help them. Fraser pulled up the hatch and threw it out. The trees below looked so close that he decided to release the pilot chute of his parachute while he was still inside the aircraft; the main chute would then open and pull him out after it. It did— like a cork out of a bottle. Within a few seconds he hit the ground, bruised but un-injured. When he saw M for Mother blow up a few moments later, Fraser thought the rest of the crew must have died. Later in prison camp, he heard that Burcher, the Australian rear gunner, had got out safely. Ken Earnshaw, the Canadian navigator, and the others didn't.

With the Möhne successfully breached, Gibson ordered Martin and Maltby to set course for home and told Young, Shannon, Maudslay and Knight to follow him east to the Eder. Young was to take control if Gibson was shot down.

The Eder was hard to find because fog was filling the valley. Gibson circled it for some time before he was certain he was there. One by one the others found it and soon they were all in a left-hand circuit round the lake. There was no flak; probably the Germans thought the Eder did not need it. The dam lay deep in a fold of hills and the ridges around it were 1000 feet high. It was no place to dive a heavy aircraft at night.

Gibson said, "Okay, Dave. Start your attack."

Shannon flew a wide circuit over the ridges and then put his nose right down, but the dive was not steep enough. He overshot and just cleared the mountain on the far side.

"Sorry, Leader," Shannon said. "Made a mess of that. I'll try again."

Five times more he dived into the dark valley but each time he failed to get into position and nearly stood the Lancaster on her tail to get out of the hills again. He called up finally, "I think I'd better circle and try to get to know this place."

"Okay, Dave. Hang around a bit and let someone else have a crack. Hullo Z Zebra. Have a go."

A minute later Maudslay was diving down the contour of the hills, only to over-shoot and go rocketing up again. He tried again but the same thing happened. Maudslay said he was going to try once more. He came slowly over the ridges, turned at the last moment and the nose dropped sharply into the gloom as he forced her down. They saw him level out very fast and then the spotlights flicked onto the water and closed quickly and he was tracking for the dam.

His red Very light curled up as Fuller called, "Bomb gone!" but they must have been going too fast. The bomb hit the parapet of the dam and blew up on impact with a tremendous flash; in the glare they saw Z Zebra for a moment just above the explosion. Then only blackness.

Gibson said painfully, knowing it was useless: "Henry, Henry—hullo Z Zebra, are you all right?" There was no answer.

He called again and, incredibly, out of the darkness a very faint voice said, "I think so . . . stand by."

They all heard it, Gibson and Shannon and Knight, and wondered that it was possible. After a while Gibson called again but there was no answer. Maudslay and his crew never came back. Among them there were two Canadians, Alden Cottam and Robert Urquhart.

Gibson called, "Okay, David, will you attack now?"

Shannon tried and missed again, came round once more and plunged into the darkness. This time he made it, curling out of the dive at the foot of the lake and tracking for the dam. He found his height quickly, the bomb dropped and Shannon

pulled his plane up over the mountain. The bomb spewed up the familiar plume of white water and as it drifted down Gibson, diving over the lake, saw the dam was still there. There was only Les Knight left. He had the last bomb. Gibson sent him in.

Knight, a young Australian, tried once and couldn't make it. He tried again. Failed. Over the radio Dave Shannon advised: "Come in down moon and dive for the point, Les."

Knight dived again. This time he made a perfect run and his bomb dropped in the right spot. Seconds later the water erupted. It seemed to Harry O'Brien, Knight's Canadian rear gunner, that the tremendous column of water was coming straight toward his turret.

Gibson, slanting down to the lake, saw the dam burst open and a torrent come crashing out. This was even more fantastic than the Möhne. The breach was as big but there were more than 200 million tons of water to pour through. The Eder Valley was steeper, and they watched wordlessly as the flood foamed down the valley. It must have been rolling at 30 feet a second. In the front turret of Les Knight's aircraft, Canadian gunner Fred Sutherland saw a bridge collapse as if it was made of matchsticks. They saw a car racing to get clear;

THE CANADIAN DAMBUSTERS

Survivors
1. Sgt. Stephen Oancia
2. Sgt. Fred Sutherland
3. Sgt. Harry O'Brien
4. Flt. Sgt. Kenneth Brown
5. Flt. Sgt. Harvey Weeks
6. Flt. Sgt. John Thrasher
7. PO. G. A. "Tony" Deering
8. Sgt. Bill Ratcliffe
9. Flt. Sgt. Don MacLean
10. Flt. Lt. Joe McCarthy
11. Flt. Sgt. Grant McDonald
12. WO2 Percy Pigeon
13. FO. T. H. "Terry" Taerum
14. FO. Danny Walker
15. Sgt. Chester Gowrie
16. FO. Dave Rodger

Prisoner of war
17. PO. John Fraser

Dead
18. FO. Robert Urquhart
19. WO2 Abram Garshowitz
20. PO. Floyd Wile
21. PO. Lewis Burpee
22. FO. Kenneth Earnshaw
23. Flt. Sgt. James McDowell
24. PO. Vernon Byers
25. Flt. Sgt. Frank Garbas
26. WO2 Joseph Brady
27. WO2 Alden Cottam
28. WO2 James Arthur
29. FO. Vincent MacCausland
30. FO. Harvey Glinz

they saw the lights, like two frightened eyes in the dark. The car was not fast enough. The foam crawled up on it, the headlights turned green as the water rolled over and suddenly they flicked out.

Hutchison tapped the code word in Morse to say the Eder was destroyed. When he had finished Gibson called, "Okay all Cooler aircraft. Let's go home."

McCarthy's plane, the sole survivor of Formation 2, had fought through to the Sorpe, south of the Möhne. The valleys were full of mist so it was a long time before he pinpointed himself over the lake.

He tried a dummy run and found there was a hill at each end. He would have to dive steeply, find his aiming point quickly and pull up in a hurry. He tried twice more but was not satisfied and came in a third time, plunging through the mist, trying to see through the suffused moonlight. He nearly hit the water and leveled out very low. Johnson, his bomb-aimer, picked up the aiming point and seconds later yelled, "Bomb gone!" They were climbing up over the far hills when the bomb exploded

by the dam wall. McCarthy dived back over the dam and they saw that the crest had crumbled for 50 yards. As they turned on course for England, they tapped out the code word that told that they'd hit the dam.

Wallis's joy was complete. Cochrane radioed G George, and asked if he had any aircraft left to divert to the Sorpe, and Hutchison answered, "None." Orders were then radioed to the reserve force which was now over Germany.

PO. Lewis Burpee of Ottawa, pilot of S Sugar, was directed to the Sorpe but he did not answer. They called again and again but there was only silence. He was dead, even as his English wife was about to have a baby. Dead with him were two other Canadians, James Arthur and Joseph Brady. Their aircraft was believed to have crashed near Hamm.

Another Canadian pilot, Flt. Sgt. Kenneth Brown in F Freddy, was sent to the Sorpe and reached it after McCarthy had left. The mist was swirling thicker and, though Brown dived low over the dam, Sgt. Stephen Oancia, his Canadian bomb-aimer, could not register his aim in time.

Brown dived back on a second run but Oancia still found the mist foiled him. They tried eight times, then on the ninth Oancia dropped incendiaries in the woods to the side of the dam. They burned dazzlingly and the trees caught too. On the tenth run Oancia picked up the glare a long way back, knew exactly where the target was and dropped his bomb accurately.

They pulled round in a climbing turn and a jet of water and rubble rose out of the mist and hung against the moon. Down in the mist itself they saw a shock wave of air like a giant smoke ring circling the base of the spout. But the Sorpe, constructed of hard-packed earth with a concrete core, had more "give" in it than the Möhne or Eder. Although damaged by the two bombs, it still held.

Miraculously, most of the aircraft dodged the flak on the way home. Lucky this, because dawn was coming and at 50 feet the planes were sitting ducks.

Over Holland, Gibson called Dinghy Young, but there was no answer and he wondered what had happened. (Group knew. They had got a brief message from

Young. He had come over the coast a little high in the air and the flak had hit him. He had struggled on a few more miles, losing height, and then ditched in the water. Dinghy had survived two earlier sea crashes—hence his nickname—but this time he and his crew, including Canadian Vincent MacCausland, ran out of luck.)

One by one the aircraft landed and the crews were driven to the Ops room where Harris, Cochrane and Wallis listened intently. Gibson came in, his hair pressed flat from eight hours under his helmet. "It was a wizard party, sir," he said. "Went like a bomb, but we couldn't knock out the flak. I'm afraid some of the boys got the hammer. Don't know how many yet. Hopgood and Maudslay for certain."

The men had bacon and eggs and stood round the bar, drinking and waiting for the others. It was an hour since the last aircraft had landed. Wallis was asking anxiously, "Where are all the others?"

Someone said, "Oh, they'll be along. Give 'em time. They've probably landed somewhere else."

But after a while Wallis knew they were all getting drunk for the eight crews not coming back. He stood there blinking back tears and said, "If I'd only known, I'd never have started this!"

The party was getting wound up. Gibson left early but not for bed; he went over to the hangar to give his adjutant and Chiefy Powell a hand with the casualty telegrams to the next of kin. Fifty-six men out of 133 were missing—among them 13 of the 30 RCAF men—and only three had got out by parachute at a perilous height to spend the rest of the war in prison. Gibson had expected to lose several aircraft over the Möhne, where the sinister installations had been spotted by the recce aircraft, but had lost only one. (It was not till after the war that they discovered what those dark shapes on top of the Möhne had been— trees, ornamental pine trees. In the middle of the war the Germans who would not send extra guns, had gone to the trouble of decorating the dam.)

When a recce Mosquito arrived with first photographs of the damage, they were breathtaking. The Möhne and Eder lakes were empty and 330 million tons of water were spreading through the western Ruhr valleys. Within a 50-mile radius of both the Möhne and Eder, coal mines were flooded and factories collapsed. One of Hitler's largest military airdromes was under water. Roads, railways and bridges had disappeared. The Unterneustadt industrial suburb of Kassel, 40 miles from the Eder, was under water, and the flood ran miles on down the Fulda Valley. Canal banks were washed away, power stations had disappeared, the Ruhr foundries were without water for making steel. A dozen waterworks were destroyed as far away as Gelsenkirchen, Dortmund, Hamm and Bochum. The communications system was disrupted. Some of the factories that remained could not work because there was no electricity. Or no water. And in the months ahead, in the Battle of the Ruhr, there was not enough water to put the fires out.

And there was a moral price: 1294 people drowned in the floods, among them 749 slaves and prisoners. There had been a Russian prisoner of war camp in the valley below the Eder.

After the raid the Germans diverted hundreds of soldiers with flak guns to guard all the other dams in Germany, and within days more than 20,000 men working on the Atlantic Wall defenses were transferred to repair the broken dams in a race to get them back in use before the autumn rains. Oberbürgermeister Dillgardt was vindicated, but too late.

For the men who were to become known henceforth as "The Dambusters," many decorations came through—34 of them. Gibson was awarded the Victoria Cross. Martin, McCarthy, Maltby, Shannon and Knight got DSOs. Four got bars to their DFCs. There were ten DFCs, 12 DFMs and two men got the Conspicuous Gallantry Medal. Nine decorations went to Canadians. Taerum and Deering got DFCs, Danny Walker a bar to his DFC, Stephen Oancia a DFM, and Kenneth Brown a CGM.

On May 27 the King and Queen visited the squadron, and the crews pressed their uniforms and stood in front of their aircraft to be presented. It was Shannon's 21st birthday. Gibson had primed the King so that when Shannon was presented the King said jokingly, "You seem to be a very well preserved 21, Shannon. You must have a party tonight."

That night Shannon had his party. At its height someone said: "Shannon, I think you're drunk," and Shannon said with hauteur: "Sir, if so, it is by Royal Command." . . .

PAUL BRICKHILL

King George VI congratulates Wing Comdr. Guy Gibson (left) as they examine photographs showing the havoc caused by the breaching of the dams. Below: the last page of WO2 Joseph Brady's logbook.

REMARKS (Including results of bombing, gunnery, exercises, etc.)	Flying Times	
	Day	Night
Time carried forward:— 133:30		
LOW LEVEL CROSS COUNTRY.	3:20	
LOW LEVEL BOMBING.	1:00	
LOW LEVEL CROSS COUNTRY.	1:40	
LOW LEVEL CROSS COUNTRY. "SPOTLIGHT"		1:20
LOW LEVEL CROSS COUNTRY. "SPOTLIGHT"		1:35
LOW LEVEL CROSS COUNTRY.	2:30	
LOW LEVEL CROSS COUNTRY.		1:40
X/C. BOMBING	2:00	
N.F.T.		:45
OPERATIONS EDER DAM MISSING —		

A sailors' place

Halifax survives six years of convoys, overcrowding, exasperation, riot and deadly danger

They said many things about wartime Halifax. In 1941 British Rear Adm. S. S. Bonham-Carter called it "probably the most important port in the world." That same year Frederick Edwards wrote in *Maclean's:* "No other Canadian city has been so profoundly affected by the war." Historian Thomas H. Raddall said Halifax had to cope with "conditions faced by no other city in North America—conditions in some ways like those of a beleaguered and refugee-crowded city in Europe." Reporters liked to call it "Canada's front-line city." Navy veteran and author William H. Pugsley wrote that it was a grim place for sailors. The sailors themselves called it that and many other things, and when the European war was over they channeled their resentments into a riot that tore the downtown section apart.

Throughout the war, under censor's orders, the press wrote many Halifax stories under the dateline "An East Coast Canadian Port." The term was used to mask the identity of the port and protect its varied and vital military functions. Halifax was headquarters and nerve center for Canadian naval operations in the Atlantic, a base for British and other Allied ships. It was Canada's and for some time the continent's main funnel for war shipments overseas. It was a coastal fortress, a naval training ground, a 3500-man base for air defense of the coast, a repair shop for thousands of Allied ships.

Here, wrote Edwards in 1941, "is a cross section of the Empire. You may hear within the space of one block Cockney, Yorkshire, Lancashire and Scottish accents. Royal Navy and Royal Canadian Navy officers and ratings mingle with men of the merchant marine. Egyptian, Malayan and Hindu seamen wait in line before theater box offices with airmen from Australia and New Zealand, Canadian soldiers, and sailors of Allied countries: Free French, Norwegians, Dutchmen, Poles. After nightfall, a civilian on Barrington, the main street, looks as though he didn't belong. And in the railway yards, beds may be made up in Pullman cars to accommodate visitors who might otherwise have to sleep in the parks."

Over the city's piers moved virtually the entire overseas army, survivors of torpedoed ships, British children being evacuated to Canadian homes, scientists on secret missions, German prisoners of war, refugees from occupied Europe, airmen going overseas, airmen coming back. They came and went in liners and freighters and tankers and tramps, from 1939 to 1945.

Yet the most memorable sight was the recurrent one of a convoy slipping out of the majestic harbor with food, men, guns and tanks and shells bound overseas. "The pageant at the harbor mouth," wrote Tho-

Well back of the anti-submarine boom (above) at the mouth of Halifax harbor, merchant ships lie safely at anchor in Bedford Basin, waiting to form into a convoy. In the background are Halifax (right) and, across the narrow harbor, Dartmouth. McNab Island is at the top, beyond that the Atlantic.

221

mas H. Raddall in *Halifax, Warden of the North,* "held its fascination until the very end. Right up to early 1945 when ships were mined or torpedoed sometimes within gunshot of outer Halifax forts, and the distant thud of depth charges could be heard through the open windows of the Nova Scotian Hotel, the sight of the gray ships plodding out to face such music all the way to Britain or Murmansk was something to catch the heart. No one could watch it unmoved."

Halifax was an incredible place, at times a maddening place, a frenetically gay, gray place packed with men who could tell a thousand tales but only wanted to relax. Primarily it was a sailors' place, a navy town. The RCN concentrated a large fraction of its strength there, up to nearly 20,000 men and women, and it employed thousands of civilians as well. It contributed, more than anything else, to overcrowding the city, whose population grew from 70,000 to well beyond 100,000.

The hostels did a marvelous job, providing inexpensive meals and beds. But they were almost as impersonal as barracks. To the sailor away from home for the first time, their lights spoke no welcome as he walked aimlessly through rain-swept streets. He knew no one, and loneliness enveloped him.

What sailors in from the sea wanted most was a good feed, a change from monotonous shipboard diet. There were only about three large restaurants and they were always crowded. So the ratings flocked to small cafés where the plates showed plainly what had been served earlier.

There were hundreds of kindly Halifax people whose hospitality and generosity won't be forgotten. And there were hundreds of women who gave unstintingly to make the canteens a haven of enjoyment for the sailor. Unfortunately there was a limit to what they could do, and they seemed to be outnumbered by citizens who were, at best, indifferent.

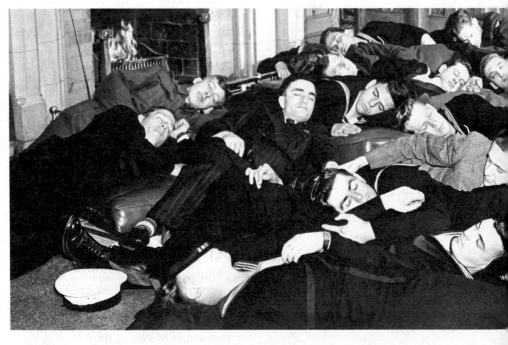

In *Saints, Devils and Ordinary Seamen,* William H. Pugsley summed up the individual sailor's reaction to the situation: . . . Halifax was grim. With all the rainy weather, you had to find something to do indoors. Rainy Sundays were particularly dreary but any day was bad enough. After looking at the queues outside the theaters, after making the rounds of the canteens—and finding either nothing going on or the place packed because something was going on—you wandered into a hostel, found an easy chair, then fell asleep.

Halifax complained about "those drunken sailors." The city itself was responsible for much of the drunkenness. With so little else to do, young seamen started drinking, and because they had no place to go they were seen intoxicated on the streets. Civilians could take liquor home but the sailors could not take theirs to barracks. So they drank it quickly in some dark corner. Moderation never had a chance. . . .

The government made no provision for housing the families of servicemen posted to Halifax. Instead, wrote Thomas H. Raddall, it tried to discourage them from going there at all. He added:

. . . Government advertisements in newspapers across Canada suggested, urged and finally commanded that people who had no business there should stay where they belonged. All this was blithely ignored. From 1939 on, trains decanted women and children eager to join their men in this strange, exciting place. Hotels, boarding houses, tenements, apartments and homes were jammed for six years

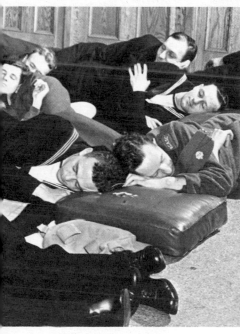

many persons had to live in filthy rooms in the slums, and a tumorous growth of shacks appeared and spread into the woods on the outskirts of the city.

There was a sharp rise in rentals. Laws to curb the rapacity of landlords had little effect. The incoming swarm were eager to pay bribes above the legitimate rent-control levels. The Halifax newspapers were full of appeals and proffered "rewards" for rooms or apartments.

Overcrowding had other unhappy results. The meager supplies of civilian goods, especially clothing, bedding and utensils, were snapped up by the enlarged population or by merchant seamen buying for their folks back home. As the war went on, the shops became bare of necessities. For years only the lucky could find a kettle, a shirt, a stove. Yet there was no dearth of luxury goods: fur coats, diamond necklaces, exquisite watches.

The food problem was severe. When large troop convoys and their warship escorts were being provisioned not only warehouse stocks in the city but all food in transit east from Montreal was subject to service priority. For days on end very little meat and few vegetables were to be had in the shops. Even fish was hard to obtain because so many Nova Scotian fishermen were at war. The inadequate fuel supply had to fill service and merchant marine demands first.

But somehow the swollen population was fed, housed and kept from freezing under conditions faced by no other city in North America. The provincial government's liquor stores, for instance, adopted a rigid rationing system. Bootleggers soon discovered that ration books could be purchased or "rented" from owners, and created a brisk black market in liquor. To feed it, stevedores stole liquor from ships. Drugs in transit to the medical services overseas were stolen too; they went inland to other cities for underworld disposal.

Prostitutes flocked to Halifax by the hundreds; the port became a courtesan's paradise. Taxicabs were scarce, and the insolence and rapacity of the average taximan became intolerable. There was a growing indifference among shopgirls, waitresses and others overworked in the incessant rush. As the war dragged on, there was an increasing *ennui* among servicemen, a steady decline in shore discipline. Four out of five men were well behaved, but theft, robbery with violence, malicious damage and assault upon women by men in uniform became matters of daily occurrence. . . .　　　THOMAS H. RADDALL

The city maintained an elaborate emergency organization just in case the Germans attacked by air. And it lived for six years in dread of something it feared even more: a repetition of the 1917 explosion of a munitions ship which took 2000 lives and injured thousands more in the greatest explosion the world had ever known. Halifax had cause to worry; the disaster almost came to pass more than once.

In April 1942, the steamship *Irongate* caught fire with a large quantity of explosives in her hold. Despite desperate efforts, the fire could not be controlled. The ship had to be sunk by a warship's guns, within a few hundred yards of downtown Halifax. Damaged ships often leaked fuel oil. In August 1943, a damaged tanker covered the harbor with thousands of gallons of high-test aviation spirit; the danger of a holocaust lasted for days.

Halifax's greatest fear was nearly realized on November 3, 1943. Terence Robertson told the story in *Maclean's*:

... The commander of the dockyard turned lazily in his bunk, groped for the ringing telephone and muttered sleepily, "Yes?" A clipped report from the duty port defense officer snapped him awake: *"Volunteer's* on fire in Bedford Basin, sir. She's carrying enough ammunition to sink the city."

Comdr. Owen Connor Struan Robertson, six-feet-seven and known through the service as "Long Robbie," scrambled into his uniform and raced to the docks. A six-man naval fire party, under Lt. Charles Spinney and Stoker Petty Officer Bill Carson, stood by in a launch. The naval fire marshal had sent fire-fighting tugs into the basin and the city fire chief had been warned. It was 7:20 a.m.

As the launch sped toward the elderly U.S. freighter, riding at anchor under a pall of smoke, Robertson realized that his handful of men would have to prevent an explosion which might blow most of Halifax off the face of Nova Scotia. The 36-year-old officer was as scared as he'd ever been.

The 12,000-ton *Volunteer* had arrived the night before and anchored in the basin to await orders to join a convoy. No accurate account of her cargo has survived, but it is estimated that she carried more than 500 tons of light ammunition, some 2000 drums of highly combustible magnesium, and about 1800 tons of heavy howitzer ammunition, an unknown number of depth charges and several cases of dynamite.

At 5:15 a.m. a stoker had attempted to raise steam in her two boilers. Working carelessly, he switched on the oil burners, let the temperature in the firebox go up to flash point and then applied the lighting torch. The burners detonated, causing a flashback of such power that the fuel pipes ruptured. Flaming oil spewed out into the stokehold, burning rapidly while the stoker ran screaming from the engine room.

Other crew members rushed to his assistance and the second officer climbed to the master's quarters to report the fire. A drunken all-night poker session was entering the stage of early morning tension and, getting no help there, the second officer

ordered the radio operator to contact the naval signal station at Turple Head while he tried to attract attention ashore with a signal lamp.

It was 5:45 a.m. The fire in the stokehold was spreading forward to No. 3 hold.

Because they were in a strange port, the radio officer sent out signals on a wrong wavelength and the second officer aimed his lamp in the wrong direction, blinking it vainly at some deserted warehouses. Thirty minutes passed before the radio began switching wavelengths and made contact with Turple Head. But his messages were so garbled that the navy signalman on duty couldn't decipher them. Twenty more valuable minutes were lost in a futile exchange of signals.

At 6:50 a.m. the American crew, by now aware that their senior officers were drunk and incapable of effective action, took to the lifeboats and abandoned ship.

Then Turple Head reported that *Volunteer* was sending out SOS signals, and naval control immediately dispatched an armed launch to find out what was wrong. Fifteen minutes later—two hours after the fire started—the launch informed naval control and the port defense officer by radio-telephone that the ship was ablaze.

The fireboat *Rouille* was the first to arrive and began pumping Foamite into the stokehold. Robertson's naval launch and the tug *James Battle,* with William Cody of the National Harbors Board's fire department aboard, drew alongside simultaneously. The two parties made their way to the master's cabin and found an unexpected scene.

"Bottles, some empty, some half-filled, were everywhere," Robertson recalled

Comdr. O. C. S. "Long Robbie" Robertson directed the struggle against *Volunteer's* fire and then to move her to a place where she could be beached before her explosive cargo could erupt. Right: some of the navy firemen after the job had been done.

later. "Poker chips were scattered about the deck and the master, chief officer and chief engineer were pretty drunk. They'd made port and they'd let their hair down. Nothing unusual about that in those days; it was a rough time for merchant seamen. I'd say these three had had a pretty good party." But Robertson had to make a snap decision. His position was delicate because he had no authority to take action aboard a foreign ship without the consent of her master. But immediate action had to be taken, and the master was in no shape to cope with the situation. Robertson decided to leave the cabin and do what he could on his own.

"When we went back to the upper deck I noticed all the lifeboats had gone and there were only two or three of the crew in sight. The rest had left the ship.

"Smoke was pouring out of the engine room and, although *Rouille's* crew had connected up the Foamite system, they refused to go below to see what effect it was having or to what extent the fire had spread."

Robertson pulled on an oxygen mask and asbestos hood and, through hot steam and blinding smoke, climbed down the engine-room ladder into the stokehold. Foamite, oil and scalding water covered its deck.

There, at least, the fire was out, but the extreme heat of the after bulkheads indicated it might have broken out in No. 3 hold. There was also the danger that with so much heat and fumes in the stokehold another fire would start at any moment.

Robertson returned to the upper deck and gave orders for *Rouille* to continue pumping in Foamite while he checked the cargo distribution. He hoped to find some way of sealing off the ammunition from the rest of the ship. He went back to the master's cabin and demanded that the officers who had supervised the loading be summoned. The master said none of his officers had been present during loading.

Robertson knew that freighters never sailed without a stowage plan. He glared at the drunken officers and said: "I'm going to search your cabins until I find it. My men are armed. If you try to interfere they'll shoot."

At that moment a series of explosions broke out below decks. The fire had reached No. 3 hold and set off the first few cases of light ammunition. Robertson looked at the master. "It's about time you pulled yourself together," he said. "This is your ship and there's a good chance that at any minute we'll all be blown to kingdom come."

He stalked away to the officers' quarters. In the chief officer's desk he found a cargo sheet showing the contents of each hold. As he read, the real extent of the danger became shockingly apparent.

In the 'tween decks of No. 3, forward of the engine room, were drums of magnesium, crates of light ammunition, some explosives and bales of tobacco. This deck led forward on either side of the engine-room well to No. 2 hold, where the bulk of the magnesium and light ammunition was stowed. Below it, in the lower hold, was the heavy ammunition.

If the light ammunition, already ricocheting around No. 3, exploded the magnesium, nothing could prevent the fire from spreading through the 'tween decks to

No. 2 and blowing up the ship, the docks and at least the north end of Halifax.

By the time Robertson returned to the bridge, Cody, Spinney and Carson had persuaded the master and his fellow poker players to leave the cabin in the hope that fresh air might help sober them.

"We have to flood No. 3," Robertson announced. "The fire's already got at the ammunition there. If we douse that there's a good chance we can prevent further outbreaks."

The master lurched forward angrily: "No you don't. This is my ship and what I say goes. I say there'll be no flooding anywhere." Robertson tried to reason with him, then gave up and turned to Carson: "Ask naval control to send out the U.S. naval liaison officer in a hurry. Then send the launch ashore to pick up some oxy-acetylene cutting gear. We may need to blow a vent in these decks."

While Robertson and his men rigged hoses to flood No. 3, Cody directed *Rouille's* men in connecting more hoses. *Volunteer's* officers went down to the saloon for a conference—with bottles of Scotch to help. It was 9 a.m. The explosions in No. 3 had become a steady, crackling roar.

Fumes and heat were building to a critical explosive level, but Robertson knew that to open up the hold to release the pressure would also give the fire oxygen and it would burn even more furiously. As he considered the problem, he was interrupted by the appearance on deck of the master and chief engineer, both wearing gas masks. They said they were going below to inspect the engine room and stokehold. Robertson, even though he had been wearing waders, oxygen mask and asbestos hood, had been burned, nearly overcome by steam and fumes and half-blinded during his brief visit below. He knew that if these two went down wearing only gas masks, the handful of fire fighters would have to leave the fire to rescue them.

He ordered two navy ratings to guard the engine-room hatch and to use force if necessary to prevent any of the ship's officers using it.

It was a brittle moment. The sweating, dirty men could barely see one another through the smoke and cordite fumes; the oil-soaked decks were becoming red hot and a sense of mounting danger gripped everyone—with the seeming exception of the drunken officers.

The master glared at Robertson, but the return of the launch, followed by a naval boarding service cutter with Lieutenant Commander Stanley, USN, aboard, eased the tension. Stanley was accompanied by Lt. Comdr. E. F. B. Watts, senior boarding officer in Halifax, who was responsible for discipline among merchant ships in port.

After a brief exchange with the master, Stanley beckoned to Robertson. Robertson explained quickly what had happened. When the master slurred a protest, Stanley recited U.S. Navy regulations that stripped an incapable captain of his authority. He announced that he was taking command and delegating control of all fire-fighting operations to Robertson.

A dull boom sounded forward of the bridge. The fire had licked along the 'tween decks from No. 3 hold, ignited a pocket of trapped fumes in No. 2 and was now burning along the entire length of the midships superstructure below the main deck.

Robertson, Spinney, Cody, Carson and four naval fire fighters rushed to the side hatches of No. 3, ripped off their covers and all but fell into the blazing hold as they ducked to keep under the ricocheting ammunition. While the others crawled to

A merchant ship loads at Halifax: in the holds, TNT; on deck, a tank.

shelter behind bales of tobacco, Robertson prowled about the hold using his flashlight to see how the cargo had been stowed. He decided that the bulk of the magnesium drums could be protected from the flying bullets by a barricade of tobacco bales. Robertson climbed back to the upper deck to instruct Watts to signal for tugs and a harbor pilot, while the other seven men remained below for more than an hour building the wall of bales.

"I had seen enough," Robertson recalled later, "to convince me the only solution was to move the ship out of the basin to McNab Island, where I knew that the sea bed off Mauger's Beach dipped into a trough. We could scuttle the ship there and let her rest in the trough with her decks awash as though in a cradle.

"The flooding would eventually extinguish the fire—providing the ship didn't blow up before we got there. I figured we had a 50-50 chance. Had the odds been any worse I'd have sunk her where she was.

"My main worry was the fire spreading to No. 2 hold and what might happen if it got down into the lower hold where the heavy ammunition was."

When he returned to No. 3 he was met by the smoke-blackened Carson. "You'd better come down quick, sir," said the petty officer. "There's a whole pile of magnesium you didn't see."

They tumbled down to the 'tween decks again and Carson led the way to where Spinney and the rest of the team were trying to drag tobacco bales around drums of magnesium stacked to the deckhead. It was an impossible task for so few men working in darkness, blinded by smoke, choked by fumes and having to keep below the level of whizzing .303 ammunition.

If the bullets penetrated the drums, the magnesium would explode, ignite the cordite fumes and set off a reaction that would blow up the ship. By then, the immense pockets of heat and fumes were as dangerously explosive as the ammunition.

There was only one thing to do—cut holes in the deck and cause a deliberate explosion which would disperse the pockets of fumes.

Robertson returned to the upper deck, gave instructions for the oxyacetylene crew to cut holes in the main deck above the magnesium and then consulted Watts and Stanley on the bridge. While they were talking, two tugs arrived, one with the

harbor pilot, Capt. John Brackett. He listened to Robertson's plan and briefed his tug skippers. Since there was no steam to drive the windlass, a naval party went forward with another cutting torch to sever the anchor cable.

Shortly after noon, the holes in the deck above No. 3 hold had been cut and, armed with a borrowed rifle, Robertson went below to join the waiting fire fighters. They had formed a screen of bales facing the eight magnesium drums and, using this as cover, Robertson took aim at the drums and began firing.

An ear-splitting explosion lifted the nearly insensible men off their feet and sent them sprawling. Flames spurted through the vent holes and shot 40 feet in the air. One stream of gases blew Carson through the open side hatch to the upper deck where he collapsed, unconscious.

"It must have been a good ten minutes before the rest of us could pull ourselves together and stumble up out of there," said Robertson. "We were just about knocked out and when we did manage to reach the upper deck we were black, blue and bruised all over.

"Carson was just coming round. He didn't remember a thing. We all suffered some internal injuries from that blast. Stoker George Shatford subsequently died of them."

The explosion had lessened the immediate danger in No. 3 hold. The major threat now was from a buildup of heat in No. 2.

Robertson went up to the bridge to see how the towing was proceeding. The ship was moving slowly with a tug on either bow and Rouille still made fast to Volunteer's starboard side. But Rouille's men, ignorant of the reason for the explosion and frightened by it, had decided to cast off and head for shore. Robertson ran to one side of the bridge and yelled: "Leave those ropes alone. We need you to keep the temperature in the stokehold under control. Keep pumping."

The fireboat's crew pretended they had not heard. Robertson grabbed a rifle from a boarding guard and aimed it down at Rouille's deck. "The first man to touch one of those ropes gets shot," he said. "And I mean it."

Robertson's blackened, sweat-streaked appearance was enough to scare anyone. The crew backed up sullenly. Robertson handed the rifle to the guard with orders to

watch the fireboat and shoot to kill if any of the crew touched a rope.

Then he clambered down to the upper deck, summoned his team and said: "We'll have to go down into No. 2 to see what's happening. If there's no danger to the heavy ammunition, we can pull more bales of tobacco round the light stuff in the 'tween decks and that should keep things under control until we reach McNab."

Using side hatches as they had done to get in No. 3, they vanished below again. Small fires had already taken a firm hold on cases of light ammunition. Again they experienced the roar of exploding ammunition, the racket of bullets clanging off the deckhead and thumping into other cases or tobacco bales. There was the added danger of the heat once again building up to flash point in the lower hold. This could prove fatal.

Robertson decided to go down into the lower hold to test the pressure. Carson got a length of rope and a piece of rubber air hose. Robertson tied the rope around his waist, wrapped rags around one end of the hose and stuffed it in his mouth. The other end led out of the hold and dangled over the ship's side away from the smoke.

While Carson held an end of the rope, Robertson lifted clear a hatch cover and dropped nine feet into the blackness of the lower hold. He crawled over the ammunition crates, feeling his way and remembering the stowage plan. To his surprise and relief there was plenty of smoke but little evidence of overheating or of cordite fumes. He was satisfied that all that could be done now was to pray that the ship could be beached and flooded before pockets of overheated fumes could accumulate.

"I reckoned we had about two hours before there was any real danger of the heavy stuff going up," he said. "And even at our slow rate of towing we would reach McNab within half an hour. So the odds were all in our favor."

He made his way to the bridge to check their progress with the pilot, just in time to see the master lurch from his cabin, climb up the bridge ladder on the far side and shout to the second officer to hand him a megaphone.

Robertson's report of the incident said: "This [second] officer was one of the few in the ship who were sober and in full possession of their faculties. To humor the master he did as he was told. The master ordered a non-existent crew on the fore-

VE-Day in Halifax. Above: a brewery is looted. Right: a male mannequin leans drunkenly in the smashed window of a clothing store—and sailors, one wearing the lady's wig, adorn a bald and armless mannequin with a Union Jack. Top right: the cleanup starts in a wrecked shoe store. VE-Day trouble was minor elsewhere. Margaret D. McLean, a navy nursing sister, wrote in *The Canadian Nurse:* "I remember the joy and unrestrained hilarity at Greenock in Scotland and the wise captain who called out the band at midnight, organized a snake dance and provided so much fun and entertainment on board HMCS *Niobe* that not one Canadian seaman went absent without leave or got into trouble in Glasgow."

castle to 'heave away when ready.' He stayed on the bridge for some ten more minutes without taking further action and then returned to his cabin."

At 3:45 p.m. *Volunteer* was nudged into position off Mauger's Beach on the south end of McNab Island. Robertson sent his men down to the engine room to open the sea cocks. The freighter began to subside.

Shortly after 4 p.m. she was beached.

It sprang out of the years of overcrowding, of gouging landlords, of slackening navy discipline, of danger, out of what Halifax —through no fault of its own—had become. It caused damage running into millions of dollars. Thomas H. Raddall in *Halifax, Warden of the North:*

. . . About midmorning May 7, 1945, the German radio announced the surrender of Germany's forces. Thousands of service-

Robertson and his men had done their job and were taken off in a launch which brought Harbor Department fire fighters to look after the flooding and to deal with any emergency.

Watts remained aboard to help Stanley maintain discipline. It was just as well. The master, who was still drinking, suddenly burst out on deck and screamed to all in sight that if their lives, the ship and the city were to be saved, *Volunteer* must be beached. She had been aground an hour. . . . TERENCE ROBERTSON

Volunteer was eventually salvaged and returned to her original private owners after the war. Her drunken master and his cohorts were removed from the ship and repatriated to the United States. There is no record of a court of inquiry into the matter by U.S. authorities, nor were any charges ever pressed against the misbehaving officers. They apparently vanished into complete—and merciful—obscurity.

Paradoxically, the explosion which did the most damage to Halifax came not from munitions but from human beings.

men and civilians gathered in downtown Halifax, wandering aimlessly through the streets. The liquor stores were closed as a precaution, but the crowds were orderly and there was no sign of trouble. Then, toward evening, a crowd of naval personnel stormed a streetcar and set it afire. They proceeded along Barrington Street, gathering followers as they went. When they reached downtown Halifax, they smashed their way into two liquor stores and looted them.

The downtown area was policed by 50 or 60 constables. The armed services provided their own police to look after men in uniform. The possibility of a riot had been discussed and some preparations made, but the riot broke before any plan could be put into effect. The well-stocked liquor stores satisfied the mob for the night. But what had begun as a lark turned overnight into a fixed determination to "take the town apart."

On the sunny morning of May 8 there were about 24,500 servicemen in the port and its defenses, including 18,000 in the navy. To celebrate the Allied announcement of victory, the city and the military services had arranged a mass meeting with band music, songs, hymns and addresses. The police hoped this would keep the crowd out of the downtown district. But some naval personnel had other plans and they were encouraged by the city's criminal element.

The mass meeting began on the Garrison Grounds as scheduled, but word quickly spread that a new riot had begun in the shopping district. The entire crowd poured over the hill to watch or take part.

The navy had managed to keep roughly half its personnel on duty but at noon about 9500 sailors were loose in the streets. Of these probably not more than a thousand took part in the rioting but many others shared in the loot, and they were joined by other servicemen, merchant seamen and loafers and petty criminals. The city was in a stage of anarchy until well into the night.

Sailors took the lead, smashing shop windows from the dockyard to the heart of the city. In the main shopping district they tore victory flags from the shops and used the poles to break the plate glass windows, leaping inside and tossing out jewelry, drugs, clothing, shoes to the mob. A police car was capsized and burned. The city police could do nothing to quell the riot. The naval police, unwilling to intervene in a riot involving so many civilians, accomplished nothing either.

Before long the downtown area was a shambles of broken glass and littered goods. Another liquor store was stormed and looted, then a brewery. Bacchanalia followed. Two shops were set afire. Sailors, waterfront toughs and women of all sorts could be seen smashing bottle necks, drinking themselves senseless and lolling amid the strewn merchandise on the sidewalks and in the gutter. Others carried their loot away. In the parks, on the Citadel slopes, drunken seamen and workmen capered and sang, sprawled with drunken or merely hilarious women, eased themselves, and made unabashed love in the full blaze of the afternoon sun. It was a scene for Hogarth.

While the riot was going on, thousands of servicemen and townsfolk looked on amazed or turned their backs and strolled away. Toward evening the senior naval officer, Rear Adm. L. W. Murray, made his way through the streets in a car equipped with loudspeakers, ordering his

men to return to their ships and barracks. Eventually most of them did, throwing away their loot or bestowing it on yelling urchins.

Murray was a keen and capable officer who had directed the greater part of the war in the western Atlantic with skill and success; it was unfortunate that the record of his command at Halifax should have been marred by this unsavory climax.

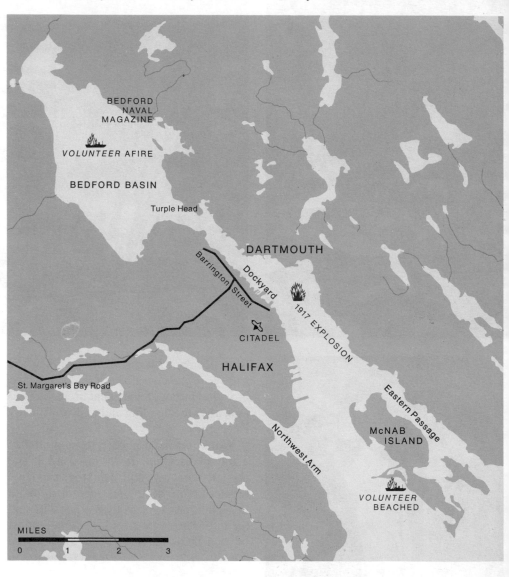

of a shortage of policemen, their "faulty direction" and the "passive conduct" of the naval command. The Kellock report said damage was done to 564 business firms: 2624 pieces of plate and other glass were smashed and 207 premises were looted. Charges were brought against 19 airmen, 41 soldiers and 34 sailors, on charges other than drunkenness, and 117 civilians.

[Navy Minister Abbott later said that

Vice Adm. G. C. Jones, Chief of Naval Staff, came from Ottawa to take over naval affairs at Halifax, and troops came down by rail from the camp at Debert, N.S. The troops found nothing to do; Mayor Alan Butler proclaimed a curfew on the evening of the 8th and the riot faded away.

[A Royal Commissioner, Mr. Justice R. L. Kellock of the Supreme Court of Canada, blamed the riots on the "failure of the naval command to put down the initial disorders." The trouble continued because

the burden borne by Admiral Murray as Commander-in-Chief Canadian Northwest Atlantic "was still his at the time of the disturbances for, however great may have been the rejoicing ashore, the U-boat war had not at that time ceased. It would be a regrettable thing if the truly great services of this officer and those under his command were to be forgotten" as a result of the riots.]

But the city's trials were not over.

By July, its Bedford Basin magazine was packed with explosives deposited by returning ships whose war was done. Much of this ammunition was stored in the magazine, but a good deal had been stacked outdoors for lack of space. The heat was stifling on July 18. As the city was sitting down to the evening meal, an ammunition barge blew up at the magazine jetty, shook the whole metropolitan area and shattered many windows. The exposed ammunition dumps caught fire and soon there was an

incessant rumbling and concussion.

That night naval headquarters warned more than half the population of Halifax to evacuate their homes. Fortunately, the city's emergency organization was still in existence. The forces sent trucks and drivers to assist in the evacuation, and civilian vehicles of every sort were put to use.

Most refugees headed out of the peninsula altogether. The St. Margaret's Bay road became a solid mass of vehicles ten miles long, crawling slowly toward the west. Some cars and trucks carried mattresses and even chairs; there were baskets of food, blankets and luggage of all sorts crammed with family valuables. Many trudged along the roadside, pushing perambulators, pulling handcarts, carrying babies or leading little troops of children. But there was no panic.

Thousands chose to remain in the north end of the city, refusing to abandon their homes. They threw open windows and doors to save them from air blast and went outside to watch the terrific fireworks. From time to time a major explosion sent up a huge flame. The worst blasts came in quick succession about 4 a.m. on the 19th, rocking buildings, shattering windows, tumbling crockery and plaster—but none had the single force of the 1917 explosion. The houses stood, shaken but intact.

With such an emergency in mind, the magazine had been designed to prevent the whole thing from going up at once. But there was a store of the powerful explosive RDX which alone could level the whole

A huge cloud of smoke hung over Bedford Basin after the first explosion at the naval magazine on July 18, 1945. Worse blasts came early the next morning. Navy volunteers helped magazine personnel put out fires and remove explosives. Above: after the disaster. The map opposite locates the magazine and the site of the 1917 explosion. Also shown are where *Volunteer* caught fire and where she was beached, and the site of much of the VE-Day rioting (Barrington Street).

north end. Naval headquarters continued to warn of a terrific blast yet to come. Still the stoics remained. The telephone, broadcasting and powerhouse staffs stuck to their posts. Household radios blared through open windows a succession of bulletins and warnings mingled with strains of music. Then toward evening the radio stations broadcast an official report that the worst was past and the people could return to their homes.

Behind this curt announcement was an epic of heroism about the men who for 24 hours had been struggling to get the fires under control. The credit was chiefly due to naval volunteers who, under the direction of the magazine staff, dragged fire-fighting apparatus to the very edge of the inferno and remained there to help. The parched woods about the magazine caught fire and burned for two days. When the fires and the explosions had ceased, navy squads began to work in the magazine area, removing explosives flung in all directions by the blasts.

Halifax soon knew how much it had been spared. The resentment against the navy over the riot vanished in admiration of the men who saved the city. Indeed, the old affection for the navy, tested by nearly two centuries of contact, good and bad, came back literally with a bang. If the magazine disaster did nothing else, it blew away in a night and a day what might have been years of bitterness between Halifax and the service to which it is bound. . . .

THOMAS H. RADDALL

Sicily: time of learning

Green troops come out of their first campaign as the "red patch devils"

The Canadian Army's long wait was at last drawing to its close. By the spring of 1943, the 1st Division had been in Britain for almost 3½ years, endlessly training, endlessly waiting and, as war correspondent L. S. B. Shapiro reported, "seeking, hoping for, finally praying for a battlefield."

Shapiro wrote in *They Left The Back Door Open:*

. . . Three years and five months! A long time to wait 3000 miles from home. Too long for the many who had rushed to recruiting offices in September 1939 in the first flush of desire to fight Nazi Germany. Much too long to spend in the bleak encampments of England. Youths of 20 had become 24. Many had married. With bitter humor they joked that the 1st Division was the only formation in the history of war whose birthrate was higher than its deathrate.

North Africa was conquered. And now the 1st Division was engaged in assault exercises and mountain training. The next battlefield must be theirs. Surely the vigil was ended!

It was. Early in June the division's heavy equipment rolled to western British ports. With it went tanks of a separate formation, the 1st Tank Brigade. On June 12 I was told by army public relations in London: "You're going on operations. We don't know what kind. They may be only maneuvers. But don't tell anybody. You're just going away for a few days, see?"

I detrained at a little town and was driven to tank brigade headquarters: a castle complete with moat, drawbridge and ghost. We waited there 11 days.

Secrecy was rigidly maintained. Although most staff officers knew details of the operational plan, no hint was dropped through long nights of conversation, cardplaying and modest drinking.

Brig. R. A. Wyman, on a last inspection of the brigade's fighting units, examined each man from head to foot, prodded pieces of equipment, tugged at belts and buckles. Then he spoke: "Men, you have been privileged to form part of the first armored formation in the history of Canada to move into active operations against the enemy."

This was the first official word that they were to go into action.

"You have everything except battle experience. That, I am confident, you will learn quickly and effectively. But feel your way. Do not move in headlong no matter how great the temptation. Be cautious. Make haste slowly. Best of luck. May God bless your efforts."

I watched for reaction in the faces of these youngsters who not long ago had been clerks and farmers and shopkeepers in Canada. I was disappointed. There was none. A Roman Catholic padre told me: "I find them no different now than before they heard the news. My services are no better attended. I suppose they're no longer men, as we know men. They're good soldiers. Pity, isn't it?"

Then, on June 26: "A vehicle will pick up your bedrolls at midnight. You will be ready to move an hour later."

Our last packs were being crammed when the door was flung open and a sergeant staggered in under an armful of equipment. "Tropical kit," he said—shirts, shorts, mosquito nets, tent poles, sun goggles, knee socks and short puttees.

"Well," said someone, "that eliminates Murmansk." . . .   L. S. B. SHAPIRO

It wasn't Murmansk. It was Sicily.

Part of the army was going to war to stay. For this big blow at the Italian island, the 1st Division and 1st Tank Brigade proudly joined the legendary British Eighth Army. They would learn about war by fighting under the renowned Gen. Bernard Montgomery, hero of El Alamein.

But it was close; they almost didn't go at all. It was not until April 24 that the 1st Division had been substituted for the 3rd British. In his official history, *The Canadians in Italy,* Lt. Col. G. W. L. Nicholson noted that this decision was not exclusively military. Canadian public opinion had come to reinforce the desire of the troops themselves, had come to demand that the government get the army into action.

Some newspapers, Colonel Nicholson wrote, suggested that the decision to keep the Canadians on the sidelines for so long had been made at Canada's request, that the blame lay with the government's wish to maintain the army intact.

In fact, Defense Minister Ralston had asked at a meeting with Prime Minister Churchill in October 1942 that "active employment" be found for Canadian soldiers as soon as possible. There were "no strings"—the army could be used in whole or in part.

The Sicilian campaign was the first hard threat to the dream of Lt. Gen. A. G. L. McNaughton that his army be kept together to carry Canada's name and reputation into the main invasion of western Europe. But there was an encouraging aspect to the decision: the 1st Division and the 1st Tank Brigade would get battle experience, then come back to salt and season the entire army. Against that background, General McNaughton examined the Sicily plan, reported it was "a practical operation of war"—and the Canadian government approved.

The plan was for the Eighth Army to land on a 50-mile stretch of coastline reaching from the Pachino peninsula, on the southeast tip of Sicily, to Syracuse, push quickly north to Messina and "shut the back door" on the enemy. Gen. George S. Patton's U.S. Seventh Army, landing to the left of the Eighth, would swing north and west, then east along the north coast. The theory was that the Germans and Italians, trapped between the two armies, would be unable to flee across the Strait of Messina into the toe of Italy.

CBC war correspondent Peter Stursberg

"Where is the action?" they asked. Canadian troops went ashore in Sicily almost unopposed. "The invasion bulletins," Beverly Baxter wrote in *Maclean's,* "set London on its ear. The usual calm, the diffidence and natural shyness of the English were swept aside. A bus driver said, 'The Canadians are in it.' The British never think of Canadians as defense troops. These sons of men who fought and won at Vimy, Ypres and Passchendaele are 'victory' troops."

was with the 1st Division on its voyage into action. In the book *Journey Into Victory,* he wrote:

. . . One morning we saw Cape Bon rise out of the sea, saw the Tunisian villages, with their mosques and minarets, as we steamed slowly in the great assembly triangle bounded by Cape Bon, Malta and Tripoli. There the mightiest armada the world had yet known was gathering: ships as far as the eye could see, big ships and little, warships and troopers, freighters and landing craft—3000 of them in all. They'd

sailed for this venture from a dozen ports in Britain, the United States and Africa. The statistics were staggering: 160,000 men, 14,000 vehicles, 600 tanks, 1800 guns.

A freak Mediterranean wind, a tricky *sirocco,* came up as we turned and headed northwest to Sicily. By afternoon the stiff breeze had become a gale. You could hardly stand, the ship rolled so. This was July 9—and we all knew the invasion was set for the 10th.

The troopers rolled and pitched, and the escort craft and small landing vessels buried their bows in the waves. The landing craft included two flotillas from the Royal Canadian Navy; scores of other Canadians were serving in RN flotillas. We thought the weather would force postponement of the invasion but we left Malta behind and kept on. The commanders were gambling that the wind would die.

One assault craft had broken loose, was banging against the chucks and had to be battened down. The signalmen were struggling with their flags. The waves washed over the bridges of a line of destroyers cutting across our bow. A little motorboat beside us would disappear, bob up and disappear again. Some planes streaked overhead, tiny silver bullets in the last rays of the sun, Spitfires on their way home to Malta, the only planes we had seen all day.

We stood on deck, listening to the wind scream through the rigging and waiting glumly in the gathering dusk for the signal which would call off our great adventure. The message came when it was almost dark: "TOMORROW."

"My God, it's on!"

At half-past ten the officers of the Royal Canadian Regiment met in the ship's lounge for the last time. Lt. Col. R. M. Crowe spoke. He expressed confidence in his men and said this was a night they would all remember: "Not only the bunch of us here. The whole world will remember it and talk about it for a long time to come."

Then "Rusty" Wilkes took over. He said he had to face the test of being a chaplain in battle, and he asked for their help and guidance. He opened a black book and we all got up and repeated a prayer.

Dieppe was in our minds. We wondered how many of us would live through the next day. After the meeting the stewards began piling chairs and shoving tables into corners. The lounge was to be a hospital.

The wind had dropped and the ship did not seem to be rolling so much. The assault troops, daubing lampblack on their faces, were noisily cheerful, but their laughter and wisecracks sounded forced. The corridors and companionways were jammed with men moving slowly to their boat stations. I felt my way forward to the bridge and realized the wind had died to a gentle breeze. The sky was studded with stars and a small moon hung like a yellow lantern. There was a tense hush on the bridge, broken now and then by the jangle of the engine-room telegraph.

Just before midnight flares pinpointed the sky ahead of us. The air force was lighting the town of Pachino as a beacon.

It was D-Day now, and not even a breeze. At half-past 12 the moon was down, and then, with a rattling roar that startled us all, the ship anchored. Two long, thin transport landing craft, LCTs, maneuvered round the ship. They were having a difficult time, but at last were alongside. I scribbled in my notebook:

1:50 LCTs alongside.

1:55 Assault troops start loading.

2:05 Mooring rope holding LCTs breaks. Another delay.

2:15 Pyrotechnics over Pachino. Looks like more flares being dropped and Italian ack-ack replying with tracer.

We could see the thin, phosphorescent wake of landing craft from other ships

Soon after the landing at Pachino, Canadians and British met stiff resistance from topnotch German troops (top). Above: tank crew commanders confer beside a Sicilian road, then a Canadian squadron (left) goes into action in support of British infantry. White dust soon covered men, guns and tanks.

leaving for the beaches. H-Hour was a quarter to three, and we were going to be late.

2:50 LCTs tied up again. Loading very slow.

3:00 Naval officer orders scrambling nets to speed up loading.

3:10 Heavy explosion on port side. Saw flash. British troops must be ashore.

3:20 Noise of gunfire on starboard side. Sounds like our warships going into action against beach defenses. Canadians on our left must be landing.

3:30 LCTs only half full.

We were almost an hour late now. A delay such as this had caused trouble at Dieppe.

The first gray light of morning was seeping across the sky when the LCTs were finally loaded. It was almost a quarter to five when the two craft left. They were going to be three hours late, for it would take at least an hour to reach the beaches.

I went in in a big LCI, an infantry landing craft. We saw the LCTs disappear in the smoke laid down by naval craft to cover the landing. A destroyer began to shell the shore. A distant crackle of small-arms fire, and a soldier said, "There they go!" Our assault troops were ashore, their rifles and automatics blazing.

A radio crackled in our landing craft. A BBC voice: "This is London calling. The Allies are invading Sicily."

The sun was bright now, and I could see the yellow-brown beach and the little white houses in the vineyards and a town spread out on the hills beyond.

But this was no invasion—where were the planes the gunnery officer had promised? There were none. Some of the landing craft were returning from the beaches, and we shouted at them, "What was it like?"

A bo'sun yelled back, "Nothing at all. Absolutely nothing at all." . . .

PETER STURSBERG

The attack surprised the Italian troops at Pachino and their meager defenses folded up with very little fighting on the beaches. Their hearts weren't in the war.

The RCR and the Hastings and Prince Edward Regiment made the 1st Brigade assault on the right sector of the Canadian beach, the 48th Highlanders following in reserve. On the left the 2nd Brigade rapidly overcame all opposition, with the Seaforth Highlanders and Princess Patricia's Canadian Light Infantry leading the way and the Loyal Edmonton Regiment in reserve. These units won the Canadian beachhead. The 3rd Brigade—Royal 22nd Regiment, Carleton and York Regiment and West Nova Scotia Regiment—came in later, with the 1st Tank Brigade's Three Rivers Regiment. All were under Maj. Gen. Guy Simonds, the 40-year-old divisional commander.

By 8 a.m. the roads winding inland were filled with Canadian troops pushing to new objectives—tanks, guns, Bren-gun carriers and trucks rolling north in clouds of choking white dust that billowed from their tires and treads like a smoke screen.

The invasion was off to a spectacular start everywhere. No one, reported war correspondent Ross Munro, had dared hope for such success.

For a while the Canadians fought mainly fleas, bugs, scorpions and mosquitoes. And the blazing sun and malaria and dust. The division and tank brigade quickly took on the grimy look of the Eighth Army's "desert rats." Guns, tanks and vehicles wore the same dusty white as the Canadians advanced through a succession of hilltop towns.

"In the distance," Peter Stursberg wrote, "they looked picturesque, like castles in the air, but they were hot and dirty and evil-smelling, close-packed gray hovels sometimes brightened by a beautiful rococo church with cupids swirling round the door. The people would stand by their houses and raise their fingers in Churchill's V sign. Peasants on the roads and refugees returning home saluted so frequently that their arms must have got tired. They apparently thought they had to do this or be shot, and we felt badly."

For the Canadians, the whole campaign changed after the occupation of a place called Vizzini. The Americans were making excellent progress in the western and southern parts of the island and the Eighth Army was in possession of the whole of the southeast. But two British divisions were blocked on the Simeto River line near the coast.

General Montgomery ordered the Canadians to advance west and north from Vizzini in the sort of left hook he'd made famous. A Canadian flying column was sent rumbling through the country between the British and the Americans, to force the Germans to release their hold on the Simeto line.

Operating on a one-brigade front because of the scarcity of good roads, the 1st Division advanced from Vizzini. Now came the great time of learning, one that all units, all soldiers had to go through. Their stories and their experiences in the squalid mountain country of Sicily had much in common. In *The Regiment,* Farley Mowat's history of the Hastings and Prince Edward Regiment, he tells the story of one unit in what has been called the most spectacular Canadian achievement of the whole campaign:

. . . The division's thrust through the mountainous heart of Sicily approached its climax. It was nearly time for the division to swing east and drive toward the coast.

But before the turn could be made there was a formidable gate to be opened.

The enemy had established himself on the Leonforte-Assoro base where the mountains swelled abruptly out of the bed of the Dittaino River and lifted steeply toward Mount Etna to the east. Of the many almost impregnable positions available to the Germans, this was by far the strongest. Astride the two roads leading out of the valley, the Assoro mountain rose nearly 3000 feet from the dead river and thrust forward from the main mountain massifs like a titanic bastion. On the slope, the village of Assoro clung precariously; a few miles to the west, the town of Leonforte guarded the back door to the citadel. As long as this position was held by the enemy there could be no further advance of the Eighth Army's 30th Corps toward Messina; and the Germans had chosen the formidable 15th Panzer Grenadier Division to garrison this natural fortress.

By July 20 the Loyal Edmonton Regiment had reached the Dittaino and established a bridgehead across it. From the valley floor the men could look up to the sheer cliff of Assoro.

The German defenders were unperturbed by the appearance of the Canadians. It was obvious that any frontal attack must be suicidal and they believed Assoro could not be outflanked. Its only open side, on the east, was a cliff face rising 1000 feet to terminate in the ruins of an ancient Norman castle on the peak.

Brig. Howard Graham, entrusted with the 1st Brigade assault, knew as well as the

Germans that a frontal assault would be disastrous. But he found hope in the prospects of an attack from the right flank and rear. The hope was faint, but he called Lt. Col. B. A. Sutcliffe and asked if the Hastings could do the job. Sutcliffe agreed to try.

[Lt. Col. H. L. N. Salmon, who had whipped the Hastings into shape in Britain, had later risen to command the 1st Division. He was killed in April in the crash of a plane taking him to Cairo to discuss plans for Sicily.]

With his Regiment committed, Sutcliffe went across the Dittaino to the most advanced positions to estimate the chances of success. With him was the intelligence officer. The two men crawled through an olive grove and far along the exposed northern slope to get a clear view of the enemy position. Crouched beside a tiny foxhole, too small to hold them both, they were soon engrossed in their study of the great mountain thrusting high out of the dun-colored earth.

On the Assoro scarp the crew of an 88-mm. gun laid their weapon over open sights. And when the cloud of yellow dust rose clear of the foxhole, Sutcliffe was dead and the IO lay dying.

Prior to this moment all soldiers of the Regiment who had been killed had died in the confusion and tumult of action. Their loss had not been deeply perceived as yet,

Brig. Chris Vokes' 2nd Brigade got the job of driving the enemy off the heights of Leonforte (left) as the 1st Brigade assaulted Assoro. With the help of an artillery bombardment, the Edmonton Regiment crossed a ravine below the town—the Germans had destroyed the bridge—and entered Leonforte. The enemy counterattacked with tanks and with machine-gun fire from rooftops and a fierce battle raged in the streets through the night. With no wireless communication, Lt. Col. J. C. Jefferson wrote an appeal for help to "any British or Canadian officer" and entrusted it to an Italian boy. It reached Vokes, who'd thought the Edmontons had been destroyed. Under heavy fire, engineers bridged the ravine and in broad daylight a "flying column" was sent across: C company of the Princess Patricia's Canadian Light Infantry, four tanks of the Three Rivers Regiment and a troop of 90th Battery anti-tank guns. They raced up the long hill, captured enemy posts on the Leonforte outskirts and, in house-to-house fighting, battled through to the Edmontons. By afternoon the town was in Canadian hands; 2nd Brigade casualties were 56 killed, 105 wounded, 1 captured.

Below: the scene of later Canadian fighting—(1) Agira, taken July 28, (2) Regalbuto, August 2, (3) Mount Rivisotto, (4) Mount Seggio, (5) Salso River, (6) Simeto River, (7) Salso-Simeto junction, (8) Carcaci.

and hatred had not grown from their graves. This new stroke of death was something else.

The tragedy had a remarkable effect. It utterly destroyed the pale remainder of the illusion that war was only an exciting extension of training. The killing of the CO *before* the battle seemed an almost obscene act, and it roused in the men an ugly resentment. Hatred of the enemy was born.

With Sutcliffe's death, the command passed to the Regiment's adopted Canadian, Maj. Lord John Tweedsmuir, son of the late Governor-General. He took over when the Regiment was faced with the toughest battle problem so far encountered. He put into effect a plan so daring

that failure would have meant not only the end of his career, but probably the end of the Regiment as well.

It was his appreciation that only by a wide right-flanking sweep through the mountains, culminating in the scaling of the Assoro cliff, could the enemy's position be reduced. Therefore the Regiment would scale the cliff.

It was late afternoon and preparations had to be hurried. Maj. Alex Campbell was ordered to form a volunteer assault force, one platoon from each of the regular rifle companies. Stripped of all gear except essential arms and ammunition, these men were to lead the Regiment, scale the cliff and, before dawn, occupy the crest.

The march began at dusk, the most difficult forced march the Regiment ever attempted. The going was foul, through a

maze of sheer-sided gullies, knife-edged ridges and boulder-strewn water courses. There was constant expectation of discovery, for it seemed certain the enemy would have listening posts on his open flank. Silence was each man's hope of survival—but silence on that nightmare march was almost impossible to maintain.

One terrifying moment came when the scouts saw a masked machine-gun post. Incredibly it was deserted, but so recently that scraps of German bread on the ground were still fresh. Hours later there was a faint sound of stones being disturbed by many feet. Men sank into the shadows, tensed for an explosion. A Sicilian boy came sleepily out of the darkness driving his herd of goats. He stared unbelievingly at the armed men, then passed on as in a dream.

There was a desperate urgency in that march for there were long miles to go and, at the end, the cliff to scale before dawn could reveal the Regiment to the enemy above. A donkey, laden with a wireless set, was literally dragged by its escort until it collapsed and died. The men went on.

By 0400 hours the assault company had scaled the last preliminary ridge and was appalled to find that at the base of the mountain was a gully 100 feet deep. Men scrambled into the great natural ditch, crossed the bottom and paused to draw breath. First light was an hour away. The cliff rocks towered 1000 feet into the dark skies.

Each man who made that climb performed his own miracle. From ledge to ledge the dark figures made their way, hauling one another up, passing weapons and ammunition from hand to hand. A signaler made the climb with a heavy wireless set strapped to his back—a thing that in daylight was seen to be impossible—yet no man slipped, no man dropped so much as a clip of ammunition. Any sound would have been fatal.

Dawn was breaking. This was the moment. If the alarm was given, nothing could save the unit from annihilation.

The alarm was never given. The two men at the head of the leading platoon reached the crest, dragged themselves over a stone wall and stared into the eyes of three sleepy Germans manning an observation post. Pte. A. K. Long cut down one German who tried to flee. The other two stood motionless, staring as children might at an inexplicable apparition.

Ten minutes later, as the sun cleared the eastern hills, the Regiment had overrun the crest and was on the western slope overlooking the whole German front. Half a mile below, in the valley leading to the front, a convoy of a dozen German trucks carried rations forward to the waiting Panzer Grenadiers.

Twenty Bren gunners on Assoro's crest vied with one another to press the trigger first.

The appearance of the Canadians must have come as a shattering surprise to the enemy and had his troops been of lesser caliber, a debacle must have resulted. But the Germans here were of a fighting breed. Although at a serious disadvantage, they had no thought of giving up.

From ditches beside their ravaged trucks, German drivers returned the Regiment's machine-gun fire with rifle shots. The crews of four light anti-aircraft pieces, sited beside the road, fired point-blank at the Canadians on the crest. Machine-gun detachments scrambled up the road, flung themselves behind stone fences and engaged the Brens. Guns concentrating on 2nd Brigade in front of Leonforte slewed around to bear upon Assoro. An hour after dawn the crest of the hill was almost hidden in the dust of volleying explosions.

The Regiment dug in: A company and the assault company on the south and southwest slopes, the rest on the north and northwest side. Narrow terraces gave scant shelter but the men, using steel helmets, scraped slit trenches in the stony soil. The enemy fire grew heavier. The Regiment's died away as realization dawned that this would be a long battle and there would probably be no new supplies of ammunition until it ended.

Before the infantry companies moved off that morning it had been agreed that two green Very flares, fired by the assault group, would indicate that the enemy position had been overrun and it was safe for the transport to move. Sometime after midnight, while the infantry was struggling through the maze of hills and valleys far from the objective, a German in a position overlooking the Dittaino sent a routine signal to his own artillery: two green flares. The transport moved out.

Before dawn it had crossed the valley and the leading carriers were halted by a crater in the road. Things were still quiet. Some men got out of the vehicles and lay on the gentle slopes.

Forty-year-old Maj. Gen. Guy Simonds (left) commanded the 1st Division in its introduction to battle. Men like these mortar crews (below) quickly became veterans and adopted what Farley Mowat called a "special type of fatalism." It led one man to say, "When you dig a good slit trench nothing can get you except a direct hit, and if it *is* a direct hit, it's because you teased your grandmother or pulled the wings off flies." Another said, "There's no use trying to hide from a shell. If it's got your name on it, it'll chase you into the house, follow you upstairs, push the pot aside and get you under the bed." Said Mowat: "The humor was not uproarious but it was adequate."

In the gray dawn the Panzer Grenadiers defending the road must have found it hard to credit their eyes as the thin light revealed 30 Canadian trucks and carriers in a neat line almost under the muzzles of the German guns.

The Canadians were rudely awakened. Some, leaping up out of a pleasant sleep, yelled horrid threats at comrades they believed had gone mad and were firing on them. Others realized the situation and did what they could. While one 3-inch mortar was put into action, the drivers tried to turn their vehicles on the narrow road. Someone threw smoke grenades around the lead vehicles and under this thin protection the carriers managed to turn and clatter down the slope. One was driven by a motorcyclist who had lost his own mount. He missed a turn and his carrier somersaulted to the valley floor. The driver, uninjured, dragged himself to his feet and stood for several minutes, in full view of the enemy, kicking and cursing his steed as if it had been a horse that had thrown him.

At this juncture the balance of the Regiment on Assoro's crest carried the battle to the enemy's rear. In the ensuing confusion, and not without casualties—four trucks destroyed and four men badly wounded—the transport group retreated to the Dittaino and beyond.

By now the 500 infantrymen on Assoro were almost surrounded on the three-acre

crest of the mountain, and could neither withdraw nor advance. Patrols were sent scuttling through the curtain of small-arms and shellfire into the village. The place was cleared but its capture brought little relief. The Regiment's threat against the enemy supply route could not be fully implemented for already the scanty ammunition supplies, carried on men's backs up the cliff, were growing perilously low. The Regiment was exposed to an increasing fury of artillery shelling which was suddenly and terrifyingly bolstered by German rocket batteries. This was the unit's first experience with the Moaning Minnie mortar and there was not a man who was not shaken by the initiation. The shells were nine inches in diameter and were fired in salvos of five or six. The screaming of the rocket motors was an intolerable sound, as if the shells were being forced through interminable and slightly too small rusty cylinders. In addition there were single 12-inch rockets, each containing 150 pounds of high explosive, that screeched slowly overhead and burst with a tremendous blast. More than 400 rockets and artillery shells crashed into the crest of Assoro in the first two hours of that bombardment.

But if the Regiment could not attack, it was not content to remain passive under this punishment. The Germans had decided that the crest must be held by a very small number of Canadians and that, under cover of the shelling, it would be safe to withdraw the many vehicles which had been at the front. It was not safe. As the armored half-tracks and open trucks came scuttling up the road the Regiment caught them in withering small-arms fire and destroyed or forced the abandonment of almost a score. The Germans prepared to counterattack the hill in force.

The Regiment, unless it could somehow silence the enemy artillery, could not hold on. Then someone remembered a captured German observation post and its fine 20-power scissor telescopes. These were hurriedly moved to the north end of the hill where Tweedsmuir and his second-in-command could sweep almost the entire area from which the enemy guns were firing. The only radio—the short-range set that had been carried up the cliff on a man's back—saved the unit.

The Regiment gave the distant Canadian artillery a series of dream targets. As each German gun fired up at Assoro, its position was radioed to the rear and within minutes salvos of Canadian shells fell on it. Every movement of the German gunners could be seen. By noon well over half the enemy's artillery was out of action; the rest was withdrawing.

The heat grew worse and water was a problem. The one well on the crest was exposed to sniping fire. There was little food. Emergency rations had long since been consumed. In C company, Private Greatrix became a hero when he produced a can of sardines and gravely offered each man in his platoon one fish.

A small cave near the well had been converted into a medical station and here the wounded lay in silent rows. The padre, Capt. Reg Lane, a man of more than 45, was not equipped either by nature or by training for the hardships he had undergone. But he performed his own private miracle of endurance as he helped the stretcher-bearers care for the living, or helped the living bury the dead.

When the CO gave up hope of relief that day, he called for two volunteers to return to the Canadian lines and attempt to guide a party with rations and ammunition during the night. The regimental sergeant major and an officer climbed down the great cliff and across four miles of enemy-dominated country, finally reaching safety in a state of exhaustion. But when darkness fell they were able to guide 100 men of the Royal Canadian Regiment, laden with food and ammunition, through the gorges to the foot of the mountain. The next morning the garrison ate its first meal in 36 hours.

While the supply party was toiling over hills and gullies, the battle situation had reached its climax. The Germans were being fiercely attacked at Leonforte by the 2nd Brigade and could not stand firm there while the threat of Assoro lay on their supply routes. Assoro must be retaken or the whole position would have to be abandoned. So at 2200 hours the enemy counterattacked. Two companies of Grenadiers came through the north end of the town, under cover of an intense mortar and artillery barrage, and met D company on the lower slopes. D company had little ammunition but when the attack broke and fell away, it had given no ground and had taken a heavy toll of attackers. It was the Germans' last effort. As darkness fell, they began to withdraw both from Assoro and from Leonforte.

At the precious well a dozen soldiers relaxed, drinking to their hearts' content and splashing cold water over their faces. Somewhere far to the north, the crew of a German rocket launcher prepared to abandon their position. Someone, in a last defiant gesture, paused to send a last rocket screaming into the quiet sky.

The indecent shriek of the projectile drifted over the brown hills. The men by the well heard it but they had time only to stiffen warily before the rocket struck. It hit the curbing of the well. When the black and acrid smoke had cleared, four dead men lay in the new crater, five others moaned in mortal agony. They were Assoro's last casualties.

While it was no great victory in terms of casualties inflicted on the enemy, Assoro was nevertheless a spectacular triumph of endurance and initiative. The spirit of the men, subdued temporarily by their first baptism of heavy shellfire, now rose to unprecedented heights. Even the taste of fear was not too bitter in their mouths, for it possessed an astringent flavor which made the battle even more stimulating in retrospect. Men looked forward, almost eagerly, to the renewal of the war and to deeds that would surpass even the epic struggle just completed.

With the loss of the gates to the inner mountain stronghold, the Germans had withdrawn—but not nearly as far as had been confidently predicted. The Grenadiers elected to fight for each mile of ground between them and their last strong-

hold, below Mount Etna. It came as an almost unbelievable surprise when the Royal Canadian Regiment, moving forward with the Salso River—20 miles to the east—as its objective, was halted and flung back bloodily at the village of Nissoria, less than five miles down the road.

Hardly had the RCR withdrawn, having lost many supporting tanks and many men, when the Regiment was ordered to renew the assault—with no tank or artillery support and no prior reconnaissance for a battle that would be waged in darkness. The lessons of Assoro were ignored. The Regiment was committed to a head-on assault against an aroused enemy.

Nissoria itself was an abject huddle of stone hovels on the road where it crossed a high col into the eastern range. Behind the village two massive hills rose north and

241

south of the road, and on these the Germans waited.

Untouched by the disaster which had befallen the RCR and filled with a mood approaching blind confidence, the Hastings companies moved up to Nissoria the night of July 24. There was a faint crescent moon, but in the shadows of the col there was complete darkness.

The northern hill seemed the more imposing bastion so Tweedsmuir ordered an attack there. B company swung clear of the road and began to climb into ominous silence. Halfway up, the scouts dropped to their bellies and behind them the twisted line froze into immobility.

Thirty yards ahead, almost invisible, human figures moved uneasily and there were coughing and muttered words. B company's commander could not be sure whether these were enemies or RCR stragglers. He did not dare order his men to open fire. Instead he ordered two platoons to swing wide and surround the mysterious figures. The platoons moved off, crawling silently, and in a few moments could identify the dim outlines: enemy.

A surprise blow might have made the difference between success and defeat but, as the platoons crawled the last few feet into battle positions, two men of another company, lost from their platoon, blundered into the German positions. A star shell illuminated the attackers, caught without cover on the slopes. More than 15 enemy machine guns swept the exposed ground with yellow and red tracer. Mortars thumped into the gullies where the balance of the Regiment lay waiting. Three tanks, dug in to their turrets, sent shells screaming over the low crest.

B company had penetrated into the advance posts of the German position, but now it paid. All three platoons were pinned down, unable to advance or to retire, and under merciless fire.

One section found a German outpost under the nose of its Bren gun and with a burst of fire persuaded the Germans to surrender. The Panzer Grenadiers came out of their slit trenches—but with their weapons held in front of them—and at the last moment tried to rush the Canadians. They were slaughtered where they stood. It was a savage and terrifying battle, with Germans and Canadians inextricably mixed up in almost utter darkness.

As dawn broke over the great mound of Etna it laid bare an entire unit under the guns of the enemy.

One section was caught in the open. Cpl. Freddy Punchard ordered the men to break away while he gave them cover, and they crawled through the appalling machine-gun and mortar fire, most of them to reach safety in the end. The Germans moved in on Punchard and called on him to surrender, but there were still two wounded men of his section in danger. Punchard cried out: "Not bloody likely!" —and fired the last of his Bren magazines. Then he picked up a tommy gun and waited for attack. It came in a few moments. When the position was cleared several days later, Punchard's body was found with those of seven Grenadiers.

Many Italians (lower right) were captured but most Germans in Sicily withdrew rather than surrender. An official history says that when news of the evacuation of Enna reached General Simonds' headquarters, the 4th Princess Louise Dragoon Guards were ordered "to take the town before the Americans." A troop set out in four carriers but five miles from Enna was stopped by a crater in the road. "Four men went forward on foot. After more than a mile of uphill plodding under the blazing sun they commandeered a donkey and rode in turn. Near the top of the long zigzag climb they saw two truckloads of American troops entering the town. The donkey was abandoned in favor of a lift in a jeep and in this manner the Canadian patrol arrived in the main *piazza* of Enna simultaneously with the American vanguard."

Private Long, first man to the top of Assoro a few days earlier, was badly wounded by a mortar bomb but would not allow his comrades to lessen their slim chance of survival by trying to drag him back. He waved them off and when they saw him last he was sitting braced against an olive tree, sucking on an empty pipe and leafing through *Macbeth*.

Casualties were mounting and it was clear the Regiment must move or be destroyed. Tweedsmuir was severely wounded. The officer who succeeded him gave the order to retire. Each man turned his naked back on the enemy and ran his own race with death. Scrambling from rock to rock, rolling down open stretches, crawling down shallow ditches, they came back—all save a section of B company under Corporal Bulliard that could not retreat without inviting destruction. Bulliard's men, most stricken with dysentry, lay for another 18 hours in a shallow depression only ten yards from the enemy. Without water and unable to move or even whisper, they suffered the Sicilian sun all that day. Having miraculously escaped detection, they came back when night had fallen.

In that brief and impassioned battle the unit had lost 5 officers and 75 other ranks dead, wounded and missing—the heaviest losses suffered in a single day by any Canadian unit during the Sicilian campaign. There was not much to show for it. A few enemy positions knocked out, a handful of prisoners taken. Nissoria remained firmly with the enemy, and the Regiment withdrew to lick its wounds.

The effect of this first failure was incalculable. Those who survived carried the knowledge of a new and terrible experience—panic. One of the most dreadful things about panic is its contagious power, and the sight of what it can accomplish is enough to break the spirit of a man. A lance corporal withdrawing through Nissoria found its meaning. Seeking refuge from shells, he dodged into a house and discovered under the stairs a soldier weeping bitterly and piercingly into cupped hands. In that instant, the lance corporal's healthy fear of shelling turned into a more dreadful fear and he ran, heedless of bursting shells, as if the devils which pursued him were more frightful than death itself.

From Nissoria onward, the men of the Regiment had not only to live with fear of death and injury, but to learn to live with, and to conquer, fear of themselves—the fear of fear.

They were also learning to be skeptical of the infallibility of higher commanders. When, on the night of July 25, the men watched the 48th Highlanders march up to Nissoria to repeat, almost identically, their own experiences, that skepticism was strongly reinforced.

These doubts of the infallibility of the staff were not necessarily bad; they tended to isolate the infantryman and to make him turn inward in search of confidence and of something he could trust. The Regiment was the gainer. It became each man's home and sanctuary, and its spirit grew large—not with love, for there is little love in war,

but with the need for faith and a belief. There was no other sufficient source for these things. Even a faith in God could not suffice for the majority of men. The soldier could be understood by, and could understand, only the men who stood beside him.

After a full-scale attack by the 2nd Brigade with massive artillery support finally cleared the Nissoria position, the division thrust eastward to bitter fighting at Agira and at last to Regalbuto, the Germans' final holding to the west of the Salso River. On July 30 and 31, a British brigade fought hard to gain this town, but was unsuccessful. On August 1, 1st Brigade moved up to the attack and the RCR clawed a foothold into the western outskirts of Regalbuto.

Conditions here were not unlike those at Nissoria: the real strength of Regalbuto lay in a commanding ridge beyond the town and in two flanking hills to the south. Here the enemy, this time units of Hermann Göring Division, sat firmly in position and no amount of frontal battle could dislodge him.

When the RCR could make no further progress, the 48th Highlanders attempted to swing in from the north, but without success, and toward evening the RCR had to be withdrawn from the town.

This was the situation when the Hastings moved forward to join the battle, but someone had learned a lesson from Nissoria. When the Regiment was ordered to attack during the night of August 1, it was given a free hand to do the job its own way. The Regiment, too, had learned a lesson

and the new CO, Maj. A. A. Kennedy, was a man to profit by experience.

Regalbuto was to be no buccaneering rush into the unknown—the sort of thing that had brought renown at Assoro and disaster at Nissoria. As far as the CO could make it, this was to be a carefully calculated action. Kennedy first sent long-distance patrols far to the east with orders to penetrate deeply into the enemy's flank and report his dispositions and the best routes of approach. The CO himself, with his company commanders, then carried out a reconnaissance and laid the battle plans with care and caution. The operation was to be a wide right flank attack, but not a blind one. Nor would it be unsupported.

trolled, fear can be a weapon of great strength and the unit had this weapon.

So the night hours passed and the companies followed the tortuous routes of the patrols until at last the heights of Mount Tiglio, the southern bastion of the enemy position, bulked large against the star-lit sky.

A and B companies were on the crest within a quarter of an hour. They reported no enemy, but found machine guns sited beside newly dug weapon pits. The Germans had anticipated a flank attack. There was no explanation for their absence now, except that they had perhaps grown careless when in the first three days of battle no southern assault had developed. It seemed

The artillery observation officers were ordered to travel with the CO, and the mortar platoon was ordered to come along on foot and manhandle its heavy weapons and ammunition over the five miles of the approach march.

It was dusk when the companies moved off. The country was at least as difficult as any traversed in the earlier days, but there was this difference—the patrols had done their task well and the long lines of marching men moved smoothly through the broken cliffs and canyons, with guides leading them and with scouts well in front.

The atmosphere was different, too. There was no exhilaration in the men's hearts. They now knew the consequences which could follow error. There was a new kind of tension that keyed each man to an almost mechanical pitch of efficiency. Con-

likely that this outpost was only manned at certain hours.

This much was luck. Now the Regiment faced the south slope of the main ridge behind Regalbuto, but dawn had broken and any premature attack might have been disastrous. Kennedy chose to wait until each company commander could assess the ground carefully and until the three-inch mortars, manhandled across country by herculean effort, were in position to support the assault. The artillery observers swept the ridge with their binoculars and picked targets for their guns, radioing the information back.

At noon D company swept forward into the broad valley to divert and focus the enemy's defense away from the main assault. The Germans reacted quickly, pouring fire down on the widely dispersed

attackers from at least ten positions. D company, its allotted role almost completed, went to ground and continued to hold the Germans' attention.

Now the battle plan bore fruit. The enemy had exposed his strongpoints, and artillery and three-inch mortars rapidly neutralized them. Under cover of the barrage, B and C companies quickly crossed the valley almost unopposed. Before the Germans on the crest could swing to meet the new threat, both companies were in among them. B company cleared the high ground overlooking Regalbuto within half an hour; C company swung east and stormed the length of the ridge. Many machine-gun posts were overrun and the remaining Germans fled.

The battle was over. Regalbuto itself was later occupied without opposition by

General Montgomery (addressing Canadians) ordered his army to dress comfortably, within reason. "On the whole," Sicily veteran Ben Malkin wrote in the Ottawa *Citizen,* "the men did not go to extremes. But one day, as he was being driven along a hot road through a Sicilian valley, Montgomery passed a truck in which stood a soldier clad only in a top hat. The soldier, obviously trying to observe military courtesy, saluted by raising his top hat smartly. Considering the dress, the gesture was suitable. But the dress itself? Montgomery thought not. He banned top hats."

the 48th Highlanders and the enemy's last stand west of the Salso was at an end. The action had gone so smoothly as to appear unremarkable. Its very excellence tended to obscure its real merits. It was probably the most important action, if the most colorless, the Regiment fought in Sicily. It differed from all previous battles in that it was fought by men with full understanding of war and with consequent skill. The capture of Regalbuto was a fitting conclusion to an arduous apprenticeship. In 20 days the unit had been blooded and hardened into a superlative machine for battle. . . .

FARLEY MOWAT

Next for the division came a march east through mountainous and almost roadless country to Adrano. By August 6 the Royal 22nd Regiment had secured a bridgehead across the Simeto River and was pushing rapidly toward Adrano—hoping to beat the British 78th Division into the town.

The Canadians were ordered to leave Adrano free for the passage of the 78th. It was a disappointment; but one patrol of the Royal 22nd did not receive the order and penetrated into the outskirts, where it found no enemy. The Canadians had another consolation: the threat to the enemy's right which they had done so much to develop had driven the enemy out of his main line of resistance; the whole front was on the move.

In four weeks the 1st Division had marched 120 miles through mountainous country, in extreme heat and in contact for most of the way with a stubborn foe. They had marched farther than any other division in the Eighth Army, and during the past fortnight had done a large share of the fighting. They had earned a rest.

On August 17, American troops entered Messina and made contact with a British armored brigade coming from the south. Sicily had been conquered in 38 days. It had taken a Canadian toll of 172 officers and 2138 other ranks. Of these, 40 officers and 522 other ranks were killed. The Canadian share in the campaign was small, only an infantry division and a tank brigade. But the Canadians performed a role more important and more difficult than the one planned for them. In the end, no division in the Allied force made a larger contribution. They were fighting their first campaign. They had much to learn, and some was learned the hard way. "But," says the official Canadian history of the

campaign, "it was to the credit of those who had trained them that they were able to perform a difficult and exacting task in a manner honorable to themselves and to their country."

They had also won the respect of the enemy, these Canadians whose 1st Division battle patch was a bright red rectangle on the upper arm of their uniform. "Red patch devils," the Germans called them.

Ross Munro reported that a prisoner taken at Nissoria said: "We see the Red Devils coming and we fire our mortars hard. But the Red Patches just keep running through the fire. I can't understand it. Other troops we fought lay down and took shelter when the mortars fired right on top of them. The Red Patches are devils. They keep on coming."

The commander of the 15th Panzer Grenadier Division, in words perhaps prompted by the Hastings' assault on Assoro, wrote that in fieldcraft *(Indianerkrieg)* the enemy was "superior to our own troops, very mobile at night, surprise break-ins, clever infiltrations with small groups between our strongpoints."

Plaudits came too from high in the Eighth Army. Lt. Gen. Sir Oliver Leese of 30th Corps congratulated General Simonds and his 1st Division for "magnificent fighting." General Montgomery called them magnificent, too, and then added the most deeply appreciated commendation of all: "I regard you now as one of the veteran divisions of the Eighth Army, just as good as any, if not better."

The division and, to a lesser extent, the tank brigade had participated in the prelude to the invasion of mainland Europe and indirectly in a major political development as well. Even as the campaign raged, Mussolini fell from power in Rome; Italy teetered on the brink of elimination from the war. In the squalid streets of Sicily, the Canadians saw the joy of an Italian people who felt little or no loyalty to the Axis cause.

But the fact remained that the trap at Messina had closed too late. Tens of thousands of German troops had escaped to mainland Italy. Under the original plan they would have been no further concern of the Canadians. But the original plan was changed. Canada's new role in the Mediterranean was destined to be not only maintained but enlarged. General McNaughton's dream had died. The army was split in two.

Scoop

It was the worst night of the blitz, Germany's bombing offensive against London through the winter of 1940-41. Newcomer Foster Barclay had been in town only a few hours that December 29, 1940, and he could hardly believe what he saw. On Fleet Street, the Canadian Press office where he had come to work was bombed out by a direct hit. Up Ludgate Hill, St. Paul's Cathedral stood with magnificent defiance amid walls of fire nurtured by tens of thousands of incendiary bombs. Beyond it, The City, the financial heart of the British world, lay in ruins.

Barclay made his way through the streets with other Canadian Press war correspondents. He finally couldn't resist asking a simple question: "Is it always like this?"

It wasn't, but Canada's war correspondents did have numerous comparable moments before the war was over.

They were a varied and colorful crew: the brilliant L. S. B. Shapiro, later a best-selling novelist, who would arise from his typewriter and proclaim, "I have just written a magnificent story"; the trenchant, red-headed Ralph Allen who agonized over every word he wrote—and wrote so well they all liked to read him; the beloved raconteur, Greg Clark; the buoyant Charles Lynch; the dramatic Matthew Halton whose throbbing CBC broadcasts brought the war into thousands of Canadian living rooms. There were dozens of them and, in their army uniforms, they followed Canada's soldiers everywhere they went.

The best-known and most respected of them all was a lean, gangling, quiet, serious reporter named Ross Munro. Wes Gallagher, an American war correspondent who later became general manager of The Associated Press, said: "Munro was not only the top Canadian correspondent but one of the best five or six correspondents of the war. He combined great personal courage with extremely lucid writing and reporting."

Like Barclay, Munro worked for The Canadian Press, the national news agency. He was 28 years of age when he went on the 1942 Dieppe raid and watched the Royal Regiment of Canada cut to pieces.

Munro was known to Canadians long before that. For years he'd covered army training and his by-line had appeared on CP stories from coast to coast. But his Dieppe story, one of the great combat reports of the war, was used around the world and made his name a household word across Canada.

He followed that with a spectacular scoop on the Allied landings in Sicily in July 1943. Elaborate communications arrangements had been made for the main force of American and British correspondents covering the invasion. But Munro and the CBC's Peter Stursberg were almost completely on their own with Canada's 1st Division. No restrictions on communications were laid down for them. No formal censorship was ordered. Their job was to cover the landing of the Canadians.

Munro went ashore in a small naval craft which led one of the assault battalions to the beach at Pachino. Just before dawn the boat stranded on a sandbar several hundred yards out. With shells from Italian shore batteries plummeting in the water, Munro swam ashore, pulling his waterproofed typewriter with him.

He trudged inland with the infantry, watched the first sporadic gun fights with the Italians, the capture of Pachino and an airfield. Late in the afternoon, through searing heat and dust, he trudged back to the beach to write his story. Through the evening, he wrote in a slit trench while Italian snipers peppered the area with rifle fire. When his story was done, Munro sent it to the Canadian headquarters ship lying off-shore. This ship was equipped with strong wireless and Munro had already arranged with the signal corps to transmit his copy to Algiers for relay to London. An intelligence officer on the headquarters ship was to check it for security.

The plan operated even better than intended. The intelligence officer checked the story and a signalman sent it off. It was picked up in Malta by an RAF wireless station and relayed immediately to London—on a priority basis. The story was simply addressed "Canapress London." The Air Ministry received it and called CP's London office. CP cabled it to Canada.

The story was a major sensation, the first word of the Canadian landing, and because no other forces were mentioned in the first cable it seemed for a while that the Canadians were winning Sicily all by themselves.

Allied headquarters in Algiers were furious. For a time there was talk of disciplining Munro until tempers cooled as more stories came in through orthodox channels. But it was a clean scoop for Munro. He beat all other correspondents by seven hours.

On June 6, 1944, Munro was attached to combat forces of the 3rd Canadian Division for the Normandy invasion. Once again he got ashore, moved inland to witness the fighting and then went back to write his story. He arranged with a Royal Navy officer to take it back on a destroyer going to Portsmouth. It was the first story to appear anywhere from the invasion beaches.

Munro covered the Canadians till the end of the war, going wherever they went, operating from an armored scout car somehow written off as a battle loss and given to him by one of his innumerable army friends.

Ross Munro, back in London, writes his great story of the Dieppe raid. He never got hardened to what he saw. "Perhaps I was too sensitive," he said after the war, "but there was tragedy in every body, in every wounded soldier."

Johnnie's wing

**The RAF's greatest ace tells of flying with Canadians
who made him one of them**

When J. E. "Johnnie" Johnson was posted to a Canadian wing in March 1943, he had his doubts. He was happy to be promoted to wing commander and to be shifting to Fighter Command's crack 11 Group in southeast England. He was happy that he'd be flying the new Spitfire IX; the 12 Group squadron he had just left had Spitfire Vs and they'd more than met their match. The Germans' new Focke-Wulf 190A had destroyed five of them in five recent days.

Johnson was 27, a frank, slender Englishman, a civil engineer by profession.

He'd flown wingman to the famous legless ace, Douglas Bader. He'd made many sorties over western Europe. He was destined to become Britain's greatest ace with 38 kills to his credit. But in March 1943, he had only eight kills, he wasn't sure about the Canadians and he suspected—correctly—that they would be just as unsure about him.

The flow of aircrew graduates from the training fields in Canada had become a flood. Thousands of them were in Britain now and Canadianization—Canadian con-

trol of Canadian men—was an issue. The RCAF had recently created its largest formation, No. 6 Bomber Group, in Yorkshire. There were those who thought there should also be an RCAF fighter group now that hundreds of Canadians had proved themselves in fighter combat.

They had fought over Malta, over Africa, in the Far East. But mostly they had fought out of the Britain which had long since passed from being an island under siege to being one big airdrome for attack. Names had emerged to take on some of the

luster of the great Canadian pilots of World War I. Names like Beurling and McLeod and McNair and Keefer, Chadburn and Houle and Hill and Ford.

They had learned the tactical lessons of offensive operations: rhubarbs (fighter attacks against enemy movements by rail and road, against munitions factories and airfields) and circuses or beehives (heavy fighter and bomber strikes at ground targets with the twofold aim of destruction and drawing the Luftwaffe into the air to fight).

But despite the large numbers of skilled pilots available, Canadianization remained only a partially-accomplished objective of Canadian government policy. Many Canadian pilots served in RCAF squadrons; many others served in RAF squadrons of mixed nationalities. The wing Johnson was taking over was an all-Canadian formation of two 12-plane squadrons. It was the RCAF's first fighter wing and it had been excellently led by Wing Comdr. Keith Hodson, also a Canadian. Now that his tour was finished, it seemed to Johnson the pilots might not be too happy about an Englishman taking over.

In his book *Wing Leader,* Johnson recounts his feelings about his new assignment:

. . . I had plenty to think about as I drove to Kenley, just south of London, to join them. A few Canadian pilots had served in my 610 Squadron, but somehow in a fighter squadron of half a dozen different nationalities it had seemed comparatively easy to mold the mixture to a common purpose. It was generally agreed among squadron commanders and wing leaders that a mixed unit was happier and more efficient than one comprised of pilots of a single nationality. The Canadians had a reputation for toughness and they required a firm hand on the reins. I thought of Douglas Bader and how he had often sworn by the Canadians he'd commanded in the Battle of Britain.

In 1943 Wing Comdr. J. E. "Johnnie" Johnson (opposite) led a formation of two all-Canadian squadrons like the one below. Each squadron had 12 Spitfires.

I wondered how the Spitfire IX would do against the 190. The engine of the IX was bigger and more powerful than that of the V, but it was mounted in the same airframe and its great tactical advantage was that, apart from its longer nose and more numerous exhaust stacks, it looked exactly like the inferior V. From the usual combat range it was impossible for the Luftwaffe pilots to distinguish between the two types. This suited me, for I had a score or two to settle.

I thought of my duties as wing leader. Fighter leadership consists not in personal victories but in success with the whole wing. My job would be to lead and to fight. To bring the greatest number of guns to bear against the enemy in the shortest possible time. To cut losses to a minimum and avoid the bad bounce. To control the engagement, to keep the wing together as a fighting force, not split up into isolated, ineffective packets—by far the most difficult task. These goals could only be achieved through a high standard of flying, perfect discipline and strict radio drill.

When I arrived at Kenley, I drove to the mess and parked my small Morris outside, much to the amusement of a party of husky Canadian pilots who were obviously comparing its size to the glittering monsters they used at home.

A smart, broad-shouldered squadron leader walked out of the mess and gave me a snappy salute. "Wing Commander Johnson?"

"That's right," I replied.

"I'm Bud Malloy. I'll take you round and introduce you to your wild Canadians."

It was a day of low cloud and drizzle, so Malloy and I made a leisurely tour of the airfield and met the two squadron commanders and upward of 70 pilots. The lean, slightly-balding Sqdn. Ldr. Syd Ford of 403 Squadron came from Nova Scotia, already held the DFC and Bar and had established his reputation as a sound lead-

Bud Malloy (above left, after promotion to wing commander) and George Keefer, two of Johnnie Johnson's Canadians. Opposite: the fiery death of a fighter plane.

er and aggressive pilot. Foss Bolton, leader of 416 Squadron, hailed from Alberta and was an open-faced, friendly character who was a relative newcomer, having spent the greater part of his flying career in Canada.

I was surprised to learn that they still flew in the old-fashioned line-astern formation. We had a long talk about this. I pointed out the benefits of the abreast, finger-four style: a more aggressive, offensive formation and so on. Syd Ford, who had flown the Spitfire IX quite a lot, favored the line astern despite my arguments. Bolton seemed to waver between the two formations.

I felt it was time for a decision: "For the first few wing shows I'll lead Foss's squadron in finger fours. You, Syd, will hold your position down sun, 3000 feet higher, and you can fly in whatever formation you like providing you do your job. We'll see how it goes the first few times and then decide one way or the other for the whole wing."

Next day I met the tall, good-looking Keith Hodson, and he told me of the wing's recent activities. "This weather of yours has been against us," he said, "and the boys are a bit restless. What they want is a few good scraps with the 190s. If you can pull that off during your first few shows they'll be right with you."

"What you mean is that I'm on approval."

"I guess that's about the size of it," grinned Hodson.

The wing had been flying the Spitfire IX for several months. I took one up for the first time to get the feel of her. She was new and very fast, the engine was sweet and she responded to the controls as only a thoroughbred can. I decided she should be mine, and I never regretted the choice. I was soon convinced that the IX was superior to both the Focke-Wulf 190 and the latest Messerschmitt, the 109G.

My Canadians, I quickly discovered, flew extremely well and their air discipline was excellent, better, I thought, than the average mixed squadron. But we needed a full-blooded scrap to weld the wing together.

Our opportunity arrived on a Saturday afternoon in early April. We were having lunch when the wing was told to come to readiness in one hour. I walked over to the Ops block to study the details. It was only a small show but far better than idling away the afternoon on the ground. A squadron of Typhoon fighter-bombers was to cross the Channel at low level, dive-bomb the Abbeville airfield and withdraw at a high rate of knots. Our job was to climb over France as the Typhoons came out and knock down any German fighters flushed by the bombing.

The weather was perfect and we were to operate under the control of a new radar station in Kent which was rapidly acquiring a reputation for excellent long-distance controlling. I telephoned Squadron Leader Hunter, its senior controller, outlined my tactics and agreed that he would not break radio silence unless he had an enemy plot on his scopes.

Crossing the French coast just south of Le Touquet, I caught a glimpse of the Typhoons well below and heading back

toward England. We climbed to 24,000 feet and leveled out. Bolton's squadron drew abreast of me in the finger-four formation. Ford's squadron were just beginning to make condensation trails and these could be seen from a great distance and would betray our position. But before I could call him, he dropped his squadron a few hundred feet and the 12 conspicuous thin white banners ceased.

Hunter broke the silence: "Graycap from Grass-seed. Twenty-plus bandits climbing up inland. Steer one-four-zero."

"Okay, Grass-seed," I acknowledged. "Any height on the bandits?"

"Well below you, Graycap. They are approaching the coast and I'll try and

bring you out of the sun. Continue on one-four-zero."

The intricate mechanics of long-range radar interception seemed to be working perfectly. Suddenly I was brimming with confidence.

"Graycap. Bandits have crossed below you at 15,000 feet. Port onto three-one-zero. Buster."

"Okay, Grass-seed."

"Graycap. Bandits now seven miles ahead. Five thousand feet below."

I put the Spitfires into a shallow dive and scanned ahead. The sky seemed empty.

"Graycap. Another strong formation of bandits behind you. Exercise caution."

Here were the makings of a perfect shambles! The Canadians clustered around me waiting for an order. Then I saw one bunch of 12 FW 190s just below us and a

mile ahead, another 10 well out on the starboard side. It was too golden an opportunity to miss. Height, sun and surprise were in our favor. I had to take a chance on how far behind the other enemy formation was.

"Graycap to wing. Twenty-plus Huns below from twelve to three o'clock. Syd, I'm taking the left-hand bunch. Come down and take the right-hand gaggle. Get in!"

I turned slightly to get directly behind the 190s, remembering to make the turn slow and easy so that our wingmen could keep well up. I put the nose down and had to fight back an instinct to slam the throttle wide open. We had to strike together.

Nova Scotian Syd Ford (above right)— "a sound leader and aggressive pilot," Johnson called him—commanded 403 Squadron, one half of "Johnnie's Wing." With him is Flt. Lt. P. T. O'Leary. It was Ford who presented the "Canada" shoulder flashes with which Johnson was "converted." Right: trailing smoke and flame, a Messerschmitt 110 plunges toward earth, seconds after taking a direct hit from an Allied fighter.

My own 190 was flying on the extreme port side of the enemy formation. We came down on their tails in a long, slanting dive. Before I opened fire I looked to the starboard. Bolton's boys were fanning out alongside and Ford's arrowhead of Spitfires were falling down on their prey about three miles away. The attack was coordinated and my task of leading the wing was temporarily suspended. Now it was up to the individual pilots to select their opponents and smack them down.

I missed the 190 with my first short burst and steadied the gun platform with coarse stick and rudder. I fired again and hit him on the wing root and just behind the cockpit. The cannon shells thudded

over Kenley. Sixteen down, four on the circuit—20. A singleton—21. A long pause and a pair—23. One to come. It seemed very important that he should swing in over Caterham and land. But we had waited too long: he was either missing or at some other airfield.

The pilots walked into the briefing room excited and full of the fight. They'd flown extremely well. We totted up the score with the Spies [Intelligence] listening silently and ever ready to reduce a claim from a destroyed to a damaged or, if they had the chance, to nothing at all. The total came to six 190s destroyed for the loss of one.

Next morning Syd Ford walked into my

and fighters could not stop them. Here and there a bomber fell burning to the ground below, but the rest pressed on, determined, irresistible, blazing a new daylight trail over Europe and somehow symbolic of the country whose star they bore.

Ford's squadron guarded the last box of bombers and I led Bolton's squadron to the third box. I heard Ford say: "190s attacking the Forts. Let's go!"

There was little point in joining him; he was ten miles away and the fight would be over when we arrived. Ford sent a 190 down in flames; Flt. Lt. Charles Magwood of Toronto, one of his flight commanders, accounted for two and saw a sergeant pilot shoot down a fourth, but the sergeant was

into him in a deadly concentration of winking explosions. He started to burn, but before he fell onto his back I gave him another long burst. Then I broke away in a steep climbing turn and searched the sky behind. Still nothing there. Below me another 190 was falling in flames, and on the starboard a parachute had opened into full bloom.

Hunter was still concerned for our safety: "Graycap. Withdraw. Strong force of bandits approaching. Almost on top of you."

I spoke to the wing: "All Graycap aircraft. Get out now. We won't re-form. Keep a sharp lookout behind!"

We poured across the Channel at high speed in pairs and fours. My section was the first to land. I lit a cigarette and counted the Spits as they joined the circuit

office. He laid a pair of blue "Canada" shoulder flashes on my desk and said: "The boys would like you to wear these. After all, we're a Canadian wing and we've got to convert you. Better start this way."

"Thanks, Syd," I replied. "I'll get them sewn on today."

A simple gesture, but for me it had a deep significance. The flashes were sewn on and two years were to elapse before it was time to take them off.

Ford did well that afternoon when we flew to Paris to escort four boxes of American Fortresses, each with 18 bombers, from the target area. We saw the glinting bombers from a great distance for the bright sun reflected from a hundred places on each silver aircraft. They made a most impressive sight, pounding their stately way through the skies in battle array. Flak

bounced himself by a couple of enemy fighters before Magwood could warn him. A fifth 190 was shot down but, in addition to the sergeant, an American was missing.

This action brought our weekend score to 11 Focke-Wulfs destroyed for the loss of three of our pilots. It was a good start. It was also typical: we were often involved with the Americans in their controversial daylight bomber offensive. The RAF had tried daylight bombing, found it disastrous and turned to night operations. Now, three years later, the Americans set out to prove that strong formations of escorted bombers could fight their way through to distant targets.

We often escorted large numbers of Forts and Liberators to targets whose selection was restricted only by the Spitfires' radius of action of less than 200 miles. We liked to fly with them for the Germans could see the writing on the wall and reacted with great determination. In one hot fight over the target area, Foss Bolton was shot down; his place was taken by the burly, assertive Buck McNair who'd scored ten kills over Malta. In another fight, our Spits passed through successive boxes of Forts to get at the 190s. When the Yanks kept firing at one and all, I waggled my wings to show them the unmistakable silhouette of the Spitfire. It only brought several well-directed bursts of machine-gun fire. I lost no time in ordering our withdrawal and I later confirmed my suspicions: the Yanks wanted their fighter escorts well out of the range of their own guns.

Meanwhile they were developing their own force of long-range fighters. Soon the twin-engined Lightnings and the sturdy Thunderbolts escorted the bombers far beyond our range. In time the single-engined Mustang made its appearance—

combining two wings to meet the Germans on equal terms but found it difficult to hold 60 planes together as a balanced fighting force. So we left it to the planners of 11 Group to see that we achieved a suitable concentration of fighters in any particular area.

There was, in addition, the flak. There was never any warning of this anti-aircraft fire. One moment you were in a serene sky and the next the flak was reaching for and bracketing your Spitfire. We always had a healthy respect for this accurate, deadly stuff.

In short, we flew hard during those summer months of 1943. The wing score mounted to a pleasing total and inscribed silver tankards were presented to the pilots who shot down the 98th, 99th and 100th Huns since the formation of the Canadian wing.

We were turning the tables on the 190s and having many experiences together in doing so. One day George Keefer had to

and it could fly as far as the bombers!

How we longed for a wing of Spitfires which could fly to Berlin and back to take part in the great aerial Battle of Germany. Fighter pilots of every nationality agreed that the Spitfire IX was the best close-in fighter of them all. But we had to confine ourselves to short-range operations while the Americans fought this distant daylight battle single-handed.

Yet there still remained plenty of Focke-Wulfs and Messerschmitts to oppose our short-range penetrations into Holland, Belgium and northern France. The men who were considered to be the elite of the German fighter pilots operated out of the Pas de Calais. We often saw formations of upward of 50 Huns. In these engagements our 24 Spitfires fought at a serious tactical disadvantage. We tried

bail out five miles off the French coast and his inseparable companion, Walter Conrad, was like a man demented until every available Spitfire was over the Channel searching for him. They had fought together in the Desert Air Force in Africa for a long time, had shared the same tent, been awarded the DFC at the same time and come to us together. George was eventually found and picked up; he was back on the job within a few hours.

Next day it was tough Buck McNair who had to be rescued from the drink. Fortresses had bombed a target in the Ruhr and we flew to Manston, an airfield near Ramsgate on the eastern tip of the Kent coast, so we'd have sufficient fuel to rendezvous with them over Rotterdam. We saw them as they flew back over Arnhem and crossed the Dutch coast without incident. They

were accompanied by a strong force of fighters, so we broke away to come home via Flushing, Ostend and Calais.

We hadn't gone far when Buck's engine began to run very rough and he radioed that he was heading straight for Manston with his wingman, Tommy Parks. This was standard procedure; we never flew over the sea alone in our single-engined Spitfires if we could avoid it.

They had only left us a short time when Parks called out: "Graycap. Red Leader's Spit has caught fire. He's bailed out. Over."

"Can you see him, Red Two?" I asked.

"Yes, sir. He's in the sea but not in his dinghy. About ten miles from the French coast. What shall I do?"

I tried to work out the best tactic before I answered. Buck was only a few miles offshore and the strong wind would drift

him nearer the enemy coast. The sea was choppy with lots of white crests, and the fact he wasn't in his dinghy sounded ominous. Parks would have a difficult task keeping sight of his bobbing head. It would be a tricky rescue.

I thought of the bitter fights we'd had with the Germans over pilots "in the drink." They usually began when a small section of circling fighters were attacked by an enemy patrol, and in this respect we were as guilty as the Luftwaffe. If you came across half a dozen Messerschmitts flying above the sea, how were you to know whether they were orbiting a dinghy or escorting one of their rescue launches? You looked for Huns in the sky and when you saw them, you went in. Both sides would reinforce the area with fighters, and a small rescue operation would often de-

"A most impressive sight," Johnson wrote of U.S. Flying Fortresses (above), "pounding their stately way through the skies in battle array." Spitfires (left) of Johnson's wing often accompanied Forts and Liberators. Right: a German anti-aircraft gun crew on watch for Allied planes.

velop into a battle. Rescue floatplanes from both sides had been shot down, launches attacked and pilots lost. Today this must be avoided at all costs.

"Red Two from Graycap. Stay over him as low as you can. Low revs and just enough power to stay in the air. Transmit for Mayday on C for Charlie and we'll get back as soon as we can. Okay?"

"Okay, Graycap."

We slanted for Manston in a long, fast dive. I called the controller at Kenley: "Graycap to Wytex. Red Leader is in the drink. I've left Red Two over him. What's the form?"

"Wytex to Graycap. Group has pushed out a section of Spits to relieve Red Two. We've got an excellent fix and the Walrus [amphibious rescue plane] is about to take off from Hawkinge."

The rescue machinery seemed to be working perfectly, but it all depended on the relief section of Spitfires finding Parks over a large expanse of sea. If he had to leave McNair alone, the chances were he wouldn't be found again.

We landed at Manston and I was soon refueled and in the air with a small section of Spitfires. "Wytex—Graycap again. What's the form now?"

"Red Two has been relieved. One section of Spits is over Red Leader. The Walrus will be there in about 40 minutes."

"Thank you," I replied. "I've got three Spits with me and we'll keep an eye on things. Any Huns about?"

"All quiet and nothing plotted. Keep your fingers crossed!"

We found the two circling Spitfires and I flew very low to have a close look at McNair. The Mae West was holding him upright in the water but he had drifted nearer the French coast. The sand dunes looked very close. Once again I zoomed down, but he made no gesture.

After half an hour or so we saw the Walrus and fretted for another ten minutes until it joined us. I called the pilot and recognized the voice of Squadron Leader Grace, CO of the Hawkinge rescue flight. Grace and his crews knew their business; they'd carried out many brilliant pickups from under the very noses of the Germans. Now he had to make a difficult landing on a rough sea, to say nothing of a dozen Messerschmitts that might suddenly wade into us. Grace carried out a wide, slow circuit to study Buck's position and then glided down. I thought he was landing, but

the pilot dropped a smoke marker and the Walrus turned for another circuit. I couldn't watch this lengthy, delicate business any longer and pulled my section away to patrol between the Walrus and the shore.

At long last the Walrus landed safely and taxied up to McNair. He was hauled on board and the plane swung into the eye of the wind to take off. It gathered speed and then bounced from crest to crest, the sea cascading from the hull. It reminded me of an old swan beating its wings along a stretch of river to get up the right speed for takeoff. Once it was in the air, I called Grace: "Graycap to Walrus. How's our pilot?"

"Not too bad. He's burned a bit and swearing a lot!"

We flew with the Walrus all the way back to Hawkinge, and I was there when McNair was transferred to an ambulance. His face looked pretty grim, but he was cheerful and recognized me.

"Don't let me lose the squadron, Chief," he said. "This is nothing, I'll be back in a day or two. Promise I won't lose the squadron."

"All right, Buck," I assured him. "Don't worry. We'll keep the job open for you."

McNair did return within a few days and was soon flying again. But unknown to the doctors who had treated him, the searing flames had damaged one of his eyes as he fought to get out of his blazing Spitfire. McNair didn't tell us, instead he fought on at the head of his squadron. [He eventually commanded a wing of his own but by April 1944 he had to be grounded because of the effects of his burns. By then he had destroyed 16 aircraft.]

It was now high summer and the headquarters of the 2nd Tactical Air Force had been formed: its subordinate groups and wings would support the Anglo-Canadian 21st Army Group in the invasion of Europe. Its 83 Group began to absorb some of our 11 Group wings, and in early

August my wing was transferred there and renumbered 127.

We left Kenley for Lashenden, a new landing strip in Kent. We lived under canvas; our food was prepared in field kitchens, our workshops and equipment were housed in special trucks so we could move on short notice.

One day in August we took off to escort a large force of Fortresses assigned to attack the Messerschmitt factory complex at Regensburg and the important ball-bearing industry at Schweinfurt. The Regensburg force would go on to land in North Africa, the Schweinfurt force would return to England. Eighteen squadrons of Thunderbolt fighters and 16 squadrons of Spitfires were sent to provide cover on part of the penetration and withdrawal.

We left the Regensburg force a few miles east of Antwerp, our limit. We hadn't seen an enemy aircraft. We flew across Holland and the North Sea, refueled at Bradwell Bay, and took to the air again to rendezvous with the raiders returning from Schweinfurt.

This was the most disastrous operation of the Fortresses yet. They were subjected to continuous attacks by squadron after squadron of Focke-Wulfs, and by both Messerschmitt 109s and the twin-engined 110s. Sixty Fortresses, almost one fifth of the total, were shot down. When we met them we saw gaping holes in their formations and a few stragglers lagging well behind, struggling home on three engines.

Individual enemy fighters were still attacking and, since the Forts sprawled over a great area of sky, I split my wing into sections of four Spitfires to look after the stragglers. Below us a Messerschmitt 110 fired rockets into the belly of a badly shot-up bomber. I half-rolled my little section of Spitfires, aileron-turned onto the tail of the 110 and missed him because my Spit was bucking in the fast dive. But the three Canadians with me made sure of the 110 and we saw him crash.

Robert Wendell "Buck" McNair (on a motorbike at a fighter base in Britain) was a top Canadian ace, with 16 victories. He twice had to bail out over the English Channel, the second time with his aircraft in flames. Below: a German trimotor flying boat crashes in the sea, victim of an attack by an RCAF Beaufighter.

The Fortresses crossed the Dutch coast and were met by more of our fighters. The combat had ceased, but I'd seen one or two damaged Fortresses break away from the main stream and fly parallel to the enemy coast. In this way their crews would not be faced with the long sea crossing; they could slip across the narrow neck of the Channel between Calais and Dover. But they would be sitting ducks for prowling Focke-Wulfs. The best thing was to fly a dog-leg route home, sweeping down the coast to Calais before turning starboard for Lashenden.

I called the section leaders: "All Graycap aircraft re-form. Over Ostend at angels 24." They came swinging in from all directions. Six sections, each of four Spitfires, jockeyed into wing formation in well under five minutes. It always pleased me to see the pilots form up in such a workmanlike manner; it was the hallmark of teamwork and good flying discipline.

We set course for Calais, and after a few minutes Walter Conrad called up: "Graycap, there's one lone aircraft behind. Six o'clock. About the same height and two miles away. Looks like he's trailing us."

"All right, Walter," I replied. "Ease out a bit and keep an eye on him." I could hardly believe this unknown aircraft would be a Hun. It was a brave man who would stalk a wing of Spitfires in a clear blue sky.

Conrad called again: "Graycap, he's gaining on us. He's not much more than 1000 yards now. It's a 190."

"Take your Number Two and break into him when you're ready," I ordered. "But don't wait too long."

A few seconds elapsed. We all continued to fly straight and level to draw on the unsuspecting Hun. Then Conrad sang out: "Blue Two, break right. Now!"

I turned the rest of the Canadians to watch the unequal fight between our two Spitfires and the bold pilot of the 190. But the enemy pilot had seen the two Spitfires break away from our main formation and he half-rolled and dived down toward Dunkirk, with Conrad and his wingman, Flt. Sgt. G. M. Shouldice, after him. We watched until they were swallowed up by the early evening haze. Then someone called up: "Graycap, two explosions on the ground."

I called Conrad: "You all right, Walter?"

An answer came back. It was Shouldice, and he spoke very quietly: "Graycap from Blue Two. I've collided with Blue Leader. I think he's gone in."

"How's your Spit, Shouldice?" I asked.

"My right aileron has gone and some of the wing tip. She's very hard to control. Over."

I had to advise him at once, either to bail out over France or to try to get back to England. If he bailed out he would probably be taken prisoner, but this didn't matter: the main thing was to save the pilot. The Spitfire was badly damaged and it was unlikely that it could be flown back to England. I called Shouldice and tried to sound reassuring: "You'd better head into France. Climb to 10,000 feet and bail out. We'll cover you. Over."

"I can't bail out, sir. The hood seems jammed. I can't get it open."

"All right then. Steer three-zero-zero for Dover. Climb as high as you can. What's your height now?"

"Eight thousand feet, sir."

I left the others flying on course and, taking my wingman, went down in search of the crippled Spitfire. On the way I called the controller at Kenley and asked him to alert a Walrus and the rescue launches.

We soon found Shouldice, just off the French coast and heading for Dover. I drew alongside. Most of his right aileron and wing tip had gone. It was a miracle the plane was still flying. The right wing

Johnnie Johnson (above, right), with ground crewmen, at the cockpit of a Spitfire. Left: off duty and under canvas, waiting for the invasion of Europe, at an advanced RCAF airfield in Britain.

was well down and the Spitfire was trying to swing to the right and back into France. Shouldice was having a hard struggle fighting this; I could see he had both hands on the stick. I spoke to him again: "We're halfway across now. Only ten miles to Dover."

There was no reply. Perhaps the stick forces were so heavy that he couldn't move a hand to the transmitter switch. Then the right wing dropped lower and I turned steeply inside him when his Spitfire yawed dangerously to the right with the wings vertical. I saw his hands reach to the rubber ball at the top of the hood which controlled the emergency release system. Then the Spitfire fell into an uncontrollable vertical dive.

It only took a second or two to reach the sea. We watched it knife cleanly, nose first into the water. A cascading ring of spray fell back, then the surging waters closed in over the Spitfire and its pilot. I called the controller and gave a fix, but I knew the rescue boys would never find a thing.

Back at Lashenden I sat down in my caravan to write letters to the next of kin

of the two pilots. I glanced through my mail and saw that two of my recent recommendations had been approved: Flight Sergeant Shouldice had been commissioned; Flight Lieutenant Conrad had been promoted to squadron leader.

In September my tour was up and, with my personal score standing at 24 kills, I was posted to 11 Group headquarters. The Canadians laid on a tremendous party to bid me farewell. Our group commander was present, the usual speeches were made, and it was strongly hinted that the Canadians would offer me another wing after I had a rest. I was presented with a beautiful gold watch and felt like an old man retiring after a lifetime with the firm.

In November, at 11 Group HQ, I got a call from Bobbie Page, the owner of the popular Kimmul Club in London. I could hear the clamor of a noisy party over the line. Bobbie said casually: "A friend of yours wants a word with you."

I waited, and then a Canadian voice said: "Is that you, Wingco? You old bastard! Guess who this is?"

"I think it's Walter Conrad. But that's impossible."

"You bet it's Walter. Right here in the jolly old Kimmul Club. Knocking back a pint of this stuff you call beer. The Spanish vino was better."

"Let's have the story, Walter," I demanded.

"Well, you saw Shouldice and me go down after that 190 last August. We were both firing and Shouldice couldn't have been watching me. The Hun went in and then Shouldice hit me behind the cockpit with his right wing. My Spit was sliced in two. I don't remember how I got out, but my parachute had just opened when I fell on a haystack just inside Dunkirk. I was pretty bruised and I'd lost my shoes when I bailed out. I hid in an old machine-gun trench for four days, feeling pretty miserable."

"How did you get out of France?"

"I got in touch with a farmer. He gave me a pair of size 12 British Army boots he'd found on the beach at Dunkirk. But he wouldn't help in any other way until I told him that if I was caught by the Huns I'd tell them who gave me the boots. It worked like a charm. I soon met the right people and spent the usual six weeks in one of Spain's lousy prisons. But here I am. Cheers." And he took a long pull at his beer. . . .   J. E. JOHNSON

259

Ortona: little Stalingrad

The 1st Division whips Germany's crack paratroopers in the first big street battle of the Italian campaign

This is Matthew Halton of the CBC speaking from an observation post in the 17th-century wall of a little old town on the Adriatic. It's 26 minutes past 3 in the afternoon. Four minutes from now there'll be a tremendous artillery barrage laid down on the enemy positions across the Moro River. The barrage will continue for an hour and at half-past four our infantry —I can't say which infantry—will move across the valley, across the little river and up the other side, to attack the enemy.

It's incredible that one should have such a dramatic view of a battle, and on such a gorgeous warm day, with the Adriatic dancing in the sunlight. War on such a day seems particularly tragic.

The other side of the valley is an enchanting patchwork of vivid reds, greens and yellows, like daubs of paint—like a painting by Cézanne—and it's hard to believe at quiet moments like this that the enemy is waiting there only a few thousand yards away. A BROADCAST, DEC. 8, 1943

The Canadians were a few miles short of Ortona, a minor Adriatic seaport whose cathedral contained the remains of St. Thomas, the 12th Apostle. Anyone who saw the tomb of the saint—so went the legend—would reach Rome safely.

The Allies *were* on a journey to Rome that December of 1943 but no legend could shake one implacable fact: there was no safe way to get there. There would be heavy fighting, Hitler had decided that. After Italy capitulated in September, he had ordered his armies to fight bitterly for Rome, for all Italy.

The Eternal City itself was a prize sought by the U.S. Fifth Army on the western side of the Italian peninsula. On the eastern side, the Adriatic side, General Montgomery's Eighth Army was fighting toward the lateral road which led to Rome from the seaside resort of Pescara, 12 miles beyond Ortona. If it got to Pescara, it might shake loose the defenses before Rome.

To reach Pescara, to break through positions the Germans hoped would hold firm through the winter, the Eighth Army had launched its fiercest attacks since El Alamein, and by December Canada's 1st Division had become its spearhead. It was a harsh and costly assignment.

The Canadians had been blooded in Sicily. They had landed in the toe of Italy on September 3 and had fought steadily north in a 400-mile march through the central mountains. Nowhere had they faced the level of violence they faced now. "Everything before this," said the division's commander, Maj. Gen. Chris Vokes, "was a nursery tale."

On the afternoon of December 8, a massive artillery barrage prepared the way for the 1st Division's infantry to attack across the Moro and, to the east, out of a bridgehead across the river won earlier in a feint near the coast. From his observation post, Matthew Halton reported:

. . . It's a terrific shelling. We get one or two enemy shells every minute on this position; the Germans get hundreds every minute on theirs. The valley of the Moro down there, through which our infantry have to attack, is one dense pall of smoke, and we can hardly see the town of Ortona, just a few miles away. It looks very ghostly now, perched on its cliffs above the sea, seen through this terrible pall of smoke. There's another gorge on our left, and our vehicles are going back and forth across it in endless streams. The gorge and a bridge are being shelled all the time, but the vehicles never stop.

In Campochiaro (left), one of many Italian towns taken by the 1st Canadian Division, a soldier of the Carleton and York Regiment is shot in a German counterattack. Between its September 3 landing at Reggio Calabria in the Italian toe and its transfer to the Adriatic in December, the division fought 400 miles through the central mountains. In a push to Potenza in mid-September it had forced the withdrawal of some German troops from the Anglo-American Fifth Army's Salerno beachhead. But by December the enemy was established in a series of deep defensive positions south of Rome. British troops forced a bridgehead over the Sangro River. Then the Canadians crossed the Moro River and fought on to Ortona (above).

Right now an ambulance is approaching the bridge from the other side. A shell has just exploded in front of it, off the road, but the ambulance is coming across. There's a military policeman. These are men with a tough job, the MPs who stand at the bridges, shellfire or no shellfire, to prevent traffic jams. A traffic jam down there could ruin the battle. The MP stands there, straight and calm and white-gloved as if on duty in a city, stopping one vehicle, giving priority to another, waving some other to come through.

The guns make a big noise, but the show really begins at half-past four when the infantry go down into the valley and through the smoke—the valley of the shadow—to the attack. Their job is to clear the enemy out of his first positions so that the engineers can bridge the Moro.

Near us are 126 German prisoners from the German 90th Panzer Grenadier Division. There were 70 of them in a huge dugout near here the other day. They wouldn't surrender. They killed the sergeant who offered them a chance to surrender. They're all dead now. The dugout is their grave.

It's half-past four now. The attack is going in. . . .

At first the attack went well, then German resistance stiffened. A staff officer wrote: "Though the two flanks of our bridgehead were secured, the enemy held a narrow corridor running downhill through the village of San Leonardo to the site of a demolished bridge. It was essential that we commence work on a bridge of our own. The enemy was known to have tanks operating in the San Leonardo area and we, as yet, had no tanks or anti-tank guns across the river. If we did not get them across by first light, we would be in for a very sticky time." The job went to the 3rd Field Company of the Royal Canadian Engineers.

Matthew Halton:

. . . One of the outstanding feats of the Moro River battle was the building of a diversion across the Moro to enable our supporting arms, ammunition, supplies and guns to get across to the infantry.

There were 120 men of the 3rd Field Company at work that night and I wish I could name them all. One man who was there, Spr. Milton McNaughton, wouldn't talk into the microphone, so I'll tell his story. McNaughton, a Manitoban, drives a bulldozer—and there's a job you can have. He had to take his great lumbering machine down to the river and level the banks before the others could start building a diversion across the shallow creek.

For two hours the shelling and the machine-gun fire and the sniping were so heavy that he couldn't start work. He got sore and went out with a gun and brought back two prisoners, German engineers. Then the shelling and machine-gun fire got worse. McNaughton shouted: "Aw, the hell with this!" and started working. He worked five hours under fire. . . .

By 6 a.m. the diversion was ready—and McNaughton had won a Military Medal. By 7 a.m. tanks were crossing the Moro. San Leonardo was won and the bridgehead was finally secured.

Then the 1st Division struck for a lateral road a mile and a quarter on. The road ran south from Ortona to Orsogna. Its military key was the crossroads where it was joined by the road from San Leonardo at a point less than two miles from Ortona.

A few hundred yards in front of the Ortona-Orsogna road ran a long ravine which came to be known as The Gully. Here the Germans held the Canadians off.

The mud on the plateau around The Gully, someone said, "was six feet deep." Amid the olive groves and vineyards, every farmhouse became a bastion. Every yard of ground was ravaged by shellfire. The rain pelted down. Mines were everywhere. The dead lay everywhere. There were repeated attacks and counterattacks, but the Germans held. They had dug deep shelters in the side of the ravine nearer the Canadians. Artillery fire couldn't reach them there, and when it stopped, they came out and manned their guns.

Matthew Halton:

. . . Soaking wet, in a morass of mud, against an enemy fighting harder than he's fought before, the Canadians attack, attack and attack. The enemy is now fighting like the devil to hold us. He brings in more and more guns, more and more troops. The hillsides and farmlands and orchards are a ghastly brew of fire, and our roads for four miles behind the forward infantry are under heavy shelling. Not as bad as our own shelling, but bad enough. Sometimes a battlefield looks like a film of a battlefield, but not this. It's too grim.

It's a very localized battle, with all hell and thousands of troops in a small area. We have fire superiority, we have wonderful soldiers—there's a dogged fierceness about the Canadians now—but the enemy is well-disciplined and cunning, and he knows all the tricks, clean and unclean. Some of his troops surrender to attacking Canadians. As the Canadian platoon advanced to take the surrender, they were mowed down by flanking machine guns. They were trapped and murdered—just one of many treacheries. Today we saw one of our stretcher-bearers killed by a German sniper.

Listen to the echo of those shells! Those are our guns far behind, in such a position that there is this wild echoing. . . .

General Vokes probed at the inland extremity of The Gully, hoping to turn the Germans' flank. On the 13th two small infantry-tank assaults gained surprise, captured nearly 100 prisoners and breached the enemy defenses. One was made by the Seaforth Highlanders, the other by the West Nova Scotia Regiment. Both were badly under strength. Both had the support of the 1st Armored Brigade's Ontario Regiment tanks.

Both made penetrations beyond The Gully, one to within 1000 yards of the crucial crossroads. They had to be withdrawn as the Germans reacted violently and reinforcement was difficult. But they had won and kept a bridgehead beyond The Gully and they had shown the way to success.

Vokes ordered the Royal 22nd Regiment to attack out of the bridgehead the following morning while other troops tried one more frontal assault on The Gully itself. The Royal 22nd's job was to take Casa Berardi, a cluster of farm buildings, and then the crossroads, three quarters of a mile along the Ortona-Orsogna road.

"I had every confidence they would succeed with little difficulty," Vokes said later, "because intercepted wireless messages indicated that the 90th Panzer Grenadier Division had been badly decimated and was not confident that it could withstand a further onslaught. Unfortunately, unknown to us, the 90th was relieved on the night of the 13-14th by the 1st Parachute Division. One company of the Royal 22nd and seven Ontario Regiment tanks would be opposed by a fresh battalion of the best German troops in Italy."

Their achievements under the circumstances, he said, were an outstanding example of "inspired leadership, tactical skill and superlative courage."

Capt. Paul Triquet of Cabano, Que., led the French Canadian Royal 22nd's C company into the attack. He had the support of the seven tanks, all that C squadron of the Ontario Regiment could muster. This is Triquet's story:

. . . As Lt. Col. J. P. E. Bernatchez briefed us, we could see the operation had to succeed. Our success was vital to the strategy of the whole Eighth Army.

Still, it was almost a shock when the CO picked my company to lead the assault. With the tanks, we were to take Casa Berardi, then the regiment as a whole would seize the crossroads and hold it until the remainder of the 3rd Brigade came up.

The object was to cut off Ortona. Then it could be attacked and occupied without destroying port installations which the navy judged essential to support the Eighth Army in subsequent operations. My company comprised 81 all ranks. With us were the tanks, an artillery officer to spot targets and his NCO to radio information to the guns.

The battle started at 0600 hours with a tremendous one-hour artillery barrage, so terrifying that some men were on the verge of panic. At 0700 hours we moved off, followed by the tanks. Across the ravine, we came upon an enemy outpost commanded by a young officer too unnerved by our barrage to resist. After progressing a few hundred yards, we were counterattacked by four tanks and a company of infantry. The tanks appeared from behind a group of farmhouses and opened up at 200 yards with machine guns and 88s. One of our tanks was destroyed but we moved two anti-tank guns up to within 50 yards and knocked one German tank out of action.

There was a sudden lull as both sides held their fire to allow an Italian woman and two little children to reach our lines. After this pause for humanity's sake, Maj. H. A. "Snuffy" Smith of the armored squadron destroyed a second German tank and the remaining two turned and fled.

Several of my men had been killed and others, including two platoon commanders, wounded. C company strength was now about 50. I reorganized as best I could and Major Smith's tanks took on the machine guns that were causing us heavy losses.

The battle raged on and soon all men of my company headquarters were killed or wounded, except my orderly. My radio was smashed and I now had to send all messages to the CO on the artillery spotter's radio or the one in Major Smith's tank.

With artillery fire to protect our flanks, we pushed on toward Casa Berardi, still a mile and a half distant. It was one long calvary. With every small gain we suffered new losses. My last platoon commander was wounded and I had to use two German prisoners to evacuate him.

It wasn't yet noon. I now had about 30 men—two platoons, each commanded by a sergeant. We were still about a mile from Casa Berardi. The Germans had worked in behind us. We were cut off from the rest of the battalion and completely encircled by the enemy. I put it to the men: "We're surrounded. The enemy is in front of us,

Canadian infantry, seen through the turret ring of a wrecked German tank, move up for a new assault. Right: officers of the Royal 22nd Regiment soon after the battle for Casa Berardi. From left: Capt. Bernard Guimond, Maj. J. G. Charlebois, Maj. Paul Triquet, V.C., Capt. Pierre Chassé, Capt. Pierre Potvin, Maj. Ovila Garceau.

behind us and on our flanks. The safest place for us is the objective." I was sure that if we could reach Casa Berardi we would be able, with tank and artillery support, to organize a perimeter defense and hold on until D company reinforced us.

In this final push, I was continually on the run between my two reduced platoons and Major Smith. I often had to jump on his tank and drop gravel in the turret to attract his attention and point out targets. My young French Canadians were superb. They showed great courage against vastly superior forces.

About 1400 hours, seven hours after we'd started, we reached Casa Berardi. There were only 14 of us, and the tanks. There were four code words to indicate C company's progress: "Monday, Tuesday, Wednesday, Thursday." Now, on Major Smith's radio, I signaled to Colonel Bernatchez: "Thursday." We were on our objective.

Twenty minutes later we were again counterattacked: artillery, then several tanks, and all the while snipers. Suddenly, down the road from Ortona came a German tank, all guns blazing. Major Smith went ahead alone, firing smoke shells. He had few high-explosive shells left and

didn't want to waste any. He fired a single HE and the German tank caught fire. All its crew were killed or wounded. Then we knocked out a second tank and two others fled.

We started to clean out the various buildings of Casa Berardi. First, we'd fire the tanks' machine guns, with two infantrymen following, then the first man at the house would throw in a grenade. We did

Canadians (below) faced some of Germany's best troops in bitter Italian fighting. Lt. R. L. McDougall of the Seaforth Highlanders wrote during a lull later that winter: "We saw a war movie depicting the Germans as barbaric fools, brutal and stupid. The boys who fought in Ortona don't take kindly to that sort of nonsense."

chase the enemy from every last house but unhappily hadn't enough men to hold the entire place. That night the Germans retook some houses.

It was a bad night. When we took Casa Berardi, we had almost no ammunition left. I informed the CO and he promised reinforcements and ammunition by nightfall. Major Smith's tank had been hit and he was immobilized by a broken track. We formed a circle with the remaining tanks and posted two riflemen in a slit trench to protect them during the night.

We were so exhausted it took superhuman effort to stay awake. I had to rest standing up, leaning against a tank; otherwise I would have fallen asleep.

During the night, the Germans sneaked back very near us and called to us in French to surrender if we wanted to get out of Casa Berardi alive. I can't repeat what our boys replied but I can say it was classic and appropriately rude! Having seen so many of our soldiers killed or wounded, we all hated the Boche and all that mattered was to pay him back in kind.

About 2300 hours I heard a strange noise from the ravine which separated us from the rest of the battalion. I ordered "Halt!" and demanded the password. "Don't worry, Paul!" It was the voice of Maj. Ovila Garceau—my good friend and his company had brought the help my shattered little group needed to hold on.

Next morning the enemy hit us hard with mortars and machine guns. Major Garceau and D company were hit as we began to push on; 50 percent were casualties. The tanks and my C company couldn't get past the start line either. All day long the Germans shelled and mortared us and casualties mounted. Strain and fatigue were overpowering.

Just before one of these shellings, I was standing near Major Smith's tank with the artillery spotter when my orderly came up with a tin of food, urging me to eat. I heard the whistle of mortar bombs. "Take cover!" I yelled, but the artillery officer and my orderly, who hadn't reacted fast enough, were almost cut in two. The officer didn't utter a word and fell back dead. My orderly crumbled to the ground, his stomach ripped open, crying, "I'm hit, Captain!" He died within seconds.

The orderly had been the last member of my original company headquarters. Now only one of the headquarters *reinforcements* was left.

Canadian tanks have broken into the main square of Ortona and remain in action as German snipers continue to fire from the nearest buildings. One first-aid man leads a wounded tank officer to cover, a second stands by to help if necessary, a third doubles away in answer to another call for assistance. At the right a group of men gather around a wounded man, who kneels half stripped while his back is bandaged.

I spent the rest of that day jumping from one hole to the next. Each time I moved there was a burst of machine-gun fire. But I always managed to reach the next trench. I told my boys, "They don't know *how* to shoot!"

My moving around was important to the men and even more so to me. Seeing all the dead littering the ground—we couldn't bury them—I could only hang on by speaking to the few who did survive.

In one hole I found a young soldier who had come to my company as a reinforce-ment. For this first battle he manned a Bren light machine gun. "Don't worry Captain," he said, "they won't get pas here."

Near a ditch, I heard someone call and discovered another young soldier almos blind from a face wound he'd suffered hours earlier. I asked why he hadn't called sooner, and he answered in all seriousnes that we were all too busy. I had him trans ferred immediately to the farmhouse where most of the other wounded were.

Toward the end of the day, I made radio

buildings and kept a harassing fire on the enemy with mortars and other weapons. *Our* snipers now had *their* turn.

Toward the end of the day on the 16th, Maj. Jean Allard joined us, succeeding Colonel Bernatchez, who left to take command of the 3rd Brigade. Major Allard sent out new fighting patrols by night and sought mortar and sniper targets by day and we retained the initiative.

On the 17th I stretched out on an old bed in the room where battalion HQ was and I slept for 20 hours straight.

As the Royal 22nd and the Ontario Regiment tanks held at Casa Berardi, the 1st Brigade mounted an attack across The Gully on December 18. The first outfit to make contact with us on the 19th was the Royal Canadian Regiment. At the famous crossroads, they were stopped temporarily, suffering 50 percent casualties. Later, the RCR dead were buried not far from our dead—French Canadians and English Canadians sleeping their last sleep side by side, reminders of a furious and heroic battle.

When we were relieved December 19, of the 81 men in my company who attacked Casa Berardi I had nine left. . . .

PAUL TRIQUET

For his valor at Casa Berardi, Major Triquet received the Victoria Cross, the first won by a Canadian in the Mediterranean theater. Lt. Gen. Sir Oliver Leese, new chief of the Eighth Army, wrote to him: "Your magnificent feat of arms made victory possible. It was essential to the army's plan that your battalion attain its objective. Your citation will be read by all in Canada and, with particular pride, by all French Canadians. In your leadership, in the bravery and sacrifice of the men who fought so courageously with you, the Canadian people will realize how much their soldiers have achieved."

contact with the CO and he asked me to try again to hold on. He would do his best to get reinforcements up soon. And he said I'd been promoted to major. (Reinforcements would have been more welcome than a promotion!)

Thirst was what we suffered most. The only well, opposite the main Casa Berardi building, was covered by German snipers. One or two men were hit trying to get to it.

A little after midnight that second night of battle, another squadron of tanks arrived with reinforcements, ammunition and food for Smith. They came in the dark at high speed, outwitting the Germans who had retaken the ground between us and the rest of the 3rd Brigade.

The clatter of the tanks had hardly stopped when I heard new noises from the ravine behind us: *our* reinforcements, with Colonel Bernatchez at their head. He had all the able-bodied men the regiment could muster. The medical officer was there, and the padre. With the arrival of these reinforcements, morale grew tremendously.

We now occupied all Casa Berardi out-

As soon as General Vokes had realized that the German paratroopers had come into the line, he knew the Royal 22nd would have difficulty getting beyond Casa Berardi. But as long as they held its farm buildings beyond The Gully, he had the Germans at a grave disadvantage.

While they held, he ordered a 48-hour pause to build up his exhausted, depleted division. Then on the 18th they moved on the crossroads. Behind a tremendous bombardment by all guns of the 5th Corps—

British, Canadian and Indian—the 48th Highlanders and the Royal Canadian Regiment attacked across The Gully. By December 19 the crossroads was in Canadian hands.

The 1st Division now controlled two miles of the Ortona-Orsogna road, and Indians and New Zealanders were across the same road in their sectors to the left. Ortona looked like a cinch—even to a diarist of the 76th Panzer Corps headquarters. With the fall of Casa Berardi, he wrote, the Allies would "bring up further forces and tanks and presumably take Ortona."

But Hitler himself had, weeks before, ordered the Gaeta-Ortona line held. Both

Ortona was an ancient town founded by the Trojans after the fall of Troy. The northern part of it was called the Old Town, a group of narrow buildings crowded together on a steep promontory thrusting out into the sea and topped by a dilapidated castle girdled with walls of great thickness. The modern part of the town, with many buildings at least four stories high, fanned out east and west over a wide tableland to the south. The town was dominated by two massive towers of the castle and by the great dome of the Cathedral of St. Thomas. Its peacetime population of 10,000 had been greatly reduced: the Germans had sent many away for slave labor; others had fled.

sides made Ortona a "prestige" battle, without being certain the tactical value was worth it. Soon the hapless town was being described in the press as a miniature version of the massive struggle the Germans and Russians had fought in Stalingrad the previous winter.

Field Marshal Albert Kesselring, the German commander in Italy, said "the English have made it appear as important as Rome. It is too bad the world press makes so much of it."

The battle for Ortona began when the 2nd Brigade moved to exploit the success at the crossroads. By December 21 the Loyal Edmonton Regiment and Seaforth Highlanders were fighting into its streets. Here, wrote Winston Churchill, "was fought the first big street-fighting battle, and from it many lessons were learned."

On one side fought the two Canadian battalions, on the other the fanatical men of the 1st Parachute Division. From the official history *From Pachino to Ortona:* . . . The paratroopers had cleverly planned their demolitions to lead an attacker along the main street to the *piazza municipale* [town square], which they had selected as the "killing ground." Houses had been toppled into the side streets to block them. Machine guns, anti-tank guns and mortars were sited in the rubble and on various floors of the buildings left standing. The result was a murderous cross fire at every corner. It was the Germans' first organized attempt in the Mediterranean to use a built-up area as a strongpoint.

There was no preliminary Allied air bombardment because the navy wanted the harbor intact if possible. The opposing

Ragged, proud Italians returned to their smashed towns to find houses demolished, streets jammed with rubble. Above: a 6-pounder anti-tank gun in action in Ortona. Twenty-four men of the Edmonton Regiment were buried in the ruins of an old stone house which retreating German paratroopers dynamited just as the Canadians entered. One man (right) was dug out, alive, three days later. Germans later fell victim to the same trick. Two dozen were lured into a block of houses and were blown up by the Edmontons.

forces were so close that artillery fire was out except against the massive walls of the castle. But mortars were used freely and with good effect. The most important artillery contribution was made by 6- and 17-pounder anti-tank guns. They were used to shoot the enemy out of his upper-story positions along the seafront.

Three Rivers Regiment tanks, firing over the heads of the infantry, blasted German paratroopers from the upper floors of houses and gave vital covering fire. Tank losses were unexpectedly light; only three were wrecked beyond repair. When the Old Town was reached, however, the streets were too narrow and the rubble too thickly sown with mines to permit tank operations.

The streets were comparatively empty. Most fighting took place inside the houses, where the Edmontons and Seaforths used a technique called mouse-holing. . . .

"Almost every one of the stone houses and tenements beside the impassable roadways held enemy infantry or gunners," wrote Ralph Allen in *Ordeal by Fire*. "The only way to get at them was to blow an opening through the connecting wall from the dwelling next door with a small explosive charge called the Beehive, or with the infantryman's portable anti-tank gun, the PIAT, and then pour through with grenades and submachine guns. Mouse-holing parties sometimes fought their way down whole blocks—often at the level of the third or fourth story—without ever seeing open air."

The paratroopers, in turn, placed demolition charges beneath the houses in the line of advance. When these houses were occupied by Canadians, the enemy would spring his trap and bury them in the ruins. A platoon of 24 Edmontons was wiped out in this way, with the exception of a lance corporal who was buried for 3½ days and finally dug out alive. The Edmontons retaliated by luring the enemy back into a block of houses from which he had already withdrawn—they blew up two dozen paratroopers.

The Ortona in which the Canadians fought was described by British war correspondent Christopher Buckley in his book *Road to Rome:*

. . . From the town came intermittent small-arms fire, but now and then the battle would fall strangely silent for no immediately obvious reason. I am not sure

that this sudden and inhuman hush is not the most awe-inspiring thing about a battlefield. It is like the passing of the angel of death.

I accompanied a Canadian patrol into the town, stealthily, in the careful precision of some macabre ballet, in single file and at well-spaced intervals down the street, taking full advantage of the cover afforded by the doorways of the houses. At each transverse road we quickened our step and darted rapidly across.

One doorway would conceal a Canadian soldier; from the next an old man or a child would tentatively emerge; then another soldier; and so on. At one point where a ruined house left a clear field of fire for an enemy sniper, I noted how the Canadians, lithe as panthers, darted past this spot.

An old woman emerged from a house. On some business of her own—heaven knows what!—she elected to follow us down the street. One could see her imitating, almost parodying, the motions of the soldiers. Then at the gap she gathered up her skirts and scuttled across the tumbled masonry. In less tragic circumstances her ungainly motions might have tempted laughter, but in shattered Ortona, among the corpses and the machine guns, their very grotesquerie suggested the horror of a dance of death.

Outside a church lay a German soldier, sprawled in the horrible convulsion of death. A packet of postcards had fallen from the pocket of his tunic and lay scattered in the roadway. Each card was smeared and dabbed with fresh blood. The portrait on every card was Hitler's.

What strikes one so forcibly about the entry of troops into a hostile town is the extraordinarily melodramatic character of the scene. The steel-helmeted Canadians, bayonets fixed, looked much more like the Hollywood version of war than the real thing. As for the bloodstained postcards of the Führer—would any novelist dare indulge in symbolism so ponderous?

We learned a great deal about street-fighting in Ortona. We learned that the attackers, even when they possess considerable superiority of firepower, are likely to suffer losses more severe than those of the defenders. Every house may be a deathtrap, every street corner an ambush. As the Germans withdrew, they left each building mined. The mine was touched off with a connecting wire when troops of our

leading sections were estimated to have entered the building. This refinement of war serves a double purpose. It renders the occupation of each separate house a hazardous and probably costly business. And the collapse of more and more buildings renders the whole town a ghastly inferno of rubble that, when the defenders are finally driven out, inevitably delays the vehicles which might be employed to speed the pursuit.

A quick, undignified scuttle across a street brought me to our most forward position. I dived through a doorway and down a couple of steps and found myself in a strange clutter of humanity: five or six Canadian soldiers, old men and women and children innumerable. A painter of genius—Goya, perhaps—might have done justice to the scene. No verbal description could. In the half-darkened room the pasta for the midday meal was simmering over the fire. Haggard and prematurely-aged women kept emerging shyly one after another from some inner chamber where an old man, the grandfather of the numerous children, was dying; he had been hit by a shell splinter.

Another old man uttered maledictions against Mussolini while his wife produced Marsala and half a dozen glasses and moved among the soldiers, filling and refilling their glasses. Marsala in the front line; how crazy it all was! (Good Marsala, too.) The children clambered around the soldiers and clutched at them convulsively every time one of our anti-tank guns fired. Soon each of us had a terrified child in his arms. And the old lady went on distributing Marsala.

Out of that medley of human beings, flung together for a half hour, there developed a singular sense of fellowship. If you want to find Christianity and human brotherhood, take a jeep and drive as far as you can toward the front line of any war (you will always find a war somewhere).

In the houses of Ortona, which they had been shelling for days, our soldiers were as welcome as if each was a new Messiah, bringing peace and security. And the soldiers, when they had a few minutes' relaxation, were entirely occupied in distributing their rations among the civilians and in comforting the children.

The firing increased in intensity, as though each side sought a final decision before the gray winter evening closed down. The smell of cordite penetrated ever

Maj. Gen. Chris Vokes, commander of the 1st Division—below, left, with General Montgomery—was a favorite butt of Monty's kidding. Col. Dick Malone, Montgomery's aide, wrote: "He would have me ask Chris why he didn't straighten out his front line; he'd 'complain' that it looked untidy on the map. Or he'd ask what was delaying the Canadians; why didn't they get a move on? Chris would roar through his enormous red mustache: 'You tell Monty if he'd get to hell up here and see the bloody mud he's stuck us into he'd know damn well why we can't move any faster!' "

more strongly into the homely little room where onions hung from the ceiling and a vividly imaginative picture on the wall showed Italian soldiers galloping into battle, brandishing sabers and mounted on snow-white chargers.

That was Ortona. It might be any town through which troops must fight their way. The details may change, but that crowded little room is the reality. . . .

CHRISTOPHER BUCKLEY

The reality was the piazza municipale killing ground too. In the simple language of a man who was there, an Edmonton lieutenant wrote this account of his platoon on the day before Christmas 1943:
. . . We had worked forward until, at about 1000 hours, we held the houses marked A and B on the diagram [opposite]. Here

we could observe the piazza municipale and exchange fire with German paratroopers in the church and school and the blocks marked D and E. The end of the school facing us was solid. So was the corner of block C. They offered no easy entrance. Our objective was the school.

I had a plan that showed the only entrances to the school were the main door facing the church and a small door at the far end. We could not get through the main door without coming under murderous fire from the church and the school itself. The alley toward E was a deathtrap, its entire length being swept by fire from both D and E. Our anti-tank guns could have knocked a hole in the end wall of the school large

it blasted down the side of the school with its 75-mm. gun. This tank then moved to position 2, a second tank to position 3 and a third to position 1. The tanks at 2 and 3 covered the church with machine-gun and 75-mm. fire, while the tank in position 1 covered the street leading to B. The fire fight was won and the stage set for my platoon. So much dust had been kicked up by the gunfire and falling masonry that smoke was unnecessary and, without further preliminaries, the first section dashed across the street, struggling over rubble, entered the school and started clearing the building. The tanks knocked down part of the front wall of the church and silenced the machine-gun post there.

section had gained a footing it moved rapidly forward, using grenades and tommy guns, clearing each room as it advanced. The enemy put up little opposition and succeeded in evacuating the building from the rear exit, taking most of their casualties. We searched the cellars rather gingerly and found no Germans. The sun was beginning to set by the time the building was cleared and I therefore ordered the tanks, which were running out of ammunition, to withdraw.

In this action my platoon sustained only one casualty. Success could not have been obtained without the invaluable assistance of the tanks. . . .   A LIEUTENANT

The fifth day of the battle was December 25, and the fighting went on. Most Canadians got a few hundred yards back from the fighting for an hour or two, long enough for Christmas dinner behind a wall or in a barn or—in the case of the Seaforth Highlanders—in the battered Church of Santa Maria di Constantinopoli. This is an extract from a diary kept by the Seaforth padre, Roy Durnford:

. . . C company came first at eleven o'clock, A company at one, and so on until seven at night. The men looked tired and drawn, as well they might, and most who came directly from the town were dirty and unshaven. "Well," I said, "at last I've got you all in church!" The floor had been cleared and tables set up, and it was heartwarming to see the tablecloths and chinaware some of the boys had scrounged, and the beer, cigarettes, chocolate, nuts, oranges and apples. There was soup, roast pork with applesauce, cauliflower, mashed potatoes, gravy, Christmas pudding and mince pies—all excellent and a credit to the cooks. Plates were heaped high with as much as any man could eat.

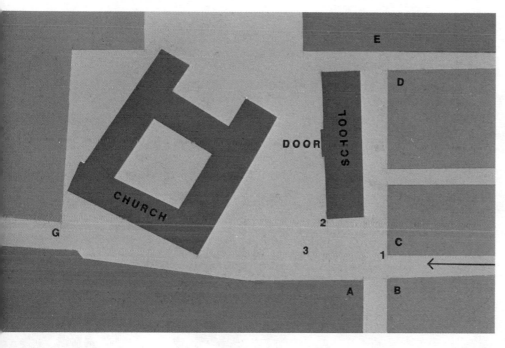

enough for a man to squeeze through, but it was essential to obtain fire superiority, to win the fire fight, before any movement took place.

This was going to be tricky; the enemy knew all our likely positions and completely dominated the square.

We decided to make a direct assault on the school, supported by tanks, with smoke if necessary. A troop of three Three Rivers tanks was made available and between us we worked out a plan to cope with the enemy machine guns. One of our problems was the block of rubble obstructing the entrance to the square between A and B. This was overcome by the tanks discovering a satisfactory bypass. Zero hour was set for noon.

The first tank came rumbling up the street to position 1. At a range of 30 yards,

After what seemed an interminable time, although it probably was no more than a half hour, the section leader signaled all was well. I ordered a second section to move to the house at C to control the back of the school and bring fire down the street toward G. I hoped, in this way, to maintain fire superiority once the tanks withdrew.

With the remaining sections, I dashed across to the school. Everything was under control. The section leader had his men at the windows, and though he had not as yet searched the cellars, the main floor was clear. There was no upper story. The section leader said he'd had little difficulty in clearing out the few Germans left in the school. We had caught them by surprise and the tank shells had driven them from the exposed end of the building. Once the

The tables filled and emptied and filled again, and I saw many a tense face relax in the warmth within the walls of the battle-scarred church. What a concert of noise! As relief and relaxation took hold, the talk became louder and greetings and jokes were shouted. The cookers hissed and sizzled behind the altar and the plates clattered as they were cleared from the tables and piled high on the altar itself. Desecration of the Lord's Table? It did not strike me so. Above the din one could sometimes hear machine-gun fire and shells. It was wonderful to hear so much laughter so close to so much death and suffering.

I don't know how many remembered Christ today, but I felt that most of these men, whether they knew it or not, remembered the things Christ stood for—compassion, faithfulness to a cause, self-sacrifice. When each company arrived, I began a little service, being careful to make it voluntary, and I was pleased to see how many gathered around. We had just a few short prayers and some carol singing—Wilf Gildersleeve played the harmonium we found in the church, with "Postie" Sinclair and Major Gowan manning the bellows.

I talked with many men. Most, I'm sure, are fearful of what lies ahead, but they are fine men and I know they will give the best that is in them. My heart grieved to see them, after their brief two-hour respite, turn their faces again to the battle. . . .

THE REV. ROY DURNFORD

There was no Christmas dinner for the 48th Highlanders. On the night of December 22-23 they had worked in behind the German defenses west of Ortona, the first stage of a move to cut the enemy's escape route along the coast road. They were under heavy fire, and mines and mud kept the Canadian tanks out of action. The Highlanders, constantly patrolling and probing, went without food for 48 hours, stopping German attempts to infiltrate into their positions. On Christmas night 60 men of the Saskatoon Light Infantry carried supplies up to the 48th, a difficult movement in the dark, under sporadic enemy fire. On December 26 a troop of Ontario Regiment tanks reached the positions.

Fighting inside Ortona after Christmas was confined to close contact by the infantry and the engineers with their explosives. Night fighting was impossible, but patrols were active amid the rubble.

On the 26th the Edmontons took the Cathedral of St. Thomas. The Germans had blown up the cathedral—and the famous tomb which had drawn pilgrims to Ortona for years. And they'd done it, ironically, on the 21st, the Feast of St. Thomas. The copper coffin, with the re-

mains that had been brought back from one of the Crusades, somehow survived.

From the cathedral's ruins, the Edmontons laid down more than 1100 three-inch mortar bombs between there and the castle. A battery of howitzers was brought up to lob 7.2-inch shells into the castle itself.

On the last day of actual fighting—December 27—the Seaforths drove close to the coast road leading out of town, and the Princess Patricias came up to relieve the Edmontons. By then the Germans knew they'd lost; the Canadians held three quarters of the town and threatened the enemy communications on the coast road with a formidable penetration of the 1st Brigade, supported by tanks. During the night of December 27-28, the enemy silently withdrew. Ortona had been taken.

The cost had been heavy. Hardest hit was the Edmonton Regiment, whose casualties for nine days numbered 172, 63 fatal. The Seaforth Highlanders lost 41 killed and 62 wounded.

The advance from the Moro River had cost the 1st Division 176 officers and 2163 other ranks killed and wounded. Sickness, including battle fatigue, had reduced divisional strength by a further 1617. Every infantry battalion had suffered 50 percent casualties in the rifle companies. Even with reinforcements—150 officers and 2258 other ranks—and the return of many of the sick, the division was still about 1050 under strength. The transition to static warfare came none too soon.

The "red patch devils" and the men of the 1st Armored Brigade had fought remarkably well. Said General Vokes: "We smashed the 90th Panzer Grenadier Division and we gave the 1st German Parachute Division a mauling it will long remember."

Reported CBC's Matthew Halton:
... With the fall of Ortona, the Battle of the Moro River is over, and there is a new name to add to the list of great deeds of the war. Call them out: Dunkirk, Tobruk, Alamein, the delaying action in Burma, Sidi Omar, the last stand at Sollum, the Battle of Tunis—call them out, and add Moro River. Measured on the scale of the last war—the Somme, for example, or Passchendaele—or the enormous scale of the fighting in Russia, this was not a big battle, but it was one of the biggest ever fought by Canadians. Neither in this war nor in any other has there been anything more bitter and intense. The Canadians beat two of the finest German divisions that ever marched in a long fury of fire and death ending in the appalling week of Ortona.

The glory and sorrow is not all Canada's. This was an Eighth Army battle; British, New Zealand and Indian troops had heavy fighting in the center and on the left. But the main role was assigned to Canada on the right flank, and the quality of this battle had something special that our race will never forget. . . .

The military correspondent of *The Times* of London put it another way. "The Canadians," he wrote, "had proved themselves the finest forged offensive weapon."

The Canadians had driven a deep salient into the coastal sector of the enemy's Winter Line, and with this they had to be content. The Eighth Army was halted, not much beyond Ortona and still short of the Pescara-Rome road the Allies coveted.

As the front became a stalemate, the 1st Division was joined by the 11th Infantry Brigade of the 5th Armored Division. It was a move with historic significance. The Canadian government had pressured London for expansion of the Canadian force in Italy into a corps—and had finally succeeded. For the first time since World War 1, Canada had a corps on a battle-front.

The 11th Brigade made one brief, bloody January attack on German positions near the Arielli River, then the corps settled into a winter of static warfare under depressing leaden skies. Cold rain filled the slit trenches and turned the coastal clay to mud. It was a winter of patrols: snatching a German from his weapon pit and dragging him screaming back to the Canadian lines; a £5 thank you from General Vokes to a patrol which brought back two particularly valuable prisoners. A winter of men dying out in no-man's-land night after tense and ugly night. A bleak and lonely winter. The only consolation was that it was just as bad for the enemy.

A wounded German prisoner, captured with his diary, had noted: "I have changed a good deal. I cannot smile now. Here one must run for one's life. We squat day and night in our anti-tank ditch. Listening posts are put forward and patrols with grenades and machine pistols. One cannot feel safe here."

The German died of his wounds in the Canadian lines.

Ortona was "the Christmas battle." Weary Canadian soldiers paused for prayer and most had Christmas dinner —in the Church of Santa Maria, near the front line, or (left) in a brigade headquarters mess. One Canadian, Maj. Alex Campbell of the Hastings and Prince Edward Regiment, was killed in action that December 25 soon after he had written a "Prayer Before Battle." It was later printed in the army newspaper *The Maple Leaf:*

When 'neath the rumble of the guns
I lead my men against the Huns
It's then I feel so all alone and weak
    and scared
And oft I wonder how I dared
Accept the task of leading men.

I wonder, worry, fret, and then—I
    pray:
O God, who promised oft
To humble men to lend an ear,
Now in my troubled state of mind
Draw near, O God, draw near—draw
    near.

Make me more willing to obey,
Help me to merit my command,
And, if this be my fatal day
Reach out, O God, Thy helping hand
And lead me down that deep dark vale.

These men of mine must never know
How much afraid I really am,
Help me to lead them in the fight
So they will say—"He was a man."

The battle of Germany

Canada's largest air formation joins in the attempt to blast the Reich into submission

There were nearly 800 bombers, manned by more than 5000 Britons, Canadians, Australians, New Zealanders. In the gathering summer darkness, they rose from their bases and crossed the tranquil face of England. Moving like some great, untidy swarm of bees, they droned eastward into the night. It was July 24, 1943. After nearly four years of war, Air Chief Marshal Sir Arthur Harris's great strategic air offensive against Germany was in full stride.

The Allied leaders no longer talked publicly of saturating whole cities to destroy morale. At the Casablanca Conference in January, they had called for unconditional German surrender. Harris's RAF Bomber Command and the U.S. Army Air Force in Europe were to help bring it about through the general "disorganization" of German industry. Yet the new instructions really made little difference. To Harris, they still added up to ravaging German cities.

What was different in 1943 was Bomber Command's ability to do so. Its planes were bigger and there were more of them. The bombs were bigger and more power-ful; the average bomb load per aircraft had increased from 2800 pounds in early 1942 to 7500. New target-finding radar aids called Oboe and H2S were coming into use. Through darkness, cloud and the industrial haze of the Ruhr, the bombers now could "see" targets they hadn't been able to see before. And with the help of these new instruments, a special pathfinder force flew into target areas first to mark them with flares for the main force. The result was substantial improvement in both accuracy and achievement. The Americans,

Bomber crews flew night after night into German skies laced with searchlights and flak. Window, strips of aluminum foil dropped from the sky, confused enemy radar and left German cities almost defenseless. Dr. Joseph Goebbels, Hitler's propaganda minister, knew many bomber men were Canadians. He wrote in his diary: "It drives one mad to think that any old Canadian boor, who probably can't even find Europe on the globe, flies here from his super-rich country, which his people don't know how to exploit, and bombards a continent with a crowded population."

too, were stepping up their daylight offensive; a new song was making the rounds, "The U.S.A. by day and the RAF by night."

For Canada, all this had special significance. Since January 1, eight RCAF bomber squadrons had been operating in their own No. 6 Group, the largest Canadian air formation of the war. In time its size would increase to 14 squadrons, one of the most powerful groups in Bomber Command.

To Harris's chagrin, the great offensive had been sidetracked for weeks while the bombers tried without much success to destroy German U-boats in great concrete pens along the coast of Europe. Then on the night of March 5 it had begun with an attack on Essen. For weeks Bomber Command struck heavily at the Ruhr Valley, the heartland of German heavy industry. Now Harris was going to try something new. In *The History of the Second World War,* RAF Flt. Lt. Alfred Price writes:

... By midnight of July 24 the bombers

had assembled over the North Sea, a mighty phalanx of 791 Lancasters, Halifaxes, Stirlings and Wellingtons sprawled out over an area 200 miles long and 20 miles wide, an airborne armada moving east at 225 miles per hour. Attentive German eyes followed their progress all the way.

Shortly before 2300 hours, a radar station near Ostend had reported: "Approximately 80 aircraft at Gustav Caesar 5, course east, altitude 23,000 feet." At the headquarters of the Luftwaffe III Fighter Division at Arnhem-Deelen in Holland, a small spot of light moved swiftly across the darkened situation map. It came to rest at position GC-5 on the German fighter grid, just to the north of Ipswich, and soon was joined by others as more and more bombers appeared over the radar horizon. The attack was obviously going to be a big one.

The Germans could only speculate where it would strike. But the men in the bombers knew. At the briefing that day, the name had dried the throat of many an experienced crewman: Hamburg. The great port had already been raided 98 times. Her defenses were formidable: she was ringed by no less than 54 heavy flak and 22 searchlight batteries, and there were 6 major night-fighter airfields within easy flying distance. The attackers had paid heavily for previous operations.

Although the flak caused damage and forced bomber crews to fly on a swerving course, making accurate bombing difficult, it was the night fighters that were the real killers. Their tactics, evolved by Gen. Josef Kammhuber, had been tested and improved in 100 battles. His system, codenamed Himmelbett, depended on a lavishly equipped chain of ground radar stations. Each station had a maximum effective interception range of 30 miles, and Kammhuber had them in a line, shaped like a giant inverted sickle, extending down occupied Europe at 20-mile intervals. The "handle" ran through Denmark, from north to south; the "blade" curved through northern Germany, Holland, Belgium and eastern France to the Swiss frontier.

The stations spotted incoming bombers and directed night fighters to them. Once the twin-seater fighters could detect a target on their own lightweight Lichtenstein radar sets, they would radio a Pauke call. Pauke, literally "beat the kettledrum," was the Luftwaffe equivalent of the RAF's

Tally Ho—the target was in sight and about to be engaged.

The fighter's radar operator gave his pilot running instructions until the latter caught sight of the exhaust flames from the bomber's motors. The hunter closed in, trying to get into firing position without being seen. The task of the night-fighter crew—of either side—amounted to cold-blooded murder. If it was possible to get to within 50 yards behind and below an unsuspecting victim, a favorite German tactic was to pull the fighter up onto its tail and open fire, raking the raider from stem to stern with cannon shells. Often the first thing the bomber crew knew of the attack was the shudder of their aircraft buckling.

By July the German defenses were knocking down more than five out of every 100 attacking bombers, and this rate was rising steadily. Three quarters of those lost fell to fighters, the rest to flak and accidents.

It was vital to the bomber offensive that some means of neutralizing the Himmelbett system be found. Technically, the answer proved amazingly simple: little strips of aluminum foil. Known by the cover name Window, the strips measured 12 inches long and three quarters of an inch wide and came in bundles of 2000, held together by an elastic band. When released from an aircraft, the bundle broke up to form a cloud of strips which gave a bomber-sized blip on a radar screen. By releasing one bundle per minute from each aircraft in a concentrated bomber stream, it was possible to saturate the area with blips and make radar-controlled interceptions impossible.

During 1942, British scientists, under the greatest secrecy, had conducted trials with these strips. Under equal secrecy, the Germans had been doing exactly the same thing. Both reached the conclusion that the new countermeasure was dynamite. It could wreck air defenses. Neither side had then felt that its bomber arm had a margin of strength sufficient to justify the risk of introducing such an innovation and inviting retaliation in kind. But by the summer of 1943 the striking power of Bomber Command had expanded beyond all recognition, while the demands of the Russian front had reduced the German bomber force to comparative impotence. On July 15, the British war cabinet finally approved the use of Window.

Now, at 0025 hours on July 25, as the

It's bombing-up time and a 4000-pound Cookie is hoisted into a Lancaster amid hundreds of smaller fire bombs. Top: Halifax bombers of the RCAF's Iroquois and Bluenose squadrons wait for darkness before taking off for Germany. Right: just dropped from a bomber, a cloud of Window aluminum foil (left) presents a mystifying new target for German radar.

leading bombers passed the island fortress of Heligoland, the first bundles were dropped into the black air below. The first German report of anything out of the ordinary came from radar station Hummer, on Heligoland, at 0040 hours: the British appeared to have 11,000 bombers! Hummer reported that it was "disturbed by many apparent targets looking like aircraft, either stationary or slow moving. The picking up of genuine aircraft is made extremely difficult. Once they have been picked up, it is difficult to follow them." A station on the southern tip of Sylt reported similar trouble. So, in turn, did the rest of the radar stations around Hamburg.

The German fighters circling over the city waited with growing impatience for instructions from their ground controllers. But below them all was chaos. The ether was thick with confused exclamations: "The enemy are reproducing themselves." "It is impossible—too many hostiles." "I cannot control you." "Try without your ground control."

When the first wave of bombers arrived over Hamburg at 0103 hours, their crews found the searchlights groping blindly. Where beams did cross, others would quickly join them, and as many as 30 or 40 beams would build up to form a cone—on nothing. Radar sets controlling both searchlights and guns were useless. The gunners loosed round after unaimed round ineffectively.

The bombers made their runs on an almost defenseless Hamburg. The pathfinders' radar-aimed yellow markers had accurately described the target. Almost immediately, these markers had been fol-lowed by reds from a visual marker force and greens from the backers-up of the pathfinder force. The waves of bombers aimed their loads at the markers: scores of 8000- and 4000-pound blockbusters, thousands of 1000-pound bombs, a veritable rain of incendiaries. In general the aircrews could make out only the flashes of high-explosive bombs and a few shimmering fires started by the incendiaries. But at 0110 hours an explosion lit the sky for miles.

Bomber Command lost only 12 aircraft that night. The normal loss for such a raid would have been about 50 bombers; 35 or more had been saved by dropping 40 tons, 92,000,000 strips, of aluminum foil. Window had clearly been a great success.

But Sir Arthur Harris had already warned that the Battle of Hamburg was not going to be won in a single night: "At least 10,000 tons of bombs will have to be dropped. To achieve the maximum effect of air bombardment, this city should be subjected to sustained attack."

Bomber Command launched another attack at 0057 hours on July 28 when 722 bombers flew across the city. Within 15 minutes the crews saw a vast carpet of fire covering almost the whole northeast quarter of the city. Into this inferno succeeding aircraft were still dropping thousands of incendiary and high-explosive bombs.

During July less than 1.7 inches of rain had fallen on the city, and the previous day had been very hot; kindling was everywhere. Under a torrent of incendiary bombs, the fires took hold. With water supplies disrupted and the civil defense headquarters blitzed in the previous raid, the blaze raged unchecked. In principle, a firestorm is horrifyingly simple. A multitude of fires heat the air above them; as the hot air rises more air rushes in to take its place; this inrushing air fans the flames to even greater heat. Then it, too, rises and the process repeats itself so that the flames grow hotter and hotter.

This was what happened in Hamburg. Soon, in places, the temperature exceeded 1800° Fahrenheit. The mighty convection currents caused winds of up to 150 m.p.h. —twice hurricane force. The air sucked into the larger fires fanned the small ones and these, too, grew in size. Quickly the fires linked with each other until a built-up area 3½ miles long and 2½ miles wide was burning itself to death, nine square miles of fire. A highly populated area was going up in flames. The Hamburg civil defense chief reported: "The scenes of terror are indescribable. Children were torn from their parents' hands and whirled into the fire. People who thought they had escaped fell down, overcome by the devouring heat, and died in an instant. Refugees had to make their way over the dead and dying. The sick and the infirm had to be left behind by the rescuers who, themselves, were in danger of burning."

The following morning, July 29, Gauleiter Kaufmann appealed to all non-essential civilian personnel to leave Hamburg. Between dawn and dusk nearly one million civilians, many swathed in bandages, streamed away.

By night, Bomber Command came back July 30 and again on August 2. By day,

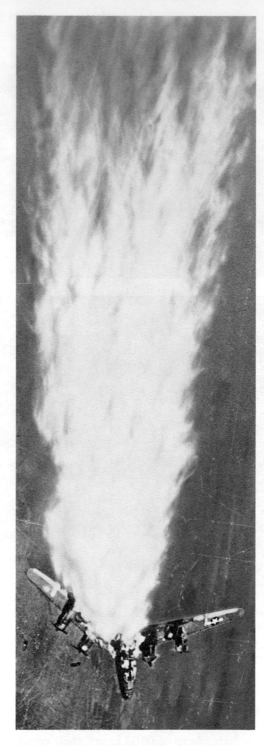

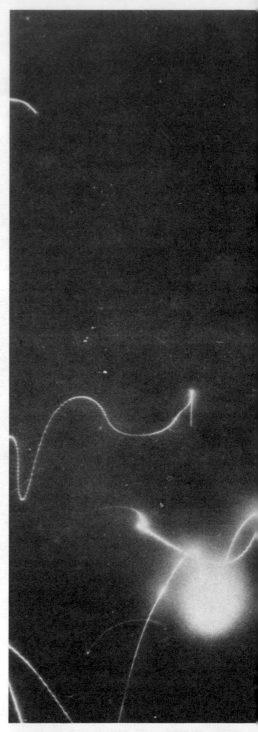

RAF Bomber Command raided Hamburg by night, the U.S. Army Air Force struck by day. Above right, the start of the July 28 Hamburg firestorm; above, an American bomber hit by German anti-aircraft fire. Gp. Capt. Johnnie Fauquier (right) was regarded as Canada's top bomber pilot.

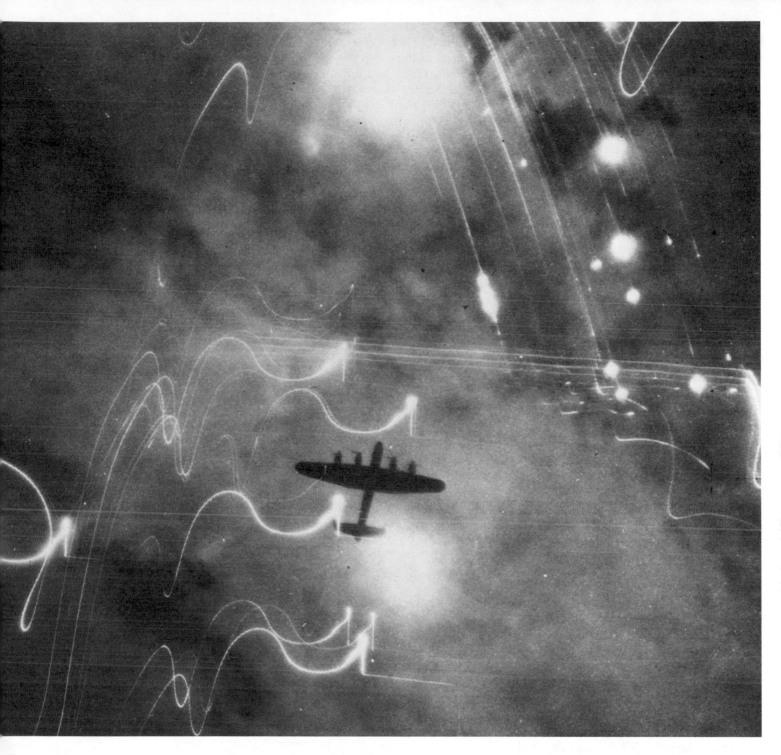

the USAAF struck Hamburg twice. Informed sources put the total number killed at about 50,000. The number of British civilians killed in German attacks up to this time was some 51,000; in one week the slate had been wiped almost clean. . . .

ALFRED PRICE

The effect of the raids went far beyond Hamburg. Adolf Galland, General of the Luftwaffe's Fighter Arm, wrote in *The First and The Last:*

"A wave of terror radiated from the suffering city and spread throughout Germany. Appalling details of the great fire were recounted. The glow of fires could be seen for days from a distance of 120 miles. A stream of haggard, terrified refugees flowed into the neighboring provinces. In every large town people said: 'What happened to Hamburg yesterday can happen to us tomorrow.' Berlin was evacuated amid signs of panic. In spite of strict reticence in official communiqués, the terror of Hamburg spread rapidly to the remotest villages of the Reich."

The Hamburg raids were a turning point in the aerial Battle of Germany. They convinced the Luftwaffe that defense of the home front must rank above all other operations. The first phase of the massive Allied bomber offensive lasted for a year and, from Hamburg on, it met top-priority resistance. The Germans found answers to Window and fought on. They not only refused to be bombed out of the war but rebuilt and revised and decentralized their productive facilities to a point where they were able to turn out more war goods in

1944 than ever before. And they fought back in the air with desperate efficiency that was fired, rather than cowed, by the threat of unconditional surrender.

Against this background, Canada's bomber men lived in two distinct worlds: one violent, the other quiet. Regularly the pilots, navigators, gunners and bomb-aimers passed from the one into the other. Night after night, in 1943, they flew to places like Hamburg and Berlin and the Ruhr. It *was* a violent world and the men who flew the bombers were, in the opinion of George Beurling, Canada's greatest fighter ace, the real heroes of the air war, the ones who did "the dirty and dangerous work." The figures bore him out. One quarter of all Canadians killed in World War II were bomber men—nearly 10,000 of them.

The survivors learned to be philosophical about it. They had to. "There were so many getting killed in those days," one Canadian pilot remembers, "that you couldn't afford to brood about it. When someone you knew got it, you just said 'too bad' and went out and had a drink for the guy."

They learned to be philosophical, too, about what they were doing to Germany. Canadian bomber ace Johnnie Fauquier, talking about the four-engine Lancaster, Britain's greatest bomber, said:

"The Lanc might be regarded as a tragic symbol. What it stood for was not a bit pleasant on either side. The German cities were massively defended. Thousands of guns ringed Berlin, Cologne, Hamburg, extending far out on all sides. Yet we burned out the guns at Hamburg in '43. We went there four times, and on the last night those guns were all burned out.

"There were sights you can't forget. Fire bombs, which set off as many as a hundred individual fires when they exploded, did the most damage. When you dropped thousands of them, the city looked like a vast pot of boiling lead.

"We were after military objectives: the seaport, armament works and so on. But there was another policy at work: demoralize the people, don't let them sleep, make them homeless, break their will. It's not a thing we bragged about. But those people were at war with us and they were very serious about it. Hitler called us 'air pirates.' Bomber pirates, ruthless, without conscience, without chivalry—unlike Hitler himself, apparently. Some of us were to

be beheaded if we were caught. It was one thing for him to bomb cities; to get it back again was something else."

By 1943, Hitler had lost much of the power he needed to bomb the cities of Britain. When the Canadian aircrews returned from their raids, they came back to a quiet world. Sixty percent of them still came back to the stations of RAF squadrons. The rest fought together in No. 6

Group, under the command of Air Vice-Marshal G. E. Brookes. Although only 60 percent Canadian at first, by the end 6 Group's air and ground crews were virtually all Canadian.

Their home bases were in the rolling hills and quiet villages of East Riding in Yorkshire. Group headquarters was Allerton Hall, a rambling old mansion known as Castle Dismal. Although the squad-

Hamburg (below) after its week of terror: 50,000 dead, nine square miles burned out in the center of the city. Purnell's *History of the Second World War* quotes from a "secret report" prepared for Germany's leaders: "Trees three feet thick were broken off or uprooted, human beings were thrown to the ground or flung alive into the flames by winds which exceeded 150 miles an hour. The panic-stricken citizens did not know where to turn. Flames drove them from the shelters but high-explosive bombs sent them scurrying back again. Once inside, they were suffocated by carbon monoxide poisoning and their bodies reduced to ashes as though they had been placed in a crematorium, which was indeed what each shelter proved to be. The fortunate were those who jumped into the canals and waterways and remained swimming or standing up to their necks in water for hours until the heat should die down."

Left: A Canadian bomber crew reports to intelligence officers after a raid.

rons were given numbers in the Canadian "400 series," they were better known by names as colorful as their adopted villages. There were the Goose and Thunderbird squadrons at Linton-on-Ouse, Moose and Ghost at Middleton St. George, Lion and Bison at Leeming, Iroquois and Bluenose at Croft, Tiger and Porcupine at Skipton-on-Swale, Swordfish and Leaside at East Moor, Alouette and Snowy Owl at Tholthorpe.

Just as soldiers of the Canadian Army became part of the life of Sussex and Surrey, the air and ground crews of No. 6 became part of Yorkshire. When the group's badge was created, it had a maple leaf superimposed on the rose of York.

Years after the war was over Peter Kirby, a Yorkshireman, recalled those days for writer David Carmichael of *The Canadian:* "On nights when the weather was too bad for flying, the bomber men would come riding on their bicycles into our village of Sutton-on-the-Forest. Some would go into the Black Swan pub but most would walk up and down the streets, talking to people, looking at the gardens and handing out gum to us kids. They were good to us. Not just the things they gave us, but the way they treated us—as if we were their kid brothers back home. They used

to take away my father's Alsatian dog and get it drunk. Once they did the same thing to our goat."

The Canadians helped gather Yorkshire's harvests, courted Yorkshire's girls, became regulars at pubs like the Punch Bowl, the Black Bull, the Shoulder of Mutton, and the Black Swan which they irreverently called the Mucky Duck. The people of Yorkshire accepted them with affection. There was, for instance, Mrs. Mudd, the self-appointed "fairy godmother" of the Canadians at Tholthorpe. Every station, wrote FO. Hugh Halliday in *The Roundel,* had her counterpart—a gentle, elderly English lady who went to great pains to lavish hospitality on the young men from far-off Canada. Mrs. Mudd even indulged in poaching to obtain fresh meat for "her boys." When the law finally caught up with her, the Canadians took up a collection to pay her fines.

They were a buoyant company, proud of their squadrons and their group and of men like R. S. Turnbull who rose from sergeant to wing commander in 11 months and Lionel Dupuis who jumped from sergeant to squadron leader in 13.

Said Halliday:

. . . Each squadron had its own form of initiation. It differed from station to sta-

tion. Sometimes a newcomer was merely spun around, sometimes he had to down a specified number of drinks. It was made tougher for westerners who were recognized as especially hardy men.

Every station had its peculiar features and its share of mascots. They ranged from stuffed rabbits and moose heads to live nanny goats. No. 427 Squadron had a lion cub, in keeping with its name, inspiring its "adoption" by Metro-Goldwyn-Mayer.

New crews quickly determined which bases in northern England served the best food. Stations were ranked as "one egg" and "two egg" bases. It was not uncommon for returning bomber crews to put down at the nearest field and some veterans claim that "two egg" bases received more aircraft than others on such occasions. U.S. Army Air Force fields, where delicacies such as ice cream and canned peaches abounded, were the most favored of all. . . .

The bomber men racked their brains for names for their planes and came up with choices like X-Terminator, Block Buzzer, Helzapoppin, Yehudi, The Champ. One was christened P for Poison and its four engines became Cyanide, Arsenic, Iodine and NAAFI Tea, in dubious honor of the facilities of Britain's Navy, Army and Air Force Institute.

But the other world, the violent world, never quite ceased to shadow everything they did. One day D. K. Findlay watched the preparations to go back to it. He wrote in *Maclean's:*

. . . Takeoff is at eight o'clock. The soft green of the English countryside is fading into gray. The sky is clear except for a bright band of pink clouds in the west. The aircraft are marshaled, stretched in a long line on the perimeter, fueled and bombed and ready. The aircrew were briefed three hours ago. They have just come over from the hangars in lorries, dressed in their flying clothes, and now they are sitting on the edge of the track with the ground crews. The bulky clothes hide the badges of rank. The lad stretched on the ground with his hands behind his head is an officer; the one stuffing a thermos flask into his boot is a sergeant. To each other they are "aircrew." They are very young, on the average about 22.

Someone says "there's the green light, boys." Without any command, they swing their bulky figures up through the belly hatches of their planes. At five minutes to eight, the motors of the lead aircraft turn over. . . .

One pilot said about takeoff, "It's funny how you take a last look around at the sun and the trees, things you ordinarily don't notice. And you think some. About your first day at school or the first time you went skating. You also think about the folks at home and how they're going to feel if you go missing."

In Sutton-on-the-Forest, Peter Kirby recalled, the village children used to go out to watch them take off. When they came back in the middle of the night, the children would lie in bed counting them. "They lost a lot sometimes," he said. "A lot."

In 2½ years, No. 6 Group lost 3500 men. In six years, another 6500 Canadians were lost with other bomber formations.

Of all Canada's bomber men, the ones who died and the ones who survived, probably the greatest, by widespread agreement, was Johnnie Fauquier. He fought in 1943 as commander of the RCAF's 405 Squadron, which had been posted from No. 6 Group to the pathfinder force. A native of Ottawa, he was a wing commander at 34 and his deeds were already growing into legend. A dapper, broad-shouldered man who preferred action to talk, he had a simple formula for leadership: he never

Alley Oop, hero of a then popular comic strip, adorns the nose of X-Terminator, a Halifax bomber of the RCAF's Snowy Owl Squadron. Ten thousand Canadians were lost in six years of bomber raids, mainly on the targets in Germany shown on the map below. Nearly 600,000 Germans died in air raids, compared with 65,000 Britons. Opposite: bomb victims in Mannheim.

asked another pilot to do something he would not do himself. The famous Australian pathfinder leader, Air Vice-Marshal D. C. T. Bennett, summed him up as "a thoroughly press-on type if ever there was one."

Unlike most Canadian wartime fliers, Fauquier was a veteran of the air long before he enlisted. Son of well-to-do parents and a former Montreal bond salesman and man-about-town, he'd turned his back on the sophisticated life to set up his own bush airline in Noranda, Que. By the time he enlisted in 1939, he'd logged more than 300,000 miles, most of them over the wilds of northern Ontario and Quebec.

He was born, people said, to fly. In the Lancaster he found the plane to match his skills. When 405 Squadron got them, he recalled, "our morale went up fantastically. The Lanc had no bad habits. You could dive her at phenomenal speeds. She flew as easily and dexterously as a Tiger Moth."

He proved it one night over Bremen in June 1942 when his squadron was trapped in the glare of searchlights and being slashed by flak and night fighters. Handling his Lancaster like a fighter plane, Fauquier dived from 12,000 feet to attack the assembly of searchlight and flak batteries. As he flew over them at 100 feet, his gunners opened up, smashing the searchlights and routing the flak crews. For weeks his feat was the talk of Bomber Command.

Over Hamburg, as part of No. 8 Pathfinder Group, his Canadians flew ahead of the main force to mark the route and the target with flares and "Christmas trees," tinsel-like phosphorus that hung in the sky like traffic lights. But Fauquier also had another job. He was deputy master bomber. His task, wrote Edmund Cosgrove in *Canada's Fighting Pilots,* was to fly over the target throughout the raid, directing the incoming streams of bombers to untouched areas. It was a dangerous job. Other planes came and went. His stayed until the last bomb had been dropped.

Within a fortnight Fauquier was doing the same thing over another target, which came to equal Hamburg in fame. Edmund Cosgrove writes:

. . . Since 1935 German scientists, under Wernher von Braun, had been experimenting with rocket-propelled guided missiles at a remote spot on the Baltic Sea called Peenemünde. The project had been top secret for years. As the war neared the end of its third year, Hitler began more and more to rely on Peenemünde to come up with the miracle weapon he needed.

But Allied Intelligence had discovered his secret. The sharp eyes of FO. Constance Babington-Smith, a photo interpreter, spotted a tiny black smudge on the runways at Peenemünde while examining photographs taken by reconnaissance aircraft. The smudge did not resemble normal runway wear and tear, so Spitfires were sent to take more pictures. These photographs showed oddly shaped aircraft around the runways. The black smudge was carbon left by the blast of burning gases ejected from experimental jets. The Allies had uncovered the Germans' robot V-1 flying bomb, The Doodlebug, which for a time was to rain death and destruction on England. The inaccurate but destructive Doodlebug was only the forerunner, however, of a far deadlier weapon, the V-2, a heavy guided missile.

The Allied Command decreed that Peenemünde must be destroyed. Six hundred aircraft were assigned to the mission, including every airworthy plane in Canada's 6 Group. Details were so secret that even the aircrews did not know what they were attacking. They were told Peenemünde was turning out improved radar sets for night fighters.

Bomber Command chose its top master bombers to conduct the raid: the RAF's fabled Gp. Capt. John Searby to lead, with Fauquier as his deputy. Their orders were simple: they were to wreck this target on the first try. If they failed, they would have to go back until Peenemünde *was* destroyed.

Accompanied by a force of light Mosquito bombers, the attackers would use the usual route to Berlin. The Mosquitos would make a feint attack on the German capital, while the main force made a last-minute turn north toward Peenemünde.

The raid took place August 17, and the deception worked at first. German night fighters were ordered inland to intercept the attack on Berlin.

Fauquier was over Peenemünde throughout the entire attack. He made 17 dangerous passes over the target, directing the waves of bombers and assessing the damage. It was a clear, moonlit night, ideal for defense. For 35 minutes Fauquier remained over the target, dodging flak, sweeping in at varying altitudes, until the last bomber was on its way home and the workshops, laboratories and living quarters at Peenemünde were blazing wreckage.

When the last plane had unloaded its bombs, Fauquier, too, turned for Britain. German fighters, fooled earlier, by now were either on the scene or lying in wait along the route home. Before the night was over 41 bombers had been shot down, 10 manned by Canadian crews. But large areas of the Peenemünde rocket site lay in ruins and many of Germany's leading experts in jet propulsion and rocketry were dead. The attack delayed the development of the V-1 and V-2 rocket bombs by a year, saving London from devastation. When the rockets were finally launched, they had neither the range nor the explosive qualities of the weapons destroyed at Peenemünde.

For his night's work, Fauquier won the DSO. He later rose to the rank of air commodore but volunteered to revert to group captain in order to do a third tour of operations as commander of the RAF's famous 617 Dambuster Squadron. His skill left even these veteran pilots a little in awe. As one put it: "He plants those bombs like he was threading a needle." By war's end Fauquier had won the DSO and two bars, DFC, two French decorations and from the British press the title "King of the Pathfinders." . . .   EDMUND COSGROVE

Pathfinders and master bombers and Window were part of a war within a war in 1943. Typically, as soon as Bomber Command used Window at Hamburg, the Germans began a sweeping reorganization of night-fighter tactics under a new leader, Gen. Josef Schmid.

They directed their twin-seater night fighters to the largest concentrations of Window and told them to forget their own radar sets and to search for bombers visually. They brought in single-seater day-fighter Messerschmitt 109s and Focke-Wulf 190s and grouped them over target areas. Like the night fighters, they sought out bombers in the glare of searchlights, of the giant fires below and of the pathfinders' markers.

These tactics worked, but they still relied for direction on the old Himmelbett Line. And there were large areas of Germany the line didn't cover. The Germans had to find some way to track the bombers that struck there.

They did it by letting the bombers betray themselves. The British and Canadian pathfinders used H2S, an advanced radar navigation device which scanned the ground below. The Germans built a chain of stations which could follow the distinctive H2S signals. Once they spotted the pathfinders' destination, they could pinpoint the target area. By late summer their toll of bombers was rising again.

The British, in turn, counterattacked. Into the wireless channels the Germans used to direct fighters to target areas, they began to broadcast a cacophony of wails, shrieks and moans to disrupt communication. Then they tried issuing fake orders in impeccable German.

The Germans responded by using more and more frequencies. And by fall they had come up with a new radar device for the night fighters which could see through Window with little difficulty. Called SN-2, it played an important role in the winter of 1943-44.

That was the winter of the Battle of Berlin. "We can wreck Berlin," Sir Arthur Harris told Winston Churchill on November 3, "if the USAAF will come in on it. It may cost us 400-500 aircraft. It will cost Germany the war."

Flt. Lt. Alfred Price writes:

. . . This was the kind of promise Churchill could not resist, and Harris was authorized to launch the Battle of Berlin. The American bomber force, however, had suffered

heavy losses in its daylight raids and could not join in the attack. Harris decided to go it alone.

The first attack was launched November 18, and only 9 of 444 heavy bombers failed to return. Losses in the next seven raids were surprisingly low, possibly because of the bad weather. But as the new year opened, they began to rise alarmingly and the appalling toll went on through January, February and March.

German exploitation of the bombers' own H2S radiations had achieved a high efficiency. By removing H2S, Bomber Command could have cut losses. But it would have deprived the force of the only radar bombing aid that could be used over Berlin, reducing its striking power considerably. If, Harris sincerely believed, Bomber Command could repeat the Hamburg pattern on five or six important cities, Germany would be bombed out of the war. The stakes were high enough to justify the greatest risks.

On March 30, Harris made his final attempt to smash a major German city before control of his force passed to General Eisenhower for the invasion of Europe. The target for 781 aircraft was Nuremberg.

Even before the leading aircraft had crossed the coast of Britain, the Germans had deduced their direction from H2S bearings. The Luftwaffe III Fighter Division assembled over radio beacon Ida, in the path of the bomber stream, in good time.

The bombers, losing cohesion because

of strong winds, advanced on a front 40 miles wide. Worse was to follow. Each minute gasoline burned in one engine produced a gallon of water given off as steam. Normally the steam dispersed, but on this very cold night it condensed, leaving long white vapor trails behind each bomber. The glow from a half moon gave the trails a phosphorescent quality.

As the bombers passed almost exactly over the Ida beacon, the waiting Luftwaffe III Fighter Division joined battle. Within minutes, horrified British and Canadian crews saw bomber after bomber going down in flames. This was the beginning of a running fight that lasted for 250 miles and drew fighter divisions from all over Germany. In all, 21 squadrons of night fighters, some 200 aircraft, went into action. They wrought fearful destruction.

The bombers' track from Ida on was clearly marked by the trail of burning aircraft on the ground.

Because of the violent winds and the night fighters, the actual attack on Nuremberg was diffuse and ineffective. For Bomber Command the cost was very high: 94 planes failed to return.

Sir Arthur Harris's daring attempt to end the war by strategic bombing had ended in failure. And the failure came close to crippling Bomber Command. In the 35 major attacks between November 18, 1943, and March 31, 1944, it had lost 1047 aircraft and had damaged 1682. Hard as it had been hit, Germany was still very much in the war.... ALFRED PRICE

By January 1, 1944, Canada's 6 Group had lost 340 planes in its first year, and the toll kept rising. It lost 52 over Berlin. Over Nuremberg, in that one disastrous raid on March 30, it lost 13.

But there was a firm new hand at 6 Group's headquarters at Castle Dismal, a man who believed that the answer to harsh challenge was stern discipline and arduous training. Air Vice-Marshal Clifford M. "Black Mike" McEwen arrived in February, a straight-shouldered, athletic-looking officer with a bristling black mustache. One of Canada's leading fighter aces of World War I—he destroyed 34 aircraft— McEwen was determined that his new command should rival the most disciplined unit in action. Edmund Cosgrove told his story:

... One of McEwen's first moves was to

order a full-scale program of flight training. For aircrews who were already veterans, this came as a surprise. Six Group had its own peculiar problems, however. Its flying fields were the most northerly in Bomber Command, the most distant from its targets. This meant its crews were in the air longer than any others. Moreover, the Vale of York was difficult for flying. Because of its rolling hills, the group's airfields were close together and landing circuits sometimes overlapped. Smog from nearby industrial towns combined with low clouds to increase the hazards of night landings.

The aircrews grumbled about the training program, but experts later credited it with the group's successes and low casualty rate.

Six Group found that Black Mike was no swivel-chair commander. Although there was a superstition about high-ranking officers riding in bombers during operations, McEwen's presence was soon taken for granted—he even became a good luck symbol. As the men saw it, when the man with the mustache was along things were going to be fine. They felt drawn to this colorful airman who wanted to share their danger and, when ordered not to, could not sleep while his men were on a raid.

McEwen changed another entrenched custom: the "50-mission look" which had grown out of the informal and sometimes sloppy attire of fighter pilots early in the war. He ordered his airmen to be properly attired, and as a result, 6 Group personnel were band-box trim in their dress. "They scorn casual attire," *Time* magazine wrote, "keep the wire in their caps, always look as if they were ready for a dress parade and consider themselves the cream of the RCAF."

It was good psychology, good for team spirit. Six Group men felt they had no need to wear the costume of combat veterans; they knew they had carried their share of the terrifying burden of the air offensive and that was sufficient....

EDMUND COSGROVE

Black Mike took over the group just as one era was ending. The attempt to bomb Germany out of the war was put aside. The time had come to attack her in another way: to destroy the German Army's communications and soften up its defenses for D-Day.

Life in the giants' shadow

After Britain's army straggled back from Dunkirk in June 1940, Lt. Gen. A. G. L. "Andy" McNaughton made the world conscious of his Canadian troops standing guard on England's south coast. They were among the few fully-trained and equipped soldiers on English soil and, in war correspondent-author Lionel Shapiro's words, their commander was "the answer to a propagandist's prayer. His iron-gray head, miraculously photogenic, was the epitome of a last-ditch fight."

Since leading the Canadians overseas in December 1939, McNaughton's popularity and prestige had kept pace with his command. This had grown from a division to a corps to the First Canadian Army of five divisions and two tank brigades. To McNaughton, it was "a dagger pointed at the heart of Berlin," and he dreamed that it would spearhead the Allied invasion that would liberate Western Europe.

By 1942 one correspondent was calling him a genius, and the *Saturday Evening Post* was extolling his army as "a motorized hell on wheels." Said *Time:* "Soldiers of Canada and elsewhere rate him the best soldier in the British Empire." Churchill consulted him, Roosevelt received him at the White House, and the Conservatives wanted him to be leader of their party. But in December 1943, this magnetic soldier was forced to retire as commander of the army he had built. It might be a small army by world standards, but McNaughton knew it was one of the best—better, he was sure, because it was all-Canadian. Convinced that Canadians fought best alongside Canadians, he refused to split their ranks to let them serve with the British. And, according to his biographer, military historian John Swettenham, McNaughton was finally ousted for this vehe-

Few generals knew as much about weaponry as Andy McNaughton. But his superiors felt the interest absorbed him too much in the field, and that perception contributed to his downfall. With McNaughton (left) is Lt. Col. J. E. Sager of the Westminster Regiment.

ment opposition to splitting his army, combined with his unhappy and, at times, bitter relations with both Canada's Defense Minister, J. L. Ralston, and Britain's top soldier, Gen. Sir Alan Brooke, Chief of the Imperial General Staff.

His brushes with Brooke went back to World War I, which was also when he came to the view that Canada should control its own army. Annoyed that Brooke and others still found it "convenient to regard us as British troops," McNaughton resolved to keep his army autonomous and intact. But to his—and Ottawa's—chagrin, the result was tens of thousands of Canadian soldiers cooling their heels in Britain. By mid-1942, they were still waiting to see action in a war they had volunteered to fight.

Then, in 1943, things came to a head. Ralston began to argue that it would be a

disgrace if at least part of the Canadian army didn't see action soon. Mackenzie King agreed, and so did McNaughton—up to a point. He accepted a role for the 1st Division and the 1st Armored Brigade in the invasion of Sicily on the understanding that both would return to his command after the Sicilian campaign. But they didn't return. Instead they were sent on to mainland Italy, where the 5th Armored Division joined them in a Canadian corps.

McNaughton became convinced that his beloved army would remain split, and spiritedly told Ralston it was wrong. He was convinced that the test of a nation's sovereignty was control of its forces. But by now his old adversary Brooke was telling Ottawa that McNaughton would not do as a field commander.

This combination of circumstances forced McNaughton out. He agreed it could be announced that he was retiring for health reasons and in fact, at 56, a medical exam did find him "below par." He came home in January 1944, bitter and angry, and promptly caused controversy by stating that there was nothing seriously wrong with him even if the government said otherwise.

McNaughton's downfall was related to the larger problems that Canada encountered in its contacts with Britain and the United States. The problems sprang from two conflicting factors.

The first was that Canada was fighting in a war of giants, but it wasn't one of them. The giants made the big decisions and ran the big battles. Even before McNaughton's removal, Canadians had to wait on the sidelines. On their own soil—at the Quebec City Conference of 1943—they watched while Roosevelt and Churchill and their advisers considered, among many other things, the role of thousands of Canadian soldiers in the D-Day invasion of Europe. The giants, as one general put it, "didn't call us to their councils."

The second factor was that Canadians were fiercely proud of a war effort that made their nation the largest of the non-giants. The nationalism that had flowered in World War I deepened and broadened in World War II.

These factors at times strained Canada's good relations with Britain and the United States. There were uneasy moments when Canada argued with both of its allies over control of Canadian forces, or became frustrated with a British tendency to speak for the Commonwealth as a whole and an American tendency to encourage the British to do so.

The Canadians fought at Britain's side, primarily with weapons of British design and in uniforms of British style. But they didn't like being called British troops; they bore Canada's name on their shoulder flashes, and they bore it like a banner.

The Canadian government stimulated nationalism with actions of its own, and suffered penalties for doing so. Primarily for reasons of national pride, Ottawa created the First Canadian Army, the first field army in Canadian history, and eventually paid for it with a bitter crisis over conscription in 1944.

The government rejected proposals for a single Commonwealth air force, then had difficulty running both a Canadian air force overseas and the British Commonwealth Air-Training Plan at home. It also rejected suggestions from its own naval advisers that most Canadian sailors serve with the Royal Navy, and set about expanding its own. The result, as one British expert put it, was that "Canadian groups were not until a late stage of the war in a state of efficiency which let them meet the U-boats on even terms."

Ironically, the navy, the smallest of the three forces, with the largest number of British-trained officers, ended up with the greatest degree of autonomy. Rear Admiral L. W. Murray became the first Canadian to command a theater of war—the northwest Atlantic and, in 1944, the whole North Atlantic.

In action, the Canadian army was completely under British command. But on occasion the British had to defer to Canada's wish to assert control over its own troops. One notable example: in July 1943, the 1st Canadian Corps joined the British Eighth Army in Sicily, but General Montgomery was unhappy that Canadian pressure had given him a corps headquarters he didn't want. When Lt. Gen. H. D. G. Crerar arrived to command the corps, Montgomery suggested he step down in rank to get battle experience. Crerar refused and Montgomery had to accept the decision.

Later, in northwest Europe, Crerar once again took orders from Montgomery, but the Canadian also gave orders to the British soldiers assigned to the First Canadian Army—a fact resented by the British. There came a time when Montgomery actually considered sacking Crerar but didn't. According to Col. Dick Malone, who served under Montgomery, there were similar "incidents when he compromised in the interests of Canada. Such tactics were completely foreign to his nature."

It was, however, the air force which caused the most problems. Despite Canada's insistence in 1939 on the creation of Canadian squadrons, there were only three overseas by 1941, and thousands of Canadians were in RAF units. So Ottawa sent outspoken Air Marshal Harold A. "Gus" Edwards to build 25 more squadrons. He found the reaction of the British apathetic or worse, and so irritated them that the more tactful Lloyd Breadner was put in his place. By the end of 1944 there were 44 Canadian squadrons overseas. But thousands of Canadians still served with the British, and the British directed all fighting operations.

Mackenzie King himself never again attained the importance he had in 1940 when he acted as intermediary between Churchill and Roosevelt. He came to regard the British leader with a mix of affection, awe and indignation. He long resisted Churchill's invitations to attend Imperial conferences and resented what Lester Pearson later called Churchill's "predilection for speaking in the name of the entire Empire and trying to integrate it more closely." Was it any wonder, King once recorded, that "Canadians began to like the Americans and were antagonized by the British"? Yet Canadian-U.S. relations also knew exasperation and concern.

Roosevelt's administration long rebuffed Canada's wish to have its own military mission in Washington. As Air Minister C. G. Power put it, "they were indifferent to or did not care to recognize Canada's status as a separate nation and full-fledged ally." Washington and London settled on their own matters in which Canada had a direct interest. Ottawa did eventually get the military mission it wanted and a larger voice but only after it was made to feel, as a diplomat put it, "like a nuisance."

At one point the Americans even wanted sweeping control of Canadian forces in Canada if they went to war. They backed off in the face of strong resistance and settled for a policy that was officially described as "mutual cooperation." This policy prevailed in Newfoundland. Both countries sent thousands of men into an island neither owned; neither took overall command, but the Canadians made sure their top officer was not of lower rank than the Americans'.

Once the United States did go to war, thousands of Americans poured into Canada to build the Alaska Highway, a northern pipeline, remote airfields and weather stations. Some U.S. establishments were finished before Ottawa even knew they were being built. The U.S. attitude, concluded American historian Col. Stanley Dziuban, was often "conditioned by amiable ignorance and disinterest" and a feeling that its needs should be accepted without challenge.

Mackenzie King never quite lost a wariness of both the United States and Britain. Whatever Canada did about fighting Japan after the defeat of Germany, he would record: "We may be sure we will get little credit" from either. He suspected that Roosevelt thought Canada should be part of the United States, and he fretted that the war might increase Canadian dependence on its neighbor. When Britain wanted to decide what the Commonwealth should do in the air war against Japan, Ottawa said Canada would run its own air force and make its own decisions. "It was," King said late in the war, "the strongest assertion yet of Canada's position as a nation."

To British overtures for a single Commonwealth postwar foreign policy, he said Canada would insist on complete sovereignty within the loose Commonwealth design. But the war taught him that Canada would have to go beyond that, into a world organization—it would become the United Nations in 1945—with more scope than the feeble League of Nations. King, and the country, had come a long way from the insular attitudes of the pre-war years.

The deadly destroyer

Haida makes dramatic war off the coast of France

HMCS *Haida* was the most famous Canadian warship of World War II and, pound for pound, as successful a fighting ship as the Allies produced. Built in England and commissioned in August 1943, she was a lean and powerful Tribal Class destroyer, designed primarily for attacks on enemy surface ships. Almost a pocket cruiser, she had a top speed of about 36 knots and tremendous firepower for a destroyer. Her armament consisted of six 4.7-inch guns in twin mountings, a pair of 4-inch high-angle guns, six Oerlikons, a multibarreled 2-pounder pom-pom gun, four torpedo tubes and 45 depth charges. Her crew of 250 was commanded by Comdr. Harry DeWolf. Like other Canadian vessels in her class—*Athabaskan, Huron, Iroquois*—she was named after an Indian tribe, appropriately the proud, seafaring Haidas of British Columbia's Queen Charlotte Islands.

After her trials, *Haida* spent four bone-chilling months escorting convoys to Murmansk in arctic Russia. Early in 1944 she and the other three Tribals joined the 10th Destroyer Flotilla in Plymouth, England, to take part in operations linked with the forthcoming Normandy invasion. In one series of patrols, the destroyers covered minelayers mining the approaches to every enemy harbor along the French coast and athwart the enemy's offshore convoy routes. In a second series of offensive sweeps, the flotilla hunted German convoys and their armed escorts and Germany's few remaining destroyers, which were a potential threat to the impending invasion.

In December, the British cruisers *Glas-*

gow and *Enterprise,* the latter commanded by Canadian Capt. H. T. W. Grant, had intercepted 11 German destroyers west of the Bay of Biscay. They sank three and heavily damaged a fourth. The Tribals were after the remaining seven. But by mid-April, *Haida* had sailed on 19 missions without contact with the enemy. Then on April 25,1944, she was made part of Force 26. With *Athabaskan* and *Huron,* the British destroyer *Ashanti* and the British cruiser *Black Prince,* she was sent to intercept three German destroyers expected to sail from St. Malo.

What happened is told by William Sclater in his book *Haida:*

. . . The wind was freshening that evening as *Haida* slipped her moorings at Plymouth. Ahead were the darkening seas of the Channel. Shrilly the pipe whistled: "Port watch to defense stations."

Guns and firing circuits were checked. "Darken ship" was piped and every man off duty headed below to get what rest he could while deadlights were screwed down on portholes, hatches were closed and thick canvas blackout curtains drawn. "Action stations" would be sounded at 10:30, if no enemy contact was made earlier. From then on the whole ship's company would be on duty till after dawn.

Ten o'clock passed and the watch below began to struggle into their heavy underwear, thick socks, sweaters, life jackets, ear protectors, steel helmets, lammy coats and other paraphernalia. Promptly at 10:30 the buzzers sounded and along the decks running figures moved with long practice to their stations. Swiftly and surely, *Haida* was readied for action.

It was quiet up on the open bridge under the stars. Visibility was good, about two miles. There was no moon. *Haida,* with *Athabaskan* close astern, formed the starboard subdivision of Force 26. To port was the cruiser *Black Prince* and beyond, screening *Black Prince* on the other side, were *Huron* and *Ashanti.*

Haida, the deadly destroyer, was commanded by Comdr. Harry DeWolf (later, above, a vice admiral and Chief of Naval Staff).

Force 26 was nearing the French coast and lookouts swept the seas and the skies through binoculars, alert for a flicker of light, a movement, the sound of aircraft.

Two hours passed and then the flash of gunfire was observed from shore batteries. A few minutes later there was more. The senior officer, in *Black Prince,* ordered a slight alteration of course off the land and almost at once the cruiser picked up radar echoes dead ahead. In a few minutes the radar contacts were confirmed by the four Tribals. There were four or five echoes and they appeared to be turning away. The time was 2:10 a.m.

"Increase speed to 30 knots," the cruiser signaled. The turbines hummed higher and the plot reported to the bridge that the enemy contacts were being held and closed. They appeared to be destroyers.

From senior officer Force 26 to destroyers: Increase to maximum speed to close and engage the enemy.

The crack of the cruiser's guns broke the darkness as she opened fire with star shell. Her role was to provide illumination while the destroyers closed in to engage. *Haida* increased speed again. The hum of her turbines rose to a high whine as she raced through the seas, with *Athabaskan* right astern. Her bridge crew watched a star shell burst and light the sea to the right of the bearing of the enemy ships. Nothing was visible.

"More left . . . more left," *Haida* signaled. The cruiser corrected and fired again. Another long, tense moment and then a star shell burst, flooding the horizon with sudden light above the indicated bearing.

Half a dozen voices blurted at once: "There they are, there they are!" Low on the horizon, five miles ahead, several little dark objects could be seen under the spread of star shell.

"Three, possibly four enemy destroyers, making to eastward under cover of smoke screen," reported the bridge.

"Open fire!" ordered the captain.

Within seconds there was a crash. The tracer track of four shells from *Haida's* two forward mountings arched across the night skies. The cruiser was firing steadily and so were the other destroyers.

Answering flashes came from the German ships and star shell burst along the horizon away over to port. The enemy seemed bewildered by the guns which had lashed at them so suddenly.

Force 26 swept on in formation, surprised to discover that it was gaining on German destroyers reputed to be much faster than the Tribals. *Haida* was abeam the enemy's smoke screen now. It was a light whitish color, about 100 feet high and some 500 yards off to starboard. Then the enemy's searching star shell found the bearing of the outer subdivision and caught *Huron* and *Ashanti* and the whole area between them in a greenish, ghostly brilliance.

Voices cried: "A hit! A hit!" as flame burst on an enemy ship and showed through the smoke screen. A few moments later the cry came again and, as the Tribals raced all out, the range slowly but inexorably decreased.

The illumination died suddenly and there was only darkness ahead. From the cruiser came a signal that her B gun turret was out of action and could fire no more star shell. Two minutes later her lookouts sighted a torpedo approaching and her captain ordered "hard aport." The torpedo passed up the starboard side. More enemy torpedoes were observed and, since her B turret was still out of action and her role was restricted to supplying illumination, the cruiser disengaged. The time was 2:48.

Command of the destroyers now devolved upon the captain of *Haida* and, by prearranged plan, illumination was provided by the second destroyer in each of the two subdivisions. At 3:01 two enemy destroyers were observed emerging windward of their smoke screen and then turning back in again. All ships in Force 26 were immediately warned to watch for torpedoes.

"E-boat at red two-five," called the officer of the watch, and every man on deck immediately looked 25 degrees off the port bow. A fast-moving object, throwing up a wide bow wave four or five feet high, could be seen approaching on an opposite course directly off the port bow. In the light of an enemy star shell, it swept past *Haida's* port side, about 400 yards off, then was lost to sight as the shell dropped into the sea. It was a British motor torpedo boat. Returning from a secret mission to France, it stumbled into the action by mistake.

Following the coastline as tightly as they could, *Haida* and *Athabaskan* found themselves in close to the enemy smoke screen and drawing ahead of *Huron* and *Ashanti*.

All four Tribals were making the same swift speed but the inside ships had the advantage of position as the coast veered south.

Heavy fire arched over the smoke screen from inshore, seemingly directed toward *Huron* and *Ashanti* as it was passing well over *Haida* and *Athabaskan*. All four Tribals were directing a furious crescendo against the enemy ships ahead, destroyers against destroyers now in equal numbers.

There was a minefield in this area but the German ships simply fled right through it and the Tribals followed. The shooting from the landward side was far astern now and seemed to be dying out. Ahead, too close, were the islands called Sept Iles.

The Canadian destroyers *Haida, Iroquois* and *Huron* steam into harbor in line ahead. The fourth Canadian Tribal, *Athabaskan,* was torpedoed and sunk in the English Channel in a battle with German destroyers.

290

Tense and alert, *Haida's* bridge watched for a sign that the German ships would try to break off the engagement. Enemy smoke floats could be seen at regular intervals, smoke pouring from them and being carried back in the wind. Farther ahead the smoke screen looked more irregular and then the bridge caught a glimpse of something, something that might be a ship trying to double back. It was a momentary glimpse, followed by a pause in which no star shell fell. *Haida* immediately altered course to allow her rear gun mounting to fire star shell. The first burst was directly over the target and revealed a destroyer streaking clear of the smoke screen. Every detail of her long hull with its high foredeck was visible in the light of the star shell; the silhouette was unmistakable to trained eyes.

"Elbing Class destroyer," barked the bridge. *Haida's* guns swung and steadied on the target.

In the eerie light, the Elbing was speeding along, apparently unmarked. *Haida's* guns crashed salvo after salvo.

The first was a direct hit. It caught the Elbing amidships, about ten feet below her main deck, and crumpled through her plates. Another crashed in aft, below deck level again, then one below the bridge, another just abaft the first.

Geysers of steam rose from the enemy's midships section. She slowed and stopped dead, red flame licking hungrily upward from where the salvo had gone home. Three fires joined rapidly to make an inferno of her main deck.

Athabaskan was firing now and hitting her, too. A salvo smashed through the high bows, and then another. More fires broke out until only the Elbing's upper bridge and afterdeck showed black in a sea of red.

Across the 2½ miles of flame-lit water, *Haida* could hear the roar and hiss of escaping steam as she and *Athabaskan* closed for the kill.

To seaward ahead of them *Huron* and *Ashanti,* having lost sight of the ships they'd been pursuing, turned and came back to the battle.

Survivors could be seen trying to get clear of the Elbing on a life raft but her guns were still being served and *Haida* had no alternative. A salvo, intended to strike below the waterline, crashed into the enemy's hull and sent raft and occupants hurtling skyward.

Her guns appeared to be silenced then.

There was only the roar and crackle of the flames and small, intermittent explosions. Circling like Indians, the Tribals sailed round her, close in.

Some men were still alive aboard the doomed destroyer. As the Tribals passed, two streams of tracer spat unexpectedly from high on her bridge and far back on her quarterdeck. They swept along *Haida's* after superstructure, spattered *Athabaskan's* length and beat on *Huron's* bridge.

Immediately a stream of colored tracer sped from *Haida's* Oerlikons and swept the enemy's decks, ricocheting over her bridge and after structure. The Elbing fired no more.

She still floated. Aflame from bow to stern, she seemed unsinkable. The Tribals closed again and salvoes rocked into her, smashing into the hull and sending up showers of sparks against the black masses of oily smoke billowing to leeward.

Then, as they watched, she rolled to port. Her bows dipped, she slipped swiftly under the sea and the darkness closed down. From *Haida's* foredeck came the sound of hoarse cheering as the gun crews watched her go. The time was 4:20.

Flashing their fighting lights, the Tribals formed up and stood away to seaward on course for England. The stars came out again and the night wind was fresh and sweet after the reek of cordite. The damaged enemy ships had probably made some protected port on the French coast. They would have to be left for another night. Dawn was near and it was time to go.

As *Haida* sped toward Plymouth, the ship was checked. There were several splinter holes through the hull and the rear gun deck; the forward messdecks were a shambles; the sick bay and the captain's day cabin, an emergency operating theater during the battle, had been swept by close-range fire. Several men had suffered wounds, all minor.

Sailing up harbor they were the subject of interested scrutiny. The word had got around, in the mysterious way it does in naval ports, and ship after ship saluted them. *Haida's* crew was happy and proud: she had acquitted herself well.

Destroyers will berth alongside to make good action damage, replenish magazines and prepare for sea.

Two evenings later, after an uneventful mission, *Haida* and *Athabaskan* were or-

dered out again. The crews would have preferred a night in port to get caught up on sleep, but minelaying craft were to operate inshore in French waters and the two Tribals were to cover them to seaward.

The order "action stations," delayed by DeWolf until midnight to allow *Haida's* crew as much rest as possible, brought all hands tumbling out. The moon was up and would not go down for another two hours. This was E-boat weather. On a moonlit sea, the bigger ships could be seen too easily from a long way off. *Athabaskan,* looking like a ship of silver as she cruised astern, was plainly visible. Like *Haida,* the lead ship, she was in the first degree of readiness.

An hour dragged by, then a second and a third. Around 3:30 a.m. a signal was received. Night radar reconnaissance had discovered two enemy destroyers making to the westward, close in on the French coast.

The captain, as senior officer, decided to steam on an intercepting course and close on them. At the point of interception, his ships would be at the western end of their area. Commander DeWolf hoped to turn the enemy and drive them eastward along the coast to prevent them escaping round the corner to Brest.

Less than 48 hours since the Tribals' last action; now the chance had come again. Heeling over as they turned, *Haida* and *Athabaskan* angled in toward the French shore, every man on the *qui vive.*

Have made contact with two enemy ships and am closing to engage.

The moon had gone down but there was a slight haze which made observation difficult. The range of the enemy ships was 7000 yards.

"Ignite," said the captain.

"Three stars, spreading left, fire!" ordered the illumination control officer, and the rear guns fired with a crack.

"There they are . . . two of them."

"Red five-oh, two enemy destroyers."

"Open fire," barked the captain.

Haida rolled with the recoil of her guns. *Athabaskan* was firing too, with star shell and main armament.

"Enemy making smoke and turning to eastward."

Haida and *Athabaskan,* with all guns bearing on the enemy, maintained their course. But after some minutes, according to plan, they turned toward the German ships to make themselves smaller targets for any torpedoes.

Through binoculars, *Haida's* bridge studied the smudges in the enemy smoke screen from which his gun flashes were coming. Enemy star shell was bursting overhead and between them. Other shells whistled overhead as the Germans brought their main armament into action.

A cry: "*Athabaskan's* hit!" Every head on *Haida's* bridge turned. From somewhere aft of the bridge a column of flame was shooting up, outlining *Athabaskan's* fore section in bold relief. As they looked, her B gun fired.

From the enemy ships came a frenzy of gunfire as they turned all their guns on the burning destroyer.

A stoker crawled out on *Haida's* afterdeck and opened a valve which turned on the chemical smoke producers. They soon put a dense curtain between the stricken ship and her enemies.

portable pump into position and started to get it ready to fight the flames rising behind them.

"After steering position out of action and ship settling by the stern, sir."

The young captain nodded. "All hands stand by their abandon-ship stations," he said.

The crew started to file off the bridge; the captain remained.

There had been no power failure. The tubes had been swung inboard and trimmed fore and aft and down there on the main deck the men still worked desperately to bring the pump into action. It was almost ready. They had put the feed line overboard and were fixing up the fairleads to the starter. There was a sudden rumble and a roar of flame blasted skyward. The after part of the ship became a holocaust. The deck tilted crazily, then collapsed. Only one man—CPO. Charles Thomas Burgess, the torpedo gunner's mate—survived. He had been flung forward from the

gashed and broken head, he looked dumbly at the rail. The ship heeled and he sat down heavily. He felt himself sliding and lay back to stop. It was no good. He went under the rail and into the sea. The cold water revived him and he turned on his side and swam with his good arm. The ship was sinking and he knew he had to get clear of the suction. He was a well-built man, in excellent condition, and a good swimmer.

About 50 yards from the ship, he looked back. *Athabaskan* was going. She had righted and now the bow was rising. Up up it came until it was nearly perpendicular, clear of the surface almost back to the first funnel. She seemed to poise there a moment and then she slipped swiftly down into the sea.

While *Athabaskan* lived her last moments *Haida* came under fire from the two German destroyers. Yet she continued to press her attack. If her gunners had been fast

In *Athabaskan* there was no panic. The propellers had ceased to function and she was being carried forward by her own impetus. The first report reached the bridge.

"Torpedo hit near the gearing room. Heavy damage aft the apron and Y gun collapsed. Steering gear out of action."

"Damage control party on the job?" asked the captain, Lt. Comdr. J. H. Stubbs.

"After pump is gone, sir. The forward pump is being taken back and rigged now."

"Try the after steering position," ordered Stubbs. "Better hoist out the sea boats but don't lower them yet. *Haida* is making a smoke screen and will try to take us in tow later."

There was feverish activity on *Athabaskan's* decks. Up forward the bosun's party rigged the towing hawser. Amidships, others hauled the heavy 70-ton

emergency pump and, dazed, thought he had landed in the forward stokehold. He staggered up again.

Great blobs of burning oil were falling everywhere. Men standing by the boats covered their heads with their arms and dashed blindly forward, trying to find shelter under the boats. Many plunged into the sea.

A signalman handed the ship's brass telescope from the bridge to one of his mates who put it in the whaler. More oil came down. The ship lurched violently and most of those who were left went over the side.

"Abandon ship!" Burgess, the TGM, heard the shout. He tried to grasp the rail to go over but his arm wouldn't move. Unaware that it was broken in two places and that blood was streaming from his

before, now they fought desperately. Far below them the lights in the forward magazines snapped out as a splinter hit came in. In the dim light of a couple of hand torches the supply parties passed heavy shells by hand to feed the guns until the emergency lighting came on.

"A hit!" The glow of fire broke out amidships on the first German destroyer and smoldered through the smoke. The second enemy ship appeared to be slowing and was falling behind the first. Commander DeWolf swung his guns to train on her.

One salvo punched out, another and another. Then a hit. High amidships flames mounted on the German destroyer's superstructure. Another salvo thudded into her and the flames spread. Then suddenly she let loose a vicious burst of close range fire—but it was directed at the other

Canadian Tribals teamed with British cruisers and destroyers in many actions in the English Channel and Bay of Biscay. Left: smoke obscures most of the ships in an engagement in Audierne Bay, between Brest and Lorient. Above: a Canadian Fleet Class destroyer, *Algonquin,* older and smaller than the Tribals, bombards German troops on a French coastal road.

fleeing German destroyer. The fire was returned. The two enemy ships were attacking each other. In the confusion they seemed unable to tell friend from foe.

Haida was surging toward one of them when a warning cry came from the officer of the watch: "Reefs ahead."

"Port 20," snapped the captain, and *Haida* heeled over and swung away from the shore. One enemy destroyer, burning furiously, had driven up on the beach, out of control. Swinging round, *Haida* let her have it again and again. When the shooting stopped, intermittent explosions burst through the smoke and flames.

Daylight was close now, too close for a long chase after other enemy destroyers up a hostile coast. *Haida* turned back toward the spot where *Athabaskan* had gone down. Smoke from the screen *Haida*

had put out was still drifting, though it was thinner now. "Fire a star shell over that bearing," Commander DeWolf ordered, "and let's see if there's anything left of the ship on the surface that we might bump."

Under the star shell, black clusters of survivors could be seen—three or four groups and numbers of small, separated figures. *Athabaskan* had left no other trace. As *Haida* closed, the flashing lights of survivors' life jackets could be seen more than three miles away.

The captain let the ship glide to a stop among the largest clusters. "All gun crews remain at their posts," he ordered. "Every man who can be spared from other positions will go to the main deck and help survivors inboard. All boats which will float are to be lowered and let go without crews. All life rafts are to be dropped. We'll wait for 15 minutes. Get as many on board as you can."

It was an eerie scene. Life-jacket lights were flashing; survivors were shouting and blowing their whistles. Inshore a red rock-buoy light was flashing. Behind that rose the low shore, a rocky promontory. And above it, a lighthouse flashed steadily.

Her engines stopped, *Haida* drifted sideways with the light wind. Survivors on the starboard side could be seen and heard, but the ship was drifting downwind faster than they could swim.

On the port side the wind was a help to the survivors. Lining the rail, *Haida's* men encouraged them to swim in. The sea was heavy with fuel oil and those who reached the ship's side were covered with it from head to foot. Few had strength left to climb up the scramble nets or the ladders and *Haida's* people went over the side and helped them. Six men formed a rescue line on one scramble net, pulling and pushing the survivors on board. Soon rescuers and rescued alike were filthy with oil. It was difficult to get a grip on the survivors since there was no handhold on the life jackets. To leave their arms free, the rescuers hooked themselves to the scramble nets with the clasps of their life preservers.

Haida's whaler went away. It was damaged but would float. The starboard motor cutter was not lowered—it had been shot full of holes. The port cutter was serviceable and three *Haida* men manned it, although they knew the ship could not wait for them. The coxswain, Leading Seaman William Maclure, directed the stoker, William Cummings, at the engine with his whistle, as if it was a routine trip. They turned away from the ship.

After 15 minutes Commander DeWolf started calling warnings: five minutes, four minutes, three, two, one minute. Then: "We are going ahead *now*." But he waited another few moments before giving the order: "Slow ahead." Men working over the side to rescue the *Athabaskan* survivors kept right on as *Haida*, alert for possible air attack, started up. The captain's first responsibility was the safety of his own ship and her company.

It was lighter now; the coast could be plainly seen. They were off Ile de Vierge. A raft came alongside with officers and men on it, and others in the water clinging to its lifelines. "Quickly now," said a voice on deck, "the ship's ready to go."

"Take the wounded first," said a man on the raft. The wounded were helped up. It was slow work for they could not help themselves. Many were burned. As *Haida* moved gently ahead, the men on the nets worked desperately to get the survivors inboard.

From somewhere at the back of the raft a voice was heard calling, "Get away *Haida*, get clear." A sailor said it was the voice of the young captain of *Athabaskan*. Other survivors said he had swum to a raft, resting his arms on it as if they were burned, and had encouraged them to sing.

A line parted with a snap and the raft swung away from the ship. One of the men on the net tried to hook it with his foot but missed, and it drifted astern. Unaware that the raft was alongside, the bridge had ordered the ship to move ahead and all men back to their stations. Daylight was imminent. It was time to go.

Unhooking themselves from the net, the rescuers scrambled up on deck. But two,

on the lowest level with water sweeping past their legs, couldn't make it. An officer climbed back down and tried to free them, but the sea was catching the boom at the foot of the scramble net and sweeping over their thighs so that they had to use both hands to hang on.

From the deck, another officer tried to haul the scramble net up. Just as others were coming to help him, the two seamen on the net let go. Torn loose by the seas sweeping past, they disappeared into the propeller-churned vortex of waters astern.

One Elbing Class destroyer hit and driven ashore in flames near Ile de Vierge. One Elbing Class destroyer damaged, escaped to eastward. Athabaskan torpedoed and sunk. Have picked up survivors and am returning to harbor. Request fighter protection—Haida.

Dawn was coming up when *Haida* cleared the land. As she sped swiftly seaward,

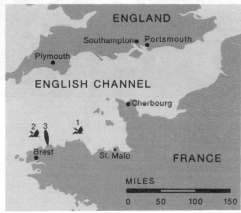

Torpedo los! (Torpedo away!) A "tin fish" is fired from a German destroyer in a battle with Allied surface craft (left) in coastal waters. The map shows where (1) *Haida* and *Athabaskan,* with *Huron* and the British destroyer *Ashanti,* sank a German destroyer April 26, 1944; (2) *Athabaskan* was sunk April 29; (3) *Haida* drove a German destroyer ashore in flames.

every man was at his action station and lookouts searched the skies.

Below decks, in the dim light of the battle lamps, survivors seemed to be everywhere. Every blanket and sheet, lammy coat and sheepskin had been requisitioned to wrap them in. In the after flats the air reeked with fuel oil. Heaps of soaked clothing lay where it had been stripped off. The surgeon and his assistants worked ceaselessly, administering morphine, treatment for burns, and a blood transfusion for a serious case in the captain's bunk. It was cold and many of the half-frozen men shivered in their blankets. All electric radiators and heating pipes had been shut off to reduce fire hazards when the ship went to action stations. Now, with everything battened down and the reek of oil everywhere, not even smoking could be permitted. Most of the men were quiet, glad to be free of the cold, oily sea. But they couldn't forget that back off the French coast were others, drifting on rafts and clinging to a few pieces of wreckage—all that remained of a good ship and her company. With them, too, were three members of *Haida's* crew in the ship's motorboat, men who had put other lives before their own. There might even be five—if the two men swept off the scramble net had been extremely lucky.

Both the sailors swept off *Haida's* scramble net had gone under as the wash of the sea along the hull sucked them down. They turned end over end in the churning water above the propellers, but their life jackets brought them up. When they surfaced they were in the wake of the ship.

They had survived almost certain death. Above them the stars still shone in the paling night sky. Inshore, France was in plain view. England and safety were over 100 miles away. They decided to float until they got their bearings.

Some distance away another man watched *Haida* go, a man with a badly broken arm and a gashed face, Charles Burgess, the torpedo gunner's mate of *Athabaskan.* He could have reached *Haida.* Why he didn't shows the stuff that makes a navy.

Swimming away from the sinking ship, Burgess had come across *Athabaskan's* coxswain in the water. They knew that if the survivors were grouped in life rafts together, there might be a better chance of survival. They set to work bringing the

295

isolated survivors, clinging to bits of wreckage, back to the life rafts.

When *Haida* returned, they were helping a young seaman get to a raft. In the semi-darkness they looked at each other, one thought in their minds. Both knew they could reach *Haida* on their own, but they would have to abandon their burden.

As if sensing their thoughts, the burned, half-conscious lad muttered, "Don't leave me." That was that. They continued toward a raft and by the time they reached it, *Haida* was preparing to go. They brought others in, all they could see, and then, worn out, sought refuge themselves.

The coxswain found a handhold on one raft but there was no place for the TGM. He swam to another. It was full and so was the cork float he came to next. Everywhere it was the same grim story. Tiring fast, Burgess swam slowly away and, with a last effort, turned over on his back and floated.

Things were getting hazy. He didn't feel the cold chill of the Channel any more. Warm slumber seemed to be creeping over him. It was pleasant and he had no strength left to fight it. Then, dimly, he heard voices

far back in his mind and a big shadowy thing seemed to loom over him. He felt strong hands haul him clear of the water. They laid him gently down by the shelter of the engine of *Haida's* motorboat.

"What ship?" he muttered.

"It's *Haida's* boat."

"Good old *Haida,*" said Charles Burgess and passed out.

The motorboat had been busy. Maclure, Cummings and Able Seaman Jack Hannam, the bowman, had decided the best plan would be to first pick up the men who had been unable to reach a raft. They had hauled in four shivering sailors when they saw *Haida* getting under way. To line up her course so they could follow later, they swung a quarter mile astern and ran in her wake. They were about to turn back toward the *Athabaskan* survivors when Hannam heard a voice hailing him.

He stared at the dark water, imagining he had heard the voice of a chum. It must be hallucination; his friend was in *Haida*. But the voice sounded again and this time it was stronger, and unmistakable. "Hi, Jack," it called. "How about a hitch."

Just before she paid the price of admiralty, *Athabaskan's* crew was addressed by Vice Adm. Percy Nelles, head of the Canadian Naval Mission Overseas. Standing on a catwalk straddling the torpedo tubes, Admiral Nelles told the men of *Athabaskan* of the pride their country felt in their achievements—and he told them of the possible price. These men had seen other ships perish. Some they had helped along the way with blazing guns. They listened—serious, attentive, knowing. But what they could not know was that in a few dozen hours they, too, would be scrambling for their lives in the oil-covered waters of the Channel and that many shown here would be dead.

from *H.M.C.S.,* by Gilbert A. Milne

The astonished bowman saw a dark blob. There, grinning up at him, was his friend from *Haida*.

It was a vigorous ghost. "Give me a hand up," it ordered. "This water's cold." It was one of the seamen swept off the scramble net. Feeling cold, he had decided to swim and had sighted the motorboat. Once aboard he quickly directed them to the other lad, still floating 200 yards ahead. Both were in good shape.

With that, their good luck deserted them. The boat's engine spluttered, stopped and refused to start again. Helpless, they drifted with the wind and tide. On the port side they discerned another floating figure and, ripping up floorboards for paddles, maneuvered the heavy motorboat toward it. They hauled in another survivor, a far-spent signalman.

It was heavy work handling the improvised paddles and they were about to give up when Hannam sighted yet another figure, floating on his back. At first they thought he might be dead, but then they saw an arm move feebly. It was Burgess, the TGM.

The men in the motorboat could see the German destroyer still burning furiously on the beach. There came a sudden flash and then a violent explosion; the flames had obviously reached a magazine. In the motorboat the crew and the survivors who could stand got to their feet and cheered.

Precious minutes were slipping away. To the eastward they could see *Athabaskan* survivors on rafts. It was full daylight now. They wondered if they could get the engine started in time to rescue some of the men on the rafts before the enemy spotted them. But the stoker, Cummings, was having a difficult time. Those who were not helping him watched the sky and the land. The wounded Burgess still lay unconscious.

"Something's coming up round that headland," said Maclure. There were ships, three of them, in line not more than four miles away.

"Minesweepers!" said Hannam.

They watched the German ships stop near the other survivors some three miles east. Two seemed to be going closer to pick them up and then, with sinking hearts, they saw the third minesweeper get under way and steam directly toward them.

Cummings lifted a hammer and, in a last frantic effort, smashed it down on the engine intake and pressed the starter button.

It caught. Coughing and spluttering, the engine started. "Give me a hand," yelled Cummings. "Hold this ruddy plug in place." Half a dozen hands reached to help him as the engine steadied into the sweetest music they had ever heard. The motorboat surged ahead, the coxswain steering directly away from the approaching enemy.

Their first quick elation was momentary. The German ship was slowly but steadily overtaking them. The original lead of 2000 yards had been reduced to almost half that. Tensely, they waited for a shot to come whistling overhead. But the minesweeper suddenly altered course and headed away. Why they did not know. Whatever it was, they thanked Providence and kept on going.

Seven miles offshore the engine spluttered and died again, but they were in better condition than they had been to start with. Sun and wind were drying their clothes. Their cigarettes had been soaked but they spread them out to dry on the engine cover. Someone produced a pipe and when the tobacco was ready, they filled it up and passed it from one to another. Then Cummings and two assistants went back to work on the engine.

It was about nine o'clock. The stoker stopped, listening. The others heard it too. Faint and distant the sound of aircraft. They could see them now, two fighters flying low. They stood up, waving and shouting. Maclure fired a red flare into the sky. The two planes thundered toward them.

Sweeping in, about 12 feet above the surface and 100 yards off, they went past on each side. The men in the boat could see the pilots looking at them.

A seaman stopped waving suddenly and, with a yell of "Krauts!", ducked down by the bulwark. Their faces grim, they watched the Messerschmitts go. At first they thought the planes would circle back to machine-gun them but the fighters made directly for land. They knew, however, that they would be reported. Without a word, they all turned impulsively toward the engine.

Cummings had done a good job. The engine started. It was a bit ragged but the motorboat started to forge ahead.

They were tired and hungry. They needed food and medical supplies. There was little they could do for the unconscious Burgess but try and keep him warm. They were a long, long way from a friendly

harbor yet they were hopeful and cheerful. *Haida*, they knew, would report them. They held course northward toward England.

Around noon the motor failed again, but they got it going. This time it ran steadily. About 6:30 in the evening they saw two planes coming from the direction of France. Believing they were the German fighters, they ducked for cover and it was not until they were almost overhead that they saw the RAF markings. They went a bit crazy, waving and signaling "Canada."

They were spotted. The two fighters stayed above them for an hour and then were relieved by two more fighters and a bomber. About ten o'clock one of the planes came in close and circled. Then they saw a ship coming. It was a rescue launch.

In all, 44 of *Athabaskan's* crew had been saved and 83 had become prisoners of war. But *Athabaskan's* captain, Lieutenant Commander Stubbs, and 128 men were lost. . . .   WILLIAM SCLATER

By the end of 1944, when *Haida* sailed home for a major refit and a warm welcome in Halifax, the 10th Destroyer Flotilla had sunk three destroyers, one U-boat and 31 other enemy ships and heavily damaged 17 others. *Haida* herself had killed two destroyers, a U-boat and 15 other ships. Her name had become famous throughout Canada. When it was announced long after the war that *Haida* was to be sent to the scrapyard, a public subscription was started to save her. Today she is berthed in Toronto harbor, a monument to the nearly 100,000 Canadians who served in the Royal Canadian Navy during World War II.

When *Haida's* own veterans visit the ship, they may recall sentiments like those expressed one time by one of her crew. "There isn't a man aboard," he said, "who would trade this ship for any other. When she's fighting, she almost seems alive."

Closeup:

Herbie

During World War I Canadians chuckled at the antics of Old Bill, the famous cartoon soldier created by Britain's Bruce Bairnsfather. In World War II they had an Old Bill of their own. His name was Herbie—a small, chinless, wistful-looking character who epitomized the "little man" ensnarled in military red tape. Hapless and harassed—and always in hot water with his superiors—Herbie was very human and very true to life. It was this that endeared him to Canadian soldiers. In Herbie they could see something of themselves, and through his misadventures they could laugh at their own troubles, at authority and at the stupidity and folly of war.

Herbie's creator was Sgt. W. G. "Bing" Coughlin who merged his talents as a professional artist with his experiences as a frontline soldier. Coughlin landed in Sicily with the Princess Louise Dragoon Guards, a reconnaissance unit, and went on with them to Italy. There his cartoons won him a job with *The Maple Leaf,* the army's daily newspaper, but he kept slipping back to the front to keep his work fresh and true. It was on the Italian battle lines that Herbie came to life.

For what he did to boost troop morale Coughlin was awarded an MBE and mentioned in dispatches. After the war, he and Maj. J. D. "Doug" MacFarlane, editor of *The Maple Leaf,* gathered the best cartoons and put out a book called *Herbie.* In it MacFarlane sums up the cartoon character who became Canada's most laughable and loveable soldier:

...Herbie *was,* in fact, the Canadian Army, the ambassador-at-large who almost missed the troop train for Halifax, got lost in the London underground and drunk in the Queen's at Aldershot, failed to salute that flag car at Leatherhead, holed up with a simply delighted English family on Exercise Spartan and was unholed by the provost. He was first in the bully-beef barter queue in Sicily, thrown for a loss by vino rosso, midwife at a bambino's birth in Italy. He stubbed his toe on a Normandy beach and became D-Day's first casualty thereby. He fought and franc'd his way through France and Belgium, fell into an Amsterdam canal, thought V-2 fluid was hopped-up calvados, was brought back to life and came home.

He was strictly an army guy. He beefed, moaned, cursed, and groaned. To him, all brass was tarnished, particularly any associated with hats. Anybody with hooks on his sleeve was a public menace and shoulder adornment was something to be shunned.

"HANG ON TO THE CAT, WE'LL TEST THIS ONE NEXT."

The grub was lousy because the cooks were morons, and anyway British rations shouldn't even happen to a dachshund. No battledress ever really fitted and web equipment was a snare and a delusion. Pay parade was such a constant source of disappointment that financing one's operations could become an excruciating experience when the bottom dropped out of the bully-beef and blanket market. The dentist jammed uppers in a mouth that needed lowers. The MO's prescriptions were limited to pills called No. 9s and a gargle that didn't even taste like alcohol. Nobody believed that he'd been sick and couldn't get back from leave . . . 14 days CB [confined to barracks].

The army was hell.

But in his own rebellious, civilian way, Herbie was known to like it at times. He got around and he had his moments. He was free with his dough and the women were free with him. He told them about his gopher ranch in Vancouver, his country home in Oxbow. He poured an unhealthy potion from the bottle he had bummed from the sergeant (liquor issue limited to rank of sergeant and above), demonstrated a brand new Canadian encircling movement, and the women loved it.

He was suitably impressed by Westminster Abbey and the Tower of London, paid his respects to equally famous characters in Madame Tussaud's, found out, on leave in Aberdeen, that at least one of his forefathers had come from Scotland, with soda. He introduced some absolutely new words into the Italian, French and Dutch languages, burped sympathetically with Mount Vesuvius, gawked at the Eiffel Tower,

"WHAT I WANT TO GIT MOST OUT OF THIS WAR .. IS ME!"

gaped at the Vatican, was awed by the opera, pub crawled, got drunk, got sick, got homesick, got home.

He had as good a time as military law would allow, and a much better time when he was breaking it. Relatively speaking, it wasn't much but he made the most of it. He was brave, fought well and hard. He was scared green at times. He was roasted. He was frozen. He gulped mepacrine tablets and turned yellow. Then he had jaundice and turned more so. He swallowed ascorbic acid tablets and had violent nightmares about corned beef and dehydrated cabbage. He had malaria and shook. He had a hangover and shook. He had a night patrol and shook. He made seven straight passes in a crap game and the boys shook.

He gave the Limeys cigarettes and stole jeeps from the Yanks. He bulldozed his way through Italy, France, Belgium, Holland and into Germany. He had a smell of Africa. And in all his travels he saw many things he didn't like, and a few he did. For the first time, he really came to appreciate his own country. He was proud to be a Canadian. He didn't like being called "British troops." He was a Canadian. He came from Canada. His first name was Herbie, his second name Canadian. Pte. Herbie Canadian.

That was important. . . .

J. D. MACFARLANE

Breakthrough

In the Liri Valley, the Canadians shatter the last great barrier guarding Rome

There were two wars in the Italian campaign: the war when the sun was hot upon the land and the war when it was not. In the sunshine there were great and splendid hopes. Then the rains fell onto the long, bony peninsula and the rivers came large and bloated down off the mountains, seething to the sea. Winter cold and wet followed and the front became a prison only spring could break.

After Ortona, the Canadians had known the winter war at its worst—static, bloody and lonely. But now the spring had come and in May 1944 the sun was high. Across the narrow land, 22 Allied divisions faced 22 German divisions in a restive quiet that masked great plans. British Gen. Sir Harold Alexander was preparing his 15th Army Group to strike for the spectacular prize of Rome, and beyond that perhaps for a larger hope: to rid Italy of the enemy before the year was out.

On the German side, there was only one question: where would the greatest blow fall? It would fall, Alexander decided, around Cassino.

In secrecy, as part of a huge deception, the Canadians pulled out of the Adriatic front and moved inland till they could look upon Monte Cassino, the 1415-foot mountain that had become one of the legends of the war. The Allies had decimated one division after another trying to get past this rock with its ancient monastery on the crest. When all else failed, they had bombed the monastery itself. But still Cassino held.

Immediately below it, to the west, lay the long, flat corridor of the Liri Valley, the one inviting avenue northward through miles of rugged hills. To get into the valley, Alexander had to break through a first, vicious defense wall called the Gustav Line, hinged on the Gari River which ran below Cassino's hill. Beyond it, in the mountains and in the valley itself, he faced a greater obstacle, the Hitler Line.

Fate had drawn the Canadians to what military men had studied for years as one of the classic defense positions of Europe. Here, near Cassino and facing into the valley, Alexander was massing the bulk of the Eighth Army—eight divisions and three armored brigades—into an area just ten miles wide. To the west, the American-French Fifth Army was set to strike through the mountains between the Liri and the sea. Farthest west of all, on the coast and actually behind the Hitler Line, Anglo-American troops waited to break out of a beachhead that had been established at Anzio in January in an abortive effort to turn the Germans' flank.

The offensive began late on the night of May 11, a night when the whole world seemed to rock with the light and thunder of thousands of guns shooting across miles of Italy, from Cassino westward to the sea. Below Cassino, the three regiments of the 1st Armored Brigade bore Canada's banner and, with the 8th Indian Division, made an assault vital to the whole offensive. Over a period of days they broke across the Gari River and through the fixed and violent defenses of the Gustav Line. Cassino held, held for days and then, outflanked, it fell too. The Eighth Army was firmly into the Liri Valley.

Rampaging French-African troops had loosened the whole front by breaking through in the mountains to the west. The Germans began to retreat to the Hitler Line; hastily they renamed it the Dora Line and, on orders from Hitler himself, prepared to defend it to the death.

The time of action had come for the 1st Division. The veterans of Sicily and the Moro, their ranks built up by reinforcements, had been held in reserve. Now they came forward to approach this miniature Atlantic Wall of steel and concrete and many guns. For the Canadians, it was an historic moment. For the first time since 1918, a Canadian corps was to attack on a European battlefield. Lt. Gen. E. L. M. Burns' 1st Corps had two divisions. Maj. Gen. Chris Vokes' 1st Division, with tank support, would assault and break the line. Maj. Gen. B. M. Hoffmeister's 5th Armored Division would drive through the hole they made.

The 1st Division hoped, at first, that there would be no major assault at all, that the Germans would withdraw from the Hitler Line in the face of the French successes. At times during their approach, they had to fight hard. At times, they didn't. Peter Stursberg of the CBC saw them in one of these lighter moments, saw infantrymen whistling and singing as they marched single file through a wheat field. "It was the first time," he said in a broadcast, "that I'd heard our soldiers singing like this. They were new troops, young men fresh from Canada although already they were bronzed by the sun of Italy. Everyone in our jeep was stirred by the happy way they were marching into battle."

There was no whistling and singing two days later. Along a 2000-yard front between the towns of Pontecorvo and Aquino, General Vokes drew up his 1st Division for a major frontal attack upon one of the toughest objectives Canadians ever faced. The Germans had not withdrawn from the Hitler Line. They were in position, ready.

"My boys move in tonight," Padre Roy Durnford of the Seaforth Highlanders wrote in his diary. "I see them off. How can one ever forget the scene? New boys with fears hidden under quick smiles and quick seriousness; old campaigners with a faraway look in their eyes. It is the hardest thing to watch without breaking into tears. I go up first thing tomorrow morning. The attack is at dawn."

The Hitler Line assault, as Canadian riflemen lived it that dawn and day of May 23, was described by Colin McDougall in *Execution,* a fictional re-creation based on his experiences as a company commander in the 1st Division's Princess Patricia's Canadian Light Infantry:

. . . Here, lashed on by the half-crazed adjurations of his Führer, Field Marshal Albert Kesselring had constructed the one last, irrevocable line beyond which the road to Rome lay open. Hitler commanded that it be held at any cost.

Forests had been felled to establish enfilading fields of fire; excavating machines had remodeled the earth; tons of concrete had been poured; steel and reinforced concrete structures had taken shape. Panther tank turrets with long snout-like guns embedded in concrete emplacements; connecting bunkers tunneled deep in the ground; anti-tank ditches scientifically sited; belts of wire planted everywhere. And mines: anti-tank Teller mines, S mines and Schü-mines. An S mine is a canister of 350 ball bearings packed round a core of explosive; on contact the canister springs five feet above ground and explodes its charge. A Schü-mine is simply a small box of picric acid designed to blow a man's foot off.

The steel and concrete were impervious to bombs or shellfire. The defenders had only to man their positions, and then kill anyone who was foolhardy enough to attack. They had built their Führer an impregnable line defending Rome, the kind of defensive position a general dreams about. And yet every general knows any line of defense can be broken—if the attacker is strong enough and willing to pay the price. Even the Adolf Hitler Line.

At 0459 hours, somewhere in the rear, an over-eager gunner fired the first round of the attack. Seconds later 800 guns were firing at once; the noise shivered, pounded and possessed the world.

The troops had been stirring for an hour. In predawn darkness they had a mighty breakfast around the cook trucks: porridge, bacon, bread and jam, burning mess-tins of tea. Then the first cigarette of the day as they trudged through the meadows to the forming-up points. There they sat and waited for the barrage to begin.

In that roaring surf of noise the churning of tanks into position was soundless. Infantry platoon commanders grinned up at tank troop commanders. Every soldier was grinning, delighted at the torrent of noise made by the guns.

As the sun topped the Apennines, the infantrymen hefted their weapons in their hands. They peered through the rolling mist toward the forest and the objective waiting beyond.

Canadian troops move up to the Hitler Line through Italy's vineyards and farmlands. A Canadian corps was about to go into major offensive action for the first time since 1918. But there was an ironic touch. The corps had been established in Italy months earlier after long, heavy pressure on Britain by Ottawa, which didn't want to wait any longer for the invasion of France. France was invaded two weeks after the corps first attacked in Italy. Many Canadians in Italy mastered enough of the language to converse with the natives—and among themselves—in something they called Vino Italian. Canadians who already spoke English and French became modestly trilingual. Said one French-Canadian soldier the morning after a heavy German shelling of the house he was in: "Ça shellait hier soir sur la casa!"

At first Capt. Bill Begg had been surprised to find so much forest still standing. But he quickly realized that the woods were tank traps: they forced the tanks to follow a predetermined route, mined and under enemy fire. In front of the line itself, he knew, the cover had been cleared for more than 100 yards on the attacking side of the wire.

Captain Begg had B company deployed beside a track, a kind of wide logging trail which led through the woods directly to the line. They were to follow behind D company, with nobody on their right flank. Bill Begg did not like the looks of that exposed right flank. It was going to feel naked being overlooked by those mountains, and once beyond the start line they would probably come under ground fire from enemy positions on the right.

He looked about him at the waiting men. The platoon commanders kept their casual glance on him, alert for signals. He looked in the faces of the men and found nothing but readiness. Some were new reinforcements, but most were veterans; many of the men had been with the company since Sicily. Begg looked at them objectively. He saw them the way the British staff officers who planned this attack must have visualized them: lean, hard, stripped for action. They knew exactly what to do at any given moment of battle; they had pride in their competence; each individual knew himself part of a superbly trained whole. They deserved the title of shock troops, assault troops. In this meadow were four companies of assault troops, ready.

In the final minute before the infantry assault the artillery fire thickened with a last, desperate outpouring. At 0559 hours Captain Begg raised his hand above his head. Everywhere his soldiers came to their feet; his platoon commanders stared at his upraised hand. Lips moving, Captain Begg was counting aloud, and then his hand started down. At 0600 hours the first wave of attackers crossed the start line.

Wherever he looked Bill Begg saw men falling—sliced down by shell fragments, bowled over by machine-gun slugs. A tank seemed to get hit every few yards and dazed troopers bailed out into the stream of machine-gun fire. The German artillery was merciless. But the worst part was the small-arms fire from the right flank.

Begg saw the end of forest. Ahead was meadow blazing in sunshine, a glimpse of wire, an ugly tank turret peering from concrete. The men of D company were out in the open meadow, running for the wire.

At the edge of the wood was a fold of covered ground. Begg threw himself down and signaled those behind to do the same.

The frontal fire alone, Begg thought, might have been surmountable; it was the fire from the flank that was murder. To the left he saw a wireless aerial in a ditch alongside the main track. There, only ten yards away, was Colonel McNabb, microphone in hand. Begg ran over.

The signaler lay dead by the set. Colonel McNabb was bleeding from small perforations in his face; a fold of his scalp dangled over one eye.

"Smoke!" Colonel McNabb roared into his microphone. "I've got to have smoke to cover the right flank. Smoke—for Christ's sake—*smoke!*" He was not in the least aware of his wounds or of Begg's presence —only of the microphone in his hand.

Yes, Begg thought, smoke would help, but it really wouldn't change things. He glanced to the front again. There were tanks out in the meadow, but none seemed to be moving; most were burning. He saw the figure of an occasional lone infantryman bob forward in the grass. He stood up then and walked back, with no appearance of haste, to his former position. Sergeant Major Mitchell and the others were lying there, waiting.

Begg cupped his hands and put his head back. "All right, B company," he bellowed, "let's get through that goddamned wire!" He plunged into the meadow. There were a lot of men lying at the edge of the wood awaiting his signal; a ragged wave of infantry got up and came charging out behind him.

Little Frazer ran with a quick, chopping step, head up, rifle across his chest, ready in an instant to sprint ahead or go to ground. Each motion was controlled. If there was such a profession as crossing a steel-swept, mine-exploding field, Frazer would be its master. He hummed as he ran while his darting glance located the chief sources of fire and calculated the distance to each available piece of cover.

Now, Frazer decided. He had been aiming for a bomb crater ten yards in front of the wire. He jumped, landed squarely in

the crater and put his head down to rest while regaining his breath.

Frazer became aware of a companion. A soldier stood peering foolishly over the lip of the crater, a reinforcement named Russo, trembling and lathered like a race horse, eyes wide, nostrils flaring, denim tunic drenched with sweat. Russo's gaze was fixed with dreadful fascination on the source of destruction ahead.

"Hail, Mary, full of Grace," he said.

Frazer pulled hard on Russo's web belt. "Why don't you learn to relax, sport?" Russo plopped into the crater beside him.

Frazer had picked the way to get over the wire—a place to the right where a tank had crashed through. The most dangerous machine gun was firing from the tank turret immediately ahead. Frazer clocked it, estimating the moment the belt would have to be changed. He slapped Russo's cheek with one hand. "Hey," he said, "it's time to git going."

"Holy Mary, Mother of God," said Russo. His eyes were glassy but he stood up obediently and tensed himself, ready to leap.

"Come on!" cried Frazer.

Together the two men hurdled the lip of the crater and went charging toward the gap in the wire. In the lee of the burning tank Frazer pulled Russo to the ground beside him. On the ground, six feet away, he saw the dead face of Simpson. Simpson, the Bren gunner, his closest friend; old Sim he had gone on leave with to Bari.

"Jesus Christ," said Frazer.

He crawled to the body. His hands went

out, gently stroking Simpson's dead limbs. Then he stopped. He lay with his head on the earth for several seconds. When his head came up, his glance darted round the battlefield. He began to empty the Bren magazines from Simpson's pouches and stuff them into his own. He picked up Simpson's Bren light machine gun and crawled back to Russo.

Frazer's face was white. "We're going again," he told Russo. "You ready?"

Russo made no reply; his gaze was still fastened to his own vision of Armageddon. But Frazer saw that he understood.

Hundreds of smoke shells were dropping from the sky. As they ran they were enfolded part of the way in comfortable white clouds. They fell into a crater only ten yards away from the tank turret. The body of someone dead yielded under Frazer's boots.

"Hail, Mary, full of Grace," Russo recited. He was trembling more than ever.

Frazer sat on the corpse and cocked his head. The volley from the machine gun in the tank turret was a cracking whip over their heads; when the big gun fired the concussion shook their crater. Frazer pulled out his cigarettes, lit one and sucked smoke deep into his lungs. Up ahead was the unmistakable bark of a Bren gun. One of the guys had got up there; it was time to be going.

"All right, Russo," he said, "just stay with me. We're going in behind that tank turret. Get it?" He slapped Russo lightly on the cheek and, obediently, Russo stood up.

Gen. Sir Harold Alexander once estimated he had 29 nationalities in his Allied armies in Italy. The Canadians, like these walking wounded (right) and the men in Charles Comfort's oil painting "The Hitler Line" (extreme right), were veterans of the world-renowned Eighth Army, which included New Zealanders (above, in the fight for Cassino) and Indians (right, two riflemen cover the advance of others). In this "British" army the Canadians battled to preserve their identity, as in this incident recorded by Farley Mowat in *The Regiment*:

A German officer under cover of a white flag approached a beleaguered section of B company and called out: "Surrender, you English gentlemen— you are surrounded and will only die." Pte. "Slim" Sanford bellowed back: "We *ain't* English. We *ain't* gentlemen —and be goddamned if we'll surrender!"

An unexpected gun cut in on them as they ran. Frazer almost tripped as Russo's body went tumbling at his feet; he saw the burst of machine-gun stitching running up his side. Frazer weaved and spurted toward a ditch. Poor Russo, he thought; poor Russo, full of Grace, poor Russo full of holes. He jumped and landed with a crash in the ditch.

One of the Mark IV tanks came rolling toward him. He had caught glimpses of them earlier this morning. They roamed behind the concrete emplacements as mobile pillboxes.

Frazer jammed the folded bipod of his Bren into the earth, the muzzle just clearing the ditch. He watched the tank. His right hand on the trigger guard held a grenade.

The tank slewed in his direction and stopped. The hatch opened and a German officer appeared. He was young, fair-haired and smiling and he wore black coveralls. One hand waved a pistol. *"Kommen Sie hier,"* the officer ordered.

Only in that moment did Frazer realize he was not the object of this command. Farther along the ditch another Canadian stood up and let his rifle drop. The soldier stood in the ditch, angry and helpless, covered by the tank and the officer's pistol.

Frazer steadied the muzzle and pressed the trigger. He fired long enough to slice off the top of the officer's head. The black-clad body slumped and fell across the hatch. In the same instant Frazer was darting forward on hands and knees, dragging his Bren. He swung up underneath the tank. He knew it wasn't going anywhere in a hurry with its dead commander hanging from the hatch.

He aimed his Bren back where he had lain a moment before. Two figures he had glimpsed at the emplacement came darting forward in a crouch, their Schmeisser machine pistols pointing at the place Frazer had fired from. He let them walk squarely into his sights, then he pressed the trigger. They went down together.

From underneath the tank, Frazer peered toward the concrete ramp of the emplacement. Now, he thought, if I can get over there and roll some grenades down.

Frazer was on the objective, and he was fighting. And therefore B company was on the objective, and fighting.

The brigadier had come forward to run his battle. In the forest clearing he came upon Colonel McNabb's body lying on top of his smashed wireless set. He knelt in the ditch for a moment, then his glance swept the open field ahead with its carpet of dead soldiers and burned-out tanks. Along the edge of the wood a few soldiers lay in firing position. There was silence along the front.

Back at divisional headquarters, the battle maps had been marked to show two companies of the Rifles on the objective and two companies of another battalion similarly forward on the left. But this information was based on reports before all the wireless sets had been knocked out. The brigadier knew differently: the edge of the woods marked the real limit of advance. The third battalion of his brigade lay in reserve a few hundred yards back in the woods. The important decision now was whether or not to commit them to the attack.

From the group at the edge of the wood a soldier came doubling over, rifle in hand. He was a stocky, powerful-looking man, bloodied and dirty. "Sergeant Major Mitchell, sir," he reported.

The brigadier regarded him steadily. "All right, Mitchell," he said, "what's the situation? Where are the forward companies?"

Mitchell knelt at the ditch. "There aren't any, sir."

The brigadier's gaze never wavered.

Another officer would doubtless have disputed the statement but the brigadier merely said: "You're sure?"

"I've been up and through the line myself, sir. Captain Begg is dead up there. Before he died he told me to bring back as many men as I could. I've got eight men from B company, a few from the others. There are no officers left. As far as I know I'm now commanding the unit."

Skillfully hidden Canadian snipers sometimes picked off attacking enemy infantrymen (right) or were pitted against German snipers. This sharpshooter uses binoculars to line up a target. In front of him is his standard army rifle, with telescopic sight.

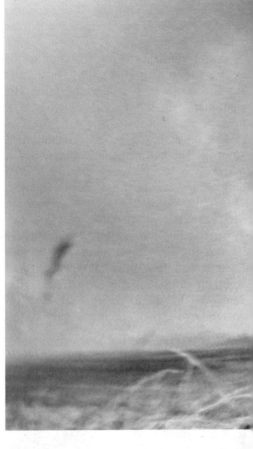

sion was supposed to exert strong frontal pressure on the Aquino defenses during our own attack. If it did so, it had no noticeable effect. The real blame may be attributed to the employment of two corps in the narrow valley instead of one. If one corps commander had planned and coordinated the assault, Aquino would have been dealt with properly and the 2nd Brigade debacle might not have occurred."

Mitchell spoke with pain and effort; until now he had not accepted the fact that his beloved battalion had been wiped out.

The padre halted at the ditch where Colonel McNabb's body lay. Since the brigadier had arrived other corpses had been added; now many of the bodies wore the name of the third, reserve battalion of the brigade, emblazoned at their shoulders. The brigadier had ordered them in.

The padre's glance touched on Colonel McNabb's face. He frowned slightly and shook his head as though to clear the frown away. He moved forward and his boot struck the dead-weight limbs of Corporal Fowler. He looked in Fowler's unseeing eyes and his frown became deeper. He saw the carpet of dead in the meadow, so thick that bodies lay on top of one another. He

recognized the faces of friends he had known in England, on shipboard, in Sicily —the young crusaders he had admired and marched with. Now they lay dead everywhere around him. . . .

COLIN MCDOUGALL

Colin McDougall's fictional account is brutally similar to what, in fact, happened that day to the 1st Division's 2nd Brigade. His unit, the Patricias, and the Seaforth Highlanders suffered heavy losses in the assault on the right. The Loyal Edmonton Regiment, brought out of reserve to support them, fared as badly.

"The brigade," General Vokes said later, "was pounded mercilessly by enfilade fire from enemy defenses sited about Aquino which lay on the front of a British division under a British corps. That divi-

It was in the center, on the 3rd Brigade front, that the Hitler Line was breached in what Vokes called "the 1st Division's most outstanding tactical success in any single day of fighting in the war."

The Carleton and York Regiment, with courageous support from the 25th British Tank Brigade, punched through during the morning. Fresh squadrons of the 1st Armored Brigade's Three Rivers Regiment tanks helped keep the hole open and finally the West Nova Scotia and Royal 22nd regiments drove through almost a mile to report "Caporetto," code for the division's final objective. On the left, the 1st Brigade—48th Highlanders, Hastings and Prince Edward Regiment and Royal Canadian Regiment—played an important if less spectacular part and fought through to Pontecorvo.

Hardest hit was the 2nd Brigade, the brigade of Ortona: 162 killed, 306 wounded, 75 taken prisoner—the heaviest casualties in a single day's fighting by any Canadian brigade during the entire Italian campaign. Total Canadian casualties were 956. But the Germans, with fewer men to lose, had lost more: several hundred killed and more than 700 captured.

Almost everywhere it had been a bad

Victoria Cross. Lt. E. J. Perkins, leader of a reconnaissance troop of Lord Strathcona's Horse, would be recommended for a V.C.—and receive the DSO, an award rarely conferred on a subaltern.

Perkins' 20-man force had four light Honey tanks, open at the top, each with a .5 Browning machine gun plus a .30 Browning, a Bren gun, a PIAT anti-tank gun, four tommy guns and demolition

was not easy to map-read but I had a good set of air photographs. I had no trouble keeping track of my position. The first enemy I saw was a half-track parked behind a house. When my troop opened fire, the crew tried to run for it. Five were hit, two got away. About 2000 yards farther on a Panther tank suddenly came across my right front at about 300 yards The crew commander was standing in the

day for the enemy. On the coast, the Anglo-U.S. 6th Corps had broken out of the Anzio beachhead toward Valmontone; the U.S. 2nd Corps had advanced rapidly along the coast; the Eighth Army, with the Canadians as its spearhead, had blasted through the toughest part of the Hitler Line and sent the enemy staggering.

The breakthrough had been made. The time had come to exploit it. The 5th Armored Division rumbled through the shattered line and on to its first offensive action as a division. All along the front the battle for Rome was rolling to a climax. But if the momentum of the Canadian attack was to be sustained, the 5th had to cross the Melfa River.

In that epic operation two Canadian officers would excel. Maj. J. K. Mahony of the Westminster Regiment would win the

charges and grenades. "In small arms weapons our firepower per man was as large as any force in the army," said Lieutenant Perkins. This is a condensation of his own account:

. . . A force commanded by Lt. Col. F. A. Vokes of the British Columbia Dragoons and including the Irish Regiment of Canada was to move through the gap in the Hitler Line, advance 2000 yards and form a firm base. My regiment was to go through, push the remaining 4000 yards to the Melfa, seize a crossing and hold it while other troops passed over and continued the advance. My job was to lead the regiment over the river. A company of the Westminster Regiment and, if possible, a tank squadron would follow.

I headed straight up the center line. The country was close and visibility limited. It

turret with most of his chest exposed. I fired with my .5 Browning and saw him slump forward out of his cupola. The Panther made no effort to retaliate and I kept going as fast as I could.

As we came to the river I saw movement in a house and opened up on it. A white flag appeared at a window, then eight Germans with their hands up. When a scout platoon carrier came up, I turned the prisoners over to them, then pushed on and reached the riverbank at about 1500 hours.

One of my tanks got lost in the difficult country. I parked the remaining three under cover, dismounted, posted three men with Bren guns to cover us and, with Sergeant Macey, searched for a crossing. About 75 yards to the right there was a ledge leading down into the riverbed. It was steep and difficult but passable. Sergeant Macey and I climbed into the stream bed and up the far bank. We came under Spandau fire from the right and one of the Bren gunners was shot in the shoulder. I got under cover on the far side and remained there to guide the tanks up. Sergeant Macey returned to guide them down the near bank, one at a time.

Getting up the bank on the far side required certain field engineering. Two men with Bren guns covered us while the remaining 13 blew up an obstruction with explosives. To widen the track in one place, we used pick and shovel to build a retaining wall of tree trunks and dirt. We were not under fire but we expected the enemy to do something soon. Everything depended on speed. In an amazingly short time the job was finished and we got the tanks into a hull-down position below the top of the bank.

About 100 yards to the left was a house showing signs of enemy occupation. Myself, Sergeant Macey and three men, carrying two tommies and a Bren gun, crept along under cover of the bank and approached the house from the rear. When I rushed in I saw eight paratroopers staring through windows and loop-holes in the direction of the crossing we had decided not to use. I shouted "Drop it!" They turned around, big well-built men armed to the teeth. First one, then all of them dropped their rifles.

We brought the three tanks into position to the right of the house and dismounted some of the smaller weapons for all-round defense. I sent one man back with the prisoners and also sent Sergeant Macey to guide the Strathcona's A squadron across. That left 13 of us to hold the bridgehead.

A sniper in a tree about 150 yards away opened up, an astonishingly poor shot but very annoying. I fired two shots from a PIAT gun; the second exploded in the branches. His rifle fell to the ground and he slumped across a branch.

It was 30 minutes since we'd reached the river. I had seized the bridgehead and now expected reinforcements. But the route we'd taken proved impractical for the Westminster scout cars. They had to feel their way over difficult ground in the face of artillery and small-arms fire. I would have to hold on by myself.

Two Panthers and a self-propelled 88 appeared to my left, the closest about 400 yards away, and began firing on the house I was in. Then they turned their attention to our A squadron on the far bank. It was

Maj. J. K. Mahony (above, left) won the Victoria Cross and Lt. E. J. Perkins (right) received the DSO for gallantry as the 5th Canadian Armored Division battled for a bridgehead over the Melfa.

Once through the Hitler Line, the Allies drove for Rome. First into the city was the Canadian-American First Special Service Force (right). Canadians in Italy felt more and more forgotten after D-Day in Normandy. They sang this song, to the tune of "Lilli Marlene":
We fought into Agira—a holiday with
  pay;
The Germans brought the bands out
To greet us on the way,
Showed us the sights and gave us tea;
We all sang songs,
The beer was free.
We are the D-Day Dodgers in sunny
  Italy.
The Moro and Ortona were taken in our
  stride;
We didn't really fight there,
We went there for the ride.
Sleeping 'til noon and playing games,
We live in Rome with lots of dames.
We are the D-Day Dodgers in sunny
  Italy.

suffering heavily. I gave command to Corporal McLean, recrossed the river and relayed the Panthers' positions to two of the tanks. They tried to knock out the targets but were unsuccessful. I returned to my position.

When Sergeant Macey got back he said he, too, realized A squadron would be unable to cross. But he had found a tank and brought it over the Melfa. I placed it below the riverbank as a rallying point in case we were forced out of our position. The situation was becoming difficult.

Spandau fire came from a house 150 or 200 yards on our left and we saw about 20 infantry. The enemy was concentrating to wipe out our bridgehead. I kept up a heavy small-arms fire to confuse him as to our strength and we caused a few casualties. I decided not to use the PIAT in order to conserve ammunition.

Only with the Westminsters' infantry could we expand the bridgehead, get tanks across and continue the advance. The tanks were fighting hard on the near bank and were not able to give me much support. The CO gave me permission to recross the river if necessary but, since we had succeeded in bluffing the enemy as to our strength, I decided to hold on.

About 1700 hours A company of the Westminsters, under Major Mahony, started to arrive. They had several casualties, including one killed, within two minutes of reaching our position. Major Mahony quickly organized an attack on the house to the left and captured it, together with 20 prisoners.

The self-propelled 88-mm. was still doing damage and a soldier volunteered to take it out with a PIAT. He crept to within 100 yards and hit it with his fourth shot. Our covering Bren shot one of the crew and the rest were captured. The two Panthers pulled back to about 800 yards.

A patrol reported the enemy massing for an attack on our right and Major Mahony asked if I could push my tanks out on this flank to give him support. I pointed out that Honey tanks were useless against Panther fire; if we kept them under cover we might bluff the enemy as to our true strength. It was hard to deny this request for fire support. On the other hand, I felt there would be no advantage in attempting the impossible. A few minutes later a Westminster carrier pushed out about 300 yards on his own initiative, apparently with the objective of securing

the infantry's flank. Before he could see his danger, the tanks swept in from the left and surrounded him.

Shortly before dusk we were attacked by three Panthers and about 100 infantry. The tanks fired high explosive as they came but most of it was high. We fired everything we had, from .5s to tommy guns. We also fired PIAT, although the range was too long to persuade the enemy we had heavy anti-tank weapons. The tanks swerved off at about 175 yards but a few minutes later they attacked again. Again we fired everything we had. Visibility was becoming very limited and PIAT ammunition was running low. But the German tanks withdrew, although they remained in the vicinity.

About this time C company of the Westminsters got across on our right, strengthening our position considerably. B company, a long way to our left, was unable to get over until after dark. We began to dig in with enthusiasm, as the enemy started to put over large numbers of Nebelwerfer bombs. Most of them overshot by about 50 yards and landed in the riverbed. This fire kept up most of the night and our slit trenches, which started out about nine inches deep, were a good four feet before morning.

A dawn attack by the Irish Regiment of Canada was postponed until 0900 hours and later until 1130 hours due to the difficulty of arranging supporting fire. At about 0800 hours the CO ordered me to return to the near bank. Our position was still not too secure and our weapons made us of greater value than our numbers would indicate. I therefore requested permission to remain until the infantry attack was completed. As the infantry attack went in, we fired our remaining ammunition to support it, and at about 1215 hours we returned to the near bank after an extremely eventful 24 hours. . . .   E. J. PERKINS

Army historian Lt. Col. G. W. L. Nicholson completes the story of the Melfa:
. . . While the Irish assaulted the main German crossing, the Westminsters' C company broke out from the left flank of the bridgehead. C squadron of the B.C. Dragoons, supporting the Irish, met the full force of the enemy's anti-tank fire and lost seven tanks. But the infantry attack went well. Within an hour both battalions were holding the lateral road 1000 yards

west of the river. The battle for the Melfa crossing was won. Much of the credit belongs to Perkins' Strathcona troop, which seized the first foothold, and to Mahony's company of Westminsters, which secured and held the bridgehead for several hours against an enemy vastly superior in armored support and firepower.

To the Westminsters, huddled in their narrow bridgehead, their numbers steadily diminishing under fire which raked them continuously and menaced at all times by the grim prospect of being overrun by armor, Major Mahony was a constant source of inspiration. He skillfully organized his defenses and even after he had received painful wounds, he was energetically on the alert, visiting each of his section posts in turn and personally directing the fire of his PIATs. He never allowed the thought of failure or withdrawal to enter his mind and infused his spirit and determination into all his men. At the first sign of hesitation or faltering, he was there to encourage, by his own example, those who were feeling the strain of battle

The Canadians advanced some miles from the Melfa, then were withdrawn. The attack moved on and Rome fell to the Allies on June 4 when flying columns from half a dozen Fifth Army formations sped into the city and seized the Tiber bridges. The only Canadians in Rome on that historic day were those of the Canadian-American First Special Service Force which had fought in the mountains of Italy and on the Anzio beachhead. The Special Force had entered Rome as the spearhead of the U.S. 2nd Corps.

The Canadians of the 1st Corps were disappointed. They had looked forward to entering Rome as a logical follow-up to their victory in the Liri Valley. But in lesser towns they celebrated, then rested and relaxed. They needed the break; they had lost 789 men killed, 2463 wounded and 116 taken prisoner.

Two days after the Italian campaign yielded Rome, its greatest prize, the excitement paled before far more sensational news. For months the Canadians and other Allied troops in Italy had felt like forgotten soldiers on a forgotten, ugly front even though they were tying up many divisions the Germans desperately needed elsewhere. After Normandy's D-Day, they were convinced of it.

A day called D

**With the greatest invasion in history,
the Allies open the campaign to free western Europe**

The battalion passed the winter in Boscombe, near Bournemouth, wrote the Rev. R. M. Hickey, padre of the North Shore (New Brunswick) Regiment. "We marched out day after day to meet an imaginary enemy or make a fake landing. We were tired of playing war and we began to fear we'd go home without having fired a shot at the enemy. We needn't have worried."

One Sunday in March 1944, Maj. Gen. R. F. L. Keller summoned all chaplains of his 3rd Canadian Infantry Division. "Gentlemen," he said, "I know that when anything serious is about to happen you want time to get the men ready. All I can say is: get ready. Good afternoon, gentlemen."

"As we drove back," Father Hickey recorded in his book *The Scarlet Dawn,* "we chaplains agreed that D-Day was near."

Soon everybody was pretty sure.

"Along the roads to the south coast of England the convoys rolled day and night," Edward Meade wrote in *Remember Me.* "Into the woods and towns, under the trees of old lanes, under camouflage nets, along hedges, in disused quarries, in the shade of houses, even into rock caves, the trucks disappeared and the earth gobbled them up and gave no clue. The Allies stood ready to launch the greatest attack in history."

As May gave way to June, over 30,000 Canadians were poised in Britain for the assault on western Europe: thousands in the 3rd Division and the 2nd Armored Brigade and a parachute battalion of the 6th British Airborne Division; thousands

in Canadian Navy landing craft, destroyers, corvettes, frigates and torpedo boats—and the minesweepers that would go first of all; thousands in the bomber and fighter squadrons of the RCAF.

Two more divisions, the 2nd Infantry and 4th Armored, would remain in Britain under Lt. Gen. H. D. G. Crerar, now commander of First Canadian Army. The invasion troops would come back under Crerar when his headquarters took the field in July. Until then, they would be part of British Second Army.

Behind the soldiers lay years of waiting and months of special training based on the lessons of Dieppe. To prevent a repetition of Dieppe's errors there were floating artillery and rocket batteries, amphibious tanks, bulldozer tanks to clear beach obstacles, flail tanks to beat through minefields —and plans for massive fire support from the air and the sea. Canadian troops who would not go until later had moved into Kent to help in a successful attempt to

The Germans were convinced that the Allies' main invasion blow would be in the Pas de Calais—across the narrow Strait of Dover. "Here, at least," wrote Brig. Peter Young in *World War 1939-45,* "the defense had some depth. But for the most part the famous Atlantic Wall (below) had no more depth than the French Maginot Line, which these same Germans had bypassed so readily in 1940." Allied military leaders (opposite) were Gen. Dwight Eisenhower, supreme commander; his deputy, Air Chief Marshal Sir Arthur Tedder, and Gen. Sir Bernard Montgomery, commanding 21st Army Group.

make the Germans suspect an attack on the Pas de Calais. Canadian troops who would go first were sealed off to the west among huge encampments of American, British and Canadian men and arms.

Ahead lay what Winston Churchill called "the most difficult and complicated operation that has ever taken place," an assault upon a Normandy coastline bristling with guns, concrete emplacements, pillboxes, fields of barbed wire and mines—all the vicious paraphernalia of the Atlantic Wall. The operation was called Overlord. Its commander was Britain's Gen. Sir Bernard Montgomery.

The Canadians were ready. Montgomery told a Canadian general: "You would not see such a body of men in any other army in the world."

During their last days in Britain, wrote Father Hickey, "secrecy was the watchword":

. . . Every letter was heavily censored and the men were warned never to mention a place name. One lad wrote: "Dear Mother, here I am in the place I came to after I left the place where I was before. Before I left the place where I was before and came to the place I came to I was at—"

We chaplains had a busy time. There was something almost heavenly in the

French beach defenses included obstacles like these, photographed from a reconnaissance aircraft just before D-Day. Below: at an invasion exercise in England, Brig. Harry Foster (helmet) of the Canadian 7th Brigade explains a problem to three British commanders—Rear Adm. Sir Philip Vian, Gen. Sir Bernard Montgomery and Lt. Gen. M. C. Dempsey. Foster described the conversation: "I had just landed, behind the Regina Rifles. 'Well, Foster,' said Monty, 'how're things going?' 'I don't know, sir,' I said. 'I was put into a landing craft three miles offshore and I've had no communication with my troops.' Vian explained that landing craft were not being risked too close to shore in exercises. 'Not good enough,' said Monty. 'How do you expect Foster to handle his reserves when he's commanding an assault for us if he doesn't know what's going on on shore?' Well, for D-Day itself we had duplicate communications—in the landing craft too—and I knew all the way in exactly where my troops were and where I could put my reserves when I needed them. So the trouble paid off."

silence around Communion time at those open-air Masses. Maybe a passing breeze would rustle the leaves, stir the priest's chasuble and make the pale candle lights tremble. Maybe a cuckoo's song, always reminding me of a sanctus bell, would echo in the woods just as the priest struck his breast and said: *"Domine non sum dignus."* But not a stir from the long line of men as they quietly moved up, received Holy Communion and as quietly came back to kneel on the grass.

One colonel called us chaplains a wolf

pack; another laddie good-naturedly christened us the morality squad. One priest told a group of men: "We're the waterproofing gang. We've come to waterproof you spiritually." . . .

Chaplain Jack Clough of the Queen's Own Rifles found he had "more requests for baptism in the last weeks than in all the years overseas."

As tension mounted behind the barbed wire of the army camps, the Allied air forces pounded rail lines, airfields, har-

bors, radar stations and factories throughout northwest Europe. German aircraft plants and other strategic industries suffered heavily. Bridges and tunnels leading to the battle area were ruined. The Luftwaffe was outfought in the air, hammered on its airfields, smashed in its factories and left powerless to interfere with the invasion concentrations in southern England.

By May 25 most assault battalion commanders had been briefed and then, as Lt. Col. W. T. Barnard wrote in *The Queen's Own Rifles of Canada,* officers and NCOs

nd riflemen were told what each had to do nd how—but still not when and where. At May 27 pay parade each man received 0 shillings in silver and 200 francs in aper money. "The next few days were ifficult," said Colonel Barnard. "Every- ne was confined to camp; everyone was at ever pitch. Only the CO knew the exact lace of attack. Men guessed and conjec- ured. No rumor was too fantastic to be iscredited. Everything possible was done o relieve the monotony: shows, lectures, uizzes. But under it all nerves jangled."

D-Day was set for June 5 but bad weath- er forced a one-day postponement—and still the storm raged. It seemed everything would be nullified by the one factor which could not be harnessed to the plan: the weather. But at 4:15 a.m. June 5, the Supreme Allied Commander, Gen. Dwight Eisenhower, listened to the final comments of his advisers, paused, then said: "Okay. We'll go." The die was cast for the 5300 ships and landing craft needed to put the invasion force ashore, the 12,000 planes assigned to cover the assault, and the

150,000 men and 1500 tanks to be landed in the first 48 hours.

They would go to the beaches of Nor- mandy between Ouistreham on the east and the base of the Cherbourg peninsula 50 miles to the west. Lt. Gen. M. C. Demp- sey's British Second Army would have the eastern half of the front (Sword, Juno and Gold beaches); Lt. Gen. Omar Bradley's U.S. First Army would have the western sector (Omaha and Utah beaches). Two American airborne divisions would land ahead of the U.S. infantry; the 6th British

Airborne Division would be in the British sector.

The British-Canadian front lay roughly between Bayeux and the mouth of the Orne River. Dempsey's Canadians were in the center, along the five miles between Courseulles and St. Aubin. Their task was to push through the gap between Bayeux and Caen and make the deepest penetration of the day, to Carpiquet airfield, 11 miles inland. By the evening of D-Day, it was hoped, two British divisions would have taken Caen and Bayeux and the Canadians would be astride the road and railway linking the two towns.

In *The Struggle for Europe,* Chester Wilmot wrote that the Canadian and British "were to land last, on the most exposed beaches, with the farthest to go, against what was potentially the greatest opposition. Because of tide and rocks, the 3rd Canadian and 3rd British divisions could not land until an hour and a half after dawn, giving the enemy ample opportunity

to prepare in a sector where his reserves were well placed to take advantage of any warning. Moreover, the outcrops of rock so divided this front that the only suitable beaches for these two divisions were five miles apart."

Three battalions of the 716th German Infantry Division defended the coast here and other divisions were close by. But, wrote Wilmot, the real enemy strength lay in the 21st Panzer Division, near Caen. And if the British and Canadians expended their strength in a slugging match with the 21st, they might be exposed to a serious reverse at the hands of another armored division, the 12th SS, a fanatical Hitler Youth formation. The proximity of these two divisions, with an estimated 350 tanks, made it unlikely Caen could be captured on D-Day, as planned.

On the afternoon of June 5, wrote Father Hickey, "I said Mass. I wish I could say all Masses like that one. My men received Holy Communion—the last for many of them. Evening came, the wind calmed and at dusk the great expanse of boats began to move. The English coast faded slowly, and we sailed to meet a scarlet dawn."

"The real maps are issued," recorded the war diary of the Queen's Own Rifles. "Grenades are primed and a good many 'last' letters written. The spirit is very high. If the Hun could see our lads tonight it would shake him."

"Moved out of Southampton harbor at 1910 hours," says a diary of the Cameron Highlanders of Ottawa. "Pipe Major Scott played the ship through the boom at the request of the captain. England gradually disappeared in the darkness by 2200 hours, most of the lads watching to the last."

"Better to ignore tomorrow," wrote Colonel Barnard, "and dwell on the past. Men thought of loved ones far away; the magnificent staunchness and charm of the British; the sheer joy of listening to skylarks with one's feet hidden in primroses and violets; the witchery of English place names—the Weald of Kent, Chelwood Vetchery, Virginia Water; all the things one has loved, consciously or unconsciously, and is aware of suddenly and acutely."

Far out in front of the armada were the minesweepers. Sixteen of them were Canadian. Ships like *Canso* and *Caraquet*, *Thunder*, *Vegreville* and *Wasaga*, little un-

sung veterans of countless sheepdog tasks in Canadian and Newfoundland waters, now were in the vanguard of the greatest combined operation in history, sweeping channels into the Americans' Utah and Omaha beaches. Scores of other Canadian Navy units were involved. Fourteen assault landing craft would be carried to the 3rd Division's Juno Beach by the landing ships *Prince Henry* and *Prince David*. Twenty-six LCIs (landing craft infantry) would deliver second-wave troops. The destroyers *Algonquin* and *Sioux* would lead the way into Juno Beach, then bombard enemy defenses. Six Canadian motor torpedo boats would patrol off the Seine estuary. Dozens of corvettes and frigates would patrol convoy routes and escort landing craft and barges.

The assault was only part of the navy's task. It had to get the troops there, then see they were maintained by a steady stream of more troops, equipment, ammunition and supplies. Joseph Schull wrote that Can-

ada's contribution to Operation Neptune, the naval part of Overlord, was 110 ships and 10,000 men – 4 percent of the total naval strength involved.

Skpr. Lt. K. W. N. Hall, commander of the minesweeper *Cowichan*, described for the CBC how the Canadian sweepers slipped in under German guns to clear the way to Utah and Omaha: "We sailed from Weymouth Bay and commenced sweeping at approximately midnight. Mine was the fourth ship, controlling the ship that laid the buoy at the beginning of the channel leading into the troop-lowering area. After sweeping the channel, we swept the bombardment area, which took us to about three quarters of a mile from the beach. It was bright moonlight with every detail of the beach completely visible. It was difficult to understand them not seeing us as we turned very slowly, one ship after the other, and went back out."

Somewhere between the minesweepers and England, the invasion fleet was on its

Canadian paratroopers had trained (opposite, top) for almost two years. Shortly before June 6, from an airfield building, the King and Queen and Princess Elizabeth (above) watched Canadian jumpers. One, Padre G. A. Harris (left) of the 1st Canadian Parachute Battalion, was killed in action on D-Day. Extreme left: bombers wear white-stripe invasion markings.

way. War correspondent Ross Munro, who was in the 3rd Canadian Division headquarters ship *Hilary,* wrote in *Gauntlet to Overlord:*

. . . I went on deck as we rounded the Isle of Wight. What a spectacle—those thousands of ships sailing south to France! Lines of LCTs carrying self-propelled artillery, infantry and tanks extended for three miles, all flying the White Ensign. And scores of landing ships. Some had been at Dieppe. Others had been on the North African landings, at Sicily, Reggio, Salerno and Anzio. Some ships were fresh from the builders in the United States, Britain and Canada.

Among the troopers, cargo boats, supply boats and hundreds of small craft were the escort ships. Behind us was the Canadian destroyer *Algonquin.* Small landing craft, carrying commandos, lurched through the sea beside her. She took each wave with a graceful bob of her bow; the little craft nearly foundered. Other destroyers weaved through the fleet while corvettes and frigates kept a vigil for submarines.

I went below and found the officers gathered in the wardroom for a drink before a good meal. There was some talk of the operation, but not much. It might have been another maneuver. I thought how similar it was to those training days when we'd made landings on the English coast. . . .

Leonard W. Brockington, a passenger in the destroyer *Sioux,* recalled the words of a senior British naval officer: "What Philip of Spain tried to do and failed; what Napoleon wanted to do and could not; what Hitler never had the courage to attempt, we are about to do, and with God's grace we shall succeed." In a CBC broadcast, Brockington quoted *Sioux's* 27-year-old captain, Lt. Comdr. Eric Boak: "This operation cannot fail. It is the greatest organization this world has ever seen." Brockington went on: "The captain showed me his instructions—printed documents two inches thick for one Canadian destroyer responsible for the bombardment of 200 yards of coast. If you multiply these instructions to cover the multitudes of operations, you will have some idea of the skill and thought British and American brains applied to this great enterprise."

On the ships, men laughed and joked and gambled and prayed and dozed and wrote intimate letters. A few looked at mail received in the last hours before leaving England. One Canadian soldier had heard from his mother-in-law: "She was glad I was doing good and writing home steady. She prayed I'd get home safe."

"We knew," said Pte. Dutch Ramsay of the Canadian Scottish, "what we had to go through. We knew some of us were going to die but we didn't know who. We were thinking about home and friends."

"That night on the *Prince Henry,*" said another Canscot, "the sailors put on stage shows and gave us as much rum as we wanted."

Capt. Bob Ross of the North Shore Regiment: "I had trouble getting to sleep. I noticed one platoon commander, Harold Day, get out of his bunk to kneel and say a little prayer. I felt pretty good when I saw that and I knew our fellows were thinking the right way."

Soon, overhead, other Canadians were en route to France.

Gwenda Thompson, in the magazine *National Home Monthly,* described the scene as the 6th British Airborne Division's Canadian battalion prepared for takeoff: "As I wandered around the field shouting questions above the roar of revving planes, a sergeant came among the paratroopers and said: 'Padre wants to know if any of you would like a few prayers before we take off.' The chaplain, G. A. Harris, was waiting with a prayer book in his hands. His face was daubed with camouflage paint, he wore a green jumping smock and there was a crash helmet at his feet. Soon he would 'jump into France with the whole of my parish.' In his kit bag, which he would strap to his leg, was a collapsible altar. The Canadians knelt and, as a stormy sun set over the woods, prayed and sang a hymn. Then after a blessing they turned, buckled the last straps and filed into the planes."

High above the Channel three divisions of paratroopers flew to France. The two U.S. divisions landed behind Utah and Omaha beaches. The 6th Airborne dropped soon after midnight on the east bank of the Orne River between Caen and the Bay of the Seine and at vital bridges over the Orne and the Caen canal. Jumping from about 300 feet, the British and Canadians came down in rivers and trees and swamps. They were badly scattered, but they seized their bridges intact and held their positions on the left flank.

When the Canadians spilled out, Padre Harris jumped with them. He died almost at once; his parachute didn't open.

For the infantry, in boats bucking a stormy English Channel, the last few hours before landing were a misery of seasickness. "I didn't care if the *whole* German Army was on that beach," said Sgt. E. D. Chandler of the North Nova Scotia Highlanders. "All I wanted was to get my feet on dry land."

But the bad weather helped the Allied cause. Alexander McKee wrote in *Caen: Anvil of Victory:* "The Germans expected a landing in the Pas de Calais but the invaders were steering for Normandy; they were expected at high tide and would land at low; they were expected in calm weather and not when the breakers were roaring on the beaches." German meteorologists had concluded there'd be no invasion for at least two weeks—and most German commanders accepted that. But at 9:15 p.m., on the BBC, Eisenhower's SHAEF head-

Swimming tanks, launched from landing craft and able to go quickly into action, were among the new weapons first used on D-Day. They were ordinary Sherman tanks with canvas flotation gear which they discarded when they reached the beach. Above: a swimming tank comes ashore. Right: camouflaged landing craft in Portsmouth harbor, awaiting the invasion signal.

A Canadian chaplain leads troops in prayer on the deck of the Canadian landing ship *Prince Henry,* en route to Normandy. Below decks, a soldier writes a letter home. The D-Day armada (below) was the greatest ever. Said Pte. Chick Daley of the North Shore (New Brunswick) Regiment: "It looked as if you could walk across the Channel on the ships and not get your feet wet."

quarters told Frenchmen: "In due course instructions of great importance will be given you through this channel. You must listen at all hours."

This alerted the Germans, wrote Chester Wilmot, and their suspicions were soon sharpened. "Radar stations between Cherbourg and Le Havre reported they were being jammed. Stations from Fécamp to Calais reported abnormally heavy shipping in the Channel. Between 10 and 11 p.m., Luftwaffe Signals Intelligence discovered that reconnaissance aircraft for American bombers were broadcasting weather information. German night fighters were alerted. At 10 p.m. Field Marshal Erwin Rommel's Army Group headquarters issued a 'most urgent' signal to all troops to be ready for action. But this alarm was directed to the Fifteenth Army alone—to the divisions north and east. To the Seventh Army, guarding the coast toward which the invasion fleet was heading, there was no warning at all."

It was almost unbelievable luck. But the men crammed in the ships knew nothing of this—and, remembering Dieppe, they'd have laughed at any report of the enemy caught off guard. The vaunted Atlantic Wall filled men's minds and each soldier lived his own hell of fear and self-doubt. Ralph Allen, who went ashore with the Canadians as a war correspondent, described in his novel *Home Made Banners* how a soldier named Mike Tully lived those last hours before landing:

. . . A sergeant came down the companionway and looked uncertainly at the sleeping men, as though he could not make up his mind to disturb them. Then loudly: "All right!" He played a flashlight around the room. He'd catch a soldier in the face and hold the light there while the man blinked his eyes open and stared vacantly until he remembered where he was. When there was room to move, the sergeant turned a switch on the wall. A single bulb winked to life, yellow and dim, and as the men

stretched and scratched and tugged the twists out of their battledress, their shadows danced between the steel ribs of the bulkheads like deformed giants in some silent tribal rite.

At first no one spoke in anything but the lowest undertone. Then, under the familiar impetus of one man's belch, the hush broke and the hold took on the half-forced, half-grumbling cheeriness of reveille. "Hey, sarge! When do we get breakfast?"

"Five minutes. Eat a good meal whether you're hungry or not. It may be a long time before you get hot grub again."

"Is it light yet?"

"Not yet," said the sergeant. "In about an hour."

"How's the weather?"

"Pretty cloudy, but not bad. They say we'll still get air support. The cloud's high enough that they'll be able to see the beach."

When they came on deck it was almost light. The low clouds were breaking and the gray sea was covered with vast reaches of gray ships. Everywhere there were ships. They could not be counted. They could only be measured by the acre.

An officer asked each man: "Water bottle full? Rations okay? Any questions about our objectives or your assignment?"

A few Spitfires sang overhead and a man near the rail yelled, "Look!" Beyond the horizon, a bleary ripple of gunflash faded and a jet of tracer cascaded up a bank of cloud, hung there for a moment, then faded too. The sound was too far away to be heard.

The officer looked at his watch. "The real stuff starts in 14 minutes."

High above, above the Spitfires and the Typhoons, they could hear the bombers. Clouds hid them from view except in brief dashes from one cloud to the next. But

after the first had gone and others were overhead, a hollow hoom-hoom-hoom rolled back across the water. They stared at the land again and saw its dingy outlines stir and quiver and finally rise like a genie in a blend of smoke and shadow.

As the ship idled closer to land they soon picked out two little towns, gleaming white against the black smoke. A battleship squirted a huge ball of flame toward the towns and before the sound reached their ship the whole fleet threw its thunder at the beaches. There was no sound of answering salvos but off their starboard bow a small craft, half the size of their own, dissolved in a single gust of flame. And as a rocket ship edged in toward

"German Intelligence," said Field Marshal Wilhelm Keitel, **"knew nothing of the real state of the Allies' preparations. The full alert was not ordered even when the Allied invasion fleet was approaching the Normandy coast."** Said General Montgomery: **"We attained a degree of surprise greater than any we could have imagined."** The landing craft rocket (LCR) (above) made its debut on D-Day. Many men in small craft (right) were seasick. Said an order from 3rd Canadian Division headquarters: **"Seasickness, alleviation—one hour before embarking, each man will be** *seen* **to take one seasickness tablet. Personnel should be sick into vomit bags, of which three are issued to each officer and other rank. The tops of vomit bags will be folded over after use and the bags will be thrown over the leeward side of the craft."**

shore, a Typhoon cut across the high gray parabola of rocket trails and disappeared in a ball of orange vapor.

Then they boarded the assault boat. Mike Tully settled on his haunches and carefully slid open the bolt of his rifle. There was a cartridge in the chamber. He closed the bolt, put the catch to safety and reminded himself that the last thing he must do before leaving the boat was to move the catch again. He felt for the handle of the trenching tool strapped to his back beneath his small pack, and wrenched at the cork of his water bottle to make sure it was tight. He opened the two ammunition pouches above his breast and closed them again. He counted the grenades hanging from his belt. Then he unscrewed the valve on his life belt and blew an extra lungful of air into it.

Mike and the men in his boat were close together, yet each was alone now. Some were gray with seasickness and some were gray with a sickness of the soul. No one talked. There was no need to talk, no need to sing or pray or curse or dredge up wisecracks. Those who were afraid had no need to hide their fears and those who were not afraid had no need to show it. There was enough fear in them all to give them the knowledge that fear or the lack of it was not a matter for shame or pride, but only a matter of chance.

"Oh God!" Mike formed the words in his mind without uttering them. "Make it now. Make the boat stop now and make the ramp open and let us out on the beach. I'm all right now. But a minute from now I might not be any good at all. I might not be any good in 30 seconds. Make it now."

The sweat lay on his face in pools, his fingers were stiff and leaden around his rifle. Beseechingly he looked across the boat. All he saw was each man's aloneness and, through it, his own. In a minute they would be pooling the unfathomable resources of their spirit in the only perfect community known to man, the community of battle. But in these last moments each was on his own. There was nothing any man could do for his neighbor or his neighbor do for him.

The boat jarred and a tremulous grating shook its hull as it came to a stop on the gravel floor off the shoreline. Mike heard the impatient clanking of the opening ramp and stumbled toward the square of daylight that had replaced the boat's flat bow, shoving at the man ahead of him in his

haste. He held himself at the crest of the ramp for an instant, then slithered into the sea, took a step on the edge of a sandbar and found himself waist-deep in water. Holding his rifle above his head, he half ran and half pushed straight ahead until he felt the heavy warm grip of the water drop from his waist to his hips and finally to his knees. He saw several dead men, and a man using his arms like flippers to drag a mash of crushed legs and shredded battledress back from the shore into the water. He saw black mines and yellow shell cases bobbing in the water on wooden stakes. He saw concrete blocks and iron tank traps at the water's edge, some broken and twisted by bombing and shelling or by the demolition parties, but many still intact.

Straight ahead and very close, he saw a straggling settlement of tall pillboxes and squat machine-gun turrets anchored to a high concrete breakwater. As his feet hit the sand he scarcely noticed the thwack-thwack-thwack of Bren guns merging with the quick slurp of German Spandaus and Schmeissers from behind the breakwater. But then a rifle bullet sang above his shoulder, a heavy mortar broke nearby with a testy crump and a German 88-mm. shell fused its warning swish with the cruel smack of its explosion. . . . RALPH ALLEN

The landing of the 3rd Division and the 2nd Canadian Armored Brigade astride the mouth of the River Seulles was complicated by offshore reefs. Because of these, wrote Chester Wilmot, H-Hour here had to be delayed until the tide was high enough to carry the landing craft clear of the reefs. This meant most craft would touch down in the mined area between the reefs and the beach. It was important that the landing not be late but the weather was worse in the Canadian sector than elsewhere. "Delayed by the choppy sea," wrote Wilmot, "the leading craft came in nearly half an hour later than intended and were borne through several hundred yards of heavily mined obstacles. Casualties on the run-in were surprisingly few, but many craft were sunk or damaged heading out to sea again. In the case of one battalion, 20 out of 24 were wrecked."

The last seven miles to shore took 90 minutes, said the Canadian Scottish war diary, and it seemed like 70 miles. "I was so sick," said L. Cpl. Fred Griffin of the Reginas, "that I didn't care whether I lived or died, but I remembered it was my mother's birthday and I thought, what a

hell of a day to die." The Canadians stumbled ashore heavily laden, cold and wet, weak and nauseated. But they were there.

"First Battalion The Regina Rifle Regiment," says one proud war diary, "on Exercise Overlord, landed at Nan Green Beach, Courseulles-sur-Mer, Normandy, France, at 0805 hours, with A company being first in, followed by B company at 0815 hours. C company landed at 0835 hours, D company at 0855 hours. Command group, with Lt. Col. F. M. Matheson, touched down at 0900 hours."

The RAF and RCAF had bombed the area all night, and in the half hour before the ground assault more than 1000 U.S. aircraft smashed at the beach defenses. Five battleships, 2 monitors, 19 cruisers, 77 destroyers and 2 gunboats joined in at

H-Hour and the ramp is down. One Canadian's good-luck touch reassures his buddy at the moment they go ashore in France. Above: an aerial photograph of part of one beach. Three tank landing craft are aground a few hundred yards offshore. Tanks and vehicles fight through heavy surf. Hundreds of soldiers have reached the beach; others swim ashore. "I'm awful glad I was there," said one Canadian soldier, "but I'll tell you this: five minutes was enough for any man." Said another: "It was a job, that's all. You're told to go and you go."

daylight. And as the assault flotillas neared shore the army's own artillery opened fire from the ships; on the Canadian front four self-propelled regiments each took on one strongpoint.

Wrote Col. C. P. Stacey: "There is no doubt this great bombardment enabled us to breach the Atlantic Wall at a cost far below what had been expected. Some positions were knocked out, others were not defended; the majority were defended with less tenacity because of the pounding they took." Even so, he noted, "many soldiers who hoped to find the defenses in ruins found them in action."

Many soldiers doubted the effectiveness of the bombardment. From the diary of the Winnipeg Rifles: "0749—in spite of the air bombardment failing to materialize, the Royal Navy bombardment being spotty,

the rockets falling short and the tanks and assault vehicles being late, C company of 1st Canadian Scottish (Maj. Desmond Crofton), under our command, landed at the junction of Mike and Love for the assault on beach defenses and the Château Vaux; D company Royal Winnipeg Rifles (Maj. L. R. Fulton), with one pioneer section under command, landed to the left of Mike Green; and B company (Capt. P. E. Gower), with No. 15 platoon and two sections No. 6 Field Company RCE under command, landed on Mike Red—all within seven minutes of one another. The bombardment having failed to kill a single German or silence one weapon, these companies had to storm their positions 'cold'—and did so."

The Winnipegs, with the Canscots, were part of the 3rd Division's 7th Brigade which made its assault on the western end of the Canadian sector, at Courseulles-sur-Mer. The Winnipegs formed the brigade's right, the Regina Rifles its left. The rest of the Canscots followed.

The 8th Brigade attacked on the east, with its North Shore (New Brunswick) Regiment on the left at St. Aubin-sur-Mer, the Queen's Own Rifles on the right at Bernières-sur-Mer. Close on their heels came le Régiment de la Chaudière. The 9th Brigade—a force made up of the North Nova Scotia Highlanders, Highland Light Infantry of Canada and Stormont, Dundas

and Glengarry Highlanders—remained offshore in reserve.

Wrote war correspondent Ross Munro:

"Soon a terse wireless message was flashed to General Keller's 3rd Division headquarters ship: 'Under fire on all beaches.' Fighting into the sand dunes, the Canadians stormed big-gun emplacements, cut a bloody path down zigzag trench systems and through a maze of barbed wire. All morning the battle raged along that precious strip of coast. Courseulles, Bernières and St. Aubin were cleared in bitter fighting. Tanks and infantry struck inland and all that day pressed on through villages, fields and groves of trees defended by determined Germans. By night a beachhead had been won."

The Canadians and British used the Funnies—special weapons developed in the aftermath of the 1942 Dieppe raid. They were Sherman tanks equipped in various ways to flail a path through a minefield, lay tracks for vehicles or span an anti-tank ditch. Some had flamethrowers or huge charges for destroying pillboxes.

The Americans did not use the Funnies. Brig. Peter Young, describing high U.S. casualties on D-Day, wrote in *World War 1939-45:* "Such devices might be all right for the cautious and war-weary British; the Americans preferred to see what could be done by straightforward frontal assault. Dieppe might never have been fought!"

But despite the Funnies and the virtual absence of German airpower, and despite the fact the Germans thought Normandy was only a feint, D-Day was far from easy for the Canadians.

Chester Wilmot in *The Struggle for Europe:* "In the attack on the defenses at the mouth of the Seulles, the 7th Brigade was assisted by DD (swimming) tanks launched only 800 yards offshore. But its engineer assault vehicles did not arrive until half an hour after the touchdown. The infantry, with superb dash and with bold support from the 1st Hussars tanks, overwhelmed or neutralized the main strongpoints on the waterfront within an hour but there was some delay in preparing exits from the beaches."

A soldier of the Winnipeg Rifles: "The first section out of the boat, everybody was hit. The second section, all hit but one. The third section out, all but two." CSM. Wilf Berry, Canadian Scottish: "We started with 138 men and at the end of the day we had 62 left." Lt. John Karasevich, Winnipeg Rifles: "I think we went in with 163. There were less than 30 by noon."

Diary, 13th Field Regiment, RCA: "Captain Else was wounded on the beach but continued on. He was again wounded but did not go to a dressing station until he had received three direct orders."

Diary, Canadian Scottish: "B company and attached troops were pinned down by

Some beaches were cleared swiftly, others had to be fought for yard by yard. Ralph Allen, in *Home Made Banners,* described some of the noises of battle: "The sound came hammering faintly through the pale air like a far but monstrous echo of the winding of a watch. First there was a multiplicity of small ratchety cogwheel noises, running so close together they could not be counted, and then a rattle, lower and steadier in tone and a little louder, with a pause after each separate note. This was the sound of a German MG42 opening fire and being answered by a Bren. It was one of the sounds of history, as much a herald to the destiny of man as the crunch of oarlocks in Caesar's galleys or the rushing hoofbeats of Mongol horses on the steppes of Asia."

mortar fire from a pillbox. It was finally cleaned out and a German lieutenant with a dozen men surrendered. One met his doom when a 'stray' bullet plugged him in the head as he stepped onto the parapet of the pillbox."

Cpl. Cal Minaker, Winnipeg Rifles: "Bull Klos took a burst of machine gun through the midsection. That would have stopped any ordinary person but he wasn't satisfied with giving up on the beach. Bull cleaned out a pillbox with his two hands. I hear he choked the very life out of his enemy. And then he died himself."

Diary, 12th Field Regiment: "The engineers worked furiously with bulldozers to clear the beach exits. In the meantime we landed and took up a gun position on the beach, in many cases engaging the enemy over open sights."

Rfn. George Haycock, Winnipeg Rifles: "I think there's still a little ridge in the sand there from my nose. I was keeping pretty low."

Diary, Canadian Scottish: "Hordes of prisoners were taken and our advance was too rapid to do anything but disarm them and send them to the beach cage under one or two escorts. The odd prisoner tried to escape and will never have the opportunity again."

Diary, Winnipeg Rifles: "Two detachments of three-inch mortars, timed to land at H-Hour, were ordered off the LCT in 12 feet of water—the craft commander refused to beach his craft—resulting in the loss of both weapons, the two carriers, one 10-cwt. trailer."

A news dispatch: "With the Canadian Invasion Forces, June 6—(CP)—The Canadian ensign—popularly known as the 'Canadian flag'—went into battle for the first time in this war. Up to now the Union Jack had been flown. A few days ago Lt. Gen. H. D. G. Crerar personally presented Canadian ensigns with instructions that they be flown at division and brigade headquarters."

Cpl. David Dumont, Regina Rifles: "I went in in water over my head. My gear weighed 50-60 pounds and I couldn't swim but the Mae West life belt kept me up. When I felt something under me I started walking and pulled my pants out of my gaiters to let the water out. There was shellfire and mortar fire and I saw an old French lady walking there right on the beach in the middle of the battle saying her prayer beads."

A Regina Rifles officer: "I had to go through a potato patch with these tracked vehicles and sure enough a Frenchman came out—shells flying in all directions and this man all upset, mad as can be at what I'd done to his potato patch."

Maj. Peter Bennett, 7th Brigade HQ: "One very excited soldier came up to me and told me he'd learned the art of war: keep your head down."

CSM. Wilf Berry, Canadian Scottish: "We were supposed to take this chalet and to get to it we had to go up a little draw.

There was a sniper, tied in a tree, and each man going by took a few shots at him. By the time we all got through he looked like a saltshaker."

Chester Wilmot: "The 8th Brigade landed a few minutes after the 7th but without any tanks. It was too rough through the rocky shallows and the tanks had to be disembarked well behind the brigade's Queen's Own Rifles and North Shore Regiment. At Bernières the assault craft of the Queen's Own were carried so far in by the tide that the men had only 100 yards to run to the cover of the high seawall but this was the beaten zone of the enemy's fire. One company lost half its strength in that dash, for it landed by error directly in front of a heavily armed strongpoint. It was taken by storm only after a flak ship ran inshore and almost aground to pour its fire into the German defenses."

Padre Clough of the Queen's Own: "I don't remember actually getting ashore. One minute we were on the ship, then we

Maj. Gen. R. F. L. "Rod" Keller (right) commanded the 3rd Canadian Division. In the British sector (below) were some "Canloan" officers, Canadians serving in British regiments. Of 673 lieutenants and captains lent to the British for service in Europe, 127 were killed and 338 wounded or taken prisoner in 11 months of action. Most Canloan officers saw fierce fighting. They won many awards for gallantry; 41 received the Military Cross.

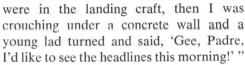

were in the landing craft, then I was crouching under a concrete wall and a young lad turned and said, 'Gee, Padre, I'd like to see the headlines this morning!' "

Pte. Robert W. Adair, North Shore: "Claude Bransfield was shot in going over the wall at St. Aubin-sur-Mer and fell at my feet. When I saw how bad he'd been hit I called the padre."

Father Hickey: "I anointed Bransfield but he died within seconds."

Diary, North Shore Regiment: "B company discovered no damage had been done to the St. Aubin-sur-Mer strongpoint by the air and naval bombardment. It appeared not to have been touched. Nevertheless the company proceeded to clear the village and allowed D company to get on with their task."

Private Adair, North Shore: "Of the three other stretcher-bearers with A company, one was wounded and two were killed. That left me. We wore the Red Cross armband until the first man got killed, then we took them off. The Germans were using them as targets."

L. Cpl. Bud Daley, North Shore: "I met Sergeant Major Poley and I asked him, 'Did you see my brother Harold?' He said, 'Yes, Buddy, I'm afraid he got it.' I came across him a little later, lying to one side of the road. I got his personal belongings and a few things to send home, and then I had to push on."

As the first French-speaking war correspondent to land, I was looking for the first meeting between a Frenchman and one of our boys. A white-haired Frenchman named Martin noticed a soldier with Régiment de la Chaudière shoulder patches. *"Hé, mon gars,"* he said, *"qu'est-ce que c'est 'la Chaudière'?"* (Chaudière to him meant boiler or furnace.) *"C'est une rivière de par cheu-nous,"* said the soldier, a river back home. And where *was* home? *"Moé, M'sieur, j'viens de Trois Pistoles."* And where was that? On the banks of the St. Lawrence. *"Au Canada?" "Oui."* Then Monsieur Martin asked, *"Allez-vous à Paris?"* The Chaudière had been warned to be careful about that kind of question. He shrugged. *"P'têt ben que oui, p'têt ben que non."* It sounded like *tet ban kwee tet ban knon,* a contraction of *peut-être bien que oui, peut-être bien que non,* which means "maybe yes, maybe no." But in Normandy too it's *tet ban kwee tet ban knon,* a pronunciation carried to Canada by our Norman ancestors centuries ago. At that Monsieur Martin grabbed the soldier by the neck, kissed him on both cheeks and said, "Look, my friend, you're not a Canadian, you're a Frenchman like me!"

Marcel Ouimet of the CBC

Cpl. Alden Daley, the third brother: "When I heard about him I had a terrible feeling of loss and a feeling of this is the real thing; there's no joke about this."

Colonel Barnard in *The Queen's Own Rifles of Canada:* "The probability that our two first-wave assault companies would be commanded by brothers was rather remote, but so it was: both Daltons had been in the regiment in militia days."

Maj. Charles Dalton: "People ask how we decided whose company would go in on the right and whose on the left. We tossed a coin. I think my brother felt there should be a farewell scene, something from *Hamlet* maybe, something appropriate. Instead we shook hands, said good luck and went to our boats."

Maj. Elliott Dalton: "We were weaving among the obstacles and mines and just before we touched down we leaned over to tell the coxswain to go slightly to the right—only to find he'd been hit between the eyes and was dead and the craft had weaved in on its own. Of the ten boats we were the only one that didn't hit a mine."

Maj. Charles Dalton: "We thought we were on the beach. Really we were hooked on an underwater obstacle. The doors went down and I very gallantly shouted, 'Follow me!' and disappeared into eight feet of water. The fire was heavy and almost every man on my right was wounded or killed. I'd have been hit too but we found later that the machine gun that was doing the damage couldn't traverse that far. The man next to me was hit four or five times. I wasn't touched."

Chester Wilmot: "So fast did the Queen's Own move that when the Chaudière began to land behind them 15 minutes later the only fire on the beach was from snipers."

Colonel Barnard: "Never did the rifleman's creed of dash and initiative reap a richer reward. Padre Clough, for example. He was everywhere, cheering the wounded, exhorting the men still fighting. While he was comforting Sergeant Morrison in his last moments a bullet inflicted a flesh wound in the padre's foot. The next day, when the opportunity came to take off his boots, the bullet fell out as the blood-soaked sock was cut away!"

The diary of Captain Clough: "Came ashore with C company 20 minutes after H-Hour. Had to keep under cover because of concealed machine guns. Made a couple of wounded comfortable. Crawled up the beach and through a fence and bandaged a lad wounded in the back and legs. Examined three others and found they were dead. With the help of another man got the wounded man to safety."

Colonel Barnard: "The medical officer, Capt. Archie Kirsch, was wounded but refused to leave. While he was giving Lt. P. C. Rea morphine to ease his pain, a mortar shell landed nearby. Captain Kirsch was wounded—and so, for the third time, was Lieutenant Rea. Kirsch dragged Rea to a more sheltered spot, dressed the wounds and carried on calmly and efficiently, the model of a medical officer in action."

Pte. Bill McGarvey, Queen's Own: "Contrary to all expectation and all the

Second-wave Canadian troops go ashore at Bernières-sur-Mer (left), close behind the Queen's Own Rifles. French civilians had a special welcome for the French-speaking Régiment de la Chaudière (far left). D-Day prisoners (above) included Russians and Poles who had been forced to serve in the 716th German Division.

briefing, this Atlantic Wall, this monster, turned out to be 3½ feet high where I landed. It was a lovely small wall, behind which I must say we crouched, and it's conceivable we'd be there yet if some sergeant hadn't booted us up and over. He showed it was possible to get over without getting killed and we took a stab at it simply because we didn't have much choice—he was a very persuasive man. We weren't soldiers really; we were all young and we had been reacting more like frightened kids than anything else. It was that first positive move into fire that changed the whole thing and we decided we were soldiers, I suppose. It was never easy but under fire it was always easier than that first time."

Diary, Queen's Own: "0900 hours, café 100 yards off the beach is open in Bernières and selling wine." Diary, Regina

Rifles: "1100 hours, civilians of Courseulles welcomed our troops with flowers." Ross Munro in *Gauntlet to Overlord:* "Old men and women, young girls and children stood in the littered street, clapped their hands, waved the troops on their way and tossed roses in their path. A girl handed me a crimson rose and there were tears of despair and joy in her eyes: 'There's my home, over there, ruined. But the Allies are here!' "

Diary, North Shore Regiment: "At 1115 hours, three hours and five minutes after landing, the strongpoint area was cleared. Thus one of the bastions of the Atlantic Wall, which had taken four years to build, was completely reduced."

gade landed without a shot fired on them. While awaiting orders to move, troops could be seen with a book in one hand reading off French phrases, to the amusement of the inhabitants. The Germans were hardly out of Beny-sur-Mer before the inhabitants began to loot their barracks. Even the parish priest was seen with a set of dishes."

Diary, Winnipeg Rifles: "By the time C and D companies had moved out from Banville and Tierceville and Creully, the remnants of B company had reported—the company commander and 26 other ranks having survived the assault on the three casemates and 12 machine-gun emplacements. Prisoners had been brought in—a

and we only found them a couple of days later."

So went this fabulous day. Despite many successes, no Allied units reached their inland objectives. But the Canadians came closest. Chester Wilmot: "It was not so much opposition in front as congestion behind—on the beaches and in Bernières —that prevented the Canadians from reaching their final D-Day objective. But this congestion was the almost inevitable result of the weather, which delayed the landing, prevented early clearance of underwater obstacles and piled wrecked craft on the narrow foreshore. It was remarkable the Canadians made as much progress as they did: more progress than any other

Chester Wilmot: "The traffic jam in Bernières became acute. The (9th) reserve brigade's three battalions were ashore by 12:30 p.m., but the beach and streets were so packed with armor and transport that it was three o'clock before they could move south. The Chaudière had advanced three miles to Beny and were still going, but the hours lost in the middle of the day could not be made good."

Diary, Highland Light Infantry (reserve brigade): "At 11:40 we made our run-in to White Beach in front of Bernières. The beach was jammed with troops and bicycles, vehicles and tanks, all trying to move toward the small exits, an awful shambles. More than one man uttered a fervent thanksgiving that our air umbrella was so strong. One gun ranged on the beach would have done untold damage, but the 9th Bri-

sorry lot—and escorted to the rear, five being turned out of a German ambulance from which they had sniped our troops."

A Canadian Scottish rifleman: "We were detailed to nail snipers and we split up, two on each side of the street. We heard a creaking noise and everybody froze. A door opened and a little old Frenchman came out. He put both arms around my neck and kissed me on both cheeks and then scurried back into his house."

The CBC's Marcel Ouimet: "We found a little inn called l'Hôtel Belle Plage—it's now l'Hôtel du Régiment de la Chaudière —owned by a most hospitable man who had a reserve of the native brew and he dished it out pretty freely. Some Canadians didn't realize that calvados is stronger than even whisky blanc. A few took too much

division on D-Day."

In a late afternoon counterattack about 40 tanks of the 21st Panzer Division struck toward the coast between the 3rd Canadian and 3rd British divisions but were repulsed. Another group of German tanks got close to the beach around Luc-sur-Mer. The other panzer division which might have further slowed the Anglo-Canadian attack, the 12th SS, was under heavy air attack as it moved forward. It saw no action on D-Day.

But the Germans did make their own contribution to the beachhead congestion—their Atlantic Wall proved a formidable obstacle. Behind it, without air or tank support, the enemy troops fought effectively. Alexander McKee sketched this vignette in *Caen: Anvil of Victory:*

"Eight tanks lay knocked out at the water's edge and at the top of the beach was the old field gun which had got them all. Behind, in newly-dug graves, the gun crew were already buried, marked only by a notice on a stick, *Six Unknown Germans.* From their country's point of view, they had not died in vain; nor had any of the defenders that day. They had been unable to stop the British and Canadian landings but they did impose a brake on the forward impetus of the invaders, both by direct fire and by flank fire which forced the attackers to funnel through a few narrow, comparatively safe gaps."

Because of the congestion, only one battalion of the 9th Brigade—the 3rd Division's reserve—had been committed by nightfall. Even so, the forward units were within sight of Caen by then, and two battalions were only three miles from the city's northwestern outskirts. On the right, Wilmot reported, the 7th Brigade had linked up with the 50th British Division, making the common beachhead 12 miles wide and 6 to 7 miles deep. But on the left there was still a strip of enemy-held territory between the 3rd Canadian and the 3rd British divisions.

A troop of 1st Hussars tanks, commanded by Lt. W. F. McCormick, probably got closer to the final objective than any other element of the Allies' seaborne assault forces. McCormick described to the CBC how, after helping the Winnipeg Rifles through Creully, they pushed to the north edge of Secqueville-en-Bessin: "We came to a sunken crossroads which offered some cover and let the drivers rest. While we were sitting there I noticed a German soldier down the road, his rifle over his shoulder, almost sauntering. I put my field glasses on him and saw him straighten up as he spotted our tanks. We couldn't quite understand what he was up to—one lone soldier marching quite smartly down the road, with our 75-mm. cannon and two Browning machine guns and my revolver trained on him. He marched right up to the tank, came to a smart halt and saluted. He'd thought we were Germans. He just hadn't expected the enemy so far inland."

Another 1st Hussars squadron, reduced to half-strength in the beach assault and now numbering only nine tanks, was severely hit when hurrying to the aid of infantry attacking Pierrepont. Alexander McKee:

. . . Swerving off the road to the attack, the force lost five more tanks. "I saw Lieutenant McLeod's tank burst high in flame,"

said Sgt. Léo Gariépy. "The troop corporal's tank suffered the same fate, and I saw several other tanks knocked out." Their end was dreadful for they had loaded the tanks with reserve ammunition, fearful that the chaos of D-Day would prevent supplies getting through.

Gariépy, who had 15 scrounged sticks of dynamite aboard, saw the muzzle of an 88-mm. rising from a hidden emplacement 30 yards ahead, the barrel pointing directly at him. "I gave rapid evasive orders to my driver and told my gunner to blast him. He fired two rounds; the second scored a direct hit. I moved up to the gun emplacement and shot all the crew of 14 cowering in the trench."

There now were only 4 tanks left of the original 18. Gariépy volunteered to look for survivors. "I was called by an infantry officer who told me a sniper had shot the commanders of three DD tanks. The sniper had not shot at the infantry; he was after tank commanders. I moved slowly toward where the other crew commanders had got hit, wrapped my beret over my earphones and waved it above the turret. The shot, when it came, was from an attic window, but the infantry were unaware of it and they were all round that house, making it impossible for me to fire into it. So I and my loader operator jumped out, hugging close against the wall, and bashed the door open. We found an old man and woman, imploring us in German, but we could not understand what they were trying to tell us. We rushed up the stairs and

there in front of the attic window, holding a Mauser low but pointed at us, was the sniper, a girl of 19. I cut her down with the Sten. Angry, irritated, probably scared, I could not hesitate. We learned from the old people that this girl's 'fiancé' had been shot by a Canadian tank that morning and she had sworn she would liquidate all crew commanders." . . .

At the end of D-Day, said Padre Clough of the Queen's Own, "we climbed to a little village where there'd been fierce hand-to-hand fighting. In a ditch I saw one of our men and a German, both dead, their hands locked on each other's throat."

That Canadian and 358 others were kill-

When resistance on the beaches was overcome, infantry and tanks pushed quickly inland (left). German snipers were left behind (above) to try to slow the Allied advance. D-Day casualties were less than expected but heavy nonetheless. "My most vivid D-Day memory," correspondent Ralph Allen said in a CBC interview, "is of a soldier caught in the wire on the beach. I knelt beside him and discovered he'd bled to death. Beside him was a pack of Canadian cigarettes—open, with one cigarette out and beside it a lighter. I tried the lighter. It was clogged. This poor man had been trying to have one last smoke and the lighter hadn't worked. Nothing had worked for him that day."

ed that day; 907 had died at Dieppe. Non-fatal casualties amounted to 715—as compared with 2460 at Dieppe. In the total picture, the Allies had gained a striking victory at a cost of fewer than 3000 lives and 6000 other casualties.

But the legend had been born that D-Day was easy. Years later Maj. Gen. Harry Foster, who commanded the 7th Brigade on June 6, was asked about it. "Well," he said, "it was *not* easy. What induces people to think so was that the wise guys and the dopesters figured we were going to have terrific casualties—which we didn't get. God knows we got enough."

But it had been an extraordinarily successful day. Colonel Stacey, in *The Victory Campaign:*

. . . On the far right the 82nd and 101st U.S. airborne divisions, although badly scattered during the drop, had helped disorder the enemy and confound his countermeasures. Of all the seaborne assaults, the one which met least resistance was the attack by the 7th U.S. Corps on Utah Beach where the bombing of beach defenses was more effective than elsewhere—and by evening a substantial beachhead had been established.

Very different was the story on Omaha Beach. Here the invading forces had more difficulty than at any other point and losses were extremely heavy. The military quality of the defenders was higher here than elsewhere; the terrain favored the defenders; the German defenses were probably stronger than at any other point on the front; and the U.S. infantry was less strongly supported than on the British sectors. On the evening of D-Day the Omaha beachhead was still narrow and precarious.

On Gold Beach, prolonged German resistance prevented the British from attaining the final inland objectives. But by evening the 50th Division had penetrated to within striking distance of Bayeux and the Bayeux-Caen road and was in touch with the Canadians on its left. The 50th Division beachhead and the Canadians' were firmly linked up, but the 50th was not yet in touch with the Americans on Omaha.

When night fell the Germans were still resisting in a portion of the beach defenses immediately east of the Canadian sector. The 3rd British had met serious resistance north of Caen and had had to deal with the 21st Panzer Division counterattack. There remained a wide gap between the 3rd British and the 3rd Canadian divisions. . . .

For Allied airmen, D-Day was one long frustration. Only in two instances did German fighter-bombers penetrate and bomb the beachhead. The Allies had absolute air supremacy, the most important single factor in the day's success. But Wing Comdr. J. E. "Johnnie" Johnson, the RAF ace who commanded the RCAF's No. 127 Wing, described in *Wing Leader* how his Spitfire pilots felt as a result:

"Four times we'd made our way across the Channel and never a sign of the Luftwaffe! We arrived back from our last patrol at dusk and had to wait a few minutes for the night fighters to take off to maintain the vigil over the beachhead. We were tired and drained and bitterly disappointed. We had geared ourselves for a day of intense air fighting; the result had been an anticlimax."

Allied bombers and fighters, wrote Chester Wilmot, flew 10,585 sorties on D-Day, in addition to the 1730 flown by transport planes in airborne operations. Not a single aircraft was lost through Luftwaffe intervention. There was no sign of the Luftwaffe over the beaches until almost dark. Then four Heinkels sneaked in and managed to scatter their bombloads near the Canadian beaches. Spitfires pounced on them. None got away.

Not many men of the 716th German Infantry Division got away either. It took the main weight of the Anglo-Canadian assault and was virtually destroyed. Of six battalions, wrote the divisional commander after the war, "there remained in the evening one battalion which had about 20 percent casualties; otherwise only remnants." Eighty percent of the division's artillery was gone.

By nightfall the Germans had to face the fact that for the first time they were under attack in Europe on three fronts: from the east, by the Russians; from the south, in Italy, by the Allies; and from the west, in Normandy, by the Allies too. Canadians were fighting on two of the three fronts.

As D-Day died into darkness, the men who had lived through the greatest invasion in history began digging in, each spading his own small slit trench in the rich Normandy soil. "And that very first night," said Pte. Angus Kearns of the Canadian Scottish, "we started burying our dead. When you start burying your buddies, you want to quit. You think, what's the use of going on?

"But we did."

Greater Love . . .

In helping breach the Atlantic Wall (right), Canada suffered 1074 D-Day casualties, including 359 men killed. That day, near Beny-sur-Mer, about three miles from the beach, two chaplains selected a plot of ground for the bodies of two North Nova Scotia Highlanders. They were the first in a cemetery which grew to have 2048 graves. Twenty years later, in a CBC program, Sgt. Alf Allen told about one of the dead at Beny-sur-Mer, a Regina Rifles stretcher-bearer named Gilbert Boxall:

"He came from Canwood in northern Saskatchewan, grew up in the Depression and had very little of this world's goods. He'd never have been the stick man in a British Guards parade but as a dedicated working man there was none better. He landed in the assault wave, gave first aid on the beach and in the battle inland. On D-plus-3, running to a chap he heard calling for help, he was cut down and killed. On his body we later found five dried shell dressings—he'd had five wounds prior to being killed. He never said a word to anybody, just crawled away somewhere, put a dressing on and went back in. People ask: Why does a man do this? Well, there are two quotations that might cover it. One was used by King George VI in a broadcast: 'If I be called upon to suffer, let me like a well-bred beast that goes out into the forest to suffer alone and in silence.' The other is from the Good Book: 'Greater love hath no man than this, that he lay down his life for his friends.' Gib Boxall was a great man. May he rest in peace."

L.27355 RIFLEMAN
G.D. BOXALL
THE REGINA RIFLE REGIMENT
9TH JUNE 1944   AGE 24

Two nights in June

In a crippled Lanc and a crippled Canso,
two airmen make RCAF history

The men of the Royal Canadian Air Force fought in many types of plane, in widely scattered parts of the world. They flew, among others, fighters and fighter-bombers, reconnaissance and transport planes, bombers and intruders and anti-submarine amphibians. They flew Spitfires and Hurricanes, Lancasters and Halifaxes, Mosquitos and Bostons, Dakotas and Cansos and Beauforts. They fought out of Britain, Canada, North Africa, Malta, Italy, western Europe and the Far East.

They fought for nearly six years and they won many medals. Yet, through sheer coincidence, the two episodes which brought their highest awards for gallantry came within 11 days of each other in June 1944.

Both began as routine missions, like hundreds of others that summer: a bomber striking at railway yards in northern France, and a flying boat doing anti-submarine patrol somewhere between Iceland and Norway. These are their stories.

The first mission was part of the bombing offensive by Canada's 6 Group in support of Allied ground operations in Europe. The bombers had prepared the way for the Normandy invasion, supported the D-Day landings and now served, among other things, as "aerial artillery" in advance of attacking troops.

It was a new kind of war for the bomber men. They were used to flying at night. Now they flew also by day. And for the time being top priority was given not to saturation raids on German cities but to precision raids against specific targets—oil refineries, railway yards, junctions and repair shops, concentrations of enemy troops, V-bomb sites along the Channel coast.

On the night of June 12-13, 6 Group was assigned to make low-level raids against rail yards and shops at Cambrai and Arras. It lost 15 planes to heavy flak and to night fighters.

George Patrick Brophy told David MacDonald of *Reader's Digest* what happened to one of these attacking planes:

... According to official records of the RCAF, I owe my life to "a miraculous escape." But was it only an amazing twist of fate that saved me from certain death? Or was there something more—another man's incredible courage—that helped me live to tell the tale? Even now, years later, I still wonder.

That night of June 12, at 419 Squadron's base in England, our seven-man crew—six Canadians and one Englishman—was sitting on the grass by our Lancaster bomber, waiting to take off for France. For us, it was a night of mixed omens. A few hours earlier we'd been briefed for a raid on railway yards at Cambrai—our crew's 13th mission. Moreover, we were due on target shortly after midnight, June 13.

Then, as if to compensate, a turret gunner named Andy Mynarski, my closest buddy in the crew, found a four-leaf clover in the grass. Twirling the good-luck token like a tiny prop, he turned to me. "Here, Pat," he said. "*You* take it."

Minutes later our black, four-engine Lanc—A for Able—was climbing into the darkness, one of 200 bombers that 6 Group sent out that night, a week after

A fleet of bombers thunders across the English Channel en route to attack railway yards in France a few days after the Normandy invasion. In one such Lancaster, on a similar raid June 12, 1944, were gunners Andrew Mynarski and George Patrick Brophy, whose story is told in this chapter. Above: another gunner in the glass-domed rear turret of the first Canadian-built Lancaster.

D-Day. I sat alone in the glass-domed rear turret, watching the evening stars pop out. As the "Tail-end Charlie," I was shut off behind the revolving turret's doors, far from all my crewmates. My only contact with them was via the intercom, on which pilot Art deBreyne's voice now crackled: "Estimating 80 minutes more to target."

"Thanks," came Andy Mynarski's reply from the mid-upper turret. "No rush."

In our crew, Andy was a relative newcomer. Four months earlier, before our first mission, he'd turned up to replace a gunner who'd gone to the hospital. At 27, Andy was a quiet, chunky fellow with a boyish grin. The son of Polish immigrants, he'd grown up in Winnipeg and left school at 16, when his father died, to help support four kid brothers and sisters. He joined the army in 1941, then switched to the RCAF because most of his friends were in it. To Andy, friends were important.

We soon became close chums. Since I was an officer and Andy an NCO, rank kept us in different quarters. But we made light of it. Splitting up on the base after a mission or a pub crawl, I'd clap him on the back and say, "So long, Irish." He'd stiffen, exaggerate a salute and reply with a hint of Polish accent, "Good night, *sir*."

In a tight spot, I could always count on him. Once, on leave with Andy and two other crewmates, I got into a late-night scrap and phoned them from a police station. They laughed and said a taste of jail would teach me a lesson. While the others went back to sleep, however, Andy got up to bail me out.

But there was one thing Andy would not do, even on practice flights. He would not go into the tail turret. Like most air gunners, he hated its cramped isolation. "Back there," he said, "you're completely cut off."

Back there now, as we crossed the French coast, I saw enemy searchlights sweeping the sky, then lazy puffs of smoke and deceptively pretty sunbursts of sparks. "Light flak below, Skipper," I reported.

Suddenly, with a blinding flash, a searchlight caught us. Others quickly converged. "Hang on!" called deBreyne. "We're coned!" He threw the Lanc into a banking dive, then swung upward trying to squirm away from the deadly glare. Then, just as suddenly, we were in the dark again.

We'd escaped—or had we? The Germans sometimes *let* a bomber shake loose,

once their fighters got a fix on it. It was too soon to tell.

Once past the coastal defenses, we began a slow descent. This was to be a low-level raid, from 2000 feet. We were down to 5000 feet when I caught a fleeting glimpse of a twin-engine fighter. "Bogey astern!" I yelled on the intercom. "Six o'clock!" Instantly, as he'd done to evade the searchlights, deBreyne began to corkscrew. Seconds later I saw a Ju 88 streaking up from below: "He's coming under us!"

As I whirled my turret around and opened fire, the white-bellied Junkers flashed by with its cannons blazing. Three explosions rocked our aircraft. Two shots knocked out both port engines and set a wing tank on fire. The third tore into the fuselage, starting another fire between Andy's turret and mine.

We began losing altitude fast. I listened for orders on the intercom, but it was dead. Then a red light flashed in my turret—the signal to bail out. A for Able was doomed. For some reason, I glanced at my watch. It was 13 minutes past midnight, June 13.

While Art deBreyne fought to keep the plane from heeling over in a spiral dive, bomb-aimer Jack Friday tugged at the forward crew's escape hatch. It flew open with the violent updraft, hit his head and knocked him out. Jack was still unconscious when our English flight engineer, Roy Vigars, dropped him through the hole, yanked his D-string and jumped after him. Navigator Bob Bodie went next, then wireless operator Jim Kelly. When pilot Art deBreyne finally jumped—from barely 800 feet—he felt sure that both Andy Mynarski and I had already got out of the rear hatch.

But he was wrong.

To fire, I'd swung my turret to port. Now I had to straighten it out so I could go back into the plane for my parachute and then jump from the rear door. I pressed the rotation pedal. Nothing happened. The hydraulic system had been shattered, locking my turret at such an angle that I couldn't get out. Meanwhile, from inside the fuselage, flames were sweeping toward me.

Don't panic, I told myself. *There's still another way.* I managed to open the turret doors a few inches, reached in for my parachute and clipped it on. Then I began handcranking the turret to the beam posi-

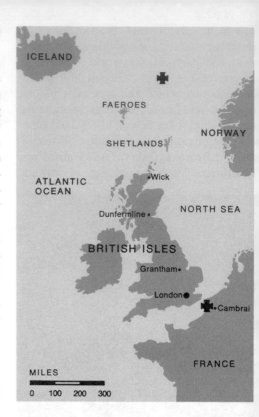

ICELAND

FAEROES

SHETLANDS

NORWAY

ATLANTIC OCEAN

•Wick

Dunfermline •

NORTH SEA

BRITISH ISLES

Grantham•

London ●

•Cambrai

FRANCE

MILES

0   100   200   300

tion, where I'd be able to flip right out into the slipstream. To my horror, the rotating gear broke off. Now there was *no* way out. At that moment, imprisoned in a falling plane, I remembered Andy Mynarski's words: "Back there, you're completely cut off."

Then I saw him. Andy had slid down from the mid-upper turret and made his way back to the rear escape hatch, about 15 feet from me. Just as he was about to jump, he glanced around and spotted me through the plexiglass part of my turret. One look told him I was trapped.

Instantly, he turned away from the hatch—his doorway to safety—and started toward me. With the aircraft lurching drunkenly, Andy couldn't keep his feet. He got down on hands and knees and crawled —straight through blazing hydraulic oil. By the time he reached the tail, his flying suit was on fire. I shook my head; it was hopeless. "Don't try!" I shouted. I waved him away.

Andy didn't seem to notice. Completely ignoring his own plight, he grabbed a fire ax and tried to smash the turret free. It gave slightly, but not enough. Wild with desperation, he tore at the doors with his bare hands—in vain. By now he was a mass of flames below the waist. Seeing him like that, I forgot everything else. Over the roar of wind and whine of our engines, I screamed, "Go back, Andy! Get out!"

Finally, with time running out, he realized that he could do nothing to help me. When I waved him away again, he hung his head and nodded, as though he was ashamed to leave—ashamed that sheer heart and courage hadn't been enough. Even then, Andy didn't turn his back on me. Instead, he crawled backward, through the fire again, never taking his eyes off me. On his face was a look of mute anguish.

When Andy reached the escape hatch, he stood up. Slowly, as he'd so often done before in happier times together, he came to attention. Standing there in his flaming clothes, a grimly magnificent figure, he *saluted* me! At the same time, just before he jumped, he said something. And though I couldn't hear, I knew it was "Good night, sir."

I turned, watched him fall away beneath the tail and saw his chute open. *So long, Irish. Good luck.*

Now I was alone. The Lanc was going down less steeply than before, but I knew it could hit the ground in a matter of

seconds, with five tons of high explosives barely 50 feet from me. I curled up in the way prescribed for crash landings and waited for death.

Time froze. While I was struggling inside the turret and Andy was fighting to get me out alive, a minute or more had flashed by like a second. Now the last agonizing seconds were like eternity. Prayers and random thoughts raced through my mind. *Hail Mary, full of Grace . . . . God, I hope Andy got down okay . . . . Pray for us sinners . . . . "Brophy? Oh, he went for a Burton over Cambrai."*

Suddenly time caught up. Everything came at once—the ground's dark blur, the slam of a thousand sledgehammers, the screech of ripping metal. Just as the Lanc went bellying into a field, a thick tree slashed away its flaming port wing, spinning the plane violently to the left—its last dying lurch. *This is it.* But in that instant, at that last possible moment, the whiplash snapped my turret-prison open.

Without knowing it—for I'd blacked out —I was hurled through the air. When I came to a few seconds later, I heard two explosions. Only when I felt the solid, blessed earth tremble under me did I realize that the crash was over and, somehow, I was alive.

Slowly, fearfully, I moved my arms and legs. Nothing hurt. Then I sat up. I wasn't even scratched! It was as if some gentle, unseen hand had swept me out of that hellish turret, now twisted and blazing a hundred feet away. Incredibly, and luckily for me, only two of the Lanc's 20 bombs had exploded.

But fear had left its mark: when I hauled off my helmet, most of my hair came with it.

After a night in hiding, I approached a farmer, who turned out to be a Resistance

leader. With six other Allied airmen, I was passed through the French underground for 11 weeks, until British troops found us near Lens. All this time I kept seeking word of my crewmates—especially Andy Mynarski.

When I got back to England, on September *13*, I finally found out what had happened. Two of the crew had been taken prisoner; three others got back via the underground and one of these was wireless operator Jim Kelly. After his parachute jump, Jim told me, a French farmer hid him in a barn. Soon another Frenchman arrived. In halting English, he spoke of a parachutist who had landed alive, only to die of severe burns. Then he held out a flying helmet. Painted across the front was "Andy."

Almost numb with grief, I realized that Jim didn't know—no one else *could* know—why Andy died. I told the story to him, and later to air force officials.

The RCAF document describing my

escape as "miraculous" went on to say that Andy "must have been fully aware that in trying to free the rear gunner he was almost certain to lose his own life." With that citation, Andrew Charles Mynarski was posthumously given the Victoria Cross, the Commonwealth's highest award for valor.

Andy was one of very few in history to get the V.C. on the uncorroborated testimony of a single witness. And I'll always believe that a divine providence intervened to save me because of what I had seen—so the world might know of a gallant man who laid down his life for a friend. . . .

GEORGE PATRICK BROPHY
and DAVID MACDONALD

While the bomber men—and Canadian fighter and fighter-bomber pilots—were ranging over the Continent, other Cana-

Double

Another Canadian airman won renown on a third night in June 1944 with a feat that was never equaled. He was FO. K. O. Moore (below), pilot of a Liberator bomber.

On the moonlit night of June 8, his Coastal Command plane was on anti-submarine patrol off the coast of France. It was just two days after D-Day and the Germans had mustered a considerable number of U-boats to try to interfere with the buildup of the forces invading Normandy.

Suddenly a report from the radar operator electrified the nine-man crew: "Contact dead ahead, range 12 miles." Moore took the Liberator down to 100 feet and there, stark in the moonlight, was a submarine making about 12 knots on the surface.

The plane's nose gunner opened fire and, on the sub's gun platform, two German sailors went down. As other Germans fired back, three depth charges exploded on either side of their U-boat. It lifted out of the sea, broke up and sank.

A few miles on the Liberator's radar picked up another contact. Soon, at 2½ miles' range, they could see a second submarine on the surface. Moore went down to 50 feet to attack. The Germans opened fire but were silenced by the nose gunner. Depth charges plunged into the sea, hiding the conning tower from sight. As Moore came in for a second attack, his crew could see the U-boat listing heavily to starboard. Then it vanished.

In the monotonous chore of hunting submarines, Allied planes often searched long without even seeing one. Moore's Liberator had killed two within 22 minutes. He was awarded the DSO and the U.S. Silver Star.

dians brought airpower to bear in the Battle of the Atlantic.

For years, RCAF squadrons on both sides of the ocean had been making their contributions to the war against submarines. From Canada's own coast and from Newfoundland, planes ranged farther and farther out to sea, often in appalling weather. From Scotland, the Shetland Islands and Iceland, other Canadian squadrons took part in the RAF Coastal Command's campaign against U-boats and other German warships and merchantmen. At one time or another, there were seven RCAF squadrons in the Command. One of them, No. 162, was posted overseas early in 1944 and soon destroyed six U-boats, four in 22 days.

In the London *Sunday Express,* Air Chief Marshal Sir Philip Joubert, former chief of Coastal Command, told this story of one attack:

. . . The pilot of the ponderous twin-engine flying boat, P for Peter, narrowed his eyes at the signs of worsening weather. The plane was 250 miles north of the Shetlands, roughly halfway between Iceland and Norway. If they couldn't get back to base at Wick, in northern Scotland, or to the Shetlands, the only possible diversion would be Reykjavik, Iceland, more than 500 miles away. The Canso had the range for it, but the weather might be no better there.

Flt. Lt. David Hornell, the pilot, called his radio operator, Flt. Sgt. S. R. Cole. "Anything from Group [headquarters] about the weather?"

"Nothing so far. They're broadcasting every half hour."

The cloud base was lowering and the sea was roughening, but the visibility was still about five miles. They still had a good chance of spotting a U-boat.

Although the submarines sometimes prowled at periscope depth, they usually stayed on the surface, guns manned, ready.

Hornell, at 34, was by far the oldest man in his all-Canadian crew. Slight and dapper, gray-haired, with a silver mustache, he had that smooth, healthy complexion which often goes with the prematurely gray. A former Sunday-school teacher, he was a man of quiet manner and mature outlook—a steady, dependable pilot. For 17 years before the war he had worked for a rubber company in Toronto. Because of his age he had been accepted as a pilot by the narrowest of margins.

On this 24th day of June, Hornell and his crew had been airborne for ten hours and had completed their patrol. FO. S. E. Matheson, the navigator, had given Hornell the course to steer for base and now Hornell was heading almost due south. FO. Graham Campbell, in the nose turret, was searching the sea for a U-boat forward to port. FO. Bernard Denomy, the second pilot, sitting beside Hornell, searched the forward area to starboard. Hornell kept a lookout straight ahead. Sgt. D. S. Scott and Flt. Sgt. I. J. Bodnoff searched laterally from the fuselage blisters.

Bodnoff made the sighting: "Fully surfaced U-boat five miles on port bow."

The U-boat had been steering northwest at full speed. On sighting the Canso it altered course to starboard, but did not dive. Its gun crews stood ready at their 37- and 20-millimeter gun mountings forward and aft of the conning tower.

Hornell sounded the warning horn and called to Campbell: "Get the attack report out." He then turned to Matheson. "What's our position, Ed?"

Matheson worked it out and gave it to Campbell. He coded it and passed it to Cole to radio back to Group with the attack report. Then Campbell scrambled down to man the forward guns.

"Action stations!"

Hornell turned to port to swing round behind the U-boat. Bodnoff, manning the

to port and starboard, undulating from 30 to 100 feet. Campbell, thrown about in the nose, still fired several accurate bursts. Scott, at the starboard blister, could also see his tracer hitting the conning tower. Denomy saw several men fall.

At 1000 yards one of Campbell's front guns jammed, but he kept firing the other. They were only half a mile from the target now, and within range of the enemy guns.

Several times they heard and felt the flak smashing through the wing of the plane. Two large jagged holes mushroomed in the starboard wing. A shell hit the fuselage, throwing a stunned Cole out of his seat at the radio. They were less than 500 yards from the U-boat when Denomy saw the Canso's starboard engine pouring oil. Then the starboard wing burst into flame.

Hornell felt the loss of power and shouted to Denomy, "Full boost!" When Denomy pushed the lever wide open, the aircraft shuddered as though it would shake itself to pieces. He cut the starboard throttle and feathered the propeller.

Three hundred yards from the target the plane was almost uncontrollable. They were undershooting badly and swerving away to starboard and the U-boat had turned broadside on, greatly reducing chances of a hit.

They could see the men on the conning tower throwing their arms about in

blister gun, lost sight of the target, but could still see its wake. Scott, at the starboard blister, picked up the sub almost dead ahead and still turning to starboard. Hornell was forced to swing back to the right.

To drop his depth charges accurately Hornell would have to fly low over the U-boat. He could take evasive action on the run in, but would have to fly straight and level for the actual drop, relying on his gunners to put the German gun crews off their aim.

At two miles' range the U-boat was still turning to make the drop difficult. Hornell corrected his approach so he could run in from astern. He wanted the whole length of the submarine as a target.

At three quarters of a mile the U-boat opened fire. Hornell threw the flying boat

In a flying boat like this one, Flt. Lt. David Hornell (top right and second from right in photo with some of his seven-man crew) killed a German submarine in a North Atlantic battle. In another engagement, a U-boat (immediately above) circles to get into position to fire at an attacking aircraft.

triumph at the blazing Canso. Denomy shared their obvious belief that Hornell would have to abandon his attack. But even with his plane aflame, almost impossible to fly and being repeatedly hit, Hornell wasn't quitting. He slowed the port engine, put the nose down to maintain speed and steadied the amphibian back on course with rudder and aileron.

As the plane dived once more, the German gun crews saw their danger too late. Fifty yards from target Hornell dropped four depth charges, spaced at 100 feet. They straddled the U-boat and exploded. One blew up a column of water underneath the submarine and lifted its bow out of the water.

There was no question of Hornell circling to see what had happened. With its starboard wing a mass of flames, the Canso was fighting for survival. For a moment, with the depth charges gone, it seemed more buoyant. Hornell coaxed it up to 250 feet, then felt a violent change of trim and saw the blazing starboard engine plunging to the sea.

He struggled to regain control, but it was impossible. Turning into the wind and across the swell, he shouted "Ditching stations."

It was a grim prospect. Even in June those northern waters were bitingly cold. Quickly the crew took up ditching positions. But Campbell, noticing that Cole had been stunned, came back from the nose to help him send an SOS.

Denomy manipulated the throttle while Hornell fought the controls. It took the two of them to keep the Canso into wind and on an even keel. They were nearing the end of a successful powered descent when the plane dropped suddenly, hit a huge wave and bounced up to 150 feet. This time Hornell decided on a glide approach, with the port engine off. He found it easier to keep straight and level, but even so the Canso breasted heavily into the water, bouncing to 50 feet before he could bring it down.

The two flight engineers, Scott and Sgt. Fernand St. Laurent, began to launch the rubber dinghies. The fuselage was submerging quickly and the plane was sinking to wing level. The starboard wing was still burning.

Hornell, Denomy and Matheson scrambled onto the wing. Scott had launched the port dinghy and was sitting in it with Bodnoff, but St. Laurent found the starboard dinghy was damaged and wouldn't inflate.

Hornell, Denomy and Matheson swam to Scott's dinghy and clung to it, helping to propel it back toward the sinking plane to pick up Cole and Campbell, who were still trying to collect food and water from the waterlogged, smoking fuselage. When they reached the wing of the Canso, Hornell shouted for Cole and Campbell and they stepped into the dinghy.

Fearing the suction from the half-submerged plane, Scott and Bodnoff paddled furiously. But when they were barely 20 yards away, Cole dived back into the water. "The dinghy radio!" he shouted. "We may need it. It's still inside."

"Come back!" shouted Hornell. "Don't be a fool." Three of them restrained Cole, and hoisted him back into the dinghy.

"The gas tanks could explode at any moment," warned Hornell. "Anyway, she's sinking." A few moments later the Canso disappeared.

Hornell turned to Campbell. "What about the SOS?"

"We sent it several times," said Campbell, "and then we clamped the key down so the transmitter was pushing out a signal until we ditched. Someone's bound to have got it."

But they couldn't be certain. It might be many hours, even days, before they were picked up. They couldn't all get into one four-man dinghy, and to stay in the water meant certain death from exposure within hours. Each man helped to close the distance to the other dinghy. As they came alongside, St. Laurent tried again to inflate it. Nothing happened. The others were about to grab it when it suddenly began to inflate on its own. Then it exploded.

Now it was eight men and one dinghy. Even if their messages had been heard, it would be eight or ten hours before a rescue launch could reach them. Already the men in the water were feeling the effects of the cold. And the weather was getting worse.

Thus there were seven men in or clinging to the one inflated dinghy. They could see St. Laurent, a quarter of a mile away, clinging to the other dinghy, which was still not inflated. The men in the water took off their flying boots and some clothes and began to push their dinghy toward St. Laurent. Scott, Cole and Campbell used the canvas paddles.

"Did you get an acknowledgment to the attack report?" Hornell asked Cole.

"I was knocked out the moment I sent it," said Cole. "But they must have got it."

U-boats sometimes prowled the northern seas at periscope depth but often remained fully surfaced, with bridge personnel (above) and gun crews at the ready. A submarine was more vulnerable to depth-charge attack (right) when on the surface but it *had* to be surfaced to fight aircraft.

"We'll have to get as many into the dinghy as possible," said Hornell. "The others can take turns hanging on. Throw everything overboard that isn't essential." They wouldn't need the food. They would die of exposure long before they died of starvation. They would keep two paddles. They must keep the rockets and the bailing bag. And one canister of water. The rest went overboard.

Hornell, Denomy and Matheson stayed in the water, hanging to the dinghy and moving as much as possible. The other five squeezed inside. Waves often broke over them, and they bailed hard.

After two hours the men in the sea were numb and blue. Scott, Cole and Campbell slid overboard, and Hornell, Denomy and Matheson climbed into their places.

As the evening wore on the light faded, the sea rose and the air turned even more chill. It became clear that no one could survive for long in the water. At the risk of capsizing the dinghy they all crowded in. Body entangled with body. Scott's legs trailed over the side.

The sea kept flooding the dinghy. Periodically one man would slip over the side, giving the others room to bail. It began to look as though their signals had not been heard.

In fact, at Group headquarters at Dunfermline, Scotland, nothing was known of the attack report or of their distress signals. But at 9:30 that night, 2½ hours after the ditching, Group sent the plane a signal diverting them to the Shetlands. An acknowledgment was requested. Twenty-five minutes later, the signal was repeated. There was no reply.

The Canso's silence could have several explanations, the most likely being radio failure. Since it was due to land shortly, it was decided that emergency action would only be taken when it was clear the plane was overdue.

In the dinghy, Hornell and his crew watched the waves increase in height. The wind had stiffened and visibility was less than a mile. Even if a plane passed near it was unlikely to see them. They were not hungry or thirsty, but they were numb with cold and aching for rest. Yet they knew that to sleep would be fatal.

Four hours after ditching, they heard engines and glimpsed a low-flying Catalina amphibian, about a mile away, on a course which would take it past the dinghy but bring it no closer. The flying boat was

from a Norwegian squadron on patrol for U-boats. Its crew did not see the dinghy.

"Fire a rocket," called Hornell.

Campbell fired one. The Catalina flew on. He fired another. Still they were not seen. "Only one more," said Campbell.

"Fire it," said Hornell.

The rocket soared upward. The plane flew on. But the Norwegian in the starboard blister had seen the third and last flare. The flying boat turned. The men in the dinghy shouted and waved as it circled overhead. The Norwegians reported to Group and were told to stay over the dinghy and await instructions.

A full-scale rescue operation was mounted at once. Two Warwick air-sea re- serve planes were sent, carrying lifeboats, and a high-speed launch was ordered to sail. Other planes in the vicinity were diverted to the scene to keep the dinghy under surveillance. The Norwegians flashed news of the rescue operation to the dinghy by signaling lamp. "Courage," they said. "Help coming." For a time the Canadians almost forgot the cold.

Soon after midnight the Norwegians thought they saw wreckage two or three miles away. After dropping smoke floats to mark the dinghy, they flew off to investigate. When they returned they signaled "U-boat killed." Thirty to 40 Germans, some dead, some alive, were floating in a patch of oil three miles away.

The news of their success inspired Hornell and his crew. They exercised, whistled and sang. But the seas now threatened to swamp them completely: the waves were 25 feet high, the wind 30 knots. To keep the dinghy on an even keel they shifted their weight from one side to the other as they rose to the top of the waves, then crashed down the far side. "Ride 'em cowboy!" they shouted to each other.

Yet hour by hour they were weakening. After eight hours on the sea, Hornell and Campbell were seasick, and Hornell was paralyzed with cold. Campbell found a number of dry cigarettes in a container in his pocket, and these were rationed out. Someone else found some squares of bar-

ley sugar, and, as they sucked them, they fancied they could feel the sugar giving them strength.

A Warwick was now approaching, a lifeboat suspended beneath its bomb bay. But low cloud and fog blanketed the area, the Warwick's radar broke down and the crew searched in vain. Two more Warwicks were dispatched later, at a time when the Canadians had been adrift 12 hours. A subchaser sailed to pick up the survivors of the U-boat.

The Norwegians continued to circle the dinghy, trying to guide the searching aircraft. The pilot, fearing he might lose touch, decided to drop his own dinghy radio. The set was wrapped in a Mae West and fell about 50 yards from the dinghy, but Hornell and his crew didn't see it. Only a moment earlier, they had been caught off balance at the top of a huge wave and the dinghy overturned. They were hurled into the sea.

Choking and gasping, their limbs feeble and numb, they somehow righted the dinghy and crawled back in. Denomy got in first and then helped the others. But Scott, with deliberate self-sacrifice, refused to get in. He supported himself with his chest and elbows on the rim.

They had lost the tin of water and the precious bailer. They were at the mercy of the sea.

St. Laurent became delirious. Hornell and Campbell complained of blindness. Then St. Laurent fell back, dead. They lowered his body over the side to make more room for Scott.

At 10:30, the Norwegian plane sighted a Warwick. The plane came in low and dropped a lifeboat. It splashed into the sea near the dinghy, but the winds were so strong that it drifted off. Soon it was 500 yards away.

Hornell announced he was going to swim for it. He was quietly preparing to go when Denomy restrained him. "You're far too weak. You can't even see properly. We're all too weak. We'll have to wait for the launch."

The Norwegians had been circling in appalling weather for over 12 hours. Without them there would have been no rescue operation at all. But now their plane had reached its endurance limit. It flew low over the dinghy in salute and left, handing the watch to the Warwick. As they left the Norwegians flew over the oil which marked the grave of the U-boat. The subchaser

heading for the German survivors would have a wasted journey—all the bodies were gone.

Meanwhile, the rescue launch was fighting through mountainous seas and near-zero visibility to the Canadians. But it still had a long way to go. Its only hope was to home on an aircraft in the vicinity. The Warwick, running short of fuel, was forced to turn for home, but not before the vigil had been taken over, first by a Liberator, then by a Sunderland flying boat.

The Canadians were near collapse. Scott was the weakest. The others tried to revive him, but it was no use. He had never been able to get properly back into the dinghy, and now, after 19 hours without com-

assistance. Only Denomy was able to climb up unaided—then he collapsed. The medical staff set to work to revive the exhausted men.

When the full story was told and analyzed, all the survivors were decorated. Denomy got the DSO, Campbell and Matheson the DFC, Bodnoff and Cole the DFM. Scott and St. Laurent were mentioned in dispatches.

For David Hornell the launch had arrived too late. He died at sea despite the most dedicated efforts to save him. He was posthumously awarded the second and last Victoria Cross won by an RCAF man in World War II. . . .

SIR PHILIP JOUBERT

plaint, he smiled at his mates and died. His body was lowered gently into the sea.

The double loss discouraged the survivors. But the sea was not quite so heavy now, and the wind was moderating. The Sunderland was still there. Surely their ordeal must end soon.

Bodnoff was the first to see the rescue launch. With the improvement in the weather, he and Cole had regained some strength. Cole was working hard to revive Matheson and bailing at the same time with his cap. Bodnoff was working on Hornell and Campbell. For the last few hours it had been Denomy who had kept them going. His cheerful, bulky figure had hardly relaxed.

The launch drew alongside. Matheson, Campbell and Hornell were hauled up; Bodnoff and Cole climbed the ladder with

An air-sea rescue launch comes alongside the dinghy to which David Hornell and his crew clung for nearly 24 hours. This historic photograph was taken from the last of a series of aircraft which kept vigil over the Canadians and guided the launch to them. Two men had died and their bodies been lowered into the sea. Hornell died soon after this picture was taken. The photo opposite, of another downed plane crew, indicates the difficulty rescuers had in spotting men adrift in the sea.

The ones that got away

Two Canadian soldiers escape from a prison train into the night and into the Maquis; two others run an escape network

The doors were bolted and padlocked, the small windows heavily wired. Day after day, trapped men huddled helplessly in the straw of the stinking boxcars as bombs rained down sporadically from high-flying aircraft bent on destroying the Germans' transportation network. The crews in the bombers were Americans, Britons and Canadians. So were the men in the long train below.

In one boxcar were seven sergeants and 24 officers, among them two Canadian Army lieutenants, Jack Veness, 21, and Jack Fairweather, 20. Both New Brunswickers, they had been among the 128 men captured on June 7, the day after D-Day, when the Germans' 12th SS Division over-ran the North Nova Scotia Highlanders at Authie and Buron.

With hundreds of other Allied prisoners, they had been moved well away from the Normandy beachhead. Now, for days, they'd been sealed into the boxcar, with inadequate food and little exercise and so many air raids that they'd begun to wonder how long their luck could last. On the sixth night, the train was on a siding near Tours. Will R. Bird in *The Two Jacks:*

... Veness wakened to the hum of aircraft. He groped his way to a window and saw flares drifting slowly earthward, lighting everything for miles. The earth seemed to shake as German anti-aircraft batteries opened up. Soon shrapnel was striking loudly on the boxcar roof and the steel rails. Above all the racket rose the mighty sound of many bombers, a thunder that struck terror to the very heart of a man.

"We're done!" someone screamed. "This is it!"

Men groveled on the floor. One chanted "Our Father who art in heaven." An officer attacked the end of the car like a maniac, striking and kicking at the boards, then trying to tear them loose.

Then came the crump-crump-crump of falling bombs—far in the rear. A voice spoke calmly: "They're after the railway yards, not us." Another five minutes of explosions, then the din ended and the sound of bombers faded.

Relief was so strong that voices were shrill or shaky. But in each man's mind was a heavy dread: could he take another attack? Escape was the only hope and Fairweather and Veness made a pact to escape together.

They found that where the crazed officer had attacked the wall, a board had been damaged and could be removed easily. If the hole could be enlarged, their hope might materialize.

After several days on the siding, the train began to move. Maj. Don Learment of the North Novas and an American pilot, William R. Fredenberg, pried and pounded away at the hole with two large spoons, a pocket knife and a hammer. The train rolled on through the night. Men drifted off to sleep.

When Veness woke it was very dark and there was no sound of pounding. He found Capt. Joe Trainor of the North Novas beside the hole. Through it came cool air and a clatter of train wheels. "Where are Learment and Fredenberg?"

"Gone!" said Trainor. "And five others have crawled out."

Veness turned quickly to Fairweather. "Wake up!"

Fairweather laced his boots and crawled to the 18-inch hole, remembering what a paratrooper had told him: "Keep your legs together with your knees slightly flexed, and roll when you fall."

Veness could see three other prisoners on the buffers between the two cars. "We'll jump five seconds apart," he said. "I'll go first."

"Okay," said Fairweather. "You walk back the way we're going and I'll do the opposite. We're sure to meet."

Veness crawled through the opening, head first. The buffers were low, the track was rough and the cars were bucking. One slip would be his last. The three men on the buffers still clung to the cars, reluctant to jump. This left little room for anyone else. Veness lunged when the train was on an upgrade and landed spread-eagled across the buffers. He caught hold of the car and gained his footing.

Fairweather, thick and broad, got stuck in the opening and for a moment felt relief: now he wouldn't have to risk his life. But then he turned and twisted until he squeezed through. He dropped onto the buffer.

The first three men took off, one by one. It was strange to see them fling out into space and not have the slightest idea where they landed. Fairweather saw Veness sitting between the car end and the pad of the buffer, one hand on top of the pad with fingers extended downward. The train had climbed a long curving grade and now began to straighten out on a level stretch. Fairweather kicked Veness's hand away just before the colliding buffers would have squashed it.

"Here goes," said Veness. He stood, and in an instant vanished.

His shoes struck sparks from stones on a roadway. He skidded a few feet and crashed hard on his chest and hands, then rolled into a shallow ditch, face down in mud and weeds. A spasm of dizziness faded and he rose gingerly and watched the red taillight of the train disappear. His chest was badly bruised. His hands were bleeding.

On the train, Fairweather thrust his glasses into his shirt pocket, then crouched and hurled himself outward. He struck heavily on his feet and pitched head over heels into a ditch filled with nettles. A bitten lip and numerous nettle stings on face and hands were his only damage. He reached for his glasses and found they were gone. As the train's taillight vanished, he groped to the rails, stood, stretched and grinned. He was free again. He turned and walked along the track.

Veness heard footsteps on gravel, some-

Guards could flee but Canadian and American prisoners were helpless when Allied bombers attacked German trains, unaware they contained captives. Some later escaped from trains, still others from prison camps —where escapers' regard for other escapers sometimes seemed to transcend nationality.

Ex-POW Kingsley Brown in *The Atlantic Advocate:* " 'Well,' said the Gestapo man, 'why did you escape?' We told him. 'Correct,' he said, 'it is your duty.' He smiled. 'I was a prisoner in the first war,' he said. 'I too escaped.' As the guards took us away, he called: 'Better luck next time!' "

Reinhart Stalmann in *Die Ausbrecherkönige von Kanada:* "In 1941 Uli Steinhilper almost made it to the still neutral United States but was recaptured at Niagara Falls. Back in the POW camp at Bowmanville, Ont., he was congratulated by the Canadian commandant: 'First class, Lieutenant. I did the same thing in Germany. Sorry you had such bad luck so close to your destination.' "

one walking with care. German patrols? He slowed and waited. The footfalls became quicker and steadier. Veness stood.

"Jack?"

"Yeah."

"Hurt?"

"No. You?"

"No. Let's go."

Veness pointed south and said, "That way."

The air was cool and clean and fresh.

"It sure is a nice night," said Veness.

It was about 2 a.m. July 22 and they were near the village of Bléré, on the Cher River east of Tours. They swam the river and talked of heading for Spain, almost 350 miles south. But German patrols were pressing the hunt for the escapers. French civilians hid Veness and Fairweather and led them from one hiding place to another —haylofts and tool sheds and for a while the steeple of a church in the village of Luzillé. After many days on the run they were still only about a dozen miles from where they'd escaped.

They joined a Maquis band near Loches, a town of about 6000 on the Indre River 20 miles southeast of Tours. The Maquis leader was Capt. Georges Le Coz, a swaggering and frequently brutal one-time Foreign Legion officer. In his 30s, he wore the Croix de Guerre and Légion d'Honneur. He commanded the respect of many, the fear and hatred of many more.

The two Jacks—Fairweather (left) and Veness—were part of a Maquis force which occupied the town of Loches, near Tours. The Maquis kept prisoners in the Château de Loches (opposite).

The guerrillas of Groupe Le Coz ate well, drank much and moved frequently. With them were more than a dozen escapers, including Learment and Fredenberg who had worked so hard on the makeshift exit from the train. Le Coz appeared to work entirely on his own, without sanction or instruction from any central command—and according to his own rules.

One night, when Le Coz and his officers were eating supper, there was a commotion at the edge of the clearing where the band was camped. As sentries herded five young Frenchmen out of the woods, Le Coz ordered his officers to "form a court." This meant to stand in line and witness what happened. A sergeant said the guard had caught the five trying to desert. Le Coz strode up and down before the prisoners, kicking their shins, pushing them, striking them with his fists, screaming his hatred of deserters.

There was no court. Le Coz was judge and jury, all others were audience. Finally Le Coz ordered three of the five shot as an example to any others thinking of desertion. The three he chose were dragged before him. He told them he had sentenced them to die. They protested their innocence, wept, shouted and pleaded, but were dragged away. One, a boy of 17, threw his arms around a tree, screamed and sobbed and called Le Coz by name. Le Coz shrugged, waved a hand in dismissal, then pointed to the woods. Two big guards tore the youth from the tree. He wrenched free and ran toward the woods. A dozen Sten guns opened fire and the lad fell, riddled with bullets.

The other two condemned men stared at Le Coz as if he were a beast. The guards caught a sign from the captain and put pistols to the youths' heads. Two shots and the bodies sprawled on the ground.

Le Coz raised a glass. *"Vive la France!"* he cried.

That night, at the height of a party under a full moon, Le Coz shouted that the two who had not been shot were to be beaten. A girl ran from the kitchen, screaming protests—she was the sister of one of the prisoners. Le Coz ignored her. She ran to the woods where they had taken the prisoners and the night was soon filled with her cries, the oaths of the guards and the groans of the two prisoners.

Her brother died of his beating. The girl's face was swollen, her eyes blackened and her head shaved as if she were a collaborator.

Veness saw Le Coz and a woman viewing the bodies of the dead youths. The woman was crying and the captain was trying to console her. He had obtained proof that the youngest of the five, the boy who had clung to the tree and begged for his life, was innocent of desertion. Le Coz detailed men to carry the bodies into the wood and bury them in a single grave.

One of Le Coz's French lieutenants once described the Maquis leader to Fairweather: "He is erratic and a show-off but he has been a terror in the underground work. It is said that he lets personal likes and dislikes rule him. It is said he has committed as many atrocities as Himmler."

On August 13 a plane came over and someone parachuted. A patrol returned with a Maquis major who said he had been sent to bring the Le Coz group into line with "the grand strategy."

"Hell take the grand strategy!" shouted Le Coz. "I am dedicated to fighting the Germans and the Milice [secret police of the Vichy-French government]. My ambition is to free Loches of Germans and capture the chief of police, who is a Milice rat."

Le Coz raved about the exploits of his group and scoffed at the idea of any outsider taking over. The major saw he could only offer advice, which might or might not be accepted.

About this time a messenger reported four large German patrols around an area the group had recently vacated and German vehicles prowling the main highway. Le Coz shrugged. This attention, he said, was proof the enemy regarded him as a dangerous opponent. "As long as they do not know where we are, the nearness means nothing."

But, as enemy activity increased, Le Coz ordered the sentries doubled. Messengers came and went to other Maquis groups. Le Coz was eager to strike at the enemy but wanted to be sure of the situation before making a move.

On August 14 dinner was just over when a nervous messenger arrived at the château where the band was camping.

"Quick!" he snapped. "You have to move. The Boche know you are here. They know how many. There is a traitor somewhere. They are coming to attack."

Le Coz ordered their trucks to be loaded. A sentry ran up.

"The Germans are coming!" he shouted. "They are on the front road!"

"To the back road then," cried Le Coz.

But sentries told him that every road had been cut off, and the Germans were in strength.

"Then we will fight them," raved Le Coz.

One of his sergeants rushed up. "They are bringing mortars," he warned. "We cannot fight bombs." They had no way to counter mortar fire; this was the underground's greatest weakness.

"Every man take what he can carry," ordered Le Coz, calm again, "and get to the woods."

The woods, not large but thick, were about 400 yards from the château. As men ran with ammunition and weapons, there came a shrill whining sound and a shell

exploded in a field a few hundred yards away. The work of getting out the weapons went on. Shells kept coming.

A rear party with provisions was approaching the woods when the Germans rushed into the château grounds, guns blazing and grenades bursting. Thinking they had trapped the Maquis, they shouted for them to come out, yelled threats and for nearly ten minutes fired bursts into the windows. Finally they risked entering the building and the shooting stopped.

The men in the woods lay still as the Germans searched the château grounds with flashlights, trying to discover tracks. They came halfway to the woods but after 20 minutes of shouting and searching they

gave up. They ransacked the château and set it ablaze. About midnight they marched away to the main road. Le Coz led his men to another château.

In the morning a committee from another Maquis group arrived and held a two-hour conference with him. Le Coz wanted a showdown, with all the Maquis joining under his leadership to attack the Germans in Loches.

To some of the escapers this seemed mad. They decided to leave and search for a secret airfield they had heard about, hoping to get from there to the Allied lines. Veness, Fairweather and three others decided to stay, believing they'd run no greater risk with Le Coz, even in an attack on Loches, than if they struck out into country infested with Germans and Milice.

Next day, August 16, armed with Bren

and Sten guns, rifles, pistols, grenades and German machine guns, the Le Coz Maquis headed for Loches in eight cars and eight trucks. The convoy stopped and the men formed into three ranks for the march on the town.

Suddenly a laughing crowd of people appeared. With their main strength in France crumbling, the German garrison had fled when they heard the Maquis were coming.

Le Coz told Veness and Fairweather to march with him at the head of the column. He seized a French flag and led the way, amid great cheering by the townspeople. The march ended before the Palais de Justice in the crowded town square. For

ten minutes the air was filled with cries of *"Vive de Gaulle!"* and *"Vive les Maquis!"* and *"Vive Le Coz!"* A phonograph and loudspeaker were brought up and Frenchmen wept as they sang their national anthem.

Then, as Le Coz walked back and forth past a line of French collaborationist prisoners, a hush came over the crowd. Le Coz slowly worked himself into a rage. He would stop before a prisoner and shout denunciation, then laugh wildly and slap or kick the prisoner. When one man denied he was a collaborator, Le Coz struck him. The man leaped at Le Coz. The prisoner was seized, carried to one side of the square and thrown to the ground. He scrambled to his feet and rushed at a Maquis guard. There was a shot from the guard's rifle and a great gasp from the crowd as the man fell. But when a French officer stepped forward to fire the coup de grâce, the man stirred, jumped up and grappled with the officer. Two men pulled him away and hurled him to the ground; one fired again. And the officer fired the official finishing shot.

There was a long sigh from the crowd. Hundreds hurried off as if to be sick. The nearest shut their lips tightly. Ugly looks were cast at Le Coz. He ordered the remaining prisoners marched to the Château de Loches and held there.

Next day Veness and Fairweather wrote postcards home, even though Loches was still behind enemy lines. Only Fairweather's made it. His card was received by his family three months later. It read in part:

"Dear Mum, Dad and Family:

"On Wednesday we arrived in Loches with the Maquis and liberated the town. They gave us a grand welcome and have been great to us ever since. Everyone wants to have us to dinner or to buy us wine.

"Now we are waiting for the Yanks and hoping that the Germans keep well away. We are pretty confident of rapid relief and hope to be in England soon. We have been with the Maquis since July 30. They are doing great work."

There was to be a parade to mark the liberation of Loches. But just as it was about to begin, machine-gun fire was heard in the distance. The Germans were coming back. Le Coz told Fairweather to lead six men to a small hill 300 yards from where a strong body of Maquis had concentrated to defend the entrance to the town. Veness, meanwhile, took a truckload of 20 men to another defensive position.

The Maquis repulsed one German attack after another but, despite heavy casualties, the enemy kept coming. The Maquis fell slowly back, then turned and retreated.

Fairweather and his group were almost isolated on their hill and were threatened from two sides. The Canadian covered the withdrawal of his six men with a Bren gun, then vaulted a fence amid a hail of German bullets. He saw his men reach the cover of some houses. The Maquis now were in full flight and it seemed inevitable that the town would be recaptured. There was nothing to do but get into Loches with the rest and fight as long as possible. When Fairweather reached the first buildings, a few Frenchmen were standing at a street corner. Fairweather set up his Bren.

All at once the mortaring was intensified and he could see bombs hitting an old castle and raising clouds of red dust. Some dropped quite near.

"Where are the others?" Fairweather asked a Frenchman.

"Gone." The man made motions with his hands. "Like scared pigeons."

"Where is Le Coz?"

"Who knows? He was here, there, everywhere. Now no one has seen him."

The mortars let up for a few minutes, and one of the Maquis drivers came by running like a madman. Fairweather shouted at him and the driver beckoned to the men at the corner to follow him.

They ran to a second street, where the driver wrenched open the doors of a small garage. Inside stood a 1928 Chevrolet, now little more than a wreck. They got it into the yard. The driver adjusted the gas and spark levers, cranked as if his life depended on it and got the motor going. Fairweather and the others piled in. The driver explained that the Germans had overlooked one road leading from the town. Le Coz had used it to escape.

The Chev stopped several times on the way out of town. Each time they got it going again. Loches was silent now, its windows shuttered.

Soon after leaving the town the Chev caught up with a group of Maquis.

"Out!" shouted the driver. "There are more to get."

Fairweather and the others piled out and the ancient car headed back into Loches in a cloud of dust. The struggling, dejected Maquis trudged along a country road. It seemed a tragedy, losing Veness, when they had been so near to freedom.

When the Germans had started their counterattack, Veness and his 20 men had crawled through a field and reached a forward slope. The Maquis formed a long line and Veness set up the Bren behind a clump of bushes. Machine-gun bullets soon told them they had been spotted. The Germans were only 200 yards away.

The Château de Loches was in full view. Suddenly Veness saw mortars bursting about it and heard the boom of artillery and the roar of vehicles: enemy reinforcements arriving.

A French officer came up and said the Germans numbered over 600, the vanguard of an armored division. A German officer had approached under a white flag

Fairweather and Veness were two of several Canadians and Americans in Groupe Le Coz (below), a Maquis band led by Capt. Georges Le Coz (extreme right), a one-time Foreign Legion officer. Right: a safe-conduct Le Coz gave to Veness. It asks Frenchmen to show Veness a safe route to the Allied lines, passing him "from farm to farm if necessary" and giving him free food and lodging. The first Maquis were small groups of young Frenchmen who took to the woods to avoid being sent to Germany as laborers. The word Maquis describes brushland in Corsica where outlaws hide.

and told Le Coz that if the Maquis would withdraw and allow the division to pass through the town, there would be no reprisals and the Maquis could reoccupy Loches afterward. Le Coz had laughed in the German's face.

"Come in and get us!" he challenged.

The officer walked away in a rage and the Germans' mortars fell with new fury. As the enemy pressed their attack, Veness and four others withdrew to the town. There a sergeant told them the Germans had cut off three of the roads leading out of

Loches. There was only one road left open and nearly all the Maquis had left by that route. Veness and his group fled too. They saw a truck ahead, with Maquis standing by it, waving in a frenzy. Veness and his men jumped aboard the vehicle just as it roared away.

The truck slowed when they saw some Maquis sitting by the road. Veness was relieved to see Fairweather among them.

headquarters for the province and a British major who had direct contact with London. The major had promised to get them a flight to Britain, but they had tired of waiting and now were going to try to reach the American lines.

The two Jacks were invited to go along but they declined. The talk did strengthen their decision to leave Le Coz and strike off on their own. In the morning they de-

"Groupe Le Coz!" exclaimed Crown. "We've been looking for him for weeks."

"He has been in St. Hippolyte," said Veness. "Do you want him for anything special?"

"To hang him, of course."

The two Jacks looked at each other. It was evident that Le Coz and his ways were well known.

"Is it true," asked Fairweather, "that

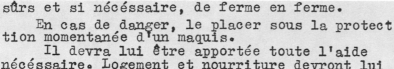

sûrs et si néccssaire, de ferme en ferme.
En cas de danger, le placer sous la protect
tion momentanée d'un maquis.
Il devra lui être apportée toute l'aide
néccssaire. Logement et nourriture devront lui
être délivrés gratuitement

Le Cdt.Militaire d'un secteur
de l'Indre et Loire

Le Coz had had nearly 300 men in Loches. Many had fought like tigers. At least 20 had been killed, more than 50 wounded. A few had been captured. Others had gone into hiding. Scarcely 50 got to the nearby village of St. Hippolyte.

Le Coz selected a farm as a temporary headquarters. At noon the escapers who had left before the attack on Loches arrived there. They had heard of the German victory and the underground had informed them of the whereabouts of the Le Coz group. They reported finding the Maquis

cided to get away before the Germans found the farm. They said good-by and were embraced and kissed on both cheeks by more than 30 unshaven Maquis. Le Coz extended his hand and wished them luck. It was evident, though, that he was not pleased by their departure.

Veness, Fairweather and an American pilot, Tom Whittimore, found the provincial Maquis headquarters. A man wearing the insignia of the Welsh Guards introduced himself as Major Crown. They told him of their experiences.

there is a secret airfield near here?"

"It is true," smiled Crown.

"Could we get to England by plane?"

"Quite possibly," agreed the major. "As soon as the weather clears."

Two days later Crown told them aircraft were due at the secret field that night, but that air force personnel had priority. The American pilot and an RCAF navigator would go first.

In the wireless room Veness put on a headset and listened to the regular BBC newscast from London. Suddenly the

French radio operator thumbed through his code book. Veness heard nothing but the news in English but the Frenchman leaped up and tried to embrace both the Jacks at once. "Two planes at 11:30 tonight," he exclaimed, "and you'll go with the second!"

In London, a military policeman stood speechless at the sight of two hatless, unshaven, long-haired tramps as they crossed Trafalgar Square on their way to Canada House. Veness had no tunic, only a German shirt. The only marks of rank were two lieutenant's pips clinging precariously to one shoulder of Fairweather's tattered jacket. The policeman shuddered, took a second look—and saluted.

The two Jacks could have been posted back to Canada. Instead they rejoined the North Nova Scotia Highlanders and saw a lot of action. Both were wounded. Both became majors.

Later, as they awaited repatriation to Canada, a letter came from friends in France: Le Coz had been arrested and tried as a criminal. There was plenty of

evidence from the relatives of those he had killed or caused to be shot. Le Coz was executed. . . .   WILL R. BIRD

Veness and Fairweather were technically escapers—captured men who'd be damned if they'd spend the rest of the war in a German prisoner-of-war camp. Not many escapers made it all the way to Britain or, after the invasion, even to the Allied lines. Most were recaptured, usually after only a few days or hours of freedom. But throughout the war, in camps throughout Germany, men never ceased plotting to get away to fight again.

There also were the evaders or, in French, *planqués,* generally airmen shot down in enemy territory but determined not to be POWs at all. "The best way to escape," wrote Eric Williams in *Great Escape Stories,* "is not to get caught."

Whether they were escapers or evaders, the ones that got away often had dramatic experiences. They hid in garbage cans, slithered across roofs and down ropes, inched through tunnels and barbed wire. They sneaked away on foot, by bus, bi-

cycle, rowboat and pony. Some ate sumptuous meals and drank fine wine; some chewed grass to stay alive. They hid in haystacks, piggeries, monasteries, ditches. They posed as German businessmen, French laborers, Hungarian technicians. Sometimes their forged papers got them past Gestapo roadblocks. Some—like Veness and Fairweather—joined the Maquis or the Polish underground. And many were lucky enough to come into contact with networks established in western Europe specifically to help them.

Two French-Canadian soldiers ran one of those networks. The story of how they spirited hundreds of Allied airmen and secret agents to safety was told by *Reader's Digest* in John G. Hubbell's *"Good Evening to the House of Alphonse"*:

. . . One night in January 1944, an announcer for the British Broadcasting Corporation voiced a cheery greeting in French from London: "Good evening to everyone in the House of Alphonse. I repeat: Good evening to everyone in the House of Alphonse."

Across the Channel in German-occu-

pied Brittany, in a small room above a café in the village of Plouha, a young man named Raymond LaBrosse, whose papers identified him as a salesman of electrical medical equipment, switched off a radio and turned to the other people in the room. "That's it," he said.

Stocky Lucien Dumais, known locally as a contractor, nodded quickly to the third man, café owner François Le Cornec. "Let's go!" They slipped into the night.

A few minutes later the rear doors of half a dozen village houses opened and small groups of young Frenchmen edged out. With them, dressed in the same sort of clothes, were 13 Americans and five British airmen who had been shot down in France. Silently, by twos and threes, led by the French, they slipped through the woods behind the village, skirting the edges of open meadows to avoid German patrols.

After an interminable time they came to a stone farmhouse—the House of Alphonse, actually the home of Resistance worker Jean Gicquel. Here, before a flickering candle, Dumais warned the airmen: "Many lives have been risked to bring you this far. There is just a mile left, and it is the most dangerous you will ever travel. You will maintain absolute silence and do exactly as you are told. There are enemy sentries and patrols in the area. If it becomes necessary to kill any of them you are expected to help—use knives or your hands. Be quick and above all be quiet; your lives and ours depend on it."

Then Dumais and the villagers led them out again through the darkness. Finally they reached a cliff that dropped sharply 200 feet to the beach. Clutching, sliding, tumbling, they scrambled down to a black cove. From a hidden perch on the cliff, a French sailor had begun blinking the letter B in Morse code on a flashlight. The signal went out over the dark Channel every two minutes. For a long time there was no answer. Then, shortly before 2 a.m., four rowboats slid into the cove to take the airmen aboard a blacked-out British corvette, standing silently offshore.

The villagers returned to the House of Alphonse where they waited for the clock to strike 6 a.m.—the hour the Germans lifted the curfew. Before going to bed in the house at Plouha, Lucien Dumais raised a wineglass to Le Cornec and LaBrosse. *Eh bien*. To our first success. It went like clockwork. But we have a busy season ahead."

Their Operation Bonaparte was the key part of a larger escape network called Shelburne Escape and Evasion Line. One of its two key men was Ray LaBrosse, a 22-year-old Canadian Army signals sergeant. In August 1942 he had been called in by a British Intelligence major in London to answer all sorts of seemingly nonsensical questions. Did he like sports? Adventure? As a boy, what games had he enjoyed most? How did he feel about the war? About the Americans? The British? The French? As LaBrosse answered, the major sized him up. A native of Ottawa, LaBrosse was of French descent and spoke the language fluently. He was young but, according to his superiors, mature, enthusiastic, strong, imaginative.

Finally satisfied, the major put the proposition: he needed two good men to set up and run an escape organization for Allied airmen shot down in France. Capture would mean torture and a spy's death. Was LaBrosse interested? LaBrosse was.

He and a partner parachuted into France in 1943, and for six months they teamed up with the French Resistance in evacuating airmen. Then the apparatus was infiltrated by the Gestapo and his partner was among those arrested. LaBrosse escaped via the Pyrenees to England. He was soon asked if he would return to help set up Shelburne—to find, hide, clothe, feed and evacuate escaping airmen. The role of Bonaparte was to get them out by sea from Brittany. He said he would.

The man selected to go with him this time was Sgt. Maj. Lucien Dumais, 38, of les Fusiliers Mont-Royal, a veteran of the August 1942 raid on Dieppe. He had been captured there but had escaped to England after making his way to Marseilles.

By the time they left England, both had had months of intensive training in jujitsu, the use of various types of weapons and explosives and the construction and operation of wireless sets. They were given fountain pens which fired a deadly gas, buttons which hid compasses, large amounts of francs, forged identity papers. For security reasons, each had his own code, unknown to the other. Finally, on a night in November 1943, a light plane landed them in a meadow 50 miles north of Paris.

The operation very nearly foundered before it got fairly started. Making their way to Paris, Dumais and LaBrosse succeeded in getting in touch with the Resistance. Soon afterward, LaBrosse went to keep a sidewalk rendezvous with one of its members, a woman. A flicker of her eye as he approached warned him that two trench-coated figures idling nearby were Gestapo agents. Shaken, LaBrosse walked on past.

Soon thereafter, immutable rules for governing the escape organization were laid down. No one involved was to know anything except his own function. Co-operating Frenchmen were to be told only that if a "package" (airman) was found it was to be hidden and "rewrapped" (given civilian clothing). Then word should be passed secretly to a reliable friend and instructions awaited. No airman was to be given more than the barest essential information.

Soon escape procedures and routes were worked out, villagers screened and recruited, hideouts arranged. Dumais and LaBrosse rented separate quarters in Paris, met only when necessary. Dumais made no pretense at working as the mortician his Paris papers said he was; he traveled extensively and let the story grow in his neighborhood that he was a successful black-market operator. LaBrosse appeared to be every inch the dutiful salesman. He picked houses known to be safe for his radio operations and exchanged coded messages with London.

As they had surmised, the season was busy. The air over the Continent was reaching its peak of violence; ever-increasing numbers of crewmen from crippled bombers were parachuting down all over France. Typical was Lt. William Spinning, a bomber pilot from Birmingham, Mich., who dropped into north-central France. Bewildered, alone, knowing that any second he might be spotted and shot, he spent days and nights hiding and walking, scavenging cabbages from farms. Once he was given a meal by a huge woodcutter who wept as he watched him eat, then wrapped him in his own worn jacket and pointed him toward Spain. There was a torrential rain, feverish illness, shelter in a barn. At last he saw two men beckoning to him from a field. They gave him hot food and drink, hid him in a warm farmhouse, told him to wait. Though he didn't know it, the Shelburne Line had picked him up.

All the airmen found were funneled first toward the organization in Paris, headed by Paul-François Campinchi. Undertaker Dumais was everywhere—watching, noting, instructing. In a wine warehouse 70 miles south of Paris, he watched while Resistance men taught four Allied airmen to act like ill-humored French laborers. They were not to look angry, just sullen, like the many French who refused to speak to the enemy. If stopped for questioning, they were to show their fake identity papers, say nothing, play dumb. "The slightest mistake can betray you," they were told. "The way you smoke, for example. You people inhale great, greedy drags and often remove a cigarette from your mouth. The Frenchman savors a cigarette. He keeps it in the

corner of his mouth and lets it build an ash. He rarely removes it and he *never* offers cigarettes to others—they are too scarce in France these days."

Next day Dumais was outside a church near Compiègne, reading a newspaper, when a farmer drove up, presented a gift of eggs to the priest, explained he was Paris-bound with a truckload of hay and wondered if Father had "packages" he wanted delivered. The priest nodded and told the man to drive his truck around back to the church cellar entrance. There the driver picked up two airmen who had been hiding in a stack of hay.

The two Canadians were in Paris one night waiting to hear if Resistance interrogators thought Lt. Manuel Rogoff, an American bombardier, was a Nazi agent. Rogoff proved he was an American: he knew that the Pittsburgh Pirates of the National League had lost no games in 1942 to the Chicago Bears of the National League because the Bears were a football team. He knew that Dizzy Dean had never pitched for the Detroit White Sox but for the St. Louis Cardinals (and that it was the Detroit Tigers, not White Sox). He knew what movies had been playing in the theaters on his base in England prior to his last raid. He was well acquainted with the adventures of Tom Sawyer and Huck Finn.

Every airman was interrogated because German agents were always probing. One night a Free Norwegian airman was brought in. Dumais himself questioned him. The man had been flying with the RAF, he said, and was desperately anxious to return to England and rejoin the fight.

He had all the right answers about his squadron, base, even personnel. But he became oddly vague and impatient when quizzed on things Norwegian, said he had not spent much time in Norway in recent years. Dumais' interrogation turned savage. The "Norwegian" panicked, confessed he was a Nazi agent, pleaded for mercy. He offered to join the organization and promised invaluable help, but no chances were taken. Shifted to a house near Versailles, he was pumped for all the information he would give. Then he was shot.

Then there was the young man who identified himself as Robert K. Fruth, an airman from Ohio. He could not answer the most routine questions: his squadron, his bomb group, the pilot of his plane, the names of others in his crew, the target his plane had last attacked. While the Resis-

Maquis guerrillas, some wearing French Army helmets, capture German soldiers after derailing a troop train. Right: Maquisards at a clandestine telephone switchboard through which information and orders were channeled. The map above shows where "the two Jacks" were captured (near Caen) and where they fought in the Maquis (near Loches). "The House of Alphonse" was near Plouha in Brittany. Allied airmen shot down in enemy territory were collected in Paris, then waited in small towns like Guingamp before being led to the coast near Plouha to be put aboard a ship and taken to Britain.

tance was considering whether to execute him, LaBrosse tapped out a short, coded message to London. Two days later a BBC broadcast keyed to the coded query established that Fruth was genuine. Newly arrived in England from the States, he had been roused from bed in predawn darkness his very first night to replace a gunner fallen suddenly ill. That explained why he had no time to acquire the most rudimentary information before he was shot down.

The transfer of airmen from Paris to the Brittany coast was tricky. Too many "packages" delivered to Plouha, the principal jumping-off point for Bonaparte escapes, might attract attention. So the disguised airmen were first sent to a num-

By the middle of March 1944, LaBrosse reported in his radio code to British Intelligence that dozens of fliers and secret Allied agents were hidden around the Brittany countryside. Thus, on three March nights, there came again over the BBC the welcome message, "Good evening to everyone in the House of Alphonse." In separate groups, the men were taken out.

Cautious and vigilant, the two Canadians nevertheless knew how to take risks. Soon after the Normandy invasion in June, they had to reach Brittany for an evacuation. Rail lines had been knocked out or commandeered by German forces, so they started out on bicycles. In Rennes, a German military policeman took Dumais'

and said it was being requisitioned for their troops. The housewife pleaded that she already was rooming several weary railroad men and had no more beds. She was given an hour to clear the rooms. That hour gave her just enough time to get rid of several Allied airmen. In François Kerambrun's truck, they were rushed somewhere else.

On another occasion, German shore batteries spotted the British corvette and opened fire. She escaped only to return hours later and complete the rendezvous. Just as dawn lit the area, the corvette slipped over the horizon with more "packages" for London.

One night the Germans themselves paid

ber of other small towns nearby. One was Guingamp, 15 miles from Plouha.

Before an airman boarded the train in Paris, he was well briefed. In his hand or stuffed in his left coat pocket he must carry a newspaper. As he crossed the Guingamp platform, a nondescript man would jostle him and give him a swift, discreet dig in the ribs. That was the sign of recognition. Guingamp's Resistance leader was Mathurin Branchoux, a thrice-wounded World War I veteran. Among his retinue was François Kerambrun, who drove a small enclosed delivery truck for the Germans. To the airmen he was carrying to a hideout near Plouha, Kerambrun would explain that the Germans allowed him to attend to his own private business in his off-hours. This was his private business—doing what he could for France.

bicycle. Dumais signaled LaBrosse to keep moving and meant to flee, himself, on foot. Then he thought better of it—boldness might arouse less suspicion than humility. He stormed into German military police headquarters, shouting that he had been robbed. "It is imperative that I be in St. Brieuc this evening," he roared at the commandant, "and you must get me there." The commandant, fearing that he had a wealthy, influential French collaborator on his hands, provided a staff car. When LaBrosse pedaled wearily into St. Brieuc next day, a grinning Dumais was waiting for him.

The Gestapo was never able to discover Operation Shelburne. But there were many close shaves. Once in Guingamp, with the town full of Germans, two Nazi officers hammered at the door of a house

French Canadians Lucien Dumais and Raymond LaBrosse ran an escape network until after the Normandy invasion, then worked with the Maquis (above, marching German prisoners through the streets of Plouha). Right: death by firing squad at Rennes. Splinters fly from the stake and the rope that bound him snaps as fellow Frenchmen execute a man who collaborated with the Germans.

a hair-raising visit to the House of Alphonse. Dumais and café owner Le Cornec had just briefed a group of airmen and left the premises when a German patrol knocked on the door and instructed its inhabitants—Jean Gicquel and his family—to come out. Instead of obeying, Gicquel slammed the door in their faces and hustled his ailing wife, his six-week-old daughter and five airmen up to the attic.

The Germans opened fire and wounded one of their own men. They brought him into the house to patch him up. Hiding in the attic, everyone lay motionless, hardly daring to breathe, ready for the fight to the death they were certain was coming. But the Germans, nervous and excited, unaccountably departed without searching upstairs. Gicquel and the airmen slipped out of the house to a nearby wheat field where

they waited out the night. Next day Dumais and Le Cornec rounded them up and later got them out.

Eight times Bonaparte's men and women led Allied airmen and agents—Britons, Americans, Canadians, Free French, Belgians, Dutchmen, Poles—through that hazardous journey to the coast. When there were no more evacuations to be made by sea, the two Canadians fought in the Maquis around Plouha.

So tightly kept was the secret of Shelburne and Bonaparte that none of the *évadés* learned a network existed. Most assumed they had just fallen in with a single escape operation. But years later one of them—Ralph Patton, a Buffalo, N.Y., businessman—tracked down the story while vacationing in France. He learned that in seven months this network

had rescued 307 downed Allied airmen and secret agents. Bonaparte alone accounted for nearly half of the total. Of all the escape networks on the European continent, Shelburne was the most successful: it never lost a single "package." The only casualty was the House of Alphonse itself—the Germans, suspecting it to be a Resistance hideout, burned it.

As a result of Patton's discovery, 50 of the American *évadés* gathered in Buffalo one night in May 1964, to honor those who so willingly had risked death for them. On hand were Lucien Dumais, now a Montreal businessman, and Maj. Raymond LaBrosse of the Canadian Army. From Brittany came Mathurin Branchoux, Guingamp's Resistance leader. It was the only noisy rendezvous Bonaparte ever had. . . .

JOHN G. HUBBELL

Troops specially trained for invasion had been so long keyed up for this great assault that they were unable (and perhaps understandingly unwilling to try) to project their thoughts beyond it. Hence, awaking cold, stiff and dirty from a night of fitful sleep in a shallow hole in French soil—in most cases their first on *terra firma* for three days—these men who had landed on D-Day had almost to pinch themselves to be assured of the astonishing fact that they were still alive. One phase of the battle was successfully completed, but to the vast majority of the soldiers little was known of the form the fighting was now likely to take, except that they had been led to expect that the Germans would recover soon and try to counterattack. The most immediate and unpleasant job for those on the ground was to resume the fighting. And this they did.

Eversley Belfield and H. Essame
in *The Battle for Normandy*

Everywhere the pale upturned faces

**Five thousand Canadians
give their lives to crush the Germans in France**

"Komm!" ordered a teen-ager in a floppy camouflage suit, a boy with cold eyes and a Schmeisser at his hip. He and another German had crawled through the wheat and slowly worked behind their enemy. Now suddenly they stood and slowly a Nova Scotian named Leon M. Rhodenizer stood too. For Major Rhodenizer the fighting war was over. It was June 7, the day after D-Day, in a field in Normandy.

The war ended that day for nearly 250 North Nova Scotia Highlanders and three-score Sherbrooke Fusiliers tankmen, killed and captured in battle a few miles northwest of Caen. Of the 110 dead, 23 were murdered after being taken prisoner by the 12th SS Division, a savage meld of young, green soldiers and tough veterans of the Russian campaign. It was as barbarous a force as the war produced, a superb fighting machine with the fanaticism of the Hitler Youth—from which the teen-agers were drawn—and the viciousness of Heinrich Himmler's SS (*Schutzstaffeln*), the elite fourth arm of the German forces.

"These Hitler Youth," wrote war correspondent Ralph Allen, "were beardless killers whose highest aim was to die, whose only god was Hitler, who came rustling through the spring wheat, a screaming curtain of mortars just ahead of them, the fearsome clanking of their tanks behind."

From that first day, the 12th SS and the 3rd Canadian Division were locked in an almost personal feud that would last until one or the other was destroyed. The Canadians were far tougher, far abler than the Hitler Youth had expected. But nothing in the long training years in Britain had prepared the Canadians for this kind of enemy. Nor had D-Day.

D-Day had been a brilliant success. Now on D-plus-1, the Germans counterattacked with the 12th SS and other divisions; the Allies tried to push inland in accordance with the 90-day master plan for the Battle of Normandy.

"We would fight inland," said Gen. Sir Bernard Montgomery, the overall ground commander, "then draw all the German strength we could—particularly armored strength—onto the British-Canadian front. British and Canadians would hold the main German strength there and I would use the American armies to break out on the western flank and sweep south and then east up to the Seine." Here the Allies hoped to trap the Germans.

As things turned out, it took not 90 days but 75. The Canadians' task was tough, thankless and unspectacular, but it contributed mightily to making the plan work. As anticipated, the Germans expected a breakout not from the American sector but from the eastern flank, the one nearer Paris, so they did concentrate their armor on the British-Canadian front around Caen.

The frontline soldier knew nothing of top-level strategy. His job on June 7, 1944, as always, was simple: clear a house or kill a sniper, reach a hedge or ditch or wall, seize a crossroads or, if he were with the 7th Brigade that day, drive to the Caen-Bayeux highway and railroad. That brigade's Winnipeg Rifles and Regina Rifles were the first Allied units to reach D-Day objectives. They met little resistance.

But it was grimly different on the left. The 9th Brigade's North Novas, with the Sherbrooke tanks in support, pushed for Carpiquet airport, three miles west of Caen. Their advance guard got beyond the effective range of Canadian artillery, and naval gunfire was temporarily unavailable because of radio failure. There were no Allied troops on the Canadians' left—a British brigade which was to have been there had been ordered to another hot spot on D-Day—and there was no contact with 7th Brigade on the right. The advance guard pushed through the village of Buron but, with no support, was seriously exposed by the time it got into Authie, the next village down the road. The Novas' Lt.

Col. Charles Petch decided to withdraw to higher ground. But before the C company platoons in Authie could get out, they were counterattacked by a 12th SS brigade led by Standartenführer (SS Colonel) Kurt Meyer.

Meyer had spotted the Canadian advance from an observation post in a turret of the Abbey of Ardenne, a cluster of medieval buildings whose name would live on in the brutal history the 12th SS was about to shape. German writer Paul Carell, in *Invasion—They're Coming!*:

. . . Meyer climbed to the lofty chapel and in his binoculars saw enemy armor [Sherbrooke Fusiliers] forming. One tank stopped only 200 yards from where his men lay behind a hedge. Not a shot was fired.

An armored unit now emerged from Buron, making for the Caen-Bayeux road. The Canadian tanks were unknowingly moving across the front of Meyer's well-hidden 2nd Battalion, exposing a long, unprotected flank. Meyer commanded: "Fire not to be opened except on my express orders." Each Canadian movement he reported by telephone from the tower was radioed to the German tanks.

As the Canadian spearhead neared the Caen-Bayeux road, Meyer barked: "Attack!" The leading Canadian tank was blown up. The second was on fire, its crew tumbling into a ditch. Tank after tank was shot up. Meyer's attack was in full swing. Already the first Canadian prisoners were shuffling into the Abbey garden, their hands above their heads. . . .

The battle the North Novas fought was described by Will R. Bird in his history of the unit, *No Retreating Footsteps,* and his book *The Two Jacks.* Excerpts from the two volumes:

. . . There were Germans everywhere in Authie. A terrific artillery barrage filled the air with earth and shrapnel and bits of wood. Tanks fired as fast as guns could be reloaded, machine guns chattered.

More and more Germans appeared in the smoke and dust. Time and again they seemed only yards away but were hurled back. Then men screamed that the enemy were coming in from the other side of Authie: C company was being surrounded. Capt. Hank Fraser and a few others determined to fight as long as possible. The rest tried to get back to positions that could be held. Some made it, across 50 yards of open ground and 200 yards of wheat field, to a hedge where A company was holding.

Fraser, some other Novas and Sherbrookes and machine gunners of the Cameron Highlanders of Ottawa took a huge toll of SS but were finally overwhelmed and killed.

Getting out of Authie, Sgt. Bill Gammon ran into two Germans, shot one and when his Sten gun jammed smashed it into the face of the other German. He ran to the wheat field and by nightfall got back to the battalion lines. Cpl. Douglas Wild, also alone, encountered three Germans. One lunged at him with a bayonet. With his rifle butt, Wild knocked the German aside, then shot the other two. He threw two smoke bombs ahead of him and used the screen to reach the grain. Pte. Freeman Wallace took six hours to get through the wheat to the battalion lines. Cpl. Walter McKillop and his brother Earl, a sergeant, were captured but escaped when machine-gun fire pinned down their captors.

A company, under Major Rhodenizer, held on back of Authie, still expecting B company to get up on the left and artillery to come to the rescue. Six German tanks appeared suddenly on the right and moved toward Buron, killing nine men as they went. More German infantry moved in around A company and, near sundown, German shelling ceased. From the wheat rose the young soldier with the Schmeisser. *"Komm!"* Major Rhodenizer and what was left of his company were surrounded. Lt. G. A. P. Smith rose, a rifle in his hands. Capt. J. A. Trainor shouted and Smith dropped his weapon just as a German was about to shoot him. More Germans came from the right. Two shot and killed two Novas who had surrendered. Still hidden, Pte. W. H. Gerrior shot these two Germans and three others; then he pulled the bolt from his rifle, threw it away, got up and surrendered without the Germans knowing where the shots had come from.

The SS shot three men as they marched the A company survivors back to Authie. Authie was littered with German bodies. As the battle smoke lifted, revealing the casualties inflicted by C company, German soldiers shot several more prisoners.

A German staff car raced by, horn blowing, and a soldier in the back seat took pot shots at prisoners. Two men staggered, hit in the stomach. The guards grinned, lined the prisoners in two ranks and searched them. One prisoner said something to a friend. As the man turned to answer, an SS guard emptied a submachine gun into his stomach.

In the square in Authie, laughing SS troops propped a dead Canadian against the wall of a house, put a German helmet on his head, a cigarette in his mouth, a beer bottle in the crook of his arm.

German vehicles were speeding both ways, some loaded with wounded who shook their fists at the Canadians. A big truck deliberately swerved into marching prisoners and two men died on the pavement. A guard said, "You bombed Germany. Can you expect mercy?"...

WILL R. BIRD

That was the savage truth of D-plus-1: little or no mercy. And on June 8 the 12th SS struck again, this time at the Canadian 7th Brigade. German tanks and infantry surrounded and cut to pieces the three forward companies of the Winnipeg Rifles.

That evening, at heavy cost, the Canadian Scottish retook the ground the Winnipegs had lost. The Regina Rifles fought a desperate night-long battle against Panther tanks; 22 tanks circled around the battalion headquarters, but the Reginas held.

Maj. Gen. R. F. L. Keller, 3rd Division commander, reported: "Two days spent repelling violent counterattacks. Losses approximately 1400-1500 all ranks, 7th Brigade restored situation in heroic manner. All of us still fighting like mad. Am very proud of them."

The losses included prisoners—and more were murdered. On the 8th, at a 12th SS battalion command post, six Winnipeg Rifles were ordered into a wood and shot. One was a stretcher-bearer with the armband of the Red Cross. Later the same day, 13 more Winnipegs were shot within 100 yards of the command post. The bodies of seven others were found close by, without arms or equipment; all had been killed by small-arms fire.

This teen-ager (left), fighting his first battle, was typical of the Hitler Youth the Canadians encountered on D-plus-1. But these fanatical youngsters were led by good officers, seasoned NCOs and other tough veterans (below) of battles on the eastern front. Together they stalled the Anglo-Canadian advance toward Caen.

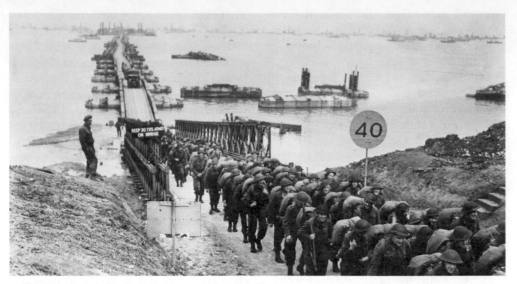

That evening, 40 Winnipegs and Cameron Highlanders were marched into a field and ordered to sit close together with their wounded in the center. German soldiers opened fire and 35 Canadians were massacred. When the firing started, the five others ran for a wheat field and escaped.

Two Regina Rifles were captured on outpost duty June 9 and interrogated by a German officer. Dissatisfied with their answers, he shot them. One Canadian was killed instantly. The other, hit in the thigh, fell to the ground, feigned death and eventually got back to his battalion. That same morning, three wounded Canadians were marched into a garden and shot by four German soldiers.

The murdering went on while the two sides jockeyed for position: the Allies building up strength, striving to enlarge their beachhead; the Germans unable to throw them back into the sea but determined not to surrender Caen. At least 18 executions occurred at the Abbey of Ardenne, Kurt Meyer's headquarters, and these formed the crux of Canada's postwar case against Meyer as a war criminal. From June 7 to 17, wrote Lt. Col. Bruce J. S. Macdonald in his book, *The Trial of Kurt Meyer,* there were 134 killings in various units and separate incidents throughout the 12th SS, some in the presence of high-ranking officers. "Indications," he said, "are that many more than 134 Canadians were murdered after capture. In 134 cases there is certain proof."

Within hours of the first killings, every soldier knew—and now sometimes Cana-

As reinforcements poured in through "Mulberry" artificial harbors (above), Germans and Canadians a few miles inland fought a battle in which some men on both sides were killed after surrendering. Maj. Gen. Kurt Meyer, many of whose 12th SS Division (right) were captured by Canadians, was held responsible for the murder of Canadian prisoners and went on trial (extreme right) in December 1945. A military court found him guilty on three of five charges and he was sentenced to be shot. Maj. Gen. Chris Vokes later ruled that the severity of the sentence was "not in keeping with Canadian justice, having regard to the degree of responsibility," and commuted the sentence to life imprisonment. Meyer was released in 1954.

dian and British soldiers shot German prisoners. Enmity, wrote Ralph Allen, soon "distilled out its last adulterant and left a pool of purest venom."

Alexander McKee said in *Caen: Anvil of Victory* that, in individual narratives and regimental and divisional histories, there are frequent reports of "no quarter given on either side from late June on." Other witnesses, wrote McKee, were "equally emphatic in declaring the opposite: they had never witnessed the deliberate execution of prisoners—deliberate, as opposed to accidental shootings or misunderstandings. But even here there were sometimes borderline cases, open to misinterpretation by any enemy who witnessed them. The men responsible were under extraordinary strain and tension, knowing they had to shoot first to stand any chance of staying alive."

McKee quotes a Canadian soldier as saying that by August "the Germans weren't too eager to surrender. We never took any SS prisoners now and sometimes dealt with Wehrmacht (regular German Army) formations in the same way."

Montgomery had hoped to take Caen on D-Day. He didn't take it for a month. He had to build up first and it was a long, laborious job. The front stayed pretty well where it was on D-plus-2 and the Germans never did mount the great tank attack they had hoped would drive the Allies into the sea. They made the deadly mistake of believing Normandy was only a feint. Their Fifteenth Army might have tipped the scales; instead, it remained in the Pas de Calais, waiting for a second assault that never came.

On the Canadian front, for weeks, there were daily barrages and nightly patrols and wounding and dying. "We dug narrow graves and lowered them to rest," wrote the Rev. R. M. Hickey, padre of the North Shore (New Brunswick) Regiment. "The men would stop a while and remove their caps as I blessed a group of graves and said the burial prayers. I often thought that somewhere a mother, a father, a wife, a sister or brother still hoped and prayed."

Padre J. C. Clough of the Queen's Own Rifles kept a diary: "June 21—Went to visit most forward company, well dug in, very close to Jerry. Suggested service in shattered farmhouse and suggestion quickly taken up. I used the parable of the man whose soul was required of him that night."

By the end of June, a half-million men were in the beachhead. The Americans hadn't broken out, the Canadians hadn't taken Carpiquet airport and the British still were not in Caen. The Germans had done what the Allies wanted: they concentrated 7½ of their 8 armored divisions and half of their 12 other divisions against the British and Canadians. With that strength the Germans might turn the British-Canadian flank and control the plain north of Caen. Then they would be in a position to command the beaches and smash the Allied buildup.

The Allies, as a prelude to any breakout, had to take Caen—and Carpiquet airport had to be taken first. It was held by 12th SS units under Kurt Meyer, recently promoted to major general and given command of the division. Carpiquet's capture was assigned to the 8th Brigade—North Shores, Queen's Own and le Régiment de la Chaudière—with the 7th Brigade's Winnipeg Rifles. They would attack July 4 with the support of tanks and flamethrowers. Alexander McKee:

. . . A concentration of 428 field guns was laid on, backed by the fire of warships, including the nine 16-inch guns of the battleship *Rodney* and the 15-inch guns of the monitor *Roberts*. Carpiquet was held by only 150 teen-agers of the Hitler Youth, 100 on the airfield and 50 in the village. They were supported by tanks and guns.

The German defense was stronger than would appear merely by counting heads or the weight of shellfire. Kurt Misch, a German artilleryman who watched from the tower of the Abbey of Ardenne, said the airfield defenders had the advantage of "very well built underground blockhouses, connected by passages." The other special factor favoring the defense, said Misch, was that "our radio intelligence had the key to the Canadian codes."

A British spotter wrote: "The Canadian attack looked like a carefully rehearsed tattoo, the only difference being that, when the first attack failed, no drums rolled, no searchlights flashed, nor did the men lying so still get up and walk away." . . .

Father Hickey of the North Shores wrote: "That first night alone, we buried 40 of our

The Love Letter

"Father," the soldier said to me, "you told us if we couldn't write you'd write for us."

"Sure," I said, "anytime."

"Any kind of letter? A *love* letter?" I assured him I was a master at love letters and I'd write just what he said.

"Dear Mary." I wrote that. "I love you." Again: "I love you." He kept repeating: "I love you."

"Yes," I said, "I have that. Now, how much?"

"I love you . . . well, I love you as much as I love the Lord."

Heresy? Not at all. That was his way of telling Mary he loved her a whole lot. Six months later they were married.

Four years later, one evening during the Battle of Carpiquet, in Normandy, I knelt and looked at the lifeless face of the boy who'd had me write that letter. I lowered him into his rough and narrow grave and, as I whispered the *Requiem Aeternam,* a voice from the past said over and over: "Dear Mary . . . Dear Mary . . ." And when I wrote to tell his wife I had prepared him for death and buried him, that same voice awoke again: "I love you, I love you as much as . . ."

From *The Scarlet Dawn* by the Rev. R. M. Hickey (above)

boys. You could fancy the wheat field had once been just like any wheat field back home. Now it was torn with shell holes and everywhere you could see the pale up-turned faces of the dead."

The Canadians took the village and most of the airport that first day—but they couldn't get it all. The cost was 117 dead and 260 other casualties. And in the ruins of Carpiquet the brigade held until the time came for Caen itself.

Caen, a city of 55,000, had been pounded by Allied fire for weeks and, on the night of July 7, it was devastated by 467 British and Canadian bombers. Next day the North Novas and the rest of the 3rd Division swept down through Buron and Authie and on into the shambles that remained. None of it was easy. At Buron the Highland Light Infantry fought its first real battle and, like the North Shores' at Carpiquet, it was their bloodiest of the entire Normandy campaign: 262 casualties, 62 fatal. Total Canadian casualties for July 8 and 9 were 1194—more than on D-Day.

On July 9, 33 days later than planned, Caen was taken by two British divisions and the 3rd Canadian. The Stormont, Dundas and Glengarry Highlanders, with Sherbrooke Fusiliers tanks, were the first Canadians into its streets.

To the CBC's Matthew Halton, the city looked like the end of the world. But "to our astonishment," he said in a broadcast, "we saw a great church, the famous Abbaye-aux-Hommes, 1000 years old, which not one bomb or shell had touched. Inside were 2000 people who'd lived there for several weeks. Babies had been born at the foot of the sanctuary and wounded people had been tended above the tomb of William the Conqueror. Hundreds of people shook our hands. All were calm and dignified but their enthusiasm was deep and touching. There was a ceremony in the square outside. The flag of France was raised and they sang 'La Marseillaise,' weeping, the broken and tortured voices of unbroken people."

Even some of the 12th SS wept in the holocaust of Caen. Their ranks were decimated by the time it was over. "A few have surrendered," Ralph Allen wrote July 9. "A few have broken under the onslaught of these last 36 hours and have become suddenly the little boys they never gave themselves a chance to be. But for the most part the pride of the Hitler Youth has died. 'They look like babies,' said a Canadian

corporal, 'and they die like mad bastards.' A Canadian major told of a German who held out in a slit trench, catching Canadian grenades and throwing them back before they exploded. Finally, one blew his right arm off. He threw back another with his left hand before he missed one and was killed."

The 12th SS now was little more than a remnant; its infantry strength was cut to that of a battalion and 65 of its 150 tanks were gone. It would withdraw to refit and it would return, but it would never be the same again.

Nor would the Normandy battle. With the fall of Caen, it was ready for a bigger, more decisive stage.

It is roughly 20 miles from Caen to Falaise. The hard, black road runs south through quiet, rustic country dotted with villages and small towns and clumps of forest and gentle ridges. That summer of 1944 it became the axis of Canadian advance—and

SLEWING POINT 8 YDS. FURTHER ON

Prisoner and guard take it easy in a shattered Norman town while awaiting transport to move the German to a POW cage. Below: Canadian troops advance toward the front.

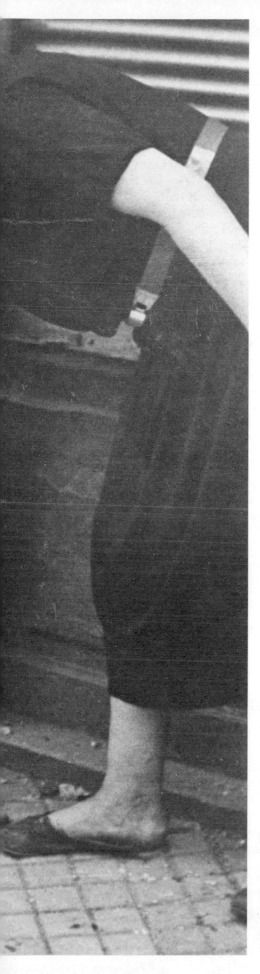

a scarlet memory in Canadian military lore.

For the 2nd Infantry and 4th Armored divisions it became a place of learning, a much more brutal place than Sicily had been for the 1st Division a year before. Here they were thrown into one of the great battles of history. They were green, and it showed, but they were brave and that showed too.

Under Maj. Gen. Charles Foulkes, the 2nd came into the line to join the 3rd and the 2nd Armored Brigade in Lt. Gen. Guy Simonds' 2nd Corps. Together, on July 18, they attacked out of Caen and across the Orne River toward Verrières Ridge, a few miles south, in support of a massive British armored thrust called Operation Goodwood. They made a few miles, with heavy air support, then were stopped by the Germans. But they had helped set the stage for a full-scale breakthrough in Normandy and they had kept the main German strength where the Allies wanted it—on the Anglo-Canadian front.

On July 25, the Canadians attacked south of Caen. They made small gains and suffered their greatest casualties—1500 men—for any single day of the war except Dieppe. One battalion alone, the Black Watch, suffered 300 casualties on the ridge of Verrières.

But, some 35 miles to the right, the First U.S. Army broke through near St. Lô. At brutal cost, the Canadians had helped the Americans begin a spectacular run.

Gen. George S. Patton's Third U.S. Army pushed toward Avranches. The new German chief in Normandy, Field Marshal Günther von Kluge, ordered to hold at any cost, told Hitler: "The moment is approaching when this front will be broken. Once the enemy has penetrated into open country, organized operations will no longer be possible to control, owing to our lack of mobility."

On July 23, eight days after his headquarters began to function in the field, Lt. Gen. H. D. G. Crerar's First Canadian Army took over the front south of Caen. For the first time in history Canada had a formation of army stature in the field, even if many of its men came from other lands. It was made up of General Simonds' 2nd Corps, including the 1st Polish Armored Division and 51st (Highland) Division, and the 1st British Corps, which had a Dutch and a Belgian brigade.

That same day Gen. Omar Bradley's U.S. Army Group broke through at Avranches. Hitler might have allowed his SS armored divisions to shepherd the rest of his Normandy forces back to the Seine. Instead, he ordered the bulk of his strength west to counterattack Bradley's spearhead. In perfect flying weather, the fighter-bombers of the RAF 2nd Tactical Air Force, many Canadians among them, reinforced

Most French civilians were pro-Allied —and showed it. Some, like this housewife, risked injury or death to assist Allied soldiers as town after town was cleared of stubbornly resisting Germans.

the Ninth U.S. Air Force and on August 7 flew 104 sorties on the American front. Together they broke the German attack. It was the first time in history, wrote German Gen. Bobo Zimmerman, "that an attacking force had been stopped solely by bombing."

Shortly after midnight that night General Crerar launched an attack into the weakened German defenses between him and Falaise.

The original plan had been to drive the Germans back on the Seine and cut their retreat by blocking the gap between the Seine at Paris and the Loire at Orléans. But the counterattack ordered by Hitler created a chance to cut off the entire German Seventh Army far short of the Seine.

Patton, at Le Mans, swung north to Alençon and drove for Argentan, forming one half of a huge pincer movement to cut off the forces Hitler had ordered into the American sector. The other half would come from Crerar's push down through Falaise. He ordered a five-division thrust called Operation Totalize.

General Simonds planned the unusual details: it would be a night attack, with searchlights providing "artificial moonlight" and tracer shells indicating enemy positions and lines of advance; heavy bombers would be used—the first bombers to support a ground operation at night; leading troops would be transported in improvised armored carriers called Kangaroos—U.S. Priest self-propelled guns from which the 105-mm. cannons had been removed.

This was a moment of opportunity, said General Crerar; a great victory might bring a quick end to the war. The only armor facing the Canadians was Kurt Meyer's reorganized 12th SS, in reserve behind the 89th German Infantry Division, and it was held there just as it was about to move to the American front.

Shortly before midnight August 7, heavy bombers blasted German positions. Then 720 Canadian and British guns opened fire. The 2nd Canadian and 51st Highland divisions, with the 2nd Armored Brigade, quickly captured the high ground so long denied them. Said von Kluge: "We must now risk everything. A breakthrough such as we have never seen is taking place near Caen."

When Kurt Meyer heard of the beginning of Totalize, he ordered 20 12th SS tanks north to block the Falaise road near

Cintheaux, then drove up himself to consult the 89th Division, which was taking the brunt of the attack. Near Cintheaux he encountered the first German soldiers he had ever seen in flight.

"I lit a cigar and stood in the middle of the road," said Meyer. "At the top of my voice I asked if they intended to leave me alone to fight the enemy. They stopped, hesitated and finally returned to their positions." Meyer had halted what might have become a rout.

The first phase of the Canadian attack broke through the first German defense line. It was a spectacular success. The second phase wasn't. Two green armored divisions, the 4th Canadian and the 1st Polish, were sent in against the Germans' second line of defense—and the Allied thrust quickly lost momentum.

The 4th had recently lost its tough, beloved Maj. Gen. F. F. Worthington. He had formed and trained the division but at 54 was judged too old for battle command and the army sent him home to a training job. Maj. Gen. George Kitching, a young officer with an excellent record but little battle-command experience, took over. Like his division, Kitching found Normandy a brutal learning ground.

The U.S. Eighth Air Force dropped close to 1500 tons of bombs as a prelude to the new attack. But two 12-plane groups—there were 492 bombers altogether—inadvertently struck the Canadian corps. The Poles and the 3rd Division were hardest hit: 65 killed, 250 wounded. The North Shore Regiment lost 100 men. General Keller, the 3rd Division commander, was among the wounded.

Once the green armored divisions got going, they made nothing like the progress planned. The impetuous Poles moved too fast—and suffered heavy losses from German tanks. The Canadians were too deliberate. General Simonds ordered them to press on that night but, wrote army historian Col. C. P. Stacey, in fact operations were largely suspended and the tanks withdrew to harbors, as in training. The 4th Division chose caution in a situation where boldness might have won a great success.

Inexperience and perhaps *lack* of caution contributed next day to virtual annihilation of the 4th's British Columbia Regiment and two companies of the Algonquin Regiment.

Sent forward before dawn to try to get

As mop-up troops (left) clear snipers from the streets of Caen, civilians (below) scramble for a psychological warfare newssheet. One Frenchman said of the liberation of the ancient Norman capital: "The joy is great and yet restrained. People have reproached us for not having fallen on the necks of our liberators. Those people forget the calvary we have been undergoing since the 6th of June." A Canadian sign went up in Caen: "Don't Loot—These People Have Suffered Enough Already."

the attack moving, the tank-infantry force apparently got lost and took up a position on high ground more than three miles northeast of its objective, Point 195. No ground help could reach it because it wasn't where it was supposed to be. All day enemy tanks, artillery and infantry tore at its positions, destroyed 47 tanks and killed, wounded and captured many men. The survivors fought courageously until dusk when, as a final attack was coming in, those who could still go slipped away. Most got to the Polish lines.

"This episode, with its tragic mixture of gallantry and ineptitude, had been appallingly costly," wrote Colonel Stacey. "Such losses would have been deeply regrettable even as the price of success. Unfortunately they were suffered in a tactical reverse which did much to prevent us from seizing a strategical opportunity of the first magnitude."

Totalize ended that day with a total gain of nine miles. With inferior forces the Germans had stabilized the situation. They had suffered a heavy blow—"ten feet gained on the Caen sector," said Supreme Allied Commander Gen. Dwight Eisenhower, "was equivalent to a mile elsewhere"—but to penetrate to Falaise, Crerar's army would have to mount another large-scale attack.

Operation Tractable started August 14, when distance between the Canadians at Potigny and the Americans near Argentan to the south had been narrowed to 18 miles. Artillery laid smoke along the flanks, then tanks swept down the Laison valley, followed by infantry in Kangaroos and for the first time using Wasps, flamethrowers mounted on carriers.

The British and Canadians bombed enemy positions south of Potigny and west of the Canadians. Some bombs fell short and Canadian troops again suffered casualties from supporting aircraft.

Advance elements of the 2nd Canadian Division got into heavy woods just north of Falaise on August 16. During the night infantry and Sherbrooke tanks battled into the devastated town—normal population 7000—and it was cleared of Germans on the 18th.

Three days before, the 4th Canadian and 1st Polish Armored divisions had thrust off to the southeast toward Trun to help seal the gap through which the German divisions were pouring in the pandemonium of retreat.

Capt. Peter Simonds wrote in *Maple Leaf Up, Maple Leaf Down:*

. . . From high ground west of Falaise, one could see German columns struggling to escape between Falaise and Argentan. Some wanted to surrender but SS troops and others wouldn't let them. So they made a hollow show of fight, hoping to get out of range of SS guns and throw their hands up before a bullet got them.

It was stupid and degrading. As one German company advanced on a Canadian platoon in an obvious bid to surrender en masse, the platoon commander told his men: "If they want to surrender, they can bloody well come in with their hands up. They're either going to disregard the SS

Canadian armor (left) and RCAF Typhoon pilots (right, at a church service in Normandy) helped make a massacre of the Falaise gap. Roads were blocked with wreckage and littered with bodies. Caen (below) was in ruins. "All day and all night," said the CBC's Matthew Halton, "the guns, blasting the way for the fighting men. Millions of shells helping to win this close, bloody and ferocious battle in Normandy, making the face of France a pitted and hideous thing, yet helping shorten the war and therefore saving lives and cities even as they destroy lives and cities."

men in those woods behind them or fight. Fire!"

The Falaise pocket became a massacre. Newspapers in Britain and North America announced in magnificent understatement: "Despite numerous counterattacks there are distinct signs of a deterioration in the German position." . . .

Deterioration had become chaos. Edward Meade in *Remember Me:*

. . . Within an ever-tightening circle, most of what remained of the German armies in France was milling in frantic confusion. Torn, battered, bleeding, disorganized, they faced surrender or annihilation.

From dawn till nightfall the air forces bombed, machine-gunned and shot up enemy transport, tanks and guns. Roads were blocked with wrecked equipment.

The dead lay everywhere, among burned tanks and in the tangled wreckage of guns, lorries and wagons, next to the grotesque swollen carcasses of horses.

The Allied noose tightened. Trapped amid their own countless dead, driven to panic, Germans surrendered in thousands. But many fought on. With the fury of caged animals, clawing over masses of their own dead, they attacked the walls of the ring that pressed in on them.

For most the position was hopeless. They lived for a day or two, prowling in the fields and woods, driven and hunted, desperate and hungry men, the fierce, fanatical followers of the mad Führer, doomed men determined to take to the grave as many of their fellow creatures as they could.

They would come out with their hands

raised in surrender and suddenly throw a grenade and die with the victors. Sometimes it was acid they threw. Sometimes they blew themselves up with their own grenades. . . .

Temperatures rose as high as 120 in the shade. "In this heat," wrote Peter Simonds, "the masses of German dead began to decompose quickly and the whole battle area

Sutherland Highlanders and a squadron of South Alberta tanks attacked St. Lambert, midway between Trun and Chambois. Major Currie was in command. After six hours of fierce fighting, they were halfway through the town. They were reinforced by a company of the Lincoln and Welland Regiment and another company of Argylls, but in the face of bitter opposition from a bigger German force, the Canadians could

developed a repulsive, fetid stench for miles around. An air force pilot told me: 'I flew over at 800 feet and the stench was all I could stand.' "

The entire Canadian corps played a decisive role in the final stages of the battle of the gap, but when it was all over one man was singled out as its greatest hero: Maj. David Currie of the 4th Division's South Alberta Regiment was awarded the Victoria Cross.

On the 19th, a company of Argyll and

make no further progress. They battled one counterattack after another, giving no ground and killing many of the enemy.

That same day the Poles of First Canadian Army and the Americans of First U.S. Army linked up at Chambois, completing a loose encirclement. At his strategic point, Major Currie found his force besieged by masses of Germans trying to break out. Many did, many others died. Bodies piled up in the fields and dirt roads around St. Lambert.

Major Currie led the infantry and tanks,

Normandy was young lives spent in freedom's name (or the Führer's) and bodies spilled on the straw of an alien stable. It was unblooded troops becoming veterans almost overnight and, like these French Canadians (right), daring to live only one day at a time.

It was comedy, too, as Lt. Col. W. T. Barnard recorded in *The Queen's Own Rifles of Canada:* "Two riflemen made a wrong turn while bringing up petrol and found themselves in a small enemy pocket. Five Germans came running up and offered 4500 francs if they could be taken prisoner. The two Canadians tumbled the Germans onto the truck, turned around and delivered the five to a prisoner-of-war cage. They split the money and made their way, petrol intact, to the Queen's Own lines."

And it was slaughter. An officer described what happened when two platoons of the Cameron Highlanders of Ottawa, a machine-gun unit, caught German attackers on rising ground, without cover, near the village of Magny on August 21: "The machine gunners had just such a target as they had often wished for. All available rifles and Brens were also in use. The machine gunners fired at whatever they could see. A host of white flags appeared and hundreds of the enemy crowded in to surrender. Many others were unable to give up, for every move toward our lines brought bursts of fire from SS troops patrolling the low ground behind them in an armored half-track."

directed the fire of his 17-pounder anti-tank guns and knocked out a Tiger tank himself. Every officer Currie had with him was killed or wounded; he led alone. The only time reinforcements got through, he took the 40 men forward. During the next German attack the reinforcements withdrew under intense fire. Currie led them back into position and they held for the rest of the battle.

When it ended and the gap was finally closed on the morning of August 21, the Canadians had destroyed 7 tanks, 12 88-mm. guns and 40 vehicles, killed 300 Germans, wounded another 500 and taken 2100 prisoners. And a Canadian Army photographer had taken a remarkable picture—"as close," said Colonel Stacey, "as we are ever likely to come to a photograph of a man winning the Victoria Cross."

When Currie's battle group was relieved, he fell asleep on his feet and collapsed. He'd had one hour's rest during the entire battle.

"If ever a man earned the V.C.," said one survivor, "it was him. It should have been posthumous, though, by all the laws of averages. He moved everywhere. He would be around the guns and something would land and kill or wound everyone within 30 feet, except him. He would be with the infantry and a mortar bomb would get everyone around him. That was happening all the time. His luck was phenomenal—like a poker player getting straight flushes and tights all evening. Everyone felt lucky when he came around."

Months later in Holland, when Currie received his Victoria Cross, war correspondents were told he had been a garage manager in Moose Jaw. Not so, said Currie: "I only worked there."

The Germans had lost a great battle and suffered tremendous losses since June 6: 200,000 killed or wounded and 200,000 captured; 1300 tanks, 20,000 vehicles, 500 assault guns, 1500 field guns and heavier artillery pieces. A few days after the gap was closed, the strength of the German forces that had fought in Normandy was listed as 18,000 men, 300 artillery pieces, 42 tanks and assault guns.

The 12th SS, 20,000 strong on June 7, got out of the gap with 300 men, 10 tanks, no artillery. Kurt Meyer escaped through the Polish lines at Trun with 60 men. Thirty of them, including Meyer, eventually got across the Seine.

Allied losses from D-Day to the end of August totaled 206,000 killed, wounded and captured—124,000 American, 82,-000 British and Canadian. Of 18,444 Canadian casualties, 5021 were fatal. First Canadian Army's casualties August 1-23 were 12,659 killed, wounded and missing: 7415 were Canadian, 3870 British, 1374 Polish. Canada had nearly as many men killed in Normandy in 2½ months as in Italy in 18. Everywhere, as Padre Hickey had said of Carpiquet, were the pale upturned faces.

For years, veterans would argue over the contribution the Canadians had made. There was no final answer. Perhaps the sternest critique of all came from the army's own historian. The Allies, wrote Colonel Stacey in *The Victory Campaign,* owed victory in great part to numerical and material superiority. A condensation of his summary:

. . . The Germans had almost no naval support and very little air support. Even on the ground, they eventually were considerably outnumbered. They also were decisively outgeneraled. Hitler's interference was a serious hindrance.

German Intelligence was extraordinarily ineffective. The Germans were completely deceived as to Allied intentions both before the landings and during the campaign. Expectation of a further assault in the Pas de

Tanks and infantry fought as teams in the series of attacks along the Caen-Falaise road. Left: men of les Fusiliers Mont-Royal take cover behind a Sherman. Below: British troops, with Churchill tanks, move through a smoke screen toward the enemy. The push to Falaise accented the brilliance of Canada's Lt. Gen. Guy Simonds. "Of all the Allied corps commanders," wrote British Maj. K. J. Macksey in *History of the Second World War,* "Simonds was among the most versatile and best equipped to deal with the wide variety of operations posed to his 2nd Canadian Corps. He had commanded, in action, an infantry division in Sicily and an armored division in Italy, was young, ruthless and aggressively intolerant. Yet his educated approach to battle made use of every possible modern aid to help reduce casualties and still achieve striking penetrations of the enemy line. No Canadian field commander had greater experience or acquired more respect from friend or foe."

Calais, and retention there of large forces, was disastrous. Their generals also failed to see the course of Allied operations. They thought in terms of a thrust toward Paris from the east and mistakenly concentrated their strength in the Caen sector.

The German soldier was courageous, tenacious and skillful. He was sometimes a fanatic, occasionally a brutal thug, but almost always formidable. German commanders and staff officers were highly competent. Man for man and unit for unit, it cannot be said we won by tactical superiority.

Canadian formations did well, but would certainly have done better had they not been learning as they fought. We had probably not got as much out of our long training as we might have. Canadian generalship in Normandy does not suffer by comparison with that of the other Allies, and the vast majority of the rank and file showed initiative, high courage and steadily increasing skill. The Canadian regimental officer at his best had no superior. There remained, however, a proportion of officers whose inadequacy sometimes had serious consequences.

It is not difficult to put one's finger on occasions when Canadian formations failed to make the most of their opportunities. In particular, the capture of Falaise was long delayed and it was necessary to mount not one but two set-piece operations at a time when an early closing of the Falaise gap might have enabled us to end the war some months sooner.

The Germans were fortunate in that the armored divisions available to the First Canadian Army had never fought before. The 2nd Infantry Division had troubles too. Its General Foulkes said: "We found that when we bumped into battle-experienced German troops we were no match for them. We would not have been successful had it not been for our air and artillery support. It took about two months to get that division so shaken down that we were really a machine that could fight."

Some German divisions also lacked experience. One suspects they got more out of their training than we did. Perhaps their attitude toward such matters was less casual.

The victory in Normandy did not end the campaign. But Hitler had lost the armies that were his best hope of staving off ultimate disaster. This, said Montgomery, was the beginning of the end....

V.C. at St. Lambert

Many pictures in these volumes were taken by Canadian Army photographers. This one, probably the most famous of them all, shows Germans surrendering to Maj. David Currie (second from left) and his small force of Canadians in St. Lambert-sur-Dives at the height of the battle of the Falaise gap. For his leadership in helping stem the German breakout, Currie was awarded the Victoria Cross. This picture, one of a series by Lt. Donald Grant, is "as close as we are ever likely to come to a photograph of a man winning the Victoria Cross," says historian Col. C. P. Stacey. Grant, using a 3¼ x 4¼ Speed Graphic, was a member of an army photo unit (stills and movie) which entered St. Lambert as Currie's force battled to close the gap.

"About 1 p.m.," Grant recalls, "we heard vehicles coming. We ducked off the road and along came a motorcycle and sidecar and an armored half-track full of soldiers—the advance party of a German convoy. They were captured and I got this picture. Before we got the prisoners and the vehicles out of the way the rest of the convoy came in sight, saw us and tried to retreat."

Some got away; many didn't. "There must have been a thousand prisoners taken that day," says Grant, "and there were so few men with Currie that they couldn't send guards with the Germans. They just headed them back along the road to Trun and told them if they stepped off the road they'd be shot by our men in the hills."

The day after Grant made this picture men of the photo unit "ran into a machine gun outside St. Lambert," says Grant. One driver suffered a head wound, another was wounded in an arm and leg. Sgt. Jack Stollery, a movie cameraman who had won the Military Medal at Ortona in Italy, was shot through the hand. Sgt. Lloyd Millen, another cameraman, was hit in the shoulder. He later was killed in Holland.

Two days earlier, at Falaise, a sniper had shot cameraman Sgt. Bill Cox in the leg. Still earlier, at Carpiquet, another driver had been killed by mortar fire. Grant, trying to get the driver's body, had been hit in the leg by a mortar fragment. He was awarded the Military Cross.

Superspy

Late in 1945 Winston Churchill was examining a list of candidates for knighthood being submitted to King George VI. Pausing beside the name of William Samuel Stephenson, whose wartime services would now be publicly honored, he wrote: "This one is close to my heart." A year later, at a private ceremony in New York, Sir William received the Presidential Medal for Merit, becoming the first non-American to be awarded this highest of all U.S. civilian decorations. Both honors were richly deserved. But it was years before the public would learn about the spectacular achievements of the superspy described as the "quiet Canadian."

From June 1940 to late 1945, Stephenson headed a British secret service network that he had set up throughout the Western Hemisphere. His organization was called British Security Co-ordination (BSC), and its headquarters were Stephenson's offices in New York's Rockefeller Center. (His cable address, INTREPID, was later popularized as his code name.) The activities were wide ranging—exposing spies and smuggling rings, infiltrating foreign embassies, training saboteurs and preparing agents for subversive missions in enemy and enemy-occupied lands.

At the height of its operation, the BSC employed more than a thousand men and women. Because Stephenson could not legally hire Americans for British Intelligence work he recruited Canadians—senior business executives and hundreds of secretaries and other female clerical staff. Some of these women came to Stephenson's New York office by answering a newspaper advertisement. It was some time before they realized that they had joined the secret service.

The director of these undercover activities was born in Winnipeg in 1896 and became a World War I fighter-pilot ace—20 enemy planes shot down in six weeks. While still a student at the University of Manitoba, he invented a method of transmitting photographs without using telephone and telegraph wires. In 1921 he moved to England to market his invention. It made him a millionaire before he was 30 years old.

Between the wars he made his home in Britain, traveled widely on business, cultivated people in high places—and listened. What he learned about Germany's preparations for war was rejected by almost everyone but Winston Churchill who was convinced of the danger. In fact, Stephenson became a main source of material for Churchill's speeches. "That," he said later, "was my only training in espionage."

Despite his lack of formal instruction, Stephenson went to the United States in April 1940 to establish top-level relations between the British Secret Intelligence Service (SIS) and the U.S. Federal Bureau of Investigation (FBI). Bureau Director J. Edgar Hoover relayed the proposal to President Roosevelt, who welcomed "the closest possible marriage" between the two organizations. But because of deep anti-British feeling in the still neutral United States, not even the U.S. State Department was informed of this cooperative effort.

Back in Britain, Stephenson suggested wide responsibilities for any secret British organization in the United States. It should not only collect secret intelligence but also strive to assure sufficient aid for Britain, fight German subversion throughout the hemisphere and bring the Americans into the war. SIS then accepted Stephenson's proposals and Churchill appointed him to take charge. His cover would be the job of British passport control officer in New York. He returned to the United States in June 1940, when France was on the verge of defeat, and Britain and the Commonwealth stood alone against the Nazis.

Stephenson lined up allies wherever he could. To establish a direct line to Roosevelt, he enlisted the aid of William J. "Wild Bill" Donovan, a New York lawyer with important connections in the Roosevelt administration. Stephenson reported to London: "There is no doubt that we can achieve infinitely more through Donovan than through any other individual." Stephenson and Donovan became the go-betweens who processed top-secret intelligence for Roosevelt and Churchill.

People who served under him say Stephenson was a man without fear. He was

Above: Gen. William J. "Wild Bill" Donovan presents the U.S. Presidential Medal for Merit to William Stephenson. Looking on are Col. Edwin Buxton, assistant director of OSS; Robert Sherwood, an aide to President Roosevelt, and Mrs. Stephenson. Stephenson's secret wartime organization recruited hundreds of Canadian women, many through a Toronto *Telegram* advertisement (right). It appeared early in 1941, on a day when "experienced operators on ladies' blouses" were needed too, as well as secretaries "to work for Britain" in Stephenson's network. Said one of Stephenson's aides: "I don't remember the name of the personnel officer but in addition to his demand for efficiency he also had an eye for beauty. This helped, especially in liaison work with young men in U.S. government offices—and with some of the older contacts who had not given up looking!"

dedicated to a task which required him to disregard many conventional rules such as the niceties of diplomatic privilege. His agents infiltrated hostile embassies and offices in Washington and elsewhere to obtain secret diplomatic codes and ciphers.

The penetration of the Italian and French embassies in Washington was the work of a woman named Cynthia whose "feminine charms," wrote H. Montgomery Hyde in *The Quiet Canadian,* "were the real instrument of her success." Cynthia was the daughter of a U.S. marine corps major, and her cover was a job with a Canadian government office in Washington. Her first coup, during the winter of 1940-41, was obtaining Italian naval ciphers from an admiral "who responded to her charms within weeks."

To Work For Britain

A Department of the British Government in New York City requires several reliable young women, fully competent in secretarial work and of matriculation or better educational standing. The chief need is for expert file clerks and for typists and stenographers able to take one hundred and twenty-five words per minute. Dependable character and satisfactory background essential. Those selected can expect to serve for the duration of the war. Wages and working conditions are good. Travelling expenses to New York will be paid.

APPLY in your own handwriting, stating your age, education and parentage, with full details of your business experience and wages received and enclosing a recent snapshot. Also give two responsible references. Address your application to Box 1087 Telegram.

AT once,

EXPERIENCED operators

ON ladies' blouses

AND ladies' neckwear.

DRESS ESSENTIALS. Ltd.,

284 KING street west.

Later, a French lover, who eventually became her husband, provided Cynthia (and Stephenson) with the Vichy French naval cipher. Within 24 hours, said Hyde, "the photostats reached the Admiralty in London. In North Africa a few months later, the elimination of Vichy naval resistance was due in large measure to Stephenson and his clever woman agent."

One of Stephenson's biggest jobs was to persuade the Americans that Britain could and would fight on after the fall of France. The U.S. ambassadors in both Paris and London said her stand was hopeless and, Stephenson said in a CBC interview after the war, most of Roosevelt's cabinet felt the same. But Donovan was convinced that, with sufficient aid, Britain would survive. "My task," recalled Stephenson, "was to inform him of Britain's foremost requirements

and furnish concrete evidence that American material assistance would not be improvident charity but a sound investment."

Without Donovan's intervention, he said, the 1940 transfer of 50 destroyers to Britain "could not have eventuated" and later the two of them were "largely instrumental in obtaining" 100 Flying Fortress bombers for the RAF and over a million rifles for the British Home Guard.

In 1941 Stephenson appointed a World War I flying comrade, Toronto stockbroker T. G. "Tommy" Drew-Brook, as his official representative in Canada. One of his projects was Station M, a laboratory set up in Toronto. Its specialty was fabrication of letters, and it had men who could reproduce the imprint of any typewriter on earth. The documents turned out were exact imitations, down to the smallest detail, of what they purported to be. Technical processes were handled by other experts, among them leading authorities on special inks and paper.

One of Station M's great achievements, wrote Hyde, was to close down an important enemy channel of communication with the Americas—the Linee Aeree Transcontinentali Italiane (LATI). The airline's planes flew regularly between Europe and Brazil carrying diplomatic bags, couriers, agents, propaganda. To stop its flights, Stephenson and his advisers faked a letter from LATI's president to its general manager in Brazil which insulted Brazil's President Getulio Vargas, abused his country, scorned his foreign policy and suggested that his political enemies be encouraged. By equally surreptitious methods, the letter came into Vargas' hands, and the infuriated president canceled LATI's landing rights, ordered its manager arrested, and took over its aircraft, landing fields and maintenance equipment. A few weeks later Brazil severed relations with Italy and Germany.

In 1941 Drew-Brook also set up Camp X, a secret establishment east of Toronto. Stephenson wanted facilities for training spies and saboteurs. London accepted his suggestion that a school be started in Canada.

To avoid creating suspicion, Drew-Brook had intermediaries purchase a 200-acre farm fronting on Lake Ontario, between Oshawa and Whitby, for $12,000. Army engineers erected barracks, converted barns and sheds and dug underground shooting ranges. Sealed off with barbed wire and heavily patrolled by armed guards, the camp went into operation in August.

Trainees wore Canadian army uniforms and received Canadian pay and allowances. The adjutant was a Canadian but the five

other officers and ten NCO instructors were Britons. Most of the school's 500 graduates were absorbed into British units, but some were RCMP and FBI men learning how enemy agents might work in Canada and the United States.

Canadians of various ethnic origins trained at Camp X. Typical of these volunteers was a man who ran a small variety store in Toronto after the war—a Yugoslav native who asked to be known only as Peter.

Peter was a shoemaker who came to Canada in 1927. He was called up for military service in 1942 and, after basic training in Sudbury, Ont., was ordered to report to a Toronto office where a major spoke to him in his own language. For two weeks the major questioned him on every aspect of his life; finally he asked if Peter would be willing to go behind enemy lines. Peter said yes.

The major asked him to find other Yugoslavs who would be willing to join the mission. Two weeks later he had five men, and together they were taken to Camp X.

"We were taught to use every type of weapon," Peter recalled. "We had to go into dark rooms, find a bag full of revolver parts, put them together and come out shooting. The same with automatic weapons." They were also taught how to use radio, explosives, invisible ink and forgeries.

The six Yugoslavs eventually went to Cairo where Peter was assigned to lead a party to link up with Tito's Yugoslav partisans. This he did. Later he went with Allied forces up through Italy, organizing partisan groups. More than these bare details Peter would not reveal, except to say that three of the Yugoslavs never returned.

After the United States entered the war, it set up the Office of Strategic Services (OSS), with a nucleus of agents trained at Camp X and directed by General Donovan. OSS maintained an office down the hall from BSC in New York, and Donovan once said: "Bill Stephenson taught us all we ever knew about foreign intelligence."

He was not alone in his praise. Hoover, the FBI chief, wrote Stephenson that his contribution would be judged among the foremost in bringing Allied victory. Ernest Cuneo, wartime liaison officer between BSC and OSS, said Stephenson was "the only man who enjoyed the unqualified confidence of both Churchill and Roosevelt." And Eleanor Fleming, a Canadian who became one of his private secretaries, would recall that they worked a six-day week and a minimum 12-hour day. Yet, she said, if Stephenson had said "we were starting a 24-hour shift, we'd have accepted it without a whimper. We'd have given our lives for him."

The time of high hope

Triumph everywhere—and dreams of peace that die too soon

On the bitter morning of the Dieppe raid of August 19, 1942, a soldier appeared in Jacques Dubost's garden. Orders had come for the Canadians to withdraw and the soldier was on his way. Strangely, Monsieur Dubost recalled later, he was cheerful and laughing. "We'll be back," he called out. "We'll be back." And he headed for a beach strewn with the dead, the wounded and the havoc of war.

On September 1, 1944, the Canadians did come back and war correspondent Ross Munro came with them as he had two years before. In *Gauntlet to Overlord* Munro recounts that triumphant return less than two weeks after the Allies' towering victory in Normandy:

. . . After several days of heavy fighting in the Forêt de la Londe, the Canadians rolled into Rouen. From morning to night on the last day of August, convoys of the 2nd Division whisked through the city. Columns of carriers and half-tracks, tanks and guns and hundreds of trucks filled with fighting men passed down the wide thoroughfares lined with ecstatic French people offering a wild, prolonged welcome. But the 2nd Division could not tarry. It had a rendezvous with history 40 miles away.

On the outskirts of Rouen the highway forks—left to Le Havre, right to Dieppe. A crowd watched the Canadians wheel to the right. *"Cà, c'est bien!"* they shouted. *"Les Canadiens s'en vont à Dieppe."*

The columns sped north up the long, straight road. Leading was the 8th Reconnaissance Regiment, with one of its squadrons under Maj. Dennis Bult-Francis of Montreal, who had been wounded in the 1942 raid. Behind came the Dieppe regi-

September 3, 1944: along streets lined by the people of liberated Dieppe, the 2nd Canadian Division parades in tribute to comrades who were killed in the August 19, 1942, raid on the French town. This, wrote correspondent Ross Munro, was "probably the most impressive and meaningful Canadian parade of the war."

ments—the Essex Scottish, the Royal Regiment of Canada, the Royal Hamilton Light Infantry, the South Saskatchewans and others. There were about 25 survivors of the raid in each infantry battalion. Neither they nor the men who had replaced the casualties of 1942 thought Dieppe would be taken without a battle. The units had been briefed for assault. Bomber Command was to raid the port in the early evening of September 1. Warships were to shell coastal positions. The plan called for a large-scale combined operation.

At Tôtes, halfway to Dieppe, there was a sharp brush with a German anti-aircraft unit withdrawing from Le Havre peninsula; there was another at Longueville. By nightfall the 8th Recce was just short of Dieppe; the rest of the division was stretched out for a dozen miles behind them.

At 10:30 a.m. on September 1 they entered Dieppe. The Germans had gone, had fled even as they approached. Instead of bullets and blood, Dieppe gave the Canadians flowers and wine. A delirious population poured into the streets to shout that the town was free.

I reached Dieppe in a scout car, my mind flooded with emotions. I was thrilled, exhilarated and moved as I had been by few sights in the war. Yet I was saddened, too, by a dozen flashbacks to the horrible things I'd seen on these beaches in 1942.

I thought of the men who died there, who were wounded, who were taken prisoner when they could fight no longer. I cursed Dieppe for the Canadian lives it had cost. Yet I also saw it as the genesis of our combined operations victories from North Africa to Normandy. The vital lessons were learned here.

As I drove through the extravagant happiness of the crowds, the flowers, the memories, an old lady tottered up to my scout car with a bouquet of flowers. A pretty girl gave us another. A hundred people crushed around, wanting to shake our hands, to kiss us, to tell us how welcome we were. The soldiers of the 8th Recce were mobbed, taken off to cafés and homes and plied with liberation wine.

I wandered around all day like a man in a dream. My guide and I went through a concrete pillbox out onto the esplanade where the fiercest fire had raged during the 1942 attack. The esplanade was covered with thick barbed wire and was mined from one end to the other. The pier jutting

out on the west side of the harbor was mined and crisscrossed with wire. The main beach was piled with obstacles and wire, and every foot of it was mined. The casino at the western end of the esplanade, in which the Canadians had fought, had been demolished to give a clear field of fire. Looking at the beach, at the towering headlands on either side of it, at the fortified houses facing it, I was appalled at the target the Canadians had raided.

I met Lt. Col. Eric Bell of Regina on the esplanade. He could hardly talk. He had gone through the hell of that main beach. Finally he turned and walked silently away. Near the esplanade, too, Major Bult-Francis found the French girl who had bound his wounds in 1942. She remembered him, and no woman of France was as surprised as she when he walked up to greet her.

In the center of town we saw the places where the infantry had fought. The buildings were still pitted with holes. The mayor pointed out a plot of grass near the church. "One of your men was hit right there," he said. "We could not reach him and he died there on the grass. We buried him with the others on the hill behind the town."

The people of Dieppe had taken the bodies of all the dead, from the beaches and the esplanade and the streets, and made a cemetery for them on the hill. Over each they placed a plain, wooden cross and for two years they had tended the graves.

I made a pilgrimage—it was that to me—to Puys, east of Dieppe. I went through the lonely, gray-brown town and down the gulch toward the beach. The mines on the road had not been lifted and I had to pick my way cautiously. When I reached the beach, I wished I had not come alone. It was like walking into a tomb. I shuddered to look at the beach, at the 12-foot stone wall across its top where so many of the Royal Regiment had been cut down before my eyes. I shuddered when I looked at the quaint houses still there on the cliff top from which fire had poured into our boats. Here one of the finest regiments in the Canadian Army had fought and died, caught in daylight under murderous fire.

The Puys defenses had been strong two years before but now they were twice as formidable. Concrete casemates had been added to the sides of the narrow defile landing from the beach. Obstacles were littered on the beach. Mines were every-

where. No craft could possibly land in the face of the new defenses.

The Channel wind eerily flapped the German camouflage on the casemates. Everything was ominous, gray and deathlike and I hurried away. After two years, Puys was still, to me, a place of death and horror. We drove along the winding road back to the friendly crowds of Dieppe. . . .

ROSS MUNRO

Two days later the entire 2nd Division marched proudly through the streets of Dieppe. It was, said Munro, "probably the most impressive and meaningful Canadian parade of the war." It was a tribute to the men who had fallen in the raid of 1942. But it also bolstered a mood that seemed now to be everywhere.

Early September was a time of high hope and the easy conquest of Dieppe reinforced it. Everywhere, it seemed, there was optimism that the war would soon be over. Everywhere the Germans were in retreat or fighting with a final desperation.

In Ottawa, Parliament had only recently concluded a session mainly dealing not with the war but with measures for the return of peace. The RCAF had stopped recruiting. War production was tapering off.

Overseas, the military machine Canada had spent five years building rolled all out. The navy ran the Atlantic's convoy escorts on its own. The ships that had participated in D-Day had gone off to other tasks. Two Canadian landing ships had just taken part in an easy invasion of southern France. The destroyer *Haida* would soon head home for refit after spectacular success in the Bay of Biscay.

In the skies of northwest Europe, three wings of Canadian fighters and fighter-bombers hammered key targets and harassed the Germans in tactical support of ground attacks; their pilots were still awed by the carnage they'd seen and made in the Falaise gap. The 14 squadrons of the RCAF's 6 Bomber Group filled similar roles with their heavy Lancasters and Halifaxes.

The army, in action on two fronts, was in high spirits. In northwest Europe, First Canadian Army's Lt. Gen. H. D. G. Crerar talked in terms of "speedy and victorious conclusion of the war"; the key, he said, would be his army's capture of the Channel ports. On the same day the 2nd Division moved from Rouen to Dieppe, the 1st

French girls greet frontline Canadian troops as they enter Rouen. In this time of high hope, even follow-up formations could count on a warm welcome wherever they went. Correspondent Ralph Allen, in a dispatch from Chartres, wrote: "Here the most outdistanced supply lorry, the rearmost echelon of the rearmost formation and the most belated newspaper jeep is greeted as enthusiastically as though its occupants were the unaided liberators of all France." Below: German prisoners glance at the body of a comrade whose boots have been appropriated by one of the living.

The Germans buried mines in fields, orchards and roads to slow the Allied advance in western Europe. Left: a mine-detecting party at work. The leader wears protective clothing. Below: a closeup of the revolving drum and thrashing chains of a Scorpion mine-beater. Flail tanks so equipped were widely used in the Normandy grain fields in the summer of 1944. Another important new weapon in France was the Wasp, a trigger-controlled flamethrowing apparatus (right) mounted in Bren gun carriers.

Canadian Corps in Italy, rested after a summer of relaxation and training, struck at the Gothic Line, Germany's last major defense barrier guarding the approaches to the Lombardy Plains and the Po Valley. The Gothic Line, the soldiers knew, meant one more costly assault. But it should open the way for a swift and crushing—and perhaps decisive—advance. The Germans in Italy *could* be whipped by Christmas.

The Gothic Line stretched some 200 miles from La Spezia on the west coast, across the northern Apennine mountains, then along a narrow coastal corridor to Pesaro on the Adriatic Sea. Gen. Sir Harold Alexander's plan called for the Canadians and the rest of Eighth Army to strike in a narrow thrust on the Adriatic side, then swing left toward Bologna once the mountain barrier had been passed. In the central sector, the U.S. Fifth Army would advance through the mountains beyond Florence in a converging attack intended to trap the German Tenth Army.

The sector assigned to the 1st Canadian

Corps lay along the Foglia Valley a short distance inland from Pesaro. The Germans had razed every house in the valley so their guns would have a clear view. Minefields in the river flats, wrote army historian Lt. Col. G. W. L. Nicholson, were sown in wide, overlapping patterns backed by an anti-tank ditch 14 feet wide. The slopes beyond the valley were thick with machine-gun positions, concrete dugouts, wire obstacles, artillery emplacements. Dug-in anti-tank guns awaited Canadian armor. Dug-in flamethrowers awaited the infantry.

The Canadians attacked this formidable wall on the night of August 30-31 under a lavish moon that spilled its light down on the hills in front of them. On the left, the 5th Division struck with two battalions of its 11th Infantry Brigade. On the right, the 1st Division's 3rd Brigade sent another battalion, the West Nova Scotia Regiment, to break into the line between the villages of Borgo San Maria and Osteria Nuovo. Quebec's Royal 22nd Regiment was alerted to follow up once the West Novas had a firm bridgehead over the river.

There were many actions in the next 48 hours. One of the most spectacular involved a company of the Royal 22nd. It was recounted by the company commander, Maj. J.-G. Poulin, in his book *696 heures d'enfer:*

...We spent August 29 and 30 on the heights south of the Foglia, cleaning our weapons and preparing for battle. With my binoculars I studied the terrain of the slopes two miles north, paying close attention to two of the higher features, points 194 and 131. Something told me there could be fierce fighting on either.

The West Nova Regiment had crossed the river and, by night, had a bridgehead on the enemy side. Were the Germans taken by surprise or were they just waiting in their fortifications? All we knew was that the Canadian regiment met little opposition, so little that it was decided to exploit the success by putting the Royal 22nd across to the enemy side without delay.

It was about 2300 hours August 30 when we got moving. Fire-charred trees stretched out thin branches as though to hold us back. Here and there lay an armored car twisted by fire. Some enemy corpses had started to bloat, their bluish flesh giving off a nauseating odor. Abandoned weapons and wrecked vehicles were strewn about, evidence of the skill of our

The high optimism of September 1944 was a doomed thing. For the Canadians in Italy, there was to be a second bitter winter against Germans like these. Padre Waldo E. L. Smith recalled in his book *What Time The Tempest* that when the Canadians opened another offensive in December it saddened him: "The unhealthy conditions were telling on them. Each infantryman carried only one blanket. They needed more for warmth so they used whatever they found in the houses, inviting whatever insects and germs were harboring there. Their blankets they spread wherever there was shelter, in pig pens, poultry houses, stables. Rolled up in blankets so contaminated, their exposure to infection was so continuous that it became a fifth column."

artillery. There was not a sign of animal life anywhere. From time to time the whine of an enemy shell was heard, then answered by our gunners on the heights behind us.

We reached the river and forded it. In the darkness, the advance was slow and unnerving. A narrow path was swept by mine detectors and we walked along it, one behind the other. It was dead quiet—too quiet. Everyone worried about what was around the next turn and whether the vines outlined against the sky concealed a machine gun, a sniper, an ambush. We worried, too, that the enemy was letting us get deep into his lines only to close in and cut us off.

We dug slit trenches behind the West Novas for shelter from the artillery that would surely open up at daybreak when

the Germans located us. German signs told of the presence of mines and we had the sector swept. I didn't like our position at all. Squeezed by a road on the right and a ravine on the left, we occupied a small triangular piece of land with its point toward the enemy. We were so tightly hemmed in that I feared a barrage would cause uncounted losses which wider dispersal would have prevented. I gave orders that no one was to leave cover.

The West Novas, a few hundred yards ahead, were due to attack at 0630 hours. Their plan was to cross a minefield, about 400 yards deep, capture point 105, which dominated the village of Borgo San Maria and then pivot and capture point 131, which controlled the whole valley as well as the main road to Pesaro.

About 0615 hours, I ordered half my

company to remain on guard while the others tried to rest. The sun was high and it was blistering hot. At precisely 0630 hours shots rang out and the air was ripped by sharp whistles. On the slope before us bursts of white smoke and clouds of black and yellow dust seemed to spring up everywhere. Our artillery was laying down a barrage, and the Germans replied with machine guns and cannon. Their fire was accurate, 88-mm. shells right on target. But the target was not the two attacking companies, it was us.

Bullets hissed and struck the branches around us with a slapping sound. Bent in a slit trench that was too short, my legs sticking out, I watched branches pirouette to the ground. From time to time, a concentration of shells landed on us. Two or three of my men were wounded; stretcher-bearers evacuated them.

I lay on my back and for the hundredth time asked myself whether I was afraid. I realized that every man knows fear some time. Some control it better than others, and that is the difference between the cowardly and the brave. The more I thought, the more I was convinced I had complete control of myself and that, consequently, I wasn't afraid. Proud of this conclusion, I smiled and lit what was probably my tenth cigarette in a half hour. Perhaps that was my reaction to danger.

The attack by the West Novas didn't succeed. The mines were so thick it was impossible to get through. I understood then why the Germans hadn't fired on the attackers. They had let their mines do the killing.

The sounds of dull detonations from the minefield told the story. Seventy-six men were killed or wounded and all the officers were casualties. The rest of the attack force came back in disorder from the massacre, some dragging wounded men who had lost a foot, a leg or even two limbs. Amid the chaos the enemy opened fire with machine guns and artillery, wounding and killing soldiers who had miraculously escaped the mines.

Worried about the effect of this disaster on the morale of my own men, I left my shelter and, trembling inwardly, walked through our positions smoking a cigarette, pretending nonchalance.

Daylight passed with spasmodic bombardments and more casualties. With no orders either for advance or retreat, we remained alert against counterattack.

As night was falling, I was summoned to battalion headquarters where Lt. Col. Jean Allard, the commanding officer, told us a company of engineers would cut three paths through the minefield. When this was done, Capt. Yvan Dubé's B company would pass through to attack point 105 and then swing to the right to occupy the village of Borgo San Maria on the road to Pesaro. Following Dubé, I would cross the minefield, take over point 105 from B company and from there carry out the attack on point 131. I would have a battery of artillery in support and Captain Howard, an artillery officer, would accompany me with a wireless operator. We would be in constant touch with his battery.

We were under no illusions. Points 105 and 131 were the first main positions of the Gothic Line and we expected to find them thick with fortifications. Point 131, by its height and strategic situation, controlled the whole valley. It had to be taken because, once it was overcome, the crust of the Gothic Line would be ruptured. The job had fallen to my company of some 85 men.

As Dubé and I made our way back to our companies, Lieutenant Belliveau of the pioneer platoon invited us to stop by his truck for a few good shots of cordial.

After two nights and days without sleep, it bucked us up a bit.

I said to Dubé: "It's all or nothing! What do you think?"

"It'll be a real slugging match," he said.

I made my way to company HQ, then issued my orders. Having done all I could, I got a bit of rest. It is curious that a man who knows he may soon be put to sleep for eternity can still lie down and doze peacefully. I slept on wet ground in an abandoned enemy redoubt until I was awakened about 0415.

Colonel Allard was seated near me. "Is everything ready?" he asked.

"Yes, sir," I said, gathering my equipment and checking my pistol.

Half an hour later we set out, again in Indian file, toward the minefield. As it grew light about 0500, we were at the edge of the mined area and my three platoons started along the paths cleared by the engineers. Ahead of us, there wasn't a sound. Dubé's company had already gone through toward 105, apparently without opposition.

The route through the minefield was marked by cotton tapes but, in the half-light, our advance was slow and difficult. Here and there were dismembered bodies, men from the West Novas who had at-

tacked the day before. A few wounded lay in the middle of the minefield, left there after several stretcher-bearers had been killed or wounded trying to reach them. Weakened by loss of blood, afraid to move for fear of setting off other mines, tortured by hunger and thirst, they called weakly for stretcher-bearers and for water and implored us not to let them die like animals. But we were on a mission; we gritted our teeth and went on. Later I learned that engineers with mine detectors were able to clear a way for bearers who rescued the wounded.

After ten minutes, we got through to the road at the northern edge. Not a shot had been fired. I deployed my men and the company started the ascent of point 105. We reached the top without incident. I spotted Dubé's company heading toward Borgo San Maria. Immediately, I ordered my men to start our own attack on point 131.

Progress was slow up the vine-covered slopes of 131. Before we had gone 100 yards, a deluge of machine-gun fire burst upon us. There were concealed fortifications on the side of the slope and at its summit and they delivered a crossfire that left little untouched.

The two forward platoons, commanded

Also the talk about the near end of the war is only an illusion.

The German soldier knows he is fighting for his home, his family and his existence. The way he is resisting to-day, he will always resist, even if it be for years. Canadians, what do you want in Europe, what is your interest in Italy? Or did you earnestly believe that the freedom of Canada was threatened by Germany?

In propaganda fired into Canadian lines (left, above), the Germans taunted the Allies' high hopes. The Allies used propaganda too. This message (left) says Hitler can no longer win; he can only prolong the war. For men like Maj. J.-G. Poulin (above, a postwar photo), the war still meant heavy fighting as in the action in Italy he describes in this chapter. In France, meanwhile, the Canadians cleared the Channel ports. Right: a German truce party meets a Canadian outside Boulogne.

by Lieutenants Hector Pelletier and François "Fritz" Laflèche, were engaging the nearest German positions. When I determined approximately where the machine-gun posts were, I got in touch with our artillery and, directing it by wireless, was able to neutralize them.

As the two platoons moved forward, they met machine-gun fire from the right flank of the slope. This murderous fire killed or wounded several men and stopped the progress of my command group and reserve platoon. The position could not be

dealt with by artillery for it was scarcely more than 50 or 60 yards from us in open territory. Our gunfire would have been as hazardous for us as for the Germans.

I turned to the light mortar section of my reserve platoon and pointed to the target, the corner of a wrecked brick house. The first few mortar bombs fell short. The fifth struck the corner of the house, and I thought it had done its work. Then with a sideways glance I saw my mortar man fling up his arms and slump to the ground. A spreading red stain marked the spot where

a bullet had struck his chest. I leaped over, picked up his mortar and fired the seven remaining bombs, shouting to Sgt. Roméo Vézina to get his reserve platoon ready to attack with grenades and bayonets.

Before the last bomb had struck, I threw the mortar aside and, clutching my pistol, dashed toward the machine-gun position. Vézina's platoon followed me. The attack was fierce and pitiless. Firing from the hip, throwing grenades, howling like demons, we ran ahead. Many of my men fell. Those of us who survived had no mercy. Firing point-blank, we didn't even give the Germans time to raise their arms to surrender.

The position had communicating trenches linking two sunken steel casemates. When we overran the trenches, we threw phosphorescent and high-explosive grenades into the ports of the casemates. The blasts killed or wounded most of the Germans inside and we cut down the few who tried to come out. Not a prisoner was taken.

The attack continued at this hellish pace, and 25 minutes after starting up point 131 we had captured, with grenades and bayonets, 13 enemy emplacements.

But heavier going lay ahead. We were stopped about 75 yards from the crest. No matter what we tried, machine-gun fire came down on us. At the top there were four reinforced concrete casemates sprouting machine guns and connected by deep trenches. The position seemed impregnable.

Pelletier and Laflèche and their platoons were pinned down. Crouched along the embankment of a sunken road, they tried to set up a defensive position against counterattack. I was at the head of my group. Bursting through the edge of a vineyard, I found myself in open territory, a perfect target. Laflèche called out to me: "Watch out, you're in their line of fire."

His voice was drowned by sharp whines and my men and I dived to the ground. Mortar bombs exploded all around us, raising clouds of dirt that blinded me for a few moments. I don't know how long I was on the ground, perhaps only four or five seconds. I scrambled up with one idea, to reach the shelter of the road embankment about 25 feet away.

The crackle of machine guns filled my ears, then a hard blow spun me around twice. I landed about 15 feet away. I got up angrily and tried again to reach the embankment. Before I had taken two steps I felt a sharp burn on my right leg. I was sure I'd been hit. I made it to the road and found myself near a redoubt the Germans had left. Inside, I found that four bullets had gone through my haversack but my leg was only scratched.

Several other men had been wounded. Langlois was hit twice in the leg; I heard him calling for stretcher-bearers. One of my wireless operators and two other members of my command group were also hit. Sergeant Vézina lost several men but got the rest of his platoon into position on the

right, so that we now formed a crescent around the Germans at the top of the hill.

Captain Howard, our artillery officer, broke out of the vineyard and raced toward us. As he threw himself down near the embankment, a bullet whistled by and he stiffened. His helmet was knocked off and rolled in the dust. I dragged him to the bottom of the embankment, turned him over and saw a small red spot at his left temple. His war was over.

I had to locate the enemy fire. By crawling about 20 feet, I could see three German casemates. The nearest was about 60 yards away and the other two, set back to back for mutual protection, were a bit farther. I crept back to the redoubt. Our situation was dangerous. I had no wireless, so I couldn't ask for artillery support or get in touch with my battalion commander.

Someone called my name from the vineyard. It was Captain Howard's signaler, who had stopped to fix his wireless set. I shouted a warning and he reached me safely.

Now that we had a wireless, my first idea was to signal for artillery fire to knock out the German positions. But on closer examination, I felt we were too close to the casemates. The spread of our artillery shelling was about 150 yards. I wondered, too, whether the shells would have any effect on the reinforced concrete casemates.

There appeared to be three choices. The first was a bayonet charge covered by smoke and explosive grenades. The second was a barrage on the German positions by heavy artillery, but this would mean withdrawing my men to safety and giving up valuable ground with no certainty that the shells would silence the powerful sunken forts.

The third choice and the best, I thought, was tank support. I was convinced the Germans, counting on the minefields below, had no anti-tank guns on the hill. The tanks could advance, using the road we were astride, and direct machine-gun and cannon fire into the ports of the casemates.

I got in touch by wireless with Colonel Allard and asked for tanks. But he said all the tanks were committed elsewhere. I pleaded until he said he'd see what he could do.

Meantime, we had to take action. Mortar fire was coming down on us and I feared we couldn't deal with a counterattack. I

told Pelletier's platoon, on our left, to assault the two left casemates. The platoons of Laflèche and Vézina would provide fire support while I laid down a smoke screen with a mortar. I hoped that with this help Pelletier and his men might get close enough to the casemates to toss grenades into their firing ports.

Assembling all available automatic weapons, we poured thick fire into the German position. Pelletier and his men attacked bravely but they were driven back twice, leaving a number of wounded behind.

Corporal Veillette, the last non-commissioned officer in Pelletier's platoon, was lying about 15 yards from one of the casemates. Two stretcher-bearers, Privates Hacault and Cloutier, holding a Red Cross flag, set out to give him first aid right under the enemy's eyes. The Germans, men of a parachute battalion, were ferocious and merciless in combat but they respected the Red Cross and stretcher-bearers.

Furious at the failure of the attack, I had the platoons regroup. Pelletier's men set up behind the Vézina and Laflèche platoons so that our company position would be triangular for better defense. Then, in desperation, I called for artillery fire, warning my men to get as low as they could in their slit trenches.

The first salvo crashed in an open space inside the German fortifications. I gave the correction "southwest 50" by wireless, and thought that the adjustment would bring the next shells down either on the western casemates or on us. At the other end of our wireless I heard the artillery officer shout: "Fire!" The second salvo landed dead on, and peering through the smoke and dust, it seemed two or three shells had struck a casemate.

"Repeat and maintain fire for ten minutes," I shouted. A deluge of fire and steel followed. The air was filled with the smell of gunpowder and pulverized masonry. Shock waves whipped my face. The blasts were so strong I thought my head would be blown in. Several shells went astray, killing one man and wounding another.

When the concentration ended, we tried another assault. This time one casemate was silent. Several shells had exploded behind it and there was no sign of life from its occupants. But the three other positions were intact and we heard from them quickly. Once again I called back the assault and just about gave up.

Then Laflèche appeared to announce: "Major, we are almost out of ammunition." We still had a few bullets but were out of grenades and mortar bombs.

I looked vainly for CSM. Irénée Roy, then picked two men to go toward Borgo San Maria with a request for reinforcements and ammunition. After an hour, they came back empty-handed. They hadn't been able to locate battalion headquarters and had been fired on by snipers.

Laflèche offered to carry out their mission. Fritz was 21, enterprising and brave, and I knew that nothing but death could stop him. Not more than ten minutes after he set out, a towering six-foot-two-inch form appeared. It was Capt. Guy Vaugeois of Montreal, sent up to command my company. Word had got down below that I had been killed.

When Vaugeois saw me, he stood open-mouthed in the middle of the road. "Aren't you dead?" he asked.

"Sorry to disappoint you," I said. "You'll be the dead one if you don't take cover."

He dashed into my redoubt, dropped down on the earth floor and offered me a cigarette. I can't say how glad I was to get it. I relaxed, waiting for Laflèche to return with ammunition. The only other thing to do was to watch for a counterattack. It would be dark by 2030 hours and somehow the German position had to be captured before then. At most, I had 50 men left of the original 85.

About 1700 hours Laflèche returned with men carrying ammunition for the whole company. I ordered it distributed immediately. Laflèche told me that CSM. Roy, realizing how perilous our situation was, had hurried to battalion headquarters to ask for tanks. Roy offered to direct them personally against the German position.

Colonel Allard had no tanks at his disposal, but he had an idea. He gave Roy a section of three armored tracked carriers, mounted with Vickers machine guns. They appeared on our sunken road at 1730 hours. I ordered them to deploy in a half-circle and advance gradually until their machine gunners could shoot right into the firing ports of the casemates. The hail of 200 bullets a minute would keep the Germans from firing. With this support, we would attack in two waves with automatic weapons and grenades. Before the Germans could recover from the carriers' fire, we would dash up, throw our grenades at the ports and fire into them at point-blank range.

The plan worked to perfection. In ten minutes we took the four German hilltop positions by assault. . . .   J.-G. POULIN

By the end of that day, Lt. Gen. E. L. M. Burns, the corps commander, reported "the Gothic Line is completely broken in the Adriatic sector and 1st Canadian Corps is advancing to the River Conca."

The swiftness of the success left the Canadians surprised and jubilant. Colonel Nicholson wrote that their mood was buoyant. Through the dust-laden air a vista of the azure Adriatic glistened, serene and refreshing in the heat. To the tired men, the end of their journey seemed in sight. A traffic sign expressed the spirit of the hour: Drive carefully if you want to see Vienna.

In northwest Europe, the Channel ports of France seemed to be the key to the same sort of quick victory as breaking through the Gothic Line in Italy. Allied supply lines had become dangerously long; harbors close to the front were urgently needed.

Ostend and Le Tréport both fell easily to First Canadian Army. But on September 3—the day armored columns of British Second Army moved into Antwerp—Hit-

One way to destroy a V-1 flying bomb before it reached its target was to nudge it with a wing tip, as this Spitfire is doing. The sensitive bomb would then plunge to earth out of control. The V-1, recalls Charles Bruce, wartime head of the London bureau of The Canadian Press, became "a common tribulation" in Britain. "Later, when the army had overrun the launching sites in the Pas de Calais and the V-2 rockets took over—until they too were stifled—a kind of debate developed in London: some reminiscently favored the V-1, which gave warning of its approach; others preferred the V-2, which was soundless until impact. 'If you hear it,' they said, 'you're okay. If you don't hear it, you're dead.'"

ler ordered the ports of Boulogne, Dunkirk and Calais held to the last.

It was decided that Dunkirk would not be attacked but placed under siege, and a truce was arranged so that the citizens could be evacuated. General Crerar sent the 3rd Canadian Division to capture Boulogne and its garrison of 10,000 men. To take Boulogne, encircled by strongly defended hills, deeply burrowed with concrete emplacements and laced with minefields, a set piece battle was required. On September 17 the assault opened with a massive artillery barrage and an attack by 690 aircraft of RAF Bomber Command, including many from Canada's 6 Group. Supported by Funnies—strange looking armored vehicles that flailed a path through the minefields and blasted and burned out defensive positions—Canadian infantry battered to the Citadel, then peeled off to clean up the coastline forts. After a nine-day fight, Boulogne surrendered with 9500 prisoners. But its harbor had been demolished.

The Canadians moved on to attack Calais and the nearby coastal guns of Cap Gris Nez. By October 1 the last defenders of the Channel ports were being mopped up. The Channel campaign had yielded 30,000 prisoners and six ports—and a rich dividend that made the First Canadian Army the toast of London. In clearing the coast, they overran the flying bomb sites from which the Germans had been bombarding southeast England for three months.

The jet-propelled V-1 pilotless aircraft, or flying bomb, was the first of Hitler's secret *Vergeltungswaffen* (reprisal weapons). It carried one ton of explosive at 400 m.p.h. With it, Hitler hoped to knock Britain out of the war or at least make her talk terms. As he said in 1943 when he gave the V-weapon development site at Peenemünde the highest priority in Germany's armament program: "Europe and the whole world will be too small from now on to contain a war. With such weapons, humanity will be unable to endure it."

The Bomber Command raid on Peenemünde in August 1943, in which 6 Group took a major part, delayed the flying bomb attacks almost a year. The first bomb fell just outside London on June 13, 1944, a week after D-Day. Soon they were arriving at the rate of 120 a day. In the first two weeks they killed 1769 people.

Allied bombers struck repeatedly at their launching sites and artillery raged at them from Britain. A band of anti-aircraft guns ringed England's southeast coast. Canadian-designed gun-laying radar sets directed them; proximity-fused shells Canadian scientists had helped design made them deadly. In one record day, 65 out of 94 flying bombs were destroyed.

Overhead, Spitfires, Tempests and Mosquito night fighters were thrown into the battle Londoners called the "baby blitz." The fighter pilots found they could safely explode the bombs in midair by firing at them from not less than 200 yards. If they ran out of ammunition, some pilots placed a wing tip under a wing of the flying bomb and tumbled it off course by quickly banking away. Another method was to fly in front of the bomb so that the fighter plane's slipstream would unbalance the missile and send it down out of control. Three RCAF squadrons knocked out 97 bombs. Of these, 82 were destroyed by the two-seater Mosquitos of 418 Intruder Squadron.

Although in the end only one bomb in seven was getting through to London, it was the capture of the launching sites that finally ended the menace. As Churchill wrote: "The victorious and rapid advance of the British and Canadian armies released London and its defenders from the intense strain of the previous three months, and on September 6 Mr. Herbert Morri-

Operation Market Garden, in September 1944, was a bid to bring the European war to a swift conclusion. Three airborne divisions were to seize bridges over vital rivers in Holland and enable the British Second Army to drive into Germany. Two U.S. divisions succeeded at Eindhoven and Nijmegen (below: a charge through bursts from German 88s) but the 1st British Airborne Division failed at Arnhem. The British, some flown in by Canadian planes, were dropped too far from the Lower Rhine bridge, ran into an SS panzer division, suffered from bad weather and poor communications and were cut off for nearly ten days. When relieved, the 1st Airborne had lost 1130 men killed and 6450 captured; only 2163 broke out. With the Arnhem bridgehead lost, hope of capturing the German Ruhr in 1944 was lost. The only Canadian soldiers in the Arnhem operation were two companies of engineers. In driving rain and under constant machine-gun and mortar fire, they helped ferry the airborne troops back across the Lower Rhine in storm boats.

son, Home Secretary, was able to announce: 'The Battle of London is won.' Although the Germans thereafter irritated us from time to time with flying bombs launched from aircraft, and with a few long-range bombs [the V-2 rockets] from Holland, the threat was thenceforward insignificant. About 8000 V-1 bombs were launched against London and about 2400 got through. Our total civilian casualties were 6184 killed and 17,981 seriously injured."

Despite the victories in Italy and on the Channel coast, the time of high hope didn't last. By the end of September, it was dying.

In Italy, the Germans quickly recovered from their defeat in the Gothic Line, flung reinforcements into the coastal corridor in front of the Canadians and slowed their thrust to a bitter step-by-step advance. It took three September weeks, and savage battles around San Fortunato and Coriano, to reach Rimini and the plains. By then, the rains of autumn had come. In the beckoning open country of the north, the 1st Corps met not swift success but thick mud and tiny streams suddenly bloated into rampaging torrents. Tanks and vehicles bogged down. The advance jerked slowly forward. In the mountains to the west, the U.S. Fifth Army's attack petered out. By mid-October, hope of swift victory had gone. Ahead, for the Canadians, lay a second costly, bloody Italian winter among the dikes, the quagmires and the rivers of the plains south of the Po.

For the Canadians in northwest Europe there would be a winter among the dikes, the quagmires and the rivers of Holland. Montgomery tried to prevent it with a daring September airborne assault to seize a bridgehead across the Lower Rhine at Arnhem. It could have opened the way into the heart of Germany, but it failed and the hopes of early autumn vanished with it.

Nor had the capture of the Channel ports solved the problem of supply. They were, it soon became obvious, too badly damaged, too small. The great port of Antwerp would have to be opened by clearing the estuary of the Scheldt River, and the Canadians would have to do it.

Cinderella
of the polders

**The prize: a route from Antwerp to the sea.
The price: 13,000 casualties**

*They had been waist deep in water—many
of them for two weeks. Impossible to over-
state their discomfort. And death had
become a daily and nightly lottery in which
each man held a ticket. Yet the Canadians
were not really unhappy, or if they were
they had a curious pleasure in it, like men
stubbing sore toes. And they had a grouse.
A peculiar sense of isolation had been
growing in them up from the Seine. It had
been noticeable in Ghent and Bruges in
late September. They felt that the main-
stream of war had turned away, and that
they were increasingly forgotten. They
heard the triumphant echoes of the armored thrusts; the tears, laughter, flowers and
champagne of the liberations: of Paris,
Brussels—even Antwerp. Their own experiences had been in a lower key. They
began to take a pride in that, the pride of
the unsung, the unappreciated, but there
was underlying bitterness. After all, they
were fighting a war, not making headlines
like politicians or actors. And they came
to believe that they were fighting it alone,
fighting it in this godforsaken corner,
this flat and flooded patch. The Canadians
had become welded together, kindred, a
tight community. The truth is that they
wanted to feel alone with the sustained and
terrible experience they clasped to themselves as something personal, and upon
which no one had a right to intrude.*
R. W. THOMPSON IN *The 85 Days*

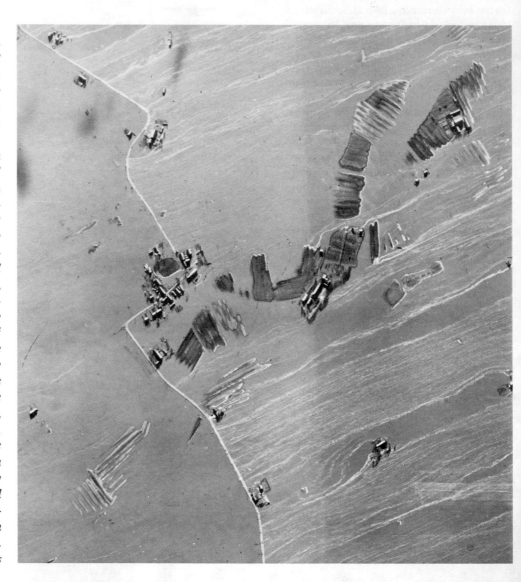

It was, the Dutch said, "land God had no
hand in," land they'd reclaimed from the
sea and had, for a century, considered an
impossible site for war. Yet through October and early November 1944, the First
Canadian Army did make war in these
polders and won a grim and major victory.

The campaign cleared the estuary of the
River Scheldt and opened the shipping
lanes to Antwerp, the second greatest port
in Europe and one that had become absolutely essential for the entire Allied front.

The price the First Canadian Army paid
was 13,000 casualties, half of them Canadian. The question that has been argued
ever since is whether the gateway to Antwerp might have been won earlier and at
considerably less cost. But in the heady,
triumphant days of September, other opportunities had held out greater attractions.

With the German collapse in Normandy,
Allied armored columns had swept across
France into Belgium, sent the Germans
reeling—and knocked Allied logistics
completely off balance. On September 3,

the British Guards Armored Division
rolled into Brussels, the Belgian capital.
The next day the British 11th Armored
Division entered Antwerp and, thanks to
Belgian Resistance fighters, found the har-
bor facilities almost intact.

Antwerp was a magnificent and badly
needed prize. Nearly 1000 ships could
berth at its ten square miles of docks. But
before the docks could be used, the 45-
mile-long Scheldt estuary between Antwerp and the sea had to be cleared of German troops, its waters cleared of mines. It

was a major task needing immediate attention if the situation was to be exploited before the Germans recovered.

Field Marshal Montgomery, however, had his eyes on a more glittering prize. He urged General Eisenhower to let him lead a "full-blooded," 40-division thrust across the Rhine to sweep into Germany. Losing his argument, he launched instead a much smaller airborne and armored attack at Arnhem, on the Lower Rhine, seeking a bridgehead for the assault into Germany. Despite great gallantry, the operation failed and, on September 25, Montgomery ordered the British 1st Airborne Division to withdraw across the river. Under constant attack, 2163 survivors were ferried back in assault boats, many of which were manned by Canadian engineers.

By then, the Allies' supply situation was critical. The French Channel ports already captured by the Canadians were still not ready or were inadequate to supply the needs of more than two million troops. Antwerp *had* to be opened. Both Eisenhower and Montgomery stressed that it must be done; from Berlin, Col. Gen. Alfred Jodl, chief of Germany's Operations Staff, warned that it must be prevented. Even so, it still took days of battle to convince the Allied leaders how big a job it was.

All through September, Chester Wilmot wrote in *The Struggle for Europe,* the First Canadian Army had been "the Cinderella" of General Eisenhower's forces. Its dogged, thankless campaign to free the Channel ports was overshadowed by the main Allied forces driving for the German frontier. In the beginning, said Col. C. P. Stacey in *The Victory Campaign,* the drive to open the Scheldt was also "a Cinderella operation," one which for a long period received from high Allied commanders more lip service than high priority.

The First Canadian Army got much less bomber support than was originally promised; it was refused airborne troops. Its Canadian divisions were sapped, as well, by a shortage of trained infantrymen. And despite these shortcomings, it tried for a time to do two things at once. Its 2nd Canadian Corps fought simultaneously on both sides of the estuary; its 1st British Corps—actually a mixture of British, Canadian, American and Polish troops—moved up on the right, assisting British Second Army in its movement toward Germany's Ruhr Valley.

The campaign to clear the estuary itself raged for a week and a half under these circumstances. No longer off balance as they had been in September, the Germans now held it in strength on both sides of the water. While Montgomery struck at Arnhem, the German Fifteenth Army, outflanked on the coast by the Allied advance to Brussels and Antwerp, had been escaping across the Scheldt to South Beveland.

To man the Scheldt and its numerous fixed coastal defenses, General von Zangen left behind the 64th Division on the south bank, in what was called the Breskens pocket; the 70th Division was to the north in Walcheren and South Beveland, an island and a peninsula which stretched, fish-shaped, out from the mainland.

The battlefield was largely in Holland, just north of Belgium. Montgomery called the terrain "appalling." The ground was dead flat and sodden, an expanse of open fields crisscrossed with dikes about 15 feet high, each a barricade the enemy could defend. Much of it was flooded or liable to be flooded by the Germans. Virtually useless for tank warfare, it was, as one soldier put it, a battleground "for men with web feet and waterproof skins." Frequent, drenching rain made it even worse.

On the eve of the operation the army's commander, Lt. Gen. H. D. G. Crerar, was invalided to England for treatment of per-

A Belgian woman takes the arm of a British soldier escorting captured Germans through the streets of liberated Antwerp. The great port was taken early in September 1944 but its docks could not be used until the First Canadian Army cleared the 45-mile-long Scheldt estuary. The flat, flooded *polders* (left) made one of the worst battlefields of the war.

sistent dysentery. The battle was directed by Lt. Gen. Guy Simonds of 2nd Canadian Corps. One of Simonds' first tasks was to clear the area north of Antwerp and close the eastern end of the South Beveland isthmus to seal the Germans in. This task he gave to the 2nd Canadian Division. In the beginning things went well, and by October 8 the division's 5th Brigade was very close to the neck of the peninsula. Then the opposition abruptly stiffened; the enemy had thrown in four battalions of paratroopers.

In his book *The 85 Days,* British war correspondent and historian R. W. Thompson describes the next, vicious phase:

... For the 2nd Division, probing toward Woensdrecht on the last lap to close the neck of the peninsula, October 9 was the beginning of a nightmare.

In the night, the rain began to beat down in a pitiless deluge that continued through four days and nights. The dawn of the 10th was full of evil. To the right of a main road, the Essex Scottish and Régiment de Maisonneuve were crawling and stumbling through the sodden woodland, cautious of trip wires and cunningly concealed mines. Their objective was to clear the enemy from strong positions round the Groote Meer Lake. There were several lakes linked together through the woodlands, but land and water had begun to lose definition. The whole earth squelched. The din of shellfire was such an accustomed background that it seemed to the men the only sounds were the high-pitched whines of rifle bullets and the roar of mines detonating. Visibility dwindled to a score of yards. Men crumpled without a cry into the soaking earth, while the enemy fought a measured withdrawal to the military training grounds a mile or two to the north, knowing every inch of the ground.

While these two battalions strove to clear the right flank, the 5th Brigade astride the main road met the full force of the enemy power before Woensdrecht. Again and again anti-tank guns halted the tanks of the 8th Reconnaissance Regiment. It was an impossible task for tanks; for men without armor it was even more impossible. The infantry lay in the shallow drains and the dikes, peering out over the ooze of the polders toward Woensdrecht. For them there was no way round this gateway to Beveland. They were without illusions in the face of the concentrated fire of 88s, anti-tank guns, Spandaus and rifles.

Woensdrecht rose on a shallow mound on the fringe of the polders, rose like some ominous hulk out of the brown water to guard the northwest corner of the isthmus. Its defenses extended for more than 1000 yards in depth to the final barrier of the railway embankment. They were held by four battalions of paratroopers, deeply entrenched and well armed, and two more battalions screened the left flank, holding up the clearance of the woods while slowly falling back on the main positions. For six days and nights the Canadians pitted themselves against that defense, paying for every yard with anonymous blood, until those who survived were aware only that they were not yet dead. Again and again, crawling, crouching, stumbling a few yards, saturated with mud and water, the leading companies strove to gain a foothold while the enemy held as firm as rock.

British historian John North wrote of it, and of the days to come: "The steel of a man's mind was to count more than the manufactured article." Colonel Stacey said: "No written record can do justice to the situation."

In the end there was nothing to record beyond the bare facts of the muddied, shapeless land and water, the dikes and drains, the embankment from which came an unfaltering, intensive, controlled fire that discovered even the men on their bellies on those open polders. The enemy, buttressed against all the firepower the Canadians could bring to bear, thankful for the rains that saved them from air attack, were men of the highest caliber Germany could still muster.

As for those in the assault, they had

The wind-driven rain seemed to join the dark evil sky to the dark evil land, so that the small space they had won resembled the inside of a tureen squelching with mud and water like some foul stew. Even the dikes had been crushed and churned into the gray muck of the featureless wilderness. There were no fires. There was no rest. Men lived and died and slept always wet and caked with ooze. The Germans had mined and booby-trapped their dead. The bloated bodies in the mud of the *polders* and the dark waters of the dikes had proved as dangerous dead as alive. Bodies exploded at a touch to destroy men in their rare moments of compassion.

R. W. Thompson in *The 85 Days*

become bearded, hungry, sleepless, muddied forms. There remained to them only the knowledge that they were a part of something, a section, platoon, company, regiment, and that it all held together.

At the end of the first three days not a yard had been gained. In battalion diaries there are entries which state simply, "mud, mud, mud—relentless rain, water everywhere."

Friday, October 13, was a day of reckoning standing out from the bleak calendar of those days. Leading their men over the polders against the dikes of Woensdrecht, every rifle company commander of the Black Watch of Canada was wounded. It was to no avail, yet the spirit of the Canadian attack brought a sense of awe and doom to the enemy. Artillery fire came down continuously on his positions, and the strain began to tell.

On the morning of the 16th, having withstood fierce counterattacks through the night, the Royal Hamilton Light Infantry at last won a foothold in Woensdrecht, and by dusk held it firm against savage counterattacks coming in with a fury that was almost berserk. At last they had something to hold to, something firmer than mud and sand and water, something that seemed almost like a "hill" in the wilderness. . . .   R. W. THOMPSON

By then General Eisenhower had realized that the double assignment given First Canadian Army was too heavy. It couldn't clear the estuary and support British Second Army simultaneously. Its 2nd

Corps couldn't send the 2nd Division westward into South Beveland until its right flank was secured. Eisenhower ordered Field Marshal Montgomery to forget the drive on the Ruhr Valley and give the Scheldt top priority in his 21st Army Group. "On our entire front," said Ike, "I consider Antwerp of first importance."

From then on 2nd Canadian Corps could turn its back to the mainland and clear the Scheldt without worrying about pressures on its inland flank; the 1st Corps took care of those in a northward drive to the Maas River in which Canada's 4th Armored Division played an important role.

With its flank protected, the 2nd Division went on from Woensdrecht to finish the sealing off of South Beveland. Then it struck westward. By October 31, after severe fighting, South Beveland was in its hands.

Through all that time, the 3rd Canadian Division was fighting on the far, southwest side of the estuary to clear the Breskens pocket, the land between the Scheldt and the Leopold Canal. Its attack had opened at dawn October 6 with a frontal assault across the canal by the 7th Brigade.

Under a searing wall of fire from 27 Wasps (flamethrowing Bren-gun carriers), the Canadian Scottish and Regina Rifles were ferried across in assault boats manned by the North Shore (New Brunswick) Regiment. Two small bridgeheads were secured but the Germans counterattacked violently. All that day and night the Canadians held on, fighting in mud and water often up to their armpits. On October 7 the Royal Winnipegs crossed over on a kapok assault bridge and a savage battle developed in the maze of dikes behind the canal. It took three days to link up the two bridgeheads, and even then the Canadians had advanced only a few hundred yards.

Then General Simonds broke the German opposition by outflanking it. On October 9, he sent the 9th Brigade, in troop-carrying amphibious Buffaloes, into an assault across the Braakman inlet to the northeast. Simultaneously, a 4th Armored Division infantry unit, the Algonquin Regiment, forced its way through the one land gap into the pocket at the south-eastern corner between the end of the Leopold Canal and the gullet of the Braakman. Pressures on the 7th Brigade soon eased.

The 9th Brigade's waterborne assault gained complete surprise and by mid-morning all three of its battalions were moving inland. On the 11th, the Highland Light Infantry captured Biervliet, the first vital objective. The same day the North Shore Regiment was ferried into the bridgehead. By October 14 the entire 3rd Division was inside the Breskens pocket.

"The countryside," writes R. W. Thompson in *The 85 Days,* "was a diabolical ruin of felled trees, craters, wire and mines, with the enemy dug in along every dike bank and their putrefying, booby-trapped dead like bait by the verges. Many of Gen. Kurt Eberding's 64th Division troops were veterans from the Russian front. They lay in the dikes and went on shooting until they were overrun and killed or taken prisoner. For the Canadians every yard seemed to hold a menace. Harmless-looking clumps of roots blazed suddenly with 20-mm. fire. Haystacks erupted. And as the Canadians floundered through the mud, men's feet were blown off by flat pancake mines that made each stride a nightmare. It was no fantasy of an inferno: it was real."

Every infantry battalion that went through the pocket came away with its own memories. Will R. Bird, historian of New Brunswick's North Shore Regiment, wrote that the campaign was "a misery they had not known before. It was like Indian war-fare, small sections taking desperate chances, probing, feeling, trying to out-guess the enemy, and advancing day after day, night after night, with nothing but courage and the hope of luck."

Bird recorded the recollections of some of the survivors:

. . . Maj. O. L. Corbett, D company commander: "After our landing on October 11 we had a rough time getting started. Although smoke had been dropped along the mouth of the estuary to hide us from big guns at Flushing over on Walcheren, the enemy knew the shoreline was being used. I was talking with Lt. Victor L. Soucisse when we heard a salvo coming. I jumped one way and he went the other—right into trouble. He was badly wounded. We moved up outside of Biervliet, which was held by the HLI, and next morning started pushing south of the town. My driver and I had just left my jeep when it received a direct hit. We reached a dike junction that was our objective and were shot up by Spitfires. These planes had just bombed A and B companies and then came over us. Our complaints to battalion headquarters were strenuous.

"The enemy now started to mortar our position from the rear of an orchard 800 yards away and, as luck would have it, along came a flight of Typhoons from our own 2nd Tactical Air Force. The flight leader came down to about 20 feet to see who we were. I stood up and used panto-mine to tell him about the enemy mortars. He was a bright lad. He got the message. The mess his Typhoon fighter-bombers made of Jerry's mortar position was beautiful to behold. The flight leader came back, waggled his wings and we cheered him on his way.

"At 1500 hours the enemy launched a counterattack with about 100 men. It was a pretty piece of work, well spaced out and controlled, but doomed. We had had time to move two .30 Brownings in on a flank to enfilade our whole front. We had our artillery well laid on to cover the area and simply waited until the enemy was 100 yards outside the fire zone and then gave the word to shoot. In three minutes the enemy formations were smashed. The men who were left took cover in small drainage ditches. My platoon commanders started using mortars, with the riflemen taking shots at anything that moved.

"I visited the platoon positions and noticed two lads lying almost on top of the dike, as if it were the firing point on a rifle range. There were two bricks between them holding down piles of francs and guilders. They were taking turns at firing. If a Jerry broke cover and one fellow fired and missed, he had to pay. But if he made a hit the other lad paid him. I went back satisfied. With morale like that it would take a strong enemy to bother us."

Canadian troops (left, behind a smoke screen) had to fight for every foot of the Scheldt estuary—against Germans defending a maze of dikes and flooded *polders* and supported by artillery, mortars and machine guns.

Lt. Osborne "Robbie" Robertson: "The Scheldt was a mixed-up mess in every way. One day shortly after we landed, Typhoons rocketed us by mistake and I had to grab a 12-foot length of yellow celanese material which we used as air markers and run across an open field toward a wood which I knew held Jerries. But I had to go that way to attract the attention of the planes. As I neared the wood the Typhoons came in again and one of their rocket bombs exploded nearby. There were seven German soldiers in the wood but I ignored them until I managed to signal the planes away. The Germans then surrendered, either grateful to me for saving them or awed by my new yellow weapon.

"On the 16th we made a fast advance and cut off a number of Jerries in a small village. Our platoon reached the outskirts and then we found we were surrounded in an orchard; the supporting arms had not followed closely enough. About 60 fanatical Jerries charged us but we beat them off, leaving half their number in the mud. Twice more they tried it, like madmen, and each time our guns cut them to pieces. Suddenly one of my men was hit and I noticed shots coming from the rear. We got out of the orchard quickly.

"I took the wounded man on my back to get him to cover, but I was hit in the leg and went down. I let the wounded lad crawl to the safety of the canal bank, covering him with a captured German automatic rifle. Then I was hit again and this time I saw the gun that was responsible. Slinging my rifle, I crawled to the canal, slipped into the cold water and moved slowly to a covered spot just opposite the Jerry machine-gun post. I hurled a grenade and wounded one of the gunners badly. The other two ran and that gun was out of action. Another Jerry gun nearby opened fire on me so I dropped down and fired, getting the gunner. I then got the second man as he tried to use the gun.

"I was able to crawl on and collect my men but it took us some hours to get back to safety. The company stretcher-bearers picked me up and put me on top of a jeep. Away we went under a farewell flurry of Jerry fire. When we reached the regimental aid post the front tire was in shreds and there were 20 holes in the jeep itself. So ended my war."

The fighting soon resolved into a pattern. Across the flat, flooded fields one company would put in a sharp attack. Immediately after the success signal, another company would push through them to deliver another blow. But always it was slow. The dikes were under direct observation and movement along them was almost suicidal. The roads were thickly sown with mines.

At one stage, when B company was cleaning out a particularly troublesome enemy light flak battery, Lt. Harry Hamley added a touch of the unusual. He ordered his men to fix bayonets, borrowed a rifle for himself and led his platoon across a lone stretch of dry ground in a wild charge that so startled and frightened the German gun crew that they threw up their hands. This spectacular charge was dictated by

Waters of the North Sea pour through a great dike at Westkapelle on the Dutch island of Walcheren after a daylight raid by RAF bombers on October 3. Near Westkapelle were German gun defenses covering the entrance to the Scheldt. Ten days later, on "Black Friday" the 13th, the Black Watch of Canada lost 183 men in an attack into the dike lands around Woensdrecht. This same 2nd Division infantry battalion had suffered over 300 casualties in a single day during the Normandy fighting three months earlier. At Woensdrecht, all four company commanders were wounded—one of them, Maj. J. R. Popham, seriously. He was evacuated, says the Black Watch war diary, "but not before he had dictated a report to be forwarded to Lt. Col. [B. R.] Ritchie." The report said the company was down to less than half normal strength. When darkness came that night, the exhausted battalion was holding on. Says the war diary: "No words can pay sufficiently high tribute to those who went out in the dark searching the flooded fields to ensure that all possible wounded had been taken out."

necessity. Flamethrowing carriers had been allotted for the job but they had come to a fiery, twisted end on mines. Steel and spirit had to take over.

Lieutenant Hamley: "In No. 4 platoon, we were very weary before the end of the first week—but morale was good. We had a dirty job—taking a place called Scherpbier—and almost had to pitchfork Jerry out of his holes in the mud. After it was over, some of the boys went into one of the few houses still intact and found a pot of chicken stewing on the stove. I said, 'Be careful boys, it may be poisoned.' That slowed them down but eventually one of them tried the stew and shouted: 'It's okay!' That big pot of stew vanished like magic.

"The morning of the 13th, Pte. Raymond Jones put on a great show. He was one of No. 4 platoon's mainstays and showed great courage and leadership that grim, wet, blustery day. He led the forward section in the attack on Kanningenhaven, and met heavy machine-gun fire and fanatical troops. Jones faced them with a Bren gun and put the Jerry gun out of commission, silencing the whole crew. This gave the platoon time to form up for a charge over the dike. The result was the capture of an 88-mm. gun, two machine guns and 14 prisoners.

"We moved to a farmhouse in the Kapitaledam area and settled down for a couple of days. In the mud and chill I was told to report to company headquarters to receive forms for selling Canada Bonds to the troops. I wonder if the politicians back home realized that many of the bonds were subscribed in foxholes in the front line.

"The North Shore went on to Ijzendijke. A couple of nights later word came through that we were not moving fast enough and must put on night attacks. Maj. Willard Parker planned every detail for each attack and we moved ahead rapidly. We captured a German major and he said: 'We can handle the Yanks and the Limeys, within reason, but you Canadians come at us at night with flamethrowers, mortars, guns, everything—yelling like hell. You simply terrify our troops!' "

Maj. O. L. Corbett: "The whole campaign was company attacks day after day. Sometimes we put in two or three attacks in 24 hours. We were soaked all the time. Along the dikes was the only place a soldier could dig in. Down on the level the water would drain in at once. We gradually worked our way along but every day saw some casualties.

"Returning from a 48-hour leave in Brussels, I learned that the battalion had become entangled in an operation and D company had suffered severely. L. Sgt. Claudius H. Jennings and Cpl. John Hollohan and several others had been killed. Jennings and Hollohan had been extremely efficient and I felt upset over the news.

"From battalion headquarters I called D company on the set and asked them to send my jeep. About midnight in came Sgt. Gordon Graham, carrying my pet automatic rifle. He said we might need the rifle the last mile or so as there were pockets of Jerries still around. He was quite correct, but with the help of darkness and fairly reckless driving we made company headquarters safely. The area held by D company was a scene from Dante's *Inferno*, lit by still burning buildings, haystacks, etc., coupled with the stench of scorched and burning men and animals and the pungent odor of high explosives. Against this weird background the company was busily digging in.

"It was here I received the finest compliment ever. My batman, Smith, guided me to the various platoon locations to see how everything was progressing. I stopped to talk with a corporal and a private digging a slit trench, and as I left I heard the private ask who I was, wandering around like that. 'Everything's all right now,' came the corporal's answer. 'It's the Old Man. He's back again.' I mentally asked God to help me justify such confidence."

Lt. Blake Oulton: "The Dutch civilians moved in behind the troops and were back in their homes—or what was left of them—almost as soon as the fighting ceased. Their chances of being killed by artillery fire did not seem to worry them. It amused us to see them leave their wooden shoes by the door and go about the house in sock feet. We were using the kitchen of a farmhouse outside Schoondijke as our headquarters, and the women waged a losing battle with the mud being tramped in by our boots. Finally they gave up trying to keep the tiled floor clean. But for a while they had even tried to keep a flagstone walk between the house and barn washed off. One thing in their favor was plenty of water. It seldom stopped raining."

Lt. Harry Nutter: "On October 22 the Highland Light Infantry captured the town of Schoondijke and we moved through their positions to beyond the town. Next day we advanced on a group of farmhouses on a crossroads, suspected of being a key point. Following our artillery barrage we went in and found nothing save dead horses and cows and some petrified civilians in a homemade shelter. We set up a defense and I slept on a pile of hay in the kitchen. Just before daybreak we got orders to advance up the main dike. We lined up for the attack, my platoon on one side of the dike and Lt. Jack Breau's on the other. We were supported by heavy machine guns and an artillery barrage was to follow. Capt. Bill Hogg, our artillery forward observation officer, went up in a windmill on the start line with his wireless

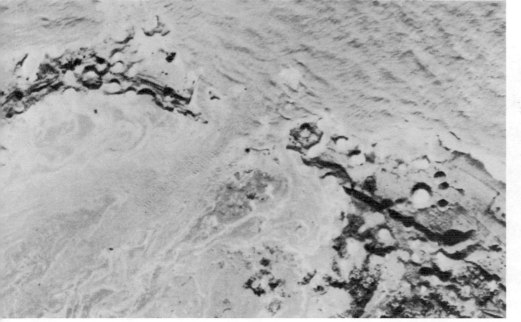

"Hardskins" (armored gun tractors) of the 6th Anti-Tank Regiment roll through Knocke in Belgium at the end of the Scheldt campaign. By November, as the First Canadian Army won the precious route to Antwerp, the last enemy troops were fleeing from France. These Germans (below) are being fired on by the SS as they try to escape toward Switzerland.

Reporter Ross Munro wrote that Antwerp went about its normal business while fighting raged in the city's outskirts. "You could get on a street car in the center of Antwerp," he wrote in *Gauntlet to Overlord,* "and go to the front in the suburban town of Merxem. I watched a couple of skirmishes and, as darkness fell, drove back to Antwerp. In half an hour I was in the lounge of the Century Hotel, listening to a string orchestra and having an aperitif before dinner, served by waiters in white tie and tails. It was fantastic! Some 2nd Division officers were in the lounge too, fresh from battle that afternoon and goggle-eyed at the splendor so close to the shooting."

operators. The windmill really got rocked by our own artillery, and Hogg was chased out—a very angry and profane officer.

"I passed Pte. Dick Sprague in the ditch on my way to the head of the platoon. We had grown up together in Sussex. He said: 'When are you going to get me transferred to your platoon?' 'As soon as this is over,' I said. He grinned and waved his hand, and was killed 15 minutes later when a gun blew up a mine right beside him.

"The dike was S-shaped and when we rounded a bend we were raked by machine-gun fire from across the fields behind us. We started heaving grenades over the dike at Jerries on the other side. Breau's platoon could not get around the bend and we couldn't go farther without being cut off. We were ordered to retire.

"The next night a second attack on a battalion scale was launched. It was most unusual to attack in the pitch-dark—and it gave you a helpless feeling to walk along expecting every minute to run into a bullet. We went up another dike nearby and took the German outposts by surprise. They were all taken prisoner before they could alert the German headquarters. It was just daylight when we arrived at the headquarters. We crouched down on one side of the dike, blasting away at the house. We

made a mess of it with our anti-tank weapons and the battle was soon over. Pte. M. A. Cooke, our Indian stretcher-bearer, was busy tending the wounded. He came to me afterward and said: 'Well, good luck. I won't see you for a while.' Then he showed me his ankle, broken by shrapnel. He had given no sign that he was injured until then.

"We took up a position at a crossroads 50 yards beyond the headquarters and started to dig in. It was easy going until an 88 gun blasted at us from 100 yards behind. Pte. John E. Rushleau was killed when the first shell hit a tree beside him. We vacated that position in a hurry—I cleared a three-foot hedge in one hop. Captain Hogg came in with his wireless set to bring down artillery support. We rushed to a small house and were just inside when the next shell from the 88 blasted the whole end of our building. We had to break a hole in the rear wall to get Captain Hogg out. His wireless operators were badly wounded.

"The 88 was perfectly camouflaged with a net. I was lying on the road staring at it when it erupted. The shell went over the road a foot above me and hit a building, a German hospital. There was a fine German medical officer in charge and he looked after the wounded all that day. We were all uneasy until our artillery took care of the 88 with a direct hit.

"That night Sgt. George Hunt, my batman, Pte. Raymond Vibert, and I decided to get some sleep in a small undamaged house on the dike above us. Anything to get out of the mud. We were joined by Lt. Jack Breau who stretched out on the floor in one corner. We had just got settled when Jerry threw over a barrage. One shell hit our house and made a three-foot hole just above Breau. He took off and fast!

"We all liked Jack Breau. One hungry day I went around a farm building and found him trying to coax a fat chicken within reach. He held a large hairbrush behind him so the chicken would not see it. That same day a soldier got some milk for my tea. It made a wonderful drink. I wondered where he got the milk—until later I saw a smashed barn with a dead cow in the timbers. She had a very full udder. You remember those days. Like the afternoon a young German lad tried to lead a counterattack against our platoon. He had to cross 100 yards in the open. His men ducked back but he came on and

Bridgehead

While the First Canadian Army was fighting on the soggy soil of Holland, the 1st Canadian Corps was fighting from dike to dike, river to river on the soggy soil of northern Italy. There, on the night of October 21-22, 1944, a 30-year-old private named Ernest Alvia "Smoky" Smith won the Victoria Cross.

He won it on the Savio, one of the seemingly endless rivers of Italy, on a night of torrential rains. He and other riflemen of Vancouver's Seaforth Highlanders managed to cross the swollen, raging stream but it was impossible to get tanks and anti-tank guns over to reinforce their bridgehead.

When German tanks and infantry attacked, Smith knocked out a tank, took on ten Germans alone at point-blank range, killed four and drove the others off. When another attack came, he drove it off. Under tank fire, he carried a wounded Seaforth to medical attention, then returned to his position to await further attacks. None came. Largely through his gallantry, the bridgehead had held.

Smoky Smith was one of 16 Canadians to win the V.C. Thirteen of them were with the Canadian forces, and their feats are described in these volumes. The other three served with the British forces:

Royal Navy Capt. Frederick Thornton Peters, 53, a native of Charlottetown, won the V.C. in leading a charge by two cutters through boom defenses in the harbor of Oran during the North African landings of November 8, 1942. He died within a few days in the crash of a plane taking him to Britain.

Maj. Charles Ferguson Hoey, 29, born in Duncan, B.C., was decorated for his leadership in capturing a Japanese position in Burma. Though twice wounded in this action on February 16, 1944, he reached the objective first and killed all the occupants. He died from his wounds.

Sqdn. Ldr. Ian Willoughby Bazalgette, 25, born in Calgary, was decorated for great courage on a bombing raid August 4, 1944. His pathfinder plane on fire, with two engines gone, he got through to the target to mark it for bombers that followed. Fighting to get his flaming Lancaster home, he brought the plane down in France, only to die when it exploded.

almost reached our position before he fell dead, simply filled with bullets. What a waste of life and courage!

"Shortly before we attacked and took Sluis, I was ordered to take a reconnaissance patrol to the outskirts of the town to detect the German positions and find out if a certain bridge was intact and if the road approaches were mined. I gathered my patrol, Lance Corporal Watson, L. Sgt. Frank "Buzzer" Cripps and Pte. Merlin Stewart, in the loft of a farmhouse shed, briefed them, checked weapons, then had them rest until it was time to go. Sergeant Hunt had listened in on the briefing and he now vanished. Ten minutes before we were to go he returned and said: 'Why are you putting on your equipment? You're not going anywhere.' He knew I had dysentery and had gone to Maj. R. B. Forbes, reporting me and asking and receiving permission to take my place. I was furious because I was all keyed up to go. I gave Sergeant Hunt hell and stamped in to see Major Forbes. He ordered me to bed. After the patrol took off I followed it a short distance from our lines, then returned and went to sleep on the kitchen floor.

"About 3 a.m. Sergeant Hunt barged in holding a German prisoner by the neck. Hunt was in a wild state. He pushed his prisoner up the hall to Major Forbes' quarters and I followed. The major got out of his bunk and took over. I think the poor Jerry thought Hunt and I would kill him. He could speak no English so Major Forbes sent for Pte. Joe Golland who spoke German fluently. He told the Jerry to start talking or have his brains beat out. How that man talked! He knew about all the defenses and was taken to battalion headquarters where he spilled all.

"Hunt then told us what had happened. He had cut across fields in front of le Régiment de la Chaudière's positions on his way to the main road leading to Sluis. He came to a small barn and house and, seeing a figure in the yard, called out: 'Chaudière?' The sentry muttered something and Sgt. Buzzer Cripps hissed, 'He's a German!' They crept up to the barn in a roundabout manner, came up behind the sentry, seized and disarmed him. Just then all hell broke loose. Germans came out of the barn and the patrol started shooting at them. The Germans, bewildered, began hurling grenades over the building. Sergeant Hunt started throwing Germans on

the exploding grenades (we found several of his victims in a hospital in Sluis when we took it), then he grabbed one German and started up a deep ditch, shouting to the others to follow. Watson and Stewart went with him but Cripps went the other way, toward the Chaudière lines. About 30 yards from the barn Stewart was shot through the stomach. Sergeant Hunt tried to help him with one hand while holding his prisoner with the other. Watson was behind acting as a covering party. Stewart said to Hunt: 'Don't bother with me. I'm done. Save yourself.' Sergeant Hunt had no choice. Stewart was a very brave man. The heartbreak—mine and Hunt's—over his death cannot be described.

"When the brilliant Lt. Gen. Guy Simonds [above] came to First Canadian Army headquarters as acting commander," says Maj. Gen. Churchill Mann, "he busied himself by infusing renewed enthusiasm in the divisions, which had been engaged in heavy and costly fighting for many weeks. His personality was responsible in large measure for the successful clearing of the Scheldt." With that victory, Antwerp (right) and its dock facilities could be used by the Allies in the final drive to destroy Germany.

"Sergeant Hunt left the ditch and circled back in the fields. The Germans were still shooting and some cattle were milling about. Hunt grabbed a cow by the horn and hung on as they raced past the Jerries. The cow was killed but neither Hunt nor his prisoner was touched. Watson also made his way back safely. What had happened was that they had run into a German fighting patrol of 40 men that later attacked and almost wiped out one Chaudière platoon.

"Buzzer Cripps stayed with a Chaudière company all night and came in the next morning, his beat-up face something to see. I took him to Major Forbes and he was given a mug of rum. 'They'll never kill old Buzzer,' gasped Cripps, when he could talk, 'but they may well scare him to death.'"

Gradually the Germans in the pocket were forced back into a smaller and smaller area. As the fighting neared the end, every soldier sensed it and was fiercely determined to finish it as speedily as possible. Time had become almost meaningless, and even day and night were indefinite boundaries. Hot food and warm sleep and being dry were things belonging to a remote past. Companies, platoons, sections, at little more than half strength, went on because they were impelled by a devotion to duty and to the regiment.

Maj. O. L. Corbett: "The steady push went on until only the town of Sluis was left in our sector. Lt. Col. J. E. Anderson decided to attack down the main road from the northeast. D company was third in and we were to pass through the two leading companies and clear the southern part of the town. We got to our sector at about 1000 hours and found we had a fight on our hands. I told the platoon commanders to play it canny and keep casualties to a minimum—shortly after that both the platoon commander and the sergeant of No. 11 platoon were casualties. Their job was to capture an important dike junction, containing a mortar battery. Cpl. Donat Savoie took charge of the platoon, did a marvelous job of leading the attack, captured the position and held it.

"The other platoons gradually forced the enemy out of the buildings. It was house-to-house fighting and savage enough at times, but our men knew every Hun trick. By 1500 hours we had the job done. The Germans' stubborn resistance had been led by an SS captain who, even when captured, would not stand with his men. He insisted he be taken prisoner as an officer. Lt. Bill Dickie was wearing a sleeveless leather jacket. He pulled the jacket off the rank badges on his shoulders and said: 'Look at those, chum!' Then he kicked the SS captain squarely on the seat of the pants and rammed him in among the other prisoners.

"When we arrived at the south end of the town and started to clear out the enemy, I picked a place for our company headquarters. It was a three-story building and normal procedure was to first check the place for enemies. This we proceeded to do and I found the door leading to the basement. In that basement we found a man, his wife, four children and two grandparents. They were afraid at first until they recognized our uniforms and then the woman started to laugh and cry. They had been in that cellar since September and all along the man kept saying: 'Cheer up. The Tommies will be here by November.' So there we were at 1030 hours the morning of November 1, and the wife was convinced that her husband was a prophet." . . .   WILL R. BIRD

The Germans had been forced back into a last refuge, the waterlogged areas around the sea end of the Leopold Canal. Here, on November 1, the North Nova Scotia Highlanders captured General Eberding near Knocke-sur-Mer; the next day Zeebrugge fell and all German resistance in the pocket ended.

The 3rd Division had cleared the pocket; the 2nd had cleared South Beveland. Only Walcheren Island remained.

The 2nd Division had to fight for three bloody days to win a narrow road-and-rail causeway leading to the island from South Beveland. From then on Walcheren was a British task. The island was taken by British commandos and infantry; Canada's chief contribution came from the imaginative General Simonds. When the plan for the attack on Walcheren was being drawn up, he had insisted that the island's huge sea dikes be bombed, even though he was told it wouldn't work. The bombing did work; it turned Walcheren into a great saucer of water and hampered enemy movements, supply reinforcements and communications. It didn't stop the Germans, however, from putting up a savage fight.

The commandos who landed at West-kapelle November 1, says Colonel Stacey, faced defenses tougher than those that the Allies encountered on Normandy's beaches. As their flotilla approached, the coastal guns sank or damaged 17 of 25 naval supporting craft. Nevertheless the commandos got ashore, won a foothold on the dikes and, after several days of violent action, linked up with another force which had landed at Flushing. On November 8 German resistance on Walcheren died. The Scheldt campaign was over.

By then the entire 3rd Division was on leave in Ghent, basking for a week in the affections of a major city. "It was good getting away from the Scheldt," said a North Shore Regiment sergeant. "We could hardly believe our luck. When we reached streets packed with cheering Belgians and fluttering flags, we forgot that we were riding war-stained carriers and muddy vehicles, that we were weary, nerve-racked, fed-up mud rats. Even the most sour among us began laughing. We laughed and shouted at each other, and waved at the kids, and got into billets that were clean and warm.

"There were four of us in the house I was in. We stopped in the kitchen and left our muddy gear there, even our boots. We had a hot bath and came down, when madam insisted, to a whopper of a hot dinner with a white cloth on the table and coffee in china cups. That night we slept between real sheets and, because it was more like a dream than reality, I went to bed about nine and slept until nine the next morning when madam came tiptoeing in with coffee to wake me.

"Boy, what a life! My boots had been cleaned! My clothes had been cleaned! Our gear in the kitchen had been cleaned! We had eggs and bacon for breakfast! It was almost too much.

"Freddie, my sidekick, got up from the table so full he looked swollen, and he swung madam around and kissed her. She clung to him and tears rolled down her cheeks. I kind of choked up, too, and got out. It was just as we were leaving that I found out she had lost both her sons in the war.

"We went to shows and heard fine music and searched the city to find presents for madam. Fred, who never could keep money in his pocket, borrowed some somewhere and bought her a dozen roses. He and I and the other two were likely the

only ones in the platoon that never got drunk in Ghent. I guess it was the shock we got at the change from the Scheldt. The last day we just sat around and got in madam's way and talked with her, and when we left it was just like going away from home. When the war was over I took part of a leave to go and see madam again. There was no one left but me: Fred got wounded and didn't come back and the other two were killed in Germany."

The 3rd—and the other divisions—richly deserved a rest. The First Canadian Army had not only cleared the Scheldt but, with the 4th Division playing a leading role, much of southeast Holland. In five weeks, it had taken 41,043 prisoners and

had lost 12,873 men, killed, wounded and missing, of whom 6367 were Canadians.

They also deserved the plaudits that came their way.

Montgomery said: "The Canadians have proved themselves magnificent fighters, truly magnificent. Their job along the Channel coast and clearing the Scheldt was a great military achievement for which they deserve the fullest credit. It was a job that could have been done only by first-rate troops. Second-rate troops would have failed."

To Eisenhower, the battle was the climax of operations of the First Canadian Army: "The end of Nazism was in clear view when the first ship moved unmolested up the Scheldt."

That first ship came as part of a convoy on November 28 and, by chance, she was the Canadian-built *Fort Cataraqui*. In Antwerp, she was given a ceremonial greeting: there were bands, national anthems, representatives of both Eisenhower's and Montgomery's headquarters, the British and American port authorities and the Belgian government and army. There was one oversight—no one had thought to invite a representative of the First Canadian Army which had made it possible.

Cape Breton Islander Albert Penny shares Christmas dinner with "Mama" in his temporary Dutch home, one of hundreds in which Canadians were billeted during the winter of 1944-45.

Showdown

The toll of battle finally forces the conscription crisis Mackenzie King had avoided for five years

On the afternoon of September 30, 1944, the Cape Breton Highlanders were manning a soggy, static front on the river Fiumicino, once known as the Rubicon. Here, 1993 years earlier, Julius Caesar had decided to cross this then-boundary of Italy to make war for power in Rome.

There was no crossing it now. After a month of fighting north from the Gothic Line, the Highlanders and the rest of the 1st Canadian Corps had broken through to the Lombardy Plain, hoping for swift, decisive progress. But the fierce rains of the Italian autumn had ended that hope, turning the countryside into a quagmire and making the tiny river a muddy torrent 30 feet wide.

Because the Germans on the far bank had the area under heavy, intermittent fire, the Cape Bretoners had been ordered to cut movement by day to a minimum. So Maj. Aird Nesbitt, the acting CO, was surprised when an NCO stuck his head in the farmhouse door of battalion headquarters and announced that an armored car had come up anyway and that it bore, of all things, a civilian.

The civilian was Defense Minister James Layton Ralston. He had rejected advice not to go up to the front. Having commanded the Cape Breton unit's predecessor, the 85th Battalion, in World War I, he wanted to visit.

Ralston asked Nesbitt about the state of the unit, passed along messages from families back in Nova Scotia and talked to men up front on the communications network. He was in a somber mood and, in an attempt at levity, Nesbitt twitted him about being unable to cross the Rubicon.

It was, in retrospect, an ironic touch. Two weeks later, when his mission to the Italian and northwestern European fronts was over, Layton Ralston *had* crossed a Rubicon of his own. Like Caesar, he came to a mighty decision and, by doing so, he pitched Canada into her greatest crisis of the war: a grim showdown over conscription. It came when Ottawa was planning how to celebrate the coming return of peace.

"For good reasons or bad," wrote Ralph Allen in *Ordeal by Fire,* "for reasons of nationalism, honest pride and politics, Canada had clung to the goal of a self-contained, self-controlled, self-administered army of its own. The army, though relatively small by world standards, still required the appurtenances and paraphernalia of a large one: a big headquarters in Ottawa, one in London, another at First Canadian Army headquarters and two substantial corps headquarters."

The armies of all the Western Allies, wrote Allen, were "clogged to the verge of smothering by their administrative overhead" and "preposterously inefficient" in their use of manpower. The Canadian Army was as bad as any. In the fall of 1944 it had 468,000 men and women in uniform; of these, about 90,000 were in the five divisions and two armored brigades fighting the enemy.

For five years Prime Minister Mackenzie King had feared that an army that was large by Canadian standards would eventually provoke a crisis over conscription for overseas service that would gravely damage national unity. There had been no serious problem as long as the army was training or had only part of its strength engaged in Italy. But in 1944, for the first time, the whole overseas army was fighting at once: two divisions and an armored brigade in Italy, three divisions and an armored brigade in northwest Europe.

When he'd foreseen this coming, King had had a discussion with Britain's Gen. Sir Bernard Montgomery shortly before D-Day in June. He'd come away reassured. He recorded in his diary that Montgomery "firmly believes that the war would be over by the month of November." If that were true, there should be no crisis.

The army had predicted casualties in northwest Europe on the assumption that the war would be over a few months after the invasion of Normandy, and on the basis of British forecasts of "battle wastage" (casualties) rooted in earlier campaigns.

It took only three months to prove both assumptions wrong. Wounded veterans returning to Canada charged that the reinforcement system was breaking down, and Ralston hastened overseas to check for himself.

Everywhere he went he got bad news. In Italy he was told that if the 1st Corps continued to be actively engaged, its reinforcement pool would soon be exhausted. In northwest Europe, he found a similar situation. The war showed no signs of ending and infantry casualties had been far higher than anticipated. This was true of all the Allied armies, but especially so of the Canadians; of the 15 divisions in the 21st Army Group, the 3rd and 2nd Canadian divisions had suffered the greatest losses.

To fill the gaps, wounded men were being sent back to fight before they should have been; men from the artillery and other arms were being hastily, and at times inadequately, trained and sent up as infantry. The flow of volunteers from home was slowing.

As early as August, during the fighting around Caen and Falaise, a shortage of reinforcements had become apparent, but the army at first had thought it could handle things. By the end of that month, says historian Col. C. P. Stacey, Canadian infantry battalions in western Europe were fighting with an average shortage of 206 men. The Defense Department says they were supposed to have some 850. But the shortage was worse than it appeared on the surface.

Four rifle companies were the core of any battalion; they required some 60 percent of its manpower. The rest—specialists in signals, mortars and other lines—existed to support them. The shortages were nearly all in the rifle companies. The situation, says Colonel Stacey, was "a serious source of anxiety throughout the late summer and autumn."

By scraping the barrel, retraining men from other arms and taking advantage of a late-summer lull in action, Ralston found the army had managed to bring considerable improvement to the picture. But now it was locked in the violent battle of the Scheldt. Beyond that, Ralston was told, loomed another major campaign: within five weeks the army could be fighting on the Rhine.

"The picture Ralston got," wrote Col. Dick Malone in *Missing From The Record,* "was that the army, assuming normal wastage rates, might squeeze through for another three months at most." And normal wastage rates would hardly apply if the Scheldt were quickly followed by major action on the Rhine.

Manpower problems weren't peculiar to Canada. By now Britain and America and especially Germany all faced shortages. The difference was that Canada alone refused to send men into battle unless they volunteered; she had conscription but only for service at home.

As these facts drummed in on Ralston, he became a depressed and shaken man. A few nights after his arrival in Belgium, a mess dinner was given in his honor by Lt. Gen. H. D. G. Crerar, commander of the First Canadian Army.

Dick Malone, a former Ralston aide who had become the army's public relations chief in Europe, was there.

"Colonel Ralston," wrote Malone, "hardly noticed what he was eating, and at times completely lost touch with the conversation. Later he and I went to his caravan. There was a single light burning and the only source of heat was a small coal-oil heater which smoked away in one corner. I kept my trench coat on but the colonel appeared not to notice the cold and sat on the edge of a bunk. He was terribly despondent and lonely. But his mind was made up. He had talked to many soldiers and had pledged that Canada would back them to the hilt. He could not let them down for political reasons. He would either force the government to bring in overseas conscription or he would resign."

Ralph Allen in *Ordeal by Fire:*

. . . Ralston came back home on a gray October day, bearing his gray and fateful news. He told King there was only one

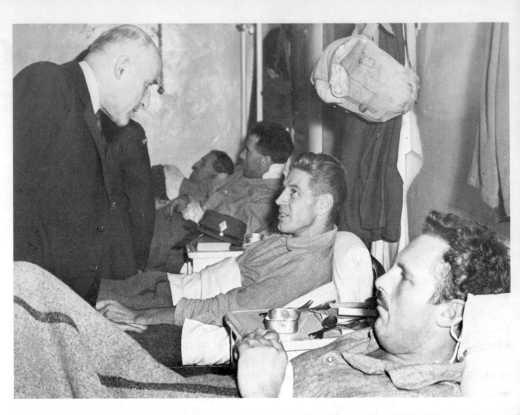

SUMMARY

1. REINFORCEMENT SITUATION.

(1) During the first half of this month the Bn. was committ times, resulting in heavy total casualties to Officers of the month we were short 17 Officers and are now shor ments received on the 15th. included two wounded office hospital. There have been no more officers forthcomin as the vacancies are largely in the rifle companies a t on the present officer slate of the fighting portion of

(2) The N.C.O. situation in the Bn. is now very serious. bottom as far as creating N.C.Os. from the ranks goes have drained the Bn. of trained privates and the reinfo are not sufficiently trained. There have been onlt th in the reinforcement flow this month (apart from a few our own), and they had been recently converted to Infa

(3) With regard to personnel in the Bn. refer to the result on training as infantry, of all ranks in the Rifle Comp shows the critical situation now existing in the Bn. r percentage of our reinforcements being personnel from R.C.A.S.C., who with very little training are sent forw This is our greatest problem and the solution is not ye necessary training time is evidently not available.

remedy: overseas conscription, at once, with no further hedging or reservations. There followed days of argument, much of it in secret meetings of the cabinet, some of it in private debate between the black hats (as the generals described the politicians) and the red tabs (as the politicians described the generals). Ralston's military arithmetic—which endorsed the demands of the General Staff—was that 15,000 trained infantry reinforcements must proceed overseas at once if the army was to recover from the wounds of summer and

autumn and be ready for the winter battles ahead. The only place to find them was among the Zombies, the 70,000 home-service conscripts who refused to volunteer for overseas.

Some Zombies were idealistic young pacifists of the kind who had recently been signing pledges and taking part in high-school debates against the whole idea of war. Others were French Canadians, whose instinct and training told them to avoid the far-off, perpetual bloodshed of Europe. Some were farm boys who wanted

action four
.   On the 14th
.   Reinforce-
rning from
 that date and
 strain is put
...
 reached rock
 casualties
ts arriving
.Os. included
ing N.C.Os. of
m other arms.
e questionnaire
   This clearly   Append. 4.
 from the great
R.C.E., R.C.O.C.,
 infantry.
ght as the

to stay on the farm, others were young men with girls they wanted to chase or marry. Many were, of course, and not unnaturally, scared stiff of being shot at. Some were willing to fight anywhere their country told them to if others like them were told the same. Whatever else they were, the Zombies were trained soldiers.

However, to Canada's shame, her great dilemma soon boiled down to a question not of military arithmetic but of political arithmetic, and the political arithmetic was at the root of all King's calculations. He had not the slightest intention of sending a single Zombie overseas, no matter what Ralston and the generals said. And so the question on which the pending decisions hinged had little to do with the bitter battle on the Scheldt. Suppose Ralston resigned; how many members of the cabinet would resign with him? Suppose conscription were forced to the floor of the House; how many Liberals would join the Opposition? Suppose there were enough to force a general election; how many seats would the government lose, how many gain, how many hold?

Day after day King fought a delaying action in the cabinet—coaxing, cajoling, calling for new plans, new figures, new explanations for the mess he insisted was of the generals' making, not his. Sometimes he threatened darkly that if hints of resignation did not cease he himself would resign.

It was a skillful exercise in stalling and if it accomplished nothing more it created a certain indecision among the four or five ministers who at first had been wholly on Ralston's side. But it was apparent that, although Ralston might compromise and even try one more crash drive for Zombie volunteers, he would no more surrender on the main issue than King would.

So King decided Ralston must go. Once that was settled, the only thing to be decided was the manner of his going. It must be on King's terms, not Ralston's, with martyrdom kept to a minimum and no suggestion that Ralston was anything less than an honorable man leaving on a point of principle. Still, it would help if his exit could be accompanied by suspicion that he was also a stubborn man being booted out for clinging to wrong and harmful policies. Most important, a strong successor must be ready to replace him at once, someone whose prestige was at least as high as Ralston's.

Such a man existed and such a man, King discovered discreetly, was available. He was the very man King and Ralston had so recently and so willingly fired, partly on the advice of the British War Office and partly because of his reluctance to divide the khaki empire that now lay at the root of all the trouble.

Andrew McNaughton was in Ottawa, retired with the rank of general. He was a declared foe of conscription. His public reputation was immense. And the Conservatives were trying to persuade him to become their national leader. If he accepted, he would be a dangerous political enemy.

After two weeks of crisis King called McNaughton to Laurier House. McNaughton assured him he could get all the reinforcements needed without invoking conscription. King offered McNaughton Ralston's job.

When the cabinet met soon after that, Ralston had no inkling of what was in store. Indeed, he held forth on the possibility—he was skeptical but willing to explore it—of solving the crisis by a last-minute appeal to the Zombies.

Then, during a pause in the discussion, King fired him. It was a discharge, as flat and peremptory as the discharge of a lackey. . . .   RALPH ALLEN

King recorded in his diary that he told the cabinet "I realized that some way would have to be found, if it could be found, to save the government and to save a terrible division at this time, and at the same time make sure of getting reinforcements if that was possible at all. That I had been asking myself was there anyone who could do this; who believed that our policy, which had worked successfully for five years, would now work for the remaining months of the war. If there was, I thought it was owing to the country that such a person's services should be secured. I said I believed I had the man who could undertake that task and carry it out. I then mentioned General McNaughton's name."

Ralston, King went on, "had clearly said that he did not believe we could get the men without conscription, while McNaughton believed we could, and he, Ralston, would have to tender his resignation, as he had said he would do if we pressed eliminating the conscription part; if Ralston felt that way, he should make it possible for us to bring McNaughton into the cabinet at once." In fact, King noted,

"Ralston had tendered his resignation to me some two years ago [during the 1942 controversy over a conscription plebiscite] and had never withdrawn it."

Ralston said he would tender a new resignation at once.

King said the defense minister "gathered up his papers and turned to me and shook hands. All the cabinet rose, formed a complete circle around the table, and shook hands with him." Then Ralston left. No one followed him.

King had won his point and his government stood firm. "But the problem," says Ralph Allen, "was still there. The army still needed infantry reinforcements and McNaughton, it became apparent almost at once, could not get them. He had misjudged the power of his own name and the temper of the Zombies. In his first week in office he made two recruiting speeches, and was booed by pro-conscriptionists. There was no increase in enlistments for overseas. King spoke over a national radio network and that appeal also failed dismally."

As he prepared to meet Parliament November 22, his prospects of success were fading.

By then the entire country was in turmoil over the issue. In 1942, King had told a Liberal caucus that if overseas conscription were imposed, "we would have to enlarge our jails and use our tanks and rifles against our own people." Air Minister C. G. Power had foreseen a catastrophe which would divide the nation into English vs. French.

As national tension grew in October and November, there was apprehension that these predictions might come true.

Lt. Gen. Maurice Pope, who was military secretary to the cabinet war committee, wrote later in his book *Soldiers and Politicians:*

"The thought of civil disturbance, even civil war, passed repeatedly through my mind. Gone was any consideration of the merits or otherwise of the conscription issue. Passions were aroused, and moderation and good sense cast to the winds. I was shocked by the violence of the views heard at every hand. Canada was divided into two angry camps. It was her rare good fortune that at the helm was the supreme politician of his generation."

English-speaking Canadians tended to equate the term Zombies with French Canadians alone. In fact, the percentage of Zombies from Quebec was not markedly greater than the French-Canadian share of the national population. But that made little difference now.

The French-Canadian press praised King for his faithfulness to his pledge against conscription and hailed his dismissal of Ralston. But growing numbers of English Canadians swung to the view

that conscription must be imposed regardless of Quebec. The Conservative party, many Liberals, the Canadian Legion, all gave voice to it. Some senior army officers violated the rule against political utterances to affirm their stand. A group of CWACs shouted abuse at King as he left his home.

Demands for "equality of sacrifice" and "an end of appeasement" intermingled with fears of conflict between Zombies and soldiers back from overseas. The Conservative press unleashed "an outpouring of unscrupulous propaganda," says Prof. MacGregor Dawson in his book *The Conscription Crisis of 1944.* "No opportunity was lost to depreciate the government's conduct of the war, to give full publicity to any soldier's grievance, to exaggerate, to harrow the public's feelings with stories of soldiers fighting at the front while the cabinet 'played politics.' The wrath of the Conservative party and press was turned especially on the French. The government

was accused of wickedly sacrificing young men's lives to retain its governing power in Quebec. General McNaughton did not escape. The man the party had wanted for its leader was now accused of betraying the army."

In *Missing From The Record,* Dick Malone says McNaughton's anti-conscription stand came "as a dreadful blow to the men fighting overseas. They simply couldn't believe the father of the army would let them down."

Amid the turmoil, McNaughton declared he must be the most hated man in Canada. The Prime Minister told him: "I could do you one better on that score." Now the two of them together had to meet Parliament.

Bruce Hutchison, in *Mr. Prime Minister,* takes up the story:

. . . Having already summoned Parliament to approve the success of his policy, King had to admit instead that McNaughton's failure had turned it into a fiasco. On

Every effort was made to man the Canadian Army with volunteers. "Come on!" says a sign in Phillips Square in downtown Montreal. "What are you waiting for?" This week the special come-on is free admittance to the Palace to see an "appropriate, timely and exciting film"—so said the caption on this wartime photograph (above). You had to sign up right there at the sandbagged recruiting office but you had your choice of navy, army or air force. But by late 1944 no come-on was enough. The Army Council (opposite page, with Gen. A. G. L. McNaughton, the new defense minister, at the end of the table) finally told McNaughton only conscription could keep the overseas army up to strength. "We all idolized the man," says one retired general, "and we were sad because we felt we were letting him down. But we could see no alternative." The essence of the reinforcement problem was symbolized by these kits (right) at a 1st Division Return Stores Depot. Their owners had been killed or wounded.

November 20 he told the cabinet he would ask Parliament for a vote of confidence anyway, would continue the recruiting campaign only two weeks more and, if it still failed, would resign in favor of some conscriptionist minister.

On the morning of November 22, the day Parliament was to meet, McNaughton still hoped to get the volunteers. He summoned the Army Council to give him its latest recruiting figures. Instead, he received a written memorandum from these top officers at headquarters saying that the recruiting campaign had failed and only conscription could provide the needed recruits. The members of the council added, verbally, that if their recommendation were not approved they would resign.

McNaughton knew that no minister, no government could survive the resignation of the Army Council. Deeply shaken, he telephoned the Prime Minister. As King recalled it later, McNaughton whispered in a voice hoarse with shock: "I have terrible news for you, Chief! A body blow."

King realized the blow could be fatal: revolt in the military high command and the specter of national disorder. Yet he also saw that, skillfully handled, the crisis might be changed into victory. Everything depended on Justice Minister Louis St. Laurent, the spokesman of French Canada. Perhaps he could persuade Quebec to accept conscription. Summoned to King's office, St. Laurent heard the news impassively and replied without hesitation that Canada was not a South American republic where the military could subvert the civil power. The government, said St. Laurent, must fight the Army Council revolt.

Revelation

For 21-year-old Paul Theodore Hellyer the conscription crisis was a time of frustration and revelation. It helped shape convictions which in the 1960s led him, as minister of national defense, to launch a program to unify the three armed forces.

From *The Search for Identity,* by Blair Fraser:

. . . Hellyer originally enlisted in March 1944 in the RCAF. He went through the basic training that was essentially the same for all three services, then passed the examination that would let him start learning to be a pilot.

By that time, there were not enough aircraft in the whole Commonwealth for the stream of young men pouring out from the British Commonwealth Air Training Plan.

Meanwhile, Defense Minister Ralston and Air Minister Power were conferring on the problem of transferring to the army some 4500 young men the RCAF did not need. It was impossible. The only way to make a soldier out of an airman, they found, was to give the airman a discharge and let him re-enlist, as a civilian, in the army. Hellyer was one of the 4500 who did.

It was explained to the young would-be pilots how urgently they were needed in the infantry, how imperative the duty to switch. But these patriotic appeals were not borne out by what happened.

First, the young army recruits were put through basic training—the same basic training they had just completed in the RCAF, but that made no difference. The book said basic training comes first, so basic training came first.

Then young Hellyer's academic record showed he was above average in mathematics. The book said recruits with an above-average aptitude for mathematics should go to the artillery. In 1944 the artillery did not need men, at least not acutely, and the infantry's need was desperate, but that made no difference. Hellyer was sent to the artillery. He never did get overseas.

When Lance Bombardier Paul Hellyer finally was discharged in April 1946, he took away a vivid impression of military organization and military thinking. According to his personal experience, it was not merely stupid, it was imbecile. . . .

"Fight!" cried King. "With what? Our bare hands?" No, said the Prime Minister, the government must surrender, impose conscription or condemn Canada to anarchy.

St. Laurent fell silent for a moment, then said he would stand beside King and face the consequences.

For the first time Canada had found a Quebec statesman prepared to defy the

deepest French-Canadian emotion, prepared to accept overseas conscription, the most hated symbol of the British conquest of New France in 1759. St. Laurent had saved King, the government and, as King thought, Confederation.

When King met Parliament and the Liberal caucus that afternoon, the secret of the Army Council threat to resign was known only to the council and to King, St. Laurent and McNaughton. It would not be revealed publicly for years.

Parliament and caucus were hastily adjourned. King explained that the cabinet must consider "important new developments." What developments? Ottawa writhed in speculation.

The conscriptionist ministers, still ignorant of the facts, decided to resign that night. King felt sure he now could hold them. He was worried about only one man: could he prevent the resignation of Air Minister Power? Ironically, this politician of Irish descent, with no French blood in his veins, had become Quebec's only significant cabinet opponent of conscription. If he supported St. Laurent, the impact of King's intended reversal of his conscription pledge would be greatly moderated in French Canada.

Power was summoned to the Prime Minister's office. "Chubby," said King, "I don't know what I'd do without you!" It was no use. Even when King had explained

that McNaughton could not recruit the promised volunteers (although he never hinted at trouble in the military command), Power refused to consider conscription.

It was unnecessary, he said. It would do nothing for the nation's war effort and it would destroy its unity. Moreover, he had given his word that he would never accept conscription. St. Laurent's position was quite different. He had never made such a promise. Power said he'd resign next morning.

The cabinet met immediately after King's meeting with Power. As McNaughton began to speak, the conscriptionist ministers expected his usual assurances of recruiting success and were resolved to resign. Instead McNaughton said the campaign had failed. He recommended that 16,000 Zombies—the number already trained as infantry—be conscripted for overseas. King and St. Laurent agreed. The cabinet approved the conscription order.

One danger remained. Ralston could still pull the government down and make himself prime minister. Everything depended on what he did in Parliament.

There, without tipping his hand, Ralston made a polite and chilling lawyer's cross-examination of the exhausted McNaughton. The Conservatives made a last hopeless attempt to upset the government and get all-out conscription. To frighten the wavering Liberals, King threatened to resign. He never mentioned the Army Council to explain his *volte-face,* but he did utter a mysterious warning which no one understood then and most of his colleagues regarded as absurd. If Parliament could not unite, he said, "we shall have to face the possibility of anarchy" and "the pillars of the temple of our Canadian life might be drawn out from under, bringing

disaster." Then he threatened that, if he did resign, he would hand the government over to a conscriptionist prime minister who might have little sympathy with Quebec.

Power announced his resignation "in sorrow, not in anger" because he would not "tear this country asunder."

Then Ralston: "I have no ambition but to be a good Canadian and I know my place is not on the dizzy heights of leadership. I neither felt nor feel any duty to take on responsibility for which I am not suited." He would accept the government decision to send 16,000 men overseas but only as a "piecemeal" second choice to total conscription of the home army. He would accept it because, if the government were defeated, an election would probably follow and reinforcements would be delayed. He did so "under protest" and only on the understanding that more than 16,000 would be sent overseas if needed. King agreed. With that, the threat of a conscriptionist government died.

Two thirds of the Quebec members voted against the government proposal but

With bitter fighting continuing in Italy and northwest Europe, the army reinforcement problem became a crisis. Soon the supply of volunteers, like these troops (right) embarking for Europe, was inadequate. Ottawa's decision to send 16,000 Zombies overseas touched off demonstrations in Quebec, this one (above) on Montreal's Champ-de-Mars. Prime Minister Mackenzie King believed his government survived only because Justice Minister St. Laurent defied French-Canadian wishes and accepted conscription. But Dale Thomson writes in *Louis St. Laurent: Canadian* that "a police guard was placed on his house and he was advised for his own safety to keep away from Quebec City until the strong feelings against him and his colleagues had subsided." It wasn't long, though, before St. Laurent could go home in perfect safety. And in four years he was prime minister.

it went through, and they soon returned to King because they still found him preferable to any other leader. Thus the crisis ended. . . .   BRUCE HUTCHISON

When conscription finally came, there was a show of resistance from 1000 armed Zombies in British Columbia who shouted "down with conscription" and tried to prevent the embarkation of reinforcements. It soon died out. So did the surface storm of anger across the land. Ralph Allen in *Ordeal by Fire:*

. . . If they had accomplished nothing else, the five years of indecision, maneuver and harangue had taken at least a little of the bitterness out of conscription. Through a sort of intellectual and emotional attrition, both sides had been worn down to the verge of reasonableness.

The new generation of Quebec nationalists, the leaders of a party called Bloc Populaire, cried predictably for "independence." Union Jacks were burned at Rimouski and Chicoutimi, and 2000 French Canadians marched through Montreal, breaking the windows of the National Selective Service office and several banks. More windows were broken in Quebec City, at the offices of an English-language newspaper and at the home of Louis St. Laurent.

But the physical outbreaks were brief and perfunctory. Even Montreal's *Le Devoir,* the most intransigent of nationalist newspapers, scolded that "burning and tearing down flags gets us nowhere and can do much harm to the cause it claims to serve." It dismissed the window breakers as silly youngsters.

Quebec City's *L'Action Catholique* came perhaps as close as any paper to expressing the province's general mood: "We like a government that is conscriptionist

'in spite of itself' better than a conscriptionist government angry because compulsion has not been used sooner; we like a government which has reluctantly sacrificed Quebec better than a government which might have sought to sacrifice us still more, if not to be revenged upon us for our anti-conscriptionist stand."

The Zombies, so long the symbol of a national schizophrenia, proceeded to war in a highly disordered and inconsistent state. Some simply went on doing what their country ordered them to do. But of

the first 10,000 warned for sailings in early January, 7800 either went absent without leave or deserted. More than half were still missing when their ships sailed. Of the first 14,500 men struck off for overseas duty, more than 4500 were still unaccounted for at the beginning of April 1945. Of these, 2400 were from Quebec and 1000 more from the prairies.

Eventually almost 13,000 went overseas and 9700 got as far as the Continent. But the war was breaking up fast, and fewer than 2500 got into the front line. Of these, 69 were killed. . . . RALPH ALLEN

The manpower situation had been righting itself even as Ottawa boiled with controversy. Though average battalion shortages did rise beyond 100 in the last days on the Scheldt, statistics indicate that the army had, in fact, seen the worst of it in August. By the time Parliament gave its decision, the Scheldt campaign had been over for a month and the average shortage was down to about 30. Then the great Rhine offensive, which Ralston had been warned to expect, was delayed for weeks; instead, the First Canadian Army found itself manning a static front at no great cost in casualties.

Wounded men had time to recover. Men from other arms kept flowing into the infantry. The supply of reinforcements—Zombies and volunteers—was greatly speeded by the opening of the port of Antwerp. Colonel Stacey says that by February, when the Rhine offensive finally did begin, the infantry shortage was a crisis no longer. As Prof. Mason Wade says in his book *The French Canadians:* "Canada had nearly split itself apart in anticipation of a situation which did not materialize."

But a final irony lies behind the reasons why. In a book entitled *Decisive Battles of World War II,* German Gen. Hasso von Manteuffel says Hitler became convinced in December that great cracks were showing in the Western Alliance and that a major German victory would lead a divided Canada "to withdraw her forces from the European mainland." He, too, had been impressed by the ferocity of the crisis.

The German try for a major victory was the Ardennes offensive, launched against the Americans on December 16. It failed, but it was the reason the Canadians' Rhine attack was postponed. It didn't knock Canada out of Europe. Instead, it gave her more time to solve her manpower problem.

Quebec: 1944

Compared to 1914-18, Quebec's military achievement is remarkable. At a conservative estimate five times as many French Canadians have volunteered for overseas service.

Yet few people in Quebec would agree with the official version that it is "as war-minded as any province in Canada." A priest said: "They're not convinced the war is for the defense of Canada, and if it isn't they're not interested."

One Quebec nationalist said: "Show me an Englishman who lives in a part of the world captured by a German empire two centuries ago and who now is compelled to put on a German uniform, take orders in German, which he doesn't understand, and be sent to fight for that empire. I'd like to meet that Englishman. We'd understand one another."

French Canadians feel their sons in uniform are treated unjustly. They say their soldiers are told to "speak white." They are aware that the navy and air force use only English.

The higher clergy have given constant cooperation in the war effort—at great cost in personal popularity. The parish *curé,* on the other hand, is often a major obstacle to recruiting.

Many French Canadians feel nothing was ever given to them by English-speaking Canada—everything had to be won. And now they feel betrayed. "They promised us a moderate war effort," said a rural *curé,* "yet expenses are *extraordinaire.*" Statements about Canada's "second to none" war effort are repeated as a reproach: "They say we're doing more than anyone else, and still they're not satisfied."

Blair Fraser in *Maclean's,*
August 15, 1944

Swift ships and daring deeds

In July 1944, as Canadian troops battled from Caen to Falaise in the Normandy campaign, the biggest convoy of the war—HXS-300—crossed the North Atlantic without loss. There were 157 merchant ships destined for Britain, nine for Russia and one for Iceland and they sailed in 19 columns, spread out over 30 square miles. The convoy encountered heavy seas and poor visibility in mid-ocean but HXS-300 met no U-boat anywhere. Victory in the great Atlantic battle was apparently in sight.

Earlier that year, the RCN had assumed responsibility for all North Atlantic escorts. For years the U-boats had preyed on convoys in mid-ocean. Now the U-boats faced not only the close escorts but also wide-ranging, destroyer-frigate support groups—four of them Canadian—and air attack from long-range, land-based planes. Almost every convoy, in addition, had available one aircraft carrier whose planes ranged ahead of the ships. The mid-ocean gap was plugged.

Thus, in 1944, the battle of the Atlantic remained the main charge of the RCN but the character of the struggle had changed.

Meanwhile, a navy which had grown from 11 ships and 1800 men in 1939 to 306 ships and 76,000 men and women was busy in many other theaters of war. Its sailors had, in fact, been busy elsewhere for a long time—in the Mediterranean, the Caribbean, in Arctic convoys to Russia's Murmansk, in the invasions of North Africa, Sicily, Normandy and southern France.

Four thousand of them had been lent to the Royal Navy. One, Lt. George Cook, twice won the George Medal for the delicate job of disarming mines. Capt. H. T. W. Grant commanded a British cruiser. Twenty Canadians served in submarines and one, Lt. Comdr. F. H. Sherwood, commanded the submarine *Spiteful* in the Pacific. Fifty Canadian medical officers were aboard RN ships. Hundreds served as pilots, observers and fighter direction officers.

At one time Canadians made up the majority of seagoing RN radar officers, and fought in almost every major British naval encounter. Canadian destroyers shared in two of the RN's greatest victories. *Saguenay, Columbia* and *Assiniboine* were part of the support force when the German battleship *Bismarck* was sunk in the North Atlantic in May 1941. *Algonquin* and *Sioux* were in the destroyer screen when the battleship *Tirpitz* was crippled by RN planes in a Norwegian fjord in 1944.

Not all the Canadians who were on loan to the RN saw big-ship action. Many served in motor torpedo boats, motor gunboats and Fairmile motor launches. Their daring deeds in these small, swift and deadly craft are the stuff of high adventure.

British Fairmiles commanded by Canadians formed part of the Coastal Forces on besieged Malta in 1942. During 1943 Canadian-commanded Fairmiles helped clear more than 400 magnetic mines from North African, Sicilian and Italian waters. Other Canadians in Fairmiles landed stores and agents on German-occupied islands. Canadians in MTBs and MGBs operated off Tunisia and Sicily in 1943 and along the Italian coast in 1944. Some of the most famous Canadian captains fought in the Adriatic and the Ionian and Aegean seas.

Of these small-ship men none was more colorful or successful than Ottawa's Tommy Fuller, a lieutenant commander who became "the pirate of the Adriatic." While based on the island of Vis, a stronghold of Marshal Tito's guerrillas off the coast of Yugoslavia, he commanded a half dozen fast and heavily armed motor gunboats, which preyed on enemy coastal convoys. Fuller's story was told by Alan Phillips:

. . . In gunboats Fuller had found his niche. "Night raiders of the sea," they were called. They were offensive boats. Successful skippers, like ace fighter pilots, were men with a flair for attack.

Fuller had fought in most coastal warfare hot spots. He won a Distinguished Service Cross one stormy night in the English Channel, his lone craft battling 22 German E-boats [motor torpedo boats], gunboats and anti-aircraft trawlers. Another time, in the Bay of Biscay, two U-boats attacked his flotilla, surfaced simultaneously, collided and sank. His midget warships once engaged a destroyer and held a squadron of Messerschmitt fighter planes at bay while fighting three E-boats. When German paratroopers captured the Greek island of Leros, off Turkey, he led an escape group, commandeering an Italian admiral's barge and winning the first of two bars to his DSC.

Then, on an April night in 1944, he led three gunboats into Komiza harbor on Vis, outermost of the islands off the mountainous Dalmatian coast. The senior RN officer ashore, Lt. Comdr. Morgan Giles, introduced Fuller to the Vis guerrillas.

A German attack on Vis seemed imminent. Fuller's gunboats were to patrol the coast and watch for signs of an invasion buildup. On his first patrol, with two boats, Fuller glimpsed the masts of a ship. "Intercept," he ordered. The gunboats leaped ahead. The shadowy shape became a small schooner. "All guns on target." The schooner held her course. "They haven't spotted us," Fuller said. He made a quick decision. "Don't fire." Then he called down the wardroom voice pipe to Maj. Tom Finn of the commandos: "We've got some fun coming up. There's a boat for you to capture."

Fuller brought the gunboat splintering into the schooner's side and Finn's boarding party vaulted over the broken rail. Two German gunners jumped and splashed away in the darkness as Finn emptied his revolver at them. The others—crying *"Italiano, Italiano!"*—raised their hands in enthusiastic surrender. "We'll tow her back," said Fuller. When he sailed into Komiza he delivered the payroll and Christmas mail for all the German troops on the islands, and a cargo of good Bavarian ale.

Fuller bet Giles he could pull the trick again. The enemy ships seemed to hug the coast, keeping watch to seaward. If the gunboats lay in wait by the shore they'd be all but invisible. Surprise would give them an edge. The Germans would hesitate to fire, wondering if they were friends and, if not, fearing their own muzzle flashes would make them a target. That hesitation would be fatal. Giles agreed.

The following dawn Fuller's two boats steamed into harbor, each with a schooner in tow. This catch was firewood and munitions. Next night they captured a shipload of wheat. On April 6 Fuller headed for Murter Island, anchored, cut his motors and waited. Soon they sighted a 400-ton brigantine under full sail. She was magnificent in the moonlight, armed with 88s and machine guns clamped to her rails.

At 16 knots, Fuller came out of the shadows toward her. He switched on the loud hailer and a guerrilla voice boomed over the water in harsh Italian: "Don't shoot or we'll torpedo you, and if anyone's still alive we'll pull you out of the water one by one and slit your throats!" The torpedo part was bluff for the gunboat carried none. When it crashed alongside, the brigantine's lifeboat burst into splinters. "Hard astern!" and the boarding party catapulted onto the brigantine's deck.

Fuller put a line on the brigantine and began the 52-mile tow to Komiza. Off Tara Island he was only 100 yards from enemy guns. But he had captured the German recognition signals and was able to pass the shore batteries unscathed.

They entered Komiza at dawn, prisoners on deck, German flag flying upside down (in distress) below the White Ensign. The Yugoslavs met them with a brass band. The brigantine proved a rich prize: sauerkraut, goulash and ten tons of Danish butter. Fuller sent three kegs "with the compliments of Tom Fuller" to every Mediterranean flag officer: "Insurance, in case anyone tried to court-martial me for looting."

In Komiza's town hall he dined with Tito and his guerrillas on pork and beans, lobster, octopus, and a red-fleshed fish baked whole. As guest of honor, Fuller was given the head of the fish.

Tito's troops received no quarter from the Germans and gave none. Following an action in which Fuller took 35 prisoners, the guerrillas announced all Germans would be hanged in the market square. This news, relayed to Britain, brought a protest from Prime Minister Churchill: under no circumstances were German prisoners to be executed in the public square. So the guerrillas hanged the prisoners from apple trees *behind* the square.

Later, in an attack on a merchant ship escorted by two gunboats, Fuller's port gun was hit. By now most MGB guns were obsolete, and he was sure his requests for new ones were filed in a wastebasket at the supply base in Italy. One day in the vice admiral's office in Malta he spotted the admiral's stamp. He surreptitiously stamped a requisition that got him some 38 Bofors.

Fuller fought his last action in July. He was hiding with three boats in a cove when a large schooner hove in sight. She had guns fore and aft. The three boats sped toward her. Then they saw that two I-boats—150-foot craft, each mounting an 88-mm. and two 36-mm. guns—guarded her stern, while ahead and to seaward were five E-boats.

Fuller closed. "Fire star shell!" As the schooner's big guns opened fire the star shell struck its deck, landing in an open bucket of fuel. The schooner burst into flame, silhouetting an E-boat and the I-boats. A few minutes later the E-boat lay burning and two I-boats were in tow.

The other four E-boats roared away. Fuller raced after them, offering one boat as a decoy—MGB-667, which was towing a blazing I-boat. The E-boats could not resist

the target. Two were hit. Fuller's boat was disabled and it seemed the E-boats would get away. But, said Fuller, "they obligingly turned on each other and carried out a spirited gun action as we lay in a grandstand seat. The crew cheered as we watched the bits and pieces fly from both E-boats."

It was, as Coastal Forces announced, "one of the most successful actions fought in the Adriatic." In September, Fuller received the second bar to his DSC. Then the RN decided he'd had enough action and sent him home. . . .

ALAN PHILLIPS

The RCN itself established two all-Canadian MTB flotillas, the 65th and 29th, to fight in the English Channel. Nightly patrols and swift, fierce, inconclusive actions formed the pattern of their work. Going where destroyers could not go, they ran in over enemy minefields to within almost a stone's throw of hostile coasts. They damaged and disrupted enemy convoys, drove away craft sent to investigate preparations for D-Day, headed off an occasional destroyer before it could do damage, and fought with minesweepers and flak ships.

In their very first action, on May 22, 1944, the crews of two MTBs of the 65th learned what sort of life they were going to lead in these tiny, darting ships. They fired 2515 rounds of ammunition at two German escort ships within three minutes. Then, racing away in the dark, one mistook the other for a German E-boat and opened fire, inflicting casualties, before discovering the error. The close range, high speed and inevitable confusion made such mistakes almost unavoidable for both sides.

The minefields off the French coast were as deadly as the E-boats. On the night of July 2, 1944, returning from a patrol, boat 460 suddenly disintegrated in a sheet of flame and a column of water 200 feet high. Six men survived; ten were killed.

That summer, a BBC report, indicating St. Malo had been taken, prompted six Canadian MTBs to look in on the ancient French port. There were no welcoming signals, radar seemed trained on them and a big range finder twitched in their direction. The order was given to retire. The boats had hardly made their turns when salvos from the port's German guns crashed all about them. Their escape, under smoke screens and at high speed, was a minor miracle.

In time, Canadian seamen were warmly welcomed in many a French port. Joseph Schull described *Iroquois'* reception by the people of Ile d'Yeu in August 1944, at a time when

she was one of four Canadian destroyers on duty in the Bay of Biscay:

. . . Lookouts reported a small boat approaching. In it were four men and a woman of about 25. *Iroquois* stopped, ropes were tossed over and they clambered aboard. Mlle Anne-Marie Gaston was a schoolteacher on Ile d'Yeu; the men were leading citizens. The villagers explained that the German garrison had left the island the night before and the French Forces of the Interior had information for the Allies.

This seemed an opportunity to learn something of German dispositions and morale, so a five-man shore party was organized. They took flour, meat, milk, sugar, chocolate and cigarettes.

As the Canadians set foot on shore they nearly went down under a deluge of greetings from a cheering, weeping, kissing multitude. They were carried shoulder-high to the town hall, where distribution of the provisions was arranged and German maps and documents were handed over.

Then, the shore party asked for a place to set up signaling apparatus and was taken to a signal tower three miles away. Here three signalmen set up and two officers spread out maps and papers they'd been given. The townspeople withdrew to let the Canadians work undisturbed. Toward 1 a.m. the Canadians heard voices, then saw Mademoiselle Gaston and 15 ladies and gentlemen of the village, all in their Sunday best. Each carried a basket with the provisions for a banquet: cake, wine, lobster, sardines, crabs and champagne "requisitioned" from the hotel of a collaborator. There were toasts to Canada, to France, to Ile d'Yeu, to *Iroquois.*

Dinner ended, the townspeople left and the Canadians worked through the night. *Iroquois* signaled that a boat would pick them up on the seaward side of the island.

The next day, the five Canadian sailors marched with French veterans and more than 1000 townspeople. They went to the graves of Allied fliers whose bodies had been recovered from the sea, then to the graves of the French war dead.

Back in town again, a boat was waiting to take them to where the ship's whaler would land. The Canadians found among their gear a huge white cake, baked with flour brought from *Iroquois* and inscribed: "Vive la France, Canada, Britain and America."

When they came to where *Iroquois'* boat was waiting, it was almost invisible under masses of flowers. Farewells were made, and a joyful wave of cheering followed the boat to sea. It was a memory to cherish, a glimpse of liberation, a foretaste of victory. . . .

JOSEPH SCHULL

A winter in the trenches

Mud, shellfire, patrols: the Canadians live the sort of warfare their fathers endured for years. An infantryman tells what it was like

The problem of keeping these notes is not just ethical but physical. Obtaining the paper to write is one of the troubles—I have even used cigarette packages and labels off cans, and my small pack is now a rat's nest of folded scraps of paper. Keeping these notes is absolutely against regulations. If I were captured I'd be a mine of local color.

Lt. Donald Pearce wrote those words in December 1944 in a frontline dugout near the Dutch-German border. His unit was in a salient captured in Field Marshal Montgomery's spectacular airborne attack the previous September. The attack had failed in its ultimate purpose of seizing a bridgehead across the Lower Rhine at Arnhem. It had succeeded in winning and holding a bridgehead over two other rivers a few

miles to the south: the Maas and the Waal (really the main arm of the Rhine). Here, for three months, from November till February 1945, the Canadians held a static front, aggressively patrolling and guarding a strategic area whose importance was symbolized by a vital bridge which had been captured intact at Nijmegen.

The following extracts cover this period and the attacks that followed on both sides of the Rhine. They come from a book by Pearce.

A native of Brantford, Ont., who had studied at two universities, he had joined the 3rd Division's North Nova Scotia Highlanders in September and fought in the campaigns to clear the Channel ports and the Scheldt estuary. He kept a diary, mainly for his own interest but also with the vague idea that it might one day "ren-

der a service to something or other back home." After VE-Day he burned much of it. The rest gathered dust for 20 years until his son asked to read it. Inspired by his interest, Pearce edited his notes into *Journal of a War,* an unsentimental, sophisticated and often amusing portrait of an infantryman's daily struggle for survival. Excerpts:

. . . November 20, Beek: We have moved to a point east of Nijmegen, and the weather is very bad. We've taken over some cramped, farm-style houses. We can't use the stoves much, as they give away our positions to the Germans across the flats. About three quarters of a mile separates us by day. At night listening patrols sometimes come within a few yards of each other, watch each other's movements, or listen for them, then draw back in the morning. Like the antennae of two insects stretching to touch, or two electrodes screwed to within spark-gap range without the current being turned on. When you're out there, you wonder if someone is going to turn on the current; it keeps you from falling asleep, it does. Normally, a couple of times a night, the Germans send over Moaning Minnies, mortar bombs fired in groups of 10 or 12, and fitted with some God-awful noisemaking arrangement that causes them to groan, howl, whine, like baying hounds, for 10 or 15 seconds; they grow louder and louder, and finally burst with one hell of a blast. They fire a few more salvos from different positions, and then nip out just in time to escape our return barrage. We welcome the dawn. Our slit trenches are one-man holes stuffed with leaves and twigs, and half full of icy water.

November 26: We have moved again, into a little pine and cedar forest in a ravine inside Germany. We are living in dugouts and caves scooped out of the wooded hills, and keep a continuous patrol to keep in touch with enemy movement. There is a telephone in my dugout, hooked up so I can communicate with company headquarters, a half mile back, or with our artillery "forward observation post," a quarter of a mile ahead of me. I often pick up the phone and listen in. The difference in voices. The people at HQ relaxed, unworried, loud (they shout over the phone), whistling, singing, joking, playing cards. The men at the observation post overlooking the enemy positions whisper into the phone, a catch in their voices; they are tense, worried, their hearts sometimes beating hard enough to make their voices quiver. They try to end conversations as soon as possible, and seem to be talking with their heads pulled down into their greatcoats. This strange dialogue goes on intermittently all night.

November 28: Without questioning the necessity of this war, or its importance, I would say there is a lot of fine-feathered talk about war by persons who are addicted to a sort of intellectual primitivism. "War reduces everything to its essentials," one writer says. I think this statement over in my wet slit trench and wonder why it seems so stupid. So maybe war does this. But what about the "essentials" to which I am reduced—not the simple discomfort of this arthritic trench, but the whole deterioration of human relations to that un-

handsome point where we spend hours trying to figure out foolproof booby traps and other devices for destroying our potential destroyers, congratulating each other on our progress? (My sergeant said to me this morning: "I've really got this re-entrant rigged this time. If a bird shit on one of them trip wires the whole place'd go up. So let them come." Naturally, I was warmly admiring. And I'll sleep a lot better tonight, too.) I can think of perhaps ten statements, all of which have the same appearance of bare factuality as the one about war reducing things to their essentials; and I know that they are just as perverted. They originate with people who are driven by something inside to embrace destruction lovingly, who are craving death, the sight of it, others' deaths, their own; with those who worship savagery because they are sick of reason.

A demented boy I used to see every day when at Ambleteuse often crosses my memory. He was dressed in a long flannel shirt, which was torn and dirty and came down to his shins. He spent his day hopping up and down the street on the rough cobblestones, his body bent over in a grotesque, crouching attitude, now and then waving his arms as he hopped, and making terrible animal noises. Sometimes he would pretend to be shooting a machine gun. His eyes were wild, his hair a mass of knotted, dirty curls, his feet scarred and calloused. A sort of maniac animal. Once he was sane and healthy, they said; but a shell landed near him one day, and he was "reduced to his essentials." There are many ways of apologizing for war, but the reduction-to-essentials way is not one of them.

One day last month we herded together a big group of German prisoners and discovered that several understood English. Somebody decided it would be a good idea if each man in the platoon gave them a piece of his mind. Four or five boys did so from a rostrum made out of crates and boxes. The speeches were mainly oaths, threats and curses. Then one lad, a well-spoken and gentlemanly boy, was forced to say his piece. He didn't want to, and acted with embarrassment. With much effort, but with his face full of passion, his eyes practically sparkling, and shaking his fist, he at last let fly at them: "You good-for-nothing individuals!" he exclaimed. He repeated this more loudly, then with an air of triumph descended the rostrum. This

Troops of the First Canadian Army take up positions in newly captured trenches during the advance to the Rhine in February 1945. The map shows the Dutch-German border area where Canadian units spent that winter, with an occasional leave in swinging Brussels, only 100 miles from the front.

ended the show, for both we and the Germans found ourselves laughing; and for an instant I saw the boy as a sort of Archimedes lever completely upending a whole world of pretentiousness and officialdom.

December 1, Imthal: In another forward position. About 800 yards now separate Jerry and us. Most of the time I study his trench system with binoculars, mark things on a map, take the ranges of mounds, scrutinize the distant houses or barns, and try to figure the location of minefields, if any. Today I saw him in the flesh again, the first time since coming out here two days ago, half-running between a barn and house, then back again, with something (eggs?) in his arms. I calculated he was about 1400 yards away, and phoned battalion HQ for mortar fire on the position. In a few minutes, four bombs dropped on our own position, blowing most of the pink tile shingles off our farmhouse, and driving us into the cellar. I phoned back pronto, said they could stop now. Later, I had another target for them, but I kept it to myself. Hope he enjoyed his eggs.

December 4: Fascinated watching Jerry run back and forth between the barn and house. He has a trench connecting the two buildings and can make this crossing invisibly—except for a little green door at the side of the barn which he has to open to get in, and always closes after he is in. Eventually, good officer that I am, I called for mortar fire; this time upping the range comfortably. Six were direct hits. The barn jumped like a scared thing, shrugged, and settled down a few feet farther into the ground. The house simply lurched forward. A bomb had gone in one window and exploded inside; smoke burst out of a dozen openings and seams, like spray from a leaky hose. The fire was irregular; as a result, the Germans thought it was all over and tried to come out. The little green door was sneaked open, pushed gently out like a fern frond uncurling. Then the whish and whine of another mortar bomb. The door was yanked shut, and a second later the barn jumped up and down—I believe the boards bent outward, giving it for an instant an almost barrel shape. But at last we finished. Five minutes after, one German ran from the barn to the house, and then two ran from the house to the barn. This afternoon I find they have merely moved down the road one house, and this is apparently all the effect our little shoot has had.

December 5: Jerry started early in the evening to mystify us with a sort of Rube Goldberg display of "psychological weapons"—leaving lanterns burning in unoccupied buildings, dragging lights on wires across roads or around the corners of houses, or causing them to be swayed to and fro at various heights, and sending up flares and sparkling smoke bombs. This had the desired effect of taking our boys' attention away from the ground and riveting it to the sky; and it was only by continually going the rounds of each section that I kept the platoon studying the fields and hills before them. Another result, and probably the one intended, was that all the telephone lines between platoons, companies, battalions and brigade were choked with reports on these goings on.

Then, at 4 a.m., he let Moaning Minnie loose. I was walking at the rear of our barn when I heard them coming—that grinding yelp and whine that means half a dozen are up there scraping the sky bare—it's like drawing your nails down a blackboard. I threw myself on the ground, in the middle of a latrine. The pink clay shingles splattered about the yard; the cement walls of the house shook with each concussion. Salvo number one. I ran for our cellar, and reached it as another six came in. In the little wine cellar it was as if you were sitting inside a bass drum which someone had begun to pound frantically. This went on for four more salvos. Then there was a pause, and we knew he was finished and would wheel Minnie away for the night. The reason is the conspicuousness of the

418

The bridge over the Waal (Rhine) at Nijmegen (left) symbolized the importance of the area the Canadians held during the winter of 1944-45. Below: camouflage suits make troops all but invisible in the snow along a Dutch dike. Canoeists of the Lincoln and Welland Regiment (lower photo) were part of a force which took Kapelsche Veer, a German-held island in the Maas River, after assaults by Polish troops and British commandos had failed. Canadian casualties totaled 234 in fighting that recalled the battle for Ortona in Italy 13 months earlier. Both struggles cost Canadians and Germans more than the objective seemed worth.

weapon. The flash from six barrels fired at once is easily picked out; and then there is the sound. Magnetic bearings on the positions were phoned in from various platoons, and it wasn't long until our artillery replied with a barrage, probably a vain one. Minnie is hit and run; and tomorrow (but we won't be here) she will fire from a new position (she did) and our artillery will reply accurately and in force, but too late (it did).

The things that enter men's minds. I visited a convalescent depot near here, and found that one of the favorite sports was racing angleworms. Bets were placed and large amounts of money were won and lost daily.

It was arranged on the model of horse-racing, with tracks, jockeys, stalls and complete regulations. The racetrack consisted of eight parallel shallow grooves cut into the ground, about six feet long and one foot apart; the grooves kept the worms racing in the right direction. Small stalls, about the size of a soap dish, were cut into the ground at the starting line for each worm. A straw was struck in front of each for a gate. The soldiers were the jockeys. Each jockey provided himself with a lighted cigarette. When the bets were laid, the timekeeper shouted "Go!" Up came the straws and lighted cigarettes were applied to the worms' posteriors. They squirmed forward along the little trenches. At the end of 30 seconds, the timekeeper called "Go!" again, and cigarettes were again touched to the worms. Again they would spurt forward until the winner crossed the finish line.

The shouting could be heard far across the parade ground. One morning, the colonel came over and stood there watching a race, fascinated. When someone finally noticed him, the men came to attention and he started to lecture them about the cruel sport; but the worms were still racing, and everyone kept watching them out of the corners of their eyes, the colonel included, till one man burst out, "My God! My worm's won!" and everybody huddled around the finish line to see.

December 12, before Den Heuvel: Back again in trenches, the December rain and hail, one day clear in four, two hours of windy sunshine per week, mud to the ankles. Some days we lie in the mud, and the warmth of our bodies keeps it soft, while the wind thickens it or freezes it where we are not lying. I keep telling myself my father's generation of soldiers did this for four years and that I have it easy. In the daytime we can't move about, as we are in full view of the Germans. We sit and wait, keeping an eye on enemy movements, report them, and watch with a sort of spectator disengagement the results of our mortar and shellfire.

We eat twice a day, morning and night. Food is brought down a slippery path, mined along the fringes, under darkness and between scattered bursts of enemy fire, for they know our habits. We pass it from dugout to dugout, so much to this, so much to that, an extra portion to those who were out on patrol last night. We try to keep the rain out of the bread, and the dirt from the

attack on their position by eight of these planes. As the target—an orchard and a small group of farm buildings—was only about 400 yards away I had a close look. Presently the Typhies were above us, circling like hawks to draw out enemy flak. Then they dropped into echelon, straight behind the leader, ready to go in. The lead plane laid three markers on the orchard, small bright indigo fountains of smoke, like mounds of mauve whipped cream flowing together. Then they bore in in a succession of power dives. As each dived, I could see the little black rockets leap toward their marks, exploding and jerking among the trees and houses, burying them in billows of black smoke. They returned

almost at once, raked and shot up everything in sight with their 20-mm. cannon, and then retired.

All I could see after the smoke cleared away was the ruined house and trees, and the loose side of a pup tent wriggling in the wind, as if in defiance; for the next day we saw several Germans moving about, as casual as ever. Somebody still has to go in there and take them out with a bayonet.

How few of the books I value can stand the test of war. Milton and Virgil are the only ones I could read in a slit trench. They hold up, and I am grateful for every word. Keats is too soft. Shelley too airy-nothing, Shakespeare too boyish and prankish—you cannot take him to war. But Virgil's slow, solid rock of writing, the lines moving like gun carriages, the people under

trench tunnels out of the mess-tins as they are passed back and forth in the slow rain, with sometimes grunts of gratitude, sometimes cursing, with ponderous oaths when the food is poor, dirty, cold or scanty. But, miraculously, the men are okay. What is called their "morale" is, in fact, really quite high. We blame everything on the Germans—muddy food, wet and soggy feet, numb fingers fumbling with rifle parts and oil, ditch-crawling with empty food containers being returned to the company office.

They are strange soldiers, the Germans. They will sit on our mortar and artillery targets for weeks. You have to lever them off with infantry. They won't budge for shells. Even Typhoon fighter-bombers will not do it.

Yesterday, for example, there was an

Men who longed for peace could enjoy Christmas fun with Dutch children but soon returned to the front and the killing of Germans. Even the infantry —"the war's firmest realists," Toronto *Globe and Mail* correspondent Ralph Allen called them—began to join in the cry of the civilians: "Why don't the Germans quit?" Allen wrote in March 1945: "The Germans have courage, they love their country and their homes and they have an appetite for causes. These characteristics keep them fighting now. The other compulsions are not yet dead—the urge for self-aggrandizement, the nation-persecution complex, the blind faith in Hitler, the fear of Himmler—but they have become secondary. The German war machine, however battered, is not yet broken."

stress. Aeneas always sighing, and Dido in the burning town—these suit our time. Milton's distortion, his violence, his chiseling power, every word biting and gripping, his marvelous compound syntax—each half of a sentence gripping the other half like a wrestler—the universe in labor, all this suits our time, too. I can hear Milton above the noise of battle. But do you think I can hear Hamlet? Or have patience with King Lear? I don't believe this is my own peculiarity. I think there is a unique virtue in Virgil and in Milton which peacetime never revealed to me.

December 13: Went to bed feeling that something ought to happen soon. So it was

machine guns and mortars would open up on known enemy posts, neutralizing them while our patrol went in after the snipers. A standard operation.

A guide took us to the edge of the battalion area, and we could make out our first objective, the dark avenue of trees looming in the faint light. We moved bent over like a line of question marks in the heavy dusk. I instinctively trailed my hand, feeling for trip wires, although the word was that the area was clear. We found two, nevertheless, and they would have disorganized things nicely if we had run into them. The air photo in my mind began to open out perfectly—holes and ditches exactly where they should be, little ridges

rendous noises. Crawling was absolutely out. It was a fantastic progress; I was never so full of aching joints. A flare. Our legs were cocked, and balancing was one hell of a job. Will someone topple before the thing goes out? It went out, and the dark flowed in around us like ink. "Stay there," I said to my Bren gunner, who was to give us flank protection as we advanced.

The field stank of rotting cattle. We put our hands into disintegrating cows' flesh as we crept along. Another flare turned the field under our hands yellow and black with sodium light. Not cattle, but dead Germans. We stopped to rest 50 yards from the avenue of trees. I looked back. No patrol. Only my corporal had followed me.

no surprise when I was called in the night and told to get ready a ten-man fighting patrol for the following night. I had to withdraw the men before daybreak, to get back to battalion HQ in darkness. The usual precautions—nobody eligible who had a cold or wore glasses. We studied air photos of our target, calculated distances, selected the best backgrounds, and embedded the photographs in our retinas till we could see them with our eyes shut.

A road ran across our front. Three hundred yards down this road was an avenue of tall elms that led into Jerry territory. A few yards past this point was an enemy outpost, containing two snipers. Our mission was to attack this outpost, capture the occupants, and bring them back. We were given an hour and a half to crawl across the 350 yards of open ground. Then our

and bushes right on schedule. We advanced slowly, crawling, rifles canted before our faces. Jerry, apparently nervous, sent up three flares in the first half hour. Each lasted 20 to 30 seconds; it must equal half an hour when you are in somebody's rifle sights. We froze in grotesque positions till they spluttered out, then went on.

We reached a wire fence. This hadn't showed up in the photograph. We crept along it, till we found a broken two-foot gap. We flowed through the fence like syrup. We should come out now in the turnip field the previous patrol had reported. There wasn't any turnip field, only rattling grass and foot-high weeds. In the darkness and silence, they crackled hideously. You had to cock your leg high, then move it slowly above the weeds, and bring it straight down to get through without hor-

Back we went through that stinking field after the patrol. I found them with the Bren gunner, having thought in their profound idiocy that they were all to stay behind. We made it back half exhausted to the junction with about one minute left, and waited for our covering fire to start. No covering fire, no attack: my basic principle of war.

I lay straining to hear. A telephone was lifted off a hook. A voice, like tissue paper in a comb, buzzed out. The receiver was put down. That telephone was directly across the road. I wondered if they knew we were here? Then horses' hoofs off to the right, perhaps 100 yards. Moaning Minnie being hauled up. But they never got a chance to use her that night, for the sky was suddenly cut by the soft whish of our first mortar bomb. It landed just where the horses had been, and the full barrage followed. Our machine guns opened up next on the woods to our front and the trees snapped with bullets like branches in a fire. Muffled shouts from the German positions, among them women's voices. No doubt of it; they had women in the front lines. We rushed the dimly outlined slit trench in a body.

Our chagrin is not to be described; it was not a trench, but an elongated embankment of manure. In the air photo it had the look of a trench. This confused us momentarily, but we probed along our side of the road for 15 minutes, hunting for their outpost. There was no enemy on this side of the road (our patrol boundary), that much

lights, hot baths, good food, whole buildings, streams of people, cafés, dives, cinemas, music; that you are going back from the tension, and the rough camaraderie of the dugouts, into easy motions and the charm of things done gracefully; back, it really feels, to the world. This world strikes everybody differently. To each one, though, it has become a sort of dreamland, made marvelous by deprivation and desire; quite and utterly mysterious.

Brussels by day is all noise and speed. Voices, horns, motors, thousands of quick footsteps, building and sustaining a flow of sound. The people and the traffic disappear at curfew. But Brussels doesn't really stop. It simply retires behind closed doors,

before a three-piece orchestra. The musicians play almost absentmindedly, and nobody seems to notice whether they are playing or not.

Champagne is 800 francs, cognac 100. We decide to try for a cheaper place. You go through several cafés of this sort, buying a drink in each, caring less and less about the price of the next one. Carefully groomed girls draw their chairs up beside you or climb on your knees, pull you onto the dance floor, order drinks for both of you, and ask to take you home for 200 francs. They are perfumed and slim; and it begins to look like a good idea. Somebody insists on visiting another café, and we leave. We become thoroughly lost among

was certain. So we took off empty-handed across the fields, dog-trotting for there were only two minutes of covering fire left. Halfway back, one stinking mortar bomb dropped short, exploding about 20 yards from us. The patrol scattered like leaves in a high wind, assuming it was German return fire, and raced individually for our lines. An absolute fiasco of a finish. When we finally reached our forward trenches, a job-happy corporal called out to us in short, sharp whispers, "Get down, get down, you're under observation!" I could gladly have separated his head from his shoulders.

December 15: Brussels leave. Forty-eight hours to do all the things you dream about in trenches. But nobody really knows what he is going to do. You only know that you are going to a place full of

and the hum and energy go underground, like a river in a cave. You can hear it leaking out of windows, doorways and alleys. A door quickly opens and shuts, and a small gust of sound leaks out into the street. If you trace it down the cobbled alley, you come upon a slit of light through a door. Knock; a head appears at the window. *"Quoi?" "Quelque chose à manger ou à boire; des filles; danse?"* The door part opens; you are hurried inside into a dim hallway where you hear voices and music gurgling farther in, like hidden, shallow water. You step between blackout curtains into the café interior. The walls glow with dim lights, barely enough to light the little groups of people clustered at tables or the polished bar. They laugh, caress each other, pour drinks from iced bottles. Others are dancing on a small square

the dark streets, wander aimlessly, vaguely in search of something but not greatly caring, until put on the route by a night policeman whose white helmet, like an August moon, suddenly looms out of the Brussels dark at 3 a.m.

December 25, Rhine [Waal] dikes: Christmas morning. Not a sound anywhere, not a shot. I have a strong sense of being able to see silence. The river, which is clearly visible beyond the icy fields, bearing a few floating branches, and the snowflakes that are rather idly falling, are the only things with any motion. A few minutes ago I was sure I could hear the snowflakes dropping onto my battle jacket. A shout would carry for miles. I have never seen such stillness. I wonder if it's the same along the entire front? Up here, at any rate, both sides seem to have decided to call

To the south of the Canadian positions, three German armies attacked along a 75-mile front in the Ardennes on December 16, 1944, striking for Liège and Antwerp and setting off the Battle of the Bulge. Twenty-four divisions, opposed by only five American divisions, cut two big holes in the Allied line. But stubborn U.S. resistance, notably at besieged Bastogne and St. Vith, and pressure from British and Americans outside the bulge, prevented a breakthrough. The Germans withdrew in January, having lost over 600 tanks and suffered 90,000 casualties. American casualties were close to 80,000. The only Canadian unit directly involved was the 1st Canadian Parachute Battalion, part of the 6th Airborne Division brought from Britain for the emergency.

everything off, as though this day were beyond the war.

Just before noon, Fraser, a slightly oddball rifleman, slipped out unnoticed; when he was pointed out to me, he was half a mile away, silhouetted against the white fields, loitering near the river edge, unarmed, head down, hands in pockets, making a deliberate target of himself for German snipers across the river. He came back an hour or so later; said he had exchanged greetings with Germans on the other bank, and that they tossed their hats into the air and threw snowballs at him, and displayed no interest whatever in shooting at him. I believed his story, and will take no action, of course.

Dinner okay—lots of milling around enjoyed by all. On the way back I dropped in to see my former anti-tank platoon. I was plied with rum and became thoroughly soused. One fact remained undislodgeable—I had to get back to the front, so I set out on foot at 4:30 p.m. in the polar cold. About halfway a warm drowsiness flooded through me, and I lay down beside a mound of frozen straw in an open field, and fell asleep. I woke up a couple of hours later. All completely dark. So cold my joints would hardly articulate. The temperature must have been below zero. I imagined myself in hospital in a day or two, delirious with fever and double pneumonia. Haven't even caught cold, damn it.

December 28, Beek and area: We have been patrolling the Rhine and guarding the bridge across it at Nijmegen for so long that they have begun to acquire a hold over our minds. Our thoughts turn to them like compasses to a magnet. This bridge is the only one over the Rhine left intact for a hundred miles, and we must keep it that way for our own no doubt imminent invasion of Germany. At the same time, if Jerry decides to counterattack in force through here, the bridge would become just as important to him. A really ambiguous prize. But he keeps sending explosives downstream at it. Damn strange. We shoot into the river at everything that moves, sometimes exploding mines tied to boards, or logs or branches. Our engineers have a net across the river about 50 yards upstream from the bridge to catch whatever floats downstream; but things get through somehow and that's what we shoot at.

December 29: In the middle of the night much waking up: German attack beginning. Word blasted along by human tele-

graph. Whole area smothered in smoke. I visited our section outposts, checked all automatics, checked the number of rounds of available ammo, checked grenades and smoke canisters, checked anti-tank and mortar-fire plans with support company. We remained at the alert till morning expecting at every minute to see attacking figures emerge out of the smoke. Then a big anticlimax when we learn what had happened: the RAF had dropped smoke canisters around the bridge to mask it from German planes which, according to prisoner information, were going to bomb it out tonight. Relaxing thought: if they are planning to bomb the damn thing, they can hardly be planning to use it.

February 10, Goch-Calcar highway: Back at the front after a month's tour of duty at a divisional school, where I instructed NCOs in garrison duties preparatory to the occupation of Germany. On the way back, we took a route that led through the Reichswald, recently captured by First Canadian Army in a major offensive. I was interested to see what 1000 guns, in 11 hours of continuous shelling, could do to a forest this size. The forest had been a strongpoint in the Siegfried Line defenses, housing a hundred guns, various stores, and crisscrossed by a maze of crawl trenches, dugouts and hidden fortifications.

I watched out the back of a covered truck and as a result saw only the incredible wake of destruction stretching behind us like a filmstrip of a forest run backwards in slow motion. It was simply a tangled mass of chewed and broken trees, blasted trenches and smashed equipment; a jungle of logs tossed this way and that, through which our tortuous road threaded around shell craters. The bent, branchless tree trunks stood like sodden celery stalks. You would think some herd of animals out of prehistory had charged the forest in line and with tusks and feet rooted it up, as if it had been a vegetable garden.

We passed German soldiers digging graves in straight rows, with their spades smoothing the edges, or patting the dirt down with their hands, as if they loved the men lying underneath. These were graves for our soldiers. The Germans' trenches were their graves, and dozens of inverted rifles stuck into mounds in the woods pointed them out.

February 15: Took up new positions on the flooded dikes and farms bordering the Rhine opposite Emmerich. Our duties purely defensive—maintaining contact with neighboring companies and, at night, patrolling the dikes.

Captain M., a beautiful, indestructible man, was killed while we were here. My former anti-tank captain, a man without fear. He had more sheer power in his compact five-foot-ten frame than I've seen in any other human being. The men were both afraid of him and loved him. He taught me a little healthy contempt for precautionary fighting, and though, I am told, he initially disliked me because I was a "college soldier," he gave me a fine break-in period when I joined the battalion. Anyway, before we left here, he led his company to

a new position and, in contemptuous defiance of merely marginal dangers (after all, he had fought all the way from Normandy without a scratch), he went stomping along in a shiny black motorcycle jacket with bright shoulder insignia flashing in the sunlight. A sniper put one through his stomach at 500 yards. He staggered 100 yards to a small barn, walked in and announced to a corporal, "Johnnie, I'm hit; and I think it's bad." He lay on the floor, and they tried to cover him with a blanket to keep him warm; but he began to thrash around and in that deep musical voice of his to curse and swear, pounding on the barn floor with his open hands and the back of his head. Four men tried to hold him down; but he fought them off and continued to roll and pound and shout in the dust. He was a full six hours dying. No medical aid was obtainable. So he gradually sank like a terrible storm to death. He had just been married on leave to a charming, gentle girl of (like himself) Scottish descent. The battalion was reduced to silence for a day over this man's death. Nobody will ever forget him that knew him. He was an intimidating man; but, by God, a marvelous field soldier.

March 2, before Udem and Keppeln: We are in new positions along the Calcar highway west of the Rhine. Jerry is directly across from us, reportedly building up for something big. He counterattacked a mile away last night, and gave the Essex Scottish a bad time. (We have orders for an attack on Udem, "a brigade show." Here we go again. I'll drop this for now.)

March 3: The city was quite heavily defended. First, a steep anti-tank ditch had to be negotiated, with covering fire from both flanks. Then we ran into a connected system of crawl and weapons trenches forming a secondary ring about the interior. Our covering artillery fire was practically saturational; so he resisted only lightly till we were more than halfway in. There followed some sporadic street-fighting and house-clearing and the city fell to us shortly after daybreak; i.e., they simply disappeared about 4 a.m.

I had a couple of close ones. On the way in, my platoon was evidently silhouetted against the night sky, and was fired on four times by an 88. (This is a vicious gun. The velocity of the shell is so high that you hear it pass or explode near you almost at the same instant you hear it being fired. You really can't duck it.) Anyway, they went past me about an arm's length away. We hit the ditches. After pointing a few more, the gun was forced off by our tank fire.

During the house-clearing, I walked from one house to another and got my helmet spun around with a close shot. There was an extremely loud, flat snap, like two hands clapped together hard beside my ear; that was all. Plus a crease in my helmet, which gave me immense prestige with the men all morning.

Two tanks with us made the assignment 100 percent easier. At one point a handful of German snipers in an attic held up the battalion for over an hour. They were finally silenced by tanks. In the half dark, we circled behind their house during the

As the final spring offensive began, civilians watched Allied soldiers pushing ever deeper into Germany. Canadians at home knew little of what men at the front suffered. "I found a kind of pattern in the letters I had to censor," wrote Lt. Jack Scott. "Soldiers are squawkers but there were few complaints in the letters. Soldiers talk endlessly among themselves about soldiering; the letters hardly mentioned the war. You ran across sudden unrelated sentences: 'Does Mrs. Hennessey still run the grocery store?' or 'Did you get the garage painted?' And one line was almost the same in every letter: 'Don't worry about me. I'm okay.'"

tank fire and cut off their escape route. Presently they came out, dangling white cloths. It was vastly disconcerting. Instead of a squad of Nazi supermen, we were confronted by five stunted, scrubby specimens. Two of them couldn't have been more than 14.

Next day I went back to look at Udem. In daylight it seemed in worse condition than the night before. Enemy shelling accounted for much of the destruction; but looters accounted for some. The houses that had not been shelled were practically turned inside out by our troops. I came across one soldier telling an admiring group how he had smashed everything he could. I turned him over to the Provost Corps.

Udem had a large church of red stone with high twin towers. German artillery scouts had stationed themselves in these towers to direct fire. So the church had had to be "neutralized." We engaged it with 17-pounders for about an hour. I went in to see what we had done. It was full of gaping holes; the stone pillars had even been shot off far within the building. The only unharmed thing was the font. The walls had had blue and gold paintings of religious scenes; one was of the Descent from the Cross. It had come loose from its frame and seemed heading for a nose dive; the pale belly of Christ had a group of machine-gun bullets through it. As I left, engineers were laying dynamite charges along the church's foundations, with the intention of using the stones as rubble for roads.

On the way back, I met a number of civilians carrying bundles. Covered with mud, they were staggering along rather than walking. One thin man was leading two children, four or five years old. The older one had a haversack strapped to his back. The man limped and was weeping. My limited German enabled me to discover that he was wounded, that his wife had been killed and that he didn't know what to do with his wet, cold and hungry children. I took them into our cellar where the stretcher-bearer dressed his wounds and evacuated him. I offered the children food but they refused. So I tried a sort of game with the names of the articles of furniture in the cellar, deliberately making silly mistakes, and after a while they laughed at my stupidity. I kept this up, and before long they gobbled whatever I put in front of them. I would like to have done more; but instead I turned them over to the Civil Affairs people, not without complicated feelings of concern and regret.

Kept rummaging around. Went to the house where I was nearly shot, and determined the window where the shots had come from. An impulse sent me inside, where I climbed to the upper room. The machine gun was still pointing out the window. I took aim on the doorway I had disappeared into at the moment I was fired on, and waited for someone to pass the spot just to see how I must have looked through his sights. No one came and I got tired of the melodrama.

March 4, before Xanten: When will it all end? The idiocy and the tension, the

dying of young men, the destruction of cities, starvation, exhaustion, disease, children parentless and lost, cages full of shivering prisoners, long lines of hopeless civilians, the endless pounding of the battle line. What keeps this war going? What do the Germans think of us, and we of them? I do not think we think of them at all, or much. Do they think of us? I can think of their weapons, their shells, their machine guns, but not of the men behind them. I do not feel as if I were fighting against men, but against machines. It is becoming hard not to feel sometimes that both sides are the victims of a common terror, that everybody's guns are against everybody ultimately.

There are times when I feel that every bit of fighting is defensive. Self-defense. If a machine-gun nest is attacked and wiped out by my platoon, I do not feel as if I had attacked somebody. It is always that I have defended myself against something that was attacking me. And how frequently I have thought there might be a poet like Rilke out there in a German pillbox. If I could only see them, as in battles long ago, at close range, before engaging them. In our wars, the sides are getting farther and farther apart and battle is getting more and more meaningless for the warriors, and more meaningful for the domestic warriors in factories and homes. Will there come a time when hundreds of miles separate the warring fronts? It is already a very impersonal thing. When a soldier is killed or wounded his buddies merely say, "Poor old Joe. He got it. Just as he was going up that hill, he got it." As if to imply that he was merely in the wrong place at the wrong time, and that life and death are only matters of luck and do not depend on the calculations of human beings at the other end of a gun. When we were in our static positions around Nijmegen, the enemy became real to me for the first time. I watched him for weeks, saw him dig, run, hide, fire, walk. I knew where he was. I knew his habits. He was real. But now when we are ripping into his body, he has disappeared and has turned into something in the papers. But the guns remain, manned by soldiers who are so meaningless to us that when they shoot a fellow, all we can say is, "He got it."

March 20: Things have cooled off along the front and we're out again for a week. We've dug ourselves comfortable caves in a more or less unmangled part of the

Scout equipment worn by a Calgary Highlanders sergeant (left) includes two hand grenades, field glasses, telescopic rifle sights, revolver, camouflaged jacket and head net. Many German prisoners (right) in the last months of the war were teen-agers and old men. Germans of a different sort, captured in Belgium, were described by Donald Pearce in *Journal of a War:*

"In Knocke we took some 200 prisoners, all packed, polished, dressed, ready for capture. They formed up in squads, happy about the whole thing —except the officers, who didn't like being ordered about by Jordan, my Negro corporal. He put on quite a show, giving them squad drill and issuing commands in a sort of comic-strip German. I let the men take all the Germans' watches.

"It appeared nothing would wipe the arrogant expression off the officers' faces—that tense, fathomless, famous Teutonic calm. Very impressive, somehow. Some urge to experiment took hold of me: how deep did this Knights Templar pose go? Perhaps under stiff questioning. . . . We worked on them for perhaps an hour but they hung on to their bitter poise. I was about ready to be convinced when young Jordan found a way to reach them. He asked permission to look through their packs—and discovered little bottles of nail polish and jars of perfumed hair-wax. That did it. They begged us to return them, promised to answer or do anything if only we gave them back their 'pomade.' One officer went down on his knees. I left the sickening business in Jordan's happy hands. I haven't yet found out what happened."

426

Reichswald. Our mattresses are spruce branches and our roofs pine logs covered with straw and clay to keep out water and keep in heat. Right fancy. We use tin cans and ammunition containers as stoves. We stretch and smoke, and loaf around. It would be hard to be dissatisfied.

I find it curious to be among the oldest fighting members of the battalion; I am the last of the platoon officers who were here when I came in almost eight months ago. The others have gone out on stretchers, or are in graves, and hundreds of men with them. But I am still without a scratch, except for some bits of shrapnel in my left index finger. What am I being reserved for? Or preserved for? How much longer can I continue to be in the right places when the shelling is on? I endorse all superstitions, honor all taboos. I hearten my men with my presence: "He knows the score," they agree, and feel much better. I know no score except that I try daily to follow what Xerxes says in Herodotus: "It is better to have a stout heart and bear one's share of evil than be always imagining the worst and suffer no evil at all."

The battalion looks different to me now. Once I thought of a battalion as a fixed fighting unit of a certain size which one joined, trained with, fought in. Now the only fixed things are the hat badge and the strangely persistent *esprit*. From week to week new faces keep appearing. Before coming to the battalion, I used to ask questions of officers back from the front, and was always dissatisfied with their laconic answers. Now I am the one giving unsatisfactory answers. All they can be told they have already been told. What they are really after is an answer to the question, "What does it feel like to be under fire?"

The almost tenderly confidential questions: "Where do you usually travel with your platoon in an attack? At the head?" "Yes." "Are night patrols very difficult?" "Oh, no. You just keep a good lookout for the enemy. Take your best men. Leave your sergeant behind. He will appreciate that. The dark is a great advantage." But it is your tone of voice he is really listening to, not your words; the tone tells him everything. Because there is actually no time for advice, only for encouragement. But he doesn't know what is going on in my head while I am looking at him. It is this: "I bet I outlive you too." Fortune has always fascinated me. As a child, I remember thinking that, among all the tor-

tuous paths human beings make through life, somebody's path must, ideally, be a perfectly lucky one, while somebody else's must be as inexplicably unlucky. My path so far has been incredibly lucky; for my platoon has been replaced four times over. Will it continue? That's a question that between operations is beginning to make me drink.

March 27: The long-awaited bridgehead across the Rhine has begun. For days, the west bank has been under smoke. The sun went down in it like a copper ball, and rose through it in the morning like a bloody head hanging over Germany. Our battalion crossed the Rhine in Buffaloes [large semi-armored, amphibious vehicles carrying about 25 men] in late afternoon, and then we marched and rested by turns all evening and most of the night, intermittently harassed by shellfire. In the morning we moved up to our objective, a small town called Bienen which was flanked on either side by released flood waters, and threaded by a single main dike road. The town constituted a serious bottleneck across an arterial road between us and the central German plains. British troops had already attacked it twice, with almost zero results. The bridgehead across the Rhine was suffering, for just beyond the town the Germans had several big guns pasting away at the crossing points, making bridging nearly impossible. Our battalion was ordered to capture the town "at all costs." Kesselring had issued orders that the town should be held. It was going to be a "rough show."

We teed up two conventional attacks, to feel the position out—infantry and anti-tank teams probing into the outskirts. We got nowhere, and had to retire behind the dike and wait for some better plan. I guessed there were at least a dozen machine-gun posts in the town, as well as scattered rifle nests. We were instructed to sit tight till 2:30 p.m. when our three companies would assault simultaneously from three directions. There would be tank and air support.

I distributed an extra rum ration to the boys (I always carry a water bottle full of rum) and we dug in along the dike, and waited. I explained the assault plan to the corporals: extended line over the dike and into three specific houses, one section per house.

At 15 minutes before H-Hour three regiments of artillery began to work on the

town. In a few minutes it was smoking like a pile of autumn leaves raked against the curb of the dike. Three tanks moved up and heavy machine guns blistered every building in sight. We crawled up the dike to just below the top, and waited.

A footpath broadened into the roadway at the top of the dike, crossed it, and led with a twist into the heart of the town. As soon as the barrage lifted, the two forward platoons dashed through this opening and made for houses about 30 yards to their left front. Cross fire from three directions cut them down like grass but with half their number they seized two of the buildings. My platoon assaulted in a single extended wave over the dike top and down the other

German children, brainwashed by Nazi propaganda to believe the enemy might slaughter them, come out with their hands up to surrender to Canadian troops. Donald Pearce (above), author of *Journal of a War*, from which this chapter is extracted, wrote: "It exceeds belief, the depth and strength of the hold which the Nazis have got. Unconditional surrender is the only possible demand."

side. Ten tumbled down, nailed on the instant by fire from two or three machine guns; we had gone broadside into their central defenses. The rest of us rolled or dropped into a shallow ditch at the bottom of the dike. The Bren gunners put their weapons to their shoulders, but never got a shot away. (I saw them after the battle, both dead, one still holding the aiming position.) I called out to my corporal, "We've got to dash for it. We've got to get that house." He raised his head to answer and dropped flat. A rifleman took aim at a German weapon pit, and collapsed on my arm. His face turned faint green, and bore a simple smile. I remember muttering to him to "take it easy."

The Germans, in a series of pits directly to our front, had now determined our position and were heaving anti-tank bombs and grenades at us as well as that steady stream of bullets. Obviously, we were on the way to extinction. But one man, Fraser, got up and incredibly walked deliberately over to two of the German weapon pits, deposited one hand grenade in each and loped back. On the way he was shot in the back. But he had left behind him three wounded and four dead Germans, each with an automatic weapon. This so reduced their firepower that we could break out and fuse with the other two platoons.

I called to the platoon to follow me, and ran up the dike. One man was left to follow. The rest we buried later that day, or dispatched to hospital. The one who did follow failed to roll when we hit the top of the dike, and was shot through the knee. The company commander, attempting to rally what was left of another platoon, was wounded as he stepped over the dike, and I was left in charge of the company. I lay the major beside a wall and called for a stretcher-bearer, but almost at once shells began to explode around us. We rolled and twisted and tugged our way around the wall and into a cement culvert.

When the stretcher-bearers didn't show up, I decided for some fool reason to nip along the dike to company headquarters, in a house 100 or so yards back, and get aid myself. This was an insane impulse, for there were snipers on our right and the top of the dike was under hot fire; but nothing seemed to matter, and I set out at a trot. I was sniped at twice and missed both times. Someone in a hole in the field to my right yelled to get under cover with him, and I did for ten minutes till the sniping stopped.

Curiously, I remember nothing about the man who befriended me. Then I crossed the dike; but by then the medical unit had already arrived at the culvert and I had made a pointless trip.

I decided to take the opportunity of giving an account of our situation to the CO. I hadn't any idea, apparently, of how far gone I was emotionally. I simply stood in front of him weeping inarticulately, unable to construct a sentence, even a single word. He approved my release from front-line platoon-leading, which I had requested two or three weeks before, when it had really begun to break me. So now, at the start of our final breakthrough into Germany, I shall be heading the other way. As a matter of fact I am too tired to care.

I shall never know why I came out of that battle; it literally did not figure. But I know it was to be my last. This I accept, and will not regret.

March 29: All my life I will be under the obligation of accomplishing something as a result of having lived through the war. Something tells me I must work hard, as if atoning for not being killed. I will doubtless outlive this feeling. But that will be because I have lost touch with the soldier's truth. Not to have been killed is unfashionable among those who are still dying. Not to have been wounded is something to do penance for. It is not that there is anything particularly desirable about being killed; in itself, even a soldier's death is not precisely desirable. It is in not being killed that the strange obligation consists. I think of the splendid ones who have died, how splendid few will know. They have made it seem as if anything short of intense labor is trifling, or shameful. I suppose their smiling eyes, perpetually young and soldierly in memory now, will be the strict judges of my leisure forever. You cannot stare them out, or turn them aside with a sleepy look. They can exact anything. Tonight I have the feeling that they will make me work. It is owing. . . . DONALD PEARCE

The indispensables

In the spring of 1940, 25 Canadian ships were put to a new and unexpected use that only the desperate demands of war could create. Originally built to carry freight on the Great Lakes, the ships were sent from the safety of mid-continental waters to the danger of Britain's shores.

The first months of the war had been a difficult time for Britain's coastal fleet. By January 1940, some 50 of her coasters had been sunk by enemy submarines and aircraft. As a result, there was a severe shortage of low-draft vessels of 1500 to 4000 gross tons. Even though they had never been intended for sea, let alone war, Canada's inland package freighters and bulk canallers looked like suitable replacements.

That January, several Canadian operators were told that the Royal Navy, with Ottawa's approval, had requisitioned certain of their ships. The 25 were the first of 133 vessels that would eventually be taken over and serve in combat zones around the world. Some of that first contingent were fated to become part of the greatest impromptu fleet in history—the ships that evacuated the British Expeditionary Force from Dunkirk in June.

Describing the hasty withdrawal from France, Leonard J. McLaughlin, former president of the Seafarers International Union of Canada, wrote: "It was quite a party, and half a dozen Canadian lakers were there with seaboots on, among them the Quebec and Ontario Transportation Company's *Thorold* and Canada Steamship Lines' *Waterloo* and *Winona*. German airmen rained fire down on the rescue ships, but still they came. Out from England, back loaded to the gunwales with soldiers, out again, back again. And they saved the British Army."

The Canadian lakers survived Dunkirk but most of them were on borrowed time. Of that first 25, only nine survived the war; 15 were sunk by enemy action.

Canada went into the war with a small merchant fleet. But the war itself eventually brought a boom to both the merchant service and to the shipbuilding industry. In 1920 there had been 82 Canadian oceangoing merchant ships of 1000 tons or more. But by 1939 there were only 38, totaling a mere 241,684 gross tons. Eleven were operated by Canadian National Steamships and 10 were Imperial Oil tankers. In the 15 years before the war, Canadian yards launched only 42 ships exceeding 150 feet in length. Some yards built only one.

In the war years, Canada produced 393 steel naval vessels (including four destroyers, 70 frigates, 122 corvettes and 122 minesweepers) and 398 merchant-men, most of them dry-cargo ships. Ninety merchant ships were sold to the United States for Lend-Lease to Britain, but most of the others were retained by Canada. Their management was supervised by the Park Steamship Company Limited, a Crown company formed in 1942, but individual private companies operated them on a fee basis.

Thousands of Canadian merchant seamen—civilians—went to sea in these ships. They ferried iron ore and cocoa from equatorial Africa, tanks from Detroit, gun carriers from Toronto, oil from Venezuela, apples from the Annapolis Valley, and fighting men from everywhere. They and their merchant-service fellows sailed Victory ships, Liberty ships, Park ships, canallers and tramps and tankers, liners like Cunard's *Queen Mary* and CNS's Great White Ladies.

Despite appalling losses, it was a mark of the men of the merchant service that, voyage after voyage, they went back for more. Although chances were never very good of surviving even one torpedoing, some seamen lived through three, four or five, and signed right back again. They ranged from boys to old men and, even though they were mostly career sailors, many had never been to sea before.

A letter received by one of these seamen says much about the remarkable men who sailed the unwarlike ships to war.

It was from 67 men, two women and a child named Janet. "We were a motley crew," it said, "but you held us together and made us think more of others than of ourselves." They were the survivors of an Atlantic torpedoing in January 1942—70 souls who lived for five winter days in an open, 60-foot boat, on hard biscuits, canned milk, two 20-gallon kegs of water, one medicine bottle of brandy and 25 ounces of rum.

The letter was to Capt. Percy A. Kelly, the only officer left after the CNS's 6370-ton *Lady Hawkins* sank 130 miles off the American coast with a loss of 250 lives. "You made terrible decisions calmly and wisely," it said. "You saw that the humblest got equality of treatment and shared what little comfort was available. You are an officer, a seaman and a Christian gentleman, a man among men. We shall never forget you."

The letter was signed:

H. E. Barrett, lieutenant, Royal Navy, for 24 RN personnel.

Vincent R. Peoples, U.S. naval base workers.

E. Thorne, CSM., for five men British Army.

Robt. Clayton, wireless operator.

A. J. Johnson, wife, and baby daughter, c/o Foreign Office, London.

O. Rivers, for West Indians.

J. M. Rozee, asst. purser, for members of Lady Hawkins *crew.*

Lady Hawkins, one of many passenger liners that became gray ships of war, was sunk a month after Pearl Harbor, at a time when German submarines were marauding all along the Atlantic coast with

little opposition. Here is Captain Kelly's own account:

. . . I was told to join *Lady Hawkins* as chief officer. It would be for one voyage only, then I would resume a command. Unescorted, we left Halifax and went by a devious route to Boston.

There passengers were embarked and we sailed again, with instructions to hug the coast to Cape Hatteras, then swing sharply toward Bermuda.

Our radio officers received one call after another from other unescorted ships torpedoed close to our course line. We saw an occasional blimp or patrol airplane but, apart from bolstering morale, they were of little value. We saw no naval craft. All a submarine had to do was move in under cover of darkness, pick off one or two vessels, then escape out to sea.

For midwinter it was a lovely night; no moon, stars shining, not too much wind, seas comparatively smooth. I checked that no lights were showing and that the lifeboats were clear of obstruction. About 10:30 I reported to Capt. H. O. Giffen that all was well, then went to bed.

Three hours later an explosion woke me. Then a second shattering explosion and the smell of cordite. Two torpedoes. It was just before 2 a.m. January 19. The ship was sinking rapidly and one after another we jumped into the dark Atlantic. I swam to a boat and hung onto the grab lines for what seemed an eternity. My hands began to lose their feeling and I thought my time had come. I was ready to let go when Bill Burton, the ship's carpenter, pulled me into the boat.

Soon I was helping save others from a sea of slimy fuel oil. We pulled them in until no more could be taken. Then I had to give the agonizing order to pull away; the sinking ship was on her beam ends and we dared stay no longer. We had to abandon living humans to suffer the fate of the lifeless *Lady Hawkins* we had left only 20 minutes before. There was nothing else we could do. The cries of people in the water rang in my ears for years.

Slowly and awkwardly, we made room for the men to handle the oars. As we moved off, we watched the grand old *Lady* disappear. Once safely away, we just stood, none daring to move for fear of capsizing, until daylight five hours later. We did not know it then but we were the only survivors; 250 people had died, Captain Giffen among them.

Daylight disclosed 76 of us in a boat certified to carry 63. There was one complete family—husband, wife and Janet, not quite three—and an elderly lady from Trinidad, a group of workers at an American base and two dozen Royal Navy men commanded by Lt. H. E. Barrett, who helped sail the boat. There were 11 black West Indians, several white members of the ship's crew and a Canadian missionary who, with her husband, had been heading for Trinidad. He had died in the sinking.

A radioman told me no distress call had been sent because one torpedo had knocked out the main transmitter. We were on our own. Up went our sails and we headed for the American mainland. I figured we were 130 miles from land. It would take 10 to 14 days. Maybe longer.

Soon water was slopping into the boat.

Capt. Percy A. Kelly (above) soon after survivors from the torpedoed passenger ship *Lady Hawkins* were rescued in January 1942. Left: merchant seamen aboard a Canadian corvette which plucked them from the North Atlantic after their ship sank.

Everybody took turns bailing. We had biscuits, condensed milk, two kegs of water and a small medicine bottle almost full of brandy. Breakfast was half a biscuit and a small amount of water; supper, the same. Lunch was milk. At first we passed the can so each individual could take a mouthful from a hole punched in the top, but some were greedier than others and it was obvious anyway that our supply would last no time if we used two or more cans for each lunch. So we used the bottom of a flashlight as a measure. When everybody had his portion, a little water was added to the empty can and it was swished around until the sticky milk which adhered to its sides became well mixed. Then it was given to Janet.

Every noon, before the milk, we bowed our heads and thanked God for our deliverance. We prayed for strength and courage. It was done simply and without emotion.

The dark nights were hardest. The winter days ended about six and we saw no daylight until seven next morning. The air temperature was around 50 but the water was quite warm.

Soon after the sun went down the first day, a wind came from the east, blowing us toward the coast but bringing bad weather. Nobody said much. It took all the tact, patience and diplomacy I knew to help those who were badly frightened. I told them that as we neared the mainland, our chances of being picked up would be much better, storm or no storm.

As we rode a particularly heavy sea, we lost control of the rudder and it became unshipped and was lost. We then steered with a long, cumbersome wooden oar. Only expert handling by Bill Burton and Charley Bolivar of the *Lady Hawkins* crew kept us from swamping.

The storm reached its height around 3 a.m. If we kept on we would surely lose both mast and sails and be helpless. Reluctantly I ordered the mainsail hauled down and we rode with our small jib and the sea anchor. With daylight the weather moderated and we hoisted full sail again. I no longer feared what the boat might do in a storm with such a heavy load; she had proved herself magnificently.

But our wet clothes did not help morale. As I thought how a hot drink would boost our spirits, a barman announced he had a bottle of *Lady Hawkins* rum—one bottle among 76 people!

I told them that here was our lifesaver and everybody must share. Each was to take a very small mouthful, neat. I implored them to be fair. When the bottle reached me, the last person, there was one small mouthful left. How wonderful it tasted! I felt it go through my entire body, even to my toes.

That day little Janet became ill with fever. We gave her brandy and placed the child and her mother in a small locker normally used for stowing gear. It was hardly three feet long, and at its widest no more than four feet. The headroom was certainly no more than three feet. But it did provide protection. We watched Janet continuously and after a few anxious hours we saw the fever leave her.

That night, in spite of all efforts, one of the West Indians died. We gave him to the sea. During the next 24 hours we lost four other people, including the barman and the old lady from Trinidad. The burials from that small lifeboat, such a dot on the expanse of water, were conducted with care and reverence. We said a prayer as each body was gently lowered over the side.

On the fourth morning I was told our spare keg of water was only half full. Somebody had helped himself. Now I had to cut the water ration even further. One or two weaker ones began to drink sea water—the worst thing they could do. Some hardier souls hid their discomfort behind banter that ranged from mild criticism of my decisions to descriptions of the big steaks they would eat when they reached land.

The fourth day started badly. The boat pitched in heavy seas and took water, keeping our feet wet. A smoke would have helped. We had some tobacco but our few wet matches sputtered out as soon as we struck them.

By now Janet's father was becoming delirious. I thought it was just seasickness but his incoherent words soon convinced me otherwise. I put him in the small locker with his wife and daughter and gave him the last sip of brandy.

By dawn the fifth day the wind had moderated and we began to make reasonable headway. Most of my people were much weaker. That night everybody bedded down quietly, wondering how much longer our ordeal would last.

I must have dozed. I was jolted awake by a shout from the man steering the boat: "A ship! A ship!"

In seconds we were on our feet. We could see the dark outline of a ship and we shouted, waved madly and played our only flashlight on the sails to attract attention. What an intense relief when the ship slowed and came to a dead stop. Many of us wept tears of joy as we took

down our sails, shipped the oars and rowed alongside.

We were all on board in 20 minutes—a long time for her captain to allow his ship to lie stopped, a sitting target for a submarine. I quickly went to the bridge to thank him.

But what sadness when I watched our lifeboat disappear into the night as the ship gathered headway. It was like leaving a faithful friend; it was the soundness and strength of that wooden boat which had weathered the storms for us.

Our rescuer was *Coamo*, bound from New York to Puerto Rico with 500 passengers.

After everybody had been fed and the most feeble ministered to, I was taken to a stateroom. They undressed me like a baby, placed me in a steaming bath, clothed me in pajamas, gave me a sleeping pill and put me to bed.

I remember closing my eyes and in a hazy sort of way trying to say my prayers of thankfulness. Then I began to cry like a child. . . .

PERCY A. KELLY

432

Captain Kelly went back to sea and only 3½ months later survived the torpedoing of a second CNS ship, *Lady Drake,* 90 miles north of Bermuda. Twelve men were killed but 274 others—and one woman—got safely away in five boats. Three days later they were picked up by an American minesweeper.

The morale of merchant seamen, wrote Joseph Schull in *The Far Distant Ships,* was "probably the greatest miracle of the Atlantic battle and certainly the basis upon which all success rested." No matter what *other* men did, no men but these could get food to the British people, raw materials to British factories, weapons to the vast armies forming in Britain. No men but these could move the gasoline and oil. Without the merchant seamen and the cargoes they nursed through U-boat-infested seas, the war could not have been won. Schull wrote:

. . . Seaborne supply from North America, a principal responsibility of the Canadian Navy, was a huge and delicate mechanism at the center of the whole war effort.

For all its ramifications, it depended ultimately on the merchant seamen. Week after week the merchant captains, many speaking just a little English and all looking in their street clothes like tired businessmen, assembled at the convoy conferences, voiced complaints, cracked sardonic jokes and departed. Accustomed to an easygoing spaciousness of sea, they now had to maneuver in crowded ranks, without lights, wireless or navigational aids, with collision and disaster the price of a moment's carelessness. They were burdened with a multitude of orders and regulations. They had to master the unwelcome art of station-keeping in convoy. Their ships' outdated engines had to be nursed and spoon-fed to avoid making smoke and betraying a convoy's presence. Bilges could not be pumped for fear of leaving trails of oil; garbage could not be heaved over the side. In the dark a pinpoint of light was likely to be doused by the bullets of an escort. Yet, week after week, the convoys sailed.

The merchant crews grumbled. Theirs

A cargo vessel, decks piled high with lumber, wallows helplessly after being torpedoed. A warship has come alongside to take the merchantman's crew on board. No task was more hazardous than ferrying vital supplies across the submarine-infested Atlantic. U-boats sank 5150 merchant ships totaling 21,570,720 tons.

was an occupation noted in peacetime for hardness and monotony, yearned for only because of the sense of freedom it gave. Now was added the prospect of death by freezing water or flaming oil in a life unrelieved by uniforms, recognition or the shoreside amenities for naval crews. And freedom was gone; behind the merchant service stood the shadow of compulsion. The ships had to be sailed and these men had to sail them.

With each voyage the odds against their ships and against themselves seemed to grow longer. There were outbursts under the strain, but these were the exceptions in a record of glum, silent, wonderful endurance. . . .

A general 24 hours a day

One night in February 1945 Prime Minister Mackenzie King and Defense Minister A. G. L. McNaughton sat chatting before the fire at Laurier House, King's Ottawa home. McNaughton had recently been defeated in a bid for a House of Commons seat in the Ontario constituency of Grey North. That was on his mind. So was something else.

The First Canadian Army, which he had forged, was fighting west of the Rhine. He was sad that he wasn't commanding it.

They had a pleasant chat, King recorded in his diary. But when King remarked that it was fortunate McNaughton was in Canada, McNaughton "said in a wistful way, 'But it is a great disappointment.' He has all along hoped he might be leading forces now being led by Crerar."

Harry Crerar had replaced Andy McNaughton as army commander a year earlier and had become the first Canadian to lead a full army in battle. On the Rhine, he commanded more than 450,000 Canadians, Britons and other Allied troops.

The two men were quite different types. McNaughton was rumpled and magnetic and colorful. Crerar was immaculate and precise. He coined no dramatic phrases. He captured no imaginations. But he was a general's general and he won the affection and the deep respect of those who worked under him and knew him well.

It was said of Crerar that "he'll never make a bad mistake." But his proficiency and his unwavering adherence to regulations made him appear cold and aloof. He wasn't, but that's how it seemed.

Crerar was born in Hamilton in 1888 and graduated from Royal Military College in Kingston, Ont. He fought in World War I as an artillery officer, returned briefly to civilian life, then joined the regular army. He became Chief of the General Staff in July 1940. In December 1941 he took command of the 1st Canadian Corps, with headquarters at Wakehurst Place, an Elizabethan house near Crawley, in Sussex, England.

Every evening Crerar strolled among Wakehurst's old trees and fed the swans. "I'd say he was a lonely man," says one aide, "but I'm positive *he* didn't think he was lonely. Being a general was a full-time job. He said, 'A commander should lead always and drive seldom—but when he does drive, drive hard.' Note that 'lead always.' He meant 24 hours a day."

Crerar was "punctual in the extreme," another aide recalls. "Regardless of traffic conditions or blackout or anything else, he expected to be brought to every meeting never one second late and within one minute of the time of appointment. He was acutely aware that a tardy general is a pain in the neck. He *respected* his troops and I think he felt that keeping them standing around was something you simply did not do." One time, annoyed that Lt. Gen. Bernard Montgomery was delaying their departure to inspect a Canadian unit, Crerar admonished: "Monty, for goodness' sake, *come on!*"

To Crerar a staff officer was "the servant of the troops, not the master." He was one of the best staff officers the Canadian Army ever produced. "A real professional," says one officer. "He knew his job cold." Another says: "He did not tolerate weaklings, negative personalities or officers who explained too much. To him a good officer was one who knew his profession and could express himself concisely and briefly."

Thomas Macdonald wasn't an officer but he knew Crerar as well as anyone ever did. He was the general's batman, with the rank of bombardier, from late 1941 on. "I'd stand outside his door, watching the second hand of my watch," says Macdonald, "and knock at the very moment of seven. I'd step in, say 'Good morning, sir,' serve him his tea and read him the weather forecast."

On visits to Canadian units, Crerar enlisted Macdonald's help: "He'd say, 'Macdonald, talk to the boys; get an idea what's bothering them. They'll talk to you.' So I'd get all the bellyaches and later I'd pass them on, but keeping personalities out of it. If some outfit didn't like its colonel, I'd keep that to myself.

"He told me once, 'You're my right arm, you know, Macdonald.' I looked after his clothing, his coughdrops—he had a little hacking cough a lot of the time—his toothpaste, his pipe tobacco and his eggs. He loved eggs and I always managed to scrounge some for his breakfast. Every evening we'd have a little chat about home, our mail and how our families were—and the things that I guess he couldn't discuss with anyone else. Like hats. He asked me once, did I think he should wear his proper hat, with the red band, and maybe draw fire on troops he was visiting—or a beret like everybody else, with no distinctive mark, and perhaps have some of the troops think he was yellow? I couldn't help much but I may have helped just by listening. Anyway, he decided to go on wearing the hat with the red band."

Macdonald once asked Crerar about the small, smooth, brown pebble he carried. "He said it went back to a bad shelling in World War I. He hugged the ground for a long time and when it was over he was grasping this pebble. He kept it and always had it with him."

When Crerar went to Italy in the fall of 1943 the tough, battle-tested 1st Division, led by Maj. Gen. Chris Vokes, came under his 1st Corps command. "We no longer stressed the spit and polish habitual to soldiering in the United Kingdom," says Vokes. "Frankly I couldn't have cared less what a man wore as long as he did his job in action. In this Crerar and I differed. He demanded the standards which pertained in the U.K. I found it no use to argue. He was a stubborn man and the 1st Division had to conform."

Weather prevented Crerar from launching any offensive that winter. When recalled to Britain in March 1944 to command the First Canadian Army, he had no experience in directing offensive operations. His later success in northwest Europe, says Vokes, "confounded those who predicted he'd fail because he lacked experience in the lower echelons of field command. He proved himself an exception to a rule which should rarely be ignored in war. In this he was like General Eisenhower."

Crerar went to France on June 18, 12 days after the Normandy landings. His army headquarters became operational July 23, taking over the extreme left flank of the Allied front. He led the drive to Falaise in August, the clearing of the Channel ports, the capture of German flying bomb sites and the beginning of the campaign to clear the Scheldt estuary and open the port of Antwerp. But then he fell ill and the army fought the Scheldt battle under Crerar's 2nd Corps commander, Lt. Gen. Guy Simonds.

Near the end of the Scheldt battle, before Crerar's return, Montgomery visited the Canadians as head of the 21st Army Group. In jocular vein, writes Capt. Peter Simonds in *Maple Leaf Up, Maple Leaf Down*, Montgomery suggested a nickname for the 3rd Canadian Division. Just as his 7th British Armored Division of El Alamein fame had been the Desert Rats, the Canadians had earned the title Water Rats because they had crossed so many rivers and fought in so many flooded areas. The division adopted the title; engineers painted a rat on 3rd Division bridging and road signs. When Crerar reassumed command, he was unimpressed. "Take that lousy rodent down," he is reported to have said. Down it came. But the division was proud of the name and went on using it.

The front was static for some months after Crerar returned. On November 16, 1944, he was promoted full general, the first Canadian to gain this rank at the front.

That same month Vokes came from Italy to command the 4th Canadian Armored Division. "When I reported to General Crerar in Holland," Vokes recalls, "he greeted me by saying he would not tolerate any slack habits learned in the 'Spaghetti League.' Then he told me the fighting in Italy had been child's play compared with northwest Europe. As a long-time member of the Spaghetti League I resented his remarks. Just as I was getting ready with a rejoinder that might have brought my career to a shuddering halt, he smiled and said he was only pulling my leg. I thought, 'Command of an army has mellowed our Uncle Harry.'"

Crerar was "an exponent of military orthodoxy," says Vokes. "His forte as an army commander was his willingness to decentralize responsibility to his brilliant corps commanders like Guy Simonds and British generals like Brian Horrocks who served under him."

Maj. Gen. Churchill Mann, Crerar's chief of staff throughout the northwest European campaign, cites this example of Crerar's reliance on key subordinates:

"About midnight one night in December 1944 I received a telephone call from the chief of staff of the British 30th Corps, which had just been placed under First Canadian Army command. He reported that the 250,-000-man corps had finished taking up its assigned positions and was ready for our impending attack west of the Rhine. Five minutes later my phone rang again.

"'I am speaking on an open line,' a voice said. 'Do you recognize me?'

"'Yes, sir,' I said, 'I do.'

"'I want them all back at once. Start them immediately. Do you understand?'

"It was Montgomery. I deduced that, because of the sudden German thrust through the Ardennes that day, he wanted the 30th Corps sent back to wherever it had come from.

"'Yes, sir,' I said. 'They will start at once.'

"When Montgomery hung up I called the 30th Corps chief of staff. 'I am speaking on an open line,' I said. 'I have just had a call from Master (our nickname for Montgomery) and you are to return to exactly wherever you came from, beginning as soon as this call ends.'

"He called me a rude name, then said, 'We will start in reverse order in five minutes.' By morning the corps was back where Montgomery wanted it."

Mann had known he had Crerar's full authority to act. Not until after breakfast did he tell him what had happened.

Crerar had good relations not only with his headquarters staff but with British commanders, both equals and subordinates. But he was an enigma to some.

"He was not the sort of man one gets to know easily," said Gen. Sir Miles Dempsey, whose British Second Army fought alongside Crerar's forces under Montgomery. "I liked Harry very much but he didn't expand easily."

Lt. Gen. Sir Brian Horrocks, British 30th Corps commander under Crerar during the month-long Rhine battle, says: "He was very patient with me because I found myself getting rather irritable toward the end of the battle. I think he suffered a bit from having Montgomery as his boss—not in a tactical sense but because Montgomery was such a personality it was difficult for his army commanders to show any personality of their own."

Crerar had two demanding bosses—Montgomery and the Canadian government. He was once overheard to tell Montgomery: "Part of the time I'm responsible to you, the rest of the time to the Canadian government." Montgomery may not always have fully appreciated Crerar's peculiar position, and there were conflicts, but generally they got along well.

Crerar once passed along to Montgomery a prisoner who had given him a good laugh. During the Rhineland fighting a German paymaster was captured by a British formation. He asked to be taken to army headquarters. Crerar saw him. General Mann tells what happened:

"The paymaster proffered a British Army message form on which was written: 'This ------- had 40,000 (Dutch) guilders. He hasn't got them now.' It was signed, 'J. Smith, Sergeant, 15th Scottish Division.' The German said he wanted this receipt validated so he could explain his discrepancies to the German authorities after the war. With difficulty, General Crerar maintained his composure, then turned to me and said, 'Have this officer taken to Field Marshal Montgomery's headquarters at once.'"

To the end of the war Crerar paid daily visits to his corps and divisional commanders, sometimes by car, sometimes in a light, unarmed plane which he occasionally flew himself.

Crerar felt deep concern for people. "It showed," says one aide, "in the personal notes he sent to the next of kin of men he knew who had been casualties in the Dieppe raid in 1942."

It showed in other things. "In mid-April 1945," Mann recalls, "Intelligence reported that a concentration camp in our area of advance was populated entirely by Polish women. General Crerar immediately ordered that the 1st Polish Armored Division be directed to overrun the camp. A few days later the Poles did liberate it and many found there the wives and sweethearts they had not seen since Poland fell in 1939."

A few weeks after that, when the war was over, Montgomery wrote to Crerar: "No commander can ever have had a more loyal subordinate than I have had in you. And under your command the Canadian Army has covered itself with glory. I am deeply grateful. If ever there is anything I can do for you or your magnificent Canadian soldiers, you know you have only to ask."

There were other letters, one from a 19-year-old Dutch girl: "It was you, General Crerar, and your Canadian troops who liberated the greater part of our country. It was your boys who gave their lives and blood and your people who had to accept, in the interest of our country, so many sad reports about sons killed in action. So many times we saw you leave in your plane, close to the front line, to carry out your hard and difficult task; we are not surprised that your soldiers give you their confidence and respect. Thank you once more for our liberation, and may God bless you."

February 8, 1945—men of le Régiment de Maisonneuve (right), ready for the First Canadian Army's thrust into Germany. Fighting for their homeland, German soldiers like this one (left) were now fighting *in* their homeland. Col. C. P. Stacey, the Canadian historian, wrote that "they displayed the recklessness of fanaticism and the courage of despair."

The savage twilight

In the drive for the Rhine, Gen. H. D. G. Crerar commands more men than any Canadian in history

Sgt. Aubrey Cosens, from tiny Porquis Junction in northern Ontario, had come to another tiny place with another unlikely name—the German hamlet of Mooshof, ten miles west of the Rhine. On the morning of February 26, 1945, Mooshof suddenly became important—it was on a slope vital for military purposes. And when the day's violence was over, it was important for another reason: the 23-year-old soldier from Porquis Junction had become a legend and Mooshof was where it happened.

Two companies of the Queen's Own Rifles attacked at 4:40 a.m. that day, advancing up the slope in darkness. D company met German paratroopers in the village—fanatical fighters with strong mortar and artillery support. Cosens' platoon twice attacked three farm buildings the Germans had turned into strongpoints. Twice the Canadians were repulsed. The Germans struck back with a fierce counterattack and by the time it was broken, the platoon was down to five men. Its lieutenant was dead and Sergeant Cosens, a former railway section hand, was in command.

German fire came from all sides. But a Canadian tank moved up across the soggy land and, with it and his four men, Cosens pressed the attack on the three strongpoints. He ran across 25 yards of open ground, climbed onto the tank, squatted in front of the turret and directed its fire against the buildings. He shattered another German counterattack by plunging the tank into the ranks of the paratroopers. Then, under intense fire, he attacked alone—he and his Sten gun.

With his four infantrymen covering him, Cosens rode the tank as it rammed into the first building. He jumped off, rushed inside the building and killed or captured the Germans there. He went on to the second building, then across a road to the third, a two-story farmhouse. His awed little platoon followed, covering him and gathering prisoners as they emerged. Cosens killed at least 20 men and captured as many more, and he broke the hard core of enemy resistance in Mooshof.

Then, within minutes, he was dead. A sniper killed him as he consolidated his position and left to report to his company commander. Posthumously, he was awarded the Victoria Cross.

Eighteen days before that morning at Mooshof, Gen. H. D. G. Crerar's First Canadian Army had broken into Germany from Holland as a crucial part of a huge Allied offensive to eliminate the Germans west of the Rhine, their last great defensive barrier.

After 5½ years that had cost millions of lives and billions of dollars, the war had come to the land where it had started. Far to the east, the Russians had crossed the 1939 frontier of Germany in late January; now they were thrusting for Berlin. South of Crerar's army, the Americans had pushed into Germany at three places.

Crerar *had* hoped to attack weeks earlier, when the ground was frozen. But the Germans' Ardennes offensive had forced delay. By the time the attack began on February 8 a thaw had turned the ground into a quagmire. Gen. Dwight Eisenhower said "probably no assault in this war has been conducted under more appalling conditions of terrain."

Across this soil, through forests and floods and waterlogged farmlands, against formidable defenses, Crerar deployed the largest force ever commanded by a Canadian: 13 divisions, nine of them British, and more than 450,000 men. Pro-

moted from lieutenant general in November, Crerar became the first Canadian of full general's rank ever to lead an army in the field.

Broadly, his role was to thrust roughly 30 miles southeast from the Nijmegen salient in Holland, clear the Germans from the corridor between the Rhine and Maas (or Meuse) rivers and, on the Rhine across from Wesel, link up with the U.S. Ninth Army coming northeast from the Roer River.

The corridor, up to 20 miles wide, had a complex series of fortified zones: a strong outpost defense screen, then the northern end of the vaunted Siegfried Line, mainly in the Reichswald forest, and finally posi-

send much of their strength north to contest Crerar's advance. There had been one division facing First Canadian Army when its attack began. At the peak there were ten, with 700 mortars and 1000 guns.

The offensive began on February 8 when Crerar's 30th British Corps, with the support of more than 1000 guns and with heavy air attack, quickly broke through the outpost screen fronting the Reichswald, a large state forest. But it took five days of bitter fighting to clear the Reichswald itself.

During this time Canada's 2nd and 3rd divisions, on the left, moved southeast between the Rhine and the Reichswald. They were temporarily under 30th Corps'

Here they encountered paratroopers as fiercely determined as the SS troops they'd fought in Normandy. It took six days to drive them out. Finally a 3rd Division battalion, the Winnipeg Rifles, attacked the enemy positions with the support of planes, guns, tanks and Wasp flamethrowers. The Wasps set fire to the trees and flames seared the paratroopers' trenches. But, says Peter Simonds in *Maple Leaf Up, Maple Leaf Down,* "the enemy troops, even with horribly blistered faces and hands, hung on and, in some cases screaming with pain, fought the Winnipegs in fierce hand-to-hand combats all through the woods." When they were subdued, Moyland Wood was won.

tions in the Hochwald forest which covered the Rhine crossings at Wesel.

Crerar had at his disposal a juggernaut of infantry, tanks, planes and guns, and although he initially caught the Germans by surprise, his men had to wage a savage, month-long struggle before the enemy was driven from his defenses. The Germans were fighting for their homeland. "In this, the twilight of their gods," as historian Col. C. P. Stacey put it, "they displayed the recklessness of fanaticism and the courage of despair."

For days Crerar had to fight many more of them than he had anticipated. When the Americans reached the last of the dams on the Roer, the Germans jammed open a sluice gate and flooded the river. The Ninth Army's offensive had to be postponed and the Germans seized this opportunity to

command. Miles of rural soil had been flooded by the waters of the river, and their amphibious Buffalo vehicles at times floated the 3rd Division over antitank ditches, wire and mines. Proudly calling themselves The Water Rats, the 3rd's soldiers also fought on foot in water up to three feet deep as they moved from village to village.

Once the area around the Reichswald was cleared, the Canadians came back under the command of Lt. Gen. Guy Simonds' 2nd Canadian Corps. On the 15th Crerar attacked with the two corps side by side. In their thrust toward the third main German defense zone in the Hochwald, the Canadians had to break through stubborn resistance centered on another forest called Moyland Wood, between the towns of Cleve and Calcar.

By February 20, the Canadians had advanced some 18 miles in 12 days and had crossed a lateral road running from Calcar to Goch. Crerar began to regroup for a new, climactic drive: first to a ridge beyond the road, then to the Hochwald and yet another nearby forest, the Balberger Wald.

While Crerar prepared for this offensive, the Roer subsided. On the 23rd the U.S. Ninth Army finally launched the attack the floods had delayed for two weeks.

Three days later General Simonds' 2nd Canadian Corps moved against the ridge running south from Calcar toward Udem. Under his command were two British divisions, one on either flank. Between them he had three Canadian divisions—the 2nd, 3rd and 4th—and the 2nd Canadian Armored Brigade.

Silhouetted against a searchlight beam (left), a Canadian soldier moves out in an early morning attack. German troops (above) fought stubbornly and well and at one stage of the Rhine offensive the First Canadian Army faced ten enemy divisions. Right: Sgt. Aubrey Cosens, V.C., and the plaque in his memory at Mooshof, a German hamlet ten miles west of the Rhine.

In Commemoration
of
SGT AUBREY COSENS V.C.
lst Bn The Queen's Own Rifles of Canada
who on the night of
25/26 February 1945
led the survivors of his
platoon in the capture of
these farm buildings which were
vital to the success of future
operations of the 8th Cdn Inf Bde
For his gallantry, initiative and
determined leadership
Sgt Cosens was posthumously awarded
the VICTORIA CROSS

Mooshof,
28 August 1963

It was in the attack on this ridge, seized within 24 hours by an able combination of tank and infantry assaults, that Sgt. Aubrey Cosens won his V.C. Three days later, and a few miles farther on, Maj. Frederick Tilston of the Essex Scottish won another in the assault on the Hochwald forest.

Despite a head wound, Tilston led his company across 500 yards of open ground under intense fire, through ten feet of barbed wire, into enemy trenches near the edge of the forest. With a grenade, he destroyed a machine-gun post that was threatening one platoon. He was severely wounded in the hip as he led his company into another complex of dugouts and trenches but he got to his feet and helped clear this position in savage hand-to-hand combat. With three quarters of his men gone, the company down to 26, violent counterattacks coming in, he moved from platoon to platoon to organize the defense and made repeated trips across bullet-swept ground to replenish their depleted ammunition. On the sixth trip, he fell wounded for the third time. He was barely conscious but would not submit to medical attention until he had given command and instructions to his one remaining officer. In his gallantry, Tilston lost both legs.

During the first days of March, the 2nd and 3rd divisions cleared the Hochwald

and Balberger Wald and the 4th Armored Division thrust through a gap between them. Together at great cost, they conquered a forested area six miles long and one to three miles deep. The U.S. Ninth Army linked up with Crerar's 30th Corps to the south and the two armies forced the Germans into a shrinking bridgehead. On March 10, the enemy blew the bridges at Wesel and withdrew across the Rhine.

In a month First Canadian Army had suffered 15,634 casualties, among them 5304 Canadians. The Americans suffered

7300. Total German casualties were about 90,000.

In this vast and complex struggle, Canadians fought in planes and tanks, in amphibious Buffaloes, in armored Kangaroos that carried them into the German lines as they had in Normandy. They used artificial moonlight, searchlights playing on clouds for night attacks; they used mountains of shells and an enormous smoke screen that blotted out targets for German guns across the Rhine. But in the end it came down, as it always did, to the courage of the in-

fantry, to men like Aubrey Cosens and Frederick Tilston.

In the mud, supply problems were a nightmare. Planes often could not fly because of bad weather. Tanks performed brilliantly but often they, too, found it hard to maneuver in the ooze of the winter thaw. The infantry battalions went forward anyway, with the skills that months of battle had taught. By now they knew their violent craft.

The battalions were a mixture of veterans and reinforcements fighting their first battles—the sort of blend that author Jean Vaillancourt told about in the following episode from his novel *Les Canadiens Errants*.

Vaillancourt's book, awarded le Prix du Cercle du Livre de France in 1954, came straight out of his own experiences. He enlisted in 1942 at 19 and fought across Europe as a corporal with le Régiment de Maisonneuve. He was a stretcher-bearer and he refused promotion so he could remain one. His height—he was six-feet-four-inches tall—didn't make his job any easier. He was wounded three times.

The platoon he describes in this episode had a hard core of veterans and a few Zombies, the conscripts who'd been forced to fight. A condensation:

. . . Corporal Dubuc and his men, attacking a mill, had been spotted by enemy artillery. Three times they were engulfed in black smoke. But the hand-picked group, well drilled in assault, always dived to earth in time. Then, as the sound of shell explosions reached us, we saw them jump up and lope ahead.

"Watch them," said Sgt. Etienne Lanthier, the acting platoon commander. "You're looking at real soldiers."

"We didn't get training like that," one of the conscripts said.

"You get it in battle by sticking your neck out every day for months," Lanthier said. "You don't learn it anywhere else or any other way."

"How often have you done it?" another conscript asked, genuinely curious, not impertinent. Lanthier glanced at him without comment and pulled out his pipe.

Just then mortar shells came in like a swarm of wasps. Everyone leaped for a slit trench. The seasoned men never ceased to marvel at the almost incredible safety of these little trenches, two feet deep or less, the length of a man, better shelter than a stone fortress. Only a direct hit could reach a man flattened out inside, the tip of his nose scarcely two inches below ground level. There was seldom a direct hit even when shells plowed up the earth all around. The slit trench was one of the miracles of the war.

Dubuc's crew got within 200 yards of the mill before the machine gun inside opened up. Now the men dashed a few yards at a time, doing startling acrobatics when they hit the ground and disappeared from view. They never reappeared where they had gone down. Each man rolled over several times to keep the machine-gun crew guessing.

Dubuc, easy to pick out because of his height, was always a few steps ahead, directing tactics with motions of his right arm that swept up and down in a wide arc. The Acadian lumberjack looked like one windmill swirling in to attack another.

Lanthier, an ex-boxer, watched Dubuc through binoculars. He yanked his pipe from his mouth and, without realizing it, coached his old comrade audibly, like a fight manager. His voice was quiet, anxious, alarmed, furious, disappointed, discouraged, resigned and then suddenly frantic. He was as involved as Dubuc himself.

"Go, Dubuc, my boy, go . . . Now!" he muttered. "Down, down, down. Down, goddammit! You sure took your time. Jesus, he's taking chances today! Look at those legs sticking up. Get those legs down, stupid! How often do I have to tell him to keep his legs down!"

Lanthier lowered the glasses, then put them up again, his concern overpowering his usual inclination to let things happen.

Now Dubuc and his men, carefully spaced out, made individual spurts forward. But finally they were immobilized. The odds against getting ahead alive had narrowed. Even crawling was perilous, the ground was so exposed. Here and there mud holes offered a semblance of shelter for experienced soldiers who could flatten and push their faces into the ooze. But the enemy had a bird's-eye view of the ground in front of them and they would be sitting ducks if they repeated their tactics.

Bursts from the Spandau searched the ground close to where Dubuc had thrown himself down. Suddenly he made two great leaps and landed near a Bren gunner. The enemy machine gun chugged nervously like an outboard motor. The Bren answered with the firm beat of a judge's gavel. When the Bren magazine was used up, Dubuc opened his cartridge pouches and tossed two more to the machine gunner. The weapon chewed into the fresh supply of ammunition.

The Spandau fell silent. The Bren gunner fired several more bursts at the mill, then started to empty a whole magazine into its high window. Instantly, Dubuc was on his feet with a gesture that brought two men up behind him. They ran for the mill. Dubuc's back was arched. His hands practically swept the ground. He moved like a great monkey. Before they had covered 20 yards, the Spandau chugged again. The three Canadians dived to the ground.

Lanthier saw two wisps of white smoke near the base of the mill just as they were vanishing in a breeze. Lanthier understood at once and wondered whether Dubuc's Bren gunner did too. And had Dubuc himself seen the wisps of smoke?

The Bren gunner resumed firing into the high window to keep the Germans' heads down. But the Germans who had taken up

Engulfed in smoke from a rapid-fire Bofors gun, artillerymen of the First Canadian Army fire over open sights in the Rhine offensive. On March 10, a month after it started, the Germans blew the bridges at Wesel (right) and took up new defenses east of the Rhine. Maj. Frederick Tilston (below) of the Essex Scottish won the Victoria Cross in the 2nd Canadian Division assault on the Hochwald forest.

the new position at the mill door would hold their fire so they wouldn't give themselves away. Dubuc, thinking he was covered by the Bren, would be cut in two in his last sprint to the mill.

Lanthier jumped out of his trench. He started to run toward Dubuc. The Bren sounded again. Lanthier stopped, dropped his Sten gun and grabbed his binoculars. He saw the Bren tracers pouring into the mill door.

Dubuc popped up again and in seconds raced to the mill. He flattened out a few feet from the door. There was one shattering explosion, then another. Dubuc got up and ran inside. Soon a German came out, his hands up. Dubuc was at his heels, urging him with kicks.

Dubuc came back in high spirits. Lanthier, biting his pipe, looked him over without a word and saw a patch of blood on one of his ears. A bullet had taken a piece of it.

Lanthier took the ear between his thumb and finger and examined it. "How was it?" he asked, faking a careless air.

"A bit hot," Dubuc said. "There were three Jerries. One got the Bren fire in the face. Another got one of my grenades in the belly. And there's this."

The prisoner was short and fat. He seemed ready to fall to his knees at the first threatening sign.

"It was damn well time you took that mill," said Lanthier. "I was going to help you."

"When Dubuc needs your help, he'll ask for it."

Dubuc's words didn't have the usual conviction. He clapped a powerful hand on Lanthier's shoulder.

They searched the captive and then pointed to the rear. The German set out as though thanking God for having delivered him.

"The bastard is luckier than we are," said Dubuc.

Lanthier sent a signal to the major about the capture of the mill and got orders for his platoon to rejoin the rest of the company.

For the moment the German artillery appeared to have forgotten them. Lanthier took advantage of the lull to get the men moving.

The sun was high. They traveled about ten minutes, then were halted by renewed shelling. They went to ground mechanically, waited for the fire to sweep by, then got up again. Lanthier swept the plain with his glasses. The glare of the sun made it hard to see. He finally located the rest of the company pinned down near a village off to the right. The smoke of bombardment rose in an oblong plume.

The northern end of the Siegfried Line (left) was among the defenses in the 20-mile-wide Rhine-Maas corridor that General Crerar's army cleared. Below: a Bren gun team gives covering fire from a shattered house as comrades advance in the street below. On March 23-24 came Operation Plunder, the crossing of the Rhine. Among the assault formations was the 51st (Highland) Division, which made the crossing in storm boats (right, lower photo). "The attack across the great river could have been a very bloody operation," wrote military historian Col. C. P. Stacey. "But in the circumstances existing March 23 it was no such thing. Only six minutes after the Highland Division launched its attack, the leading wave reported its arrival on the far bank." Right: Jean Vaillancourt, author of *Les Canadiens Errants,* an episode from which is condensed in these pages.

Since morning, the enemy cannonade had been intermittent and erratic. Now it started to come in long echoing rolls, like thunder behind a storm cloud. Suddenly, about 75 yards ahead on the plain, the men saw a line of smoke puffs and, shortly after, there was a series of sharp explosions. They exchanged anxious looks. Two minutes later, another line of black smoke balls sprang up, only 50 yards in front. When the sound of the shell explosions reached them, a third line rose from the ground like a wall, about 40 yards away.

"Down!" Lanthier shouted. They went to ground and shells struck among them in five waves, aimed with great precision. This time the barrage didn't move on. Corporals Lanoue and Dubuc, crawling furiously, got to Lanthier's side. "That's not random fire," said the sergeant. "It's a son of a bitch to get pinned down out here without cover. No time to dig either. Do the two-inch mortar guys have smoke bombs?"

"No," said Lanoue. "No. 6 platoon has them."

"Well, get back to your sections," said Lanthier. "Tell the men to lie low and wait. I'll talk to the major."

The 88-mm. shells and mortar bombs came in at an increasing rate. The German gunners in the village must have calculated that the company would attack when Lanthier's platoon arrived. They were doing all they could to stop it.

The Allied artillery, after escorting the company to the edge of the village, was engaged in other business, pounding a cluster of farm buildings.

Lanthier reported to the major that his platoon was pinned down. The major replied that the shells came from the village and that the platoon should wait until they stopped. In fact, there was nothing else to do. The major said he would find out whether the artillery could help with the village. Lanthier was to keep in contact and if the situation got worse, the major would take charge of the platoon himself.

In a brief pause in the shelling, Lanthier scanned the village. To be caught by chance in unobserved fire—after dark, for example—was one thing. It was quite different to know that every movement was watched by an unseen, inaccessible enemy. The most experienced men started to sweat. Shell fragments fell among them. The bursts raised thick curtains of dirt. It was astonishing that anyone survived.

Corporal Lanoue, thinking back, could recall only one bombardment of such devilish precision, back in Normandy. He raised himself on his elbows. A barrage

like this had to have forward observation. He studied a grove to the right. He didn't expect, from this distance, to make out anything among the trees, but he was convinced there was activity in there. He crawled over to Lanthier.

By now the ground looked like a volcano crater. The shells howled in among men clutching at ground they would have liked to crawl into. The explosions seemed to lift them, surround them with flame, envelop them in frightful black smoke. They pressed arms, legs, their bodies to the earth. Their mouths opened convulsively and cries, pleas, groans and the gasps of the wounded could be heard. The bombardment got heavier until the entire plain seemed to shudder.

Suddenly a gasp: "Mama!" The word clutched at the heart of every man who heard it.

It came from a young conscript. He raised himself, arms upstretched, mouth open, eyes staring. He stood motionless. Then his legs failed and he slowly crumpled into the drifting smoke of the shell that killed him.

A feeling of madness seemed to sweep over the men. Lanthier rose and cried: "Up. Up. Everybody up. Out of here. Follow me to the woods."

All the men still able to hold themselves up set out on the run behind Lanthier. They dashed through the fury of hell. The German gunners had only to adjust the angle of their fire slightly to keep up with the moving targets. The torrent of steel and fire followed all the way.

The men, at a mad gallop, thought of nothing, saw nothing but the bounding shape of Lanthier vanishing in smoke, reappearing, waving them on. "On the double. On the double. Keep going," he kept shouting over his shoulder.

It was hard to judge the distance to the

trees in the brilliant sunlight but it was a long way. Corporal Lanoue thought every step would be his last. When he looked back he saw that six or seven men, including two conscripts, were with him. He gestured to them to keep up. The next time he looked back only three or four were left, spread out according to the strength of their legs.

Lanoue made no further sign to them. He knew how soldiers were. He knew a man might say, "I won't move" or "I can't" or "I'm going to die right here." He could then give a command, but if he did he took responsibility for the man's life. The three or four still following him did so because they thought it was right. Others had taken their chances another way. That's all there was to it.

Nothing could be done for the dead or wounded. Those who had stayed behind instead of making the dash may have been the wise ones. It was no safer where he was than where they chose to stay. No one could tell the right thing to do. Death was waiting everywhere, so Lanoue made no more signs to anyone.

They ran for several minutes, yet the grove seemed to stay maddeningly out of reach. Sweating, panting, stumbling to their knees, falling flat, pulling themselves up, the men reached the limits of their breath and the point of stress at which human consciousness turns into madness.

Instead of escaping hell, they had run into it. Flaming and smoking craters appeared wherever they turned—in front, behind, on every side. Explosions flung them to the ground. They rolled and twisted, eyes wild, arms and legs thrashing. Then they got up and tried once more to escape.

Perhaps only Lanthier knew any longer what he was trying to do. The men were driven forward by panic alone; thought had been swept away. Each man saw into the very bottom of his spirit, and beyond into some abyss.

Lanthier, driven to fury, imagined himself to be a lion at the bottom of a deep trench where the whips of 20 trainers cut at him. Then his practical side got the better of the nightmare. Running, although no longer conscious of the movement of his legs, he relived in a lucid flash his last boxing match. Every moment was felt in every muscle and with all his senses. He heard the roar of the crowd, saw the sweating, scowling face of his opponent, heard

Wounded and defeated, but at least alive, a German soldier (opposite page) is marched off to a prisoner-of-war cage, escorted by a swash-buckling Canadian. Allied troops had strict orders not to fraternize with German civilians (above and right). "Troops entering Germany," wrote Blair Gilmour in *The Pictorial History of Canada's Army Overseas 1939-1945*, "were amazed at the prosperous farmlands. Lush green fields, fat cattle, chickens and hogs presented a maddening contrast after the vacant pastures and barns of plundered Holland. There was contrast in the attitudes of the people—the almost delirious joy of the liberated Netherlanders; the stark fear or apathy of the conquered Germans.

"Nearly every city home and certainly every farm was well stocked with food and it was not unusual to come upon larders of fresh meat and dairy butter. Stores displayed luxury goods unseen for years in England and France. Conquering troops lived well, commandeering what food they desired. On many occasions the servility of the beaten 'super race' was embarrassing."

the hysterical scream of a woman in the crowd that took his attention for a fateful fraction of a second. He saw triumph in the eyes of his opponent unleashing blows that sent him down into the dark pit. After the fight, he had never been able to remember what had happened and, night after night, he had tossed in bed, trying to recollect. Now, for the first time, it was clear; nothing in the past of Etienne Lanthier eluded him any longer.

Laurent Hurtubise saw the tender face of his mother leaning over to put him to sleep at the age of four. He felt an immense security and peace. His spirit seemed to have detached itself from the body he was conscious of no more. His soul, aflame with religious fervor and mystical love for God entwined with love for his mother, bounded over plains, rivers, forests and hills. "Praise the Lord on High," Hurtubise chanted within himself. Tears he was unaware of flowed down his face.

Corporal Dubuc, running, foaming at the mouth, had forgotten where he was and where he was headed. A Bren gun was on his shoulder and his hand gripped its barrel. The stock pounded his shoulder with every leap, but he felt nothing.

He thought he was among a band of giants, in a forest where the trees were so tall their tops disappeared in the clouds. Legs widespread, he swung an axe as high as a house. The trees toppled in a slaughter that filled him with fierce joy. Then he saw the tallest tree coming down on him with a noise that filled the forest. He threw himself down and hid his head between his arms.

Corporal Lanoue, after his 15th, 16th, 17th fall to the ground, felt his strength ebbing. But he rose and started off again because he *had* given the order "follow me" to the one or two men still behind him.

A shell shrieked louder than any he had heard. He made two or three wild, instinctive leaps. The shell struck behind him. He was lifted, then thrown to earth. Mud rained on him.

He thought it was the end. There was a hammering in his skull. He bled from the nose. He couldn't tell whether he was wounded but he felt demolished. His face sank into the mud. He felt relieved forever of the need to think.

With the cold mud on his face, he slipped into an indescribable euphoria. He dreamed he would never get up again, that he would play dead and stay there until the war was over. His will had never failed before. He hadn't the physical stamina of Lanthier or Dubuc, but his source of pride had been that his courage matched theirs. Now he had given in. All the courage had been pointless. What was God thinking when He cruelly mocked the courage of these men? Their unique dignity, their highest quality, had been crushed. Lanoue was broken and his life had lost its meaning. He dreamed he would melt into the soil and belong to it. When summer came the green grass would grow around him. It would become tall, encircle him and finally cover him.

For a long time he lay there. Then life stirred faintly again within him. His spirit made its way out of the abyss. He was young and his source of life was inexhaustible.

Either the Germans ran out of ammunition or the Allied barrage finally located them because the bombardment gradually died.

Lanthier, the first to get up, slowly found his platoon. He counted 6 dead, 9 wounded and 18 men intact. Not one had reached the grove. But he had saved half the platoon. The men hadn't bunched up as soldiers often did, they had dispersed in spite of themselves. Otherwise, the platoon would have been wiped out. Lanthier sent one man to the rear to bring up vehicles and stretchers for the wounded. Then, at the head of the platoon, he set out for the grove.

Two Germans, their hands up, awaited them. Searching a concrete shelter, Lanthier found the wireless set that had been used to direct the artillery.

In the undergrowth a soldier found a second dugout, perfectly camouflaged between two trees. He fired into it. Out came a yelping German, slightly wounded. He got free of his captor and assumed a proud attitude, like a wrestler at a fair. As Lanthier asked him a question in English, he spotted the man's SS insignia. The German called Lanthier a *Schweinhund*, then spat in his face.

Holding his Sten gun by its sling, Lanthier crashed it down in the German's face and knocked him to the ground. Then he stuck the barrel of the Sten against the German's stomach and pressed the trigger until the magazine was empty. The body gave a start and for several moments it was hideously convulsed. Then it was still. . . .

JEAN VAILLANCOURT

447

The "angel" that came too late

The world's first jet fighter fails to stem the Allies' final air offensive

One day in October 1944, a strange, incredibly fast plane swooped over a front-line airfield at Grave in Holland. It let loose a shower of fragmentation bombs, wounding seven pilots and numerous ground crew of Canada's 127 Spitfire Wing. Seconds later it climbed and disappeared. It was a Messerschmitt 262. With a top speed of 540, it was a good 100 miles an hour faster than the latest piston-engine Spitfire.

The world's first operational jet fighter might have changed the course of the war in the air. German fighter ace Adolf Galland described its performance as not just a step forward but a leap. Given the right priority, it could have been in action in 1943—in time to ravage Allied bombers over Germany, regain ascendancy for the Luftwaffe, and perhaps force the Allies to postpone D-Day. But short-sightedness, low priority and Hitler's interference doomed it to a minor role.

This attitude changed only after General Galland flew a prototype in May 1943. "It's like flying on the wings of an angel," he said and at once reported to

Reichsmarshal Göring that the Me 262 was of prime importance. Yet series production did not begin even then. Hitler was against it. He did not want a new defensive fighter. He wanted bombers, for attack. After a further six months delay, the Me 262 was demonstrated on November 26, in Hitler's presence. "So," he cried, "there at last is our blitz bomber!"

The people about him were stunned, wrote Cajus Bekker in *The Luftwaffe War Diaries,* but they could not persuade him to change his resolve. The jet fighter was to be weighed down with bombs, eliminating its superiority. A whole string of technical difficulties arose. But by August 1944, nine Me 262 jet bombers were ready for combat. Two broke up due to faulty servicing; two were lost in landings; five reached the front.

Galland's "angel" did appear two months later. Hitler had relented and permitted his blitz bomber to be produced also as a jet fighter. It had "complete superiority" over the Spitfire, wrote Wing Comdr. J. E. "Johnnie" Johnson, British flying leader of the Canadian wing

at Grave. The few rounds he fired at a 262 on October 5 "were more an angry gesture at our impotence than anything else." But that same day Spitfire pilots of the RCAF's 401 Squadron in 126 Wing did combine to destroy a 262.

Shortly after noon, over Nijmegen, Holland, Sqdn. Ldr. Roy Smith sighted the jet 500 feet below and coming head-on. The Me 262, painted green with a yellow decoration on its long nose, went into a climbing turn, then dived, twisting and turning and half-rolling. Smith and other pilots made strikes before they saw it crash. A pilot who circled the wreckage reported debris scattered for 150 yards. Investigators sent one of the cannons to the squadron as a souvenir.

Canada's fighter pilots fought fewer air battles than they'd have liked that autumn, either with the new jet or conventional fighters. The two Spitfire wings and Canada's 143 Typhoon fighter-bomber wing flew mostly strafing missions against road convoys, trains and barges as part of a plan to paralyze German transport. One reason for the lack of air combat was that General Galland was building a fighter reserve for what he hoped would be the largest and most decisive air battle of the war: *Der Grosse Schlag* (The Great Blow). He planned to use more than 3000 aircraft against Allied bombers and their escorts. The object: to shoot down 400 to 500 planes and thus cripple the Allies' air offensive against Germany. By mid-November Galland had 18 fighter wings ready. All he needed was suitable weather.

But the Great Blow was never delivered. On November 20, Galland was ordered to use his fighter force to provide air support for a great land battle. Only a few days in advance did he learn that it was to be Hitler's astonishing three-army counterattack through the Ardennes, aimed at splitting the Allied forces and capturing Antwerp. Galland confessed later that, when he learned his reserve was to be sacrificed for such a futile assault, "I lost all spirit for the further conduct of hostilities."

The Ardennes offensive opened December 16 and for a week bad weather grounded all aircraft. By December 23 the German breakthrough, 50 miles deep in some sectors, had been stemmed. The skies cleared and Allied aircraft, Canada's Spitfires and Typhoons among them, took to the air to seek out the Luftwaffe and strike at German troops and transport. A few days later, a 22-year-old Canadian Spitfire pilot, Flt. Lt. Dick Audet, made air force history.

In the two years since he'd won his wings, the tall, handsome Albertan had never fired at an enemy aircraft. Then on December 29, in the most exciting ten minutes of his life, Audet scored more victories than most pilots *ever* do. At 1 p.m., as enemy fighter activity was reported over Osnabrück, the pilots of 411 Squadron scrambled. As they cruised toward Osnabrück at 10,500 feet, Audet spotted a dozen enemy fighters off his starboard wing. From his combat report:

"The enemy were four Messerschmitt 109s and eight Focke-Wulf 190s, flying line astern. I attacked an Me 109, the last aircraft in the formation. At 200 yards I opened fire and saw strikes all over the fuselage and wing roots. The 109 burst into flames and trailed black smoke.

"I now went around in a defensive circle until I spotted an FW 190. I attacked from 250 yards down to 100 yards and from 30 degrees from line astern. I saw strikes over the cockpit and to the rear of the fuselage. It burst into flames. I saw the pilot slumped in his cockpit.

"Ahead was a 109 going down in a slight dive. It pulled up sharply into a climb, and the cockpit canopy flew off. I gave a short burst at about 300 yards and the aircraft whipped down in a dive. The pilot attempted to bail out, but his chute ripped to shreds. I saw the 109 hit the ground and smash into flaming pieces.

"I next spotted an FW 190 being pursued by a Spitfire, pursued in turn by an FW 190. I called to this pilot—one of my Yellow Section—to break, and attacked the 190 from the rear. We went down in a steep dive. I opened fire at 250 yards and it burst into flames. I saw it go into the ground and burn.

"Several minutes later, while attempting to re-form my section, I spotted an FW 190 at about 2000 feet. I dived on him and he turned into me from the right. He then flipped around in a left-hand turn, and attempted a head-on attack. I slowed down to wait for him to fly into range. At about 200 yards I gave a short burst. I could not see any strikes but he flicked violently and continued to do so until he crashed."

Five in a row! Enough to make Audet an ace. Plus three more scores in the same dogfight by others in the squadron. There was quite a celebration that night, but Audet wasn't in it. He didn't drink and went to bed early, a very tired man.

He was awarded a DFC for his five-in-one victory and then went on to prove that it was no fluke. On New Year's Day he destroyed two more FW 190s. By late February when he went to England to spend leave with his wife, he had brought his score to 11. The day after his return to action he was killed when his Spitfire was hit by anti-aircraft fire during a low-level strike on a railroad siding in Germany.

In its record book, 411 Squadron paid Audet a high tribute: "March 3, 1945: a gloomy and very expensive day . . . modest and unassuming, Dick Audet was just one of the boys and a real credit to Canada. He was a leader, respected and admired by all. Just one swell guy."

By late 1944, as the Germans fell back along the Ardennes front, the Luftwaffe still had plenty of sting. Early New Year's

German fighter ace Adolf Galland (below) and the world's first jet fighter, the Me 262 (left). After testing the prototype in May 1943, Galland said: "It was like flying on the wings of an angel." Hitler rejected a plan to produce 1000 of the new jets each month. He insisted the superb fighter should be used as a bomber. Later, he relented, but the Me 262 came too late to halt the Allied air offensive.

Day it launched a 700-plane strike at Allied airfields in Holland, France and Belgium. The low-flying fighters came in four great waves, two from the east, the others from across the Zuider Zee. Strict radio silence was enforced and the Germans flew wherever possible up snow-covered valleys to escape radar detection. They achieved tactical surprise.

They struck three RCAF airfields, causing particularly heavy losses at Eindhoven, where a Canadian fighter reconnaissance wing and the Typhoon wing were based. Leslie Roberts in *There Shall Be Wings:*

. . . It was 9:20 a.m. Two waves of FW 190s, Me 109s and jets flashed across the field, coming out of the sun. Men dived for ditches, slit trenches, anything that would give cover. Flt. Sgt. W. Large brought down a Focke-Wulf with a Bren gun. Flt. Sgt. Ron Beatty, an armorer, mounted a Bren on a wall and was thought to have brought down another. Other ground crew helped bring in wounded. Seven ground crewmen were killed and 15 wounded.

An RAF officer who was testing his aircraft destroyed a German plane but was shot down a moment later. A Canadian, Flt. Lt. P. Wilson, had begun a takeoff as the enemy swept in. He pulled off the runway, was hit as he climbed out of his aircraft and died shortly after. His No. 2, FO. R. W. Keller, was hit just after becoming airborne. He was found dead in his aircraft at the edge of the field where he crashed. FO. S. Angelini engaged the enemy but was shot down. Flt. Lt. R. F. Gill was wounded while preparing for takeoff.

The attack lasted 22 minutes. Ammunition and bombs exploded for more than an hour. Many aircraft were destroyed, others badly damaged. That afternoon the dead were prepared for burial, including four enemy pilots brought down on or near the field. . . .

At Heesch, the Germans had no luck. When some 40 fighters swept over the field, most of 126 Wing was already in the air. Swiftly recalled to base, the Canadian fighter pilots struck back, destroying 17 German aircraft for the loss of two. Johnson's wing at Evère was less fortunate. "The enemy completely dominated the scene," he wrote. From Johnson's *Wing Leader:*

. . . We could do little except shout with rage as our Spitfires burst into flames before our eyes. Despite the strafing, our airfield controller remained at his post and warned our two airborne Spitfire sections to get back. When they arrived over Evère, the highest Messerschmitts and Focke-Wulfs curved to meet them. Three of our pilots shot down six; Steve Butte got three. But they were too few to drive off 60 Germans, and after using all their ammunition the Spitfires took to their heels. The Luftwaffe withdrew abruptly and we were left to our burning airfield.

One airman had been killed and another nine wounded. Eleven Spitfires were destroyed and 12 damaged.

The operation was a bold stroke. But the Germans could not exploit their advantage. Their shooting was atrocious. They reminded us more of beginners on their first solos than experienced pilots. Strategically, the operation should have been the prelude to the Ardennes offensive. . . .

Adolf Galland agreed with this verdict. In *The First and The Last* he wrote: "The

Luftwaffe received its death blow in the Ardennes offensive. In unfamiliar conditions, coupled with insufficient training and combat experience, our numerical strength had no effect. It was decimated during transfer, on the ground, in large air battles, especially during Christmas, and was finally destroyed. With the large-scale, well-prepared attack on Allied airfields January 1, the enemy's air force was to be paralyzed in one stroke. About 400 Allied planes were destroyed but we lost nearly 300 fighter pilots, including 59 leaders."

A few weeks later, after a stormy confrontation with Göring, Galland was relieved of his post. His request to return to the air as leader of a fighter squadron of Me 262 jets was granted.

In the last months of the war Canada's fighter wings flew sortie after sortie, strafing German strongpoints and airfields, shooting up enemy trains and road convoys. Many missions were in support of First Canadian Army. Other Canadians in RAF wings were also in action. Wing Comdr. George Keefer was now flying leader of 125 Spitfire Wing under the command of Johnnie Johnson who had just been transferred from 127 Wing and promoted to group captain. They made a good pair. From Johnson's *Wing Leader:*

. . . We found a lot of Huns during the latter half of April. We destroyed fighters, bombers, transports, Stuka dive-bombers, trainers and a bunch of seaplanes we found floating on a lake. We could not catch the jets in the air, but we knew they were operating from Lübeck, on the Baltic coast. We paid special attention to this

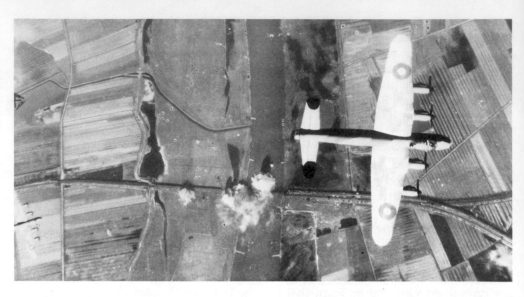

Canadian Spitfire pilot Dick Audet (right) shot down five German aircraft in ten minutes. Six later victories pushed his total to 11. In March 1945, he was among the Allied fighter pilots attacking enemy roads and railways. "Strafing trains," wrote Tom Coughlin in *The Dangerous Sky,* "was especially dangerous since flak cars attached to the trains were heavily armed. On March 3 Audet was flying an armed reconnaissance in the Münster area. He spotted a train and started down. A roar from the train's guns met Audet's oncoming Spitfire. His body was found in the wreckage of his aircraft." Above: a Lancaster commanded by Canadian Gp. Capt. Johnnie Fauquier—"King of the Pathfinders"—hits a bridge with a Grand Slam bomb. Above, right: an RCAF Spitfire squadron, led by Wing Comdr. James F. Edwards of North Battleford, Sask., just before take-off from an airfield near Hamburg, Germany.

airfield, shooting the jets down when they took off or came in to land. Some of the enemy leaders showed flashes of their old brilliance, but the rank and file were poor.

One evening George Keefer led one of the squadrons on a sweep round the far side of the Elbe and I led a finger-four down sun from him. We swung toward an airfield neatly camouflaged in the midst of woods. Heavy flak bracketed us and George led us into the cover of the low sun. On the airfield I saw a squadron of Messerschmitts about to take off.

Five minutes later we returned in a fast dive from the sun. The 109s were still there. Hundreds of light flak guns joined the heavy barrage against us.

I twisted my neck for a final look at the airfield. All 11 Messerschmitts were burning fiercely. It was the best and bravest strafing attack I had ever seen. . . .

J. E. JOHNSON

For Bomber Command, the last year of the war provided a payoff for the grim night battles over Germany in the winter offensive of 1943-44. Despite massive destruction in German cities, that offensive had neither broken German morale nor crippled German war production. In its last phase—the Battle of Berlin—German night fighters and anti-aircraft gunners had inflicted such heavy casualties that the bombers could not have sustained such losses much longer.

In the spring and summer of 1944 Bomber Command largely broke off the offensive to provide tactical support for the invasion forces and to hit flying bomb sites. In September it girded for the second round of the Battle of Germany. But the position now was different. Germany's air defense was crumbling and effective command of the air had passed to the Allies. Protected by packs of long-range fighters, American daylight bombers hit German targets with greater accuracy. The Allied advance through France and Belgium had robbed the Germans of their frontline night-fighter defense and early-warning radar posts along the Channel. So night-raiding Bomber Command formations, too, were able to strike harder and more often.

In the summer of 1944 the Americans began a systematic air offensive against Germany's fuel supplies—the lifeblood of its military forces. In September, Bomber

My heart sank. Probably we all thought the same thing: the war could only last a few more days. The pilots of the 109s below had probably left their cockpits for the engines had stopped. What were the chances of getting through the flak now that the gunners were roused? I reckoned they were about 50-50.

George said: "Graycap, I'm going in with my No. 2. Cover us, will you?"

I wanted to say "Is it worth it?" but only muttered: "Okay, George."

The two Spitfires got smaller and smaller as they went down in a fast dive. Their gray-green camouflage merged into the spring greenery below and for a second or two I lost them. But the gunners on the ground still saw them, and the whole airfield seemed to sparkle with flashes from the guns.

We saw the Spits again when they streaked over the boundary of the airfield. We saw George's cannon shells bouncing on the concrete. I shouted into my microphone: "Up a bit, George, you're underdeflecting!"

Then his shells ripped into the last Messerschmitt in the line. It caught fire, its ammunition exploded and the cannon shells slammed into the next 109. In a matter of seconds the whole lot were blazing and a great spiral of white smoke curled up from the airfield.

"You all right, George?"

"Fine, Graycap. Am climbing up."

"Red 2?"

"I've been hit, sir, but she's flying," replied the wingman.

"Lead him home, George, and we'll cover you," I instructed.

Command joined the offensive, starting with attacks on ten synthetic oil plants in the Ruhr. German roads, railways, canals and bridges had been hard hit during the invasion and now took further punishment. At the same time the Command continued its attacks on German towns and industrial centers. Canada's 6 Group was in the thick of it. Leslie Roberts in *There Shall Be Wings:*

. . . The group put a record 293 four-engine bombers into the air the night of October 6 as part of a 523-plane attack on Dortmund. The German ground controllers were confused by the attackers' clouds of aluminum foil called Window, which jammed their ground-to-air communications, and by a diversionary air strike. Only two 6 Group crews were lost.

A week later the group took part in two raids in which 2000 aircraft hit Duisburg with 9200 tons of bombs—only slightly less than all the bombs dropped on London during the whole war. The Canadian group's contribution was 501 Lancasters and Halifaxes. The fires of Duisburg could be seen for 180 miles as the crews flew home to Yorkshire. Canadian losses were only five aircraft—one percent.

All the targets of 1943 were hit again during the winter of 1944-45: Cologne, Essen, Stuttgart, Düsseldorf, Bochum, Münster, Karlsruhe, Nuremberg, Hanover, Bremen—and always Hamburg. Hamburg had been pulverized in 1943, but had restored a good deal of its capacity to make war. The last vicious defense encountered by the Allies occurred over that crippled port city in daylight March 31, 1945. Thirty Me 262 jet fighters intercepted the bombers over the target and were skillfully directed by ground controllers to stragglers and to formations not protected by fighter cover. The last Canadian Lancasters were ten minutes behind schedule and made their bomb runs under heavy attack from jets. Eight Canadian aircraft were lost. . . .

In these final months of war, Canada's "King of the Pathfinders," Johnnie Fauquier, was on his third tour of operations and winning his third DSO.

When he heard the RAF's celebrated Dambuster Squadron, No. 617, needed a new leader, he was an air commodore in a staff appointment. He took a demotion to group captain to get back into battle in December 1944. When the weather

cleared, they made war against enemy convoys off Norway, against attacking fighters, against U-boat pens along the coast of Europe.

Their Lancasters were now dropping 12,000-pound Tallboy bombs. For maximum effect, they had to be delivered with superb accuracy from about 20,000 feet. With the aid of a new gyroscopic sight, the Dambusters were soon knocking out whole factory complexes.

After Fauquier arrived, they got an even more devastating weapon, the 22,000-pound Grand Slam, the biggest bomb of the war. It was so big—more than 26 feet tall and up to 3 feet 10 inches in diameter—that the planes had to be strengthened and the bomb doors taken off to accommodate it.

In March, the Allied air forces made an all-out assault on German communications to cut the country into "islands" that could be taken one by one. The Dambusters went after bridges and viaducts. In *The Dam Busters,* Paul Brickhill describes one attack:

. . . One day they went to the Nienburg Bridge, near Bremen, over which the Germans were taking oil to the front. It was not heavily defended, so Fauquier evolved a plan to try and save some of the precious new bombs. He ordered four aircraft to start their runs and told the others to circle nearby and wait for orders in case the first four missed. It was an unprecedented idea, and the very fact that Fauquier considered it possible speaks eloquently of their phenomenal accuracy. He himself dived low to watch.

The results were fantastic. The four Lancasters made a steady run in loose formation and bombed almost in the same second. Fauquier saw the first two bombs hit simultaneously (one of them a

Grand Slam) on each end of the bridge. The bridge span lifted bodily and still intact into the air, seemed to hang there a second, and in that very moment a third bomb hit it fair and square in the middle. When the smoke had cleared there was no visible sign of the bridge and the squadron turned for home, taking their 15 remaining bombs with them. Fauquier said when he landed, "Hell, I'd hate to have to do *that* again to prove it."

When there were no worthwhile bridges left, 617 went back at the U-boat pens. Then a recce plane reported that Germany's last pocket battleship, *Lützow,* was sheltering in Swinemünde, in the Baltic, where fighters could be expected. The Dambusters slogged up there April 13 only to find it smothered under cloud. They went back two days later; ten-tenths cloud again. By this time it was obvious they were after *Lützow.* Fauquier guessed the German fighters would be alerted and he asked for, and got, an escort of long-

Many German factories had gone deep underground and managed to maintain production despite Allied bombing. Right: accompanied by government, party and local officials, Hitler inspects bomb damage in a German town.

range fighters. Next day they went back again with the fighters and found the target clear but the flak waiting for them.

They picked out *Lützow* far below, a microbe on the water beside the quay, and as they turned on her, the flak burst with deadly accuracy on the unwavering formation. Puffs blotched the patch of sky in which they moved so that nearly every one of the 18 bombers was hit and holes opened in wings and fuselages as shrapnel ripped through. A heavy shell got a direct hit on one plane; it spun down dragging a tail of flame like a comet. One parachute came out.

Then the gaggle was peeling off out of the flak as the bombs went down. Three hit close together, straddling the ship. Other bombs vanished into the spray and smoke that enveloped her.

They flew back unmolested and next morning were stood down completely. After the flak only two aircraft were serviceable, and the ground crews toiled

over the others. The aircrews were content to relax and await news of *Lützow*. The recce aircraft landed with photographs, and such was the squadron's self-confidence that a howl of incredulity went up as they saw *Lützow* still by the quay, apparently untouched. The recce pilot swore there was no mistake. He had flown right over her, and there, indubitably, she lay, decks clearly visible.

It was two days before they found that *Lützow* had sunk as far as the seabed would let her. A near miss had torn out her bottom. Later someone in the navy claimed she was not *really* sunk because her decks were still above water. . . .

PAUL BRICKHILL

By mid-April, with armies engulfing Germany from west and east, there were no major targets left. For the bomber crews the war was over. How effective had they been? Cajus Bekker in *The Luftwaffe War Diaries* gave a German viewpoint:

"Bomber Command's decision to end the war by carpet-bombing German cities was unsuccessful. The morale of the inhabitants stood up to the test, and the decentralization of factories enabled war production to reach its highest output in 1944, at the peak of the bombardment. Victory was due much more to the overwhelming superiority of the Allies' tactical air forces during and after the invasion, and to the strategic bombing of fuel-production installations and transportation—all of which hastened the collapse of the German armed forces. Attacks on military targets, not those on the civil population, decided the issue."

A British historian, Dr. Noble Frankland, came to the same conclusion. In the *History of the Second World War*, Frankland wrote:

. . . It took longer to get effective results than most prewar advocates of bombing had expected. Effective damage required a more sustained and greater weight of attack than expected. This was because the Germans were much more resilient than had seemed likely, and because repair, recovery and substitution was more efficient than expected.

The effectiveness of anti-aircraft guns and fighters had a greater impact on bombing efficiency than experts had envisaged. So much so that Allied bombing had little effect upon Germany until her air defenses were overcome. Even then, an all-out Allied effort in the air was prevented not only by weather, but also by disagreements within the high command as to the best targets. Thus, the bombers' efforts were divided between a variety of aims to an extent that delayed the fulfillment of any. . . .

Of the men who had no say in such decisions, whose job was to fly the missions, Sir Arthur Harris, chief of Bomber Command, said in *Bomber Offensive:*

"There are no words with which I can do justice to the aircrew under my command. There is no parallel in warfare for such courage and determination in the face of prolonged danger, at times so great that scarcely one man in three could expect to survive his tour of 30 operations. Of those who survived their first tour, between six and seven thousand undertook a second, and many a third. It was a clear and highly conscious courage. Such devotion must never be forgotten."

The lonely years

**Escape attempts, futility, despair, a forced march:
the war that prisoners knew**

Above: an International Red Cross official and the camp commandant watch as Allied soldiers peel potatoes in a German prison in August 1940. These men faced nearly five years of imprisonment and suffered the whims of sometimes brutal guards. Left: an illicit photograph of a guard at Stalag III, part of remarkable photographic documentation of prison-camp life by Canadian Flt. Sgt. Kenneth Hyde. The longer the war lasted, the greater were the privations the POWs suffered. "A man's eyes betray his hunger," Flt. Lt. Robert Buckham of Montreal wrote in a prison camp in January 1945. "Watch them recede and narrow as they probe within for the taste of remembered meals. Watch them again as the rations are served, comparing size of portion, measuring width of bread slice. An empty belly is a very basic thing."

Thousands of Canadians spent some part of the war behind barbed wire in prisoner-of-war camps. "Not a few," says one ex-POW, "came out better than they entered, an achievement that must be regarded as a triumph of the human spirit." But many, as one of them wrote, were men "alternating between hope and despair till their numbed hearts could feel no more; fighting without encouragement

against approaching lethargy, with the blight of futility on all they did."

They combated the blight with lectures, athletics, theater, correspondence courses, religious services, talk of home—and often with dreams and hopes and plans of escape. Each camp had its escape committee and each made its own plans. In the majority of cases the prisoners decided to try tunnels. A man wasn't apt to be shot digging a tunnel and, if it got through, it might be used by many men.

Just such a mass break was being planned at Stalag Luft III's north camp when Rod Ball of Kitchener, Ont., got there in late 1943. It was destined to become famous, in books and movie, as *The Great Escape.*

Ball was an airman who had been shot down. A former trapper and Mountie, he'd survived, almost incredibly, on the night of June 12-13, 1943, when his gunner's glass turret was thrown free in the crash of a bomber shot down by flak near Caen, France. One leg broken, one arm useless, he crawled to the burning wreckage. The first three men he found were

dead. The pilot, terribly injured, was jammed into the fuselage. Ball had just worked him free and was trying to help him when the Germans came.

Ball was eventually sent to the central camp at Stalag Luft III, a prison halfway between Berlin and Breslau (now Wroclaw, Poland) for Commonwealth and American air force officers. Later he was transferred to the north camp.

Chances of escape from such a stronghold seemed hopeless. Set in a thick dark forest, it was surrounded by two high barbed-wire fences, seven feet apart. Great rolls of barbed wire were packed in the space between. A safety wire was 40 feet inside the inner fence. One foot past this wire would draw machine-gun fire and searchlights from the many guard towers.

In *Men of Valour,* Mabel T. Good tells what happened:

. . . When Rod Ball learned that plans for an escape attempt were well organized, he volunteered and was accepted. The idea was to dig a tunnel—under the hut, under the prison yard, under the very guard towers—which would emerge into the forest. Each man was given the task best suited to him. Civil engineers planned the tunnel [Canadian Wally Floody in charge of building it], miners dug, tailors gathered pieces of cloth to make civilian clothing. Identification papers were forged, maps traced. Getting rid of the earth and sand from the tunnel was a problem. It was solved by sewing long sacks inside the men's trousers. The sacks were filled and tied with drawstrings. The carriers wandered off to join groups watching softball or volleyball games. Men crowded about them. The carriers released their loads and dozens of feet stamped the spilled earth into the ground.

So the work went, month after weary month. Finally the tunnel measured 240 feet. One day in March 1944, the diggers bored upward until they came to tree roots. They built makeshift ladders into the shaft and two days later all was ready.

Although nearly 600 men had worked on the project, only about 200 could hope to get through in one night. About 50 of the leaders were to go first; 20 others were chosen by secret ballot and another 140 names drawn from a hat, Rod Ball's among them.

The night of March 24 was dark and windy. Snow covered the ground. Each

man had been supplied with a map showing his route. Tense with excitement, Ball and the others waited.

Finally the signal to start. One by one, the men worked down into the earth. When the first man pushed through the earth covering the opening at the end of the tunnel, he discovered the passageway was not long enough. Instead of being hidden by the woods, the outlet was ten feet short of the forest. Not 15 yards from the gaping hole, a guard tower loomed against the sky.

It was too late to turn back. The leader climbed out and wriggled toward the forest. He let out a rope behind him to signal to the second man when to start. One by one the men emerged, slithered across the snow and vanished into the trees. There they struck off in different directions.

Rod Ball and 75 other prisoners escaped before a guard came upon the tunnel's exit and raised the alarm. Thousands of German troops and police were turned loose in the hunt.

Rod Ball's route led him straight through the woods. He walked all night and by morning had traveled quite a distance. His years as a Mountie had taught him many of the tricks of flight. Yet all his skill could not hide his tracks in the soft snow when daylight came. Before the sun was high in the sky, his pursuers had overtaken him. In a short time, he was back in Stalag Luft III.

Only three men made good their escape. Others who, like Rod Ball, were taken by local guards, were returned to prison. But 50 were not so lucky. They were captured by the Gestapo. A few days later the commandant of Stalag Luft III announced that they had all been shot elsewhere.

Rod Ball was present when the badly shaken survivors joined in a memorial service for their executed comrades. Then the ache of prison life resumed again. . . .

The murder of the escapees was ordered by Hitler himself, in violation of the Geneva Convention governing prisoners of war. Among the slain men were six Canadians: James Wernham, George Wiley, Patrick Langford, George McGill, Henry Birkland and Gordon Kidder.

Of the many other escape attempts, few succeeded. Only three RCAF airmen, for instance, broke out of prison camps and reached Britain or Allied lines: Warrant Officer H. E. Brooks who got to Poland, fought with its underground and eventually came out through Russia; Sgt. C. E. Macdonald who got to England via Spain and Gibraltar; Sgt. J. L. N. Warren who reached Allied lines in Holland.

Probably the worst treated of all Canadian prisoners were the nearly 1700 captured at Hong Kong in 1941 and kept in camps on that island until 1943. Primarily because of wretched conditions there, 128 died. Four others were shot by the Japanese without trial when captured after escaping. A diphtheria epidemic in 1942 took 50 lives, mainly because of the refusal of proper medical facilities by the Japanese. Of the remaining Canadians, 1184 were taken to Japan and forced to work, chiefly in mines. The conditions were so bad that 136 men died.

The nearly 1900 Canadians captured at Dieppe on August 19, 1942, suffered the indignity and discomfort of shackling because the Germans discovered that the

bitter wind. Snow on the roof, ice on the windowpanes. Door, windows sealed with ice. Candlelike flames struggle pitifully in the stove, feed reluctantly, miserably on practically uninflammable lignite. Smoke and gas ooze through the cracked top of the stove and mingle with the cold, sour air of the hut.

Everyone's in his bunk hiding from the depressing externals, covering up from realities, the cold, the wind, the gloom, the squalor; they're cuddling private thoughts, carousing on memories, banqueting on hope, fermenting petty grievances, rubbing the sheen back on faded yesterdays, limelighting those fantastically pleasant tomorrows that never come. On winter Sunday afternoons you crawl under the blankets with melancholy and hate and love. Someone comes in and four men yell together: "Shut that bloody door!" A bugle goes. It's four o'clock. Hitler's Third Reich gives us our evening meal, a jug of boiling water. . . .

below zero—noon 29/1/45

Dieppe military plan contained this instruction: "Wherever possible, prisoners' hands will be tied to prevent destruction of their documents."

"We were in shackles for one year, 44 days and 45 minutes," said Lt. Col. R. R. Labatt of the Royal Hamilton Light Infantry. Then, following conversations with the International Red Cross, the Germans stopped all shackling.

Sgt. Kenneth N. Laing, a Spitfire pilot who had crash-landed in France in November 1941, was among Canadians who were imprisoned. He kept a logbook. One entry, written by a fellow prisoner, is entitled "Stalag Sunday":

. . . It's quiet, one of those few occasions in the hut when someone isn't shouting, arguing, whining, quarreling, bragging. Men are whipped, cowed by frost and a

For tens of thousands, imprisonment reached a grotesque climax in the last winter of the war. Over large areas of Germany that January, great masses of prisoners were on the move away from the advancing Russians. One was Flt. Lt. Robert Buckham, an artist from Montreal who was a prisoner at Stalag Luft III. Buckham stood six-feet-four-inches tall and weighed 214 pounds when he was shot down on a bombing raid in April 1943. Here are extracts from his diary of a march that left him weighing 164 pounds. It begins in prison camp:

. . . **January 25:** The camp is tense tonight. The Russians are only 46 miles distant. Tomorrow could be our day. Packs to carry what we need are in major production under the guidance and supervision of Rod Ball. Iron ration is being pre-

Two visual records of the great forced marches of 1945 as the Germans herded prisoners away from the advancing Russian Army. Top, left: one of Flt. Lt. Robert Buckham's fine sketches. Above: a photograph that Flt. Sgt. Kenneth Hyde of Calgary made with camera and film smuggled into and out of Stalag III.

pared as well: a "dry" cake made with finely ground biscuits, chocolate powder, raisins, prunes (pitted) and black-bread crumbs. These are mixed with warm margarine which hardens as it cools. The finished product looks like chewing tobacco and resembles it in other ways too.

Near panic tonight at an unconfirmed rumor that the goons [German guards] were pulling out and leaving us behind.

January 27, 11:30 p.m.: We have been

waiting to leave for over two hours. The room is a shambles. Torn bedding, broken glass, splintered bunks, discarded clothing and boots. Brod is semi-reclining on the remnants of his bed, full pack bulging over his greatcoat collar, cursing the goons. Steve is portioning the iron ration. Pappy Crozier and Cliffe are swearing in frustration as they attach straps to their hurriedly completed packs. Les is searching for better boots. Buckholz and Bruce, two Americans, are creating a sled from the two sideboards of a bunk by nailing bed boards to them.

12:30 a.m.: Still waiting. The CO has issued orders that no one is to attempt to escape during the march.

We are to be the last to go. West camp is still moving out through the wire in an unbroken line, four abreast. Searchlights probe the camp. Doors and windows are open, ignoring the blackout. The night is clear and very cold, with strong wind.

Eight of us plan to travel as a group. Each will carry a bag. Extra food is in a canvas bag roped to our sled. I have a change of underwear, socks and shoes. We carry as many cigarettes as possible. For personal use and for barter. Prolonged waiting has sapped our strength. Utterly weary.

January 29: We are resting in a pub in a hamlet named Priebus. Yesterday was rough. We left camp at 4 a.m. Food parcels were issued, one per man. The added weight and bulk had not been reckoned for. The cartons were torn open, a few items selected, the remainder cast aside. Guttural shouts harried us as packs and sleds were readjusted.

The road disappeared into the darker mass of the forest, the trees soft in silhouette and taller than imagined from inside the camp. We passed a farm wagon, canvas-covered, hauled by a dejected horse. We heard a woman's soft laughter from within. Why laughter?

Roadside ditches were littered with castoffs. Jettisoned clothing, boots, food, blankets and even cooking grates half-projected from the snow. The guards and a few civilians followed us, scavenging.

We left the forest, the sheltering forest. At dawn our line of march stretched to the horizon. The wind mingled with driving snow. From midday on, we marched in below-zero temperatures. Food froze in the cans. Bread snapped into granular chunks. The column trudged on for an estimated 36 kilometers [23 miles].

Feet froze. A limp became commonplace.

We halted in the bitter night, barely aware of the snow and wind. Too cold to light a cigarette. Gp. Capt. Larry Wray, senior Canadian officer, walked the length of the column and back, offering advice and encouragement.

At last we were shouted into a farmyard. In the stable, I fell to the straw-covered floor and leaned against the steaming side of a reclining horse. Unfrozen biscuits provided my meal. Someone vomited, groaned and vomited again. I had no reaction.

Miserably cold, I walked to a barn in the swirling snow and picked my way through the confusion of shouting figures and abandoned sleds. Climbing a ladder, I found space in the hay and, wrapped in everything I possessed, I slept.

On leaving the barn this morning, we stumbled over a snow-covered mound near our sled—an American named McLachlan wrapped in a frozen blanket. Semiconscious, he mumbled only a few words. We fed him hot coffee and lashed him to our laden sled. He thrashed about in his delirium and we gradually fell back with the lame and the stragglers at the end of the column.

There are about 15 of us in this pub, plus guards. The others have gone ahead. We rub McLachlan's ankles, wrists and feet in an attempt to restore circulation.

Difficult to stay awake in this warmth. An old woman and three girls have provided hot water and beer. They seem quite unaware of the Russian advance.

January 30, Muscau: Seated in warm dry straw, well fed and with an antiquated bathtub gurgling a few feet away. McLachlan was left at the pub with a lame RAF type. A German doctor gave him medicine and left instructions for nursing.

Extremely tired, we pressed on into a

> "A roar of cheers.... Laughter and tears.... Thousands of men in a state of hysterical, bewildered, blessed release. We were free...."

blinding snowstorm. In midafternoon we were hailed by three Americans who had been hiding in some deserted barns. All three were miserably cold and lame. We added their loads to our sled and pushed on. Our guards seemed indifferent to their presence. The Americans said three men in their column were shot last night while attempting a dash to the woods.

At dusk we came upon a large beer hall and were greeted by about 40 men spread out on the straw-covered floor. After a brief meal I washed my feet, more for the heat than for cleanliness, changed my socks and found a place on the floor as near as possible to the stove.

A horse-drawn, two-wheeled vehicle appeared this morning into which we placed about 30 sick or lame men. We walked until noon in weather which grew steadily milder. At Muscau, we were directed to the stableyard of a castle. The main stable is a multi-storied building and there are various one-story buildings, some of them combined stables and living quarters. I discovered a small room at the rear of a stall. It contained a four-legged bathtub with hot running water, and a straw-covered floor large enough to sleep eight.

A heated discussion as to who would first enjoy our first hot bath in years. Eight men in various stages of undress, reclining, standing, voices raised, periodi-cally obscured by clouds of steam. Hot water gushing from the pipe. A happy, humid hell!

A carpentry shop was made available and individual sleds were built for future marching. Food was divided as it appears that the American prisoners will leave us shortly.

The weather is becoming increasingly mild and the slush has disclosed leaks in my boots. Pappy is limping from a lame knee, but otherwise we are in fair shape.

This afternoon I went outside the camp area with a New Zealander named Christensen. We went to a house to bar-ter for food. A teen-age boy answered

our knock and called his mother. We exchanged cigarettes for bread. They appeared to be quite friendly.

Christensen went back to the castle but I walked into town. No undue attention was paid me, although I was in uniform with "Canada" patches on my shoulders. Some children did ask for cigarettes. I ignored them. The streets were filled with troops.

When I got back, the gate guard met me with loud language. But there seems to be little organization among the goons.

·**January 31:** Our blankets exactly filled the floor space of our room. Eight men, a small room, no open window and hot-steam pipes combined to make an over-warm atmosphere, but we slept well.

This morning I extended the hospitality of our bath to Group Captain Wray. The tub has seldom been empty, but its use is by invitation only, else we'd be forced to repel another D-Day invasion.

The Americans are leaving us today, bound for Bremen. We "British" are scheduled to depart tomorrow, to march 29 kilometers to Spremberg where we are to entrain.

Evening, same day: I returned to the house which had proved so hospitable yesterday. I was asked into the living room and, after trading cigarettes for bread, I asked if some beer, wine or schnapps were available for trade. The mother returned with a bottle of Jamaica rum and poured me nearly a full glass. I drank it while attempting conversation with them. The boy let me out through the cellar in a very cautious manner.

My return to the camp was as ludicrous as yesterday's. How absurd to have to talk one's way into a prison camp!

February 1: In the night I was violently sick. A large cup of powdered milk for breakfast improved my condition. Later some of us went foraging. We acquired two eggs at one house, but at the next we received a thorough tongue-lashing. We came upon a tiny cottage in the woods. We were greeted by an old lady who invited us in with birdlike motions. The room was so low that I couldn't stand erect. Seated at a table beneath an oversized chandelier, she served us two glasses of milk into which we broke our eggs. She accepted some instant coffee in exchange and, after shaking her hand, we headed back to camp. In our absence, one

sixth of a food parcel per man was issued. Food is becoming scarce.

At 10:30 p.m. we marched out in ragged order. The streets were bare and pocketed with slush. I began to sweat freely. Warmth turned to fever and then to chills and nausea.

Outside the town we faced a steep cobblestone hill which climbed for a mile or more. I found myself stumbling, unable to drag my sled or lift my feet. Vomiting, retching, I sank to the roadside. It was decided to have me wait for the sick wagon. Pappy elected to remain with me, but a guard struck him repeatedly with a rifle, forcing him to move on.

Dazed, retching, I remained on the roadside until the column had disappeared. Three guards hauled me to my feet. Two supported me for several yards, the other pulled my sled. A motorcyclist in leather uniform approached and I was placed on the pillion, my pack in the sidecar. The sled was abandoned. I hung on dizzily until we stopped at the front of the entire column.

I felt better but severe cramps began when I resumed marching. My side trips to the pines bordering the road became frequent but provided only momentary relief from diarrhea. Weakness eventually overcame pride, and I asked Minnie Walker to carry my pack while I pushed his possessions, which were lashed to a bicycle.

Within a few kilometers I collapsed. Some time later I moved on, half crawling, and stumbled to a farmhouse. I sat on the doorstep while the column passed by. No one saw me in the darkness, and I had no desire to call for assistance.

A few stragglers, vague silhouettes, slowly followed the others. Then deep silence, broken only by the sound of distant explosions. Time passed unheeded until the realization filtered through that further delay would be pointless. I shrugged into my packstraps and began to walk up the empty road. I overtook a few stragglers and went on with them.

At the approach of dawn, word was passed back that our destination was about one kilometer ahead. My legs gave away again. I collapsed and lay there utterly spent, unable to raise my head from the slush.

February 2 (recorded at a later date): I lay on the floor of a barn this morning. I was helped to my feet and told to wait for

the sick wagon. The column walked past, unshaven, bedraggled and weary.

The wagon carried us about 18 kilometers, then stopped at an army barracks. I rested briefly in a garage before a recurrence of diarrhea and vomiting. In the waning afternoon we walked three kilometers. We passed large numbers of tanks, gray shapes in the dusk.

The column came to a halt in a train yard. We were ordered into wooden boxcars, barely distinguishable in the light of flickering lanterns. The doors closed and the eerie light vanished. The bolts were shot. The train moved off. We had no water, no light, no straw for bedding. Forty men crowded into dark confinement, attempting to create order from the jumble of gear, bedrolls, clothing. A lamp was lit. Some men lay down, some slept sitting, some just stood. The Australian alongside me grew violent during the night. We could do little for him. Dysentery.

February 4: The train stopped at Tarmstedt, about 160 miles northwest of Berlin, at 4 p.m. We formed up and began to march in a drizzling rain, which developed into a downpour by the time we arrived at a navy camp two hours later. The column halted at the gates. Not unlike cattle, we turned our backs to the wind and rain. Minutes became hours. The probing lights revealed a squalid scene: men tightly packed together from the gates to the end of the rutted cinder roadway half a mile distant. We became more silent as the hours went by. Word filtered back that each man must be searched prior to entry into the camp. We waited six hours in the rain.

We had another forced march in April and reached Lübeck, near the Baltic, in two weeks. Then on May 2 the British came. From a parapet around our barracks prison we watched aircraft attacking, saw the nearby city gradually disappear in smoke. In late afternoon a tank stopped outside the camp. The turret opened and a khaki figure waved.

A roar of cheers. Crudely made flags waving. Laughter and tears. The guards running off, weaponless. Men embracing one another, shouting incoherently. Men kneeling to pray. Thousands of men in a state of hysterical, bewildered, blessed release. We were free. . . .

ROBERT BUCKHAM

Outfits of quite superior individuals

Throughout the winter of 1944-45, the Allied forces fought to get to the Rhine River, Hitler's last major defensive barrier. Finally, on the night of March 23, thousands of British and American assault troops crossed the swift, 500-yard-wide waterway with all the help that planes and guns, rockets, amphibious tanks and vehicles could provide. The attack was concentrated on an 18-mile front around Wesel. Success would mean the isolation of the great but battered Ruhr industrial complex immediately to the south and Allied penetration deep into Germany. As reinforcements, including troops of Canada's 3rd Division, pushed across, the stage was set for the climax—an airborne strike beyond the bridgehead.

The core of this attack was two divisions, the 17th U.S. and the 6th British, and their craft—nearly 3,000 planes and gliders—came from Britain and France to rendezvous at 10 a.m. on March 24. Suddenly the clear morning sky was vivid with parachutes, with gliders drifting into the morning haze, with masses of fighter planes flying protection. It was the largest airdrop of the war and, reported correspondent Ross Munro, "Never in this war has there been such a spectacle. From the banks of the Rhine, we watched it spellbound."

Somewhere in this spectacular assault was the 600-man 1st Parachute Battalion, a Canadian unit with the 6th British division. The battalion was one of two units that had made outstanding contributions to Canada's fighting record. The other was the First Special Service Force—or the Force, as it was called—an elite unit of both Canadians and Americans.

Although these two units never saw action together, less than two days separated their roles in two historic events. On the morning of June 4, 1944, the First Special Service Force became the first Allied unit to enter Rome and early on the morning of June 6, the Canadian paratroops were among the first Allied soldiers to land in France on D-Day.

Both units were formed in 1942. The parachute battalion included officers and senior NCOs handpicked from army units across Canada and Britain. The First Special Service Force had some 700 Canadians and 1700 Americans of all ranks distributed throughout three regiments. It was a tough outfit, trained to drop by parachute and fight in mountains or on skis.

The Force had its first taste of mountain fighting in Italy in December 1943, when it helped take a group of German-held hills barring the Allied advance on Rome. Two battalions scaled the sheer face of a 3000-foot peak and drove the enemy from their caves and pillboxes around the summit. Within four days, all the neighboring ridges were also cleared. The Force had done superbly in its first action, but it had suffered 400 casualties. Canadian losses totaled 27 killed and 64 wounded.

Later the same month, the Force was sent to fight alongside U.S. troops on the approaches to Cassino. And, in February 1944, the unit was committed to the Anzio beachhead, which the Allies had established in an attempt to outflank German forces south of Rome.

Churchill called the Force's leader, U.S. Maj. Gen. Robert Frederick, "the greatest fighting general of all time." The Force itself won the nickname "The Devil's Brigade," a term apparently inspired by the blackened faces members wore on patrols and in battle. A German officer's diary recorded: "The black devils are around us every time we come into the line, and we never hear them come."

In May 1944, after breaking out from Anzio, the black devils teamed up with an armored task force to lead the final drive on Rome. They entered the city limits at 6:30 a.m. on June 4 and, by nightfall, they had broken German resistance and captured six bridges intact. Between the beachhead breakout and the capture of the Italian capital, 185 Canadians were injured or killed.

The Force ended its fighting days in August in the largely unopposed invasion of southern France and was disbanded later that year. The Americans were formed into an infantry regiment; the Canadians went back to their own army, some of them to the 1st Parachute Battalion.

That unit was still in action in France in August, something it hadn't expected. On D-Day one company had landed in Normandy just after midnight with an advance party assigned to secure a main drop zone. The rest of the battalion came down about an hour later but some planeloads were badly scattered and 84 Canadians were captured. Nevertheless, one company covered a British attack on a coastal gun battery; another destroyed a vital bridge. Then they came together to establish the 6th Airborne Division on the eastern flank of the Allied invasion. They expected to be withdrawn to make another parachute drop. Instead, they fought as infantry for three months, and their ranks were badly depleted before they got back to Britain.

The paratroops' second jump into combat was the spectacular drop behind the Rhine on March 24, 1945. Under severe fire, they suffered 65 casualties. But they also killed and captured hundreds of German soldiers and saw Cpl. Fred Topham win a Victoria Cross.

Then, once again, the battalion fought as infantry, advancing on the right flank of Field Marshal Montgomery's 21st Army Group, and penetrating deeper into Germany than any other Canadian unit. Their easygoing attitude was admired. One British soldier reported overhearing a Canadian sergeant giving orders: "I guess we gotta get this bridge and if we hit anything don't you guys sit around. Let's go." They won the respect, too, of the British officers who led their brigade and their division. Just as the First Special Service Force had, they also considered themselves a crack unit, and with justification. As Sgt. R. F. Anderson remarked, the 1st Parachute Battalion was "an outfit of quite superior individuals."

As the war drew toward its close, those superior individuals found German soldiers pouring into their lines. Sometimes they outnumbered the Canadians 50-1, were fully armed and angry that nobody would take them prisoner. Capt. Russell Harrison obliged one group. He found one German who understood English, gave him a map and told him where they could all go to be officially captured.

Behind the fleeing German soldiers came the victorious Russian armies. In Wismar the Canadians became the first troops of any British formation to meet them on the battlefield—and the only Canadians to do so. In the next few days there were many handshakes and many vodka toasts to Stalin and King George.

Then camaraderie and friendship gave way to growing Russian hostility and belligerence. On May 7, the day before VE-Day, Sergeant Anderson made a sad but prophetic entry in his platoon diary: "On the surface and at our level at least, the Russians seem more like an enemy than an ally."

A victory won, a nation renewed

Canada liberates Holland, loses a hero in the Pacific, and the troops return home to a nation transformed by war

When Mrs. C. Hilsum-Beuckens looked out her window one morning in April 1945, there were Canadian soldiers in the streets of the little Dutch town of Delden. Six tired men stood on her doorstep looking for a place to sleep. She took them in and later told about it in a book called *Thank you, Canada:*

. . . We examined them with interest and called them Tommies. Smiling tolerantly, they said that they weren't Tommies but Canadians. Six! Where was I going to find room for them all? We still had four people with us who had been hiding from the Germans. "Put a couple of beds side by side," the Canadian lieutenant advised us. "They're not hard to please."

A few minutes later our house was unrecognizable. Machine guns, rifles, shovels, grenades, kit bags lay everywhere and the soldiers were stretched out in our chairs.

One, Lesage, was of Belgian descent. He spoke a little Flemish and, at 21, had a wife and two children. He proudly showed us a snapshot of them. There was a boy who looked like Mickey Rooney. His name was Hearst and he was 19. Kelly and Garnett were the names of two others. When they saw we had little to eat they immediately gave us food. Both had just had a birthday. Kelly was 29 and beginning to grow bald, Garnett was 19. The corporal, Podolski, was a friendly good-looking boy. I have forgotten the name of the sixth.

Lesage discovered our violin and scraped away happily on it. They took our children off to their unit's cookhouse, brought back a large jug of tea, sugar and milk and thick slices of dazzlingly white bread. They sat talking about "back home" and what they were going to do when the war was over. Then they went to bed.

They'd been on the go for 40 hours without a break. I was to call them at seven o'clock. And I did. I shouted and knocked until my knuckles were red. At last one answered. While dressing they joked about my attempts to wake them: "I thought I was in heaven when I heard a woman's voice" and "Just like being back home." They washed and shaved all over the house as if they had lived there all their lives. They sang, punched and kidded one another, and laughed at me for asking whether they had slept well.

They did all sorts of things for us that day. Lesage scraped away on the violin, and the corporal had various jobs to do. Hearst slept. One wrote letters. Kelly and Garnett rustled up firewood and food, heaven knows where from, and we all felt completely at ease with one another.

In the evening a message came that they were to be ready to leave on five minutes' notice. Two went to bed fully dressed, four sat up with us. We told them about our Resistance movement, they told us about their homes. I had to promise to write to their families.

We sat in the dark, our glowing cigarettes signaling our positions like tiny beacons. Now and then we heard guns in the distance. My heart ached as I listened to their stories, plans and fears. All of them were afraid. Afraid that even now, at the eleventh hour of the war, something might happen to them.

Next morning the dreaded message came: they had to leave. Without a word they picked up their gear and put on their camouflaged tin hats. "Keep your fingers crossed," one of them said, and they left. . . .   MRS. C. HILSUM-BEUCKENS

The Canadians were crowning their war with the liberation of Holland, a country about the size of southwestern Ontario and with a population then of nine million. And they came just in time. The Dutch were facing the threat of starvation following the worst winter in five bitter years of German occupation. The winter had been terrible in itself but it was made worse because the Dutch *had* hoped for freedom by the end of 1944.

When Montgomery threw his airborne attack at Arnhem in September, aiming for victory before the year was over, the Dutch had called a general railway strike to try to help. But the attack had failed. In reprisal for the strike and growing Dutch resistance, the Germans brought horror to the land. In *Holland and the Canadians,* J. Nikerk wrote:

. . . Even as the fighting at Arnhem rages, the Germans in western Holland threaten to put the "lowlands by the sea" entirely under water. They begin to inundate many a *polder* [land reclaimed from the sea].

Around the harbors of Rotterdam and Amsterdam a police cordon is drawn. Explosion after explosion can be heard. Cranes tumble into the water. Elevators and docks are smashed. The Germans plunder the great warehouses. Trainloads of machinery are taken away. Everyone realizes that when liberation does come there will be widespread poverty.

When it is clear that the Allied attack on Arnhem has failed, things get worse. Angered by the rail strike, the Germans stop the distribution of food supplies for six weeks. Still the locomotives remain idle. New tactics are used—arrests, hand grenades thrown into homes of leaders of the strike. Only when German railway hands are brought in does the transportation system partly operate. The Germans loot factories and warehouses, loading the materials into the trains. Our diesel trains and even the copper cables of the electric railway power system are taken to feed the German war machine.

In October the electricity goes off and town after town stops the supply of gas. Millions of housewives are forced to cook with scarce coal and wood. Candles or oil lamps provide the only illumination and matches to light them are increasingly scarce. Holland lives in chilly rooms, without light. Streetcars run no longer. Worst of all, the secret radio receivers of the Resistance are silent because of lack of power.

In the towns, prices rise to fantastic heights. The rationing system falters, the signal for a mass exodus from town to country. Thousands throng the roads and prowl the countryside in the hunt for food.

The Germans hunt for men to work in Germany. A village is surrounded. Whoever does not stand in front of his home ready to go into slavery will be summarily executed. Rotterdam is besieged by Nazi press gangs for three days. District after district is cordoned off and more than 50,000 men are trapped. Packed into bar-

The fertile *polders,* reclaimed by the Dutch in their ancient battle with the sea, were flooded anew when the Germans smashed the dikes of Holland. Canadian troops used tracked, armored amphibious vehicles called Buffaloes.

ges like herrings in a barrel, they are sent to the eastern front to dig trenches.

Terror and distress increase. The underground organizations become more daring. Not a week passes without some incident. In the dead of night automatic weapons beat out. The body of a German or a collaborator is found. The Germans shoot groups of 10 or 20 political prisoners in reprisal. Eventually the relatives receive a watch or some other personal belonging with a message from the security police that the owner was shot or died of a "heart attack." The climax is reached when Resistance forces raid the German police headquarters. Many Netherlanders are killed during the fighting and in reprisal.

North Nova Scotia Highlanders (below left) enter Zutphen under heavy fire in a breakthrough to northeast Holland. Below: a platoon of the South Saskatchewan Regiment is pinned down by enemy fire in a Dutch farmyard.

As the new year begins temperatures drop. But it is not cold enough for the great rivers in the south to freeze. They remain a barrier to the Allies. Always Holland has thought of her rivers as her protection. Now they favor the enemy. The Germans clear the banks far inland, evacuate the population, loot and destroy.

Shops are almost empty, yet queues still form. Thousands line up outside communal kitchens. Potatoes disappear. Raw beetroot becomes the mainstay of the national diet. The bread ration drops to one slice a day. The death rate multiplies three or four times.

Nor is there peace even for the dead. Coffins of cardboard replace those of

wood. Then neither wood nor cardboard are obtainable. At one time 235 dead are waiting in one of the old churches of The Hague. A label is attached to a meager arm, a sheet is wrapped around the starved frame; it is ready for a common grave.

People hew down trees and tear up wooden paving blocks even at the risk of being shot. On the streets women, old men and children beg for a slice of bread. Then comes news that the Allies are on the move again. The people wait for liberation with throbbing hearts and empty, gnawing stomachs." . . .   J. NIKERK

Holland's liberation coincided with an historic period for Canada: the entire First Canadian Army fought as Lt. Gen. A. G. L. McNaughton had wanted it to fight, together under Canadian command.

The Canadian government had pressed for months to have the 1st Corps transferred from Italy. In January, Allied leaders agreed. In a massive move known as Operation Goldflake, the corps sailed from Leghorn to Marseilles, then drove up through France and on into Belgium and Holland. When spring came, its men were eager and ready to show their abilities on the western front.

Gen. H. D. G. Crerar ordered them to deal with the Germans occupying western Holland north of the Maas River. To the 2nd Corps, simultaneously, he gave the job of liberating northeastern Holland, then sweeping into Germany to clear the coastal belt eastward to the Elbe River.

Against a demoralized but far from beaten enemy, 2nd Corps pushed forward against savage pockets of resistance. Deventer fell, then Zwolle. By April 13 its men had reached Groningen by the North Sea, and after four days of bitter house-to-house fighting the town was taken. Meanwhile the 4th Canadian and 1st Polish Armored divisions swung east in thrusts across the flat north German plain toward Emden, Wilhelmshaven and Oldenburg. They were soon joined by 3rd Division, which also moved on Emden. On May 3, as 2nd Division took Oldenburg,

1st Canadian Parachute Battalion crossed the Elbe River to link up with the Russians at Wismar, more than 50 miles east of Hamburg.

In western Holland, 1st Corps attacked Arnhem on April 12 and captured it two days later. Apeldoorn fell April 17. In a week's fighting the enemy had been pushed back nearly 30 miles from his defenses along the River Ijssel. Maj. Norman Phillips, co-author of *Holland and the Canadians,* wrote:

"Jubilant were the scenes as town after town was freed. Even while German shells were falling, the people would come out to welcome the Canadians. One moment the streets would be full of people. Then the whistle of a projectile, and troops and civilians alike would take shelter. Reports from Resistance groups brought a flow of information about German dispositions and plans. Some plans had been stolen from waylaid enemy couriers, others had been copied, drawn or photographed from originals. Even telephone service was maintained between occupied and unoccupied territory. On one occasion a Netherlands woman telephoned a description of German demolition work she could see as she spoke."

Often a cruel price had to be paid for such resistance. On a road between Arnhem and Apeldoorn a small Dutch group attacked a German car, killing and wounding its passengers. Among the wounded was SS Gen. Hans Rauter, commander of German police in Holland. Soon 117 Dutch prisoners—none of whom had anything to do with it—were taken to the site of the attack and shot. The Germans revenged themselves in other places, too. In Zutphen, Apeldoorn, Zwolle and Deventer, Dutch prisoners were murdered just before the Canadians entered.

By April 18 the Germans in western Holland had withdrawn into what they called "Fortress Holland"—a pocket of land, much of it below sea level, bounded on the south by the great rivers and on the east by the river defense barrier called the Grebbe Line. In this pocket was concentrated nearly 40 percent of Holland's population, mostly in the cities of Amsterdam, Rotterdam and The Hague. These people faced the threat of the Germans opening the dikes and flooding the countryside—and the more ominous threat of death by starvation. A Red Cross official reported: "In the struggle for existence, men even eat flower bulbs. Horses killed in bombardments are immediately cut up by passersby. The bread wagons can only circulate at four in the morning; if they go about in daylight, crowds threaten to plunder them."

For the Allies, saving Dutchmen's lives now took priority over killing Germans. On April 22 operations in western Holland were halted. A report had come through that Nazi Reichskommissar Arthur Seyss-Inquart was ready to negotiate and had stated that if the Allies halted at the Grebbe Line, he would refrain from ordering further destructive flooding, would permit food supplies to come in and would surrender his forces if Germany capitulated. Negotiations were started, a temporary cease-fire was agreed on and a section of the front was demilitarized to allow food to be brought in.

The first airdrop of supplies was made April 29, even before the truce was final. On May 2 Canadian and British truck convoys rolled into no-man's-land. A roadside depot was set up by Dutch civilians and 1000 tons of food and fuel began to pour daily through the narrow gap in the battlefront. The supplies arrived none too soon. Subsequent reports showed that more than 100,000 people in Holland were suffering from starvation edema (dropsy). Thousands had already died. A Canadian Army report said acute general starvation had been avoided by only a few weeks.

On May 4 all German forces facing 21st Army Group surrendered unconditionally. For the Canadians the war in Europe was over. The formal surrender on the Canadian sector took place the next day. Historian Col. C. P. Stacey wrote:

. . . In the shell-scarred hotel in the small village of Wageningen, Col. Gen. Johannes Blaskowitz, tired and disconsolate,

received from Lt. Gen. Charles Foulkes of 1st Corps his orders for the disposition of the defeated Twenty-Fifth Army. The terms of surrender were read by General Foulkes, and Blaskowitz hardly answered a word. The German delegates looked like men in a dream, dazed, stupefied and unable to realize that for them their world was utterly finished.

At Lt. Gen. Guy Simonds' 2nd Corps headquarters at Bad Zwischenahn, Gen. Erick Straube was more wordy and less dignified. He is reported to have been particularly shaken by information received from Brig. J. A. Roberts of the 8th Brigade, who escorted him. Straube asked Roberts the age of the corps commander. Learning he had just surrendered to a man of 41 unnerved him; and learning that Brigadier Roberts was also

| 16 | You will continue to assist in the arrangements for feeding the Dutch civilian population. | 16 | Sie fahren weiter mit hilfe an Einrichtungen für die Ernährung des Holländischen Zivilbevölkerung. |

| 17 | These orders are issued to you without prejudice to, and will be superseded by, any general instrument of surrender applicable to GERMANY and the German Armed Forces as a whole. | 17 | Diese Befehle werden Ihnen übergeben vorbehaltlich einer allgemeinen Urkunde der Uebergabe von Deutschland und der gesamten deutschen Wehrmacht, und werden von einer solchen Urkunde überholt. |

Charles Foulkes

Commander — Lieut-General, GOC 1 (Signature of Allied Cdn Corps Commander)

Befehlshaber (Unterschrift des alliierten Befehlshabers)

| 18 | I acknowledge receipt of a copy of the above orders at WAGENINGEN | 18 | Ich bestätige den Empfang einer Abschrift der obigen Befehle |

The Germans surrendered on May 5, 1945. The instrument of surrender was signed by Lt. Gen. Charles Foulkes of the 1st Canadian Corps and Col. Gen. Johannes Blaskowitz of the Twenty-Fifth Army in a ceremony at Wageningen.

years younger than himself and not even a regular soldier but a manufacturer in civil life was the final blow to the dignity of the German General Staff. . . .

News of the surrender came almost as an anticlimax to the fighting troops. They felt not so much exultation as intense relief. The war diary of the Queen's Own Rifles recorded simply: "There is no celebration but everybody is happy." It was much the same with the men of the North Shore (New Brunswick) Regiment in the German village of Ostersander. In *The Scarlet Dawn* their padre, R. M. Hickey, recalled:

"On the evening of May 4, I gathered my men into a large barn and said Holy Mass. I gave a general absolution and one by one the men came up to Holy Communion. I could see a ray of hope in every face. I finished Mass and was unvesting when a babble of voices and some cheering started outside. Then someone rushed in and shouted: 'The war is over, it's over!' The news of the German surrender on the Canadians' front had been picked up on wireless. Everyone took it quietly. One fellow said: 'Well, I guess that's it, eh, Father?' Most of the lads just stood there, watched me take off the vestments, then quietly walked away. Like myself, they were thinking hard; memories rushed in fast and stilled expression."

There were many things to remember,

above all the deaths of good men. Four-teen hundred Canadians had died since the crossing of the Rhine in March, many of them in Holland. They included two of the men who had left the home of Mrs. Hilsum-Beuckens in April with fears that, in the dying days of the war, they might not make it. Lesage had been slain by a sniper. When Garnett rushed out to help him, he was killed too. Three others were wounded by shellfire. Only Kelly survived unhurt.

May 8 was VE (Victory in Europe) Day. The war in Europe was over. Major Phillips wrote:

. . . The day before this the liberation of western Holland formally began with the entry into Utrecht of British and Canadian forces. The same day General Foulkes sent his troops into Amersfoort, Hilversum and Amsterdam. The next day 1st Division arrived at The Hague and Rotterdam. With the fields of tulips in full bloom, this was the Holland Canadians had always imagined. But the joyous reception was more than the most veteran troops had dreamed of. There were flags flying on every building. In towns and cities the streets were full of singing, dancing people. Military vehicles were bombarded with flowers. Crowds closed in until military traffic could scarcely move. Happy men, women and children hung on the sides of jeeps, trucks, tanks and cars.

In the midst of these throngs walked some of the 160,000 men of the conquered Wehrmacht. Day by day they were gathered into concentration areas, stripped of their arms and of their plunder. "I want to make it perfectly clear," said General Foulkes, "that you Germans are leaving Holland with an absolute minimum. None of the loot you have stolen through Europe will accompany you."

The ignominious departure of the Wehrmacht was routed across the great causeway spanning the Zuider Zee. Horse-drawn carts carried rations, fodder, medical supplies and kitchen equipment for the 300-mile trek to Germany. The Germans were searched and searched

Jubilant crowds throng the streets of liberated Amsterdam to welcome the first elements of the Canadian army entering the city on VE Day.

again. From them more than 15,000,000 guilders were taken, plus jewelry, fur coats, valuables of every description. . . .

The liberation celebrations were climaxed by a big parade of Canadian and Netherlands troops before Queen Wilhelmina in Amsterdam. Then the Canadians set to work to help Holland get back on its feet. In addition to delivering 3000 tons of food a day to major cities, Canadian soldiers volunteered to work on farms. Others cleared rubble in war-damaged towns or sawed up trees felled by Germans in retreat. Canadian engineers helped drain flooded areas, cleared canals of broken bridges and built new ones.

The Canadians built human bridges, too. Perhaps the most touching were the friendships between Canadian soldiers and Dutch children. In *Thank you, Canada,* a Dutch boy, Wim Alings, Jr., recalled:

. . . The grown-ups believed that one day the war would be over, but I was quite sure they were mistaken—until suddenly, one evening, everybody knew the Canadians would come the next morning. Here and there flags were put out, but within an hour cars with loudspeakers were driving through the streets, the air-raid warning was sounded and Germans in armored cars were emptying their guns into the flags.

Early the next morning I was awakened by shouts in the house: "They will be here in an hour!" They came in jeeps, tanks and trucks—fellows in funny uniforms. They waved. Everybody waved. Now and then the column was held up and people jumped on the cars, but the children were not so daring that first morning. It was hours before we began to run after them, shouting, hoping to draw the attention of just one Canadian or to catch just one of the cigarettes they were throwing by handfuls into the streets. Then I ran home. My father looked as if he had been crying. But he laughed when I showed him my cigarette. He took me up and swung me over his shoulders.

That same week we got bread and chocolate and chewing gum. Everybody started trafficking: small silver coins were exchanged for cigarettes, stamps were exchanged for cigarettes, anyone who still had a watch could exchange it for cigarettes. Only the children had nothing to exchange, but we found another way to get our share. "Can I show you the way?"; with these words we accosted every Canadian we met and often one would take us by the hand. After five minutes they would say good-by and pay with candy for our services as a guide. After a week every child that lived near a barracks had singled out his own Canadian, whom you might take by the hand and accompany on his way, and whom the others would leave alone. . . .

The bonds of affection between Canadians and Dutch would endure for years, through friendships, marriages and everlasting gratitude that would make the liberation of Holland perhaps the most meaningful, lasting chapter in the history of Canadian arms.

But even as millions celebrated VE Day in Holland and elsewhere, there remained another war to be won. Japan's forces were reeling back from one Pacific island after another, preparing for a last-ditch stand in the homeland itself. To reinforce its credentials as a Pacific power, Canada aspired to be in on the kill. The effort wouldn't be large, Ottawa decided, but it would involve all three forces.

Yet even within this limited design there were problems. Ottawa, wanting no part of any role that would smack of Canadian assistance in restoring lost Asiatic colonies to the British Empire, rejected proposals for two ships to serve off southeast Asia. Canada's contribution would have to be against Japan itself.

But it soon became obvious that the United States wasn't interested in any contribution at all. When Col. Dick Malone was assigned to do advance planning for Canadian press coverage in the Pacific, he found obstacles in his way. In *Missing From The Record,* he says Washington "indicated that an official party would not be welcomed. One American was frank enough to tell us the real reason was that the United States wished to handle Japan itself without further assistance from Canada or Britain."

The Americans eventually relented. Malone did get to the Pacific, and Canada made plans to dispatch an army division, an eight-squadron RCAF bomber force and a fleet that would reflect her wartime naval growth: two light aircraft carriers and two cruisers as well as destroyers, frigates and corvettes.

Time ran out before most of this force could be mustered in the Pacific; only the cruiser *Uganda* got into action. In fact, Canada's most remembered blow in the three months between victory in Europe and victory in Asia was struck by one man: Lt. Robert Hampton "Hammy" Gray, a 27-year-old, steel-nerved, crap-playing Canadian flier from Nelson, B.C. As a Fleet Air Arm pilot aboard the Royal Navy aircraft carrier *Formidable,* he won the DSC in July for leading a series of actions against Japanese airfields and shipping. Then, on August 9, Gray took off at the head of a force attacking shipping in Onawaga Bay on the island of Honshu, Japan.

When they got there, they found a number of ships in the bay and prepared to attack. But a fury of fire came up at them from shore batteries and five warships. "Taking the destroyer first," Gray reported by radio. As he dived, his Corsair was hit. "Going in low." The Corsair was hit again and burst into flames. Gray never altered course. When he got down to 50 feet, he released his bombs. At least one was a direct hit. The destroyer sank.

Gray was killed—five days before Japan's surrender. He was posthumously awarded the Victoria Cross.

The day Gray made his last attack, the 8000-ton cruiser *Uganda,* obtained from Britain in 1944, was en route to Canada after four months' Pacific service with a powerful British task force. The cruiser had acted as part of an anti-aircraft screen for *Formidable,* three other aircraft carriers and three battleships.

She went home under unique circumstances, as probably the first ship in history to vote herself out of a war. Ottawa had decreed that all Canadian service in the Pacific be voluntary. It caused endless, bitter debate aboard *Uganda* but eventually her crew voted 605 to 300 to go home. They were three days away from Esquimalt, B.C., on August 7, when they received word that the first atomic bomb had been dropped on Hiroshima. Three days later a second bomb fell on Nagasaki. On August 15, Japan surrendered, ending almost six years of war.

Already thousands of Canadian veterans had returned from Europe and more were coming each week. Entire regiments were cheered as they marched through the streets. But for 42,000 there would be no cheering. They were the dead, the men who had made the ultimate sacrifice in what Winston Churchill called Canada's magnificent war effort. They lay in the soil of Italy, France, Holland, Belgium and other lands, and in the eternal sea. They and their comrades, they and their country, said Ralph Allen in *Ordeal by Fire,* had made major contributions to Allied victory:

. . . The army, which reached a peak strength of nearly half a million men, fought all the major campaigns of western Europe. It suffered total defeats at Hong Kong and Dieppe, the first to no purpose, the second redeemed by the lessons it provided in amphibious landings. Its casualties numbered 81,000, including 23,000 dead.

The navy played a part second only to that of the British Navy in keeping the lifeline to Britain open during the dark and almost fatal years of the Battle of the Atlantic. It expanded its strength fiftyfold to almost 100,000 and built, bought and borrowed more than 400 cruisers, destroyers, frigates, corvettes, minesweepers, gunboats, torpedo boats and landing craft. It convoyed 25,000 merchant ships and nearly 200 million tons of supplies, either part or all the way to the United Kingdom. It sank 27 U-boats and lost 24 warships. More than four in every five of 2000 casualties were fatal. There were not many second chances in the Battle of the Atlantic.

The air force put nearly a quarter of a million Canadians into uniform, steadily stepping up its overseas striking power to 48 squadrons. Of its 18,000 casualties, more than 17,000 lost their lives.

Canada brought into being, ran and largely paid for a work of genius, cauldron of discord and essential implement of victory called the British Commonwealth Air Training Plan. This program was a magnificent success.

From what amounted to a standing start, the country developed into a major supplier of munitions and war machinery of all kinds, not only for itself but for other nations. It accomplished this without financial help from outside, and while extending $3.4 billions in various kinds of aid to its allies.

The three armed services enlisted more than a million men, one and a third times as many as in 1914-18, and lost only two thirds as many dead. . . . RALPH ALLEN

The war had taken tens of millions of lives, cost hundreds of billions of dollars, destroyed Nazi Germany and Fascist Italy, and brought forth two new superpowers, the United States and Russia. But even though Canada came through physically unscathed, the war changed every aspect of Canadian life.

Military contracts had stimulated the country's economy and, as a result, unprecedented prosperity had supplanted the Depression. Between 1939 and 1945, the gross national product doubled, from $5.6 billion to $11.8 billion. The population rose by 7 percent and the consumption of goods and services by 78 percent in the same period. As Maj. Gen. E. L. M. Burns put it: "We had, emphatically, butter as well as guns."

The war, in fact, transformed Canada into an industrial state. In an economic effort as remarkable as its military achievements, it made a host of things it had never made before: roller bearings, optical glass, high-octane gas, synthetic rubber, not to mention tanks and heavy bombers.

By 1945 Canada was producing $8 billion worth of goods, more than double the 1939 figure. The St. Lawrence Valley–Great Lakes corridor was becoming even more firmly entrenched as the nation's industrial heartland—and Canada ever more dependent on world markets.

The war diminished Britain's importance to Canada, which began shifting into the economic orbit of the United States. Prime Minister Mackenzie King ended the war worrying over growing American influence. Despite this concern, Canada greeted peace with self-assurance and sought to play an important political role on the world stage. Universally liked and respected, it took its place in the United Nations, an organization that won its wholehearted support. Before long, Canada was one of the foremost champions of a North Atlantic Treaty Organization, which was established to counter Russian expansion.

During the war, the power of the federal government increased, creating an ever-growing bureaucracy. By war's end, Canadians were prepared to accept massive state intervention in their lives.

Sensing the mood of the country, Mackenzie King's Liberals won a June election by promising to use the state's financial power to achieve full employment.

With government intervention, too, came family allowances, to be added to such earlier measures as unemployment insurance and old age pensions. The welfare state with its high taxation had arrived.

Even the Canadian trade union movement was affected by the war, gaining strength when Ottawa, worried about wartime labor unrest, acted to prevent employers from discriminating against workers for joining unions. Union membership was 359,000 in 1939; by 1947 it was 912,000, of which many were women. From 1939 on, great numbers of women went into jobs in business and industry and, by war's end, it was clear that many would be staying in the workplace.

The Veterans Charter which, among numerous other benefits, sent thousands of servicemen to college who would never have gone otherwise, drew Ottawa into the field of education. The charter became a prelude to such later federal moves as student loans and aid to universities.

Finally, the war saw Canadian science come of age. Canada had become involved in the war's scientific dimension— from synthetic rubber and new explosives to mass production of penicillin. Most significantly, the war teamed Canada with Britain and the United States in the development of atomic power.

In brief, World War II and its aftermath broadened Canada's horizons. Everything changed. By 1945, in the words of Ralph Allen, "no country in the world was more confident than Canada, or had better cause to be."

Under the impetus of civilian demands that war had held in check, and of ravaged Europe's need for reconstruction, Canada's economy took off on an expansion beyond anything it had ever known. It would for a time inflate Canada's importance and feed its vanities. And it would go on for years.

Canadian veterans themselves, and the 43,000 wives they brought home, were soon swept away in the new prosperity. Few doubted that they had served in a just cause. The revelations about Hitler's concentration camps gave proof that they had fought not only an enemy but an evil. But they had few illusions about the world they'd raise their families in. The atomic bombs that forced Japan to surrender had clearly ushered in a new and terrifying age.

Index

A page number in **bold type** indicates that the reference is in a picture caption or a short feature story on that page.

A

Abbaye-aux-Hommes: 362.
Abbeville: 149, 250.
Abbott, Douglas: 312.
Aberdeen: 113.
Action Catholique, L'. 413.
Adair, Pte. Robert W.: 327.
Adams, Ian: 103, 109.
Addis Ababa: **7**.
Adler Tag: 63.
Admiralty: merchant ships pass under its control, 21; *St. Laurent*, 45; *Saguenay*, 91; Dieppe, 134; U-boats near to disrupting communications between New World and Old, 174; loans Canada senior Wren officers to help organize Canada's Wrens, 196; acquires Vichy French naval cipher, 377; Canadian lake ships, 430.
Adrano: 328.
Adriatic Sea: 382, 389, 414.
Aegean Sea: 414.
Africa: 248, 268, 430.
  North: 151-2, 155, 232, 377, 414.
  South: 48.
Agira: **237**, 243.
Aircraft—
  Anson, Avro: 82-3, **82**, **86**.
  Beaufighter: 192, **357**.
  Beaufort: 192-3, 335.
  Bisley: 192-3.
  Blenheim: 59, 64.
  Boston: 335.
  Canso: 335, 338-41.
  Cant: 153, 204-5.
  Catalina: 341-2.
  Dakota: 335.
  Defiant: 59-60.
  Dornier: 34, 59, 63, 72, **73**.
  Fleet Finch: **84**, 85-7.
  Flying Fortress: 253, **255**, 377.
  Focke-Wulf: 254;
    FW/190: 250, 252-3, 284, 449.
    FW/190A: 248.
  Halifax: 276, **276**, 335, 380, 452.
  Harvard: **80**, 82-3, **84**, 87, 88;
    AT-6: 86;
    Mk II: 86.
  Heinkel: 69, 332.
  Hudson: 89, **89**.
  Hurricane: 22, 34, 58-9, 60, 335.
  Ju 87: **65**.
  Ju 88: 64, 205-6, 336.
  Lancaster: 201, 207, **208**, 214, 276, **276**, 308, **335**, 452.
  Liberator: 153, 253, 255, 338, 343.
  Lightning: 254.
  Link Trainer: **82**.
  Lysander: 58, 163.
  Macchi: 153.
  Messerschmitt: 153, 254, 297;
    Me/109: 60, 65, 72, 284.
    Me/109G: 250.
    Me/110: **66**, 67, 257.
    Me/262: 448, **449**.
  Mosquito: 284, 335, 390.
  Mustang: 153, 254.
  Nieuport: 86.
  Spad: 85.
  Spitfire: 152, 255, 257, 320, 332, 390, 449.
    V: 248, 250, 271.
    IX: 248, 250, 254.
  Stearman: 86.
  Stirling: 276.
  Stuka: **65**.
  Sunderland: 41, 343.
  Tempest: 390.
  Thunderbolt: 254, 257.
  Tiger Moth: 82-3, **84**, 85.
  Typhoon: 250, 320, 396, 398, 420, 448-9.
  Vibrator, Vultee: 86.
  Walrus: 256, 259.
  Warwick: 342-3.
  Wellington: 193, 276.
  Zero: 102.
Aircraft Production, Ministry of: 209.
Air Fighting Development Unit: 63.
Air Force—
  British: *see* Royal Air Force.
  Canadian: *see* Royal Canadian Air Force.
  Chinese: 152.
  German: *see* Luftwaffe.
  United States: *see* United States Air Corps; United States Army Air Force.
Air Ministry (British): 82, 247.
Alamein, El: 261.
Alaska: 186, **187**, 189.
Alaska Highway: 180, **187**, 287.
Aldergrove: 89.
Aldershot: 27-8, 33, 169.
Aleutian Islands: 186.
Alexander, A. V.: **38**.
Alexander, Maj. Gen. R. O.: 114.
Alexander of Tunis, Field Marshal Earl: 164, 299, **304**, 382.
Alexandria: **274**.
Algiers: 247.
Algonquin Regiment: 366, 395.
Alings, Wim, Jr.: 469.
Allard, Lt. Col. Jean: 367, 386, 388-9.
Allen, Sgt. Alf: **332**.
Allen, Ralph: 10, 13, 33, **50**, 151, 188, 247, **331**, 357, 361-2, **381**, 408, **420**; *Home Made Banners*: 319, **325**; *Ordeal by Fire*: 6, 8, 28, 133-4, **172**, 269, 405-7, 412-3, 470.
Allerton Hall ("Castle Dismal"): 280.
Allison, Carlyle: 186.
Allister, William: 103, 114.
Alphonse, House of: 351, **352**, 354-5.
Aluminum Company of Canada: 186.
Amersfoort: 468.
Amsterdam: 463, 466, 468-9, **468**.
Ancienne Lorette: 88.
Anderson, Lt. Col. J. E.: 402.
Anderson, Sgt. R. F.: 461.
Angelini, FO. S.: 450.
Annapolis Valley: 88.
Anticosti Island: 122, 127-8.
Antwerp: 389-90, 392-3, **400**, 404, 413, 423, 435, 449.
Anzio: 151, 299, 307, 461.
Apeldoorn: 466.
Apennines: 300.
Aquino: 299, 306.
Arcachon: 35, 37.
Arcand, Adrien: 8, 47, **48**.
Archdeacon (Resistance operation): 160.
Archer, Mme Thérèse de Salaberry: 197.
Ardenne, Abbey of: 357, 360-1.
Ardennes: 413, **423**, 435, 437, 449-50.
Argentan: 366-7.
Argentia: 118-9.
Argentina: 7.
Argyll and Sutherland Highlanders of Canada: 370.
Arielli River: 273.
Armentières: 157.
Armored Units—
  British Columbia Dragoons (9th Armored Regiment): 307, 309. British Columbia Regiment (28th Armored Regiment): 366. Calgary Regiment (14th Armored Regiment): 130, 135, 140-1. 14th Canadian Hussars (8th Reconnaissance Regiment): 379-80, 394. 1st Hussars (6th Armored Regiment): 324, 331.
Lord Strathcona's Horse (Royal Canadians) (2nd Armored Regiment): 307, 308-9. Ontario Regiment (11th Armored Regiment): 272. 4th Princess Louise Dragoon Guards (4th Reconnaissance Regiment): **242**, 298. Three Rivers Regiment (12th Armored Regiment): 236, **237**, 269, 271, 306. Sherbrooke Fusiliers (27th Armored Regiment): 357-8, 362, 367.
Army—
  British: 28, 58, 76;
    ATS: 195.
    Second: 311, 313, 389, **391**, 393, 395, 435.
    Eighth: 1st Canadian Division and 1st Canadian Tank Brigade join, 232, 388; Sicily, 236, **244**, 246, 287; Pescara, 261-2; Ortona, 273; Liri Valley, 299; Hitler Line, 307; Gothic Line, 382.
  Canadian: Non-Permanent Active Militia, 23; Permanent Force, 23, 26; personnel in SOE, 155, 160; long wait ends, 232; soldiers become part of the life of Sussex and Surrey, 281; conscription crisis, 405, **410**; Crerar, 434-5; first elements enter Dutch capital, **199-200**, **203**, 409; CWAC, 195-6, 299, 409.
  First Canadian: formed, 287; Caen, 365; Ostend and Le Tréport, 389; Scheldt estuary, 392-401, **400**; improvements in manpower situation, 413; advance to the Rhine, 417, 437-8, 439, 440, **441**; Reichswald, 423; closeup of commander, 434-5; 1st Corps reunited with, 465; *other refs*, 311, 374.
  Council, Canadian: 410-1, **410**.
  French: 29, **31**.
  German: 12, 59, 209, 361, 468-9.
    Seventh: 319, 366.
    Tenth: 382.
    Fifteenth: 319, 361, 393.
    Twenty-Fifth: 467, **467**.
  Groups—
    12th U.S. Army: 365.
    21st Army: 256, 395, 405, 435, 461.
    First: 313, 365, 370.
    Third: 365.
    Fifth: 261, 299, 309, 382, 391.
    Seventh: 232.
Arnhem: 254, 391, **391**, 393, 416, 462, 466.
Arques: 135.
Arques River: **133**.
Arras: 335.
Arthur, WO2 James: **217**, 218.
Artificial Moonlight: 366.
Artillery—
  Anti-Tank Battery, 90th: **237**.
  Field Battery, 8th: 21, 23.
  Field Regiment—
    1st: 33.
    3rd: 76.
    12th: 326.
    13th: 324.
  Royal: 105.
Artois, Guy d': 165, **165**.
Aruba: 122.
Arvida: 186.
Asdic: 97, **99**, 170.
Associated Press, The: 247.
Assoro: 236-41, 243-4, 246.
Astell, Bill: 210-2.
Astor, Lady: 30.
Atkins, Vera: 155.
Atlantic Advocate, The: **345**.
Atlantic, Battle of the: 90-101, 118, **122**, 166-79, 338.
Atlantic Wall: 301, **311**, 319, 323, 329-30, 332.
AT-6 Harvard, The: 84.

ATS (Auxiliary Territorial Service): 195.
Audet, Flt. Lt. Dick: 449, **450**.
Audierne Bay: 293.
Ausbrecherkönige von Kanada, Die: **345**.
Australia: 48-9, 88, 119.
Austria: 8.
Authie: 344, 357-9, 362.
Avranches: 365.
Aylmer: **84**, 86.
Azores: 172.

B

Babington-Smith, FO. Constance: 283.
Baby Blitz: 390.
Bader, Douglas: 60-62, **62**, 65, 67, 69, 71-75, 248-9.
Bad Zwischenahn: 467.
Baffin Island: 164.
Bairnsfather, Bruce: 298.
Baldwin, Harry: 17.
Ball, Eric: 62, **62**, 69.
Ball, Rod: 455-6.
Balloons: **58**.
Baltic Sea: 283.
Bancroft: 24.
Banville: 330.
Barber Pole Brigade: **170**.
"Barber Pole Song, The": **170**.
Barclay, Foster: 247.
Barnard, Lt. Col. W. T.: 312-3, 315, 328, **370**.
Barnett, Capt. James: 113.
Barrett, Lt. H. E.: 431.
Barrow-in-Furness: 90.
Barthropp, PO. Patrick: 75.
Bartley, PO. Anthony: 72.
Bassin du Canada: 146.
Bassin Duquesne: 146.
Bastogne: **423**.
Baxter, Beverley: 8, **233**.
Bayeux: 199, 314, 332.
Beaches—
  Dieppe: Blue (Puys): 134, 136, **141**, 149, 150.
    Green (Pourville): 134, 137.
    Orange 1 (Varengeville): 134, 136.
    Orange 2 (River Saane): 134.
    Red (Dieppe, East): 134, 140, 142, 144, 147.
    White (Dieppe, West): 134, 140, 144, 147.
    Yellow 1 (Berneval): 134, 136.
    Yellow 2 (Belleville-sur-Mer): 134, 136.
  Normandy: Gold: 313, 332.
    Juno: 313, 315.
    Love: 324.
    Mike: Green, 324, Red, 324.
    Nan: Green, 323, White, 330.
    Omaha: 313, 315, 332.
    Sword: 313.
    Utah: 313, 315, 332.
Beardmore, Eric: 65.
Beatty, Flt. Sgt. Ron: 449.
Beaverbrook, Lord: **63**, 89, 186.
Bedford Basin: **221**, 224, 230, **231**.
Beek: 416, 423.
Beekman, Yolande "Mariette": 224-5, 230.
Bekker, Cajus: 448, 453.
Belfield, Eversley: **356**.
Belgium: 28, **29**, 76, 88, 134, 155, 254, 276.
Bell, Lt. Col. Eric: 380.
Bell, Ralph P.: 81.
Belle Isle, Strait of: 123, 125, 127.
Belleville-sur-Mer: 134, 136.
Bennett, Al: 86, 88.
Bennett, D. C. T.: 89, 283.
Bennett, Maj. Peter: 326.
Bennett, R. B.: 6, 10.
Beny-sur-Mer: 330, **332**.
Berkenkopf, Father: 214.
Berlin: 254, 279-80, 284, 437, 451, 455, 460.

Berliner Illustrierte: 75.
Bermuda: 37, 48, 56, 116.
Bernatchez, Lt. Col. J. P. E.: 262, 264, 267.
Berneval: 134, 136, 150.
Bernières-sur-Mer: 324, 327, 329-30, **329**.
Berry, PO. "Razz": 72.
Berry, CSM. Wilf: 324, 326.
Beurling, FO. F. George "Buzz": 152-3, 249, 280.
Beveland, South: 393-5, 403.
Bieler, Maj. Gustave "Guy": 154-64, **155**, **157**, **159**, **162**, **164**.
Bieler, Jean-Louis: 164.
Bieler, Mania: 157, 164.
Bieler, Marguerite: 157, 164.
Bieler, René-Maurice: 157, **162**, 164.
Bieler Lake, Baffin Island: 164.
Biervliet: 396.
Biggar, Col. O. M.: **54**.
Biggin Hill: **71**, 72-3.
Birchall, Sqdn. Ldr. Leonard J.: 102.
Bird, Will R.: 344, 357, 396.
Birkland, Henry: 455.
Biscay, Bay of: 35, 289, **293**, 380, 415.
Bishop, Edward: **80**.
Bishop, Air Marshal W. A. "Billy": 83, **88**.
Bishop, Maj. W. A.: 111.
Black Watch (Royal Highland Regiment) of Canada: 130, 134, 136, 365, 395, **407**.
Blaskowitz, Col. Gen. Johannes: 466-7, **466**.
Blenheim Castle: 76.
Bléré: 346.
Bloc Populaire: 413.
Blodgett, Fern: 205.
Bloody Winter: **90**, 167, **167**, 172, **176**.
Boak, Lt. Comdr. Eric: 316.
Bochum: 219, 452.
Bodie, Bob: 336.
Bodnoff, Flt. Sgt. I. J.: 338, 340, 343.
Bofors: **442**.
Bohain: 164.
Bolivar, Charley: 432.
Bologna: 382.
Bolton, Foss: 250, 254.
Bomber Offensive: 453.
Bombs: atomic, 469, 470; Grand Slam, 452; Tallboy, 452.
Bonaparte, Napoleon: 316.
Bonaparte, Operation: 351, 354-5.
Bonham-Carter, Rear Adm. S. S.: 221.
Bordeaux: 34-5, 38.
Borgo San Maria: 383-4, 386, 389.
Borneo: 102, 122, **160**.
Boscombe: 310.
Boston: 120.
Boulogne: **386**, 390.
Boury, Camille: 159.
Bowmanville: **44**, **345**.
Boxall, Gilbert: **332**.
Braakman Inlet: 395.
Bracken, Brendan: **441**.
Brackett, Capt. John: 227.
Bradley, Lt. Gen. Omar: 313, 365.
Bradwell Bay: 257.
Brady, WO2 Joseph: **217**, 218, **219**.
Branchoux, Mathurin: 354-5.
Bransfield, Pte. Claude: 327.
Brantford: 377.
Braun, Wernher von: 283.
Brazil: 377.
Breadner, Air Marshal L. S.: 197, 287.
Breau, Lt. Jack: 399, 401.
Bremen: 283, 452.
Bren: 26, 31, 107, 111, 201, 238, 266, 347-8, 441-3, **444**, 446.
Breskens Pocket: 393, 395-6, 402-3.
Brest: 30-31, 33-34, 58, 291.
Breyne, Art de: 336.
Brickhill, Paul: 60, 62, 65, 69, 452; *see also The Dam Busters*.

471

Brigades—
Barber Pole Brigade: **170**.
East: 108, 111.
West: 108, 111.
Armored—
1st: 262, 273, 286, 299.
2nd: 311, 322, 365-6, 438.
Infantry—
1st: 28, 30, **31**, 33-4, 235-6, **237**, 243, 267, 273, 306.
2nd: 235, **237**, 238, 241, 243, 268, 306-7.
3rd: 76, 236, 262, 267, 306, 383.
5th: **394**.
7th: **312**, 324, 327, 331-2, 357, 359, 395.
8th: 324, 327, 361.
9th: 324, 330-5, 395.
11th: 273, 383.
Tank—
1st: 232, 236.
25th British: 306.
Briggs, Mrs. David: 164.
Brighton: 130.
Bristol, Adm. A. L.: 119.
Britain, Battle of: 58, **60**, 71, **73**, 74-5, 77.
Britain, Great: **11**, 12, 58, 103, 106, 117, 222, 248.
British Army: see Army, British.
British Broadcasting Corporation: 159, **199**, 235, 316, 349-50, 354.
British Columbia Dragoons (9th Armored Regiment): 419, 422.
British Columbia: 114-7, 186.
British Columbia Regiment (28th Armored Regiment): 366.
British Commonwealth Air Training Plan: 23, 48, 97, 287, **411**, 470.
British Empire Medal: Irene Vivash, 195.
British Expeditionary Force: 28, **31**.
British Intelligence: 354.
British Navy: see Royal Navy.
British Secret Intelligence Service: 376.
British Security Coordination (BSC): 376.
Brittany: 29, **31**, 33-34, 58, 351, 354.
Brockington, Leonard W.: 316.
Bromley: 74.
Brooke, Field Marshal Sir Alan: 35, 132, 286.
Brooke-Popham, Air Chief Marshal Sir Robert: 78-9, **79**.
Brookes, Air Vice-Marshal G. E.: 382.
Brooks, WO. H. E.: 455.
Brophy, George Patrick: 335, **335**, **336**.
Brown, Ben: **62**, 63.
Brown, Flt. Sgt. Kenneth: 210, **217**, 218-9.
Brown, Kingsley: **345**.
Brown, Wing Comdr. Mark "Hilly": **62**.
Brown, Stoker William: 97-8.
Bruce, Charles: **389**.
Bruchési, Msgr. Paul: 12.
Bruges: 392.
Brussels: 392-3, **417**, 422.
Bryson, PO. Johnnie: 59.
Buchenwald: 155, 161, 164.
Buckham, Flt. Lt. Robert: **454**, 456, 456, 460.
Buckingham Palace: 73-4.
Buckley, Christopher: 269-70.
Buckmaster, Col. Maurice J.: 155, 163, 165.
Buffalo, N.Y.: 87-8.
Buffalo: 395, 427, 438, 440, **463**.
Bulge, Battle of the: **423**.
Bult-Francis, Maj. Dennis: 379-80.
Burgess, CPO. Charles Thomas: 292, 295-7.
Burns, Lt. Gen. E. L. M.: 299, 389, 470.
Buron: 344, 357-8, 362.
Burpee, PO. Lewis: 210, **217**, 218.
Burton, Bill: 431-2.
Burton, Richard: 83, 190.
Bush, Roy: 63.

Butler, Mayor Alan: 230.
Butt, Sonia "Tony" (Mrs. Guy d'Artois): 165, **165**.
Butte, Steve: 450.
Buxton, Col. Edwin: **376**.
Byers, PO. Vernon: 210-1, **217**.

C

Cabot Strait: 129.
Caen: D-Day, 314-6, 331-2; battle for, 357, 360-2; beyond, 365-6; mop-up troops clear snipers from, **367**; other refs. 199, 405, 455.
Caen: Anvil of Victory: 316, 330, 361.
Café du Moulin Brûlé: 159, 164.
Calais: 28, 72, 254, 258, 319, 390.
Calcar: 424, 438.
Calgary: 15, **88**, 207.
Calgary Highlanders: 130, **426**.
Calgary Regiment (14th Armored Regiment): 130, 135, 140-1.
Cambrai: 335, **336**, 337.
Cambridge, Ont.: **188**.
Cameron Highlanders of Ottawa (M.G.): 315, 358, 360, **370**.
Campbell, Maj. Alex: 238, 273.
Campbell, Sgt. Bob: 86-7.
Campbell, Sir Gerald: 51, 54, 56, 78.
Campbell, FO. Graham: 338-43.
Campbell, Neil: **62**, 63.
Campbell, Sir Ronald: 35.
Camp Borden: 80, 82.
Campinchi, Paul-François: 352.
Campochiaro: **261**.
Camp X: 377.
Canada: isolationist mood, 6; officially at war, 13; population and gross national product, 17; doubts about leadership, 17-8; sets up navy and army commands on Atlantic coast, sends troops to Newfoundland, Iceland and West Indies, 47; called "linchpin of peace", 48; interpreter role, 57; Battle of Britain, 58; Air Training Plan, 78; air crew graduates, 88; receives seven U.S. "four-stackers", 95; declaration of war, 106; aftermath of Hong Kong, 116; Dieppe, 133, 151; fourth largest producer of weapons, 180.
Canada Bonds: 399.
Canada House: 350.
Canada Steamship Lines: 430.
Canada-United States Permanent Joint Board on Defense: 54, **54**.
Canada's Fighting Pilots: 152, 283.
Canadian, The: 281.
Canadian Army 1939-45, The: 139.
Canadian Army: see Army, Canadian.
Canadian Auxiliary Territorial Service (CATS): 195.
Canadian Broadcasting Corporation: declaration of war, 13; sinking of Repulse and Prince of Wales, **107**; Wallace Reyburn on Dieppe, 137; Lt. Col. R. R. Labatt interview on Dieppe, 147; Forbes West on Dieppe, 149; Peter Stursberg, 232, 247, 299; Matthew Halton, 247, 260-2, 273; Leonard W. Brockington and Sioux on D-Day, 316; Marcel Ouimet and le Régiment de la Chaudière, 328, 330; Ralph Allen on D-Day, **331**; Lt. W. F. McCormick on D-Day, 331; William Stephenson, 377.
Canadian Legion: 409.
Canadian Medical Services, The: 198.
Canadian National Railways: 81, 201.
Canadian National Steamships: 127, 430.

Canadian Nurse, The: 198, **228**.
Canadian Officers Training Corps: 155.
Canadian Pacific Railway: 89.
Canadian Power Boat Company: **204**.
Canadian Press, The: 130, 197, 247, **389**.
Canadian Scottish Regiment: 324, 326, 359, 395.
Canadian Women's Army Corps (CWAC): 195-6, **199**, **200**, **203**, 409.
Canadian Women's Auxiliary Air Force: 195-7, 200.
Canadian Women's Service Force: 195.
Canadianization: 248-9.
Canadians, The: 22.
Canadians in Italy, The: 232.
Canapress London: 247.
Canloan: **327**.
Cannell, Augustus: 190.
Canterbury: 72.
Canton: 105.
Canwood: **332**.
Cap-Chat: 125, 128.
Cap-de-la-Madeleine: 125.
Cap-des-Rosiers: 128.
Cap Gris Nez: 390.
Cape Bon: 233.
Cape Breton Highlanders: 405.
Cape Hatteras: 120, 431.
Cape Horn: 122.
Cape Race: 166.
Cape Ray: 122.
Cape Town: 94, 101.
Cape Verde Islands: 94.
Carcaci: **237**.
Cardin, P. J. A.: 18, 117.
Carell, Paul: 350.
Caribbean: 120, 122, 125, 414.
Carleton and York Regiment: 76, 236, **261**, 306.
Carmichael, David: 281.
Carpenter, Supt. Joan: 196.
Carpiquet: 314, 357, 361-2, **362**.
Carr, Emily: 13.
Carr, W. G.: 197.
Carson, Stoker Petty Officer Bill: 224-7.
Casa Berardi: 262, **263**, 264-8.
Casablanca: 274.
Cassino: 198, 299, **304**, 461.
"Castle Dismal": 280.
Casualties: Battle of Britain, 75; Hong Kong, 132-3; Dieppe, **143**, 148-9; North Atlantic in 1942, 169; Convoys SC-107 and ONS-154, 173; Atlantic in February and March 1943, 174, 178; May 1943, 178; total in Battle of the Atlantic, 179; Ortona, 273; breakout at Anzio and to Rome, 461; bomber crews, 280; 6 Group/RCAF, 282; civilian in air raids, 283; Athabaskan, 297; Hitler Line, 307; Liri Valley, 309; on run-in to Normandy, 322; U.S. on D-Day, 324; Canadian on D-Day, 324, 331-2, **331**, **332**; among Canloan officers, **327**; in 3rd Division to June 8, 1944, 359; Verrières Ridge, 365; from bombing by supporting aircraft, 366-7; Allied from D-Day to end of August 1944, 372; German, 372; from flying bombs, 390-1; Arnhem, **391**; Scheldt estuary, 404; and lack of reinforcements, **407**; Kapelsche Veer, **419**; Battle of the Bulge, **423**; Lady Hawkins, 432; Lady Drake, 433; in drive for Rhine, 440; losses in aircraft in Ardennes offensive, 450; Canadian aircraft losses in raids on Duisburg, 452; in 1st Parachute Battalion drop over Rhine, 461; total losses, 470.
Casualty Clearing Station, No. 5: 198.
Catania: 198.
Caterham: 253.
Catto, Lt. Col. D. E.: 137.
Caza, Roger: 155.
Ceylon: 102.

Chalmers, Rear Adm. W. S.: 94-5.
Chamberlain, Neville: 9-10, 28, 47, 77.
Chandler, Sgt. E. D.: 316.
Channel Ports: 380, 389, 391, 393, 435.
Charlebois, Maj. J. G.: **263**.
Chartrand, Gabriel: 155-6, 163-4.
Chassé, Capt. Pierre: **263**.
Châteaubriant: **31**.
Châteaudun: 34.
Château Laurier Hotel: 91, 180.
Château Vaux: 324.
Checkmate in the North: 197.
Cherbourg: 313, 319.
Cher River: 160, 346.
Chiang Kai-shek, Generalissimo: 103.
Chichester: 63.
Chicoutimi: 413.
China: 6, 103-4.
Chinese Fifth Column: 105, 107.
Chloridorme: 124.
Christie, Kathleen: 197.
Christmas, FO. Bev E.: 63, 65.
Churchill, Clementine: 73.
Churchill, Winston: is Prime Minister, 28, **29**; "long night of barbarism", 33; Canada's relationship between Great Britain and U.S., **46**; oratory stirs free world, 47; calls Canada "linchpin of peace", 48; speech of June 4, 1940, 49; would never enter into peace negotiations with Hitler, 51; quote when Italy entered war, **53**; negotiations with Roosevelt on bases and destroyers, 54, **55**; "we shall never surrender", **58**; assessment of Beaverbrook, 63; at 11 Group HQ at Uxbridge, 71-2; Battle of Britain, **74**, 75; air training scheme, 77; names Beaverbrook Minister of Aircraft Production, 89; Battle of the Atlantic, 90, 92; Hong Kong, 103, 112; Dieppe, 133, **148**; Ceylon, 135; Canada's war effort, 180; SOE, 154; Ortona, 268; "We can wreck Berlin", **284**; forecast of D-Day, 312; William Stephenson, 376; looked on as a hero, **390**; protest to Tito hanging prisoners in public square, 415; refers to Canada's magnificent effort, 470; other ref, 390.
Cintheaux: 366.
Citizen, The (Ottawa): 210, 218, **246**.
Clarence Decatur Howe: 25.
Clark, Greg: 247.
Clark, W. C.: 182.
Clayton, Robert: 431.
Clough, Rev. J. C.: 312, 327-8, 331, 361.
Clyde, River: 26, 40.
Cochrane, Air Vice-Marshal Ralph: 209-11, 214, 218-9.
Cody, William: 224-6.
Cohen, Leonard: 153.
Cole, Flt. Sgt. S. R.: 338-41, 343.
Coleman, Jim: 190.
Collier, Richard: 63-4, 71, 75; see also Eagle Day.
Collingwood: **92**.
Collins, Robert: 195, 197, 200, 203.
Cologne: 280, 452.
Colombo: 135.
Colony to Nation: 8.
Coltishall: 66, 75.
Combined Operations: 131-2, 149.
Commands—
Allied: 283.
Anti-Aircraft: 75.
Bomber: 207-8, 274-8, **278**, 283-5, 380, 390, 451.
Canadian Northwest Atlantic: 178, **179**, 230.
Coastal: 64, 91, 338, **338**.
Fighter: 59, 60, 63, 75.

Newfoundland: 118-9.
Southeast: 131.
U-Boat: 167.
Commons, House of (Canada): 82, 116, 407, 434.
Commonwealth: 58.
Compiègne: 37, 352.
Conca, River: 389.
Congress, U.S.: 54, 56-7.
Conrad, Sqdn. Ldr. Walter: 254, 258-9.
Conscription: 12-3, 18, 23, 48, 116-7, **117**, 287, 405-13.
Conscription Crisis of 1944, The: 409.
Conservative Party: 90, 407, 409, 411.
Conspicuous Gallantry Medal: 219.
Convoy—
Atlantic: **118**, **169**.
HX-1: 22, **23**.
HXS-300: 414.
ONS-154: 171-3.
SC: 118.
SC-42: 97.
SC-107: 173.
TC-1: 21.
Cook, Lt. George: 414.
Cooke, Pte. M. A.: 401.
Cookridge, E. H.: 161.
Corbett, Maj. O. L.: 396, 399, 402.
Corbett, FO. Vaughn: 65.
Cordelette, Eugène: 157-60, **157**, 164, **164**.
Coriano: 391.
Cornwall: 209.
Corps—
British—
1st: 365, 393, 395.
5th: 267.
30th: 235, 246, 435, 438, 440.
Canadian: 23.
1st: leaves Britain for Italy, 287; Liri Valley, 299; disappointment over not entering Rome, 309; Gothic Line, 382-3; advance to River Conca, 389; Rimini, 391; Lombardy Plain, 405; at Wakehurst in 1941, 434; moves to Holland, 465; Holland, 466-7; other ref, 132.
2nd: 365, **373**, 393-4, 438, 465, 467.
German, 76th Panzer: 268.
United States—
2nd: 309.
6th: 307.
7th: 332.
Corvettes: 92, 95, 97, **101**, **118**, 430.
Cosens, Sgt. Aubrey, V.C.: 21, 437, 439, 440-1.
Cosgrove, Edmund: 152, 283, 284-5.
Cottam, WO2 Alden: 216, **217**.
Coughlin, Sgt. W. G. "Bing": 298.
Coughlin, Tom: **450**.
Courseulles-sur-Mer: 314, 323-4, 330.
Cowburn, Ben: 158.
Cramon-Taubadel, Major von: 72.
Creery, Rear Adm. Wallace B.: 35, 37-9, 38.
Crerar, Gen. H. D. G.: Chief of General Staff, 51; Dieppe, 132-3, 147, 150-1; the McNaughton-Ralston affair, 286; Montgomery, 287; Commander of First Canadian Army, 311; presents Canadian ensigns, 326; takes over front south of Caen; Falaise, 366; Channel ports, 380, 390; invalided to England, 393; mess dinner for Ralston, 406; closeup, 434-5; drive to Rhine, 437; promoted general, 438; discussing newspaper with Montgomery, **441**; Maj. Gen. C. C. Mann's assessment, 441; army reunited, 465; other ref, **388**.

Crerar, T. A.: 56.
Crete: 112.
Creully: 330-5.
Cripps, Sgt. Frank "Buzzer": 402.
Croft: 281.
Crofton, Maj. Desmond: 324.
Crowe, Lt. Col. R. M.: 233.
Crowley-Milling, Denis: **62**, 63, 69.
Croydon: 63.
Cryderman, Laurie: 63.
Cuffe, Air Commodore A. A. L.: **54**.
Culioli, Pierre: 160.
Cummings, Stoker William: 294, 296-7.
Cuneo, Ernest: 377.
Curaçao: 122.
Currie, Maj. David, V.C.: 370, 372.
Czechoslovakia: 88.

D

D-Day: 150-1, 285, 287, 311, 313-5, **318**, 324, 330-2, **331**, 357, 448, 461.
Dachau: 155, 164.
Dafoe, John W.: 6, 8.
Daily Express (London): 75.
Daily News (New York): **143**.
Daily Packet and Times (Orillia): **101**.
Dale, Mrs. Hartas: 154.
Daley, Cpl. Alden: 328.
Daley, L. Cpl. Bud: 327.
Daley, Pte. Chick: **318**.
Daley, Harold: 327.
Dalongeville, Maurice: **164**.
Dalton, Maj. Charles: 328.
Dalton, Maj. Elliott: 328.
Dambusters: 206-219, 452.
Dam Busters, The: 210-9, 452.
Danard, Wren Jean: 197.
Dangerous Sky, The: **450**.
Dartmouth: **221**.
Darragh, Cpl.: 111.
Daudelin, Pte. N.: 145-6.
Davey, Dr. Jean: 196.
Davidson, Hal: 192.
Dawson, MacGregor: 409.
Dawson Creek, B.C.: 180, 186, **187**.
Day, Lt. Harold: 316.
Debert: 88, 230.
Decisive Battles of World War II: 413.
Deering, PO. G. A. "Tony": 207, **208**, 211-3, **217**, 219.
Defense, Continental: 47.
Defense, Department of National: 405.
Defense, Canada-United States Permanent Joint Board on: 54, **54**.
Defense Headquarters: 47.
Delden: 462.
Dempsey, Lotta: 195.
Dempsey, Gen. Sir Miles C.: **312**, 313, 435.
Den Heuvel: 419.
Deniset, François: 155.
Denmark: 47, 276.
Denomy, FO. Bernard: 338-41, 343.
Depression: 6, 470.
Desert Rats: 435.
Desloges, FO. Jean-Paul: 65.
Destroyers: American, 51; *see also* Ships.
Detroit: 88.
Deventer: 465-6.
Devil's Gorge: 169.
Devil's Peak Peninsula: 107.
Devoir, Le: 413.
Dewar, Douglas: 183.
DeWolf, Vice Adm. Harry: **36**, 40, 43, **44**, 288, **289**, 291-4.
Dexter, Grant: 182, 184.
Dhuizon: 160.
Dibnah, Roland: 71.
Dickie, Lt. Bill: 403.
Dicks, Cpl. Bud: 112-3.
Dieppe: raid, 130-53; in minds of troops invading Sicily, 233; Ross Munro, **247**; lessons, 311; 2nd Division parade, **379**; liberation, 379-80; Crerar, 435; *other refs*, 72, 470.
Dieppe at Dawn: 135, 149, 151.
Dieppe: August 19: 149.
Dieppe: The Shame and The Glory: 140.
Dillgardt, Oberbürgermeister: 209, 219.
Distinguished Flying Cross: 219; awarded to—
Flt. Lt. Dick Audet: 449.
FO. Graham Campbell: 343.
Sqdn. Ldr. Walter Conrad: 254.
PO. G. A. "Tony" Deering: 219.
Air Commodore Johnnie Fauquier: 284.
Sqdn. Ldr. Syd Ford: 250.
Wing Comdr. Guy Gibson: 206.
FO. S. E. Matheson: 343.
FO. T. H. "Terry" Taerum: 219.
FO. Danny Walker: 219.
Distinguished Flying Medal: 219; awarded to—
Flt. Sgt. I. J. Bodnoff: 343.
Flt. Sgt. S. R. Cole: 343.
Sgt. Stephen Oancia: 219.
Distinguished Service Cross awarded to—
Lt. Tommy Fuller, 414.
Lt. Robert H. Gray, V.C.: 469.
Distinguished Service Order awarded to—
Guy d'Artois: 165.
Maj. Gustave "Guy" Bieler: 164.
FO. Bernard Denomy: 343.
Air Commodore Johnnie Fauquier: 284.
Wing Comdr. Guy Gibson: 207.
Les Knight: 219.
Dittaino River: 236-8.
Divisions—
British—
Guards Armored: 395.
1st Airborne: **391**, 393.
3rd Infantry: 314, 330-2.
6th Airborne: 311, 313-4, 316, **423**, 461.
7th Armored: 435.
11th Armored: 392.
15th Scottish: 435.
50th: 331-2.
51st (Highland): 36, 365-6, **444**.
52nd: 28, **31**.
78th Infantry: 246.
Canadian—
1st Infantry: to England, 21, **23**; and B.E.F., 28-9, **31**; troops march to board ship to Brittany, **33**; only whole and reasonably equipped division in U.K., 58; Sicily, 232-3, 236-7, **239**, 246-7, 286; Ortona, 260-73; Campochiaro, **261**; Liri Valley, 299; Return Stores Depot, **409**; Holland, 467; *other refs*, 86, 434.
2nd Infantry: elements sent to Britain, 47, 58; Dieppe, 130-2; Falaise, 365-7, 374; return to Dieppe, 379-80, **379**; Oldenburg, 465; *other refs*, 311, 405.
3rd Infantry: D-Day, 310-1, 314, **320**, 330-2; 12th SS Division, 357, 362; Boulogne, 390; Scheldt, 395-6, 403-4; "Water Rats" nickname, 435; drive to Rhine, 438, 440, 461; Emden, 465; *other refs*, 247, 365, 405.
4th Armored: **120**, 311, 365-7, 395, 404, 435, 438, 440, 465.
5th Armored: 273, 286, 299, 307, **308**, 383, **420**.
German—
Hermann Göring: 243.
1st Parachute: 262, 268, 273.

12th SS Panzer: 315, 330, 344, 357, 359, **360**, 361-2, 366, 372.
15th Panzer: 236, 238-9, 241-2, 246.
21st Panzer: 315, 330, 332.
64th Infantry: 393, 396.
70th Infantry: 393.
89th Infantry: 366.
90th Panzer Grenadier: 261-2, 273.
302nd Infantry: 134.
716th Infantry: 315, **329**, 332.
Indian: 8th Infantry, 299.
Polish: 1st Armored, 365-7, 435, 465.
United States—
17th Airborne: 461.
82nd Airborne: 332.
101st Airborne: 332.
Dobson, Lt. Comdr. A. H.: **169**.
Dodecanese Islands: 155.
Dönitz, Grand Adm. Karl: 118, 167, 169, **170**, 178; *see also* U-Boats.
Donovan, Gen. William J. "Wild Bill": **55**, 376, **376**.
Dora Line: 411.
Dortmund: 219, 452.
Douglas-Jones, Wing Cmdr. Eric: 72.
Dover: 28, 258-9.
Dover, Strait of: **311**.
Dowding, Air Chief Marshal Hugh: 75.
Dress Rehearsal: **150**.
Drew, George: 113.
Drew-Brook, T. G. "Tommy": 377.
Drillio, Pte. Edward G.: 308.
Dubost, Jacques: 379.
Dubé, Capt. Yvan: 386.
Dubuc, Sgt. Pierre: 145-6.
Duff, Chief Justice Sir Lyman: 113.
Duisburg: 452.
Dumais, Lucien: 351-2, **351**, **354**, 355.
Dumont, Cpl. David: 326.
Dunfermline: 341.
Dunkirk: 28, 31, 37, **143**, 188, 259, 390, 430.
Duplessis, Premier Maurice: 18-9, **18**.
Dupuis, Sqdn. Ldr. Lionel: 281.
Durnford, Rev. Roy: 271-2, 411.
Düsseldorf: 452.
Dutch East Indies: 122.
Duxford: 67, 70, 75, 78.
Dziuban, Col. Stanley: 287.

E

E-Boats: 37, 101, 136, 290-1, 414-5.
Eagle Day: 63, 71; *Adler Tag*: 63.
Earnshaw, FO. Kenneth: 216, **217**.
East Anglia: **210**.
East Moor: 281.
Easton, Alan: 99, 101, 166-7, 171.
Eberding, Gen. Kurt: 396, 403.
Eden, Anthony: **79**.
Eder Dam: 206-7, 210, 216-9.
Edmonton: 117, 209.
Edwards, Frederick: 221.
Edwards, Air Marshal Harold A. "Gus": 287.
Edwards, Wing Comdr. James F.: **450**.
Edwards, FO. R. L.: 64.
85th Battalion (C.E.F.): 405.
85 Days, The: 392, 394, 396.
Eindhoven: 211, **292**, **391**, 449.
Eisenhower, Gen. Dwight: Dieppe, 130, 133, **148**; Bomber Command, 285; McNaughton, 303; Allied commanders, **311**; D-Day, 313; Caen, 367; Scheldt, 393, 395, 404; Crerar likened to, 434.
Elbe River: 465-6.
Elections: 1917 Federal, 13; Quebec, 18; 1940 Federal, 19; 1945 Federal, 470.

Elizabeth, Princess: **315**.
Elizabeth, Queen: 219, **315**.
Ellis, Jean: 199-200.
Ellis, R. L.: 45.
Emden: 465.
Emmerich: 424.
Engineers—
3rd Field Company: 261.
6th Field Company: 324.
English Channel: evacuation of BEF, 28, 37, R. W. "Buck" McNair, **257**; Canadian destroyers, 289, **290**, **293**, 296; D-Day, **318**, 319, 332; Canadian MTBs, 415; *other refs*, 40, 58, 250, 253-4, 258.
Enna: **242**.
Espionage: 47.
Esquimalt: 265, 469.
Essame, H.: **356**.
Essen: 275, 452.
Essex Scottish Regiment: 130, 135, 140, 142, 147-8, 380, 394, 424, 440.
Ethiopia: 6-7, **7**.
Evère: 450.
Evening Telegram, The (St. John's): 15.
Ewell: 154, 156.
Execution: 299.

F

Face Powder and Gunpowder: 199.
Fairbanks: 180, 186, **187**.
Fairweather, Lt. Jack: 344, 346-50, **346**.
Falaise: 151, 362, 367-74, 405, 435.
Falaise Gap: 163, **369**, 374, 380.
Falentin, Emile: **164**.
Falloon, Capt. Tom: 414.
Far Distant Ships, The: 21, 37, 90, 118, **128**, **169**, 174, 433.
Far East: 100, 105, 155, 248.
Fauquier, Air Commodore Johnnie: **278**, 280, 282-4, **450**, 452.
Feasby, Lt. Col. W. R.: 198.
Fécamp: 319.
Federal Aircraft: 82-3.
Fifth Column: 34, 105, 107.
50 North: 99, **101**, 166.
Fighter Command, RAF: 59, 60, 63, 75.
Financial Post, The: 13.
Findlay, D. K.: **115**, 282.
Finn, Maj. Tom: 414.
First and The Last, The: 279, 450.
Fiumicino River: 405.
Flame of Power: 183.
Fleet Aircraft Limited: 83.
Fleming, Eleanor: 377.
Flin Flon: 201.
Floody, Wally: 455.
Florence: 382.
Flossenbürg: 155, 160, 163-4.
Flushing: 254, 396, 404.
Foch, Marshal Ferdinand: 11.
Foglia Valley: 383.
Folkestone: 60.
Fonsomme: 157, **162**, 164, **164**.
Foot, M. R. D.: 160, 164.
Foote, Maj. John W., V.C.: 15, **147**, 148.
Forbes, Maj. R. B.: 402.
Ford, Sqdn. Ldr. Syd: 249-50, 253.
Forêt de la Londe: 379.
Förster, Hugo: **99**.
Fort Nelson: 186.
Fort St. John: 186.
Fortune: 83, 180, 183.
Foster, Maj. Gen. Harry: 312, **312**.
Foster, Merle: 201.
Foulkes, Lt. Gen. Charles: 365, 374, 467-8, **467**.
"Four-Stackers": 92.
Four Winds Farm (trench system): 139.
Foxlee, Toby: 211.
Franco, Generalissimo Francisco: 10.
Frankland, Dr. Noble: 453.
Frankland, Sqdn. Ldr. Roger: 72.
Fraser, Blair: 411, 413.

Fraser, Capt. Hank: 358.
Fraser, Helen Gray: 201.
Fraser, PO. John: 214, 216, **299**.
Fredenberg, William R.: 344, 346.
Frederick, Flt. Lt. Gordon: 99.
Frederick, Maj. Gen. Robert T.: 461.
Free French: 134.
French Army: 29, **31**.
French Canadians: 12, 46, 48.
French Canadians, The: 413.
French Fleet: 51.
French National Railways: 157.
Friday, Jack: 336.
From Pachino to Ortona: 268.
Fruth, Robert K.: 352, 354.
Fulda Valley: 219.
Fuller, Lt. Tommy: 414-5.
Fulton, Maj. L. R.: 324.
Funkspiele: 160.
Fusiliers Mont-Royal: 130, 135, 140, 144-6.

G

Gallagher, Wes: 247.
Galland, Gen. Adolf: 72, 75, 279, 448-50, **449**.
Gallipoli: 149.
Galt: **188**, 196, 197.
Gammon, Sgt. Bill: 358.
Gander: 53, 89.
Garbas, Flt. Sgt. Frank: 211, **217**.
Garceau, Maj. Ovila: **263**, 265.
Gariépy, Sgt. Léo: 331.
Garigliano River: 299.
Garner, Hugh: 169, 171.
Garshowitz, WO2 Abram: 211, **217**.
Gaspé: 122, 124-5, 128.
Gaston, Mlle Anne-Marie: 415.
Gathering Storm, The: **29**.
Gauntlet to Overlord: 130, 136, 316, 330, 379.
Gazette, The (Montreal): 13.
Gee, Flt. Lt. "Auntie": 192.
Gelsenkirchen: 219.
General Engineering Company: 203.
General Motors of Canada: 189.
Gennep: **441**.
George VI: Canada answers call by, **19**; urged to go to Bermuda, 48; William J. "Wild Bill" Donovan, **55**; congratulating Guy Gibson, **219**; visiting Dambuster Squadron, 219; 1st Canadian Parachute Battalion, **315**; knighthood for William Stephenson, 376; *other refs*, 50, 78-9, 152, **332**, 461.
George Cross awarded to—
LAC K. M. Gravell, **82**.
LAC K. G. Spooner, **82**.
George Medal. Lt. George Cook: 414.
German agents: 17.
German Air Force: *see* Luftwaffe.
German Army: *see* Army, German.
German Intelligence: 372.
German Navy: 59, 178; *see also* Ships.
Germany: 49, 51, 103, 254, 276, 279, 376-7, 393, 461.
Gerrior, Pte. W. H.: 358.
Gestapo: 155-6, 158-61, **159**, **160**, 164, 350-1, 354, 455.
Ghent: 392, 404.
Gibraltar: 94, 153, 173.
Gibson, Wing Comdr. Guy, V.C.: 206-14, **208**, 216-9, **219**.
Gicquel, Jean: 351, 355.
Giffen, Capt. H. O.: 431.
Gildersleeve, Wilf: 272.
Giles, Lt. Comdr. Morgan: 414.
Gill, Flt. Lt. R. F.: 450.
Gilmour, Blair: **446**.
Gilze-Rijen: 211.
Gin-Drinkers Line: 107.
Glace Bay: 180.
Glasgow: **228**.
Glinz, FO. Harvey: 211, **217**.
Globe and Mail, The (Toronto): 13.
Gobeaux, Mlle Odette: 159.

Goebbels, Joseph: **275**.
Goldflake, Operation: 465.
Golland, Pte. Joe: 402.
Good, Mabel T.: 455.
"Good Evening to the House of Alphonse": 350.
Goodwood, Operation: 365.
Goose Bay: 89, 123, 126, 197.
Gordon, Donald: 183, **185**.
Göring, Hermann: 58, 75, 448, 450.
Gort, Lord: 28.
Gossoin, Simon: **164**.
Gostling, Lt. Col. A. C.: 140.
Gothic Line: 382-3, 386, 389, 391, 405.
Government of Canada: 232, 273, 435.
Government House: 79.
Gowan, Maj. J. H.: 272.
Gower, Capt. P. E.: 324.
Gowrie, Sgt. Chester: **217**.
Graham, Sgt. Gordon: 399.
Graham, Brig. Howard D.: 236.
Graham, Pte. T. W.: 145.
Grant, Capt. H. T. W.: 289, 414.
Grantham: 211, 214.
Grassick, Bob: 63.
Grave: 448.
Gravell, LAC K. M.: **82**.
Gravesend: 65.
Gray, Lt. Robert H., V.C.: 15, 469.
Great Bear Lake, NWT: 187.
Great Escape, The: 455.
Great Escape Stories: 350.
Grebbe Line: 466.
Greece: 129.
Greene, Lorne: **107**.
Greenland: 47, 51, 94, 117, 125, 169, 178.
Greenock: 27, 40, 43, **99**, **228**.
Gresham, Maj. A. B.: 112.
Griffin, L.Cpl. Fred: 322.
Griffiths, Cpl. Daphne: 72.
Groningen: 465.
Groote Meer Lake: 394.
Grosse Schlag, Der: 449.
Groups: *see* Army; Royal Air Force; Royal Canadian Air Force.
Grubb, Lt. F. E.: **99**.
Guildford: 76.
Guillet, Edwin: 186.
Guimond, Capt. Bernard: 263.
Guingamp: **352**, 354.
Gully, The: 262, 267-8.
Gustav Line: 299.

H

H-Hour: 322, **323**, 326.
Haakon, King: 205.
Haase, Gen. Konrad: 140.
Hague, The: 465-6, 468.
Hahn, Hauptmann Hans von: 72.
Haida: 288-97.
Haidas: 288.
Hailey, Arthur: 83.
Haiti: 122.
Halifax, Lord: 103.
Halifax: 21, 49, 178, 221-31, 297, 431.
Halifax, Warden of the North: 211, 229.
Hall, Skpr. Lt. K. W. N.: 315.
Halliday, FO. Hugh: 281.
Halton, Matthew: 247, 260-2, 273, 362, **369**.
Hamburg: 58, 276-80, **278**, **281**, 283-4, 452, 466.
Hamilton: 434.
Hamley, Lt. Harry: 398-9.
Hamm: 211-8, 218-9.
Handful of Rice, A: 103.
Hanlon, Betty: 199.
Hannam, Able Seaman Jack: 296-7.
Hanover: 452.
"Happy Time": 167.
"Happy Valley": 206.
Harderwijk: 211.
Harris, Angus K.: **415**.
Harris, Air Chief Marshal Sir Arthur: 208, 211, 214, 219, 277, 284-5, 453.
Harris, Rev. G. A.: **315**, 316.
Harrison, Connie: 199-200.
Harrison, Capt. Russell: 461.
Hart, Norrie: 63.

Hartwig, Lt. Comdr. Paul: 125-6, 128-9.
Harvison, RCMP Commissioner C. W.: 47.
Hastings and Prince Edward Regiment: 24-33, 169, 235-43, 246, 418.
Havilland Aircraft of Canada Limited, de: 83, 201.
Hawkinge: 256.
Haycock, Rfn. George: 326.
Hayworth, Margaret: **25**.
Hearn-Phillips, Norman: 192.
Hebrides: 209.
Hedgehog: 178.
Hedges, Sqdn. Ldr. G. P.: 196.
Heeney, Arnold: 78-9.
Heesch: 450.
Heligoland: 277.
Hellyer, Paul Theodore: **411**.
Henderson, Leon: 183.
Hepburn, Premier Mitchell: **18**, 19, 115.
Herbie: 298.
Hero, The "Buzz" Beurling Story: 152-3.
Hewitt, PO. D. A.: 59.
Hibbard, Lt. Comdr. J. C.: **36**, 97.
Hickey, Rev. R. M.: **25**, 310-2, 315, 327, 361, **362**, 372, 467.
Hickson, Sgt. George: 145.
Highland Light Infantry of Canada: 324, 330, 362, 396, 399.
Highlanders of Canada, 48th: **31**, 235, 243, 246, 268, 272, 306.
Hilsum-Beuckens, Mrs. C.: 462, 468.
Hilversum: 468.
Himmelbett Line: 276, 284.
Himmelpforten: 214.
Himmler, Heinrich: **420**.
Hiroshima: 469.
History of the Second World War: **281**, **373**, 377, 453.
Hitler, Adolf: and Mackenzie King, 8; Britain's declaration of war, **11**; Stalin, 12; Poland, 12; Paris, **48**; peace feelers after fall of France, 58; postpones Operation Sea Lion, 75; invades Russia, 92; Channel defenses in 1942, 134; orders Malta neutralized, 152; orders armies to fight for Rome and Italy, 260, 299-300; Ortona, 268; calls Allied bombers "air pirates", 280; miracle weapons, 283, 390; Normandy, 365-6, 374; Ardennes, 413; Messerschmitt, 448, **449**; inspects bomb damage, **452**; orders murder of escapers, 455; *other refs*, **44**, 98, 192, 316, **420**, 461.
Hitler Line: 151, 299-300, **300**, 306-7, **308**.
Hitler Youth: 357, **359**, 361-2.
Hochwald: 151, 438, 440, **442**.
Hodkinson, Maj. E.: 112.
Hodson, Wing Comdr. Keith: 249-50.
Hoffmeister, Maj. Gen. B. M.: **244**, 299.
Hogg, Capt. Bill: 399, 401.
"Hole, The": 72.
Holland: 28, **29**, 76, 88, 134, 218, 254, 276, **391**, 462.
Holland and the Canadians: 462, 466.
Hollingsworth, Sgt. "Holly": 415.
Hollohan, Cpl. John: 399.
Holmes, Sgt. Ray: 74.
Home, Lt. Col. W. J.: 103.
Home Made Banners: 319, **325**.
Hong Kong: 103-4, 114, 116, 198, 456, 470.
Honshu: 469.
Hoover, J. Edgar: 376.
Hopgood, John: 206, 210-2, 214, 216, 219.
Hornchurch: 72.
Hornell, Flt. Lt. David, V.C.: **336**, 338-43.

Horrocks, Lt. Gen. Sir Brian: 435.
Horsemen, The: 47.
Hospitals: *see* Medical.
Houde, Mayor Camillien: 8, 48, **50**.
Houlton: 56.
Howe, Clarence Decatur: 47, **50**, 51, 81-2, 180, 183, 185-6.
Howley, Richard: 59-60.
Hubbell, John G.: 350.
Hudson, Christopher: 165.
Hughes-Hallett, Capt. John: 134, 144.
Hull, Cordell: 49-50.
Huls: 211.
Hunt, Sgt. George: 411-2.
Hussars 1st (6th Armored Regiment): 324, 331.
Hutchison, Bruce: 8, **46**, 182-3, 188, 191; *The Incredible Canadian*, 48, 57; *Mr. Prime Minister*, 18, 409.
Hutton, Eric: 13, 17.
Hvalfjord: **92**.
Hyde, FO. George: 65.
Hyde, H. Montgomery: **55**, 377.
Hyde, Flt. Sgt. Kenneth: **454**, **456**.
Hyde Park, N.Y.: 182.
Hyde Park Declaration of 1941: 183, 213.

I

I-Boats: 415.
Iceland: 47, **53**, 91, **92**, 94, 118-9, 335, 338.
Ijssel River: 466.
Ijzendijke: 399.
Ilsley, James Lorimer: 47, **50**, 181-2, **181**.
Imperial Airways: 89.
Imperial Oil Limited: 122, 430.
Imthal: 418.
Incredible Canadian, The: 48, 57, 182.
India: 88, 115, 119.
Indianerkrieg: 246.
Indian Ocean: 122, 135.
Infantry—
  British—
    Middlesex Regiment: 105, 108, 110, 112.
    Royal Scots: 105, 107-8, 112.
    Welsh Guards: 349.
  Canadian—
    Algonquin Regiment: 366, 395.
    Argyll and Sutherland Highlanders: 370.
    Battalion, 85th: 405.
    Black Watch (Royal Highland Regiment): 130, 134, 136, 365, **407**.
    Calgary Highlanders: 130, **426**.
    Cameron Highlanders of Ottawa (M.G.): 315, 358, 360, **370**.
    Canadian Scottish Regiment: 324, 326, 359, 395.
    Cape Breton Highlanders: 405.
    Carleton and York Regiment: 76, 236, **261**, 306.
    Essex Scottish Regiment, 130, 135, 140, 142, 147-8, 380, 394, 424, 440.
    First Canadian Special Service Battalion: 461.
    Fusiliers Mont-Royal: 130, 135, 140, 144-6, **373**.
    Hastings and Prince Edward Regiment: 24-33, 235-43, 246, 306.
    Highland Light Infantry of Canada: 324, 330, 362, 396, 399.
    Highlanders of Canada, 48th: **31**, 235, 243, 246, 268, 272, 306.
    Irish Regiment of Canada: 309, 410.
    Lincoln and Welland Regiment: 307, 370.

Loyal Edmonton Regiment: 28, 236, **237**, 268-9, **268**, 270, 272-3, 306.
North Nova Scotia Highlanders: 324, **332**, 344, 350, 357-8, 362, 403, 464.
North Shore (New Brunswick) Regiment: **25**, 310, 324, 327, 330, 361, 366, 395-6, 399, 467.
Parachute Battalion, 1st: **315**, **423**, 461, 466.
Princess Patricia's Canadian Light Infantry: 28, 235-6, **237**, 273, 299, 306.
Queen's Own Cameron Highlanders: 130, 134-5, 137, 139-40.
Queen's Own Rifles: 312, 315, 324, 327, **329**, 361, 437, 467.
Régiment de la Chaudière: 324, **329**, 330, 361, 402.
Régiment de Maisonneuve: 130, 154-5, 163, 394, **436**, 441.
Regina Rifle Regiment: **312**, 323-4, 326, 329-30, 357, 395, 459-60.
Royal Canadian Regiment: **31**, 233, 241-3, 267-8, 306.
Royal Hamilton Light Infantry: 130, 135, 140, 142, 144-8, 380, 395, 456.
Royal Regiment: 130, 134, **134**, 136-7, **137**, **141**, 144, 148-9, 247, 380.
Royal Rifles: 103, 108, 111-2.
Royal 22nd Regiment: 76, 236, 246, 262, **263**, 267, 306, 383.
Royal Winnipeg Rifles: 323-4, 326, 330-1, 357, 359-61, 395, 438.
Saskatoon Light Infantry: 272.
Seaforth Highlanders: 235, **244**, 262, **265**, 268-9, 271, 273, 306.
South Saskatchewan Regiment: 130, 134, 136-40, **139**, 380, 464.
Stormont, Dundas and Glengarry Highlanders: 324, 362.
Toronto Scottish Regiment (M.G.): 130.
Westminster Regiment: 421-2.
West Nova Scotia Regiment: 76, 236, 262, 306, 383-6.
Winnipeg Grenadiers: 103, 107-8, 110, 112.
  Indian—
    14th Punjab Regiment: 105, 108.
    7th Rajput Regiment: 105, 107-8, 110-1.
  United States: 1st Ranger Battalion: 130, 134, 143.
Inside SOE: 161.
Intelligence: Allied, 283; German, 372.
Invasion—They're Coming!: 357.
Ionian Sea: 414.
Ipswich: 276.
Irish Regiment of Canada: 309.
Ironside, Sir Edmund: 28.
Italy: 6-7, 47, **48**, 103, 232, 260, 377, 434, 461.

J

Japan: 6, 103, 469, 470.
Japanese Canadians: 114-5.
Japanese spies: 105.
Jaques, Edna: 186.
Jardine's Lookout: 110-1.
Jarvis: 83.
Jasperson, Lt. Col. Fred K.: 140, 142.
Jefferson, Lt. Col. J. C.: **237**.

Jenner, Pte. F. E. A.: 145.
Jennings, L.Sgt. Claudius H.: 399.
John Inglis Company Limited: 201.
Johnson, A. J.: 431.
Johnson, Gp. Capt. J. E. "Johnnie": 248-59, 332, 448, 450.
Jones, Vice Adm. George C.: 230.
Jones, Pte. Raymond: 399.
Joube, Marcel: **164**.
Joubert, Air Chief Marshal Sir Philip: 338.
Journey Into Victory: 233.
Journal of a War: 416, **426**, **429**.

K

Kammhuber, Gen. Josef: 276.
Kangaroo: 366-7, 440.
Kanningenhaven: 399.
Kapelsche Veer: **419**.
Kapitaledam: 398.
Karasevich, Lt. John: 324.
Karlsruhe: 452.
Kaslo: 115.
Kassel: 219.
Kaufmann, Gauleiter: 278.
Kearns, Pte. Angus: 332.
Keefer, Wing Comdr. George: 249, **250**, 254, 450.
Keenleyside, Dr. Hugh L.: 50, **54**.
Keitel, Field Marshal Wilhelm: **320**.
Keller, Maj. Gen. R. F. L.: 310, **327**, 359, 366.
Keller, FO. R. W.: 450.
Kellock, Mr. Justice R. L.: 230.
Kelly, Jim: 336-7.
Kelly, Capt. Percy A.: 431-2, **431**.
Kemptville: 189-90.
Kenley: 249-50, 253, 256-7, 259.
Kennedy, Maj. A. A.: 244.
Kennedy, Mrs. Joan: 195.
Kennedy, Joseph: 55.
Kent, Flt. Lt. J. A. "Johnnie": **69**, 71.
Keppeln: 424.
Kerambrun, François: 354.
Kesselring, Field Marshal Albert: 268, 412, 427.
Kidder, Gordon: 455.
King, Adm. Ernest J.: 177.
King, Mackenzie: League of Nations, 6-8; meets Hitler, 8, **9**; "appeasement", 10; cables Chamberlain, 10; cables appeals to Hitler, 12; broadcasts September 3, 1939, **13**; conscription not necessary, 13; wins 1940 election, 19; why Canada went to war, **19**; link between Churchill and Roosevelt, **46**, 48, 56, 287; private belief that Chamberlain would have been a safer guide for Britain, 47; expresses opinion U.S. should get bases, 51; meets with Roosevelt at Ogdensburg, 51, 53-4, **54**; air training plan, 77-80, **80**; conscription plebiscite, 116-7, **117**; Dieppe, 133; wartime cabinet, 180; Lend-Lease and Hyde Park Declaration, 182-3; removal of McNaughton, 286; conscription crisis, **408**, **412**; *other refs*, 160, 434, 470.
Kingston: 434.
Kirby, Peter: 281-2.
Kirsch, Capt. Archie: 328.
Kitchener: 195.
Kitching, Maj. Gen. George: 366.
Kluane Lake: 186.
Kluge, Field Marshal Günther von: 365-6.
Knelman, Dr. F. H.: 204.
Knight, Les: 210, 216-7, 219.
Knocke-sur-Mer: 403, **426**.
Komiza: 414.
Kootenay Valley: 115.
Kowloon: 104-8.
Kretschmer, Otto: **44**.

474

L

Labatt, Lt. Col. Robert R.: 140-1, 144, 147, 456.
Labelle, Placide: 155.
LaBrosse, Maj. Raymond: 351-2, **351**, 354-5, **354**.
Lacroix, Second Officer André: 127.
Laflèche, Lt. François "Fritz": 387-9.
LaGuardia, Mayor Fiorello: **54**.
Laing, Sgt. Kenneth N.: 456.
Laison Valley: 367.
Landing Craft Infantry (LCI): 235, 315.
Landing Craft Rocket (LCR): **320**.
Landing Craft Tank (LCT): 148, 234-5, 316, 326.
Landymore, Sub Lt. William: 38.
Langford, Patrick: 455.
Lane, Capt. Reg: 241.
Lapointe, Ernest: 7-8, 13, 15, 46, 48, 56, 117.
Large, Flt. Sgt. W.: 449.
Larichelière, PO. Joseph: 63.
Lashenden: 257-9.
La Spezia: 382.
Latta, John: 63.
Laurendeau, André: **19**, 46.
Laurier House: 367.
Laval: 30, **31**.
Law, Maj. A. T.: 140.
Lawrence, Lt. Harold: 98, **99**, 122.
Lawson, Brig. J. K.: 103, **105**, 108, 112.
Lay, Capt. H. N.: **36**.
Leacock, Stephen: **111**.
League of Nations: 6-7, **7**.
Learment, Maj. Don: 344, 346.
Leather, Flt. Lt. Jack: 73.
Le Cornec, François: 351, 355.
Le Coz, Capt. Georges: 346-50, **348**.
Leeming: 281.
Leese, Lt. Gen. Sir Oliver: 246, 267.
Leghorn: 465.
Legionary, The: **101**.
Le Havre: 37, 319, 379-80.
Leigh-Mallory, Air Vice-Marshal Sir Trafford L.: 65, 134.
Le Mans: 165, 366.
Lemon Creek: **157**.
Lend-Lease Act: 118, 183, 185, 430.
Leonforte: **237**, 241.
Leopold Canal: 395, 403.
Lens: 337.
Leros: 414.
Les Canadiens Errants: 441, **444**.
Liberal Party: 407, 409, 470.
Liège: **423**.
Lille: 75, 157-8, **162**.
Lincoln and Welland Regiment: 370, **419**.
Lindbergh, Col. Charles: 22.
Linee Aeree Transcontinentali Italiane: 377.
Linton-on-Ouse: 281.
Liri Valley: 299, 309.
Lisbon: 160.
Little, FO. Tom: 63, 65.
"Little Chief": 26-7, **27**, 33.
Liverpool: 40, 45.
Loches: **346**, 347-9.
Lochnan, FO. Phil: 70.
Lockheed Aircraft Corp.: 89.
Loire River: 34, 366.
Lombardy Plains: 382, 405.
London: 59, **66**, 103, 247, 284, 349-50, 377.
London, Battle of: 391.
Londonderry: 52, 119.
Long, Pte. A. K.: 238, 243.
Longueuil: 189.
Longueville: 380.
Lord Strathcona's Horse: 307-9.
Louis St. Laurent: Canadian: **412**.
Lovat, Lord: **145**.
Lovett, Agnes: 198.
Lower, A. R. M.: 8, 13.
Loyal Edmonton Regiment: 28, 236, **237**, 268-9, **268**, 270, 272-3, 306.

M

Lübeck: 450, 460.
Lucas, "Laddie": 152.
Luc-sur-Mer: 330.
Luftwaffe: 40, 58-9, **62**, 63, 72, **74**, 134, 149-50, 255, 279, 332, 448-50.
  1st Wing, 3rd Fighter Group: 72.
  Signals Intelligence: 319.
  III Fighter Division: 276, 285.
Luftwaffe War Diaries, The: 448, 453.
Luxembourg: **29**.
Luzillé: 346.
Lye Mun Passage: 111.
Lynch, Charles: 247.

Maas River: 395, 416, **419**, 438, 465.
Macalister, John: 155, 160-1, **160**, 162.
McCarthy, Flt. Lt. "Big Joe": 209-11, **217**, 218-9.
MacCausland, FO. Vincent: **217**, 219.
McComb, Sqdn. Ldr. James: 73-74.
McCool, Maj. Brian: **134**, 142.
McCormick, Lt. W. F.: 331.
McCourt, Pte. Hugh: 141.
Macdonald, Angus L.: 6, 47, **50**, 181-2, 196.
Macdonald, Lt. Col. Bruce J. S.: 360.
Macdonald, Sgt. C. E.: 456.
MacDonald, David: 335.
McDonald, Flt. Sgt. Grant: **217**.
McDonald, Margaret: 201.
McDonald, Mickey: 201.
Macdonald, Bdr. Thomas: 434.
McDougall, Colin: 299.
McDougall, Lt. R. L.: **265**.
McDowell, Flt. Sgt. James: 211, **217**.
McEwen, Air Vice-Marshal Clifford M. "Black Mike": 152, **284**, 285.
Macey, Sgt. C. N.: 307-8.
MacFarlane, Maj. J. D. "Doug": 298.
McGarvey, Pte. Bill: 328.
McGill, George: 455.
McGill University: 210, 213.
McGregor, Flt. Lt. Gordon: 63-64, 71.
MacKay, Ida: 198.
McKee, Alexander: 316, 330-1, 361.
Mackenzie King Record, The: 48, 51, 78.
Mackenzie River: 117.
McKillop, Sgt. Earl: 358.
McKillop, Cpl. Walter: 358.
McKnight, Willie: 34, **62**, 63, 69-70.
Macksey, Maj. K. J.: **373**.
McLaughlin, Leonard J.: 430, **433**.
McLaughlin, R. S.: 189.
MacLean, Flt. Sgt. Don: 217.
McLean, Margaret D.: **228**.
Maclean's: 8, 13, 40, 95, **103**, **108**, **134**, 161, 165, 180, 186, **188**, 190, 195, 200, 203, 221, 224, 282, **315**, **413**.
McLeod, Sqdn. Ldr. Henry Wallace: 249.
Maclure, L/S William: 294, 296-7.
McNab, Sqdn. Ldr. Ernest: **60**, 63, 70, 75.
McNab Island: **221**, 226, 229.
McNair, R. W. "Buck": 249, 254, 256, **257**.
McNaught, Lt. Jack: 122, 126, 128, 171-2.
McNaughton, Gen. A. G. L.: in 1935 deplores lack of equipment, 10, **18**; proposals to send 1st Division to France in 1940, 28-9; defense of U.K., 33; Dieppe, **131**, 132; Sicilian campaign, 232; difficulties with Ralston and events leading to being relieved of command, 286-87; with Lt. Col. J. E. Sager of Westminster Regiment, 286;

conscription crisis, 407-11; his great disappointment, 434; his dream fulfilled, First Canadian Army reunited, 465.
McNaughton, Spr. Milton: 261.
McNaughton's Flying Circus: 58.
Macneill, Lt. Comdr. Isabel: 196.
McRae, Lt. R. F.: 145.
MacRitchie, Comdr. Peter: **101**.
Madoc: 24.
Magee, John Gillespie, Jr.: **88**.
Magee, Willa: 196.
Maginot Line: 22, **311**.
Magny: **370**.
Maguire, Eric: 149.
Magwood, Flt. Lt. Charles: 253.
Mahony, Maj. J. K., V.C.: 21, **308**, 309.
Maida Barracks: 27.
Maidstone: 75.
Maison, Ivy: 195.
Malan, Adolph "Sailor": 55.
Malaya: 102, 106, **107**.
Malkin, Ben: 76, **246**.
Malloy, Wing Comdr. Bud: 250, **250**.
Malone, Col. Dick: **270**, 287, 406, 409, **441**, 469.
Malta: 152, 153, 233, 247, 248, 415.
Malta Spitfire: 152.
Maltby, Maj. Gen. C. M.: 105, 112-3.
Manchester: 155.
Manion, R. J.: 19.
Manitoba: 190.
Manitoba, University of: 376.
Mann, Maj. Gen. Churchill C.: 134, 435, **441**.
Mannheim: 283.
Manning, PO. Ralph: 192-3, **193**.
Manston: 254, 256.
Manteuffel, Gen. Hasso von: 413.
Maple Leaf, The: 298, 408.
Maple Leaf Up, Maple Leaf Down: 367, 435, 438.
Maquis: 165, **165**, 346-9, **346**, **348**, **351**, **352**, **354**, 355.
Maracaibo: 122.
Marais, Colin Bain: 35.
Maritime Commission, U.S.: 126.
Market Garden, Operation: **391**.
Marmora: 24.
Marolle, Ambroise: **164**.
Marne River: 179.
Marsoillos: 351, 465.
Marsh, Sgt. Tom: 110-3.
Marshall, Gen. George C.: 120, 133.
Martin, Mickey: 210-1, 213-4, 216, 219.
Massey, Vincent: 8, **79**.
Matheson, Lt. Col. F. M.: 323.
Matheson, FO. S. E.: 338, 340-1, 343.
Mauger's Beach: 227, 229.
Max Horton and the Western Approaches: 94.
Maxwell, Flt. Sgt. (Old Bloody Nerves): 84-6.
MBE: Sgt. W. G. "Bing" Coughlin, 298.
Meade, Edward: **21**, 311, 369.
Mears, F. C.: **13**.
Medal for Merit: 376, **376**.
Medical—
  Casualty Clearing Station, No. 5: 198.
  Hospitals—
    No. 7: 199.
    No. 14: 198.
    No. 75 (British): 199.
Mediterranean Sea: 94, 119, 122, 414.
Meighen, Arthur: 116.
Melfa River: 308, 309.
Men of Valour: 455.
Ménard, Lt. Col. Dollard: 144.
Merchant seamen: **95**, 101-2, **179**, 430, 433.
Merritt, Lt. Col. Cecil, V.C.: 138-40, **139**.
Mersey River: 40.
Messina: 232, 236, 246.
Meuse River: *see* Maas River.
Mexico, Gulf of: 120.
Meyer, Standartenführer Kurt: 357, 360-1, **360**, 366, 372.

MGB (Motor Gun Boat): 414-5.
Middleton St. George: 281.
Military Cross: **327**.
Military Medal: Spr. Milton McNaughton, 261.
Militia, Non-Permanent Active: 23.
Minaker, Cpl. Cal: 326.
Minches: 43.
Mines: "S", 300; Teller, 300.
Misch, Kurt: 361.
Missing From The Record: 406, 409, **441**, 469.
Mitchell, PO. Harry: 63.
Moaning Minnie: 240, 417-9, 421.
Mobilization: 15, 23.
Moffat, Pierrepont: 53-4.
Möhne Dam: 206-19.
Mölders, Werner: 72.
Molson, Hartland: 63.
Moncton: 21, 23, 189, 197.
Monnet, Mme Marie-Louise: 157, 164.
Montargis: **162**.
Montebello: 56.
Monte Cassino: 411.
Montgomery of Alamein, Field Marshal: Dieppe, 131-2; Sicily, 232, 236, **244**, 246, **246**; relations with Maj. Gen. Chris Vokes, **270**; D-Day, **311**, 312, **312**, **320**; Normandy, 357, 361, 374; Operation Market Garden, 391, 393; relations with Crerar, 287, 434-5, 441; Scheldt, 393, 395, 404; his prediction that war would be over by November 1944, 405.
Montreal: 89, 123, 126, 187, 189-91, **204**, 223.
Montreal, University of: 155.
Moore, FO. K. O.: **338**.
Mooshof: 437, **439**.
Morale: 27, 108.
Morcourt: 164.
Morel, Maj. Gerry: 161.
Morgan, Len: 83, **84**, 88.
Morgenthau, Henry: 56.
Morison, Samuel Eliot: 118, **148**.
Moritsugu, Frank Akira: 114-5.
Moro River: 260-1, **261**, 273.
Morrison, Herbert: 390-1.
Mossbank: 82-3.
Mountbatten, Lord Louis: 130, 133, **148**, 149.
Mount Butler: 111-2.
Mount Etna: 236, 241-2.
Mount Houston: 112.
Mount Nicholson: 112.
Mount Parker: 111.
Mount Rivisotto: **237**.
Mount Seggio: **237**.
Mount Tiglio: 244.
Mowat, Farley: 24, 28-9, 33, 236, **239**, 246, **303**, **304**.
Moyland Wood: 438.
MTB (Motor Torpedo Boat): 414-5.
Mulberry: 149, **360**.
Munitions and Supply, Department of: 47.
Munro, Hugh: 209.
Munro, Les: 210-1.
Munro, Ross: Dieppe, 130-2, 136-7, 151, 247; Lt. Helen-Marie Stevens, 197; Sicily, 236, 248; Sicily and Normandy landings, 247; D-Day, 316, 324, 330; return of 2nd Division to Dieppe in September 1944, 379-80; Rhine crossing, 461.
Münster: 209, 450, 452.
Murmansk: 119, 222, 232, 414.
Murray, Rear Adm. L. W.: call up of RN reservists, **15**; public apathy between wars, **38**; member of Canada-United States Permanent Joint Board on Defense, **54**; at sea in *Assiniboine*, 92; command of Canadian ships and establishments in the U.K., 92; Commodore Commanding Newfoundland Escort Force, 94; tribute to merchant seamen, **95**; corvettes, **101**; relations with U.S. Navy, 119; presents reward for sighting

U-boat, **169**; C-in-C Canadian northwest Atlantic, 178, **179**, 287; Halifax riots, 230; *other ref*, **44**.
Murter Island: 414.
Muscau: 458-9.
Mussolini, Benito: 7, 10, 112, 246, 270.
Mutual Aid Bill: 185.
Mynarski, PO. Andrew Charles, V.C.: 335-7, **335**, **336**.

N

NAAFI (Navy, Army and Air Force Institute): 282.
Nagasaki: 469.
Nantes: 34.
Naples: 200.
Narvik: 28.
National Harbors Board: 224.
National Home Monthly: 316.
National Research Council: 172.
National Resources Mobilization Act: 48.
Naval Service of Canada, Its Official History, The: 173.
Navy—
  British: *see* Royal Navy.
  Canadian: *see* Royal Canadian Navy.
  French: 51.
  German: 59, 178.
Navy at War, The: 178.
Nelles, Vice Adm. Percy: **101**, **296**.
Nelson, FO. W. H.: 59.
Neptune, Operation: 315.
Nesbitt, Maj. Aird: 405.
Nesbitt, Deane: 63, 73.
Neutrality Act (United States): 46, **56**, 57, 89. Neutrality Patrol: 118.
New Canadian, The: 114, 115.
New Forest: 155.
Newfoundland: 15, 47, 51, 53, 56, 89, 94, 103, 120, 190, 338.
Newfoundland Command: 118-9.
Newfoundland Escort Force: 94, **97**.
Newhaven: 135.
Newman, Peter: 183.
New Territories: 105-7.
New World Illustrated: 111, 189.
New York: 178, 197, 376, 432.
New York Times, The: 75, 180.
New Zealand: 55, 88.
Niagara Falls: 87, **345**.
Nicholson, Lt. Col. G. W. L.: 232, 309, 383, 389.
Nijmegen: **391**, 416, **419**, 423, 438, 448.
Nikerk, J.: 462.
Nimerovsky, "Nimmy": 192.
Niseis: 114-5.
Nissoria: 241-4.
Noble, Adm. Sir Percy: 94.
Nolan, Brian: 152-3.
Nolan, Capt. Dan: 127.
Noorduyn Aviation: 82.
Noranda: 283.
No Retreating Footsteps: 357.
Norfolk: 62.
Normandy: 150-1, 247, 312-3, **315-6**, **320**, 324, 332, **332**, 357, 362, 365, 372, 374, 392, 414, 461.
North, John: 394.
North Africa: *see* Africa.
Northampton: 76.
Northolt: 63-4, 71.
North Nova Scotia Highlanders: 324, 332, 344, 350, 357-8, 362, 402, 416, **464**.
North Sea: 45, 257, 276.
North Shore (New Brunswick) Regiment: **25**, 310, 324, 327, 330, 361, 366, 395-6, 399, 467.
North Weald: 64, 67, 69.
Northwest Territories: 187.
Norway: 7, 88, 334, 352, 452.
Norwich: 60-1.
Nova Scotian Hotel: 222.
Nuremberg: 387, 452.
Nursing Sisters: 194, **203**.
Nutter, Lt. Harry: 399.

O

Oancia, Sgt. Stephen: **217**, 218-9.
O'Brien, Sgt. Harry: 209, 217, **217**.
Observer Corps: 72, 74.
Office of Strategic Services: 377.
Ogdensburg: 51, 53-4, **54**, 57.
Ogilvie, PO. Keith: 74.
Oldenburg: 465.
Oldfield, Pte. A. W.: 145.
Onawaga Bay: 469.
Ontario: 81, 115, 186.
Ontario Regiment: 262, 267, 272.
Opposition: 19, 82-3, 113, 116, 407.
Ordeal by Fire: 6, 28, **172**, 177, 269, 405-6, 412, 470.
Orléans: 366.
Orne River: 314, 316, 365.
Orsogna: 262, 268.
Ortona: 151, 260-3, 266, 268-73.
Osborn, CSM. John R., V.C.: 112-3, **112**.
Oshawa: 377.
Osnabrück: 449.
Ostend: 254, 258, 389.
Osteria Nuovo: 383.
Ostersander: 467.
Ott, Wolfgang: **126**, 174, 178.
Ottawa: 47, 87, 103, 114-5, 132, 180, 184-5, 195, 203.
Ouimet, Marcel: **328**, 330.
Ouistreham: 313.
Oulton, Lt. Blake: 399.
Overlord, Operation: 312, 315.
Oxford: 76.

P

Pachino: 232, 234-5, **235**, 247.
Pacific Coast: 117.
Paddon, Surgeon Lt. W. A. "Tony": **170**.
Page, Bobbie: 259.
Panama Canal: 120.
Parachute Battalions: 1st Canadian, **315**, **423**, 461, 466.
Paris: 30, **31**, 34, 154, 351-2, **352**, 354, 366, 374, 392.
Park, Air Vice-Marshal Keith: 71.
Park Steamship Company Limited: 430.
Parker, Maj. Willard: 399.
Parks, Tommy: 254-6.
Parliament of Canada: debates what Canada should do, 12; dissolved in January 1940, 19; Air Training Plan, 78; Royal Commission on Hong Kong, 114; approves overseas conscription "if necessary," 117; concludes measures for return of peace, 380; conscription crisis, 408-12.
Pas de Calais: 254, **311**, 312, 316, 361, 372-4.
Passchendaele: 23, 78, **172**, **233**.
Pathfinder Force: 274.
Patton, Gen. George S.: 232, 365-6.
Patton, Ralph: 355.
Pearce, Lt. Donald: 429.
Pearl Harbor: 102, 106, 114, 116-7.
Pearson, Lester B.: 287.
Peenemünde: 283-4, 390.
Pelletier, Lt. Hector: 387-8.
Pembina: 89.
Penfield Ridge: 83.
Penicillin: 470.
Pentland Firth: 43.
Peoples, Vincent R.: 431.
Pepper, Nursing Sister Evelyn: 198.
Perkins, Lt. E. J.: **308**, 419, **420**.
Permanent Force: 23, 26.
Perri, Rocco: 17.
Persian Gulf: 122.
Pesaro: 382-4, 386.
Pescara: 261.
Pétain, Marshal: 35.
Petch, Lt. Col. Charles: 357.
Peterborough: 195.

Peterson, FO. O. J.: 70.
Petit Appeville: 140.
Pevensey: 72.
Philippines: 102.
Phillips, Alan: 414.
Phillips, Maj. Norman: 466.
PIAT: 269, 308, 309.
Pickersgill, Frank: 155, 160-1, **160**, **162**.
Pickersgill, J. W.: 48, 78, 160.
Picton: 24, 26.
Pictorial History of Canada's Army Overseas 1939-45, The: **446**.
Picture Post: **199**.
Pierrepont: 331.
Pigeon, WO2 Percy: 211, **217**.
Pitcher, FO. Paul: **60**, 70.
Placke, Joseph: 160-1.
Plebiscite: 116, **117**, 408, **408**.
Plouha: **352**, 354-5, **354**.
Plunder, Operation: **444**.
Plymouth: 29, 33, 37, 288-9, 291.
Po River: 382, 391.
Pointe-aux-Trembles: 155.
Point 105: 384.
Point 131: 383-4, 386, 388.
Point 194: 383.
Point 195: 367.
Poland: 7, 12-3, **15**, 85, 97.
Poling: 72.
Ponsford, George: 26.
Pontecorvo: 411, **420**.
Pope, Lt. Gen. Maurice: 103, 408.
Population: 17.
Porquis Junction: 437.
Port Alberni: 180.
Port-aux-Basques: 129.
Porter, McKenzie: 161-2, 165, **165**, 375.
Portland: 59.
Port Menier: 122.
Port Radium: 187.
Portsmouth: 64, 135, 247, **316**.
Post, Robert: 75.
Potenza: **261**.
Potigny: 367.
Potvin, Capt. Pierre: **263**.
Poulin, Maj. J.-G.: 383, **386**.
Pourville: 134, 137, **139**, 140, 144.
POW (Prisoner of War): 115, **454**, *see also* Stalag.
Powell, Petty Officer A. J.: 122.
Powell, Chiefy: 219.
Powell-Sheddon, George: 62, 67.
Power, C. G. "Chubby": 18, 47, **50**, 53, 78-82, 88, 181, 287, 408, 411-2.
"Prayer Before Battle": **273**.
Prentice, Comdr. J. D.: 97.
Price, Flt. Lt. Alfred: 275, 284.
Priebus: 457.
Prien, Capt. Gunther: 40, **44**.
Priest: 366.
Prime Minister, Mr.: 18, 409.
Prince Edward County: 24.
Prince Rupert: 189.
Princess Louise Dragoon Guards, 4th: **242**, 298.
Princess Louise's (New Brunswick) Hussars, 8th: 408.
Princess Patricia's Canadian Light Infantry: 28, 235-6, 237, 273, 299, 306.
Provost Corps: 425.
Pruner, Alice: 195.
Pugsley, Lt. William H.: 167, 169, 221-2.
Punchard, Cpl. Freddy: 242.
Punjab Regiment, 14th: 105, 108.
Purcell, Capt. Gillis: **23**.
Purkis, Sgt. Maj. Fred: 196.
Puys: 134, 136-7, **141**, 144, 150-1, 380.
Pyrenees: 351.

Q

Quebec: 12-3, 18-9, 81, 191, 410, 412, **413**.
Quebec and Ontario Transportation Company: 430.
Quebec City: 125, 128, **412**, 413.
Conference: 287, 395.

Queen Charlotte Islands: 288.
Queen's Own Cameron Highlanders of Canada: 130, 134-5, 137, 139-40.
Queen's Own Rifles of Canada: 89, 114, 312, 315, 324, 327, **329**, 361, 437, 467.
Queen's Own Rifles of Canada, The: 312, 328, **370**.
Quiet Canadian, The: **55**, 377.
Quinte, Bay of: 24.

R

Radar: **60**, 166, 390.
Allied—
Aids: 233, 274.
H2S: 274, 284-5.
Oboe: 274.
German—
Lichtenstein: 276.
SN-2: 284.
Station Hummer: 277.
Raddall, Thomas H.: 221-3, 229, 231.
Radio Berlin: 125.
Raeder, Adm. Erich: 75.
Rajput Regiment, 7th: 105, 107-8, 110-1.
Ralston, J. L.: finance minister: 23; defense minister, 47; supplies from U.S., 53; cabinet war committee, 56; air training scheme, 78-9; conscription, 117; characteristics, 180; asks "active employment" for Canadian Army, 232; McNaughton, 286; conscription crisis, 405-13; resignation, 408; *other refs,* **50**, **120**.
Ramsay, Pte. Dutch: 316.
Ratcliffe, Sgt. Bill: **217**.
Rationing: 17, 188.
Rauter, SS Gen. Hans: 466.
Rawicz: 161.
Raymond, Maxime: **31**.
Rayner, Lt. Comdr. Herbert S.: 43, 45.
RDX (Research Department Explosive): 207, 231.
Rea, Lt. P. C.: 328.
Reach for the Sky: 60, 65.
Reader's Digest: 43, 335, 350.
Reconnaissance Regiment, 8th: 379-80, 394.
Recruiting: 15; RCAF: **16**.
Red Cross: 190, 199, **203**, 327, 359, 454.
Redfern, Sir Shuldham: 78-9.
Red Patch Devils: 246, 273.
Red Sea: 119.
Regalbuto: **237**, 243-4, 246.
Regensburg: 257.
Reggio Calabria: **261**.
Regiment, The: **24**, 236, **303**, **304**.
Régiment de la Chaudière: 324, **329**, 330, 361, 402.
Régiment de Maisonneuve: 130, 154-5, 163, 394, **436**, 441.
Regina Rifle Regiment: **312**, 323-4, 326, 329-30, 357, 359-60, 395.
Reichswald: 423, 427, 438.
Remember Me: **21**, 311, 369.
Rennes: 354, **354**.
Resistance (Movement): 154-5, 157, 159, 337, 351-2, 355, 392.
Revelstoke: 115.
Reyburn, Wallace: 137.
Reykjavik: 101, 338.
Reynaud, Paul: 46.
Reynolds, Quentin: **150**.
Rhine River: 391, **391**, 393, 406, 413, 416, **417**, 423-7, 434-40, 461.
Rhodenizer, Maj. Leon M.: 357-8.
Ribbentrop, Joachim von: **11**.
Rice, Geoff: 210-1.
Richardson, Fran: 197.
Richibucto: **88**.
Riddell, Dr. Walter A.: 7-8.
Rideau Hall: 164.
Ridge, CPO Sam: 44-5.
Rimini: 391.
Rimouski: 413.

Riverdale, Lord: 77-9, **79**, **80**.
Rivers, O.: 431.
Road to Rome: 269.
Roberts, Brig. J. A.: 467.
Roberts, Maj. Gen. J. H.: 33, 130, **131**, 134, 142, 144, 147, **147**, 151.
Roberts, Leslie: 13, 80, 82, 135, 186, 449, 452.
Robertson, Lt. Osborne "Robbie": 398.
Robertson, Comdr. Owen Connor Struan "Long Robbie": 224-7, **224**, 229.
Robertson, Terence: 40, 95, 98, 140, 146, 148, 224, 229.
Rockcliffe Airport: 196.
Rockcliffe Airport: 196.
Roer River: 438.
Rodger, FO. Dave: 209, **217**.
Rogers, Norman: 47, **50**.
Rogoff, Lt. Manuel: 352.
"Roll Out the Barrel": 21, 40, 196.
Romania: 7, 374.
Rome: 260-1, 268, 299, 309, 461.
Rommel, Field Marshal Erwin: 319.
Roosevelt, Franklin D.: pledges aid to Canada in case of attack, 6; Churchill, **46**; hobbled by Neutrality Act, 46; announces all possible aid for Britain, 47; Mackenzie King, 48; Churchill's message of June 1940, 50; "common defense for North America", 51; meets King at Ogdensburg, 51, 53, **54**; advised by William "Wild Bill" Donovan, 55; "airdrome of democracy", 88; Pearl Harbor, 116; McNaughton visit, 286; possibility of "sacrifice" landing in 1942, 133; Lend-Lease and Hyde Park Declaration, 182-3; William Stephenson, 377.
Rosendaal, 211.
Roskill, Capt. S. W.: 174, 178.
Ross, Capt. Bob: 316.
Ross, Irwin: **63**.
Rosyth: 40, 43, 45.
Rotterdam: 254, 463, 466, 468.
Rouen: **33**, 163, 379-80, **381**.
Roy, CSM. Irénée: 389.
Royal Air Force: 56, 58-9, 75, 86, 89, 149, 247.
Commands—
Bomber: 207-8, 232-3, 274-85, 380, 390, 451.
Coastal: 64, 91, 338, **338**.
Fighter: 59, **60**, 63, 75.
Flight, No. 1474: 233, **238**.
Forces—
Pathfinder: 274; No. 8 Group, 283.
Tactical Air: 2nd, 256, 365, 396.
Groups—
No. 5: 211.
No. 8: 283.
No. 11: 60, 63, 65, 67, 71-4, 248, 254, 256, 259.
No. 12: 60, 65, 72, 248.
No. 83: 256.
Squadrons—
No. 1: **62**.
No. 72: 72.
No. 74: 59.
No. 87: 63.
No. 92: 72.
No. 111: 63.
No. 141: 59, 63.
No. 162: 338.
No. 213: 63.
No. 235: 64.
No. 242 "All Canadian": 34, 59-60, 62, **62**, 65, 67, 70-1, 75.
No. 302: 73.
No. 303: 59, 69.
No. 501: 59.
No. 504: 59.
No. 609: 74.
No. 610: 74.
No. 617 (Dambuster): 206, 210, 219, 284, 452.
Women's Auxiliary: **60**, 195-6, 206-7.

Royal Air Forces Escaping Society: **351**.
Royal Artillery: 105.
"Royal California Air Force": 85.
Royal Canadian Air Force: 63, 78-9, 84, 335, 380, 469.
Group, No. 6 Bomber: 248, 275, 280-5, **284**, 335, 380, 390, 452.
Schools—
No. 9 Elementary Flying Training: 84-5.
No. 14 Service Flying Training: 86.
Squadrons—
No. 1: 58-9, **60**, 63, 70, 72, 74-5.
No. 115 Auxiliary: 63.
No. 401: 448.
No. 403: 250.
No. 405: 282-3.
No. 408 (Goose): 281.
No. 413: 135.
No. 415 (Swordfish): 281.
No. 416: 250.
No. 418: 390.
No. 419 (Moose): 281, 335.
No. 420 (Snowy Owl): 281, **283**.
No. 424 (Tiger): 281.
No. 425 (Alouette): 281.
No. 426 (Thunderbird): 281.
No. 427 (Lion): 281-2.
No. 428 (Ghost): 281.
No. 429 (Bison): 281.
No. 431 (Iroquois): **276**, 281.
No. 432 (Leaside): 281.
No. 433 (Porcupine): 281.
No. 434 (Bluenose): **276**, 281.
Wings—
No. 125: 450.
No. 127: 332, 448.
No. 143: 448.
Women's Division: 195-7, **200**.
Royal Canadian Legion: 409.
Royal Canadian Mounted Police: 17, 47, **48**, 115, 377.
Royal Canadian Navy: prewar strength, 21; Canadian ships under its control, 21; using mainly corvettes, 94; strength at end of 1941, 98; formed main strength in western Atlantic, 119; adjustment in command, April 1943, 178; credit for victory in Atlantic, 179; strength at Halifax, 222; Sicily, 233; *Haida* a monument, 297; assumes responsibility for all North Atlantic escorts, 414; strength at end of war, 470; *other refs,* 122, 173; *see also* Ships.
Escort Group C5: **170**.
MTB Flotilla, 29th: 415; 65th, 415.
Newfoundland Command: 118-9.
Newfoundland Escort Force: 119.
Wrens: 194-5, **200**.
Royal Canadian Regiment: **31**, 233, 241-3, 267-8, 418.
Royal Commission on Hong Kong: 114.
Royal Hamilton Light Infantry: 130, 135, 140, 142, 144-8, 174, 380, 395, 456.
Royal Military College: 434.
Royal Navy: reservists in Canada, **15**; escorts Convoy TC-1, carrying 1st Division to U.K., 21; rescues British Army from Dunkirk, **31**; Roosevelt and fate of, 48; contribution to Newfoundland Force, 94; losses in Colombo Harbor, 102; strength diluted in 1942, 119; Battle of the Atlantic, 173, 178-9; C-in-C Western Approaches, 171; bombardment in Normandy, 323; Home Fleet, 40; *other ref,* 247; *see also* Ships.
Force 26, 290.
10th Destroyer Flotilla, 288, 297.

Royal Regiment of Canada: 130, 134, 136-7, **137**, **141**, 144, 148-9, 247, 380.
Royal Rifles of Canada: 103, 108, 111-2.
Royal Scots: 105, 107-8, 112.
Royal 22nd Regiment: 76, 236, 246, 262, **263**, 267, 306, 383.
Royal Winnipeg Rifles: 323-4, 326, 330-1, 357, 359-61, 395.
Rozee, J. M.: 431.
Rubicon River: 405.
Rudellat, Yvonne: 160.
Rudeltaktik, Die: 167.
Ruhr: 206-8, 209, 211, 219, 254, 274-5, 280, **391**, 393, 395, 452, 461.
Rushleau, Pte. John E.: 401.
Russel, Dal: 63-65.
Russia: 89, 92.
Rutherford, Lt. Comdr. C. A.: **95**, 167.
Ruttan, Lt. "Fats": 27.
Rye: 72.

S

Saane River: 134.
Sablé: **31**.
Sabourin, Roméo: 155, 161.
Sager, Lt. Col. J. E.: **286**.
Saguenay River: 186.
Ste. Anne de Bellevue: 196.
St. Aubin-sur-Mer: 314, 324, 327.
St. Brieuc: 354.
St. Catharines: 102.
St. Hippolyte: 349.
St. Jean-de-Luz: 37-8, **38**.
Saint John: 187.
St. John's: **92**, 94, **179**, 190.
St. Lambert: 370.
St. Laurent, Sgt. Fernand: 340, 343.
St. Laurent, Louis: **408**, 410-3, **412**.
St. Lawrence, Battle of the: 122, 125, 129, 167.
St. Lawrence, Gulf of: **117**, 122, 125, 128.
St. Lawrence River: 92, 99, 173.
St. Lô: 365.
St. Malo: **31**, 289, 415.
St. Margaret's Bay: 231.
St. Paul's Cathedral: 247.
St. Quentin: 157, **157**, 159-60, **162**, 163-4.
St. Stephen's College: 113.
St. Thomas (Apostle): 260.
St. Thomas: 115.
St. Thomas, Cathedral of: 268, 272.
St. Valéry-en-Caux: 37.
St. Vith: **423**.
St. Yvon: 124.
Saints, Devils and Ordinary Seamen: 167, 222.
Sai Wan Hill: 111.
Salerno: 151.
Salisbury Plain: 28, 76.
Salmon, Lt. Col. H. L. N. "Harry": 27, **27**, 31, 237.
Salso River: **237**, 241, 243, 246.
Salvation Army: 190.
Sanford, Pte. "Slim": **416**.
San Fortunato: 391.
Sangro River: **261**.
San Leonardo: 261-2.
Sansom, Charmian: **199**.
Sansom, Lt. Gen. E. W.: **199**.
Santa Maria, Church of: **273**.
Santa Maria di Constantinopoli: 271.
Sarnia: 180.
Sarthe: 163.
Saskatoon Light Infantry: 272.
Satchell, Sqdn. Ldr. Jack: 73.
Saturday Evening Post, The: **46**, 286.
Saturday Night: 151, 182.
Savoie, Cpl. Donat: 402.
Scampton: 206, 209, **210**.
Scapa Flow: 40, **44**.
Scarborough: 203.
Scarlet Dawn, The: 311, **362**, 467.
Scheldt River: 151, 391, 392-404, 406-7, 435.
Schepke, Joachim: **44**.
Scherpbier: 399.

Schmid, Gen. Josef: 284.
Schnösenberg, Maj. Richard: 150.
Schoondijke: 399.
Schull, Joseph: 39, 92, 99, **118**, 120, 122, 129, **174**, 178, 315, 415, 433; *see also Far Distant Ships, The*.
Schweinfurt: 257.
Scie River: 134, 137, 140.
Sclanders, Pat: 70.
Sclater, William: 289, 297.
Scott, Sgt. D. S.: 338-41, 343.
Scott, Lt. Jack: **425**.
Scott, Pipe Maj. Samuel: 315.
Seafarers International Union of Canada: 430.
Seaford: 131.
Seaforth Highlanders of Canada: 235, **244**, 262, **265**, 268-9, 271, 273, 418.
Sea Lion, Operation: 58, 75.
Searby, Gp. Capt. John: 284.
Search for Identity, The: **411**.
Seigniory Club: 56.
Seine River (France): 357, 365-6, 372, 392; Bay of, 316.
Selassie, Emperor Haile: **7**, 8.
Selsey Bill: 64.
Senlis: 157.
Seulles River: 322, 324.
Seyss-Inquart, Reichskommissar Arthur: 466.
Sham Shui Po: 105.
Shannon, Dave: 206, 210, 214, 216-7, 219.
Shapiro, L. S. B.: 191, 232, **241**, **247**, 286.
Sharks and Little Fish: **126**, 174.
Shatford, Stoker George: 227.
Shaw, Chief Officer Frank: 127.
Shelburne, Operation: 354-5.
Shelburne Escape and Evasion Line: 351-2.
Sherbrooke Fusiliers: 357-8, 362, 367.
Sherwood, Lt. Comdr. F. H.: 414.
Sherwood, Robert: **376**.
Shetland Islands: 338.
Shipbuilding: 256.
Ships—*see also* E-Boats; Liberty Ships; Park Ships; U-Boats.
    Aeas: 128.
    Akagi: 102.
    Alberni: 97.
    Algonquin: **293**, 315-6, 414.
    Annapolis: 92.
    Aquitania: 21, **23**.
    Arandora Star: **36**, 40-3, **43**.
    Arlyn: 126.
    Arrowhead: 128.
    Ashanti: 289-90, 295.
    Assiniboine: 37, 91, **92**, **122**, 414.
    Athabaskan: **203**, 288-97.
    Athenia: **13**.
    Awatea: 103-4.
    Baddeck: 99.
    Battleford: 172.
    Berwick: 22.
    Biter: 178.
    Black Prince: 289.
    Bogue: **43**.
    Calcutta: 38-40.
    Calgarolite: 122.
    Calgary: 98.
    Calpe: 134, 142, 147.
    Canadolite: 122.
    Canatco: 127.
    Canso: 315.
    Canterbury Belle: 31, 33.
    Caraquet: 315.
    Caribou: 129.
    Chambly: 97, **97**, **99**.
    Charlottetown: 128.
    Chatham: 125.
    Chilliwack: 119, 171.
    Clayoquot: 128.
    Coamo: 432.
    Columbia: 92, 414.
    Conestoga: 196, **197**.
    Cornwallis: **90**.
    Cowichan: 315.
    Cygne, Le: 35.
    Dauphin: 119.
    Donald Stewart: 126-8.
    Drumheller: 178.
    Duchess of Bedford: 21.

E. G. Seuber: 171.
Empress of Australia: 21.
Empress of Britain: 21, **41**.
Enterprise: 289.
Ericus: 127.
Fernie: 142.
Formidable: 469.
Fort Cataraqui: 404.
Fraser: **36**, 37-40, **38**, 91.
Galatea: 35, 37.
Galt: 98.
Gentian: 119.
Glasgow: 288-9.
Haida: 288-97, 380.
Hamilton: 92.
Heina: 119-20.
Highlander: 90.
Hilary: 316.
Huron: 288-91, **290**, **295**.
Invicta: 136.
Irongate: 223.
Iroquois: 288, **290**, 415.
James Battle: 224.
Kenogami: 97.
Kitchener: **170**.
Lady Drake: 433.
Lady Hawkins: 431-2, **431**.
Lagan: 178.
Laramie: 126.
Leto: 125.
Lützow: 452-3.
Margaree: 91.
Mayflower: 95.
Monarch of Bermuda: 21.
Monterey: 198.
Montrolite: 122.
Moose Jaw: **92**, 97-8, **99**.
Mosdale: 205.
Mount Pindus: 128.
Mount Tayegetos: 128.
Nelson: 41.
Niagara: 92.
Nicoya: 123-5.
Niobe: **228**.
Oakton: 128.
Oakville: 122, 125.
Orillia: 97.
Ormande: 26-7.
Prince David: 315.
Prince Henry: 315-6, **318**.
Prince of Wales: 106, **107**.
Prince Robert: 104.
Proserpina: 192-3, **193**.
Queen Mary: 431.
Raccoon: 128.
Repulse: 106, **107**.
Restigouche: **36**, 37-40.
Roberts: 361.
Rodney: 361.
Rouille: 224-5, 227.
Royal Oak: 40, **44**.
Sackville: 166.
Saguenay: 22, 37, 90-1, **90**, 414.
St. Clair: 92.
St. Croix: 92, 169, **169**.
St. Francis: 92.
St. Laurent: 22, **36**, 37, 40-5, **43**, 171-2.
Samaria: **23**.
Santa Elena: 198.
Scottish Heather: 171.
Shawinigan: 127-8.
Shediac: 171-2.
Sioux: 315-6, 414.
Skeena: **36**, 37, 40, 43-4, 97.
Spikenard: 119-20.
Spiteful: 414.
Thorold: 430.
Thunder: 315.
Tirpitz: 209, 414.
Toward: 171.
Trail: 127.
U-47: 40, **44**.
U-94: 122.
U-210: **122**.
U-501: 97-8, **99**.
U-517: 125, 128-9.
U-553: 122, 125.
Uganda: 469.
Vegreville: 315.
Victolite: 122.
Victorious: 129.
Ville d'Angier: 29-30.
Ville de Québec: **188**.
Viscount: 45.
Volunteer: 224-5, **224**, 227, 229, **231**.
Wasaga: 315.
Waterloo: 430.

Wetaskiwin: **97**.
Windflower: 95, 98.
Winona: 430.
York: 22.
Shipshaw Project: 186.
Shoreham: 135.
Shouldice, Flt. Sgt. G. M.: 258-9.
Sicily: 151, 232-7, **233**, **244**, 246-7, **272**, 286-7, 414.
Siegfried Line: 22, 423, 438, **444**.
Singapore: 102, **109**, 115.
Simeto River: 236, **237**, 246.
Simmons, Lt. Edward T.: 97.
Simonds, Lt. Gen. Guy G.: 236, **239**, **242**, 246, 365-6, **373**, 394-5, 403, 435, 467.
Simonds, Capt. Peter: 367, 370, 435, 438.
Sinclair, Adelaide: 196.
Sinclair, "Postie": 272.
696 heures d'enfer: 383.
Skelton, O. D.: 49, 54.
Skinner, Comdr. E. G.: 128.
Skipton-on-Swale: 281.
Slocan Valley: 115.
Slovakia: 12.
Sluis: 402.
Smellie, Col. Elizabeth: 195.
Smith, A. W.: 59.
Smith, Brig. Armand: 29.
Smith, Sgt. Basil: 33.
Smith, Pte. E. A. "Smoky", V.C.: 15, **401**.
Smith, Lt. G. A. P.: 358.
Smith, Maj. H. A. "Snuffy": 262, 264-5, 267.
Smith, Sqdn. Ldr. Roy: 448.
Smith, Rev. Waldo E. L.: **384**.
Smither, FO. Ross: 65, 73.
Smiths Falls: **82**.
SOE: *see* Special Operations Executive.
SOE in France: 160.
Soest: 211.
Soissons: 157.
Soldiers and Politicians: 103, 408.
Soldiers' Summit: 186.
Somme: 23.
Sorbonne: 160.
Sorpe Dam: 206-7, 210-1, 218.
South Africa: *see* Africa.
Southampton: 135, 315.
Southeast Command: 131.
South Saskatchewan Regiment: 130, 134, 136-40, **139**, 380, **464**.
Spafford, "Spam": 212.
Spain: 7, **38**, 352.
Spanish Republicans: 10.
Spark, Flt. Sgt. Norm: 192, **193**.
Special Operations Executive (SOE): 154-65.
Special Service Force, First: **308**, 309, 461.
Spinney, Lt. Charles: 224-7.
Spinning, Lt. William: 352.
Spooner, LAC K. G.: **82**.
Sprague, Pte. Dick: 401.
Spremberg: 460.
Sprenger, Bill: 65.
Stacey, Col. C. P.: lack of equipment, 16; six Canadians left behind in France in 1940, 33; Dieppe, 133, 139, 150-1; D-Day, 323, 332; Operation Totalize, 366-7; Maj. David Currie winning V.C., 372, **374**; Scheldt, 393-4, 404; conscription crisis, 405-6, 413; Germans fighting for homeland, **436**; crossing Rhine, **444**; Lt. Gen. Charles Foulkes reading surrender to Gen. Johannes Blaskowitz, 467.
Staggs, Lt. A. A. G.: 157.
Stalag Luft III: **454**, 455.
Stalin, Joseph: 12, 150, 392, 461.
Stalingrad: 268.
Stalmann, Reinhart: **345**.
Stanley, Lt. Comdr.: 226-7, 229.
Stanley Mound: 111.
Stanley Peninsula: 111-2.
Stansfeld, Noel: 62.
Stapleton, CSM. Cornelius: 142, 144.

Station M: 377.
Stavoren: 211.
Steel Company of Canada: 201.
Steep Rock: 186.
Steinhilper, Lt. Uli: **345**.
Stephenson, Sir William: **55**, 376-7, **376**.
Stevens, Lt. Helen-Marie: 197, **203**.
Stewart, Pte. Merlin: 402.
Stimson, H. L.: 53, **54**, 133.
Storm Below: 169.
Storm from the Sea: 150.
Stormont, Dundas and Glengarry Highlanders: 324, 362.
Story of Canadian Roads, The: 186.
Stratford-on-Avon: 208.
Struggle for Europe, The: 314, 324, 393.
Stubbs, Lt. Comdr. J. H.: 292, 297.
Stursberg, Peter: 232, 235-6, 247, 299.
Stuttgart: 452.
Sudbury: 377.
Sudetenland: 10.
Sumatra: 102.
Sunday Express (London): 338.
Sunde, Fern: 205.
Sunde, Gerner: 205.
Sun Life Assurance Company of Canada: 155, 159.
Supreme Court of Canada: 230.
Surrey: 281.
Sussex, England: 130, 281.
Sussex South Downs: 130.
Sutcliffe, Lt. Col. B. A.: 237-8.
Sutcliffe, Lt. Col. J. L. R.: 103.
Sutherland, Sgt. Fred: 217, **217**.
Sutton-on-the-Forest: 281-2.
Swettenham, John: 286.
Swinemünde: 452.
Swinggate: 72.
Switzerland: 7, 155.
Sydney: 100, 118, 125-6, 129.
Sylt: 277.
Syracuse: 232.

T

Tactical Air Force: *see* Royal Air Force.
Tacrum, FO. T. H. "Terry": 207, 210-2, **217**, 219.
Tail-end Charlies: 70, 336.
Takàli: 152.
Tamblyn, PO. Hugh: 59-60, **62**, 63.
Tangmere: 64.
Tanks (and Armored Vehicles): 16, 150.
    Buffalo: 395, 427, 438, 440, 463.
    Churchill: 130, 135, **373**.
    Flail: **382**.
    Funnies: 324.
    Honey: 307, 309.
    Kangaroo: 366-7, 440.
    Panther: 300, 307, 308-9, 359.
    Scorpion: **382**.
    Sherman: **316**, 324, **373**; DD, 324, 331.
    Tiger: 372.
    Wasp: 367, **382**, 395, 438.
Tara Island: 415.
Tarmstedt: 460.
Tashme: 115.
Taylor, E. P.: 183.
Tecumseh: 26.
Tecumseh Canning Factory: 26.
Tedder, Air Chief Marshal Sir Arthur: **311**.
Telegram (Toronto): **376**.
Terre Haute: 39.
Thames Estuary: 63.
Thank you, Canada: 462, 469.
Their Finest Hour: **53**, 57.
Their Finest Hour: The Story of the Battle of Britain 1940: **74**.
There Shall Be Wings: 80, 102, 449, 452.
They Left The Back Door Open: 232, **241**.
Tholthorpe: 281.
Thompson, Gwenda: 316.
Thompson, R. W.: 135, 149, 151, 392, 394-6.

Thompson, Inspector Walter: 75.

Thomson, Dale C.: **412**.

Thorne, CSM. E.: 431.

Thorney Island: 64.

Thrasher, Flt. Sgt. John: **217**.

Three Rivers Regiment: 236, **237**, 269, 271, 306.

Thurmann, Lt. Comdr.: 122-3.

Tierceville: 330.

Tillsonburg: 87.

Tilston, Maj. Frederick, V.C.: 440-1, **442**.

Time: 285.

Times, The (London): 75, 273.

Tito, Marshal: 377, 414.

Tixier, Georges: 159, **159**, 164.

Tixier, Mme Georges: 160, 164.

TNT: 44.

Tobruk: 192.

Tojo, Gen. Hideki: 103.

Tokyo: 102.

Tooke, Capt. Paul W.: 127-8.

Topham, Cpl. Fred, V.C.: 461.

Toronto: 17, 97, **107**, 130, 187, **260**, 377, 430.

Toronto Daily Star: 11, 195.

Toronto Scottish Regiment (M.G.): 130.

Totalize, Operation: 366-7.

Tôtes: 380.

Tours: 344, 346.

Tractable, Operation: 367.

Trafalgar: 179.

Trafalgar Square: 350.

Trainor, Capt. J. A.: 342, 358.

Transport, Department of: 81.

Trenton: 24-5, 80, 82.

Tréport, Le: 389.

Trial of Kurt Meyer, The: 360.

Trinidad: 431.

Triple Alliance: 103.

Tripoli: 233.

Triquet, Maj. Paul, V.C.: 262, **263**, 267.

Trondheim: 28.

Trotobas, Capt. Michael A.: 157-8, **162**.

Trun: 367, 372.

Tucker, Gilbert Norman: 173.

Tunisia: 414.

Turkey: 414.

Turnbull, Elsa: 198.

Turnbull, Wing Comdr. R. S.: 281.

Turner, Gp. Capt. Stan: 34, **34**, 60-2, **62**, 69, 75.

Turple Head: 224.

Tweedsmuir, Lord: 8, 78-9, 238.

Tweedsmuir, Maj. Lord John: 238, 240, 242-3.

Two Jacks, The: 344, 357.

U

U-Boats: Command, 167; *Saguenay* torpedoed, 90-1; in Mediterranean, 94; *Sackville*, 166-7; forbidding odds, **176**;
Drumheller and *Lagan* share kill, 178; *Haida* credited with one, 297; No. 162 Squadron sinks four U-Boats in 22 days, 338; FO. K. O. Moore and crew destroy one U-Boat, **338**; Flt. Lt. David Hornell, V.C.: 338-43; *other refs*, 37, 40, **44**, 56, 97-8, **99**, 122, **122**, 125, 128-9, 414, **433**, 470.

Udem: 424-5, 438.

United Nations: 287, 470.

United Services Center: 190.

United States Coast Guard: 125, 172-3.

United States of America: 47, 49, 106, 116, 229.

  Air Corps: 85.

  Army: *see* Army.

  Army Air Force: 274, **278**, 279, 282, 284, 366.

  Congress: 54, 56-7.

  Constitution: 57.

  Federal Bureau of Investigation: 376-7.

  Maritime Commission: 126.

  Medal for Merit: 376, **376**.

  Navy: 118, 173, 178; Pacific Fleet, 173; liaison officer at Halifax, 225; *see also* Ships.

  Neutrality Act: 46, **56**, 57, 89; Patrol, 118.

  Office of Strategic Services (OSS): 377.

  Ranger Battalion, 1st: 130, 134, **143**.

  Silver Star: **338**.

  Special Service Force, First: 461.

Unknown Country, The: 188, 191.

Uranium: 186-7.

Urquhart, FO. Robert: 216, **217**.

Utrecht: 468.

Uxbridge: 71.

V

V-1 Flying Bombs: 283-4, 390-1.

V-2 Rockets: 283-4, 391.

Vaillancourt, Jean: 441, **444**.

Valençay: 160, **162**.

Valmontone: 307.

Vancouver: **82**, 83, 104, 113, 115.

Vancouver Island: 83, 114.

Vanier, Lt. Col. Georges P.: 35, **36**, 54.

Vargas, President Getulio: 377.

Vaugeois, Capt. Guy: 389.

VE-Day: **228**, **231**, 461, 469.

Veness, Lt. Jack: 344, 346-50, **346**, **348**.

Venezuela: 122, 430.

Verdun: 152.

Vergeltungswaffen: 390.

Vermilion: 195-6.

Vernon: 187.

Verrières Ridge: 365.

Versailles: 352.

Versailles, Treaty of: **11**.

Veterans Charter: 470.

Vézina, Sgt. Roméo: 387-8.

Vian, Rear Adm. Sir Philip: **312**.

Vibert, Pte. Raymond: 401.

Vichy, France: 160.

Vickers: 107, 389.

Victoria, B.C.: 17, 191, 194.

Victoria (Hong Kong): 107, 113.

Victoria Cross: 15, **336**.

  Sqdn. Ldr. Ian Willoughby Bazalgette: **401**.

  Sgt. Aubrey Cosens: 15, 437, **439**, 440-1.

  Maj. David Currie: 370, 372, 374.

  Wing Comdr. Guy Gibson: **219**.

  Lt. Robert H. Gray: 15, 469.

  Maj. Charles Ferguson Hoey: **401**.

  Flt. Lt. David Hornell: 343.

  Maj. J. K. Mahony: 15, **308**, 309, **420**.

  Lt. Col. Cecil Merritt: **139**.

  PO. Andrew Charles Mynarski: 337.

  CSM John R. Osborn: 112, **112**, 114.

  Capt. Frederick Thornton Peters: **401**.

  Pte. E. A. "Smoky" Smith: 15, **401**.

  Maj. Frederick Tilston: 440-1, **442**.

  Cpl. Fred Topham: 461.

  Maj. Paul Triquet: **263**, 267.

Victory Bonds: 181, 184.

Victory Campaign, The: 332, 372, 393.

Victory Troops: **233**.

Vienna: 389.

Vierge, Ile de: 294.

Vigars, Roy: 336.

Vimy Ridge: 23, **233**, 389.

Vis, Island of: 414.

Vivash, Irene: 195.

Vizzini: 236.

Vlieland: 211.

Vokes, Maj. Gen. Chris: **237**, 261-2, 267, **270**, 273, 299, 306, **360**.

Vokes, Lt. Col. F. A.: 307.

W

WAAFs: **60**, 195-6, 206-7.

WDs: *see* Royal Canadian Air Force, Women's Division.

Waal River: 416, **419**.

Wabana: 173.

Wade, Prof. Mason: 413.

Wakehurst Place: 434.

Walcheren: 393, 396, 403-4.

Walker, FO. Danny: 207-10, **217**, 219.

Walker, Kay: 196.

Walker, Minnie: 460.

Wallace, Pte. Freeman: 358.

Wallis, Barnes: 207-11, **207**, 214, 218-9.

Wallis, Brig. C.: 108.

Wanborough Manor: 155.

Wan Chai Gap: 112.

War Office: 28, 154, 160, 407.

War Supplies Limited: 183.

War Supply Board: 81.

Warren, Sgt. J. L. N.: 456.

Warsaw: 72.

Wartime Prices and Trade Board: 183, 196.

Washington: 47, 49, 51, 87, 197, 377.

Water Rats: 435.

Waters, Capt. John M., Jr.: **90**, **101**, 167, **167**, 172-3, **176**, 178.

Waters, May: 198.

Watson, Edna: **204**.

Watson, L.Cpl.: 402.

Watson Lake: 186.

Watts, Lt. Comdr. E. F. B.: 226-7, 229.

Weeks, Flt. Sgt. Harvey: **217**.

Wehrmacht: 12, 76, 209, 361, 468; *see also* Army, German.

Welsh Guards: 349.

Werl: 211.

Wernham, James: 455.

Wesel: 438, 440, **442**, 461.

West, Forbes: 149.

West Brigade: 108, 111.

Western Approaches: 167; C-in-C, 171.

Western Isles: 43.

Western Local Escort Force: 119.

West Indies: 47, 51, 103.

Westkapelle: 404.

Westminster Regiment: 308, 309.

West Nova Scotia Regiment: 76, 236, 262, 306, 383-6.

Wetaskiwin: **97**.

Weygand, Gen. Maxime: 35.

Weymouth Bay: 315.

What's Past Is Prologue: **79**.

What Time The Tempest: **384**.

Whitaker, Capt. Denny: 145.

Whitby: 377.

Whitehorse: 117, 186.

Whittimore, Tom: 349.

Wick: 338.

Wight, Isle of: 63, 134, 316.

Wild, Cpl. Douglas: 358.

Wile, PO. Floyd: 211, **217**.

Wiley, George: 455.

Wilhelmina, Queen: 74, 469.

Wilhelmshaven: 465.

Wilkes, Rev. Rusty: 233.

Wilkinson, Pte. R. W.: 145.

William of Normandy: 33, 362.

Williams, Eric: 350.

Willis, Austin: 13, **107**.

Wilmot, Chester: 314-5, 319, 322, 324, 327-8, 330-2, 393.

Wilson, J. A.: 81.

Wilson, Morris: 89.

Wilson, Flt. Lt. P.: 450.

Windeyer, Lt. Comdr. Guy: 171.

Window: **275**, 276, **276**, 284, 452.

Windsor: 189.

Wing Leader: **199**, 249, 332, 450.

Wings Parade: 88.

Winnipeg: **16**, 130, 190, **191**, 197.

Winnipeg Free Press: 6, 182.

Winnipeg Grenadiers: 103, 107-8, 110, 112.

Winnipeg Tribune, The: 186.

Wismar: 461, 466.

Woensdrecht: 394-5.

Woking: 64.

Women's Royal Canadian Naval Service (Wrens): 194-7, **200**.

Women's Service Club: 194-5.

Wong Nel Chong Gap: 108, 110-3.

Woodhall, Wing Comdr. A. B.: 67, 73.

Woodsworth, J. S.: 10, 12.

Wooler, Maj. J. R. "Ray": **160**.

World War 1939-45: **109**, **311**, 324.

Worthington, Maj. Gen. F. F.: **120**, 366.

Worthington, Larry: 120.

Worthy: 120.

Wray, Gp. Capt. Larry: 458, 460.

X

Xanten: 425.

Y

Yard Creek: 115.

Yellowhead: 115.

Yeo-Thomas, Wing Comdr. F. F. E.: 161.

Yeu, Ile d': 415.

Yorkshire: 281, 452.

Young, Sir Mark: 105.

Young, Melvyn "Dinghy": 210-1, 213, 216, 218-9.

Young, Brig. Peter: 104, 150, **311**, 324.

Young, Lt. Col. Sherman: 24.

Ypres: 23, **172**, **233**.

Z

Zeebrugge: 403.

Zombies: 406-8, 411-3.

Zoot suit: 189.

Zuider Zee: **210**, 211, 449, 468.

Zwolle: 465.

Acknowledgments

The publisher thanks the many people and organizations who have helped in the preparation of *The Canadians at War 1939/45.* The publisher is also grateful to the following authors and publishers whose works are quoted or excerpted in this book.

Alings, Wim, Jr., "Every Child his own Canadian," in *Thank you, Canada,* published by *Stichting Wereldtentoonstelling,* Montreal, 1967.

Allen, Ralph, *Home Made Banners,* by permission of Academic Press Canada Ltd., Don Mills, Ont., copyright, Canada, 1946.

________ *Ordeal by Fire,* by permission of Doubleday and Company, Inc., New York, copyright © 1961 by Ralph Allen.

Barnard, W. T., *The Queen's Own Rifles of Canada 1860-1960,* by permission of The Queen's Own Rifles of Canada. Published by the Ontario Publishing Company Limited, Don Mills, Ont., copyright 1960 by The Queen's Own Rifles of Canada.

Bekker, Cajus, *The Luftwaffe War Diaries,* by permission of Macdonald & Co. (Publishers) Ltd., London, copyright © 1964 by Gerhard Stalling Verlag. Translation copyright © 1966 by Macdonald & Co. (Publishers) Ltd.

Belfield, E. M. G., and Essame, H., *The Battle for Normandy,* by permission of B. T. Batsford Ltd., London, copyright © 1962.

Beurling, George F., and Roberts, Leslie, *Malta Spitfire,* by permission of Oxford University Press, Toronto, copyright 1943 by George F. Beurling and Leslie Roberts.

Bird, Will R., *No Retreating Footsteps,* published by Kentville Publishing Company, Limited, Kentville, N.S.

________ *North Shore (New Brunswick) Regiment,* published by Brunswick Press, Fredericton, N.B.

________ *The Two Jacks,* published by The Ryerson Press, Toronto.

Bishop, Edward, *Their Finest Hour,* published by Ballantine Books, Inc., New York, N.Y., copyright © 1968 by Edward Bishop.

Brickhill, Paul, *The Dam Busters,* by permission of David Higham Associates Ltd., London. Published by Evans Bros. Ltd., London, 1951.

________ *Reach for the Sky,* by permission of David Higham Associates Ltd., London. Published by William Collins Sons & Co. Ltd., Glasgow, 1954.

Buckham, Robert, *Forced March to Freedom,* by permission of Canada's Wings Inc., Stittsville, Ont., copyright © 1984.

Buckley, Christopher, *Road to Rome,* by permission of Hodder and Stoughton Limited, London, 1945.

Carr, W. G., *Checkmate in the North,* published by The Macmillan Company of Canada Limited, Toronto.

Chalmers, W. S., *Max Horton and the Western Approaches,* published by Hodder and Stoughton Limited, London, England.

Churchill, Winston S., *Closing the Ring,* by permission of Houghton Mifflin Company, Boston, copyright © 1951 by Houghton Mifflin Company. Copyright © renewed 1979 by the Hon. Lady Sarah Audley and the Hon. Lady Soames.

________ *The Gathering Storm,* by permission of Houghton Mifflin Company, Boston, published in association with The Co-operation Publishing Company, Inc., copyright © 1948 by Houghton Mifflin Company. Copyright © renewed 1976 by Lady Spencer Churchill, the Hon. Lady Sarah Audley and the Hon. Lady Soames.

________ *The Hinge of Fate,* by permission of Houghton Mifflin Company, Boston, copyright © 1950 by Houghton Mifflin Company. Copyright © renewed 1978 by Lady Spencer Churchill, the Hon. Lady Sarah Audley and the Hon. Lady Soames.

________ *Their Finest Hour,* by permission of Houghton Mifflin, Company, Boston, copyright © 1949 by Houghton Mifflin Company. Copyright © renewed by Lady Spencer Churchill, the Hon. Lady Sarah Audley and the Hon. Lady Soames.

________ *Triumph and Tragedy,* by permission of Houghton Mifflin Company, Boston, copyright © 1953 by Houghton Mifflin Company. Copyright © renewed by the Hon. Lady Sarah Audley and the Hon. Lady Soames.

Ciano, Count Galeazzo, *The Ciano Diaries,* published by Doubleday & Company Inc., Garden City, N.Y.

Collier, Richard, *Eagle Day,* by permission of Curtis Brown Ltd., London, copyright © 1966 by Richard Collier.

Cookridge, E. H., *Inside S.O.E.,* by permission of Arthur Barker Limited, London, copyright © 1966 by European Copyright Limited, London.

Cosgrove, Edmund, *Canada's Fighting Pilots,* by permission of Irwin Publishing Inc., copyright © 1965 by Clarke, Irwin & Company Limited.

Coughlin, Tom, *The Dangerous Sky,* by permission of McGraw-Hill Ryerson Ltd., Toronto, copyright © 1968 by Tom Coughlin.

Dawson, R. MacGregor, *The Conscription Crisis of 1944,* by permission of University of Toronto Press, Toronto, copyright, Canada, 1961 by University of Toronto Press.

Easton, Alan, *50 North,* by permission of Paperjacks Ltd., Markham, Ont., copyright © 1980 by Alan Easton.

Ellis, Jean, *Face Powder and Gunpowder,* by permission of Saunders of Toronto Ltd., Don Mills, Ont., copyright © 1947.

Feasby, W. R., *The Canadian Medical Services 1939-45,* by permission of the Minister of Supply and Services Canada, Ottawa, crown copyrights.

Foot, Michael, *S.O.E. in France,* by permission of the Controller of Her Majesty's Stationery Office, London, copyright © 1968.

Frankland, Noble, "Bombing: The RAF Case" in *History of the Second World War,* by permission of Purnell & Sons Ltd., Paulton, England, in cooperation with the Imperial War Museum, copyright © 1968 by Purnell & Sons Ltd.

Fraser, Blair, *The Search for Identity,* by permission of Doubleday & Company, Inc., New York, copyright © 1967 by Blair Fraser.

Galland, Adolf, *The First and The Last,* by permission of Kurt Hellmer, New York. Published by Henry Holt and Company, Inc., copyright 1954 by Henry Holt and Company, Inc.

Garner, Hugh, *Storm Below,* by permission of McGraw-Hill Ryerson Ltd., Toronto, copyright © 1949 by Hugh Garner.

General Staff, Canadian Military Headquarters in Great Britain, *From Pachino to Ortona,* by permission of the Minister of Supply and Services Canada, Ottawa, crown copyrights.

Good, Mabel T., *Men of Valour,* by permission of the author and Macmillan of Canada (A Division of Canada Publishing Corp.), Toronto, copyright © 1948.

Guillet, Edwin C., *The Story of Canadian Roads,* by permission of University of Toronto Press, Toronto, copyright © 1966 by University of Toronto Press.

Harris, Sir Arthur, *Bomber Offensive,* by permission of David Higham Associates Ltd., London.

Hickey, R. M., *The Scarlet Dawn,* by permission of Rt. Rev. R. M. Hickey. Published by UNIPRESS, Fredericton, N.B., copyright 1949 by R. M. Hickey.

Hilsum-Beuckens, Mrs. C., "Liberation" in *Thank you, Canada,* published by *Stichting Wereldtentoonstelling,* Montreal, 1967.

Hutchison, Bruce, *The Incredible Canadian,* by permission of Harcourt Brace Jovanovich Canada (formerly Longmans Canada Limited), copyright © 1952.

________ *Mr. Prime Minister,* by permission of Harcourt Brace Jovanovich Canada (formerly Longmans Canada Limited), copyright © 1964.

________ *The Unknown Country,* by permission of Harcourt Brace Jovanovich Canada (formerly Longmans Canada Limited), copyright © 1942.

Hyde, H. Montgomery, *The Quiet Canadian,* by permission of Hamish Hamilton Ltd., London, copyright © 1962 by H. Montgomery Hyde.

Johnson, J. E., *Wing Leader,* by permission of Chatto & Windus Ltd., London, copyright © 1956, 1957 by Ballantine Books Inc., N.Y.

Kelly, Percy, and Hannington, Felicity, *The Lady Boats,* Canadian Marine Transportation Centre, Dalhousie University, Halifax, N.S., copyright © 1980.

Laurendeau, André, *La crise de la conscription 1942,* by permission of the estate of André Laurendeau, copyright 1962.

Lower, A. R. M., *Colony to Nation,* by permission of Harcourt Brace Jovanovich Canada (formerly Longmans Canada Limited), copyright © 1946.

MacFarlane, J. D., *Herbie,* by permission of the Minister of Supply and Services Canada, Ottawa.

Macksey, K. J., "Top Generals of the Western Front" in *History of the Second World War.* Published by Purnell & Sons Ltd., Paulton, England, in cooperation with the Imperial War Museum, copyright © 1968 by Purnell & Sons Ltd.

Maguire, Eric, *Dieppe: August 19,* by permission of Jonathan Cape Ltd., London.

Malone, Dick, *Missing From The Record,* by permission of the estate of Richard S. Malone, copyright © Canada, 1946 by Col. R. S. Malone.

Manteuffel, Hasso von, *Decisive Battles of World War II,* published by G. P. Putnam Sons, New York.

Massey, Vincent, *What's Past Is Prologue,* published by The Macmillan Company of Canada Limited, Toronto.

McDougall, Colin, *Execution,* by permission of Macmillan of Canada (A Division of Canada Publishing Corp.), Toronto, copyright © 1958 by Colin McDougall.

McKee, Alexander, *Caen: Anvil of Victory,* by permission of Souvenir Press, London, copyright © 1964 by Alexander McKee.

Meade, Edward, *Remember Me,* by permission of Curtis Brown Limited, London. Published by Faber and Faber Limited, London, copyright 1946, 1965 by Edward F. Meade.

Milne, Gilbert A., *H.M.C.S.,* by permission of the author and Thomas Allen Limited, Toronto, copyright © 1960 by Thomas Allen Limited.

Morgan, Len, *The AT-6 Harvard,* by permission of the author, copyright © 1965 and © 1965.

Morison, Samuel Eliot, *The Battle of the Atlantic,* published by The Atlantic Monthly Press, Boston, copyright © 1947 by Samuel Eliot Morison.

Mowat, Farley, *The Regiment,* by permission of McClelland and Stewart Limited, Toronto, copyright © Canada, 1955 by McClelland and Stewart Limited.

Munro, Ross, *Gauntlet to Overlord,* by permission of the author, copyright © Canada, 1945.

Newman, Peter, *Flame of Power,* published by Longmans Canada Limited, Don Mills, Ont.

Nicholson, G. W. L., *The Canadians in Italy,* by permission of the Minister of Supply and Services, Ottawa, crown copyrights, 1956.

Nolan, Brian, *Hero: The Buzz Beurling Story,* by permission of Lester and Orpen Dennys Ltd., Toronto, copyright © 1981 by Brian Nolan.

Ott, Wolfgang, *Sharks and Little Fish,* by permission of Pantheon Books, Inc., New York. Translation by Ralph Manheim, copyright © 1957, 1958 by Pantheon Books Inc.

Pearce, Donald, *Journal of a War,* by permission of Ann Elmo Agency Inc., New York, copyright © 1965 by Donald Pearce.

Phillips, Alan, *The Living Legend,* by permission of Curtis Brown Associates, New York, copyright © 1954 by Alan Phillips.

Phillips, Norman, and Nikerk, J., *Holland and the Canadians,* by permission of Contact Publishing Company, Amsterdam, Holland.

Pickersgill, J. W., *The Mackenzie King Record,* Volume I 1939-1944, by permission of University of Toronto Press, Toronto, copyright, Canada, 1960 by University of Toronto Press. This volume is based on William Mackenzie King's diaries, held by Public Archives Canada, Ottawa. Permission also granted by Public Archives Canada, crown copyright 1977.

________ and Forster, D. F., *The Mackenzie King Record,* Volume 2 1944-1945, by permission of University of Toronto Press, Toronto, copyright © 1968 by University of Toronto Press. This volume is based on William Mackenzie King's diaries, held by Public Archives Canada, Ottawa. Permission also granted by Public Archives Canada, crown copyright 1977.

Pope, Maurice A., *Soldiers and Politicians: The Memoirs of Lt. Gen. Maurice A. Pope, C.B., M.C.,* by permission of University of Toronto Press, Toronto, copyright © 1962 by University of Toronto Press.

Poulin, J.-G., *696 heures d'enfer avec le Royal 22e Régiment,* by permission of the author. Published by Editions A-B, Quebec, distributed by Beauchemin Ltd., Montreal.

Power, C. G., *A Party Politician: The Memoirs of Chubby Power,* edited by Norman Ward, published by The Macmillan Company of Canada Limited, Toronto, copyright © 1966 by Charles G. Power.

Price, Alfred, "The Duel over Germany," in *History of the Second World War,* by permission of the author. Published by Purnell & Sons Ltd., Paulton, England, in cooperation with the Imperial War Museum, copyright © 1967 by Purnell & Sons Ltd.

Pugsley, William H., *Saints, Devils and Ordinary Seamen,* by permission of the author. Published by Collins Publishers, Don Mills, Ont.

Raddall, Thomas H., *Halifax, Warden of the North,* by permission of the author. Published by McClelland & Stewart Limited, Toronto, copyright 1965 by Thomas H. Raddall.

Reynolds, Quentin, *Dress Rehearsal,* by permission of Random House, New York, copyright 1943 by Random House, Inc.

Roberts, Leslie, *The Life and Times of Clarence Decatur Howe,* by permission of the estate of Leslie Roberts.

________ *There Shall Be Wings,* by permission of the estate of Leslie Roberts.

Robertson, Terence, *Dieppe: The Shame and The Glory,* published by McClelland and Stewart Limited, Toronto, copyright © 1962 by Terence Robertson.

Roskill, Stephen Wentworth, "The Navy at War," in *White Ensign, The British Navy at War, 1939-1945,* by permission of William Collins Sons and Co., London.

Schull, Joseph, *The Far Distant Ships,* by permission of the Minister of Supply and Services Canada, Ottawa, crown copyrights.

Sclater, William, *Haida,* published by University Press, Toronto, copyright © 1947 by Oxford University Press (Canadian Branch).

Shapiro, L. S. B., *They Left The Back Door Open,* published by The Ryerson Press, Toronto.

Simonds, Peter, *Maple Leaf Up, Maple Leaf Down,* published by Island Press, New York, copyright 1946 by Island Press Cooperative Inc.

Smith, Waldo E. L., *What Time the Tempest,* published by The Ryerson Press, Toronto, copyright, Canada, 1953.

Speelman, Ap, "I am 17," in *Thank you, Canada,* published by *Stichting Wereldtentoonstelling,* Montreal, 1967.

Stacey, C. P., *The Canadians 1867-1967,* edited by J. M. S. Careless and R. Craig Brown, by permission of Macmillan of Canada (A Division of Canada Publishing Corporation), Toronto, copyright © 1967.

________ *The Canadian Army 1939-1945,* by permission of the Minister of Supply and Services Canada, Ottawa, crown copyrights, 1948.

________ *Six Years of War,* by permission of the Minister of Supply and Services, Ottawa, crown copyrights, 1955.

________ *The Victory Campaign,* by permission of the Minister of Supply and Services, Ottawa, crown copyrights, 1960.

Stalmann, Reinhart, *Die Ausbrecherkönige von Kanada.* Published by Verlag der Sternbücher, GmbH., Hamburg, Germany, copyright © 1958 by Verlag der Sternbücher.

Stursberg, Peter, *Journey Into Victory,* by permission of George G. Harrap & Co. Ltd., London, copyright © 1944.

Thompson, R. W., *Dieppe at Dawn,* by permission of David Higham Associates Ltd., London.

________ *The 85 Days,* by permission of David Higham Associates Ltd., London.

Tucker, Gilbert Norman, *The Naval Service of Canada, Its Official History,* by permission of the Minister of Supply and Services, Ottawa, crown copyrights, 1952.

Vaillancourt, Jean, *Les Canadiens Errants,* by permission of Le Cercle du Livre de France, Ltée, Montreal, copyright 1954 by Jean Vaillancourt and Le Cercle du Livre de France.

Wade, Mason, *The French Canadians 1760-1967,* by permission of Macmillan of Canada (A Division of Canada Publishing Corporation), Toronto, copyright © 1968 by Mason Wade.

Waters, John M., Jr., *Bloody Winter,* by permission of Wadsworth Inc. Published by D. Van Nostrand Company Inc., Princeton, N.J., copyright © 1967.

Wilmot, Chester, *The Struggle for Europe,* by permission of William Collins Sons and Co., London.

Worthington, Larry, *Worthy,* by permission of the author, copyright, Canada, 1961 by Clara E. Worthington.

Young, Peter, *Storm from the Sea,* by permission of William Kimber & Co. Ltd., London.

________ *World War 1939-45,* by permission of Arthur Barker Limited, London, copyright © 1966 by Peter Young.